GATEWAYS TO UNDERSTANDING MUSIC

Gateways to Understanding Music, Second Edition, explores music in all the categories that constitute contemporary musical experience: European classical, popular, jazz, and world music. Covering the oldest forms of human music making to the newest, this chronology presents music from a global rather than a Eurocentric perspective. Each of 60 "gateways" addresses a particular genre, style, or period of music. Every gateway opens with a guided listening example that unlocks a world of music through careful study of its structural elements. How did the piece come to be composed or performed? How did it respond to the social and cultural issues at the time, and what does that music mean today? Students learn to listen to, explain, understand, and ultimately value the music they encounter in their world.

New to this edition is a broader selection of musical examples that reflect the values of diversity, equity, and inclusion advocated by North American universities. Eight gateways have been replaced. A timeline of gateways helps students see the book's historical narrative at a glance.

Features

- **Values orientation**—Diverse, equitable, and inclusive approach to music history.
- **All genres of music**—Presents all music as worthy of study, including classical, world, popular, and jazz.
- **Global scope within a historical narrative**—Begins with small-scale forager societies up to the present, with a shifting focus from global to European to American influences.
- **Recurring themes**—Aesthetics, emotion, social life, links to culture, politics, economics, and technology.
- **Modular framework**—60 gateways—each with a listening example—allow flexibility to organize chronologically or by the seven themes.
- **Consistent structure**—With the same step-by-step format, students learn through repeated practice how to listen and how to think about music.
- **Anthology of scores**—For those courses that use the textbook in a music history sequence.

Gateways to Understanding Music continues to employ a website to host the audio examples and instructor's resources.

Timothy Rice is Distinguished Professor, Emeritus, and founding director of the Herb Alpert School of Music at the University of California, Los Angeles (UCLA).

Dave Wilson is Senior Lecturer in Music at the New Zealand School of Music—Te Kōkī, Te Herenga Waka—Victoria University of Wellington.

GATEWAYS TO UNDERSTANDING MUSIC

Second Edition

Timothy Rice
University of California, Los Angeles

Dave Wilson
Te Herenga Waka—Victoria University of Wellington

Routledge
Taylor & Francis Group

NEW YORK AND LONDON

Cover image: Boogich/E+/Getty Images

Second edition published 2023
by Routledge
605 Third Avenue, New York, NY 10158

and by Routledge
4 Park Square, Milton Park, Abingdon, Oxon, OX14 4RN

Routledge is an imprint of the Taylor & Francis Group, an informa business

First edition published by Routledge 2019

Library of Congress Cataloging-in-Publication Data
Names: Rice, Timothy, 1945- author. | Wilson, Dave (David R.),
    1980- author.
Title: Gateways to understanding music / Timothy Rice, Dave Wilson.
Description: Second edition. | New York : Routledge, 2022. | Includes
    bibliographical references and index.
Identifiers: LCCN 2022020750 (print) | LCCN 2022020751 (ebook) | ISBN
    9781032216300 (hardback) | ISBN 9781032216294 (paperback) | ISBN
    9781003269304 (ebook)
Subjects: LCSH: Music appreciation.
Classification: LCC MT90 .R53 2022 (print) | LCC MT90 (ebook) | DDC
    780.9—dc23/eng/20220427
LC record available at https://lccn.loc.gov/2022020750
LC ebook record available at https://lccn.loc.gov/2022020751

ISBN: 978-1-032-21630-0 (hbk)
ISBN: 978-1-032-21629-4 (pbk)
ISBN: 978-1-003-26930-4 (ebk)

DOI: 10.4324/9781003269304

Typeset in Univers and Optima
by Apex CoVantage, LLC

Visit the companion website: www.routledge.com/cw/gateways

To the many people who have taught us to love all the world's music, and to those at the institutions where we have taught who have allowed us and inspired us to experiment with the ideas in this book, with gratitude.

BRIEF CONTENTS

DETAILED CONTENTS

              Symphony No. 7 ("Leningrad"), Mvt. I ("War"), by Dmitri
              Shostakovich

                  Music and politics
                  Olivier Messiaen
                  Viktor Ullmann
                  Arnold Schoenberg, twelve-tone serialism

Gateway 45   **Trinidadian Steel Pan Music**   328
              "Mystery Band" by Renegades Steel Orchestra

                  Calypso
                  Music and Carnival
                  Lord Kitchener
                  Music and class
                  Music and patronage

12   **Music from an Age of Disenchantment and Protest (1950–1975)**   337

Gateway 46   **Rhythm & Blues and Soul**   339
              "(You Make Me Feel Like) A Natural Woman,"
              by Aretha Franklin

                  Sister Rosetta Tharpe
                  James Brown and funk
                  Motown
                  Gender and music
                  Civil rights and Black Power movements

Gateway 47   **Rock**   346
              "All along the Watchtower," by Jimi Hendrix

                  Rock and roll
                  Rhythm & blues
                  Chuck Berry
                  Bob Dylan
                  The British invasion

Gateway 48   **New Directions in Jazz**   355
              "Acknowledgement," from *A Love Supreme*,
              by John Coltrane

                  Modal Jazz
                  Miles Davis
                  Hard Bop, Art Blakey and Horace Silver
                  Cool jazz
                  Jazz fusion, Herbie Hancock, Wayne Shorter
                  Free jazz
                  Ornette Coleman
                  Association for the Advancement of
                  Creative Musicians (AACM)
                  Charles Mingus
                  Jazz as protest

TIMELINE

Nomadic Pastoralists   Buddhist Chant   China   North Indian Classical   Javanese Court Music

Balinese Gamelan

K-Pop

Horticultural Societies   Qur'anic Chant   Middle East   Rennaisance Sacred Vocal   Baroque Sacred

Classical Music at Century's End

Rhythm & Blues and Soul   Rap & Hip-Hop

Christian Chant   European Village   Rennaisance Lute   Baroque Orchestra   Classical Period Symphonies   Programmatic Orchestra Works   European Musical Nationalism   Classical Music of the New Century   American Symphonic Nationalism   Classical Music & WWII   Experimental Music   Post-Modern Classical Music   Classical Music Today

Small Scale Societies   Ancient and Medieval Religious Music   Ancient and Medieval Secular Music   European Age of Discovery   Age of Global Commerce   Age of Enlightenment & Revolution   Early Nineteenth Century   Late Nineteenth Century   Turn of the Twentieth Century   Interwar Period   World War II and its Aftermath   Age of Disenchantment and Protest   Music and Community   Music Today

| 1500 | 1600 | 1750 | 1815 | 1850 | 1890 | 1918 | 1939 | 1950 | 1975 | 1994 |

Key
- Asia & the Pacific
- Africa
- Europe
- North America
- Latin America & the Caribbean

Rennaisance Secular Vocal   Baroque Opera   Classical Period Opera   Early 19th Century Opera   Late 19th Century Opera   Ragtime   Early Jazz   Bebop   New Directions in Jazz   Neo-traditional Jazz   Jazz Today

Baroque Keyboard   Classical Period Chamber   Romantic Period Piano   Native American Pow-wow   American Band Music   Swing   Country Music   Rock   Electronic Dance Music   Pop Today

Foragers   Africa

Atlantic Slave Trade   Early American Popular Music   African American Religious Music   The Blues   Mariachi Music   Trinidadian Steel Pan Music   Salsa   Reggae   Regional Mexican Music

PREFACE TO THE SECOND EDITION

Gateways to Understanding Music is designed for introductory music appreciation and music history courses dedicated to the principles of diversity, equity, and inclusion. Traditionally, these courses have placed the history of European classical music at the center of the narrative and either omitted or placed on the margins popular music, jazz, and the music of communities defined by ethnicity, race, nationality, and religion. In this book we retain the historical approach of most textbooks that serve these kinds of courses, but we decenter European classical music, placing it in an equitable relationship to all the other kinds of music that contribute to musical and cultural life today.

To achieve our goals, we have integrated music from various traditions into a chronological narrative that includes European classical music, jazz, pop, rock, country, reggae, regional Mexican music, North Indian classical music, Javanese and Balinese gamelan, soul, salsa, and much more. This approach yields many exciting and unexpected pairings and juxtapositions of musical styles and genres. These juxtapositions illustrate fascinating similarities and differences in the way musicians have responded to the cultural, social, political, and economic conditions of their time and place. It allows us to make the case that all forms of human music making are worthy of careful listening and study. And it provides timely and relevant choices for today's students.

MUSIC APPRECIATION courses with the history of European classical music at the center too often carry with them implicit claims about white supremacy in the musical domain. These courses suggest, often explicitly, that the classical music composed by European men is more worthy of study, more beautiful, more sophisticated, and superior to the kinds of music left out of the course or placed on its periphery. These claims are not tenable in university settings and can cause harm in the context of the social and political life of multicultural, multiethnic, multiracial societies. In this book, we provide the theoretical perspectives and pedagogical tools that instructors need to transform these traditional music appreciation courses from harmful ones into ones that serve the common good and the shared values needed to live peacefully and thoughtfully in these kinds of societies.

MUSIC HISTORY courses for music majors need a similar restructuring. They should begin by asking this question: the history of what music? For most music students today the answer would typically be "the history of the music you are studying to play, compose, and teach," unless you are a jazz major. But this is the wrong answer for instructors, courses, and departments and schools of music seeking to expand their approach to music study to make it more diverse, equitable, and inclusive. It is the wrong answer because it closes off the possibility of recruiting a diverse group of music majors from all the many communities that form a multicultural nation and who might be interested in the full range of music being made in the world today.

An answer that would improve the chances of recruiting a diverse student body would be "the history of the music of our time and place." That repertory would include virtually every kind of music in the world, not because it is over there, not because it is "world music," but because it is performed and valued by some segment of the population in many countries today. The diversity of music included in this book, and the even-handed, equitable approach we take to each example, create the ground on which an ethical study of music can be built both for majors and nonmajors.

We as authors and teachers believe that the ethical study of music must be inclusive. It needs to include all the music of the society in which students and instructors live and, we would argue, all the music of a world defined by its interconnections. When instructors base their courses and curricula on an aesthetics that excludes vast amounts of music, they end up with an ethics that excludes all the people who make those excluded kinds of music. This book begins with an ethics of inclusion. As a matter of principle, we think all of humankind, all of society, should be welcome to study music in music departments and schools. But if potential students' music is excluded from the curricula of music departments and schools, they won't come to study music in those institutions. This book transforms our inclusive ethical principle into an inclusive aesthetics. We believe all music is worthy of study, and we include as much of it as we can. Instead of advocating for the study of beautiful music, we advocate for the study of the music that makes all of humanity beautiful.

NEW IN THE SECOND EDITION

This second edition makes clear our dedication to the principles of diversity, equity, and inclusion. New gateways on rhythm & blues and soul and on Native American pow-wow drumming, singing, and dancing fill two gaping holes in the first edition. A revised gateway on experimentalism in classical music and a new one on electronic dance music allow us to include African American contributions to these musical styles and to highlight the musical life of LGBTQ+ communities to a greater extent. New gateways on American pop music of today and K-pop bring the narrative up to date and extend it out into the world. The second edition contains the same number of chapters and gateways as the first edition. To make room for the new gateways, we moved a few gateways dealing with European classical music to the book's website. We think the result of these choices is an even more interesting and equitable story about musical life today in many countries of the world.

THE NARRATIVE STRUCTURE

Presenting this vast range of music in a historical narrative presented us with a number of interesting challenges. One problem is that some musical traditions have a detailed written history captured in musical notation and written commentaries while other traditions lack a history that predates the advent of sound recordings in the late nineteenth century. We solve this problem in two ways. First, our historical narrative centers on recordings rather than written compositions. Where we can, we foreground the performers and performances of music in written traditions along with the composition they are performing. So we analyze a modern recorded performance of Beethoven's Fifth Symphony as much as or more than we analyze the composed structure of the score from 1808. Focusing on recordings puts written and aural traditions on a similar footing and solves one problem associated with bringing this vast array of music together in one book.

Second, our focus on recordings means that all the music in this book is, in an important sense, contemporary music. No matter when a piece was, or might have been, composed, today the recordings of it mentioned in this book are accessible to listeners nearly everywhere in the world. Even if the recordings are part of "the music of our time and place," we think historical narratives are still valuable, not least for the easily understood storytelling arc they provide. But creating a historical narrative around the date of the selected recordings makes no sense. To solve that problem, the musical recordings are presented in the order in which some important aspect of the tradition they represent entered human history. For example, we use a newly composed song by Rhiannon Giddens recorded in 2017 as a gateway to the fiddle-and-banjo tradition so important to early nineteenth-century American musical life. We could have used a recording of an old fiddle tune notated in the 1840s in a fiddler's handwritten tunebook, but we think the Giddens recording allows us to tell a more interesting story. In another example, we begin our historical narrative with a recording from the 1980s of Central African foragers not because we believe this song or their way of singing is the oldest in the world, but because foraging, and the kind of social and musical life it supports, is the oldest extant form of human food production in the world.

Bringing this array of music together in one book creates problems not only for us, its authors, but for instructors who are not experts in all of these traditions (and doesn't that include all of us?). To solve this problem, this book uses a modular structure and a consistent pedagogy that enables trained musicians, no matter their specialty, to teach effectively using this book. Our modules are called "gateways." There are three to six gateways in each of fourteen chapters. Every gateway has the same structure and takes the reader on a path toward understanding the music of a particular time or people or place or genre.

Each gateway is unlocked by a single recording of music. By beginning with listening, we mimic and formalize the informal and direct way everyone encounters and learns about music in their everyday lives: hearing it on the radio or watching it on TikTok, attending a concert or music festival, or having a friend introduce a favorite artist or musical genre on YouTube or Spotify. Listening carefully to a gateway recording opens up a world of music and all of its rich meanings, histories, and legacies, whether that world is the European Classical period, Chinese music, country music, or an improvisation by John Coltrane.

FIVE QUESTIONS

In everyday life, listening to a new recording or attending a concert often leads the curious to ask questions about this new experience, and that is what each gateway of this book does. Each gateway asks—and answers—the same five questions:

- What is it?
- How does it work?
- What does it mean?
- What is its history?
- Where do I go from here (to explore this world of music)?

Every gateway is organized with the same step-by-step format, starting with listening and moving to musical, cultural, and historical explanations. As the content changes, the similarity of structure creates a welcome sense of familiarity and reinforces the basic analytical and descriptive methods the book conveys. This gateway model, with its consistent and repeated pedagogical structure, allows us to achieve one of the book's goals: to teach students how to ask and answer questions about music. We hope to stimulate curiosity about music by, first of all, asking questions about it. Asking questions is, after all, the first act of a curious mind.

The five questions that organize each gateway are ones that mirror the ways that students encounter and discover music in their lives today. Each gateway, instead of starting with pages of historical context or explanation, begins with listening. Instead of prompting students to ask questions that might be typical of their everyday listening practice (for example, do I like it or not?), we guide them through questions that move beyond taste and aesthetic preference. These questions unlock new understandings, help students acquire knowledge, and cultivate in them an attitude of openness to new ways of making and listening to music. We believe these goals provide the foundation of an ethical approach to courses in music appreciation and music history today.

The instructor's main task becomes helping their students navigate through this familiar and repeating structure and understanding the many links between the book's text and the gateway recording. The answers to the first two questions—What is it? and How does it work?—don't demand that the instructor has deep historical and cultural knowledge of the world of a particular genre or style or recording. Instructors with musical training in any area can help students answer these questions. That training is the only necessary prerequisite for teaching effectively with the assistance of this book. These first two questions guide students through deep and detailed listening as they learn to describe and explain musical sound using the elements of music (timbre, melody, rhythm, and so on). Instructors can help their students understand the book's explanations of the elements of music and help connect these elements and related terms to the students' listening experience. Equipped with this new understanding of ways to listen to music, students can read on their own the answers to the next two questions in the gateway: What does it mean? and What is its history? The fifth question is Where do I go from here? In other words, what else can I listen to or read about if I am interested in this kind of music, and how can I learn more about the world of music opened up by this gateway? The suggestions for further study in this section are ideal prompts for students to journey farther down the path into a musical world in class discussions and writing assignments. This modular structure allows instructors with widely varying expertise in the musical traditions, genres, and styles we introduce in the book to be successful teachers with this book as their aid. The structure also provides instructors with a useful model for structuring their own lectures. Doing so could add to the coherence of a course.

SUPPORTING MATERIALS

To help instructors use this book, we have included a COMPANION WEBSITE, with the following supplementary material located on www.routledge.com/cw/gateways:

- Gateway musical examples delivered on a Spotify playlist (and other sources) or on the book's website.
- Multiple-choice and short-answer quiz and exam questions.
- Suggestions for essay questions and in-class discussions.
- Gateways for traditions included in the first edition but omitted from the second edition.
- PowerPoint slides for each gateway with an outline of the main points, photos, and links to the gateway recording and related recordings.

For instructors in Music History courses, our colleagues Samuel N. Dorf, Heather MacLachlan, and Julia Randel have created an accompanying ANTHOLOGY OF SCORES, with composers' scores, ethnomusicologists' transcriptions, and other graphic and written representations of the "gateway" recordings. This anthology facilitates the integration of score study and music theory into the (ethno)musicology curriculum, a necessary focus in the training of professional musicians, and it provides one more opportunity to go beyond the textbook to examine our gateway musical examples in even greater depth. The anthology is available at www.routledge.com/9780367485382.

We trust that the rich set of materials, the exemplary pedagogy, and the goals and values we provide in this book and in its associated website and anthology of scores will serve the interests of instructors committed to diversity, equity, and inclusion and of their students, who are in the process of discovering their place in the world.

Timothy Rice
Dave Wilson
February 2022

ACKNOWLEDGMENTS

Thank you to the reviewers who read, discussed, advised, and commented on various sections of this book.

Ric Alviso, California State University, Northridge
Paul Berliner, Duke University
Tara Browner, University of California, Los Angeles
Elizabeth Clendinning, Wake Forest University
Larry Crook, University of Florida
Jeffrey Cupchik, Independent Scholar
Regina D'Amico, Independent Scholar
Kevin Delgado, San Diego State University
Mike D'Errico, Albright College
Noe Dinnerstein, John Jay College of Criminal Justice, CUNY
Jacqueline Dje Dje, University of California, Los Angeles
Ryan Dohoney, Northwestern University
Stephanie Doktor, Temple University
Shannon Dudley, University of Washington
Stephen Epstein, Te Herenga Waka— Victoria University of Wellington
Sam Girling, University of Auckland
Nancy Guy, University of California, San Diego
Deonte Harris, Duke University
Michael Iyanaga, College of William and Mary
Stephen Jones, Independent Scholar
Michele Kisliuk, University of Virginia
Kelsey Klotz, University of North Carolina at Charlotte
Mark Lamson, Musician
Theodore Levin, Dartmouth College
Scott V. Linford, University of California, Davis
Olivia Lucas, Louisiana State University
Maureen Mahon, New York University
Peter Manuel, The Graduate Center, CUNY
Alyssa Mathias, Knox College
Timothy J. McGee, University of Toronto
Eddie Meadows, San Diego State University
Matthew Mendez, Yale University
Heather Moore, University of Southern California
Anna Morcom, University of California, Los Angeles
Inna Naroditskaya, Northwestern University
Jocelyn Neal, University of North Carolina at Chapel Hill

Daniel Neuman, University of California, Los Angeles
Rahul Neuman, University of California, Los Angeles
Nancy November, University of Auckland
Samantha Owens, Te Herenga Waka—Victoria University of Wellington
Eftychia Papanikolau, Bowling Green State University
Jann Passler, University of California, San Diego
John-Carlos Perea, San Francisco State University
Leonor Xóchitl Pérez, Independent Scholar
Marianne Pfau, University of San Diego
Howard Pollock, University of Houston
A. J. Racy, University of California, Los Angeles
Anne K. Rasmussen, College of William and Mary
Helen Rees, University of California, Los Angeles
Alex W. Rodriguez, Independent Scholar
CedarBough T. Saeji, Pusan National University
Lauryn Salazar, Texas Tech University
George Sawa, Independent Scholar
Anthony Seeger, University of California, Los Angeles
R. Anderson Sutton, University of Hawaii at Manoa
Richard Valitutto, Cornell University
Inge van Rij, Te Herenga Waka— Victoria University of Wellington
Patrick Warfield, University of Maryland
Louise Wrazen, York University, Toronto
Tyler Yamin, University of California, Los Angeles
Hugo Zemp, Centre national de la recherche scientifique, Paris

We thank those who graciously helped us think through the new ideas, thoughts, and challenges of this second edition, including Matthew Allison, Jonny Avery, Chris Buckland, Eli Elinoff, Sarah Hoskyns, Connor Krohn, Dawn Mack, Doug McIntyre, Gus Reece, Camryn Rice, JR Wilson, and Lainie Wilson. We also thank the instructors and teaching assistants of M10 at UCLA who helped us develop many of the perspectives and pedagogical strategies at the heart of this book: Julius Reder Carlson, Lindsay Johnson, Hojoon Kim, Eric Schmidt, Luke Storm, and Ty-Juana Taylor. From UCLA we also thank Donna Armstrong from the Department of Ethnomusicology and Aaron Bittel from the Ethnomusicology Archive. Aleisha Ward served as research assistant for the second edition, with support from a Victoria University of Wellington Faculty Research Grant. Ann Rice acted as our ever-faithful and indefatigable editorial assistant, researching figures, managing our files, checking for consistency, and innumerable other tasks, all with unlimited patience and good spirits. Finally, we thank Constance Ditzel, our Routledge editor, whose faith in the worthiness of this project has meant the world to us.

AUTHOR PROFILES

Timothy Rice has taught undergraduate courses based on the content and principles of this book since 1981. A Distinguished Professor, Emeritus, at the University of California, Los Angeles (UCLA), he is the author of *Ethnomusicology: A Very Short Introduction* (Oxford University Press, 2014) and many books and articles on Bulgarian traditional music. He was founding co-editor of the *Garland Encyclopedia of World Music*, served as president of the Society for Ethnomusicology (2003–2005), and was founding director of The UCLA Herb Alpert School of Music (2007 to 2013). Since 2015 he has been the president of the Center for World Music in San Diego, California.

Dave Wilson is Senior Lecturer in Music at the New Zealand School of Music—Te Kōkī, Te Herenga Waka—Victoria University of Wellington, where he has also served as Jazz Performance Program Director. A specialist in jazz and popular music, he has been consistently teaching courses based on the approaches of this book since 2014. His research integrates ethnography, performance, and composition and has been published in journals such as *Commoning Ethnography, Ethnomusicology, Leonardo Music Journal, Music & Politics*, and *Popular Music*. As a saxophonist and clarinetist, he frequently performs in jazz and other styles of improvisatory music, including on his collaborative albums *SLANT* (2019) and *In Passing* (2017).

INTRODUCTION

OUR GOAL IN WRITING THIS BOOK is to introduce readers to the vast range of human music making today. We believe that music is a fundamental aspect of our humanity. It is a form of human expression every bit as central to our social and personal well-being as language and speech. So rather than focusing on a particular type of music, like classical music or jazz or popular music or some of the world's many musical traditions, we believe there is much to be learned by thinking about all the ways human beings have chosen to make and listen to music no matter when or where they have lived or what kinds of music they love. From this broad selection of music we hope that our readers will learn how to:

- value all kinds of music for the ways they make us human;
- describe and analyze music through careful listening;
- interpret the psychological, social, and cultural meanings of music;
- ask and answer questions about any music; and
- understand the importance of music in human life.

Our approach to the study of music in this book is captured in the book's title, *Gateways to Understanding Music*. This introductory chapter explains the words in the title—music, understanding, and gateway. Grasping the distinctions, concepts, and questions that guide the organization of the text will help launch our exploration of some of the fascinating music people are making in the world today.

MUSIC

The book focuses on sixty recordings of music in three large and commonly used categories—classical music, jazz, and popular music—as well as the music of a number of communities that define themselves by their ethnicity, nationality, race, or religion. All the recordings are from the last 100 years. The earliest was released in 1927 and the most recent in 2021. They are not introduced in the order they were recorded or in the order the compositions were composed. The recordings are introduced in an order based on when some aspect of the musical tradition represented by the recording entered human musical experience.

The chronological narrative of the book is organized into three eras:

- Part I: the premodern era up to 1500 CE;
- Part II: the modern era from 1500 to 1890; and
- Part III: the age of recordings from 1890 to the present.

During the premodern era, no single country or empire dominated the world. Music developed in different ways in different places depending on geography, modes of economic production,

DOI: 10.4324/9781003269304-1

political control of land, and unique cultures and religions. The book divides this era into two periods:

1. the period from about 10,000 BCE to 3500 BCE, when human food production supported only small-scale societies; and
2. the Ancient and Medieval period from about 3500 BCE to 1500 CE, when kingdoms, empires, large cities, and the so-called Great Religions spread across many parts of the globe.

Representing small-scale societies are recordings of music by contemporary foragers (people who hunt for and gather their food) from Central Africa, nomadic pastoralists from Siberia, and horticulturalists from the Solomon Islands in the Western Pacific. One chapter in Part I is devoted to the music of three religions that emerged in the Ancient and Medieval periods: Buddhism, Christianity, and Islam. Another chapter is devoted to secular music with roots in the Ancient and Medieval periods: the court musics of China and the Middle East and rural traditions from Zimbabwe in Africa and Bulgaria in Europe.

Part II covers what historians call the modern era in world history, from 1500 to 1890. It is defined partly by European domination in global affairs through colonization and trade. As a consequence, the five chapters in Part II focus on European music, with excursions to other parts of the world where new traditions were being created simultaneously:

1. the European age of discovery (1500 to 1600);
2. the age of global commerce (1600 to 1750);
3. the age of Enlightenment and revolution (1750 to 1815);
4. the early nineteenth century (1815 to 1850); and
5. the late nineteenth century (1850 to 1890).

During the European age of discovery, Christian religious music developed new approaches to music composition at the same time that the roots of the court music traditions of India were being planted. During the age of global commerce, famous composers like Johann Sebastian Bach and Antonio Vivaldi were composing the first important works for string orchestra at the same time that wealthy sultans on the island of Java in present-day Indonesia were patronizing the formation of large orchestras of gongs and other metallic instruments. The age of Enlightenment and revolution witnessed the height of aristocratic patronage of such composers as Franz Joseph Haydn, Wolfgang Amadeus Mozart, and Ludwig van Beethoven at the same time as enslaved Africans in the Americas were recreating their musical traditions under the harshest imaginable conditions. During the nineteenth century, as the power of the European aristocracy crumbled in the wake of the French Revolution, composers like Frédéric Chopin and Richard Wagner performed and composed for the newly wealthy beneficiaries of the Industrial Revolution, while people in the United States created music that responded to slavery, the Civil War, postwar Reconstruction, and end of Native American sovereignty and control of traditional lands.

Part III, covering the age of recordings, examines the era of mechanical, electrical, and digital reproduction of music. It began around 1890 with the sale of the first phonograph recordings. During this era, the United States replaced Europe as the center of global geopolitical power and cultural influence, and so in Part III American music becomes the focus of the narrative. Part III is divided into six chapters:

1. the turn of the twentieth century (1890 to 1918);
2. the interwar period (1918 to 1939);
3. World War II and its aftermath (1939 to 1950);
4. an age of disenchantment and protest (1950 to 1975);
5. music and community (1975 to 1994); and
6. music today (1994 to the present).

The invention of recording technology has preserved the history of music transmitted in both aural and written traditions for the past century and a quarter. Each chapter in Part III discusses recordings of European or American classical music, American popular music, jazz, and some kind of community-based music from the United States or abroad. European composers Igor Stravinsky and Dmitri Shostakovich, American composers Julius Eastman and Julia Wolfe, jazz pioneers Duke Ellington and John Coltrane, and popular music stars Jimi Hendrix, Public Enemy, and Olivia Rodrigo share the stage with innovators in mariachi, salsa, reggae, and K-pop.

UNDERSTANDING

People without musical training sometimes say, especially when they talk to musicians, "I don't understand anything about music." But in fact they understand a lot about music, especially the music they love. Nearly everyone has their favorite songs and pieces of instrumental music. They listen to them all the time, watch videos of them online, and, if they can, they go to live performances of their favorite musical artists. If they really didn't understand music, they wouldn't spend so much time listening to it, enjoying it, and being moved emotionally by it. **Understanding music** simply means that we find some of it orderly rather than chaotic, pleasant rather than unpleasant, predictable rather than unpredictable, meaningful rather than meaningless, and familiar rather than unfamiliar.

We gain these understandings of music through repeated listening over a lifetime. Each of us has a different collection of music we understand. What kinds of music do you understand? Rock or rap? Classical or jazz? EDM or K-pop? Chinese traditional music or Irish dance music? Soul or Tex-Mex music? Music for guitar or *sitar*? Your answers to these questions depend on your already having spent many years of your life listening to some of these kinds of music. During your lifetime of listening, the music you have listened to has become orderly, pleasant, predictable, meaningful, and familiar to you. Unless you have been living in a cave, isolated from the world of human-made sound, you already understand some significant part of the world's music. One of our goals is to transform and expand your understanding of music. This book will help you to understand the music you already love even more deeply. It will also help you to understand music that hasn't yet become part of your experience but that is just as important to other people as the music you understand and love is to you.

Our method for deepening and expanding your understanding of music involves explanation. **Explaining music** means to describe it, classify it, label it, and interpret its meanings. Explaining happens in words and also in diagrams and musical notation. Musical explanations provide the path along which you will move from your current understandings to new, deeper, and expanded understandings of music, including the music you already understand, the music that you may understand hardly at all, and the music you have never heard before. Probably the most satisfying result of explaining new and unfamiliar music will be that, through repeated hearings, you will come to understand it and find it orderly, pleasant, predictable, meaningful, and familiar.

While music will always remain a source of personal enjoyment, this book suggests that there are real intellectual, aesthetic, and ethical rewards in broadening the horizons of our listening experience and our current understanding of music. Reaping those rewards involves asking fundamental questions about the nature and meaning of music for all human beings, not just for ourselves. Why is music so important that virtually everyone in the world loves it in some form or other? What do differences in musical taste tell us about other individuals and about other groups of people? How does music function in our personal and social lives and in the lives of others? This book challenges the reader to understand the full range of music today, including the music you already know, love, listen to, and perform and the music that you don't know much about or have never heard. Taking up the challenge by reading this book involves an aesthetic commitment to opening your mind to new musical possibilities and an ethical commitment to hearing and caring about all the people who make this music in your locality, your region, your nation, and the world.

GATEWAYS

Our explanations of each of the sixty recordings featured in the book are contained in short sections called gateways. A **gateway** is a portal to a world of music. Such a world might be the music of a composer like Ludwig van Beethoven, a songwriter like Bob Marley, or a performer like Louis Armstrong; a genre or category of music such as Italian opera, salsa, or the blues; or the music of a nation or ethnic group such as Mexicans, Arab Americans, or the Shona people of Zimbabwe. **Genre** is a term for a category and type of music that is associated with a community of musicians and listeners. All the gateways ask the same five questions. Answering them in each gateway takes the reader on a path from initial understandings of the recording through explanations of it to new understandings of the recording and the world of music it opens up. The five questions are: What is it? How does it work? What does it mean? What is its history? and Where do I go from here?

In each gateway, the path from an initial understanding through explanation to a new understanding takes time. The journey begins by listening to the first thirty seconds or so of the recording to gain your first impression, your first understanding. Then you will read about how the music is put together, and we ask you to listen again for up to a minute to hear the features of the music that you have just read about. Then we ask you to listen a third time to the entire recording while following a timed listening guide with detailed explanations of important sections and moments in the recording. At the end of that third hearing of the recording, you will be familiar with the recording and have a new and significantly richer understanding of the recording and the world of music it represents than after your initial hearing. Don't miss this journey. You can't get this kind of understanding of music by reading about music. You can only get it by listening a few times to a recording and thinking a bit about it. You will get the most out of this book if you follow the path (the listening instructions) we give you in each gateway. We invite you to join us on the exciting journeys to new worlds of music that we have prepared for you.

Listening to music is the key that unlocks each gateway and begins the path to new understanding. Part of walking that path is engaging with musical explanation. That requires some new concepts and vocabulary. Here is an introduction of the basic concepts and terms necessary to answer the five questions in each gateway.

What Is It?

One of the first things humans do when they encounter something in the world is identify, label, or name it. What is it? What is this thing in front of me? Does it resemble anything I've encountered before? Do I have a category I can place it in? In the case of music, we typically name particular pieces and recordings, identify the composer and performers, and place the piece or performance within groups of pieces and performances: for example, Symphony No. 40 by W. A. Mozart; "Summertime" by George Gershwin; "Rokudan" for Japanese *koto*; "Formation," from *Lemonade* by Beyoncé; and a video recording of us singing "Happy Birthday" at my sister's party last Tuesday.

Answering the question "What is it?" sometimes requires identifying and labeling the category or genre or style to which it belongs. We use four categories or genres as one way to tell our story about all the world's music: American popular music; classical music; jazz; and the music of ethnic, national, racial, or religious groups.

Musical style is another way to label and categorize music. Musical **style** refers to the manner in which musical elements like melody and rhythm are deployed and combined in a large number of pieces or performances. We can speak, for example, of a composer's style, a performer's style, a national style, the style of a particular period in music history, or the style of a musical genre like R&B or disco. Analyzing musical elements helps us characterize the common features of many related pieces and performances.

Distinguishing among category, genre, and style can be tricky. For example, jazz is a named genre with its circle of players and fans, but a classical composer or an American popular songwriter or a Turkish performer might employ some elements of jazz style to create a certain effect in the genre they are working in. With that caution in mind, the terms "category," "genre," and "style" appear frequently throughout this book.

How Does It Work?

Asking how a recording of music works is the second step in explaining music and moving from old to new understandings of it. Music, like every field of study, has a vocabulary specific to it, and to explain how music works will require some specialized terms. We will introduce many of these terms as we go along, but for now, we'll lay out some of the basics used to answer the question, "How does it [this recording of music] work?"

The most basic concept in music is the musical tone. Metaphorically, musical tones might

FIGURE 0.1
The popular singer Madonna in 1987
Source: Olavtenbroek, Wikimedia Commons.

FIGURE 0.2
The Chicago Symphony Orchestra
Source: Jordan Fischer, Wikimedia Commons.

be called the atoms of music. A tone is perceived when an event in the world causes air to vibrate, that vibration hits the eardrum, and those vibrations are processed by the brain as sound. Musical tones are those sounds that human beings make and interpret as music. A musical **tone** has five components: overtone structure, pitch, duration, envelope, and loudness.

Overtone Structure

Every tone consists of a **waveform**, a complex set of waves vibrating in air. The slowest vibrating wave in a tone, the one with the longest wave form, is called the **fundamental**. It is perceived as the pitch of the tone. The set of faster vibrating waves of the tone are called **overtones**. They are typically not heard as pitches but unite in our perception as an impression of tone color or tone quality or timbre. Different timbres allow us to distinguish one musical instrument or voice from others: to tell the difference, for example, between a clarinet, a flute, and a trumpet.

Pitch

Our perception of the slowest vibrating wave in a tone, the one with the longest wavelength, is called the **pitch** of the tone. We call slow-vibrating waves low pitches and fast-vibrating waves high pitches.

Duration

Each musical tone also exists for a period of time, called its **duration**. Durations can be long or short.

FIGURE 0.3
A jazz combo: Art Tatum (piano), Sid Catlett (drums), Oscar Pettiford (bass), and Billie Holiday (vocals)
Source: Pictorial Press Ltd/Alamy Stock Photo.

FIGURE 0.4
Japanese court orchestra performing in Ukraine in 2010
Source: Antanana, Wikimedia Commons.

Envelope

Tones vary over their duration, forming the tone's **envelope**. Key moments in the envelope are its onset, called the **attack**, and its **decay** into silence. Plucked string instruments like the acoustic guitar have a sharp attack and a rapid decay. Bowed string instruments like the violin and wind instruments like the oboe can produce sustained tones over a long period of time.

Loudness

The **loudness** of a tone depends on the amplitude of the waveform. Musicians use Italian terms to describe loudness: soft is **piano**, and loud is **forte**. The difference between the loudest and softest tones in a piece of music is called its dynamic range, and changes in loudness are called **dynamics**.

One final comment: Some musicians, especially those who read musical notation, commonly refer to tones as notes. Technically, **notes** are visual representations of tones in musical notation. Musicians also refer to tones as pitches when the pitch of the tone is the topic of conversation. In this book we tend to use note and pitch rather than tone when describing music because that is what most musicians do.

Musicians combine musical tones in a nearly infinite variety of ways. To understand how they do this, to explain "how the music works," requires the use of a somewhat specialized vocabulary. These terms break music down into its composite "elements." Viewing music as made of "elements" derives from the many philosophical and religious traditions that believe that the world consists of fundamental and irreducible elements, essences, powers, or atomic particles that underlie everything in the universe. Such a view was expressed in the Ancient Greek classification of the world into four elements: earth, air, fire, and water. Modern physics, with its theories of atoms made up of tiny subatomic particles, and modern chemistry, with its notion of chemical elements consisting of pure forms with one type of atom, are legacies of these traditions, as are explanations of music that claim it consists of musical elements.

In each gateway of this book we use seven elements to describe "how music works": timbre, texture, rhythm, melody, harmony, form, and performance technique.

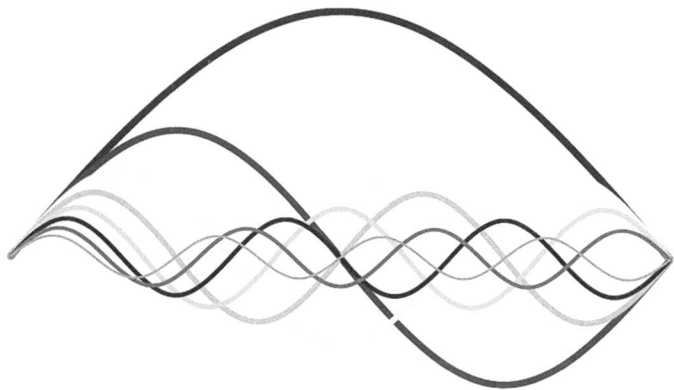

FIGURE 0.5

The fundamental and multiple overtones of a vibrating string producing a musical tone
Source: Alex Sawicka-Ritchie.

FIGURE 0.6

Pitches of tones indicated on the piano keyboard (with low pitches to the left and high pitches to the right) and in notation (with low pitches low on the music staff and high pitches high on the musical staff)
Source: Alex Sawicka-Ritchie.

Timbre

The timbre or sound quality of a musical tone is a function of its overtone structure and its envelope. Studies of music perception and cognition show that one of the first things we recognize when we listen to music is its sound quality, which we often associate with the source of the sound. Is it a man or a woman singing? An adult or a child? What instrument is playing? Naming the musical instruments and vocal sounds in a musical example is one way to describe its timbre.

🔊 Listen to example 1, "Someone Like You" by Adele. There are just two timbres in this recording. What are they?

Other than naming the instruments we hear, we have no systematic way of describing timbre, tone quality, or tone color. Instead, we use metaphors that link our listening experience of sound to other sensory experiences. So, for example, linking tone quality to taste, we might describe a sound as sweet or rich. Linking timbre to touch, we might say a sound is smooth or rough. Linking tone color to sight, we might call a sound bright or dull. Linking timbre to smell, we might call a sound fragrant or fresh. Sometimes we link the timbre of musical instruments to other aural experiences, saying, for example, that the sound is noisy or buzzing. We also sometimes link tone quality metaphorically to other experiences, calling the sound clean or dirty, pure or distorted, warm or cold. Beyond the naming of the source of the sound (the instrument creating it), descriptions of the element of timbre are notably subjective.

🔊 Listen to example 2, Jimi Hendrix performing "The Star-Spangled Banner," and example 3, Kenny Burrell playing "But Not for Me." What adjectives would you use to describe and compare the tone quality of these two examples of electric guitar? (Hint: there is no correct answer!)

Texture

The word texture is a metaphor that connects the sound of music to the feel of woven cloth. Just as threads in a cloth interweave to create different sensory impressions when touched (smooth or rough) or looked at (shiny or dull), musical **texture** refers to the way the elements of a musical performance are woven together at one moment in time. There are two fundamental types of musical textures: those with a single musical line or threads and those with many interweaving musical lines or threads. A performance with a single musical line or part has a **monophonic texture**. A monophonic part may be performed **solo** (one performer sings or plays the part) or in **unison** (all the performers sing or play the same part). A texture with many lines or parts has a **polyphonic texture**. **Monophony** derives from Greek words meaning "one sound" and **polyphony** from Greek words meaning "many sounds."

🔊 Listen to the difference between the monophony of the solo male singer and the polyphony of a choir of male voices in example 4, a recording by the South African vocal group Ladysmith Black Mambazo called "Unomathemba."

FIGURE 0.7
Adele performing with a pianist in 2016
Source: Getty Images/Christopher Polk.

Rhythm

Music is an art that unfolds in time, and the word **rhythm** refers to the temporal dimension of music in the broadest sense. Rhythm has two features: rhythm and meter. Rhythm in this more specific sense refers to the duration of tones and their organization. The rhythm of some performances might consist principally of long tones, another of short tones, and another of a combination of short and long tones. **Meter** refers to the organization of the pulsation or the beat of tones. There are two types of metrical organization in music: **nonmetrical** music lacks a beat or pulse; **metrical** music has a beat or

FIGURE 0.8
Soloist with choir (Ladysmith Black Mambazo) in 2017
Source: Joe Mabel, Wikimedia Commons.

pulse. Most metrical music organizes its beats into groups of two or three or more pulses, with the first pulse receiving the most emphasis as the "strongest" beat. If the music is organized into groups of two beats, the music is said to be in **duple meter** or in two. If the beats are organized into groups of three, then the music is said to be in **triple meter** or in three. (In European musical notation, such groupings of beats or pulses are called **measures** or **bars**.) Figuring out the meter of a musical performance is one of the most important steps in explaining the music. Musical tones can be emphasized, or accented, "on the beat" or in between beats. When they are accented in between beats or on "weak" beats rather than on the regularly emphasized (strong) beats in a given meter, they are said to be **syncopated**. **Syncopation** may characterize individual parts in a performance, sections of a performance, an entire performance, or a style or genre of music.

 Listen to example 5, "Let's Go Crazy" by Prince. He begins by speaking nonmetrically over a sustained instrumental background until, around 0:38 seconds, the drums introduce a beat organized in a meter of four (or in four-beat measures).

Melody

Melody is the term used for the most important line in a musical texture. A melody consists of a series of pitches performed over time. We hear these pitches strung together in time as a coherent melody, **melodic part**, or **melodic line** in the musical texture. If we think in spatial terms of pitches moving through time in the horizontal direction and from low to high in the vertical dimension, then we can describe the shape of the melodic line, the **melodic shape**, as ascending, descending, undulating, and flat.

 Listen to example 6, the Duke Ellington Orchestra playing "The Mooche." The opening melody at 0:08 has a descending shape.

Harmony

Harmony refers to the systematic combination of simultaneously sounding tones over the course of a section or piece of music. Usually harmonic systems produce pleasant, harmonious,

FIGURE 0.9
Five saxophones playing jazz in harmony
Source: René Clement, Wikimedia Commons.

consonant sounds, but not always. This musical term has been borrowed to describe people, objects, and ideas that go well together as being "in harmony." On instruments like the piano and guitar, a musician can easily produce simultaneous pitches, that is, harmony. On instruments that produce one pitch at a time, like the voice, trumpet, and violin, musicians have to play together in ensembles to produce harmonies. Two or more simultaneously sounding pitches is called a **chord**.

Listen to example 7, a 2013 composition by Caroline Shaw titled Partita for 8 Voices (No. 4: "Passacaglia"). For the first minute and a half, the ensemble of male and female voices sings a progression of different chords, where all of the parts sing different lines simultaneously.

Form

Form refers to the "shape" of a musical performance as it unfolds through time from beginning to end. Form is an important aspect, in addition to rhythm, of the temporal dimension of music. Listening for the form of a piece or a performance means keeping track of how the elements of music change or stay the same from the start to the finish of the performance. Listening for the form of a performance means understanding whether what you are hearing now is a repeat of something you heard before, a variation of something you heard before, or something different from what you heard before. The "something" in this formulation is usually the melody or a melodic phrase, and descriptions of form are often descriptions of melodic form. In principle, however, a performance of music may have timbral form, textural form, rhythmic form, and harmonic form.

One way to notate and describe form involves the application of uppercase and lowercase letters to the "somethings," let's say melodies. So the letter A applies to the first melody in the performance, and it is applied to any repetition or return of A. The notation A' (read "A prime") is applied to a varied repetition of A. The letter B is applied to a new melody, and after that successive letters of the alphabet are given to yet new melodies. Here are a few possibilities:

A A: a single melody is repeated exactly;

A A': a melody followed by a varied repeat of it;

A B: a melody is followed by a second, different melody.

Forms can also be analyzed at two or more temporal levels. So, for example, the A melody may consist of, say, four melodic phrases indicated with lowercase letters, for example, A = a b a c.

 Listen to example 8, a recording by Irish accordionist Sharon Shannon and her group of the song "Norwegian Wood" by John Lennon and Paul McCartney of the Beatles. How many different melodies do you hear in the course of the song? How many times is each of them repeated? Can you describe the form of the song at two different levels?

Performance Techniques

Performance techniques are a mixed bag of performance practices that musicians use. Musicians can manipulate the timbre of their voice or instrument. They may also change the loudness of the tones (**dynamics**), sometimes abruptly and sometimes getting gradually louder (**crescendo**) or gradually softer (**decrescendo**). A melody may be performed with or without **ornamentation**, which are short tones between the main melody pitches. **Articulation** refers to the ways musicians connect the tones of the melody: smoothly (**legato**) or with spaces between them (**staccato**). Musicians can vary the **tempo**, that is, the speed of performance, from fast to slow.

🔊 Listen to example 9, Whitney Houston's recording of "I Will Always Love You," a song by Dolly Parton. Notice how Houston ornaments the melody and progresses from soft to loud over the course of the performance.

What Does It Mean?

Music is a type of art and entertainment made up of musical tones and the seven musical elements outlined above. But music also is a human behavior with deep psychological, cultural, social, economic, and political significance. In this book we interpret the meaning of music in seven categories: (1) aesthetics; (2) emotional resonance; (3) cultural linkages; (4) social behaviors; (5) politics; (6) economic activity; and (7) use of technology.

Aesthetics

Part of the meaning of the music is revealed when we describe and explain the way composers and performers put the seven elements of music together and the way listeners hear them. These descriptions are at the root of understanding people's musical tastes. **Aesthetics** is the area of philosophy that deals with what is beautiful and appealing in the arts based on an analysis of the elements of the art. When, in a particular gateway, we speak of a composer's aesthetic or a cultural aesthetic, our understanding of that aesthetic depends on our descriptions of music in the "how does it work" section.

> AESTHETICS

Emotional Resonance

Humans also sing and play music to express and communicate emotions in a controlled way. Many listeners enjoy music for the emotional response it can generate in them. Music functions in this way because it is, like language, a system of signs that signal our thoughts to others. A **sign** or **signal** is an object or an action that has meaning to a person or a group of people. Musical performances are signs with meaning, just as stop signs, national flags, a smile, or a tattoo are. Every aspect of our life in society, our social life, is suffused with signals and signs. Without them we could not live together in social groups. Music is a particularly effective sign system for conveying and generating emotion.

Music conveys its meanings and emotions in a different way from language and speech. **Language signs** convey their meanings in precise, detailed, and clearly understood ways that everyone who speaks a particular language can understand. All speakers of English agree on the meaning of the word "tree," for example. Language signs are useful because they allow us to communicate our thoughts and feelings rather exactly to those around us who speak the same language.

Music does not communicate or act as a sign or convey meaning in the same way that language does. The meaning of music is not conveyed by language signs but by two other types of signs: indexes and icons.

FIGURE 0.10
Singer Janis Joplin (1943–1970)
Source: Keystone Pictures USA/Alamy Stock Photo.

FIGURE 0.11
Fans and football players with different responses to the indexical meaning of the U.S. national anthem
Source: Keith Allison, Wikimedia Commons.

An **index** or **indexical sign** is named for the index finger that points to things. The national anthem is a tune that points to and thus is associated with patriotic events, lyrics, and feelings. Whenever the tune is played, even at a sporting event with no patriotic significance, it points to or indexes pride in one's nation. However, not everyone may understand this musical sign the same way. Those disaffected and alienated by the gap between a nation's ideals and its realities may have more complex feelings.

While a national anthem is a shared sign for the people of a nation, some musical indexes are very personal and even unique to a single person or a few people. One example is the "our song" phenomenon. Two people in love may decide that a particular song they heard on their first date is "our song." From then on that song will be associated with the lovers' relationship. While they are together, they may like the song, but if they break up, they may come to hate the song because of its negative associations with a failed relationship.

Musical indexes are very powerful signs and are the bearers of many of the

EMOTIONAL
RESONANCE

strong feelings we experience when we listen to music. Indexical musical signs generate strong emotions without our thinking about them in words. Because not all of us share the same associations between a musical sign and its references, a given piece or performance of music may generate rather different emotions in different listeners. A musical index is thus a very different type of sign from a language sign, in which agreement as to its meaning is basic to the communicative function of language. Throughout this book we use certain phrases as synonyms for stating that something is an indexical sign of something else. We might say that it "is an index of," "indexes," "points to," "is associated with," or "is linked to" something else. All these phrases are driving at the same idea: one way music has meaning and generates emotion is through its association with previous experience, whether outside music or within the music itself.

The other type of musical sign conveys meaning through similarity. These musical signs are called **iconic signs** or **icons** by analogy with religious icons, paintings in a church that portray in two dimensions the features of a three-dimensional person, typically a saint. In symphonic music, for example, a fast, low-pitched drum roll and a cymbal crash can be icons of thunder and lightning, which the composer may hope will generate a corresponding feeling of dread in the listener. In heavy metal rock music, loud, distorted guitar chords called power chords may generate a feeling of social power among fans of this music, many of them teenagers who might feel otherwise powerless. Musical performances can also be iconic of social relationships, both real and imagined. When, in the 1930s, the white jazz bandleader Benny Goodman included Black musicians in his small combos, the ensembles became icons of an imagined racial equality and integration in a segregated society. They may have generated a feeling of hope in some audience members.

Like indexical signs, iconic musical signs are sometimes shared by a culture or subculture and sometimes are individual in their meaning. Certain phrases in this book are synonyms for saying something is an iconic sign of something else. We might say that it "is an icon of," "is a metaphor for," "is similar to," "resembles," "imitates," "is coherent with," or "paints" something else. All these phrases are driving at the same idea: one way music has meaning and generates emotion is through its similarity to previous musical, cultural, and social experience.

Cultural Linkages

Music is also a cultural expression. As such, its elements are nearly always coherent with (icons of) other modes of cultural expression such as cosmology, religion, poetry, painting, sculpture, and theater. Commonly, musical elements amplify the meanings of these other expressive forms. A high-pitched descending melodic phrase can add emotional power to a sad song lyric. Musical performances tell us stories about ourselves and others in ways different from language. They are metaphorical texts that we can read to understand our fellow human beings, whether they are sitting next to us in the classroom, come from another part of the country or the world, belong to a different ethnic or social group, or live in a faraway city we someday hope to visit or a rainforest that we may never visit.

> **CULTURAL LINKAGES**

Social Behavior

Music is also a social behavior. As such, it participates in the production of social difference along lines of class, race, ethnicity, gender, and sexual orientation. Of these issues gender and sexual relations are fundamental. Love songs are part of musical experience nearly everywhere in the world. And music enables dancing, the archetypal arena for displaying gendered selfhood and sexual attraction. But just as important, gender in many societies limits who makes what kinds of music. Men and women may each have their own specialized repertoires and styles. Men may be accorded more freedom to move about in the public square and thus to perform music there, while women may be encouraged to make music only in domestic circles. In some communities gender non-binary individuals may find little space for their music making, while in others they may be highly valued and centrally important performers.

> **SOCIAL BEHAVIOR**

Male musicians throughout the history of classical music, jazz, and many popular music and other genres have had profound social advantages over women, and so gateways on J. S. Bach, Ludwig van Beethoven, Duke Ellington, Charlie Parker, Bob Marley, Jimi Hendrix, and others are unavoidable when telling the stories of those traditions. But we intervene in various ways to illuminate this mostly male history of music by focusing on women performers and composers whenever we can. Today we understand that composing, singing, arranging, playing instruments, producing recordings, and much more are legitimate pursuits for people of any gender.

Politics

Politics, from the Greek for city, concerns the exercise of power in governance and decision-making, particularly in the public sphere. Because of music's emotional resonance, its indexical links to other aspects of culture, and its iconic enactments of social behavior, authoritarian governments have often thought it necessary to control music making in support of its control of society. Those without

FIGURE 0.12
Siebenbürgen, a goth metal band from Sweden, in 2008
Source: Levidark, Wikimedia Commons.

FIGURE 0.13
Brittney Howard singing and playing guitar with her blues rock band Alabama Shakes in 2012
Source: Fred Rockwood, Wikimedia Commons.

FIGURE 0.14
Drummers march with Indigenous activists in Seattle, Washington, in solidarity with the Standing Rock Sioux in their fight against the Dakota Access Pipeline, 2016
Source: John Duffy, Wikimedia Commons.

POLITICS

power have often used music to support nascent feelings of national sentiment, rage against the powers that be, champion a political movement, or amplify the sound of mass demonstrations. Music's significance as an aid to the exercise of power and political action will appear in quite a few gateways.

Economic Activity

ECONOMIC ACTIVITY

In some cultures music is a pastime and something that nearly everyone does for the fun of it and to contribute to successful social interactions. But in stratified societies with divisions of labor, musicians may be specialists or professionals who are paid for their labor. Patronage, that is, the question of who provides musicians with the means to support themselves, is an important factor in the creation of music. The significance of music as an economic activity suffuses many of the gateways in this book.

Technology

We tend to think of technology as the latest electronic gadgets in our world (smartphones, computers, medical devices), the software that runs on them (apps, programs), and the computer networks they use (the internet, Wi-Fi). But in a broader sense technology refers to the tools humans have always used for tasks in their lives: hunting, farming, cooking, building, healing, communicating, thinking, and making music. Nearly every gateway contains a discussion of the musical instruments and the electronic technology that musicians have invented or used to make the music they want to make.

What Is Its History?

Each gateway recording is also explained by its history. That history includes the origins of the genre or style it represents, the social and cultural conditions that produced the particular gateway recording, and the history of that music since the recording was first created. No matter the place or historical time period that originally produced it, this section also discusses the way this type of music resonates in our culture and our listening experience today. In other words, although our narrative is broadly historical, we are not consigning any of the musical worlds we introduce to the past. Each one is alive in the present and has its own history.

Where Do I Go from Here?

The book answers this question by providing a few suggestions for listening to audio recordings, watching videos, or doing some additional reading to expand your understanding of the world of music opened up by the gateway example.

FIGURE 0.15
Country singer Dierks Bentley performs at the White House in 2011
Source: The White House, Wikimedia Commons.

Learning to ask and answering the five questions asked about each gateway recording in this book should enable you to apply this explanatory apparatus to all the music you encounter in the future. You should be able to understand and explain what any music you hear means to you and to those who make it and love it no matter where in the world they live. Let's get started.

THINGS TO THINK ABOUT

- Think of a recording of music that you react to emotionally and, using the concepts of index and icon, explain why you think it has that effect on you.
- Explain why you like a particular song or genre of music either in terms of the way it expresses your social identity (class, race, ethnicity, gender) or in terms of the way it reflects your political values or the cultural worlds you live in, or both.

NEW TERMS

articulation	chord	decrescendo
attack	crescendo	duple meter
bar	decay	dynamics

envelope
explaining music
form
forte
fundamental
gateway
genre
harmony
icon/iconic sign
index/indexical sign
language sign
legato
loudness
measure/bar

melody, melodic line, or melodic part
meter
metrical
monophony/monophonic texture
nonmetrical
note
ornamentation
overtones
piano
pitch (low, high)
polyphony/polyphonic texture

rhythm
sign/signal
solo
staccato
style
syncopated/syncopation
tempo
texture
timbre
tone, musical
triple meter
understanding music
waveform
world of music

Music History to 1500 CE

UNTIL ABOUT 1500 CE no single cultural, economic, or political center dominated world affairs. Political power was either local or limited to particular areas of the world such as China, India, and Mesopotamia. Part I examines some of the musical traditions in the world today with roots in this period of history before 1500. Chapter 1 looks at music of the oldest social formations still in existence today. These are small-scale societies that sustain themselves by foraging (hunting and gathering plants), caring for domesticated herd animals (nomadic pastoralists), and planting small gardens (horticulturalists).

Chapters 2 and 3 examine music with roots in the Ancient and Medieval periods of human history. The Ancient period begins around 3000 BCE with the invention of writing and the advent of large-scale agriculture based on growing wheat, rice, and other grains. The ancient Egyptian, Chinese, Indian, Greek, and Roman Empires appear during this period, as well as four major religions (Hinduism, Buddhism, Judaism, and Christianity).

European histories name the time after the fall of the Roman Empire in 476 CE the Medieval period. Formed from the roots "medi" meaning between and "eval" meaning time, it was the time, the "Middle Ages," between the Ancient period and the beginning of European dominance in world affairs, which historians call the modern period. Islam and many secular musical traditions today have their roots in this Medieval period between 476 and 1500. Chapters 2 and 3 cover both the Ancient and Medieval periods: Chapter 2 on Ancient and Medieval religious music and Chapter 3 on Ancient and Medieval secular music.

DOI: 10.4324/9781003269304-2

PART I

MUSIC OF SMALL-SCALE SOCIETIES

EVERYONE IN THE WORLD today lives in a complex web of national, regional, and local governments, economies, and media information. About half live in cities and half in rural areas. In the United States about 80 percent live in cities. In rural areas around the world there are a very few small-scale societies that continue to sustain themselves with the oldest still-extant modes of human food production on the planet: foraging, nomadic pastoralism, and horticulture. The gateways in this chapter provide a portal to the musical worlds of these types of societies.

Foraging societies hunt wild game and gather plants, nuts, and seeds to sustain themselves. Human forager societies date to the late Paleolithic Period (Old Stone Age), which began around 2.5 million years ago. Around 10,000 BCE, humans began a transition from food gathering to food producing. At that time humans learned how to domesticate plants and animals, a set of practices known collectively as agriculture. Horticulture refers to the domestication of plants for food, but in small quantities that support only small groups of people. This "Agricultural Revolution" or "Neolithic Revolution" first took place in four regions of the world: grain farming in the Fertile Crescent, the area along the Tigris and Euphrates Rivers in present-day Iraq and along the Nile River in Egypt; rice growing in the Yangtze and Yellow River basins of China; maize growing in Central America; and root crops in Papua New Guinea. From these regions it took until about 2000 BCE for agriculture to spread to most regions of the world.

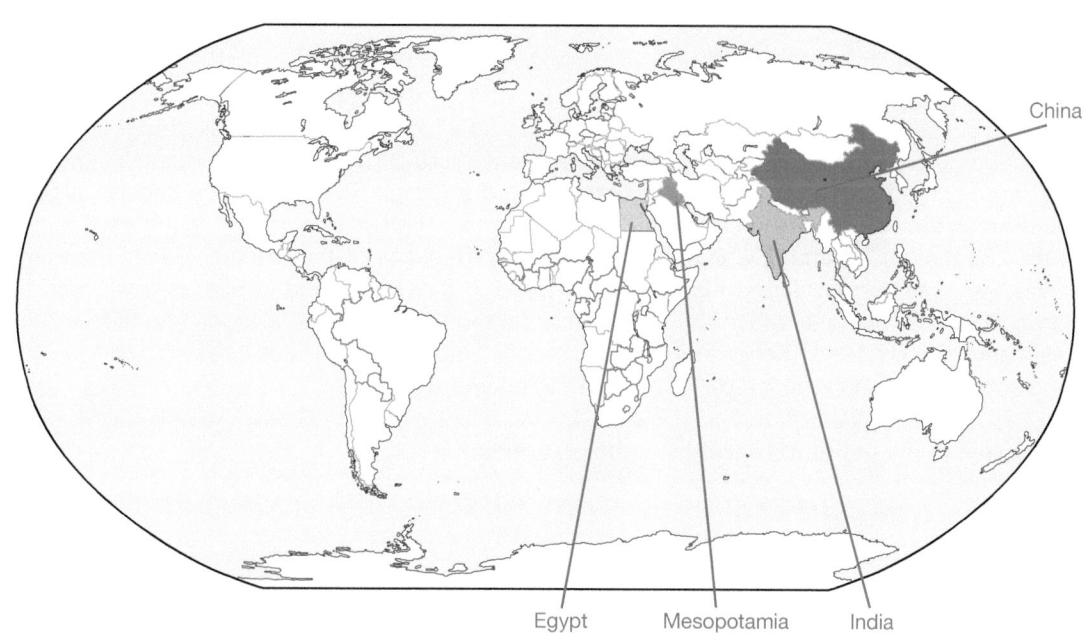

FIGURE 1.1
Map of Ancient civilizations

DOI: 10.4324/9781003269304-3

The music of these still-extant social formations is mainly known today through recordings made by ethnomusicologists who have lived in these isolated places for a year or more to study their music. In a few cases musicians from these cultures have toured around the world and played with musicians from the classical and jazz scenes. Sometimes these musicians, seeking new sources of inspiration, have used or referenced ethnomusicologists' recordings in their own creations. This chapter contains three gateways, one example from each of these three types of societies: Central African foragers; nomadic pastoralists from Inner Asia (Siberia); and horticulturalists from the Solomon Islands in the Western Pacific. In all these cases the music making of these foragers, nomadic pastoralists, and horticulturalists is intimately linked to the natural environment in which they live. Their music contributes in important ways to the social organization, psychological well-being, and work patterns of these societies.

Because the histories of these musical traditions were not written down before their contact with explorers, missionaries, ethnomusicologists, and tourists, we do not claim that the actual music in these recordings is thousands of years old. But we place them first in our chronology because the social formations that these musical practices contribute to and draw from are the oldest on earth today. And some of the general elements of the musical cultures we observe today may, indeed, be very old:

- the understanding of the resonant potential of found and made objects for making music, for example, from a hollow log, a piece of bamboo, a cooking pot, or a hunting bow;
- the prominent use of the human voice to create social harmony and communicate across social barriers;
- the iconic and therefore expressive, emotional link between singing and crying;
- the intimate relationship between the sound of music and the sound of the environment; and
- the belief that singing can be more effective than speech for contacting the supernatural world of ancestors, spirits, and gods.

These very old understandings of the nature of music form the bedrock of all human musical cultures today.

GATEWAY 1
MUSIC OF FORAGERS

What Is It?

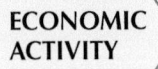

ECONOMIC ACTIVITY

Our gateway to the music of extant forager societies is a recording of the BaAka people of the Central African Republic singing "Bisengo Bwa Bolé" in a dance form called *mabo*. It was recorded in the 1980s by ethnomusicologist Michelle Kisliuk. The BaAka live in small bands of fifty to a hundred people in a huge rainforest along the Congo River basin, the second largest rainforest in the world after the Amazon River basin, near the borders of four countries: Central African Republic, Cameroon, Congo, and Democratic Republic of the Congo. *Mabo*, a hunting dance that was current during Kisliuk's visits there in the 1980s and 1990s, is sung before, during, and after hunts in which the community spreads nets in a circle around an area of the forest and then chases and ensnares animals, mostly antelopes of various sizes, into them. This song accompanies dancing led by men but including women.

 Listen to the first thirty seconds of the recording.

How Does It Work?

Timbre

This performance includes men's and women's singing with yodeling, along with low- and high-pitched drum sounds and a stick beating time.

FIGURE 1.2
**Map of Africa
(BaAka people)**

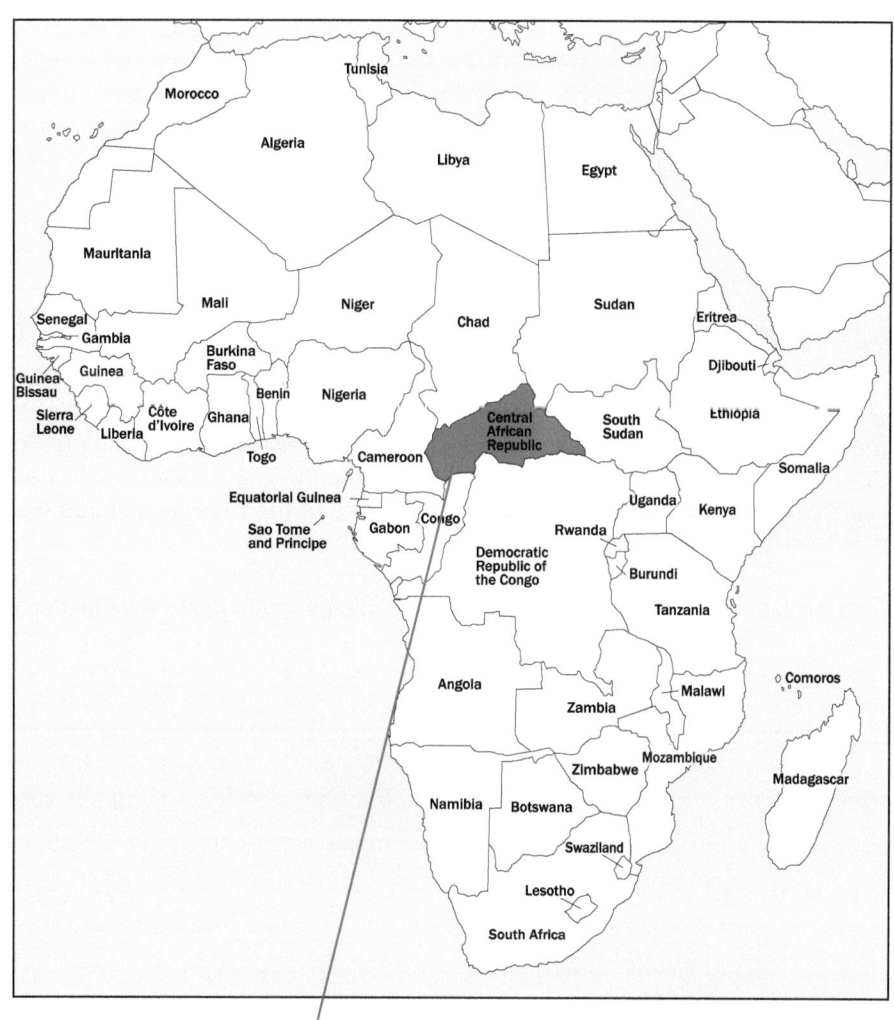

Home of the BaAka people

Texture

The texture is polyphonic, consisting of many people singing different rhythmically independent melodic lines.

Rhythm

The drums play a pattern of four strong beats, each subdivided into three pulses by a pattern of low- and high-pitched sounds (L-H-H-L-H-H) to create a meter of six beats. Notice that the pulses are not absolutely even but have a slightly lilting character. The melodic lines interlock with the drum rhythms but in a way difficult to hear.

Melody

A prominent feature of some BaAka songs is yodeling. **Yodeling** is an alternation between chest-resonated tones and high-pitched, head-resonated tones, which produces melodies with disjunct or leapwise melodic motion.

Harmony

The harmony is the result of the simultaneous singing of many melodic lines.

Form

The basic form consists of fixed melodies, some of which are repeated and treated to improvised melodic variations. As a new song gets older and becomes familiar, singers stop singing

FIGURE 1.3
BaAka women dancing *mabo*
Source: Michelle Kisliuk.

the main theme. With the main themes silent but in their ears, they sing variations on them. The singers listen carefully to each other and echo, repeat, and vary what they sing in response to what they hear. Careful listening is a skill necessary for survival in the forest and interpersonal and social well-being. The loudest melodic line in the texture is not the melody but the voice of the person, named Mokpake, who was sitting closest to the ethnomusicologist's microphone. The text is a single line of text plus a variety of **vocables**, nonlexical syllables like "i yay i oh."

Performance Techniques

The most striking performance techniques are the yodeling by some of the singers and melodic variations in their singing.

 Listen to this recording with these elements in mind and while following this timed listening guide.

LISTENING GUIDE 1.1

TIME	DESCRIPTION
0:00	The recording fades in.
0:04	A woman close to the mic starts a yodeling melody; other melodies are heard in the background.
0:30	The yodeling line is no longer heard, but a melody line without yodeling is prominent.
1:12	A yodeling melody returns.
1:45	The yodeling line again disappears.
1:58	The yodeling line returns.
2:18	And so on to the end.
5:27	End

What Does It Mean?

SOCIAL BEHAVIOR

The equality of voices in a performance of *mabo* during a BaAka music-and-dance event mirrors the social organization of BaAka society and the physical activity of the hunt. BaAka and other forager societies are often described as egalitarian, meaning that they value and maintain a social order that makes few if any of the distinctions that most large-scale societies have between leaders and followers, high and low classes, and occupational categories. They own very few things except hunting nets, spears, machetes, cooking pots, and some clothing, and these are routinely shared, traded, and even swiped when the swiper claims it is common property. When they want drums for a *mabo* dance, they quickly make a temporary drum from a rotting log and an animal skin or, if circumstances allow, they borrow more substantial drums from village horticulturalists who live on the edges of the forest and where the BaAka live during some parts of the year.

Every able-bodied man and woman participates in food-gathering activities, although men usually take the lead in net hunting while women gather roots and seeds on the way to help with the hunt. To ensure the success of the hunt, men start and lead the *mabo* dancers just as they start and lead the hunt, but women soon join in both activities, helping with the hunt and singing and dancing enthusiastically for the success of the hunt. Women also have dances that they control entirely, some of which mock men as a way of restoring the balance of power.

Although BaAka society is closer to an egalitarian ideal than most societies in the world, they single out four important social categories: (1) eldest sibling, (2) lead hunter, (3) healer, and (4) expert teacher of songs and dances. The lead hunter and healer are usually men, an indication of some inequality between men and women. Both men and women may be the eldest sibling and act as expert teachers of songs and dances. Children learn the songs and dances by watching adults, but adults sometimes invite master teachers from other camps to teach them new songs and dances. Some of these songs and dances are attributed to particular individuals, who have some heightened status on that account.

Circular forms permeate their lifeways. The nets are spread in a semicircle in the forest just as, in their forest camps, people's small, one-room, dome-shaped houses, made by women out of forest materials, are arranged in a circle. *Mabo* dancers dance counterclockwise in a circle within a circle of spectators within the circle of houses constructed in circular form. The iconicity of these circular architectural, social, and dance structures creates a feeling of familiarity, comfort, and coherence for the BaAka.

AESTHETICS

Although they are taught new songs and learn old songs by watching, they are not taught fixed parts to sing in the polyphonic texture. Instead, they develop the ability to create numerous variations, which they are free to sing at will, on the melody of each *mabo* song. Sometimes, as in the recording, they drop out for a while, only to enter again when they feel like it. Consistent with their egalitarian social structure, no one leads the performance and tells others what to do. If they try, they are usually ignored. All the lines in the polyphony are equally important. Their ability to create polyphony spontaneously stands in striking contrast to spontaneous group singing in American culture, where singing, say at a birthday party, is typically monophonic. The inability to sing polyphonically in relatively egalitarian social settings is consistent with American society's stratified social structure, which includes a specialized category of trained musicians who have the ability to sing and play polyphonically, but often only under the direction of a leader who organizes them. The specialization of labor characteristic of many modern societies results in a distinction between the few people who perform polyphonic music very well and most people, who perform monophonically and not always very well.

For the dancers, the drumming provides the rhythm for their dance movements. They hold their bent arms close to their bodies, while their feet move in a step-touch-step-touch pattern on the main low-pitched drum beats as they move around the circle. Their hips articulate the subdivisions of the beat, which they may hear in groups of two or in groups of three. Hearing these groups of two is aided by the way the players of the small drum play the triple-sounding L-H-H pattern. They do not use their hands to mirror the sound pattern, however. Instead, they play the sound pattern by alternating their two hands like this:

Pitches   L -H-H-L-H-H
Hands   R -L -R-L-R-L

This difference between the sound and the motion that produces them creates a **polymeter**, the simultaneous presence of two meters, in this case duple meter in the hand motion against triple meter in the sound that results from the hand motion. The dancers hear the two meters and, bent at the waist, move their feet, knees, and buttocks in response to what they experience as a rich polymetric texture. These two parts yield what seems to be a single monophonic drum part, but the polymeter of the duple hand movements against the triple pattern of the drum sounds creates an **inherent polyphony**, an experience of polyphony that results from a monophonic line or part played by the drummers.

Polyphonic singing also sounds literally natural to the BaAka, not least because it is iconic of the polyphony of forest sounds (birds singing and calling, leaves rustling, cicadas buzzing, insects chirping) that they hear all around them. Unison singing probably would sound rather unnatural to them and not in harmony with nature. When they are alone, walking or gathering food in the forest, they sing monophonically the solo yodeling melodic lines that make up the

EMOTIONAL RESONANCE

texture of *mabo* singing. Each person's particular way of singing these lines is their personal signature and an index of their presence in the forest. During the hunt they use their personal yodeling melodies to signal their position to the other hunters, creating a rich polyphonic texture of yodels and calls that help with the hunting. Melodic yodeling lines, as signatures or indexes of particular individuals, may touch those who hear them as they recognize friends. The texts also may be touching, as they express incidents in ordinary life, memories of people who have died, and accusations of bad behavior.

CULTURAL
LINKAGES

The genre *mabo* and solo singing in the forest are but two of a number of BaAka genres. Others include music for spear hunting, women's dances, solo lullabies, and songs included in stories that tell of the BaAka's relationship to the animals and the natural and supernatural worlds. They believe, for example, in a benevolent forest god that brings them good fortune. Both men and women sing net-hunting and spear-hunting songs, and the women have their own dance-and-song forms that serve their emotional and social needs and exclude men.

What Is Its History?

ECONOMIC
ACTIVITY

Foraging, which refers to both the hunting of game and the gathering of edible plants, and forager societies arose toward the end of a long era called the Paleolithic (Old Stone Age). It began about 2.5 million years ago when protohuman hominids began using stone tools, and it ended around 10,000 BCE, when humans invented agriculture. Forager societies typically operate in small bands, some perhaps no larger than the nuclear family. Such bands need to be just the right size, not too small or too large, to hunt and gather food efficiently enough to feed the group.

Today, only a few forager societies, like the BaAka, still exist. They can be found among some American Indian groups, especially in California and the Great Basin between the Rockies and the Sierra Nevada; the Arctic people known as Inuits; Aboriginal Australians; the San people of the Kalahari Desert in Namibia (southern Africa); the Amazon basin; and societies of forest dwellers in Central Africa like the BaAka. The small stature of these Central African foragers led writers in the past to refer to them collectively as Pygmies. Because this label comes from outside the culture and has developed pejorative connotations, scholars today prefer to call them by the names they give themselves: BaAka, BaBenzele, BaMbuti, and so forth.

TECHNOLOGY

In nearly all cases the music of forager societies is primarily vocal. They rarely have dedicated or permanently constructed musical instruments. Rather, they transform hunting and cooking tools or objects found in the environment into musical instruments. They do not mind discarding these found instruments and rebuilding them when they need them.

It is possible to imagine, but not prove, that some of the principles behind their music making today are among the oldest on earth. Probably the specific melodies and musical elements heard today in their music are not the same as they were thousands of years ago. And yet some elements of their music may be thousands of years old, including the emphasis on vocal rather than instrumental music and their performance of both solo and polyphonic singing. Other Central African foragers use flutes made from small sections of bamboo and trumpets made from hollow logs, and it is probable that they discovered long ago the music-making capacity of these objects from their environment. Foragers, including the BaAka, turn hunting bows into musical instruments by placing the string in their mouths and resonating overtones of the vibrating bow string, which they pluck. Making a link between present-day and millennia-old musical elements depends on the hypothesis that musical elements are always embedded in social, cultural, political, and economic structures, some of which, like hunting and gathering, have been with us for millennia. So perhaps some elements of foragers' music making today have their roots in millennia-old ways of making music.

EMOTIONAL
RESONANCE

The BaAka and other contemporary foragers do not live in the past, however. They live in the modern present and are connected to nearby local groups and Christian missionaries from far away. Possibly for as long as there have been village agriculturalists living near them, foragers may have been exchanging musical styles and musical instruments with them, as the BaAka now borrow drums from nearby agriculturalists for their *mabo* dance. The BaAka live part of the year in isolation in the forest and part of the year in or near a village of nearby cultivators, where they may cultivate a small garden for food. They like exchanging the meat they hunt for some of the products, like drums, the villagers can offer, but living in the stratified village society, where they are low in social status, can make the men anxious. They are happiest in the forest. Their performances of songs and dances can express the pleasure or anxiety they experience in these two different living spaces. They also have to deal with intrusions from the modern world, such as the poaching of elephants in the forest and challenges to their world-view from Christian missionaries. In response, they invent new genres of music and dance and learn new songs all the time to deal with new challenges in their lives. The *mabo* net-hunting songs became prominent when the diminishing number of elephants made spear hunting, and spear-hunting songs, less efficient than net hunting for small game. When ethnomusicologist Michelle Kisliuk returned to visit the BaAka a decade after her original research, they were singing another new song-and-dance style. BaAka music today is thoroughly modern, but we include it at the beginning of our music history because we believe it has some iconic links to very old ways of living and making music.

BaAka music could only enter into the global musical soundscape with the invention of sound recording technology and its use by anthropologists and ethnomusicologists. As a result, part of the history of the music of the BaAka and other Central African foragers has been its use by musicians from other cultures who have heard those recordings. In one striking example, the jazz keyboardist Herbie Hancock recorded his composition "Watermelon Man" in 1973 with references to a recording of forager music from a subgroup of the BaAka, the BaBenzele. Instead of yodeling, this recording documents a young woman alternating a low-pitched sung tone with a high-pitched tone produced by blowing over the edge of a hollow twig to create a flute. (A **flute** is an instrument type on which a sound wave in a vibrating column of air is ini-

> CULTURAL
LINKAGES

tiated by blowing over an edge, either on the end or the side, of a hollow tube.) "Watermelon Man" begins with one member of Hancock's band, the Headhunters, mimicking this sound on a beer bottle to produce a syncopated **ostinato** (short, repeating) pattern. Eventually a second beer bottle-and-voice part enters after which a bass and jazz drum set enter, increasing the number of parts in a polyphonic texture, which in this case is similar to African ways of making music. Herbie Hancock's "Watermelon Man" was created during the civil rights movement of the 1960s and 1970s. Because slavery had denied African Americans the ability to trace their genealogy further back in history than the slave markets of the New World, many of them, then and now, asserted their African roots through the creation of artistic and cultural forms that recover those origins. Herbie Hancock's imitation of this BaBenzele recording was one of many such creative acts, in his case linking jazz to its African roots.

FIGURE 1.4
Djembe **drums for sale in Ghana**
Source: ZSM, Wikimedia Commons.

WHERE DO I GO FROM HERE?

• Find the recording of the BaBenzele young woman playing her voice-and-flute music and compare it to Herbie Hancock and the Headhunters' 1973 recording of "Watermelon Man." (There is an earlier 1962 recording of "Watermelon Man" that does not include the reference to BaBenzele music making.)

• Find and listen to other recordings of the BaAka and other Central African foragers such as the BaBenzele and the BaMbuti.

• Find and read all or part of the book on which this gateway is based: *Seize the Dance! BaAka Musical Life and the Ethnography of Performance* (New York: Oxford University Press, 1998/2001) by Michelle Kisliuk.

GATEWAY 2
MUSIC OF NOMADIC PASTORALISTS

What Is It?

Nomadic pastoralists move large herds of domesticated horses, cows, sheep, and other animals across vast plains in search of food and water. Our gateway to the music of nomadic pastoralists is a performance titled "Borbangnadyr with Stream Water" by Tuvan throat-singer Anatoli Kuular. Tuva is a republic in south-central Russia on the northern border of Mongolia. Tuvans speak a Turkic language and herd goats, sheep, yaks, and reindeer across the southern steppes (grasslands) of Siberia, part of a large area known as Inner Asia. Tuvan **throat-singing** involves a single singer producing a drone pitch and, at the same time, using their mouths to amplify the set of overtones in the drone that results in high-pitched melodies. *Borbangnadyr*, one of many genres of Tuvan throat-singing, is associated with the sound of water. Anatoli Kuular sang along the banks of a river for the recording.

 Listen to the first fifteen seconds of the recording.

FIGURE 1.5
**Map showing the
Tuvan region in
Russia**

How Does It Work?

Timbre

One male singer produces a wide variety of vocal timbres from low-pitched raspy sounds to high pitches that are clear and flute-like. He sings in duet with the variety of timbres of a shallow river.

Texture

The singer sings both monophonically and polyphonically by producing a vocal drone with overtones. He varies the pitch of the overtones to produce a melody. He is able to do this because the drone tone, like every tone, consists of a fundamental pitch and a set of overtones. He and other Tuvan throat-singers have found a way to amplify those overtones by shifting the position of their tongues, raising and lowering their soft palates, moving their lips, and singing different vowel sounds. The changing vowels are clearly audible in this recording.

Rhythm

The rhythm lacks a clear beat or meter.

Melody

The melody uses just two pitches in the beginning until the drone begins and five different overtone pitches are heard with the drone. If the fundamental pitch is C, then the overtone series looks approximately like that shown in Figure 1.6.

FIGURE 1.6
The overtone series. Solid notes are approximations, as these overtones sound noticeably higher or lower than the pitches indicated.

The singer produces his melody by amplifying overtones in the overtone series.

Harmony

The simultaneous sounding of the drone and overtone melody does not constitute harmony in a systematic way. Rather the harmony Tuvans hear is a timbral harmony consisting of a changing "spray" of overtones. In other words, they engage in "timbral listening" rather than harmonic listening.

Form

The singer sings four sections suggesting the form of a strophic song with nonverbal refrains.

Performance Techniques

Although the timbre of the melody may suggest whistling, the singer is not whistling. Rather this performance features throat-singing or **overtone singing**: two sounds from one voice, one produced by the vocal cords and the other by resonating the overtones of the throat-produced drone tone in such a way as to create simultaneous high-pitched sounds.

FIGURE 1.7
Anatoli Kuular on the bank of the "Singing River"
Source: Theodore Levin.

Listen to this performance with these elements in mind, following this timed listening guide.

LISTENING GUIDE 1.2

TIME	SECTION	DESCRIPTION
0:00	Prelude	The sound of running river water.
0:09	A (first phrase)	The singer sings words on one pitch.
0:19	second phrase	The singer imitates the gurgling sound of rushing water.
0:32	third phrase	The singer sings words on one pitch and then imitates the sound of gurgling water.
0:43	fourth phrase	The singer sings a drone underneath a changing high-pitched overtone melody.
1:05	A'	The singer sings a two-phrase variant of the first strophe.
1:47	A''	The singer sings another two-phrase variant.
2:26	A'''	The singer performs just one phrase, ending after the gurgling.
2:43	End	

What Does It Mean?

CULTURAL LINKAGES

This performance is part of a rich sound world connecting Tuvan pastoralists to the natural environment in which they live. That environment is filled with the sounds of animals, rivers, wind, and echoing caves and cliffs. Their sound culture is devoted to responding in at least five ways to those sounds. First, they employ a rich set of vocal and instrumental sounds to mimic animal calls to aid in the hunt, much as duck hunters do. Second, they make sounds to soothe their domesticated animals and encourage them to suckle their offspring. Third, they believe that animals, rivers, mountain cliffs, and certain locales have spirits, a belief system called animism, and they engage in throat-singing to honor and appease those spirits. Fourth, they throat-sing for fun and to entertain the spirits, as in this recording. Fifth, they sing songs about their experiences in the natural world.

Their throat-singing is a creative imitation, an icon but not a perfect copy, of the sounds they hear in that spot or that they hear a particular animal make. When they want to sing near a river, they seek out a place where the water babbles over rocks and makes a nice sound, perhaps with an echo off a nearby cliff, and where they can produce a lovely harmony with the river. They prefer such places to wide, slow-moving spots without an interesting sound or to rushing rapids that drown out their singing. They believe that the river has a voice and sings and that they are singing in duet with the sound of the river.

The genre of throat-singing called *borbangnadyr* means "rolling." The subtle inflections of the drone and the overtones roll and flow in ways similar to water rolling over river rocks. The Tuvans have other throat-singing genres with names and sounds that respond to the sound of a particular bird, of boots clacking in stirrups, and of places where steep mountain peaks rise out of the steppes. They distinguish genres based on the sound quality, for example between one that uses a drone lower than *borbangnadyr* and another that features higher-pitched harmonics than *borbangnadyr*. Some of these styles avoid manipulating the overtones to create melodic structures, as Anatoli Kuular does in this *borbangnadyr*. Rather, they luxuriate in the timbre of the overtones combined with the timbre of the drone, inviting the listener to listen timbrally to human sounds that are creative mirrors of the timbre of sounds they hear in the natural world.

Tuvans are not taught throat-singing by their elders; they learn it on their own. Some claim that they learned while riding a horse or that the river was their teacher. As a Tuvan singer said, "The river is alive. Rivers sing." While their throat-singing depends on the physical properties of sound waves, the Tuvans carefully select just a few pitches from all that is available to them in the overtone series, that is, in the natural world, to create their music culture. In other words, for Tuvans, and indeed all humans, music making is a fact of culture as much or more than it is a fact of nature.

EMOTIONAL RESONANCE

Tuvan throat-singers are able to imitate not just the general sound of a river, or a cave, or a mountain cliff. They can evoke with great specificity the sound of a particular place, distinguishing in the sound of their singing between high and low mountains, one cave and another, or one river and another. When others hear their singing, they are able to recognize these different locales because they have been there too, and they may weep or laugh or respond emotionally in some way to the singing depending on their associations with that place.

The Tuvans also have quite a variety of musical instruments, all of which are played to empha-size the overtones inherent in their sound. They include a hunting horn to attract wild animals, a two-stringed bowed fiddle that accompanies songs about life on the steppes, and an end-blown, rim-blown flute whose sound mediates between the human and spirit world, bringing healing, success in hunting, and advice from the spirits about what to do in human affairs.

> **TECHNOLOGY**

What Is Its History?

As with BaAka music, it is impossible to recover the ancient history of music that only existed in face-to-face aural tradition until the advent of sound recordings. We place this example near the beginning of our music history because nomadic pastoralism is one of the earliest forms of human subsistence and social organization. Nomadic pastoralism depends on the ability of humans to domesticate animals, that is, bring them under human control. Humans first domesti-cated dogs about 10,000 BCE and somewhat later wild sheep and goats, which added important and reliable sources of protein to hunters' diets. The domestication of the horse allowed herders to move large herds over vast distances, creating the possibility of nomadic pastoralism on the steppes of Inner Asia sometime around 3000 BCE. This region does not support agriculture, and so the pastoralists have it to themselves, moving from place to place with the seasons in search of better pastures. They listen for the sounds of insects and birds in their environment as signals of the changing seasons: crows indicate the coming of winter, cuckoos the end of spring, mat-ing calls of bull yaks the beginning of summer, and crickets the start of autumn. The largest and most famous group of nomadic pastoralists in Inner Asia are the Mongolians, who share many aspects of culture and music with their neighbors, the Tuvans, but who speak a different lan-guage. Although there is a long history of the movement of peoples across the steppes of Inner Asia that surely influenced some aspects of Tuvan music making today, it does not seem unrea-sonable to conclude that Tuvans for many millennia have engaged in musical interactions with natural and animal sounds similar in some respects to what ethnomusicologists have recorded in the last few decades.

> **ECONOMIC ACTIVITY**

The Tuvans began to live in cities only after the Russians built one in their territory just before World War I. As part of the Soviet Union in the second half of the twentieth century, professional folklore ensembles and schools were formed to train musicians in Tuvan traditional musical styles. It is possible that these schools and ensembles encouraged some of the extravagantly virtuosic throat-singing we hear today. With the fall of the Soviet Union in 1991, the metaphorical iron curtain between communist eastern Europe and the capitalist world disappeared, easing contact between musicians from that formerly closed-off part of the world and the rest of the world. Musicians in Rus-sia were free to form small folklore ensembles, and entre-preneurs from western Europe and the United States started organizing concert tours for them. On January 1, 1993, Tuvan musicians Anatoli Kuular, Kaigal-ool Xovalyg, and Kongar-ool Ondar were known well enough in the United States to ride in the Rose Parade in Pasadena, California.

> **CULTURAL LINKAGES**

Later in 1993 Kaigal-ool Xovalyg joined three other musi-cians in an ensemble called Huun-Huur-Tu and recorded their first album, a CD called *Sixty Horses in My Herd*. Huun-Huur-Tu literally means sunpropeller, or sunbeam, and refers to the spray of light sometimes seen through clouds at sun-rise and sunset. In giving their group this name, the Tuvans were making a metaphorical connection between their visual and aural experiences: a spray of light and a spray of over-tones, on the steppes of Inner Asia.

FIGURE 1.8

Left to right, Kaigal-ool Xovalyg, Anatoli Kuular, and Kongar-ool Ondar holding a long-necked plucked string instrument with a carving of a horse head on top of the neck

Source: Theodore Levin.

Huun-Huur-Tu and other Tuvan musicians in the 1990s became the darlings of the popular and classical music worlds, admired by and performing and recording with eclectic composer-performer Frank Zappa, traditional Irish band the Chieftains, Mickey Hart of the Grateful Dead, and the Kronos String Quartet. Among them Kongar-ool Ondar (1962–2013) became so well known that, like many pop stars, he was known by one name, Ondar. In 1999 he appeared in the Oscar-nominated documentary film *Genghis Blues* and on the TV show *Late Night with David Letterman*, who promoted his CD *Back Tuva Future*, which includes a duet with country singer Willie Nelson. More recently, the Tuvan throat-singing band Alash has continued Ondar's cross-genre approach by collaborating with musicians from jazz and bluegrass styles, and even with a beatboxer. Some might criticize Alash, Ondar, and other Tuvan musicians for selling out to commercialism and debasing the supposed purity of an ancient tradition. Although they certainly make money from their performances and recordings, they, like so many traditionally trained artists today, have sought to find a meaningful connection between musical styles that are icons and indexes of very old ways of making music and the life experiences of cosmopolitan listeners in Tuva and around the world.

WHERE DO I GO FROM HERE?

- This gateway is based on a book by ethnomusicologist Theodore Levin, together with Tuvan researcher Valentina Süzükei, called *Where Rivers and Mountains Sing: Sound, Music, and Nomadism in Tuva and Beyond* (Bloomington: Indiana University Press, 2006). Read chapter 2, "The World Is Alive with the Music of Sound," and listen to the CD/DVD that comes with the book.

- Find and listen to recordings and videos of Huun-Huur-Tu, Kongar-ool Ondar, and other Tuvan throat-singers, both with and without collaborators from other musical styles. In what ways do the musical and other elements of their performances change when they collaborate? In what ways do they remain the same?

GATEWAY 3
MUSIC OF HORTICULTURAL SOCIETIES

What Is It?

Horticultural societies grow root crops and plants in gardens carved out of forests with fire and tools. They live in small settlements for significant periods of time, but they may move when the soil's nutrients are exhausted. Our gateway to the music of horticultural societies is a recording made by the ethnomusicologist Hugo Zemp in the 1970s of a panpipe ensemble of the 'Are'are people from the island of Malaita in the Solomon Islands off the northeast coast of Australia. The Solomon Islands, where about 10,000 'Are'are (the primes indicate glottal stops) live in small villages in the interior mountains and near the coast, gained their independence from Britain in 1978. One of the islands, Guadalcanal, was the site of a famous World War II battle between the United States and Japan. A **panpipe** is a type of flute that consists of a set of tubes of unequal length, each of which plays one pitch. The panpipes in this 'Are'are ensemble are organized in a straight line, side by side in a wing formation, from low-pitched to high-pitched. The players blow across the top edge of each pipe to produce the sound. This ensemble, called *'au tahana*, consists of four panpipes, two small ones playing high pitches and two large ones playing an octave lower. The piece is titled "Pisi Ni Tootora." *Pisi* is the name of a sacred bush used to attract an abundance of people, food, and shell money. When this piece is played for a ritual feast, the musicians hope it will have this effect.

 Listen to the first thirty seconds of the recording.

How Does It Work?

Timbre

These panpipes, open at one end and closed at the other, have a breathy flute sound.

Texture

"Pisi Ni Tootora" has a polyphonic texture consisting of two rhythmically independent melodic lines. Each line is played in octaves. An **octave** is the interval between two pitches whose frequency of vibration has a ratio of 2:1. Pitches an octave apart are perceived as higher and lower versions of the same pitch.

Solomon Islands, home of the 'Are'are people

FIGURE 1.9
Map of the Western Pacific (Solomon Islands, 'Are'are people)

Rhythm

The rhythms of each of the two parts are different from one another in a four-beat meter.

Melody

The polyphonic lines use a heptatonic scale. A **scale** is the set of pitches in a melody arranged from low to high. **Heptatonic scales** have seven pitches. The intervals (an **interval** is the distance between any two different pitches) between adjacent pitches of the scale in this recording are approximately equal.

Harmony

The contrapuntal lines create a variety of harmonic intervals.

FIGURE 1.10
Four 'Are'are men play panpipes in an *'au tahana* ensemble
Source: Hugo Zemp.

Form

The performance is in AA form. Each A section consists of three subsections: a b c.

Performance Techniques

The end of each subsection is marked by slowing down, called **ritardando** or simply **ritard**. Occasionally a player plays a harmonic second by blowing across two adjacent pipes simultaneously.

Listen to this performance with these elements in mind following this timed listening guide.

LISTENING GUIDE 1.3

TIME	FORM		DESCRIPTION
0:02	A	a	After a very soft chord, the panpipes play a series of chords with the pitches sounding simultaneously, a texture referred to as **block chords**.
0:09		b	The players split into two rhythmically independent parts, each part consisting of a four-beat melody of just three pitches repeated many times before a ritard and the playing of the chords in the a subsection.
0:39		c	The players continue, each part consisting of an eight-beat melody with more pitches than the b subsection. The melody is repeated several times before a ritard and the playing of the chords in the a subsection.
1:18	A	a	The A section is repeated almost exactly.
		b	
		c	
2:33	End		

What Does It Mean?

Unlike foragers, sedentary horticulturalists like the 'Are'are live in permanent houses and subsist on domesticated pigs, taro, and other crops. They do not need to hunt every day as the BaAka do when they live in their forest camps. As a result, the 'Are'are have the time to construct permanent musical instruments that serve only one function, making music, a luxury not available to foragers. The 'Are'are have a more hierarchical social system than the BaAka do. The political hierarchy of leaders known as "big men," who manage the economic life of the community, is mirrored by a hierarchy of music specialists. Among them is a man named 'Irisipau, one of the best musicians and a specialist in making panpipes and explaining the elements of 'Are'are music. The 'Are'are have developed an astonishing array of panpipes and panpipe ensembles, made from bamboo tubes, on which they play their polyphonic music. Bamboo (called *'au*) is a ubiquitous material in their environment, and they use it to make both their houses and their musical instruments, which they call by the generic name *'au*.

The 'Are'are play and sing in twenty different genres of music, including four types of panpipes ensembles, four kinds of solo flute music, and panpipe ensembles that are struck rather than blown. The *'au tahana* ensemble heard in this gateway plays in two-part polyphony. In the accompanying photo one part, called "to braid," is played by 'Irisipau with closed eyes. On his right Warahane plays the same part on a small panpipe an octave higher. The other part, called "head of music," is played by the two musicians at right, Kinipa'a and Ooreana. They always play the two polyphonic parts face-to-face. Another ensemble of six players plays in three-part polyphony an octave apart and another one of ten players plays in four-part polyphony over three octaves. Since the higher-pitched panpipes are easier to play than the large ones playing an octave lower, beginners play the higher-pitched panpipes and learn their part by standing next to a senior player, who plays the part on the larger panpipe an octave lower.

The 'Are'are have the most elaborate music theory yet discovered in a nonliterate culture. Ethnomusicologists used to believe that elaborate music theory existed only in the literate cultures of Europe, the Middle East, and Asia. The music of the 'Are'are disproves that assumption. Their ensemble panpipe music employs different kinds of polyphonic textures, and they have names for each one. 'Are'are melodies are based on a heptatonic (seven-pitch) scale. In that scale they have names for two sizes of intervals between adjacent pipes, just as European music theory names two different sizes of adjacent intervals on the piano: whole steps and half steps. A **half step** is the distance or interval between two adjacent keys on the piano. A **whole step** is the distance or interval between every other key on the piano. The sizes of the intervals between adjacent pipes in the music of the 'Are'are are not related to the whole steps and half steps on the piano. While literate cultures can use writing and musical notation to illustrate their understanding of musical scales and intervals, 'Irisipau turns the panpipes he constructs upside down, and there for all to see is the scale of 'Are'are panpipe music in the relative sizes of the tubes.

The 'Are'are panpipe ensembles play during death and funeral rituals and major feasts. Some ensembles, like those played at funerals, have a great deal of spiritual power. Other ensembles with lesser power are used to attract gifts of seashell money and a large audience, especially of young girls, and to ward off illness and death. Women occasionally play struck panpipes, not the blown ones, for entertainment. Men use solo panpipe playing as indexes of their presence in a village and as secret signs to a lover. The ensembles play compositions and, because of their spiritual power, they take great care to play them exactly correctly. They regard some of the compositions as especially beautiful, and these are able to generate the greatest emotional response, including sadness when they remind people of a deceased loved one and feelings of love toward someone they are flirting with. Some ensembles have vast numbers of pieces in the repertoire. Some titles refer abstractly to the content of the piece, some the origin of the piece, or what the piece expresses, such as the sound of birds, the sound of human speaking, and so on.

> **EMOTIONAL RESONANCE**

What Is Its History?

There are many such small-scale agricultural societies in the world today. In the Pacific, where the Solomon Islands are located, agriculture developed in Papua New Guinea around 7000 BCE. Pig raising may have been introduced around 500 BCE. The 'Are'are live in small villages, where they subsist on taro, yams, sweet potatoes, domesticated pigs, and fishing. In forested areas of the world, such as the Solomon Islands, the agricultural potential of the land is limited and can only support small-scale societies, some no larger than a few hundred people living in a single village. An early form of this agricultural practice, slash-and-burn horticulture (gardening), involves clearing, with fire, spaces in dense forests where edible root crops can be planted. This type of farming provided a family or a community's subsistence, but did not allow the accumulation of much wealth. Villages are interwoven into larger social groups united by trade, and the hierarchical social structure of so-called 'Are'are big men developed to manage these relationships. Among horticultural societies, the 'Are'are of the Solomon Islands stand out for the complexity of their musical culture. We cannot know when the 'Are'are invented these panpipes. They believe that their first flutes were made to imitate bird sounds, and they think that the 'au tahana ensemble is the oldest of their panpipe ensembles.

> **ECONOMIC ACTIVITY**

In recent years the 'Are'are have been exposed to Christian and international popular music. They and other Solomon Islanders have created their own popular music for "bamboo bands," some of blown panpipes and some of struck panpipes. Some of these bands have toured internationally. In turn, their music has entered global culture through the media of recorded sound and the internet. The recordings made by ethnomusicologists who travel to such isolated societies

> **CULTURAL LINKAGES**

have made it possible for cosmopolitan popular musicians to include these recordings in their mixes of contemporary dance music such as house, techno, and electronica. European and American music producers and their audiences often find music from parts of the world distant from them to be a meaningful and attractive addition to their own musical creativity and enjoyment. Very often the recordings fit into romantic notions of a lost natural world and ways of life untainted by industrialization and urbanization. Sometimes these producers treat the recordings they sample as if the people who made the recordings have no rights to their own deeply meaningful music traditions. Views on copyright and ownership of music and musical traditions can vary widely from community to community. In our interconnected world, usually those working in cosmopolitan centers of music production have been able to impose their views on those on the periphery, often in economically exploitative ways. The resulting ethical problems have cast a shadow over the otherwise celebratory or positive aspects of such borrowings.

WHERE DO I GO FROM HERE?

- This gateway is based on Hugo Zemp's ethnographic research, including academic articles, two books, and many LP and CD recordings and films. Watch a six-minute preview of a 141-minute documentary film of all twenty genres of 'Are'are music.

- Read about and listen to the music of another horticulturalist society. Two excellent examples are Steven Feld's study of the Kaluli people of Papua New Guinea, *Sound and Sentiment: Birds, Weeping, Poetics and Song in Kaluli Expression*, 3rd ed., (Philadelphia: University of Pennsylvania Press, 2012) and Anthony Seeger's study of the Suyá Indians of the Amazonian basin, *Why Suyá Sing: A Musical Anthropology of an Amazonian People* (Urbana-Champaign: University of Illinois Press, 2004).

- Listen to and read about the panpipe tradition of Indians in the Andes Mountains of Peru. A modernizing tradition, it can be heard on the streets of virtually every major city in the world. Thomas Turino's *Moving Away from Silence: Music of the Peruvian Altiplano and the Experience of Urban Migration* (Chicago: University of Chicago Press, 1993) documents this tradition.

CLOSING

The three gateways in this chapter illustrate the close connection between music and the environment typical of many cultures, but especially of those where people live and work outdoors all the time. The BaAka match their polyphonic singing to the sounds of the forest in which they live. The 'Are'are make their panpipes from the vegetation in the forest around them and take the very idea of flute sounds from the sounds of birds. The Tuvans model an entire sound culture on the sounds of animals, rivers, and mountains.

All three cultures make music polyphonically but in different ways. The BaAka improvise variations that signal each person's uniqueness within a social setting. The 'Are'are play fixed compositions collectively in two-, three-, and four-part polyphony. Tuvans have found a way for single, isolated herders, alone with their flocks, to entertain themselves with their own polyphonic singing. All these cultures believe that music is a fundamentally important way to connect to the supernatural world. In one form or another these three basic principles—music in harmony with environmental sounds, polyphonic music making in social settings, and music as a pathway to the supernatural world—have deep roots in human music making and are important components of many music cultures of the world today.

THINGS TO THINK ABOUT

- Compare the ways that BaAka, 'Are'are, and Tuvans respond musically to their natural environments and their patterns of work.

- What are some of the ways that musicians living in urban environments today make music in response to the sound environments in which they live?

NEW TERMS

block chords	octave	scale
flute	ostinato	throat-singing
half step	overtone singing	vocables
heptatonic scale	panpipe	whole step
inherent polyphony	polymeter	yodel, yodeling
interval	ritardando, ritard	

ANCIENT AND MEDIEVAL RELIGIOUS MUSIC

2

THE ANCIENT PERIOD (also called Antiquity and the Classical period) covers nearly 4000 years, from about 3500 BCE to 500 CE, when the Roman Empire fell. The thousand-year period from about 500 CE to 1500 is called the Medieval period, from the Latin roots *medi* ("between" or "middle") and *eval* ("time" or "age"). Thus, another name for this period is the Middle Ages. It is a term developed in Europe to label the period between the end of the Ancient period of Greece and Rome and the modern period, when European ideas, economic power, and people spread around the world. For the purposes of this chapter, and the next, we treat the Ancient and Medieval periods as a single time period.

Around 3500 BCE, having domesticated plants and animals millennia earlier, communities living along the world's major rivers learned to smelt metal for tools and irrigate their crops. These inventions facilitated large-scale agriculture and the production of surpluses of grain, rice, and maize beyond the needs of day-to-day subsistence. An excess of foodstuffs supported greater population densities than ever before, including large cities. Through war, trading, and thievery, some individuals and families acquired and controlled vast areas of land, establishing themselves as rulers over large numbers of people. New specialized occupations arose to serve the needs of these large societies and their rulers. Master builders constructed huge temples and palaces. Craftsmen made tools and decorative objects from metal (bronze, iron, copper, and gold). Priests controlled religious life, their prayers assuring the welfare and success of the ruler. With the invention of writing, scribes recorded trades of goods and services and the proclamations and histories of their rulers. Traders invented money. Artists memorialized religious and courtly life. And professional musicians provided the rulers' entertainment and sang of their heroic deeds in epic ballads.

The four oldest city cultures, called **civilizations**, depended on the fertility of river valleys: the Nile River in Egypt; the Tigris and Euphrates River basin in present-day Iraq, an area known as Mesopotamia ("between the rivers" in Greek); the Indus River basin in South Asia where present-day India, Pakistan, and Afghanistan meet; and the Yellow and Yangtze River basins in China (see the map of ancient civilizations in Chapter 1). In addition to these four riverine cultures, the Greeks developed an urban culture supported by trading along the shores of the Mediterranean Sea. These societies were at the forefront of the technological, cultural, and social advances that, millennia later, spawned the modern societies we know today.

In addition to agriculture, the Ancient and Medieval period witnessed three other important developments: (1) the invention of writing; (2) the spread of five religions (Hinduism, Buddhism, Judaism, Christianity, and Islam) to many

FIGURE 2.1

Entrance to the temple at Luxor along the banks of the Nile River, built around 1400 BCE

Source: MusikAnimal, Wikimedia Commons.

DOI: 10.4324/9781003269304-4

corners of the world; and (3) the formation of the first large empires. The three principal musical legacies of these ancient empires and religions were (1) the invention of stringed instruments still played today; (2) the development of written theories about the nature of music; and (3) religious rituals with chanting. **Chant** and **chanting** are terms used to refer to religious melodies and singing. This chapter contains gateways to three Ancient and Medieval religious traditions: Buddhism, Christianity, and Islam.

GATEWAY 4
BUDDHIST MUSIC

What Is It?

Siddhartha Gautama, the founder of Buddhism and known as "the Buddha," lived in India from *c.* 563 to 483 BCE. Buddhism today flourishes mainly in Tibet and East and Southeast Asia with an estimated 500 million adherents. Our gateway to Buddhist music is a recording of a short excerpt of ritual practice by eight Tibetan Buddhist monks from Drepung, which was once the largest Buddhist monastic university in Tibet. To convey the underlying meaning of this portion of ritual practice, the recording is titled "Invoking the Spirit of Kindness through Sound." Opening and closing instrumental sections bracket a middle section with chanting. It is one of thousands of chants performed during daily rituals and ceremonial occasions at this institution of higher learning.

The recording is the opening section of a much longer ritual. The instrumental ensemble performs an offering of sound, an invocation of a Buddha deity to come to the site of the ritual. Simultaneously, practitioners and ritual music performers visualize the universe resounding with pleasant sound offerings vastly more extensive that what is audibly experienced. Other offerings, described in the written and chanted liturgical texts, accompany the sound offerings: water to wash the body with, water

FIGURE 2.2
Map of Tibet, today part of China

to drink, incense to please the olfactory sense, and deli-
cious foods and other offerings to please the senses of
smell and taste.

 Listen to the first fifteen seconds or so.

How Does It Work?

Timbre

The instrumental ensemble consists of four pairs
of instruments: two very long horns that rest on
the ground or are carried by assistants, two double-reed wind instruments, two cymbals, and
two double-headed frame drums. We also hear
a male **chorus** (a group of singers) of specialist
ritual performers who are expert instrumentalists
and trained vocalists. The vocalists create tones
extraordinarily rich in overtones, an aural sheet of
rippling sound.

Texture

The instrumental texture consists of a very low-pitched
drone played on the two long horns, a few middle and
high pitches played by the double-reed aerophones, a
nearly continuous shimmering sound on the cymbals,
and a rhythmic pattern on the drums. (**Aerophones**
are instruments whose sound is produced by a vibrating column of air. In this case the vibration in the column of air is started by a **double reed**, two thin reeds
striking one another.) The vocal texture consists of a
very low-pitched drone sound with a few high-pitched
overtones.

Rhythm

The rhythm varies from nonmetrical to beats that
speed up and slow down. There is little sense of meter.

Melody

Discrete pitches are nearly absent in favor of sliding
from pitch to pitch.

FIGURE 2.3
**Tibetan Buddhist monastery in India near the border with
Tibet and Bhutan; it has links to the Drepung Monastic
University which was built in Lhasa, Tibet (est. 1416) and
re-established in South India during the 1960s**
Source: Vikramjit Kakati, Wikimedia Commons.

FIGURE 2.4
**Instrumental ensemble of Buddhist monks from another sect,
playing instruments similar to those in this recording**
Source: Getty Images.

Harmony

Many pitches sound simultaneously. Each set of two instruments is tuned to play slightly different pitches to create a highly valued resonant beating or oscillation between them.

Form

The recording has an ABA' form, where A refers to the instrumental sections and B to
the vocal chant. Each of these sections features very small changes in pitch, timbre, and
loudness.

Performance Techniques

The ability of the singers to create sounding overtones from a fundamental requires extensive
training.

Listen to the entire recording with these elements in mind, following the timed listening guide.

LISTENING GUIDE 2.1

TIME	SECTION	DESCRIPTION
0:00	A (Instrumental ensemble)	A pair of long horns play a very low pitch with slight variations in pitch, loudness, and timbre.
0:38		Cymbals enter with shimmering sounds.
1:10		The cymbals begin playing beats that speed up until they become a continuous shimmering sound.
1:20		Drums enter and the ensemble begins to play a very slow beat.
1:40		A pair of double-reed aerophones enter playing distinct pitches but with a lot of ornamental variation that colors the sound. The beats get faster and then slower, diminishing to just the cymbals and then silence.
3:02	B (Vocal chant)	The monks begin singing a very low pitch with variations in timbre from a relatively pure tone to one rich in overtones that sounds a bit like a growl. The monks produce a pitch high in their range, an overtone of the fundamental tone they are singing. **Range** refers to the span of possible pitches on a given instrument or voice. It also refers to the distance between the highest and lowest pitches in a section or piece of music. The pitches and the vowel change slightly, and phrases end when the singers take a breath from time to time. There is a marked descent in pitch at the end of the singing.
6:04	A' (Instrumental ensemble)	All the instruments of the ensemble enter nearly at the same time. The beats they play speed up throughout this section and the pitch rises.
6:44		The beats nearly disappear and then enter slowly, becoming slower and softer until the music dies out.
7:20	End	

AESTHETICS

What Does It Mean?

This recording challenges many basic understandings of the way music works. This music appears to be extraordinarily slow moving with little in the way of a beat or a melody, two fundamental elements in the way many people typically understand music. The basic pitch is extraordinarily low, one almost impossible for most men to sing. That suggests that these monks have had extensive training to learn to produce these low-pitched sounds. The sounds of cymbals and drums are familiar, but the low-pitched trumpet and double-reed sound may be rather unfamiliar. Knowing that this is religious music is an important part of understanding it. The sound, as part of a religious ritual, has deep spiritual significance. It is also intended for entertainment and pleasure.

Initial understandings of this tradition are, of course, based on previous musical experience. Tibetan Buddhists trained in monastic universities likely have a completely different understanding of the music than most students studying in a North American university. For example, they would know that the apparently slow tempo of this chant is part of a huge corpus of chants with many different styles, including some that are quite fast with singable melodies. Some instrumental music has a strong, rapid beat and accompanies masked ritual dancing in sections that contrast with slow, graceful, and subtle movements of arms, hands, legs, and feet. And these trained experts would be able to read thousands of volumes of notated chant melodies using a line-based graphic notation that conveys the subtle and meaningful nuances of melodic movements. Explaining and understanding Tibetan music at something like this level of detail requires many years of study.

Early Buddhists worried that instrumental music, singing, and dancing could create the very earthly desires they sought to eliminate through study and meditation. However, the Buddha sanctioned chanting as a desirable and pleasurable middle ground between the dry asceticism of merely reciting his teachings and the distracting pleasures of secular music. The chanting and instrumental music in this example are considered a "sensually pleasing offering" to the

Buddha and to other deities, for the monks and nuns who recite them, and for the lay people who hear them. Thus, the music in this recording is in fact a serious and demanding practice developed, through years of training, into music even more beautiful and entertaining than any secular music. "This music," one Tibetan monk said, "is more beneficial than a hundred years of meditation."

Buddhism consists of a highly varied set of principles and practices based on the teachings of Siddhartha Gautama, who was born and raised about 2500 years ago in the foothills of the Himalayas near the border between present-day India and Nepal. He grew up in a religious culture based on the idea of reincarnation, endless cycles of life that could only end with enlightenment or *nirvana*, a state of release from the troubles of the world and the cycles of life. Gautama achieved this state at the age of thirty-five and spent the rest of his life, until he died at age eighty, as an itinerant beggar, teaching the wisdom he had gained as Buddha, the Enlightened One. His teachings in the form of sermons called *sutras* were preserved by his disciples, who chanted them communally until they were

FIGURE 2.5
Tibetan statue of the Buddha
Source: Daderot, Wikimedia Commons.

CULTURAL
LINKAGES

written down as scripture in the first century BCE. To this day, monks preserve the Buddha's teaching and learn his path to wisdom and enlightenment, called *Dharma* ("Law" or "the teaching of Buddha"), by chanting his *sutras*. In Tibetan Buddhism, the chanting of later texts called *tantras* and *mantras*, magical formulas representing deities, is also important. With the goal of achieving wisdom and ultimately *nirvana*, some monks spend as much as twenty to thirty years memorizing all these texts, which contain an encyclopedic body of knowledge.

When the Buddha was enlightened, he achieved vast knowledge and understanding, which included the ability to see all his previous lives in cycles going back billions of years; a clairvoyant power to see the death and rebirth of all living beings "according to their good and bad deeds"; and the capacity to eliminate or transcend all his human cravings and desires. In the wake of his Enlightenment, his teachings focused on Four Noble Truths: (1) the diagnosis that life is suffering; (2) the explanation that suffering is caused by craving; (3) the insight that suffering can end; and (4) treatment as a path leading to the end of suffering. Thus, as one scholar put it, "the ultimate goal of Buddhism is to put an end to suffering and rebirth . . . by fulfilling the human potential for goodness and happiness."

The surest path to Enlightenment is through a lifetime of monastic devotion to the study of, and meditation on, the teachings of the Buddha. In Tibetan Buddhism, study and meditation are brought together in the chanting of a vast repertoire consisting of the *sutras* of Buddha, *tantras*, and *mantras* and in the playing of instrumental music. Through meditation and extensive philosophical study under the guidance of qualified teachers, monks explore their bodily experiences and mental life (feelings, moods, perceptions) with the help of *mudra*, *mantra*, and *mandala*, ritual practices representing the Body, Speech, and Mind of the Buddhas (awakened ones) and the other practitioners. *Mudra* is bodily gesture, stance, hand gestures, and imagery representing it. *Mantra* can be anything from repetition of a short formula to a lengthy descriptive liturgy or recitation of a *sutra*. The descriptive liturgy is connected to visualization practices that generate mental changes through meditation. The descriptions are materialized in *mandala*, which can be either individual deity images or an array of them in circular or tree-shaped or three-dimensional images. The richness of visual and aural practices and sacred dances in Tibetan music may be the result of a fusion of Buddhism from India with local animist practices called Bon, which recall in some ways Inner Asian nomadic pastoralists' beliefs in spirits.

Ritual performances of chants and instrumental music take up an enormous amount of time in monastery life. The largest Tibetan monasteries may have as many as 10,000 residents, with 2000 of them being music specialists. They recite some texts, chant others in a melodic style, and perform still others in the long, drawn-out manner emphasizing subtle pitch and timbral changes heard in this recording. Many Tibetans are semi-nomadic pastoralists with herds of yak, sheep, goats, horses, cows. The earliest descriptions of these sounds suggest a link to animal sounds of the sort imitated by Tuvan pastoralists. The Buddha was said to be able to imitate the voices of birds and wild animals, and the Bon religion acknowledged "nine vocal modulations," including "the dog's voice, barking and growling, . . . the beautiful-voiced parrot, . . . [and] the fluctuating voice of the lark." Monks learn to meditate on the sounds actually heard in their chanting and instrumental music and those that exist only in the imagination. They distinguish between four types of vocal production: a throat voice, a mouth voice, a nose voice, and in this recording a "body-cavity voice." Produced by tensing muscles in the throat and diaphragm and applying great breath pressure, it is considered the most beautiful and ritually significant of all the voices. They distinguish two styles of "tone-color chants": the "voice of the hybrid yak-bull" and the "roaring voice of the [slayer of the] Lord of Death." These are considered particularly fierce chants.

The monks also learn to play musical instruments, which in addition to the ones heard in this recording, famously include trumpets made of conch shells and human thigh bones and small drums made from human skulls. The instrumental music iconically represents a combination of the melodic style of chant, which is played on the double-reed instruments, and the tone-color, deep-toned chant of the body-cavity voice, which is played on the long trumpets. Even absent the words of the chant, they form an aural field that aids meditation and pleases the perfect hearing of the Buddha and other deities and those monks initiated into the beauty of this style of musical performance. They recognize the music as sounding fierce, the sort of sound necessary to destroy the evil forces arrayed around them.

What Is Its History?

Buddhism adopted ideas of the cycle of rebirths and the law of causation through deeds (*karma*) prevalent in ancient India. Between 100 BCE and 100 CE, a schism developed between adherents of older forms of Buddhist teaching, now known as Theravada Buddhism, and a newer form, Mahayana (Great Vehicle) Buddhism, which teaches that some beings on their way to Enlightenment, called *bodhisattvas*, can transcend their own personal concern for Enlightenment to help others achieve it. In India such teachers are known as *gurus*; in Tibet they are called *lamas*.

Theravada Buddhism is the type found today in Southeast Asia (Burma, Thailand, and the Indonesian island of Bali). It spread south throughout India until it reached Sri Lanka in about 250 BCE. There, in about 80 BCE, the Buddha's *sutras* were written down for the first time. From the fifth to the fifteenth century CE, Theravada Buddhism spread to Burma and Thailand, where it coexisted for a time with Hinduism, which today is the principal religion of the Indonesian island of Bali. Mahayana Buddhism spread north into Inner Asia and to China during the Han dynasty (206 BCE to 220 CE). It arrived in Japan from Korea in the sixth century and entered Tibet between 700 and 900 CE. Wherever Buddhism took root in Asia, it had a slightly different character and different ideas about how to combine the study of scripture with meditation to traverse the path to Enlightenment.

Although we introduce Buddhism at this point in our music history because of its beginnings in the life of Buddha, Buddhism and Buddhist music in Tibet and elsewhere have their own histories of development since then. Buddhism was introduced to Tibet in the seventh century. After the fall of the Tibetan Empire in the ninth century, new sects arose in the eleventh and fourteenth centuries. The drawn out "body-cavity" chant style in this recording has been traced to the eighth century. The cymbals and drums are the oldest of the instruments in the ensemble. The long horns were introduced in the eleventh century, written musical notation in the thirteenth century, and the double-reed instruments in the fifteenth or sixteenth century. Monasteries became an important institution in the sixteenth century, in some ways rivaling and threatening secular governmental structures.

The political ruler of Tibet was, with a few exceptions, the leader of the Gelugpa sect of Tibetan Buddhism, a Dalai Lama ("Ocean of Wisdom") believed to be a reincarnation of the *bodhisattva* of compassion. From 1642 to 1912 Tibet was a protectorate of the Qing emperors of the last imperial dynasty of China. After the fall of the Qing Empire in 1912, Tibet maintained its independence until 1951, when a military invasion forced it to incorporate into the newly created People's Republic of China. The Chinese communist government, officially atheistic, took a malign view of this religion. The 1950s until the later 1970s saw the destruction of temples, monasteries, and sacred art. The Fourteenth Dalai Lama (b. 1936) decided to leave Tibet for his own safety in 1959. Since then, Tibetan Buddhist monasteries have been reestablished in neighboring Nepal, India, Sikkim, and Bhutan. Monks have also established learning centers in many countries around the world. In Tibet in the late 1980s many monasteries and temples were rebuilt atop old ruins. In recent years there has been official but measured tolerance of Buddhism in some regions, but repression continues in many ways.

Recordings of Tibetan Buddhist music were part of the "world music" scene in the 1960s and found a following among musicians who championed their music and sponsored concert tours. One of them, Mickey Hart, drummer for the Grateful Dead, said of these monks' chanting, "They will rattle your bones."

WHERE DO I GO FROM HERE?

- Watch some videos of Tibetan Buddhist rituals and ritual dancing.
- Read about and view Tibetan Buddhist art and architecture on the internet, in online galleries, or books you find in the library.
- Listen to Japanese *shomyo* Buddhist chant. It is different from Tibetan Buddhist chant but shares a similar element, namely, sliding between pitches.

GATEWAY 5
CHRISTIAN CHANT

What Is It?

From its origins in the territory of present-day Israel, Christianity spread rapidly throughout the Middle East, North Africa, and Europe. Different styles of liturgical chanting developed in each part of the early Christian world. In the western part of Europe governed by the Roman Catholic church, written notations of chant with pitches began to appear during the eleventh century. Most of the notated chants preserved from this period were transmitted in oral tradition. But some were composed by individuals. Our gateway to Christian chant is a composition in the Roman Catholic tradition from the twelfth century called "Quia ergo femina" (Since therefore a woman) by Hildegard von Bingen (1098–1179). A nun and founder of a convent near the small town of Bingen on the Rhine River in Germany, she wrote the music and text, which praises the Virgin Mary as the greatest example of the female form or idea since God made Man. In "Quia ergo femina," Mary is depicted as greater than Eve, who could not conquer death, as the Virgin did, through her son. Although the piece was composed for nuns to sing during religious services, this modern performance, by a small ensemble of women singers called the Mediatrix Ensemble, is intended for secular concerts.

Listen to the first thirty seconds of the recording.

How Does It Work?

Timbre

Women's voices sing with a relatively clear, pure, relaxed tone quality.

Texture

The texture is monophonic, sung in unison by a choir. A **choir** is a chorus of singers supported by a church, school, or other institution often with a leader or conductor.

Rhythm

The rhythm is nonmetrical and relatively free, with some mix of short and long tones.

Melody

The melody moves mainly in **stepwise motion** or **conjunct motion**. These phrases are used to describe melodies that mainly move through adjacent pitches of a scale. The melody occasionally employs **leapwise motion** or **disjunct motion**, that is, leaps from one pitch to nonadjacent pitches in the scale. The melody employs a seven-tone, heptatonic scale.

Harmony

Since the texture is monophonic, there is no harmony in this example.

FIGURE 2.6
Hildegard von Bingen receives divine inspiration and passes it on to her scribe
Source: Rupertsburger Codex, Wikimedia Commons.

Form

The form consists of a series of melodic phrases, each with new musical material (a b c d, and so on). However, the stepwise motion using a scale of seven pitches creates a sense of unity. Against that unity, each melodic phrase has a unique character, some rising, some falling, some arc-shaped, some undulating, some with a few leaps, some with mainly stepwise motion. The form is also shaped by the way the music is matched to the text. Some syllables are set on just one or two pitches (called **syllabic singing**); other syllables have many pitches (called **melismatic singing**). A **melisma** is a single syllable set to many pitches.

Performance Techniques

The singers perform straight tones without **vibrato** (a pulsating slight raising and lowering of the pitch of a tone), ornamentation, or changes in dynamics.

Listen to the first thirty seconds of the recording and pay attention to the unison monophonic texture and the stepwise melodic motion.

Listen to the entire recording following this timed listening guide.

What Does It Mean?

AESTHETICS

The calm, relaxed sound of monophonic Christian chanting echoing through a large church or cathedral creates a sonic icon of otherworldliness. For believers, it suggests that the chanting of the monks or nuns is resonating in heaven and that God is listening to the praises in the sacred Latin texts, many of them taken from the Bible. Its pure vocal quality, moderate tempo, nearly

TIME	LATIN	ENGLISH	DESCRIPTION
0:00	*Quia ergo femina*	Because therefore a woman [Eve]	The melody ascends with two leaps.
0:10	*mortem instruxit,*	battled death,	The melody descends mainly stepwise, but with some leaps.
0:24	*clara virgo illam interemit,*	a bright virgin defeated it.	The melody descends before leaping through two large intervals to a pitch an octave above where it started.
0:45	*et ideo est summa benedictio*	And so the greatest blessing	The melody undulates in stepwise motion.
0:57	*in feminea forma,*	in the female form,	The melody descends in stepwise motion and then continues with an undulating motion.
1:10	*pre omni creatura,*	before every creature	The melody stays in a narrow range.
1:18	*quia Deus factus est homo*	since God made man,	The melody rises and falls in stepwise motion through an octave range.
1:31	*in dulcissima et beata virgine*	is the sweet and blessed Virgin.	The melody moves in stepwise motion through a narrow range.
1:52	End		

equal-length tones, and relatively smooth, stepwise motion lend dignity to the ceremonial events of the **liturgies** (the ritual rules and practices for sacred services) of the Roman Catholic Church. The sound of chanting is as important as the meaning of the text for the spiritual efficacy of the liturgy.

Hildegard's musical compositions were intended for the two main types of services developed in the Church governed from Rome. One was for the Mass, the celebration of Christ's Last Supper with his disciples before his death and resurrection. Performed for lay people in church and by monks and nuns in monasteries and convents, the Mass liturgy includes a prescribed succession of chants, prayers, sermons or homilies, and lessons (readings from the Bible). The chants, like ceremonial processions, the priests' elaborate vestments, the smell of incense, the chiming of bells, and the opulence of church architecture, were designed to amplify the meaning and emotional impact of the prayers and lessons on those in attendance. The chants for the Mass are of two types: the **Proper of the Mass**, those for a particular day in the church calendar; and the **Ordinary of the Mass**, those sung during every Mass.

The second type of liturgy was developed for the ceremonial life of monasteries and convents, where monks and nuns spend many hours each day, from before dawn into the night, in a set of eight prayer services called Divine Offices (Duties) or "hours." Hildegard's "Quia ergo femina" is for these services, whose texts were based on the Old Testament book of Psalms. During one week of offices the monks and nuns perform all 150 **psalms** (biblical poems in praise of God). The Old Testament psalms were introduced by newly composed chanted texts, called **antiphons**. Antiphons in general, and Hildegard's antiphon "Quia ergo femina" in particular, were more musically elaborate than the psalms, each line of which was often recited mainly on a single tone with a short opening and closing melodic gesture. Some antiphons asked for God's mercy and help with such practical matters as the weather and the fertility of animals and crops. Others related the message of the Old Testament psalm to ideas in the New Testament, especially veneration of Jesus and the Virgin Mary. Hildegard's "Quia ergo femina" is just such a composition, linking New Testament Mary to Old Testament Eve.

Hildegard's artistry and her expression of emotion and meaning are carried in the variety of melodic motions she creates and her use of melismas on certain syllables of the text. Her use of melodic leaps, especially an upward leap on the first syllable of *virgo* (Virgin) is, in this context, an ecstatic expression of joy and admiration. In each line, one syllable of an important word is singled out for expressive treatment with a long melisma: *femina* (woman); *mortem* (death); *virgo* (Virgin);

two syllables of *feminea* (female) in the line "*in feminea forma*"; *Deus* (God); and, in the last line, all three syllables of *virgine* (Virgin). Hildegard, using the monophonic texture of her time, creates music with deep emotional resonance from what may seem like the tiniest of melodic gestures. It is tempting to interpret the ascending melodies of the first and third phrases, which mention women and the Virgin, as musical representations of celebration and the descending melody of the second phrase, "battling death," as a musical icon of struggle against the inevitable. Such text painting was common in later centuries, and it seems to be a characteristic feature of Hildegard's musical style.

SOCIAL BEHAVIOR

Meaning in this example also comes from the simple fact that a woman composed it and women are singing it, in what was and remains a strongly patriarchal tradition. Hildegard herself disclaimed authorship of the text and music and believed that she was a mere conduit for divine creativity. The text juxtaposes and exalts the two most important women in Christianity, Eve and Mary, praising Mary in terms analogous to the way the Church praises Jesus. In the context of a religion that only allows male priests, Hildegard's person and compositions argue for the perfection of women as well as men.

CULTURAL LINKAGES

The tenth child of a noble, landowning family, Hildegard was given to a Benedictine monastery as a tithe at the age of eight. There she came under the influence of an anchoress, a woman who lived in contemplative isolation in a cell in the monastery and who taught her the biblical psalms. At fifteen she became a nun, and soon her and her mentor's teaching attracted a growing number of women to the monastery. At thirty-eight, after the death of her teacher, she was elected the head of the assembled nuns. At the age of forty-two, she experienced her first mystical vision, in which

> the heavens were opened to me and a blinding light of exceptional brilliance flowed through my entire brain. And so it kindled my whole heart and breast like a flame, not burning but warming. . . . Suddenly I understood the expositions of the books . . . of the Old and New Testaments.

Although she also received a command from God to write down her vision, she was at first reluctant, due to "a low opinion (of myself)." Eventually, she began to write them down with the aid of a male secretary. When the pope read them, he interpreted them as authentic "secrets of God" and commanded her to transcribe what she, and he, believed to be the word of God. They both considered her to be, like Jesus and some other biblical figures, a prophet.

As her fame grew, the number of nuns at the monastery increased until, at fifty-two, she took them, over the objections of the abbot, to a spot on the Rhine River near the town of Bingen, where she founded a convent. At sixty-seven she founded a second convent across the river from the first. She composed much of her religious poetry and music for services at those nunneries. She also wrote extensive volumes on a wide range of matters including natural history, medicine, theology, and music. She was one of the most prolific writers and composers of the period, at a time when most women were not literate. In a patriarchal church, her success as a writer was possible because her knowledge and insights were "divine secrets," not her own insights. For this reason, she refused the sort of agency and authorship that men claimed for their writing. She preached publicly in several cities, where she helped with exorcisms and cured the blind using water from the Rhine. After her death, she was proposed for sainthood, which the Church refused. She was beatified instead. Although she was called St. Hildegard for centuries, she was canonized as a saint only in 2012, when Pope Benedict XVI declared her a Doctor of the Church for her contributions to theology and doctrine and added her name to the list of the original Four Doctors: St. Augustine, St. Benedict, St. Ambrose, and St. Gregory.

What Is Its History?

Christian chanting has roots in Jewish chanting. The Old Testament book of Psalms, the basic text of the Divine Offices, contains songs composed over many centuries after about 500 BCE. Some are attributed apocryphally to King David, who reigned around 1000 BCE and was a singer and poet (psalmist) and player of the lyre. (The **lyre** is a stringed instrument with a resonating body and a frame holding five or six strings, which are plucked.) The Christian liturgy, including the chanting of psalms, may have been shaped by Jewish liturgy and chants, but making any precise link is difficult. This early Christian chant tradition is also historically important because some music terminology and musical notation were developed to serve it.

Christian liturgical practices developed slowly following Christ's crucifixion. They grew in complexity after Emperor Constantine adopted Christianity as the official religion of the Roman Empire in 324 CE. Sometime around 500 CE these liturgies began to take the shape they have today, aided by the foundation of monastic orders. St. Benedict (480–543) developed the first one in central Italy and wrote the first rules for monastic behavior around 530. Huge numbers of chants developed to serve the Divine Offices and Masses, which were performed daily as well as special ones on Sunday and important events in the Christian calendar such as Christmas, Easter, and saints' days. The chants were created and transmitted in oral tradition, and monks and priests had to learn and memorize hundreds of chants. Large churches supported schools where young boys were trained for a decade or more before they took up the priesthood or became monks. It helped that many chants were formulaic, that is, they were based on relatively short melodic passages sung over and over in many chants and, as a result, easily remembered. Still, some traditional chants were elaborate and unique and had to be memorized, as did new compositions such as Hildegard's antiphons.

Today we know this repertoire of music because it began to be notated in the ninth century at the court of the Emperor Charlemagne in northern Europe. After the fall of the Roman Empire in 476, Charlemagne's family of Germanic language-speaking people known as Franks established in 751 the first large-scale political entity in western Europe, known as the Holy Roman Empire. Charlemagne was an able administrator, directing reforms in virtually all domains of life from governmental, economic, and military matters to culture, literacy, and religion. Anxious to establish his empire as the legitimate successor to Rome and its Christian heritage, he supported monastic life, schools, and *scriptoria* (manuscript-copying rooms). Musical notations, copied in *scriptoria*, were a way to regulate and preserve the liturgical practices of his empire.

These early notations were graphic in form. They consisted of curved lines and dots called **neumes** that indicated how many syllables were sung to a pitch and hinted at the melodic shape of a melisma, a

FIGURE 2.7
Achilles playing a lyre, *c.* 480 BCE
Source: Marie-Lan Nguyen, Wikimedia Commons.

FIGURE 2.8
Map of the Holy Roman Empire around 1000
Source: Owen Blacker, Wikimedia Commons.

kind of graphic representation of the shape of the chant melody. Written above the text, neumes were used as an aid in learning and remembering the chants, but they failed to register the intervallic relationships between pitches, as modern notation does. During the ninth century these early musical notations helped to regularize and discipline the singing of monks and priests.

Hildegard's writings and compositions are a legacy of Charlemagne's support of Latin literacy and the Roman Church in a rebirth of learning after the fall of the Roman Empire. Eager to invest the religious practices of his dynasty with the prestige of Rome, his reforms of chant singing and their preservation in notation were given the name **Gregorian chant** in honor of Pope St. Gregory I, who had reigned two centuries earlier from 590 to 604. Enormously successful in theology and church politics, Pope Gregory was apocryphally credited with writing these chants. More likely, they were traditional chants with no known authors.

CULTURAL
LINKAGES

Medieval Christian theologians read Ancient Greek explanations of music's scalar structure and applied them to their repertoire of chants. The Greeks gave letters to pitches, used them as a musical notation, and constructed an elaborate classification of melodic scales called modes. **Modes** are seven-pitch, heptatonic scales with one pitch defined as the final or most important pitch. They named the scales after various Greek ethnic groups such as the Dorians, Ionians, and Phrygians and assigned ethical qualities to each mode based on stereotypes about the behavior of these groups. The philosopher Plato (c. 428–348 BCE) famously argued that some scales should be avoided because they caused the bad behaviors associated with particular ethnic groups, while other scales could be used fruitfully for the education of philosopher-kings.

Christian scholars adapted these Ancient Greek ideas about scales to a set of four scales to which they gave the Greek names Dorian, Phrygian, Lydian, and Mixolydian but without assigning ethical qualities to them, as the Greeks had. These four scales are called modes because they are, in a sense, different manners of making melodies. Each pitch in a scale is called a **scale degree.** Each mode has a **final**, that is, the pitch on which a chant ends, and it is assigned the first scale degree. The first scale degree is also indicated with the Arabic numeral one (1). Other pitches in the scale are assigned numbers in ascending order: second degree (2), third degree (3), and so forth. Christian scholars gave each step in a heptatonic scale a letter name: A B C D E F G. Each of the four modes has a final on a different step of the collection of seven pitches:

Dorian mode	=	D	E	F	G	A	B	C	(D)
Phrygian mode	=	E	F	G	A	B	C	D	(E)
Lydian mode	=	F	G	A	B	C	D	E	(F)
Mixolydian mode	=	G	A	B	C	D	E	F	(G)

These modes based on scales consisting of whole steps and half steps are called **diatonic scales**. The distances between these scale degrees are not equal, as they are in 'Are' are music.

FIGURE 2.9
Christian chant notation using neumes
Source: Codex Sangallensis 359/Unbekannter Schreiber,
Wikimedia Commons.

These heptatonic scales have two sizes of intervals, whole steps and half steps. If the number 1 equals a whole step and 1/2 equals a half step, then here are intervals in a heptatonic scale, starting on A:

1	1/2	1	1	1/2	1	1
A	B	C	D	E	F	G	(A)

Hildegard's "Quia ergo femina" has a final on E, so it is in the Phrygian mode. Its intervallic pattern is:

1/2	1	1	1	1/2	1	1
E	F	G	A	B	C	D	(E)

Much later, during the sixteenth century, modes on A, C, and B were added to complete this system. Later still, the mode on A came to be known as the minor mode and the mode on C as the major mode. Those two modes, rather than the original four, became the basis for European music after 1500 and popular music and jazz in the twentieth century. Around 1960 jazz musicians developed a style that became known as "modal jazz." It explored the melodic and harmonic possibilities of these Medieval Christian modes.

The composers of early Gregorian chants are not known. They were transmitted in oral tradition until they were written down in the ninth century. Beginning in the tenth century, the names of composers of new chants, such as for local saints, began to be notated. Not technically Gregorian chant (because they cannot be attributed to Gregory), they were somewhat more elaborate in musical style than the older traditional chants. Hildegard's compositions from the twelfth century fall into this category. Today the term Gregorian chant is commonly used to encompass all monophonic Christian chanting, including the chants of Hildegard.

As the size of the chant repertoire grew with new compositions, problems of transmission and memorization grew with them. Guido of Arezzo (*c.* 991 to *c.* 1033), a Benedictine monk from central Italy, solved these problems in two ways. Earlier music theorists had given letter names to the seven pitches in a heptatonic scale: A B C D E F G. To aid the teaching of chant, Guido invented a system of note names based on the first syllables of a six-line poem (*ut-re-mi-fa-sol-la*). Singers could sing these syllables more conveniently than the letter names for pitches. Called **solmization** or **solfege**, the system later changed *ut* to *do* and added a seventh pitch name, *ti*. This modified eleventh-century pedagogical technique is still used today to train musicians. It was famously the basis for the song "Do-Re-Mi" from the Rodgers and Hammerstein 1959 Broadway musical *The Sound of Music*. Second, to specify the intervals of chant more precisely, Guido created a four-line **staff**, a set of four equally spaced lines. He placed one of two **clefs** (keys) at the beginning of the staff to indicate which pitches were assigned to which lines: the letter C, the C clef, was placed on the line for the pitch C; the letter F, the F clef, was placed on the line for the pitch F. Guido claimed that his pedagogical techniques would eliminate the poor performances he observed during

FIGURE 2.10
Guido of Arezzo's four-line staff notation (1335–1345)
Source: Codex Sangallensis 359, Wikimedia Commons.

FIGURE 2.11
The modern Grand Staff

services and the variations he heard from church to church and monastery to monastery. He wrote,

> Who does not bewail . . . that when we celebrate the Divine Office we are often seen rather to strive among ourselves than to praise God? One scarcely agrees with another, neither the pupil with his master, nor the pupil with his colleague.

And he claimed that, whereas teaching the entire repertoire of a monastery's chants in oral tradition could take ten years, he and his "helpers . . . can produce a perfect singer in the space of one year, or at the most two."

In the thirteenth century, as the range of music expanded, a fifth line was added to form the five-line staff used today. A G clef was added to the C and F clefs, and today the G and F clefs are combined in the **Grand Staff**, two parallel five-line staves linked together. The top staff uses the **treble clef** (also the G clef); the lower staff uses the **bass clef** (also the F clef). The C clef, called the **alto clef** or **tenor clef**, can be placed on any line of the staff and is used for instrumental parts in the middle range.

From the Medieval period to the present, composers have drawn on some of the melodies and Latin texts of Gregorian chant new music in new styles of religious music (Chapter 4, Gateway 11). The central role of Gregorian chant in the Roman Catholic liturgy ended with the Second Vatican Council (1962–1965), which allowed vernacular (that is, local) languages to replace Latin in the Mass and popular and local traditional music styles to replace Gregorian chanting. Reformers hoped to make the Mass more attractive to modern congregations. In 2015 a recording of Gregorian chant called *Benedicta: Marian Chants from Norcia* by the monks of St. Benedict's Monastery in Norcia, Italy, reached the top of the *Billboard Magazine* classical music charts. One chant, "Dies irae" (Day of Wrath), performed as part of the Proper of every funeral Mass and during three days set aside for honoring the dead—in the United States Halloween, All Saints' Day, and All Souls' Day and in Mexico the Day of the Dead or *Día de los Muertos* (October 31 to November 2)—has lived a long life as an index of death in many secular classical compositions and in popular music and film, including *The Exorcist* (1973) and *The Shining* (1980).

WHERE DO I GO FROM HERE?

- Listen to examples of monastery choirs such as *Benedicta: Marian Chants from Norcia* singing traditional Gregorian chant, and compare their style of Gregorian chant to Hildegard's "Quia ergo femina."
- While Roman Gregorian chant has been the most influential in the history of European classical music, other early Christian chant traditions are well worth listening to. Listen to some of these and compare them to each other and to Gregorian chant: Ambrosian chant, from northern Italy and named for St. Ambrose, the fourth-century bishop of Milan; Byzantine chant of the Greek Orthodox Church, noting their use of ornamentation and drone; Armenian chant; Syriac (Syrian) chant, sung in a dialect of Aramaic, Jesus's language; or Ethiopian Orthodox chant.
- Listen to Jewish chant of the Ashkenazic (European) and Sephardic (North African and Spanish) traditions.

GATEWAY 6
QUR'ANIC CHANT

What Is It?

The Qur'an is the holy book of Islam. Muslims believe it contains the word of God as revealed to the Prophet Muhammad, who lived near Mecca in present-day Saudi Arabia, over a period of many years during the early seventh century. Although compiled into a book in the decades after the Prophet's death in 632 CE, devotees learn to recite large parts of it from memory, and specially trained chanters recite it during prayer services. Our gateway to Qur'anic chant is a passage from the Qur'an recited by Sheikh Hamza Shakkur (1947–2008) from the Great Mosque in Damascus, Syria.

 Listen to the first thirty seconds of the recording.

How Does It Work?

Timbre

The reciter chants in a relaxed, resonant low-pitched voice in the beginning and then moves slightly higher in his range.

Texture

The texture is monophonic, a solo male voice without accompaniment.

Rhythm

The meter is nonmetrical, without a beat. The rhythm varies from one tone for each syllable of text (syllabic singing) to a few tones for each syllable (melismatic singing).

Melody

The melody is based on a seven-tone scale with a few additional pitches. The melody moves principally in a smooth, stepwise motion.

Harmony

This is monophonic chanting, so there is no harmony.

Form

The form consists of many improvised phrases. The performance begins with just two pitches and very gradually adds higher and higher pitches until it reaches its highest pitch two octaves above the final about two-thirds of the way through the recitation.

FIGURE 2.12

Qur'anic reciter Sheikh Hamza Shakkur
Source: Al-Kindi Ensemble.

Performance Techniques

The reciter starts by chanting rather plainly but then begins to add subtle ornaments as he proceeds through the text. At the ends of phrases the reciter clearly pronounces the consonant and guttural vowels of the Arabic language in the Qur'an.

 Listen to the first sixty seconds for the increasing phrase lengths and the gradual addition of pitches.

All Qur'anic recitations begin with the same line of text (in Arabic): "In the name of God the compassionate, the merciful." This particular recitation is an excerpt from Book 3 of the Qur'an: "The Family of 'Imran." After the formulaic opening, it begins, "God chose Adam and Noah and the family of Abraham and the family of 'Imran above all his creatures." It goes on to tell the story of the wife of 'Imran, who dedicated her child, Mary, to God's service. An angel tells Mary that, although "no man has touched" her, she will give birth to a child whose "name is the Messiah, Jesus." Qur'anic portions always end with these words: "In the name of God the most merciful, the most compassionate. God, the Great, has spoken the truth."

Listen to the first three minutes or so of the recording following this timed listening guide.

LISTENING GUIDE 2.3

TIME	SECTION	PHRASE	DESCRIPTION
0:00	Section A with a low-pitched tonal center.	1	A short phrase on two pitches a whole step apart. He ends on the higher pitch, establishing it as the final, also called the **tonal center** or **tonic**.
0:12		2	Another short phrase, this one with two new pitches (the second and third degrees of the scale) above the tonal center.
0:23		3	A longer phrase with four pitches and with some slight melodic ornaments toward the end.
0:45		4	A slightly longer phrase that begins with a leap to the fourth degree of the scale, later adds the fifth degree, and ends on the fourth degree.
1:04		5	Begins on the seventh degree of the scale and descends in a rapid stepwise run to the third degree and continues with mostly stepwise motion to a cadence on the tonal center. A **cadence** is a musical marker of the end of a section or piece of music.
1:15		6	Repeats familiar pitches in a short phrase emphasizing the fourth degree of the scale.
1:30		7	A long phrase on the middle pitches of the scale, again emphasizing the fourth degree of the scale.
1:52		8	Begins on the fifth degree of the scale, adds a new pitch, the sixth degree of the scale, and then sings a new descending interval before descending to the tonal center.
2:11		9	A short phrase on familiar pitches.
2:23	Section B with higher-pitched tonal center on the fourth degree.	10	Adds the higher octave seventh degree of the scale and engages in extensive melodic runs (melismas) on a single syllable, ending on the fourth degree. From here on the fourth degree of the scale is the new tonal center.
2:41		11 and beyond	Sings in the high part of the range, on the fourth, fifth, sixth, and seventh degrees of the original scale.
4:04			Rises to a new high pitch, the octave above the original tonal center, and for the rest of the passage sings predominantly on five pitches between the fourth degree and the octave with the fourth degree continuing as the tonal center.
5:52		End	

What Does It Mean?

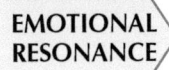

CULTURAL LINKAGES

The sound of Qur'anic chanting is ubiquitous in Muslim societies. It is recited in Friday prayer services throughout the year, at daily prayers during Ramadan, for secular events to celebrate family rituals such as weddings and funerals, to celebrate the opening of a shop or restaurant, and in gatherings of aficionados to listen to a skilled reciter. Always performed in Arabic, it is chanted wherever Muslims gather regardless of their native language.

EMOTIONAL RESONANCE

Muslims believe the Qur'an is the final revelation of God's will for humankind, succeeding and perfecting earlier ones to Adam, Abraham, Moses, Jesus, and some others not known to the Jewish and Christian traditions. The angel Gabriel recited its verses to the Prophet Muhammad (*c.* 570–632 CE), who lived in the cities of Mecca and Medina on the Arabian Peninsula, in a series of revelations between 609 and 632. Muhammad preached the lessons of the Qur'an during his lifetime, starting with family and friends and then to a widening circle of pagans and Jews on the Arabian Peninsula. In the late seventh century, after Muhammad's death, the recited revelations were compiled into a book of 114 chapters containing 3 to 286 verses each, plus an opening prayer of seven verses. Muslims around the world study the Qur'an translated into their local language. But it is always recited in Arabic, and its recitation fills the soundscape of the Islamic world: in mosques, on the radio, and on the streets.

The word Qur'an comes from a root word meaning "to recite," and it is in this recited form, more than through study of the written text, that it has its most powerful effects on the faithful. Children are taught to memorize parts of the Qur'an as a pathway to understanding. Someone who memorizes the entire Qur'an is called a *hafiz*. Some become professional reciters like Hamza Shakkur. The Qur'an proclaims monotheism and opposes paganism; tells stories of earlier prophets like Abraham and Jesus; prescribes righteous behavior, including submission to God's will and obligatory acts (the pillars) of worship (recitation of its creed, daily prayers, giving alms to the poor, fasting during the holy month of Ramadan, and a pilgrimage to Mecca); and warns of the fate of believers and nonbelievers on Judgment Day. The simplest statement of its creed is "There is no God but God, and Muhammad is his prophet." The text of the Qur'an is considered the standard for the vocabulary and grammar of classical literary Arabic. The way reciters pronounce the words is the model for speaking classical Arabic.

FIGURE 2.13
Map of the Arabian Peninsula with the cities of Mecca and Medina

To believers, both the words of the Qur'an and the sound of its recitation are profoundly moving because together they recreate the moment of God's revelation to Muhammad. The words and their recitation represent "divine and inimitable beauty," and they must be performed with absolute accuracy. Since the very sound of the words comes from God, many rules, called *tajwid*, govern pronunciation and require lengthy study. Reciters also spend years studying the meaning of the words. Even the pauses in the recitation, so prominent in this recording, are crucially important and subject to the rules of *tajwid*. They signal the reciter's understanding of the text and give the listeners time to absorb and reflect on its meaning. Because of the prestige of the Qur'an's language, some secular singers practice Qur'anic recitation to improve their pronunciation of Arabic song texts.

Muslims have taken two contrasting positions on the musical qualities of the recitation, which include its melody, ornamentation, rhythm, and the voice quality of the reciter. Some Muslims consider musical performance an evil that distracts from proper religious observance, a view captured in the English expression "wine, women, and song." Conservative Muslims censor excessive displays of musical skill on the part of a reciter and insist on a clear distinction between singing a song and reciting or chanting the Qur'an. Other less conservative but also devout Muslims acknowledge the power of music to affect the human spirit (it "calms the child and refreshes the camel on the long journey") and value highly the musicality of reciters' performances. They argue that "the beautiful melody is a spirit from God which revives burning hearts" and makes people kinder and gentler. Both camps agree that music is powerful, but one takes a negative and the other a conditionally positive view, the condition depending on intent: the musical qualities of the recitation must serve devotion to God in both the reciter and listener.

Reciters must manage this tension in their performances. If they try to please the first group with a spare, barely musical performance, others may find it boring and unmoving. But if it is too beautiful, it may distract listeners from the meaning of the text. Navigating this divide is a source of excitement for discerning listeners.

To enhance the musical qualities of their recitations, many professional reciters study, in addition to the meaning and rules of the text, the Arab secular classical music system, which forms the musical foundation of their recitations. This system was codified in the tenth century and includes an extensive set of melodic modes, called *maqamat* (s. *maqam*). A **maqam** is a melodic mode that specifies intervals between pitches, characteristic melodic gestures, the addition of chromatic pitches, and typical modulations to other *maqamat*. (**Modulation** refers to changes in one or another element of music: a modal modulation, a key modulation, a metric modulation, and so forth.) Unlike early Christian chant, with its heptatonic modes with intervals of whole steps and half steps, the *maqam* system has more than fifty heptatonic modes, each with its own name. The modes use all the twelve pitches of the Europe musical systems plus an additional set of "microtonal" intervals. A **microtone** or **microtonal interval** may be smaller than a half step, the smallest interval in the European musical system, or between a half step and a whole step.

Qur'anic reciters have some leeway in choosing the *maqams* they use for particular verses based on their interpretation of the meaning of the recited verses. Arab musical theorists of the tenth century associated emotions with particular *maqams*. In doing so they followed in the footsteps of Ancient Greek music theorists, who had assigned the ethical qualities of ethnic groups to the melodic modes they used. Given the association of emotion and meaning of a *maqam*, reciters' choices of *maqams* therefore signal to listeners their understanding of the text. Proper choices are said to "extract" the meaning of a verse and "bring the listener closer to the Qur'an." On the other hand, a poor choice may be criticized by knowledgeable listeners. One reciter sang a text about hell and damnation so beautifully that a critic commented, "If hell is so lovely and pleasant, take me to it."

The link between the meaning of a properly chosen *maqam* and the meaning of a verse is called "picturing the meaning," a statement that transforms the indexical link between the emotion and *maqam* into a musical icon of textual meaning. For example, one verse of the Qur'an has a person reflecting on their fate on the Day of Judgment: "Ah, would that I had sent forth [good deeds] for [this] my [future] life." To express the meaning, one singer might choose a *maqam* associated with "grief and pain." Another might choose a *maqam* associated with "self-reproach and repentance."

The *maqam* system allows both secular singers and Qur'anic reciters to improvise during their performance. So, for example, a reciter may change between lower and higher pitch ranges within the *maqam*, as Hamza Shakkur does in this recording, to signal the voices of different figures in dialogue. He might recite on higher pitches to signal particularly important moments in the text. These formal principles guide Qur'anic reciters, as well as respected singers and talented instrumentalists, in Arab secular music traditions.

What Is Its History?

During his lifetime Muhammad managed, despite significant opposition from pagan tribesmen, to unify politically the Arabian Peninsula based on Islamic principles. By 750, little more than a century after his death, a succession of leaders of the faithful, called caliphs, had succeeded in spreading Islam west across North Africa to Spain, north to much of the present-day Middle East, and east to southern Pakistan. Ruled from Damascus in present-day Syria, this caliphate, the area ruled by a caliph, was the largest empire in the world to that date. In 750 the capital of the caliphate moved to the city of Baghdad in present-day Iraq, where science, art, music, and literature flourished in a golden age of Islamic culture. Qur'anic recitations based on secular Arab classical music may date to this period. The capital of the caliphate shifted to Cairo in 1261 and to Istanbul in the Ottoman Empire in 1517 where it remained until 1924, when the president of the new Republic of Turkey abolished the caliphate.

As early as the ninth century Islam spread into sub-Saharan Africa, including present-day Mali and Sudan. Today nearly half of Africa's population is Muslim. By the tenth century Islam had also spread to Central Asia. Between the thirteenth and the seventeenth centuries it traveled east to parts of southeast Asia, including Malaysia on the mainland and some islands of Indonesia and the Philippines. Today Indonesia has the largest Muslim population in the world, more than 200 million out of an estimated total of 1.7 billion Muslims. It is the second-largest religion in the world after Christianity with its estimated 2.4 billion believers.

Since the early twentieth century, recordings and radio and television broadcasts have transmitted the Arab style heard in this recording to many parts of the world. International recitation competitions contribute to the standardization of oral practices. Nevertheless, it is difficult to know how Qur'anic recitation has changed through the centuries since it was revealed to the Prophet Muhammad. The chanting style seems to have molded itself to the *maqam* practices of secular classical music (Chapter 3, Gateway 8). The history of maqam practice has historically documented roots going back at least to the tenth century, but those practices have changed in some details over time. Also, in each of the many societies where Islam has taken root, Islam has accommodated local social and cultural views, particularly with respect to the position of women in society and in Islam. In Indonesia, for example, women may become skilled reciters and work alongside men.

> CULTURAL
> LINKAGES

WHERE DO I GO FROM HERE?

- This gateway is based on Kristina Nelson, *The Art of Reciting the Qur'an* (Austin: University of Texas Press, 1985). Read chapter 4, "The Ideal Recitation of the Qur'an," pp. 52–100.
- Listen to, and compare, the Qur'anic chanting of reciters from Egypt, Saudi Arabia, Turkey, and female reciter Maria Ulfah from Indonesia with the recitation of Hamza Shakkur in this gateway.
- For an account of gender in Qur'anic chanting, read chapter 6, "Rethinking Women, Music, and Islam," in Anne K. Rasmussen, *Women, the Recited Qur'an, and Islamic Music in Indonesia* (Berkeley: University of California Press, 2010), pp. 211–243.

CLOSING

The religious chanting of the major world religions enhances religious experience and the meanings of liturgical texts by adding elements associated with music: melody, rhythmic recitation, special timbres, and performance techniques, and in the case of Tibetan Buddhism, musical instruments. Since religious music often supports the recitation of a great deal of text, they all employ syllabic singing, a good way to focus attention on the meaning of the text. When worshippers want to express the mystical and emotional nature of religious belief, they amplify the aesthetic quality of the sound in special ways: Tibetan Buddhists with their two-tone vocal production and raucous instrumental music; Christians and Muslims with their melismatic singing.

Buddhists, Muslims, and Christians share a concern that too much emphasis on the musical elements of religious chant will lead believers away from true devotion to the serious obligations of their faith toward distracting and lascivious thoughts associated with secular music. In all cases, believers in these religions with roots in the Ancient and Medieval period share with small-scale societies a belief that music has special powers that enable humans to communicate effectively with the supernatural world.

Buddhism, Christianity, and Islam have all spread over wide areas of the world with the support of secular political power, sometimes via crusades and holy wars (jihad) and sometimes as the adopted state religion of kings, emperors, and sultans. Under the umbrella of state protection, all have developed strong institutions to teach and support religious devotion and music: Buddhist and Christian monasteries; Buddhist temples, Christian churches, and Muslim mosques; and full-time ritual specialists (lamas, priests, and imams), some of whom are chanting and music specialists.

THINGS TO THINK ABOUT

- How do modern religious believers amplify the meanings of religious texts with musical elements? How is what they do similar to, and different from, the Medieval practices described in this chapter?
- Historically, many religions have spread with the support of secular political regimes. To what extent are the political and the musical interconnected in religious settings today?

NEW TERMS

aerophone	double reed	neumes
alto clef	final	Ordinary of the Mass
antiphons	Grand Staff	Proper of the Mass
bass clef, F clef	Gregorian chant	psalms
C clef	leapwise motion	range
chant, chanting	liturgies	scale degree
choir	lyre	solmization, solfege
chorus	*maqam*	staff
civilization	melisma, melismatic singing	stepwise melodic motion
clef	microtone, microtonal interval	syllabic singing
conjunct motion	mode	tenor clef
diatonic scales	modulation	treble clef, G clef
disjunct motion		vibrato

ANCIENT AND MEDIEVAL SECULAR MUSIC

SOME SECULAR MUSICAL TRADITIONS alive today can trace their roots to the Ancient and Medieval period, which begins with the rise of cities and empires along rivers in Mesopotamia, Egypt, India, and China. The rich soils along these rivers produced unprecedented wealth for the rulers who controlled these terrains. Their wealth and power grew in tandem with the vastness of the land they controlled. Those who had domains large enough to contain diverse populations not united by language or ethnicity were called emperors, and their territories were called empires. On the peripheries of empires, some city-states, notably those of the Ancient Greeks, thrived culturally and politically. Though each of these empires controlled a large area, none of them dominated the globe militarily, economically, intellectually, or artistically.

During the Medieval period, the empires of the Middle East, East Asia, and Africa shone especially brightly. Court music, some still performed today, was brilliant and impressive. Europe, by contrast, was a relative backwater. After the fall of the Roman Empire in 476 CE, Europe was a wasteland of small-scale agriculturalists, a few warlords claiming control of extended territories here and there, and a growing number of isolated Christian monasteries. Around 1350 the largest city in Europe was Paris (200,000). Rome (15,000) and London (25,000–50,000) had much smaller populations. At the same time the four largest cities in the world were Baghdad (one million), Beijing (400,000), Cairo (300,000), and Kyoto, Japan (300,000). Delhi in India and Timbuktu in West Africa had populations of about 100,000. Beyond these large cities, religious chanting in monasteries and churches and singing, playing, and dancing in rural villages and small aristocratic courts were the most important forms of musical expression during the Medieval period.

This chapter contains gateways to four of many traditions around the world that can trace their beginnings to the Ancient and Medieval periods: (1) the music of Chinese literati; (2) the court music of the Middle East; (3) an African tradition with roots in the Medieval city of Zimbabwe; and (4) the rural music of Bulgaria.

DOI: 10.4324/9781003269304-5

GATEWAY 7
MUSIC OF CHINA

What Is It?

China is the largest country in the world by population and the third largest by area. It contains a vast array of musical styles including rural village music, traditional forms of urban popular music, music with roots in its long history of imperial court music, new music created to serve its Communist government, European classical music, and global popular music. Our gateway to the music of China is a recording of a composition associated with the Ancient and Medieval court tradition entitled "Three Variations on Yang Pass" played on a plucked zither called *qin* (pronounced "cheen"). **Zithers** are stringed instruments with a resonator but no neck. The *qin* has seven silk strings stretched along the top of a one-meter-long wooden box with an arched top and a flat bottom with two "sound holes." Along the top of the resonator are thirteen inlaid circles indicating where the player is to stop the strings (to press them down with a finger against the wooden resonator). "Yang Pass" refers to a melody associated with a poem about a passage through the mountains in western China. The phrase "three variations" indicates that the piece consists of three versions of a melody. The performer on this recording, released in 2000, was a highly respected scholar and teacher at the Shanghai Conservatory of Music named Lin Youren (1938–2013).

 Listen to the first thirty seconds of the recording.

How Does It Work?

Timbre

The player produces a variety of timbres, including plucked open strings, harmonics, a contrast between tinny, thin tones and full, rich ones, and scraping sounds on the strings.

Texture

The texture is mainly monophonic with occasional octaves and **perfect fifths**. **Perfect fifths** are intervals with a frequency ratio of 3:2, for example, C to G. (**Perfect fourths** are intervals with a frequency ratio of 4:3, for example, C to F.)

Rhythm

The rhythm has an elastic beat with an irregular meter.

Melody

Five of the *qin*'s seven strings are tuned to a pentatonic scale. A **pentatonic scale** has five pitches in an octave. The other two strings double two of the five pitches at the octave. The melody employs a pentatonic scale and moves mainly in stepwise motion among the five scale degrees.

Harmony

Except for the occasional perfect fifth, harmony does not play a role in this performance.

Form

The piece has three main sections, each a variant of others: A A' A". Each section contains a through-composed set of melodic phrases. The piece ends with a short **coda** (the tail

FIGURE 3.1

Lin Youren plays the *qin* at a gathering of *qin* aficionados, Suzhou 1987. With beard, the great *qin* master Wu Zhaoji.

Source: Stephen Jones.

or ending added at the end of a musical composition or performance) that repeats one characteristic melody from the main part of the piece.

Performance Techniques

The player's manipulation of timbre is a striking performance technique in this piece.

Listen to the first thirty seconds of this recording for its pentatonic scale and the timbre of the instrument.

Listen to the entire recording following this timed listening guide.

TIME	SECTION	DESCRIPTION
0:00	Intro	Five low pitches are plucked.
0:09	A	The player plays the melody with different timbres on repeated pitches, various attacks and slides into pitches, and the sliding sound of the hand stopping the strings as it moves. The player repeats the melodic phrase played near the beginning and continues with some short melodic phrases until he ends by repeating one pitch a number of times.
1:38	A'	The melodic phrase played twice in the previous section starts the second variation, this time played as harmonics. A **harmonic** is produced when the sound of an overtone, rather than the fundamental, is heard. In this case the harmonic produced is the overtone an octave higher than the fundamental for each of the pitches played. The short melodic phrases of the previous variation return. The section ends in the same manner as the previous section.
3:10	A''	The third variation begins with the now-familiar melody in harmonics, as the previous section did. The short melodies return as well. Sometimes only the sliding of the finger on the string is heard after the tone decays. The section ends as the previous two did.
5:09	Coda	This section begins a bit differently and then the familiar opening melody is played. But this section doesn't continue with the other melodies and ends rather quickly with a single sounding of a pitch, rather than with repetitions of a pitch as in the previous sections.
5:41	End	

LISTENING GUIDE 3.1

What Does It Mean?

The poem "Yang Pass" was written in the eighth century CE by one of China's most famous poets. It is about travelers leaving China for unknown and dangerous lands in Central Asia beyond the Great Wall of China. Knowledgeable players and listeners associate this instrumental melody with the poem's wistful sentiment of parting with loved ones, because "going west through Yang Pass there will be no acquaintances." They also listen for how carefully the performer brings to life the timbral richness of a composition that first appeared in notation in 1491. This latter interpretation flows from the position of the *qin* in Chinese culture, where it has long been associated with the ancient Chinese sage Confucius (c. 551–479 BCE). In that tradition, careful performance on the *qin* is a sign of the musician's great learning and discipline.

> EMOTIONAL
> RESONANCE

Qin players have historically been scholars who devoted their lives to learning across a wide variety of disciplines, including not only the reading of classic texts but also the arts of music, painting, calligraphy, and archery. They used this learning to serve the state as well-educated rational, knowledgeable administrators, as Confucius said they should. Thus a performance on the *qin* can be read as a metaphor for the player's education and refinement. The player uses performance on the *qin*, and other artistic practices, for training the mind and disciplining the body. As a consequence, the performance is meant most of all for the performer, not for an audience. Practicing, not performing for others, is what is crucial. Occasionally, the performer might play for another scholar or a few friends and students who are equally dedicated to the scholarly life Confucius modeled. Two elements of the sound are essential to this intimate performance

> SOCIAL
> BEHAVIOR

context. First, the silk strings produce a very faint sound. Second, the timbre of this quiet sound, including sliding on the strings, requires the complete attention of the players and listeners.

"Three Variations on Yang Pass" is one of nearly 3000 pieces in the *qin* repertoire. Collected in books of notation for more than a millennium, they are, along with neumatic notations of Gregorian chant, among the world's earliest examples of written music still performed today. *Qin* notation is a type of **tablature**, a notation method that indicates how an instrument is to be played rather than the pitches to be played. (Guitar tablatures are a well-known example.) In *qin* tablature, each tone is indicated by a complex written figure that is a composite of four Chinese characters: (1) the number of the string to be plucked (1 through 7); (2) the number of the marker on the sound board to be stopped (1 through 13); (3) the manner of holding down the string (for example, to produce a harmonic or not); and (4) the finger and the direction (in or out) of the pluck. Notating the way each tone is to be played clearly places a great deal of emphasis on the timbre of the resulting tone. As in Chinese writing, directions for each tone are written down the page in columns beginning on the right side of the page and proceeding to the left. The tablature does not specify the rhythm of the tones, and players either create their own rhythmic interpretation after careful study or learn one from their teachers in aural tradition.

In addition to musical notation, the Chinese also have a long history of music theory. They were probably the first to classify musical instruments, invent a system of fixed pitch, and create the theory of an **equal-tempered scale**. An equal-tempered scale is one in which all the half steps of a twelve-pitch scale are exactly the same size (see Gateway 9 for a discussion of non-equal-tempered scales). Already around the time of Confucius, Chinese music theorists recognized five-tone (pentatonic), seven-tone (heptatonic), and twelve-tone (dodecaphonic) scales and had names for each of the pitches in them. A few centuries later they discovered that the interval of an octave was the result of the ratio of 2:1 between pitch frequencies and that the interval of a fifth (between, say, C and G) was the ratio of 3:2 between pitch frequencies. They then figured out that the series of intervals a fifth apart didn't go on forever but was a closed circle, the **circle of fifths**. The first five notes of the circle of fifths result in a pentatonic pitch set: starting on F, the circle of fifths yields F C G D A and, when rearranged into a scale, the pitches F G A C D. The next two pitches in the circle of fifths, E and B, create a diatonic, heptatonic scale: F G A **B** C D **E**. The next five pitches in the circle of fifths, F♯ C♯ G♯ D♯ A♯, close the circle to create a **dodecaphonic** or **chromatic** or twelve-tone scale: F F♯ G G♯ A A♯ B C C♯ D D♯ E. On a piano keyboard the white keys play diatonic scales, the black keys play pentatonic scales, and black and white keys play a dodecaphonic scale.

The Chinese were also the first to create the idea of fixed pitch, that is, the setting of a pitch to a particular number of vibrations per second (in European music, for example, the idea that the pitch A equals 440 cycles per second). In keeping with Confucian ideas about the importance of music for the stable functioning of society and the state, the measurement of the exact pitch of notes was a matter of importance to the state, and each dynasty maintained a bureau of weights and measures where standards for pitch were kept alongside exact measurements of weight, length, and volume (in American terms, the exact weight of a pound, the length of an inch, the volume of a gallon, and so forth). These measurements were believed to be so fundamental to political and social functioning and stability that when a dynasty was overthrown and replaced by a new one, the new dynasty

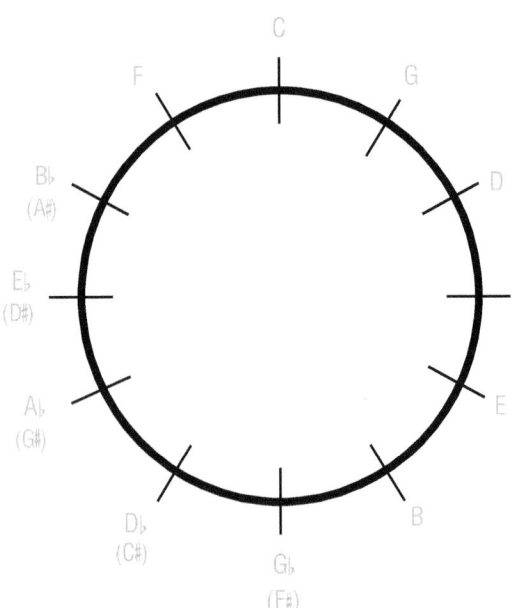

FIGURE 3.2
The circle of fifths
Source: Alex Sawicka-Ritchie.

FIGURE 3.3
The piano keyboard with pitch names
Source: Alex Sawicka-Ritchie.

would reset the standards of weights and measures, including the fixed pitches of their music, to new levels.

The Chinese also have a long history of giving pitches meaning. For example, the five pitches of the pentatonic scale were associated with five bodily organs, five directions (north, east, south, west, and center), five elements (earth, fire, water, wood, and metal), five flavors (sweet, spicy, bitter, sour, and salty), five known planets, five colors, and five odors. The twelve pitches were associated with the twelve hours of the day, the twelve months of the year, and the twelve signs of the zodiac. Similarly, the Chinese often give compositions names that suggest a mood, an image from a painting or from nature, or the text of a poem or story. These symbolic associations of Chinese music with other elements of human experience are one indicator of the central importance the Ancient Chinese placed on music in human life. It may also be part of a heritage, from earlier agricultural and pastoralist ways of life, that connects music to the natural environment. The Chinese also classified musical instruments according to the primary material producing the sound: metal, stone, silk, bamboo, gourd, earth (pottery), hide, and wood. The *qin* and all stringed instruments are members of the silk class of musical instruments.

CULTURAL LINKAGES

What Is Its History?

Historical records suggest zithers resembling the *qin* existed in China as early as 1000 BCE. One of the earliest representations in art of a similar instrument is a terra-cotta figurine made between 100 BCE and 100 CE. The *qin*, its repertoire, and its players constitute a 2000-year tradition of Chinese education and political organization associated with the teachings of Confucius. And legend has it that Confucius played the *qin*.

POLITICS

Confucius lived before China was first unified into an empire during the Qin dynasty (220 BCE–207 CE). He devoted his early life to reading and studying the growing body of Chinese literature. In middle age, after failing at government service, he traveled to many kingdoms searching for the keys to a well-lived life. As an older man he taught students what he had learned from his studies and travels. They transmitted his lessons in oral tradition until they were written down as his *Analects* (edited conversations) during the Han dynasty (206 BCE–220 CE). From that time to the present his philosophy has formed the foundation of much of Chinese culture. His principal insights are ethical and moral rather than metaphysical or theological, as religious beliefs are.

Raised in a time of conflict among small states, he believed that social organization at the family and political levels could be peaceful and successful if individuals, from ordinary peasants to the ruler, followed three ethical principles: (1) benevolence and kindness to others; (2) the righteous and just treatment of the ruled by rulers; and (3) filial piety and brotherly love within the family. The paths to achieving these qualities were learning and ritual, both of which trained the mind and body to overcome base instincts such as greed, cruelty, and selfishness. Learning to play the *qin* and performing music during state rituals helped achieve these ethical goals, which Confucianists call the Way of Heaven. Rulers who followed the Way would not act despotically but in the interest of their subjects, who would flourish as a consequence of wisdom and benevolence of the ruler. All would seek a balance between Heaven and Earth through ritual and its music. Once China was unified into a vast empire by the Han dynasty and successor dynasties, emperors claimed they were Sons of Heaven and so detached from those they ruled. To rule benevolently their vast land, they created a bureaucracy administered by scholars who studied the classics of Chinese literature, music, and art.

FIGURE 3.4

Terra-cotta figurine of a musician playing a *qin* or *qin*-like instrument (100 BCE–100 CE)

Source: De Agostini Picture Library/ Getty Images.

Confucius is said to have believed that training in proper or good music, like that for the *qin* and that played during state rituals, could cultivate good qualities in the ruling class and in the state itself. Confucianist ideas about the importance of music, in the context of their influential views on state management and ethical behavior, meant that music appeared at the center of political and social processes as one of the contributors to political and social stability.

FIGURE 3.5
The Imperial Vault of Heaven at the Temple of Heaven, Beijing, constructed in the fifteenth century
Source: Philip Larson, Wikimedia Commons.

For 2000 years, during a time when a large meritocracy of highly educated Confucianist scholars (called mandarins by the Portuguese) ruled China on behalf of its emperor, music was central to the life of Chinese society.

The *qin*, as one of the important symbols of this educated elite's learning and political power, enjoys considerable prestige in Chinese culture. That prestige continued even after the fall of the last Chinese emperor in 1911 and the formation of the Republic of China. The People's Republic of China, founded in 1949, has supported the *qin* tradition not as a symbol of imperial class hierarchy but as a valued historical achievement of Chinese culture. However, they mandated that it should enter the musical life of all classes through public concerts, commercial recordings, instruction at music conservatories, and the composition of new works for *qin* in ensembles with other instruments. To produce a louder, more audible sound in these new settings, some players, like Lin Youren in this recording, have substituted metal strings for silk strings, which change the timbre and some of the playing techniques on the instrument. By the 1980s some *qin* players were professional musicians, a status at odds with their traditional position as highly educated amateurs who made their living in service to the emperor and the state.

WHERE DO I GO FROM HERE?

- Listen to Lin Youren's other recordings of compositions for the *qin*.
- Find and view recordings of Chinese musical instruments representing the eight classes of Chinese musical instruments: silk—*erhu*, a two-stringed bowed lute; bamboo—*xiao*, end-blown, notched flute; earth (pottery)—*xun*, globular flute; gourd—*sheng*, a set of reed pipes in a resonator once made of gourd; hide—a large variety of Chinese drums; wood—clappers; metal—bells and bell chimes; stone—chimes made of slabs of jade.
- Read more about Chinese music in the *Garland Encyclopedia of World Music: Volume 7: East Asia: China, Japan, and Korea* (New York: Routledge, 2002).

GATEWAY 8
MUSIC OF THE MIDDLE EAST

What Is It?

Many musical traditions of the Middle East have roots in the Medieval period, when Islam spread rapidly out of the Arabian Peninsula after the Prophet Muhammad's death in 632. Some of

FIGURE 3.6
**Map of the Middle
Eastern musical
world**

these traditions are considered to be forms of Middle Eastern "classical music" because of their long histories as court music with elaborate systems of melodic and rhythmic modes. Middle Eastern classical music includes musical traditions from a vast and varied region encompassing present-day Turkey, Iran, the Arab countries east of the Mediterranean, the Arabian Peninsula, North Africa, and the countries of Central Asia. Besides Islam, another unifying cultural feature of this region is the presence of classical and other musical traditions based on elaborate systems of melodic and rhythmic modes that are performed monophonically or with a drone and featuring melodic improvisation with many local variations.

Our gateway to secular musical traditions of the Middle East with roots in the Medieval period is a performance of classical Arab music titled "Taqasim and Sama'i Bayyati Al-Arayan," played on the *'ud* by A. J. Racy, with the accompaniment of a *riqq* (a small frame drum with jingles). The *'ud* is a fretless, short-necked, pear-shaped, plucked lute with a vaulted (that is, rounded) back and a pegbox bent away from the neck. It has five double courses and one single-string course (the lowest-pitched string). (A **course** is one string or a set of close-together strings tuned to the same pitch and simultaneously stopped or pressed onto the fingerboard by one finger.) The musician plucks the strings with a plectrum. The title of the piece refers to two important musical forms in Arab music. A *taqsim* (pl. *taqasim*) is a nonmetrical improvisation in a particular melodic mode (*maqam* in Arabic). A *sama'i* is a composed instrumental form in a meter of ten beats. *Bayyati* in the title is the name of a *maqam*. The combination of an opening nonmetrical improvisation followed by a metrical composed piece, both in the same melodic mode, is a common formal principle in Arab and other Middle Eastern musical traditions. Al-Arayan in the title is the family name of the composer of the *sama'i*, Ibrahim Al-'Arayan (1892–1953) from Cairo, Egypt.

 Listen to the first thirty seconds of the performance.

How Does It Work?

Timbre

The sound of the *'ud*'s plucked strings, with their characteristic rapid decay, and the thump of a drumhead and jingles on the *riqq* create the timbres of this performance.

FIGURE 3.7
A. J. Racy playing the *'ud*
Source: Barbara Racy.

Texture

The texture combines a single ornamented melodic line with occasional drone effects and drum accompaniment.

Rhythm

The opening section is nonmetrical followed by a metrical section that features a meter of ten beats. The meter is marked by a repeating pattern of drum strokes played on the *riqq*. Toward the end of the metrical section the meter shifts from a ten-beat meter to triple meter, or a meter of six beats, before returning to the ten-beat meter at the very end. The tempo varies from rather slow to quite fast.

Melody

The melody moves mainly in stepwise motion through a seven-pitch melodic mode. The mode resembles the European minor mode (A B C D E F G), but some of the pitches are microtones between the whole steps and half steps of European music.

Harmony

Aside from the occasional sounding of octaves and drones, harmony is not an element in this performance.

Form

The form consists of two parts defined by rhythmic treatment: the first part is nonmetrical and the second part is metrical. Within the metrical section new melodies alternate with a **refrain** (R). A **refrain** is a melody that regularly returns during a performance: A R B R C R D R. In European music this form is quite common and is called **rondo form**.

Performance Techniques

The performance features rapid strumming, rapid melodic runs from time to time, and ornamentation.

Listen to the performance from 2:30 to 3:30 and pay attention to the shift from a nonmetrical to a metrical approach to rhythm.

Listen to the entire performance following this timed listening guide.

LISTENING GUIDE 3.2

TIME	PART	SECTION	DESCRIPTION
0:00	***taqsim* (nonmetrical melodic improvisation)**	first section	The melody, consisting of a series of short phrases marked by pauses, begins near the middle of the scale before descending to a cadence on the tonal center.
0:34		second section	The melody moves to higher pitches in the scale.
1:04		third section	The melody is played in the lower octave with a drone above the melody. The drone then ceases and the melody works its way through a series of short phrases and fast scale passages to cadence again on the tonal center.
1:48		fourth section	The melody, based on melodic sequences, is played in the middle and high registers with punctuating low pitches. A melodic **sequence** is a melodic phrase repeated at different pitch levels.
2:51	*sama'i* (metrical composition)	first section (A)	The melody consists of five measures of ten beats each.
3:22		refrain	A five-measure melody in a meter of ten beats is based on a descending sequence.
3:51		second section (B)	A new five-measure melody in a meter of ten beats.
4:20		refrain	A repeat of the refrain.

TIME	PART	SECTION	DESCRIPTION
4:47		third section (C)	A new five-measure melody in a meter of ten beats.
5:15		refrain	A repeat of the refrain.
5:42		fourth section (D)	The meter shifts to six beats per measure and two melodies are played in the form AABBA'A'.
6:39		refrain	The refrain melody returns in its original ten-beat meter.
7:09		End	

What Does It Mean?

Musical performances in all traditions gain aesthetic meaning from the musical system of which they are a part. This performance exists within Middle Eastern systems of musical theory dealing with melodic and rhythmic modes that date from the Medieval period. It also has meaning in relation to other musical instruments common in this style of performance and in relation to a variety of social settings and their associated genres of music.

The gateway on Qur'anic chanting introduced the Arab *maqam* system of fifty or so hepta-tonic modes. Although fifty or more modes exist in theory, in practice there are nine common *maqamat* (plural of *maqam*). The theoretical system has so many modes because they are con-structed from a theoretical system of twenty-four equally spaced pitches, twice as many as in the European system of twelve pitches. The twelve additional pitches in Arab music are, in theory, a quarter-tone above or below those in the European pitch system. They are said to be half-flat or half-sharp. The result is that Arab musical modes have half steps and whole steps and also microtones of three-quarter steps. In fact, Arab musicians play some smaller microtones than this theory explains. *Maqam bayyati*, heard in this recording, is written with the tonal center on D: D E-half-flat F G A B-flat C D. It has four whole steps (F to G, G to A, B-flat to C, C to D), one half step (A to B-flat), and two three-quarter steps (D to E-half-flat, E-half-flat to F). To further compli-cate matters, in *maqam bayyati* the B-flat sometimes shifts to B-half-flat. Although the intervals of *maqam bayyati* are fixed in music theory, skilled musicians on the *'ud*, which lacks frets, have an even more refined sense of the exact pitches they should play depending on the direction of a melody or the location of a pitch in a phrase. Sophisticated listeners hear these tiny differences in pitch, and they judge musicians on their ability or inability to bring them out in performance.

Listen one more time to the first minute or so of this recording and try to identify the sec-ond degree of the scale as an E-half-flat between E-flat and E-natural.

A composed *sama'i* has a relatively fixed form with four sections, each ending in a refrain, and a change of meter in the fourth section. The *sama'i* in this performance provides a degree of aesthetic pleasure just by meeting audience expectations and providing a particular instance of an ideal form that listeners are expecting to hear in such a performance. While the *sama'i* and its characteristic rhythm are meant for listening, other types of short composed pieces, especially in duple and quadruple meter, can accompany dancing, including so-called belly dancing meant for the entertainment of the audience.

The meter of ten beats is heard not only in the melody but in a repeating rhythmic cycle played on the *riqq* in a succession of low strokes (called *dumm*) and high strokes (called *takk* and *takka*) on the drum head. Arab music employs many of these rhythmic cycles, which are called *iqa'at* (s. *iqa'*) in Arabic. The ten-beat cycle in this recording is called *sama'i*. It features this repeating pattern of *dumms* and *takks* (||: :|| are repeat signs indicating that the musical material between them should be repeated):

||: 1 2 3 4 5 6 7 8 9 10 :||

   D - - T - D D T - -

AESTHETICS

The drummer fills in the pauses (-) in the skeleton rhythmic structure with improvised drum strokes. The cycle of six beats in the fourth section is called *sankin sama'i* and has this set of *dumms*, *takks*, and *takkas*:

‖: 1   2   3   4   5   6 :‖

D   TK T   D   T   -

Maqamat are associated with different emotions. For example, some listeners associate *maqam rast* with masculinity and pride and *maqam bayyati* with femininity and joy. Other *maqamat* are linked to love and sadness. One *maqam*, called *maqam hijaz*, is named after the "distant desert" of the Arabian Peninsula where Islam was born in the cities of Mecca and Medina (see the map of the Arabian Peninsula in Chapter 2), and is particularly evocative. Its scale is written as follows: D E-flat F-sharp G A B-flat (also half-flat) C D. The defining interval of this maqam is the augmented second between E-flat and F-sharp. An **augmented second** is an interval of one and a half steps. In *maqam hijaz*, musicians reduce its size by slightly raising the E-flat and slightly lowering the F-sharp, creating a microtonal interval not explained by Arab musical theory. In European and American music composers often use the *hijaz* scale when they want to index the "exotic" Middle East.

Sophisticated listeners also gain pleasure from hearing this performance as a manifestation of a well-known musical form. So, for example, they expect a musician improvising in *maqam bayyati* to begin his (and they are traditionally men) *taqsim* near the middle of the scale before descending to the tonic, as A. J. Racy does in this recording. They also expect a performer to improvise melodies and explore the *maqam* using a full octave range and, for an instrument like the *'ud*, a variety of plucking techniques just as Racy does. In a concert setting or an intimate performance in someone's home, the musician's goal is to tell an emotional story, to take listeners on a musical journey they are already somewhat familiar with. As they pass along a familiar yet unique route, listeners seek to enter an ecstatic emotional state known as *tarab*. Rather than sitting quietly, as audiences for European classical music do, they signal their pleasure at particularly delightful moments during the improvisation (a clever modulation to a new *maqam*, an interesting cadence, a subtle variation in intonation) with short cries and subtle body motions. The performer, in front of a knowledgeable and engaged audience, also enters a state of inspired ecstasy, called *saltanah*, and plays with even more emotion. In this tradition, becoming a master musician and a masterful listener requires practice and experience.

Like European classical music, Middle Eastern classical music requires close listening and appreciation in courtly and concert settings. This performance on the *'ud* also gains meaning within a set of familiar Arab instruments. The *'ud* has been, since the Medieval period, a favorite instrument of singers to accompany their performances. Since singers in this tradition have long enjoyed more prestige than instrumentalists, probably because of their ability to express the sentiments in song lyrics, the *'ud* shares in the vocalists' high regard. The *nay*, an end-blown, rim-blown reed flute, is held in high regard because its sustained tones mimic the sound of the human voice. The *qanun*, a plucked zither, and the *buzuq*, a long-necked plucked lute, are other important Arab melodic instruments. Today the *'ud* is probably the most highly regarded instrument in the Arab world. Sometimes called the prince (*sultan* or *emir*) of instruments, it is seen as an index of high Arab culture and a sign of musical pleasure as well as intellectual and scientific sophistication. Today a performance like this one sounds very different from the Arab popular music heard in nightclubs and recordings and performed on amplified instruments like synthesizers.

What Is Its History?

This performance is part of a classical musical tradition going back to the ninth and tenth centuries. The *'ud* may have even deeper roots in human history. It belongs to a family of **chordophones** (stringed instruments) called **lutes** (chordophones with necks and a resonating body). Among the earliest lutes in the historical record are long-necked ones shown in Egyptian paintings of

FIGURE 3.8

A. J. Racy playing the *nay*

Source: Daniel Neuman.

the second millennium BCE. Played by women, the resonating body is a gourd covered by animal skin. Short-necked lutes like the *'ud*, with bodies covered by a wooden face, may have developed from these ancient long-necked lutes. (The word *'ud* means "twig" or "wood" in Arabic.) Short-necked lutes like the *'ud* traveled east to China, where similar short-necked lutes are called *pipa*, and west into Europe, where they are called lute, from the Arabic *al-'ud* meaning "the *'ud*." The *riqq* is the inspiration for the tambourine.

During the Medieval period a fabulous musical, artistic, and intellectual life flourished in the courts of the caliphs in Baghdad. The cultural and musical life of this city easily outshone that of Paris and Rome in Europe during this period, not least because it was, in some sense, the capital of the Silk Road: goods and ideas flowed into and out of it from the west and the east.

Medieval musical style and practice in the Middle East is known today because the caliphs commissioned scholars and philosophers to write in detail about all branches of knowledge, including musical theory. These scholars, writing in Arabic, had access to Greek manuscripts about music. They borrowed many ideas about musical scales and modes and rhythm and meter from Greek writings. The music the Middle Eastern scholars describe consisted of monophonic, ornamented melodies with rhythmic accompaniment on drums. It was passed down in aural tradition rather than written tradition. It featured improvisation as an art equal to and even more valued than composition. Scholarly writings on music from the Medieval period document both the rich musical life of professional court musicians and an elaborate system of melodic and rhythmic modes. The descriptions of this life in the past are consistent in many ways with the musical life and musical structures heard today in the Middle East.

Islam spread quickly through the modern Middle East, North Africa, and Central Asia. In this unified religious environment, similar traditions of music based on extensive use of melodic modes accompanied by drums developed among the Persian- and Turkic-language groups of this huge region. Today Iran, Turkey, and the countries of Central Asia and North Africa each have their own related but distinct musical traditions. The same sorts of instruments, a similar music theory, and the patronage of professional musicians typical of Medieval Arab courtly music reverberate in these and many other kinds of Middle Eastern music today.

In Middle Eastern musical traditions, the history of music is not recorded in musical notation as it was in Europe. Rather, it is carried in theoretical treatises, paintings, and musical relics dating from the Medieval period. It has also been passed on for centuries in an aural tradition that included improvisatory practices and that has changed in many difficult-to-document ways through time. Notated compositions appear rather late in the history of this tradition. What is known of Arab composers comes mainly from the twentieth century.

One such twentieth-century Arab composer is A. J. Racy. He was born into a well-educated family in Lebanon in 1943. His father was a famous poet and folklorist. His mother, who played violin, and her brothers, who played *'ud* and violin, introduced him to music. As a child he made musical toys including flutes out of reeds cut from his family's garden. After learning to play violin and *'ud*, he began to play *nay* and *buzuq* during his early teens. After graduating from the American University of Beirut in 1968, he came to the United States, received a Ph.D. in ethnomusicology from the University of Illinois at Urbana-Champaign, and became a professor at the University of California, Los Angeles (UCLA). Respected as

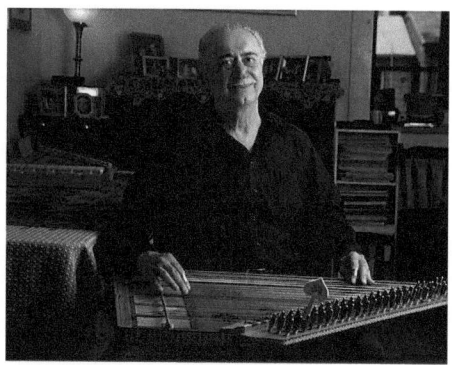

FIGURE 3.9
George Sawa, originally from Alexandria, Egypt, playing the *qanun*
Source: Pedro Bonatto de Castro.

FIGURE 3.10
A. J. Racy playing the *buzuq*
Source: Daniel Neuman.

FIGURE 3.11
Ancient Egyptian long-necked lute and harp on papyrus from c. 1400 BCE (a reconstruction)
Source: De Agostini Picture Library, Wikimedia Commons.

both a performer and scholar, he has composed pieces in the Arab tradition and for symphony orchestra and string quartet. He has performed with many popular singers and for film composers. In the United States and Canada, immigrant communities in major cities continue to support this kind of Arab music and prominent musicians such as A. J. Racy. One noteworthy institution is the National Arab Orchestra in Detroit, Michigan.

WHERE DO I GO FROM HERE?

- Watch video recordings of A. J. Racy playing *'ud, buzuq,* and *nay.*
- Listen to a recording of A. J. Racy's composition "Ecstasy" commissioned by the Kronos Quartet for string quartet, *nay,* and Arab hand drum.
- Listen to recordings of the most famous Arab singer Umm Kulthum (c. 1904–1975). Trained by her father to recite the Qur'an, she moved vast audiences to emotional heights with her perfect pronunciation of classical Arabic, the delicacy of her melodic embellishments, and orchestral accompaniments that eventually combined European and Arab instruments to create the iconic sound of a modernizing Arab, and specifically Egyptian, tradition.
- Listen to a recording of the Turkish or Persian *ney,* a flute deeply important in the Sufi tradition of Islam. Ripped from a bed of reeds as humans are separated from God, *neys* are believed to yearn for their origins just as humans yearn for connection to God's love.

GATEWAY 9
AFRICAN MUSIC

What Is It?

Traders and scholars from the Medieval Caliphate, with its capital in Baghdad, very quickly spread across the Sahara Desert of Africa to the southwestern coast of sub-Saharan Africa and along the East Coast of Africa as far south as present-day Kenya. During the Medieval Period the Mande people of West Africa formed the Mali Empire around 1000 CE. The Shona people of East Africa formed the kingdom of Great Zimbabwe at about the same time. Both the Shona and Mande developed great wealth from the mining of gold, which they exchanged with Arab traders from the north. Today Africa is home to the descendants of these empires, to modern nations, and to a host of ethnic groups, each with its own distinct types of music.

Our gateway to African music is a recording from Zimbabwe in southeastern Africa, where about ten million Shona live. The musician plays an *mbira,* an **idiophone** (an instrument whose wood or metal or other natural material vibrates) found in many parts of Africa in a multitude of forms. The ***mbira*** in this recording has twenty-two tuned, plucked metal keys mounted on a flat soundboard. It is called *mbira dzavadzimu* (also *mbira huru*) and is one of several types of *mbira* played in Zimbabwe. The composition's title, called "Nyamaropa" ("Meat and Blood"), references a hunt. The instrument is often placed inside a gourd resonator to amplify its sound. The singer on this recording, originally released in 1973, is respected elder Hakurotwi Mude.

 Listen to the first thirty seconds of the recording.

How Does It Work?

Timbre

The plucked metal keys of the *mbira* produce a sound rich in overtones. The rattles on the *mbira* and the *hosho* (rattle) add a buzzing sound. The singer commands a variety of vocal timbres, including a raspy quality at times.

FIGURE 3.12
Map of Africa (Shona people)

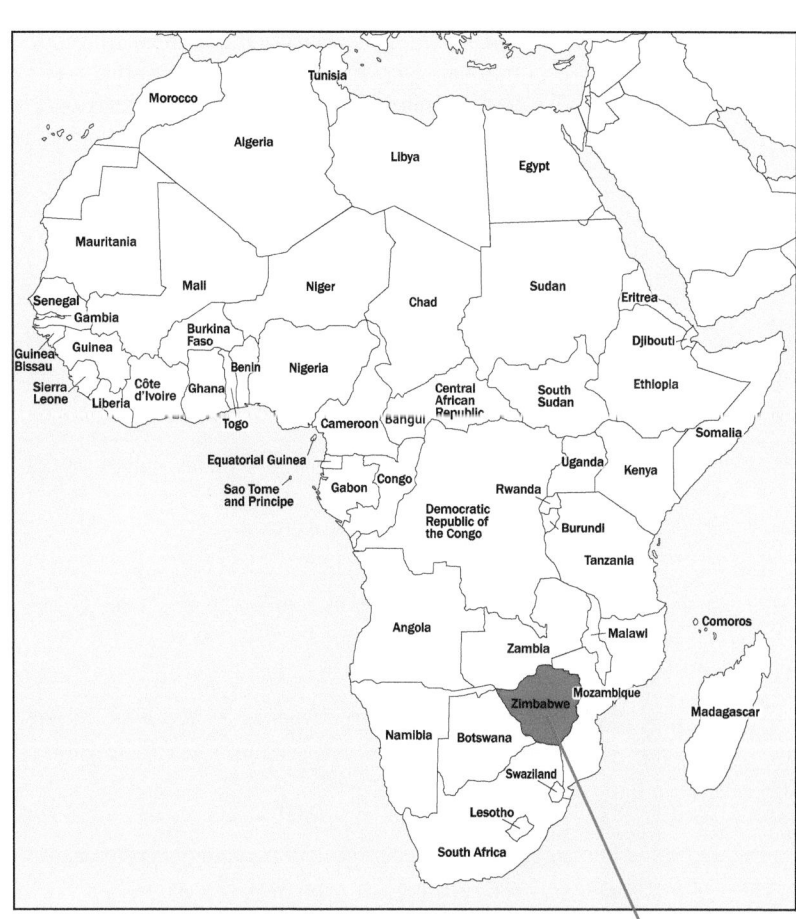

Zimbabwe, home of the Shona people

Texture

The *mbira*s play different polyphonic patterns in an interlocking style: high-pitched melodic lines produced by the thumb and forefinger of the right hand; mid-pitched melodic lines produced by the left thumb on the high row of keys on the left side of the *mbira*; and low-pitched melodic lines produced by the left thumb on the low row of keys on the left side of the instrument. The *hosho* adds another strand to the texture, as does the singer with his melodic lines.

Rhythm

The piece is based on a rhythmic cycle of four phrases. Each phrase is four beats long, and each beat is subdivided into three pulses for a total of forty-eight pulses. The *hosho* articulates the three-pulse divisions of the beats.

Melody

There are many melodies inherent in the *mbira*s' polyphonic texture, which the musician brings out in his singing. Melodies fall into high, middle, and low ranges.

Harmony

The harmonic structure is created by interlocking melodies, which sound a variety of intervals.

Form

The form consists of a forty-eight-beat pattern on the *mbira*. One complete cycle consists of four progressively altered four-beat phrases, which suggest a harmonic sequence. The four-phrase forty-eight-pulse pattern is repeated over and over with improvised variations on the *mbira* and improvised vocal lines.

Performance Techniques

The singer employs three different styles of singing, which the performer inserts at will in an improvised fashion.

1.   Vocal style #1, called *huro*, consists of high-pitched, descending melodic lines sung with yodeling on syllables like "wo-i-ye, i-ye, i-ye."

FIGURE 3.13
Cosmas Magaya, a member of Hakurotwi Mude's ensemble, models the *mbira*'s playing technique
Source: Paul Berliner.

FIGURE 3.14
Hakurotwi Mude playing the *mbira* inside a gourd resonator
Source: Paul Berliner.

2. Vocal style #2, called *mahon'era*, is sung softly on "yah" in the lower part of the vocal range. It is usually a series of ascending phrases using somewhat disjunct melodic motion.
3. Vocal style #3, called *kudeketera*, carries improvised lines of poetry sung syllabically. The singer reflects on the context of the performance, the people listening, and his personal life.

Listen to the first forty-five seconds of this recording for the triple feel of the pulses of each beat and the shift from *huro* vocal style to *mahon'era* style around 0:30.

Listen to this recording following this timed listening guide.

LISTENING GUIDE 3.3

TIME	DESCRIPTION
0:00	Fade in on the sound of the *mbira* and the *hosho*.
0:06	*Mbira*s play the repeating pattern, and the singer enters in an ornate, descending exclamatory style that includes yodels (*huro*).
0:30	The singer changes to a low, bass style with ascending phrases (*mahon'era*).
0:54	The singer changes to *huro* style.
1:20	The singer changes to *mahon'era* style.
1:36	Melodic variation in the *mbira* part.
1:44	The singer alternates between *huro* and *mahon'era* styles.
3:18	Melodic variation in the accompaniment part. The singer changes to *kudeketera* vocal style (improvised poetry in Shona).
4:07	The singer alternates between *mahon'era* and *huro* styles.
5:28	The singer drops out and the *mbira*s play melodic variations.
5:43	The singer re-enters in *huro* style.
6:01	The singer changes to *mahon'era* style and the recording fades out.
6:20	End

What Does It Mean?

> SOCIAL
> BEHAVIOR

The Shona constitute the majority ethnic group of the country of Zimbabwe in southeastern Africa. In addition to gifted, specialist performers, like Hakurotwi Mude, Shona music making is distributed among the population, which mainly consisted of farmers before modernization and urbanization in the twentieth century.

> TECHNOLOGY

The Shona possess a wide variety of musical instruments, including drums, flutes, and stringed instruments. They are most famous for the many types of *mbira* they play, including a number, like the *mbira dzavadzimu* (*mbira huru*) that are played for the amusement of the ancestral spirits. The *mbira dzavadzimu* has twenty-two metal keys organized in three manuals with a three-octave range. The keys in the lower left manual are an octave lower than those in the upper left manual. The left thumb (LT) plays both these manuals. The right manual plays an octave above the upper left manual. On the right manual, the right thumb (RT) plucks down and the right forefinger (RF) plucks up.

An important characteristic of the *mbira*'s sound is its buzzing tone quality. This is created by the *hosho* and also by a set of bottle caps (in the old days snail shells and imported seashells) attached to the soundboard or to the gourd resonator in such a way as to rattle in sympathy with the plucked metal keys. This rattling sound is a highly desired quality of musical sound in much of sub-Saharan Africa and may well help musicians and listeners hear the many potential, inherent polyphonic lines in the musical texture.

> AESTHETICS

The *mbira*'s keys are tuned to a seven-tone, heptatonic scale. Instead of a fixed scale and set of intervals, however, musicians employ a variety of tunings. By sliding the metal keys forward and back over the instrument's bridge, they can change intervallic relationships of the *mbira*'s tones to slightly shift the character of the tuning. When two *mbira*s play together, they take great pains to tune them very precisely to each other, so they "sound as one," but the precise intervallic relationships within an octave are not measured against an external standard such as half steps and whole steps. Musicians sometimes delight in changing the tuning system they use from time to time, and they say that such retuning has the effect of refreshing their entire repertoire.

Musicians play fixed patterns and improvised variations by alternating the right and left hand in this pattern: LT on the lower left manual—RT on the right manual—LT on the upper left manual—RF on the right manual. This sequence of finger movements is repeated throughout the performance. This four-pulse movement cycle creates a polymeter with the three-pulse sounding beats and helps musicians hear the polyphony inherent in the monophonic musical line they are playing. Improvisations on the basic pattern involve more complicated fingering patterns. Since the pitches of the piece are spread over three octaves, the brain chunks the resulting pitches into at least three mentally constructed melodic lines. Complicating the inherent polyphonic texture even further, the brain can chunk pitches at the top of one octave with pitches at the bottom of the next higher octave to create even more mentally constructed melodic lines. The musician playing the instrument listens intently to the instrument to pull out these inherent lines. Some players affectionately personify the role of their instruments in the process, as if the instrument itself is suggesting musical ideas to the player.

The form of a performance consists of the repetition of a cyclical pattern, which is then the basis for instrumental and vocal improvisations. As a result, in this tradition, the *mbira* is not accompanying a song. Rather, the voice accompanies an instrumental tune in various ways. Musicians say that the *huro* and *mahon'era* styles are "molded to the voice of the *mbira*," that is, they articulate some of the inherent polyphonic lines the musician is hearing on the instrument. All three styles establish the reflective mood of most Shona *mbira* music.

The third vocal style, *kudeketera*, carries a highly coded form of the Shona language known as "deep Shona," which suggests a variety of meanings subject to interpretation in a way that captures profound truths. Such singing was very important to the Shona people at the time of this recording during the 1960s and 1970s, when the Shona fought a war to liberate the country, then known as Rhodesia, from the control of British colonists. The three vocal styles alternate in a fashion that is completely up to the musician. In this recording of "Nyamaropa," the singer sings a series of improvised single lines of poetry in *kudeketera* style about a wide variety of topics, which include flirting with a woman in the audience, complaining about his troubles with women, praising his mother, lauding his own performance, reporting a bit of local news, worrying that he is getting too old to play well, and voicing concern about an ancestor's interference in his life.

> EMOTIONAL RESONANCE

Mbira music and its accompanying vocal styles are sung for entertainment, including self-entertainment, for dances, and for spirit-possession ceremonies. It seems to have been mainly a male instrument, though today fine female players are well known. The most spectacular occasions for performance of the *mbira dzavadzimu* are spirit possession ceremonies, called *biras*. *Biras* attract ancestral spirits who act as intermediaries between the living and the Creator. *Biras* are held when a person becomes sick and traditional healers believe that a social problem rather than a medical one has caused the illness. In these cases the healer suggests that a *bira* be held so that an ancestor spirit can appear and identify the cause of the mysterious illness. At the *bira* a group of *mbira* players is hired to play for a large gathering of family members and neighbors of the patient. They lead the assembled group in skillful and energetic singing, dancing, and hand-clapping in the hope that an ancestor will like what he or she hears and be tempted to appear at the *bira* by taking possession of the ancestor's human medium or, occasionally, an unsuspecting attendee. Two factors seem to determine success. One is that

> CULTURAL LINKAGES

FIGURE 3.15
Thomas Mapfumo
Source: Jeremy Hogan/Alamy Stock Photo.

the musicians and attendees have to play, sing, and dance well and with enormous energy, and they have to find a piece that the ancestor really likes. Sometimes the ancestors never appear, and other times it can take nearly all night for them to do so. "Nyamaropa" is part of a repertory of traditional pieces believed to be old and thus especially popular with the ancestors and effective in bringing them to the *bira*. Once the ancestor appears by taking possession of a person, the performance ends. The ancestor is consulted and provides a solution that will cure the illness.

What Is Its History?

Though we have no way of knowing the age of Shona *mbira*s, it is likely that zithers and *mbira*-type instruments with idiophonic keys made of wood and bamboo and other natural materials have existed in sub-Saharan Africa since the formation of village agricultural life there many millennia ago. The Shona developed iron smelting and thus the potential to make iron *mbira* keys before 1000 CE. In 1589 a European missionary provided the first written reference to a *mbira* with nine iron keys. The buzzing sound of the *mbira* contrasts strikingly with the European notion of "pure tones" favored in classical music. Enslaved Africans transported this buzzing sound aesthetic, which is common to much African music, to the New World, where it found its place in the vocal effects of jazz singer Louis Armstrong's voice, James "Bubber" Miley's trumpet solos for the Duke Ellington Orchestra in the 1920s, and the gritty guitar aesthetic of early rhythm & blues recordings, among many other examples in African American music.

POLITICS During the nineteenth century the British, French, Germans, and Dutch colonized Africa. Cecil Rhodes (1853–1902), a British businessman, invaded Shona lands in the 1890s, and the territory was named Rhodesia. In 1965 a white rebel coup, anxious to head off progressive changes in the country involving greater parity for Africans, declared independence from Great Britain. That act ignited a fifteen-year guerrilla war that ended with Black majority rule in 1980 and the renaming of the country as Zimbabwe. During the war traditional *mbira* music became an important symbol of resistance to white rule, as did popular music based on the *mbira*'s sound and repertoire.

For decades Zimbabweans, like Africans across the continent, have been listening to recordings of American popular music and creating popular music that either imitates it or alters it in ways to suit local musical taste. The most famous Shona musician in this regard is Thomas Mapfumo (b. 1945), "the lion of Zimbabwe," and his band, The Blacks Unlimited. Mapfumo began his musical life playing covers of rock and soul music, but in the 1970s, during the war for independence from white rule, he turned away from this foreign music and toward traditional Shona music to create a new style of popular music he dubbed *chimurenga* ("struggle"). His guitarist performed the patterns of *mbira* music, and after independence Mapfumo added *mbira*s to his bands. The effect is an aural icon of a combined Shona traditional and modern identity. A decade after Zimbabwe's independence in 1980 he released an album called *Corruption*, which criticized the government of Zimbabwe's former president Robert Mugabe, the person Mapfumo had supported during the war against the British colonists. The album engendered Mugabe's wrath, and ten years later, in the face of increasing pressure, Mapfumo left Zimbabwe for the United States.

AESTHETICS The musical traditions of the Shona people have found new life in the United States. Shona music thrives throughout the Pacific Northwest, with many active ensembles and eager students from Berkeley to Seattle. This is due largely to the influence of Dumisani Maraire (1944–1999), a Zimbabwean *marimba* (xylophone) and *mbira* teacher who settled in the region in the late 1960s. Maraire taught at the University of Washington from 1968 to 1972 and again from 1986 to 1990, and a number of his American students have carried on his legacy in the region, including Seattle *marimba* groups Kutamba and Musango and the Mahonyera Mbira Ensemble, among others.

ECONOMIC ACTIVITY Shona musicians today often find greater opportunities abroad than at home. They have extended their horizons and recast traditional models of patronage, performance, and transmission with a global audience in mind. No longer limiting their opportunities for patronage to ceremonial *bira*s, these artists have forged productive relationships with everyone from government officials and academics to cosmopolitan musicians and world music promoters across the globe. Shona *mbira* players have offset the grinding poverty they face in Zimbabwe and resistance by the country's charismatic churches by turning to their many enthusiastic students and sponsors abroad. The expansive growth of the "world music" recording and concert promotion industries in the United States and U.K. during the 1980s saw ever-increasing opportunities for Shona and other African musicians to perform for large audiences outside of academic and community contexts. With their extended patronage networks, new lines of transmission, and successful popular hybrids, the Shona *mbira* tradition has been strengthened at home. Over the last forty years, it has begun taking new shape as Shona music entered into the global, cosmopolitan, mediated world of recordings and concerts.

WHERE DO I GO FROM HERE?

*   Find and watch a video of the *mbira* being played.
*   Listen to a recording by Thomas Mapfumo that references traditional Shona music and singing styles. "Ngoma Yarira" or "Bukatiende" are two of the many examples.
*   Read about Thomas Mapfumo in Thomas Turino, "Stars of the Seventies: The Rise of Indigenous-Based Guitar Bands," in *Nationalists, Cosmopolitans, and Popular Music in Zimbabwe* (Chicago: University of Chicago Press, 2000), pp. 262–310.

GATEWAY 10
EUROPEAN VILLAGE MUSIC

What Is It?

Until the twentieth century most Europeans led an agrarian life. They lived in small villages and sustained themselves with small-scale agriculture on small plots of land. These rural cultures,

FIGURE 3.16
Map of Bulgaria

while poor and fragile in economic terms, enjoyed a rich musical life full of singing, dancing, and playing on homemade instruments. Starting in the nineteenth century, many of these old traditions began to fade as villagers in western Europe moved to cities to work in the new factories of the Industrial Revolution. But some of these traditions, many with roots in the Medieval period, have continued into the present. The countries of southeastern Europe were among the last to modernize because, from the fifteenth to the late nineteenth centuries, they were part of the Ottoman Empire. At its height the Muslim Ottoman Turks ruled a vast multiethnic territory including southeastern Europe, the present-day Middle East, and much of north Africa.

Bulgaria, a land of Slavic-language-speaking Eastern Orthodox Christians on the Balkan Peninsula in southeastern Europe, absorbed many influences from the Middle East before gaining independence in 1878. Our gateway to European village music with roots in the Medieval period is a performance of Bulgarian dance music titled "Kopanitsa." **Kopanitsa** is a dance genre in a meter of eleven (2+2+3+2+2). This performance was recorded in the 1950s by a small ensemble of five homemade traditional instruments: *gaida* (bagpipe), *kaval* (end-blown, rim-blown flute); *gadulka* (short-necked, fretless bowed lute), *tambura* (long-necked, fretted plucked lute), and *tapan* (double-headed bass drum).

 Listen to the first thirty seconds of the recording.

How Does It Work?

Timbre

The timbre of this recording is created by the five instruments sometimes playing solos and sometimes in combination. The *gaida*, like all bagpipes, is a reed instrument, so describing the timbre as "reedy" is appropriate. The *gaida* is a single-reed instrument. The *kaval* is an end-blown, rim-blown flute with a flute's characteristic pure tone quality. The *gadulka* has a rich but somewhat dull or muted timbre. The *tambura* has a high-pitched, somewhat thin, metallic sound. The *tapan* plays both low-pitched and high-pitched sounds.

Texture

The texture consists of the *gaida, kaval*, and *gadulka* playing melody accompanied by rhythmic strumming on the *tambura* and a drum part. The melodic instruments play together with very slight differences mainly in ornamentation, a monophonic texture called **heterophony** or **heterophonic texture**.

Rhythm

A *kopanitsa* is a fast-tempo dance piece in an additive meter of eleven pulses grouped into measures of five beats counted 1-2-3-4-5 or short-short-long-short-short. The short beats are divided into two pulses and the long beat has three pulses for a total of eleven pulses counted 1-2-1-2-1-2-3-1-2-1-2 or 2+2+3+2+2. The beginning of each measure may be difficult to distinguish in the first sections of the recording, but it is frequently marked by a low accented beat on the drum, the first one appearing at about 0:05. **Additive meters** combine beats of two and three pulses that add up to meters of five (2+3), seven (2+2+3), nine (2+2+2+3), eleven

FIGURE 3.17
The small ensemble of Bulgarian traditional instruments in the recording. Left to right: *kaval* **(Stoyan Velichkov),** *gaida* **(Kostadin Varimezov),** *gadulka* **(Neno Ivanov),** *tambura* **(Yordan Tsvetkov), and** *tapan* **(Ognyan "Jimmy" Vasilev).**
Source: Ivan Varimezov.

(2+2+3+2+2), and so forth. The rhythm consists of almost constant pulses with only a few long tones here and there.

Melody

The melodies in this piece cover a range of about an octave in a number of different modes on different pitch levels. They move mainly in stepwise, conjunct motion.

Harmony

The harmony is based on the sound of a strummed drone.

Form

The form consists of opening and closing sections in which all the instruments play together. Between these sections, each melody instrument plays a solo.

Performance Techniques

The principal performance technique is the ornamentation. Between the main tones of the melody the players add all sorts of short ornamental tones.

Listen to the first thirty seconds of the recording and count along to the five main unequal beats: short-short-LONG-short-short.

Listen to the entire recording following this timed listening guide.

TIME	FORM	DESCRIPTION
0:00	A	The full ensemble plays a narrow-range melody that consists of four eleven-pulse measures.
0:07	A	The A melody repeats.
0:11	B	A new melody similar to the first, also four measures long.
0:18	B	The new melody repeats.
0:23	CC	A new melody based on just three pitches.
0:35	DD	A new melody with a wider range of nearly an octave.
0:46	EE	A new three-pitch melody, similar to C.
0:56	FF	A new melody with an ascending leap is introduced.
1:07	G	The *gaida* changes mode and plays six different short four-measure repeating melodies.
1:37	H	The *kaval* changes mode, signaled by two held pitches, and plays three eight-measure repeating melodies.
2:10	I	The *gadulka* changes mode and plays three eight-measure repeating melodies.
2:37	AA, BB, CC, DD, EE, FF	The entire ensemble enters and repeats the opening section.
3:41	End	

LISTENING GUIDE 3.4

What Does It Mean?

This performance gains some of its meaning as an expression and symbol of an ethnic group. Bulgaria is a small country of eight million people in southeastern Europe. Bulgarians speak a Slavic language written in the Cyrillic alphabet. They are ethnic cousins of Russians, Czechs, Poles, Serbs, and other Slavic-speaking ethnic groups. Their name comes from a group of Turkic-language speakers from Central Asia called Bulgars. They moved into southeastern Europe in the seventh century CE and were absorbed culturally by the Slavs who already lived in the region. Among

CULTURAL LINKAGES

the most distinctive features of Bulgarian musical style are the homemade musical instruments heard in this recording, dances and songs in a variety of additive meters like five, seven, nine, and eleven, and a distinctive type of women's singing with a sharp, loud vocal timbre.

SOCIAL BEHAVIOR

Until the second half of the twentieth century most Bulgarians were subsistence farmers living in rural villages. This recording represents an instrumental musical practice deeply embedded in that rural, agricultural, and pastoral lifestyle. The *gaida* and *kaval* have long been the instruments of shepherds, who entertain themselves, and their herds, during many hours spent in pastures outside the village. The *gadulka* and *tambura*, on the other hand, are often used to accompany singing at weddings and other family celebrations and gatherings.

EMOTIONAL RESONANCE

This recording of a *kopanitsa* also gains meaning from the types of performance contexts it references. Bulgarian listeners would immediately understand it as dance music, especially wedding dance music. Weddings in Bulgarian villages involve long hours of feasting before and after the marriage ceremony at midday on a Sunday. During wedding feasts, while guests eat and drink, a bagpiper plays nonmetrical melodies that evoke the sadness the bride's family feels at losing their daughter, who will move to the home of the family of the groom. As an important moment in the ongoing history of a family, a village, and a people, a wedding recalls past weddings and family members, living and dead, going back as far as memory allows. The *gaida*'s nonmetrical melodies amplify feelings of nostalgia on such occasions. On the other hand, weddings are joyful occasions celebrating a promising future of children and grandchildren and continued family prosperity. These feelings are expressed in energetic music and dancing.

Bulgarian dancing is done mainly in long lines of people holding the hands of those on either side of them. Called *horo* from the Greek word for chorus, meaning a group of people (not a group of singers), the dancers often arrange themselves socially. A man leads the line, reflecting the patriarchal nature of village society, and men dance as a group near the front of the line. Women dance together farther down the line with children at the end. Sometimes young men dance in one part of the line, their energetic, large movements an icon of their youthful masculinity. Women dance with smaller, more careful movements to signal their modesty. Traditionally, everyone watched others dancing in the line, young people checking out potential marriage partners, and older people noting any flirting for future reference in a society where arranged marriages were once the norm.

SOCIAL BEHAVIOR

In Bulgaria, instrumental music, especially the playing of the *gaida* and *kaval*, carries a strong gendered association. All traditional Bulgarian musical instruments are played almost exclusively by men, while women are the best singers. In traditional village culture, women spent all their time raising children, cooking, spinning wool into yarn, weaving yarn into cloth, sewing cloth into clothing, and embroidering the clothing to make it beautiful. Their hands were never free to practice and play a musical instrument. Men, on the other hand, built and maintained homes, plowed and planted fields, and shepherded animals. During long hours in pastures, they had time to develop the virtuosic instrumental skills demonstrated in this recording.

AESTHETICS

The musical form of dance performances is not fixed, but neither are they completely improvised. The performers begin by playing melodies from a stock of familiar tunes they all know. At an actual dance this pattern would repeat many times for as much as an hour of continuous dancing. The musicians change the character of their tunes either at a signal from the lead dancer or by observing and sensing what they think the leader might enjoy at that moment. This performance is constrained by the conventions of recordings and lasts only a few minutes.

Bulgarian dance pieces are given genre names according to the meter of the dance. *Kopanitsa*s are all in a meter of 11 = 2+2+3+2+2. The dances in a meter of 5 = 2+3 are all called *paidushka*, and so forth. Each dance genre has a huge number of melodies, and some of them are named for the village or region where they are popular or for a person who loves the particular opening melodies.

What Is Its History?

The musical instruments in this recording from Bulgaria are early examples of the kinds of the instruments that make up the modern European classical symphony orchestra. A few of these instruments are native to Europe, but many of them entered Europe through contact with the Ottoman Empire. European orchestral musicians divide musical instruments into four groups: the strings (bowed lutes of various sizes called, from high-pitched to low-pitched: violin, viola, cello, and bass); the woodwinds (clarinet, flute, oboe, and bassoon); the brass (buzzed lipped aerophones called trumpet, trombone, horn, and tuba); and percussion. Percussion refers to instruments that are struck. There are two kinds in the orchestra: idiophones such as cymbals, gongs, and **xylophones** (instruments with multiple struck wooden keys); and **membranophones** (instruments with stretched skins or "heads" such as **timpani** [single-headed, bowl-shaped **kettle drums**], snare drum, bass drum, and tambourine). In addition to the Bulgarian *tapan*, virtually all the orchestral percussion instruments came into Europe from the Ottoman Empire, where they contributed to court and military music. Bowed string instruments in the shape of the Bulgarian *gadulka* are the predecessors of orchestral strings. The predecessor of the double-reed oboe and bassoon is a Turkish outdoor double-reed aerophone called *zurna*, played by Ottoman military bands. In Medieval Europe its successor was called a **shawm**. Single-reed bagpipes like the Bulgarian *gaida* are among the antecedents of the clarinet. The *kaval* has no analogs among modern European instruments, but the ancestors of orchestral side-blown flutes are found in Medieval European court cultures that predate the Ottoman invasion of European lands. Brass instruments have their roots in European shepherds' wooden trumpets and animal horns and the Roman military's large metal *tuba* and *cornu* (horn). The European orchestra doesn't employ lutes that are primarily plucked or strummed, but the precursor of the classical guitar is the Arab *'ud* featured in the previous gateway. The long-necked plucked lute called *tambura* is widespread throughout the Middle East. It is popular in the village music traditions of southeastern Europe, but it never found a home in Europe's classical music.

The archetypal symbol of European village music is the bagpipe, made as it is from the skin of one of the villagers' herd animals. Bagpipes are found in virtually every European culture. There are suggestive references to them in the plays of the Ancient Greek dramatist Aristophanes from the fourth century BCE. The bag of the *gaida* is made from a goatskin turned inside out, and the word *gaida* probably has a Germanic-language root meaning goat (*gaid*). The instrument and its name may survive from a time in the fifth century CE when the paths of migrating Germanic and Slavic people crossed in central Europe. In the industrialized countries of western and central Europe, bagpipes have largely disappeared in European village music, replaced by two other **reed instruments**, the clarinet and the accordion. They have flourished mainly in a few peripheral areas of Europe with strong rural cultures. Scottish bagpipers at some point added two additional drone pipes

TECHNOLOGY

FIGURE 3.18
Swiss alphorn
Source: Hans Hillewaert, Wikimedia Commons.

FIGURE 3.19
A Medieval, thirteenth-century manuscript illustration of two players of a bowed lute called rebec or *rebab*, which had entered Europe from Arab North Africa
Source: Cantigas de Santa Maria, Wikimedia Commons.

to the older single drone, which the Bulgarian *gaida* preserves. Sometime in the eighteenth century Irish bagpipers added keys to the melody pipe and a set of pipes called regulators that could play chords in addition to a drone. To play the regulators, Irish bagpipers sat down while they entertained the upper classes in their salons. They pump air into the bag from a bellows under one arm, rather than blowing into the bag as most bagpipers do. At some unknown time in the past, Bulgarian bagpipers reduced the size of the top hole on the melody pipe, making it possible for them to play a fully chromatic scale on the instrument without using keys.

CULTURAL
LINKAGES

The Scottish bagpipes are the best-known bagpipes. They suffuse the culture of Britain's former colonies in North America and the western Pacific: pipe bands play in holiday parades, and solo pipers play at funerals for soldiers, firefighters, and the police. They were brought to North America by Scottish and Irish immigrants, for whom bagpipes are a symbol of national identity and resistance to English domination. As a consequence they have a long association with the military. But for an even longer time bagpipes have been part of European pastoral culture, where they have none of the links to the military that Scottish bagpipes do.

AESTHETICS

Bulgaria's history helps explain why the Bulgarian bagpipe and the instruments in this recording continue to flourish today. During the ninth and tenth centuries the Kingdom of Bulgaria was one of the largest countries in Europe. Its rulers had adopted Eastern Orthodox Christianity as their national religion. By the fifteenth century the Turkish Ottoman Empire had conquered Bulgarian lands and occupied most of southeastern Europe. Although the Slavic population remained Christian, Bulgaria was part of the Islamic Caliphate ruled from Istanbul until Bulgaria re-emerged as an independent kingdom in 1878. For 500 years under the Ottoman Empire and until the 1950s, most Bulgarians missed out on the industrialization, modernization, and religious and philosophical changes going on in central and western Europe. Bulgaria's agrarian society preserved features of Medieval European rural, peasant culture, including bagpipe playing and traditional singing and dancing during this long period.

Widespread education and urbanization, which are threats to traditional village culture, began in Bulgaria after 1944, near the end of World War II, when a communist regime under the influence of the Soviet Union came to power. Although the communists fostered dramatic changes in traditional ways of life that undermined the foundations of Bulgarian traditional music and dancing, to their credit they adopted those same threatened Bulgarian traditions as symbols of the Bulgarian nation. To keep these rural traditions from dying out completely in the face of mass urbanization and universal education, they established schools and conservatories where young people could study these traditions. Graduates of the schools were hired to play in professional folklore ensembles, which presented these waning traditions to the nation's people and to audiences abroad. And they directed and coached village amateur groups, which performed in government-sponsored local, regional, and national festivals. The continuing strength of the Bulgarian instrumental music tradition heard in this recording is the product of this history of preservation, first by a rural society largely untouched by modernity for the past 500 years, and second by a totalitarian government that institutionalized its performance as a symbol of the nation.

Small ensembles like the one heard in this recording first began to appear and record in the 1930s. From the 1950s on, classically trained composers began to arrange village instrumental music using European harmony for an orchestra of Bulgarian village instruments, including *gaidas*, *gadulkas*, *kavals*, *tamburas*, and the *tapan*. These orchestral arrangements of traditional village music were heard every day on the radio, transforming what Bulgaria's urban, educated elite interpreted as a backward, muddy village tradition into a clean, modern sound suitable for a modernizing society.

CULTURAL
LINKAGES

These composers made similar changes to village songs, which were sung mainly by women. They transcribed them into musical notation and arranged them in three-part harmony for professionally trained village singers to perform. That choral sound also became an important symbol of Bulgaria's modern national identity. In the late 1980s a Swiss music producer happened on these recordings and released three LP/CD albums of them under the title *Le mystère des voix bulgares* (The Mystery of the Bulgarian Voices). The striking village vocal timbres and the interesting harmonies captured the attention of the burgeoning audience for the newly named "world music" genre in western Europe, North America, and Japan. Bulgarian music rose to the top of the world music charts.

When Bulgaria entered the European cultural orbit after becoming an independent country, musicians, including village musicians, began to play European musical instruments like violin, clarinet, and accordion. They competed with players of Bulgarian traditional instruments for jobs at weddings and other celebrations. Virtuoso players of these instruments plus saxophone, synthesizer, and drum set developed among a minority group in Bulgaria called Roma (also known disparagingly as Gypsies). In the 1990s their recordings also started appearing abroad, and a few of them, notably those of clarinetist Ivo Papazov and saxophonist Yuri Yunakov, became quite well known. Today the tradition of Bulgarian rural village music is still taught in Bulgarian schools and music conservatories, and musicians showcase their virtuosity in competitions, festivals, and on the radio and television.

WHERE DO I GO FROM HERE?

- Listen to Bulgarian traditional instruments playing solo or in communist-era orchestral arrangements on an album entitled "Great Masters of Bulgarian Instrumental Folklore—vol. 1."
- Listen to recordings of modern arrangements of Bulgarian village songs sung by women's choirs on albums entitled *"Le mystère des voix bulgares."*
- Find videos of "Bulgarian folk dance" and "Bulgarian weddings" and watch professional folklore ensembles as well as videos of modern weddings.
- Listen to Bulgarian virtuosos on modern instruments, especially clarinetist Ivo Papazov, saxophonist Yuri Yunakov, and accordionist Petar Ralchev.

CLOSING

The gateways to Ancient and Medieval secular music in this chapter include two examples of music supported by elegant and wealthy courts, those of China and the Middle East, and two with origins in preindustrial, subsistence farming societies, those of the Shona of Zimbabwe and of Bulgaria. Some historical sources describe Shona *mbira* players who were retained in courts of "kings" and "spirit mediums." Taken together, these gateways make the point that wonderful music can be created when musicians can devote themselves to music because they are paid handsomely for their labor, and when they must labor on the land to feed themselves, making music in their spare time in exchange for little more than the gratitude and admiration of their friends and family.

These gateways all focus on one or a small group of specialized musicians: a Chinese *qin* player; an Arab *'ud* virtuoso and composer; a quintet of Bulgarian traditional instrumentalists; and a trio of two *mbiras* and rattle. While solo and small-ensemble playing were important during this period, imperial courts of Ancient and Medieval China, Korea, and Japan had large court orchestras. *Gagaku*, the music of the Japanese court orchestra, survives from this period. In agrarian cultures, most people could play and sing to some extent because these were socially necessary skills. Large groups of people often sang together on special occasions and during social gatherings. The Bulgarian instrumentalists and Shona *mbira* players featured in these gateways represent a small fraction of the wealth of musicality in these societies.

The music and the ideas about music in the gateways of this chapter are known to historians in different ways. Compositions for the Chinese *qin* are preserved in musical notations, some of which date to the Medieval period. Ancient Chinese philosophical treatises contain ideas about the meaning of music and its aesthetic and social value. Arab music, dependent as it is on improvisation rather than composition, was not recorded in notation. Instead, Medieval Arab philosophers wrote extensively about music theory and musical life, some features of which are preserved in modern compositions and performances. In contrast, Bulgarian and Shona musical traditions possess little or no written record from the Ancient or Medieval period. The histories of these traditions are based in part on historical inferences and analogy with modern musical practices. Frescoes and paintings from the Medieval period suggest that bagpipes have long been part of the European pastoral tradition. The Bulgarian word for bagpipe, *gaida*, probably dates from a time more than a thousand years ago when Slavic and Germanic tribesmen came in contact. But the actual music in the gateway example is a modern manifestation of Ancient and Medieval ways of making music in Europe. The metal keys of the Shona *mbira* may date from the Medieval period, and we can assume from the similarity of this instrument to African instruments with cane and reed keys that it derives from Ancient instrumental technologies. But the actual age of the tune, which the Shona regard as very old because of its links to the ancestors, is unknown. Even though all four gateways in this chapter tell us much about Ancient and Medieval ways of thinking about and making music, they are all modern manifestations of those ways of thinking and show us some of the ways that people today are making music with Ancient and Medieval roots in the modern worlds they inhabit.

THINGS TO THINK ABOUT

- Compare the ways musicians in each of the musical traditions in this chapter have used new technologies to change something about their tradition.
- How are the societies described in this chapter organized with regard to social categories like class, gender, race, ethnicity, or age? How do those social divisions affect music making in each one?

NEW TERMS

additive meters
augmented second
chordophone
chromatic scale
circle of fifths
coda
course
dodecaphonic scale
equal-tempered scale
gaida
harmonic

heterophony, heterophonic texture
idiophone
kopanitsa
lute
mbira, Shona
membranophone
pentatonic scale
perfect fifth
perfect fourth
qin
reed instrument

refrain
rondo form
sama'i
sequence
shawm
tablatures
taqsim
timpani
'ud
xylophone
zither

Music History from 1500 to 1890

THE WORLD'S HISTORY CHANGED DRAMATICALLY after 1492, when the Italian navigator Christopher Columbus set sail with three ships and a crew of Spanish sailors from Andalusia (southern Spain) in search of fabled India. Throughout the sixteenth century dozens of other Spanish, Portuguese, English, and French explorers inaugurated a new era of European influence in world affairs. Between 1500 and 1890 Europeans, their culture, their Christian religion, and their economic and political power came to dominate large areas of the world.

Part II of this book reflects this era of European influence by placing European music at the center of the narrative without losing sight of other musical traditions around the world. It includes a good deal of music that today is typically called classical music. **Classical music** commonly refers to music that was composed for churches, courts, and concerts in Europe from about 900 CE to the present (so it includes the compositions of Hildegard von Bingen featured in Part I). Classical music is commonly heard today played by large ensembles like symphony orchestras, opera companies, concert bands, and choirs in large concert halls. Small ensembles and soloists play recitals, often in smaller halls. The central figure in European classical music is the composer, whose compositions have been preserved in musical notation. Its fans today are typically middle- and upper-class patrons wealthy enough to buy expensive concert tickets, contribute to non-commercial, listener-supported classical radio stations, and pay for their children's private music lessons. The genre also gains support from national governments in some countries and from high schools and universities with elaborate music training programs.

Much of the classical music performed in these settings today is from the period between 1500 and 1890, when Europe was at the height of its influence in the world. Chapter 4 deals with music from 1500 to 1600. It is the height of the European age of discovery, a period called the Renaissance in Europe and a time when the North Indian classical music tradition was taking shape. Chapter 5 examines music from 1600 to 1750, a period of global commerce when a style of music and art called Baroque flourished in Europe and large gong orchestras called gamelans appeared in present-day Indonesia. Chapter 6 explores music from 1750 to 1800, the age of Enlightenment and revolution in Europe and the Americas but also the height of the transatlantic slave trade. In Europe art and music were under the sway of neoclassicism, while enslaved Africans were reimagining their religious traditions in strange and horrible conditions. Chapters 7 and 8 look at European music during the nineteenth century and introduce, for the first time, the music of the United States.

DOI: 10.4324/9781003269304-6

PART II

MUSIC FROM THE EUROPEAN AGE OF DISCOVERY (1500–1600)

THE PERIOD FROM ABOUT 1500 to 1600 was a European age of discovery. During this century, Europeans expanded their maritime exploration of the world around the Horn of Africa to the shores of Asia and across the Atlantic Ocean to North and South America. But Europeans were not only discovering what they called the New World in the Americas. They were also intensely engaged in scientific investigation. Astronomers demonstrated that the earth must revolve around the sun, not the other way around. This conceptual reorganization of the cosmos dislodged humans from the center of God's creation and challenged a millennium of teaching by the Catholic Church.

These discoveries in geography and astronomy followed a century of rediscovery of the art and philosophy of Ancient Greece and Rome, which had been lost to Europeans after the fall of the Roman Empire in 476 CE. A pre-Christian heritage of humanism—that is, the notion that humans, not God, are the source of meaning and value in the world—began to animate European intellectual and artistic life. In the nineteenth century a French scholar labeled this phenomenon a *renaissance*, a rebirth of Ancient Greek and Roman philosophy and art. Since then this period in European art, literature, and music has commonly been known as the **Renaissance**.

Historians of literature also find in this period a renaissance of Ancient Greek and Roman stories, myths, and characters. Historians of art see a rebirth of Greek and Roman realistic representations of the nude human body and individual faces after centuries of Medieval Christian art that covered the body and abstracted the face to represent ideal religious sentiments. In striking contrast to the Gothic cathedrals of Medieval France, with their jumble of gargoyles and spiky towers and buttresses, St. Peter's Basilica in Rome, begun in 1506 and completed in 1590, exhibits the colonnaded regularity and simplicity of the Parthenon in Ancient Greece.

The ferment in science, literature, and the arts undermined the Catholic Church's previously unquestioned authority and prepared the ground for a critical assessment of its activities and teachings. In 1517 one of its priests, Martin Luther (1483–1546), nailed to a church door in Germany a document with ninety-five indictments of the Catholic Church's doctrines and practices, thus igniting the Protestant Reformation and a new chapter in Christian history, one in which priestly authority gave way to interpretations by individual literate readers of the Bible.

Reconfiguring the world from a human-centered point of view led to important innovations in literature and art. Miguel de Cervantes (*c.* 1547–1616) wrote what some consider the first modern European novel, *Don Quixote*, to narrate the adventures of an individual. William Shakespeare (1564–1616) told stories of the full range of human emotion and experience in his plays. Artists learned to paint scenes as humans see them, in three dimensions. Medieval painters had represented the world as God might see it, from a great distance through

DOI: 10.4324/9781003269304-7

FIGURE 4.1
The Parthenon in Greece
Source: Steve Swayne,
Wikimedia Commons.

FIGURE 4.2
St. Peter's Basilica in Rome
Source: Jean-Pol Grandmont,
Wikimedia Commons.

a metaphorical telephoto lens that flattened humans and their world into a single plane. Renaissance painters discovered a way to represent the world in two dimensions with close objects larger than distant objects to create the illusion of three-dimensional space. Called **perspective**, this technique allowed painters to paint the world from a human point of view, or perspective.

Music of this period is less notable for its renaissance of Ancient Greek musical ideas than for its stylistic innovations based on the humanistic spirit of the times. They invented new harmonies and counterpoints that the human ear judged pleasant, and they found ways to express human emotion. In other words, they created music based on the same humanistic principles that painters, novelists, and playwrights were using.

In this chapter we examine gateways to three important European musical genres of this period:

- polyphonic sacred vocal music, a continuation of the Gregorian chant tradition introduced in Chapter 2;
- polyphonic secular music sung at the courts of the nobility; and
- music for the precursors of the modern guitar.

We also provide a gateway to the classical music tradition of North India, also called Hindustani music. Although the instruments in this gateway recording acquired their present form only recently, we introduce them in this chapter for two reasons: first, the most "serious" forms of today's Hindustani instrumental music appeared during the sixteenth century; and, second, nearly all modern North Indian classical instrumentalists trace their musical lineage to a single sixteenth-century musician and his son and daughter.

GATEWAY 11
RENAISSANCE SACRED VOCAL MUSIC

What Is It?

The written record of European sacred music begins in the ninth century with the earliest notations of monophonic Gregorian chant. While these early notations do not record polyphonic music, a few ninth-century manuscripts give rules for the way a soloist could add a second voice to the choir's chant melody in parallel motion with the original chant melody. **Parallel motion** refers to two polyphonic lines that maintain the same interval between them. In this case the two lines proceed in parallel perfect fourths or perfect fifths. Another Medieval polyphonic practice involved the addition of a drone pitch to the chant melody creating a texture called **oblique motion**. For the next 500 years priests, monks, and nuns developed a number of styles of polyphonic singing to enhance the religious and aesthetic effect of their liturgies.

Over these centuries composers began to write polyphonic parts in contrary motion. **Contrary motion** refers to two polyphonic lines that move in opposite directions. They also wrote voices with different rhythmic values. To aid singers in the singing of these developing styles of polyphonic music, the notation of music developed as well to record the precise way the pitches and rhythms that two, three, and four voices were supposed to sing together. This polyphonic practice of writing many melodic lines in parallel, oblique, and contrary motion, sometimes with the same and sometimes with different rhythms, is called **counterpoint**, and the results are referred to as **contrapuntal textures**. **Counterpoint** takes its name from the "points," the notes of musical notation, and refers to the simultaneous singing or playing of two or more melodic lines.

The harmonies that contrapuntalists (an old name for composers) developed during the 500 years from about 1000 to 1500 used many different kinds of harmonic intervals and chords. Some were based on the frequency ratios of the "perfect" intervals of the octave (2/1), fifth (3/2), and fourth (4/3) in the belief that they represented the perfection of the Christian Trinity. Over time the harmonic intervals of **major thirds** and **minor thirds** were introduced. For example, the interval from C to E is a major third; the interval from E to G is a minor third. Some found these intervals pleasing to the ear. The use of thirds in counterpoint signaled a shift from a religious perspective to a human one. By around 1500, contrapuntalists began to rely on these intervals of a third to create harmonies based on chordal triads. A **triad** is a three-pitch cord build from low to high on the interval of a third, for example, A-C-E and C-E-G. This triadic harmony was typical of polyphonic music during the Renaissance and provided the fundamental harmonic basis for European classical music until the early twentieth century, when composers began to experiment with other harmonic systems. Triadic harmony continues to provide the basis for harmony in jazz and popular music.

Our gateway to sixteenth-century European sacred vocal music based on triadic harmonies is a motet called "Sicut cervus" (As a deer) composed by Giovanni Pierluigi da Palestrina (*c.* 1525–1594) and published in 1584. For Renaissance composers, many of whom were from France and Belgium, a **motet** (from the French *mot* meaning word) was a sacred work composed on a Latin text, either newly created or taken from the Bible, and sung during the Catholic liturgy. The poem "Sicut cervus" is an excerpt from the text of the book of Psalms in the Bible's Old Testament. It expresses the passionate nature of faith:

Sicut cervus desiderat ad fontes aquarum ita desiderat anima mea ad te Deus.	As a deer thirsts for spring water, so thirsts my soul for you, God.

This performance by the Cambridge Singers is directed by the renowned English choral conductor John Rutter (b. 1945). His choral compositions and arrangements are frequently performed by school and church choirs.

 Listen to the first thirty seconds of the recording.

How Does It Work?

Timbre

Male and female voices across a wide range from low pitches to high pitches sing with a relaxed vocal quality.

Texture

The texture is based on imitative polyphony or imitative counterpoint. **Imitative polyphony** involves each part in the choir singing the same melodic phrase in succession, entering one after the other. When all the parts have entered, the result is four-part harmony created by four rhythmically independent voices. Each such succession of entrances is called a **point of imitation**. The pitch range of Renaissance music includes four parts from low to high called **bass**, **tenor**, **alto**, and **soprano**.

Rhythm

The rhythm of each part combines long and short tones in a slow-tempo, four-beat meter.

Melody

The melodic lines feature mostly conjunct, stepwise motion.

Harmony

The harmony features chordal triads.

Form

The form is through-composed with two main sections (A B) corresponding to the two lines of the poem.

Performance Techniques

The singers sing long tones without vibrato or ornamentation.

FIGURE 4.3
Giovanni Pierluigi da Palestrina. Lithograph (1828) by Henri-Joseph Hesse (1781–1849)
Source: Wikimedia Commons.

Listen to the first twenty-five seconds of the recording for the entrance of each voice (tenor, alto, soprano, bass) in succession in imitative counterpoint.

Listen to the entire recording following this timed listening guide.

LISTENING GUIDE 4.1

TIME	SECTION	TEXT	ENGLISH TRANSLATION
0:00	First point of imitation: the melodic line enters first in the tenor, then the alto, then the soprano, and finally the bass. The melody has a graceful, singable, slightly ascending melodic contour. Each part's melodic line is a variant of the tenor's melody, altered slightly to create pleasing triadic harmonies.	*Sicut cervus desiderat ad fontes aquarum*	As a deer thirsts for spring waters
0:25	Second point of imitation: just after the bass enters, the tenor repeats the text on a variant of the first melody before the other parts have finished their first version of the melody. When they finish their first line, they follow the tenor for a second time in another point of imitation. This point of imitation is rather buried in the texture until the bass part enters on this repeated text at 0:38.	*Sicut cervus desiderat ad fontes aquarum*	As a deer thirsts for spring waters
1:09	The music on the first line of text cadences on a long-held tone, and the basses begin a third point of imitation on a descending melody, followed in order by the tenors, sopranos, and altos.	*ita desiderat*	so thirsts
1:34	The basses initiate a fourth point of imitation, repeating the words. The tenors, sopranos, and altos follow.	*ita desiderat*	so thirsts
1:54	The tenors initiate a fifth point of imitation, repeating the words. The basses follow.	*ita desiderat*	so thirsts
2:03	Almost immediately, the sopranos initiate a sixth point of imitation with a descending melody on new words overlapping with "ita desiderat." The alto, tenor, and bass parts each follow in turn.	*anima mea ad te Deus*	my soul for you, God
2:30	The sopranos initiate a seventh point of imitation, repeating the words. The basses and the tenors follow while the altos complete the first time through the words. The section and the motet end on a cadence formed of two long-held chords, the last a perfect fifth recalling the perfection of Medieval harmony.	*anima mea ad te Deus*	my soul for you, God
3:07	End		

What Does It Mean?

A number of elements combine to create a dignified, reverential effect appropriate for a religious service:

- the relaxed, pure voice quality and slow tempo;
- the slow declamation of the words, repeated during each point of imitation, focuses attention on the words;
- the harmonies based on triads create a soothing, pleasant effect;

- the stepwise ascending and descending melodies consisting of long-held tones create a calm effect;
- for sixteenth-century listeners, the text in Latin linked this performance to more than a thousand years of *a cappella* singing, that is, choral singing without instrumental accompaniment, enhancing the sense of the continuity and authority of the church's teaching;
- the text evokes religious belief in a poetic and emotional way that inspired both Palestrina and worshippers;
- a choir singing in four-part harmony in this manner would echo rather grandly through the large churches of western Europe, creating an aural image of the Catholic Church's rich traditions, which were also expressed in its extravagant buildings, paintings, and sculptures by the best Renaissance painters, and the elaborately embroidered vestments of the clergy.

Listen to the recording one more time with these effects and sentiments in mind.

An important feature of this new style of Renaissance harmony and polyphony, and of much jazz and classical and popular music ever since, is its regular use of cadences (a **cadence** is a musical gesture marking the end of a phrase of music) that move from triads based on the fourth or fifth degrees of the scale to a triad or perfect fifth on the first degree of the scale. (The first degree of a scale is called the **tonic**.) The most common cadence in this new harmonic style is called an authentic cadence. (An **authentic cadence** moves from a triad on the fifth degree [V] to a triad on the tonic [I] and is often written V-I.) Another common cadence is called a plagal cadence. (A **plagal cadence** moves from a triad on the fourth degree (IV) to one on the tonic (I) and is written IV-I.) Because the plagal cadence came to be associated with the singing of "amen" at the end of hymns, it is sometimes called an amen cadence.

For much of "Sicut cervus" the moving contrapuntal parts create the harmonic impression of rocking between the tonic triad (I) and the triad on the fourth degree of the scale (IV). The first section ends with a V-I authentic cadence (at 1:09), and the second ends with a IV-I plagal cadence (at the end). Using these two cadences to end sections of a composition became the new method for organizing musical forms and remains in use today, especially in popular music.

Listen one more time to "Sicut cervus" with attention to the V-I cadence at 1:09 and the IV-I cadence at the end.

CULTURAL LINKAGES

This historical change from harmony based on fourths and fifths to harmony based on thirds can be interpreted as one aspect of the larger humanist impulse of the fifteenth and sixteenth centuries. Harmonies based on perfect fourths and fifths were linked metaphorically to God's creation and what the Ancient Greek philosopher Pythagoras called "the harmony of the spheres." Fifth and fourths were God's harmonies or nature's harmonies. Harmonies based on thirds seemed to be based on what humans preferred to listen to, at least humans in western Europe. In that sense, harmonies based on thirds proceeded from the same aesthetic framework that led artists to create the illusion of three-dimensional perspective in their paintings.

Palestrina composed his sacred polyphonic choral music during a period called the Catholic **Counter-Reformation**. The pope, church leaders, and musicians sought to restore the dignity and sanctity of the church in the wake of the Protestants' attacks on both. Popes, accused of corruption and licentiousness, adopted modest, ascetic habits as a sign of their renewed dedication to the Christian value of humility. A nearly twenty-year-long (1545–1563) conclave of cardinals and archbishops convened in the northern Italian town of Trento. At this gathering, known as the Council of Trent, delegates reconsidered every aspect of church doctrine, including the liturgy and its music. They rejected the Protestant practice of singing in local languages to educate their congregations in biblical lessons and Christian theology. Instead, they reaffirmed the use of Latin in the liturgy. They considered rejecting polyphonic music and returning to monophonic Gregorian chant to focus worshippers' attention on the text and not distract them with the pleasures

FIGURE 4.4
"The Delivery of the Keys" (1481) by Pietro Perugino (c. 1450–1523) demonstrates the technique of perspective through depicting the lines of the city square all receding to a single point in the distance
Source: Sistine Chapel, Wikimedia Commons.

of music, a concern echoing those of Buddhists and Muslims about music's seductive powers. They abandoned this proposal, not least because Palestrina and his contemporaries adopted the contemplative, slow-moving style, with appropriate attention to textual clarity, exemplified by "Sicut cervus."

What Is Its History?

Composers began to move away from Medieval harmonies based on the "perfect" fourths and fifths and write music based on triadic harmonies about a century before Palestrina. The most important composer of this transition to Renaissance harmonies based on thirds was Guillaume Dufay (c. 1397–1474), who lived through most of the fifteenth century. Born in northern Europe near Brussels, he was educated in the church and may have been paid as a church composer as early as age sixteen. Throughout his life he traveled between the French-speaking area of northern Europe and the Italian cities of Rome, Florence, and Bologna, where he taught Italians these new French polyphonic techniques. Among his many compositions was a set of lamentations on the fall of the Eastern Orthodox Christian city of Constantinople to the Ottoman Turks in 1453. He wrote in many genres including motets, secular French *chansons*, and settings for seven complete mass ordinaries.

Dufay is perhaps most famous for his masses based on a ***cantus firmus*** (fixed song) taken from popular, secular music to make church music more engaging for worshippers. Sometimes the chosen song melody appears in all the movements of the ordinary of the mass, providing it with a unifying musical element and creating what is called a **cyclical mass**. Using a secular song as a *cantus firmus* connected religious worship to everyday secular experience, the same impulse that has led the Catholic faithful since the mid-twentieth century to compose folk masses, mariachi masses, and African masses. One of Dufay's most famous works is his *Missa L'homme armé* (Mass [based on the song] "The Armed Man"). The song "L'homme armé" may have been composed in 1453 at the fall of the city of Constantinople, capital of the Eastern Christian church, to the Ottoman Empire. A call for a crusade against the Ottoman Empire in 1460 may have inspired Dufay to write this *cantus firmus* mass based on it.

Fifty years after Dufay's birth, another important precursor of Palestrina was born in northern France or Belgium: Josquin des Prez (c. 1450/1455–1521), often called simply Josquin. During his lifetime he worked at the courts of a number of French dukes, but also traveled to Italy, where he worked for a time at the papal chapel. Twenty of his complete masses survive, including one using "L'homme armé" as the *cantus firmus*. He is also well known for his polyphonic secular *chansons*. His works were among the first to be published in musical notation on the new printing presses invented in Germany by Johannes Gutenberg in 1453. Printed music allowed musical

CULTURAL LINKAGES

scores to be reproduced in greater quantities than ever before. Printed versions of Josquin's music circulated widely around Europe, making him famous and amplifying the influence of his innovative compositional style.

Born around the time of Josquin's death, Palestrina lived his whole life in service to the Church, most of it in Rome as a singer, choirmaster, and composer for various papal chapels, including for a time at the Sistine Chapel, the pope's chapel famous today for its frescoes painted by Michelangelo (1475–1564). Palestrina could not stay there long, however, because he was not a priest. He married twice and had a number of children. "Sicut cervus" is one of 375 motets he wrote during his lifetime. Some critics consider these motets his greatest works, perhaps because of the marriage of his sensitive music with religiously enthused texts. Even more important historically are the 104 polyphonic Masses he wrote based on the ordinary texts of the Mass (Kyrie, Credo, Gloria, Sanctus, Agnus Dei). Compositions for the Ordinary of the Mass have continued to attract composers from Palestrina's time to the present, including Protestant and Jewish composers. A great deal of Palestrina's music survives largely due to his long-lasting employment at St. Peter's in the Vatican. A century or so later, eighteenth-century Austrian composer Johann Joseph Fux (1660–1741) codified Palestrina's style in his highly influential treatise *Gradus ad Parnassum* (figuratively, "steps to the loftiest peaks of art"). The book introduced the concept of "species counterpoint" (types of counterpoint, that is, ways of writing polyphony), a pedagogical tool still used today in some university music theory classes.

During the late nineteenth and early twentieth centuries, *a cappella* sacred singing in the tradition of the harmonic innovations of Palestrina and other Renaissance composers was an important feature of American cultural life, taking both sacred and secular forms in barbershop quartet singing, college glee clubs, and African American spirituals (Chapter 8, Gateway 30). Today choral singing like that of "Sicut cervus" occupies a somewhat peripheral place in American musical life. Today European-derived choral singing finds its home principally in school and university music programs, churches, and synagogues, and a few professional ensembles devoted to its performance. These choral singing institutions have in turn incubated the current interest in *a cappella* singing on college campuses and on TV shows like *The Sing-Off* and films like *Pitch Perfect*.

WHERE DO I GO FROM HERE?

- Listen to the "Gloria" from Palestrina's *Missa Pater Noster* (Our Father). Notice the way each of the first three voices enters in imitation after just two syllables of the previous voice. The bass voice enters with the same melody just a bit later. Listen also for the harmonies in thirds.

- Compare "Sicut cervus" to other recordings of other Palestrina motets such as "O magnum mysterium" (1569) or "Jubilate Deo" (1575).

- Listen to the "Kyrie" from Josquin's *Missa L'Homme armé super voces musicales*, composed about 1502. How is it similar to and different from "Sicut cervus"?

- Listen to and read about African American composer Mary Lou Williams's *Mary Lou's Mass* (1970, originally titled *Music for Peace*). Commissioned by the Vatican, it integrates elements of jazz with the Catholic liturgy, a combination of sacred and secular that echoes Josquin's *Missa L'Homme armé*. How does it demonstrate a connection between religious experience and everyday secular experience?

GATEWAY 12
RENAISSANCE SECULAR MUSIC

What Is It?

During the sixteenth century secular rulers and landowning members of the hereditary nobility hired professional musicians to entertain them. These aristocrats also learned to read musical notation and play musical instruments, sing, and dance for their own amusement and as an important part of refined behavior at court functions. They, as well as professional entertainers, sang together in the new four-part triadic harmony introduced in Gateway 11. And they, or the professional musicians they hired, played dance music harmonized in that same harmonic style.

Our gateway to Renaissance secular music in this new harmonic style is an example of vocal music. It is a madrigal called "Fair Phyllis I Saw Sitting All Alone." John Farmer (*c.* 1570–1601), an English composer, published it in 1599. **Madrigals** first appeared in Italy around 1530 as a genre of polyphonic love songs in Italian, the secular counterpart of the sacred motet. The term may derive from the Latin *matri* (*lo*) *quela*, meaning mother tongue, that is, Italian rather than Latin. When the English began composing and singing them in English later in the sixteenth century, they kept the Italian name madrigal. "Fair Phyllis" is a cheeky song about a shepherd boy named Amyntas in search of his lost lover, Phyllis, a shepherdess. Well-educated sixteenth-century singers of madrigals knew Phyllis and Amyntas as the names of a shepherdess and shepherd from their study of Latin literature from Ancient Rome. The Roman poet Virgil, famous for his epic *Aeneid*, wrote that Amyntas played a reed pipe, perhaps a bagpipe like those that shepherds all over Europe have played since antiquity. The performance is by four members of The King's Singers, a group of six male vocalists formed at King's College, Cambridge, founded in the 1960s.

FIGURE 4.5
The King's Singers in 1970
Source: United Archives/Alamy Stock Photo.

 Listen to the first fifteen seconds of the recording.

How Does It Work?

Timbre

Four male singers sing relatively pure tones over a wide range from bass to soprano.

Texture

The texture changes from monophonic to polyphonic, including imitative counterpoint.

Rhythm

The meter changes back and forth between duple and triple.

Melody

The melodic motion is conjunct.

Harmony

The harmony is based on triads, with authentic cadences (V-I) at the end of each line of text.

Form

The form can be described, using letters, as AABCC.

Performance Techniques

To reach the high pitches in the soprano voice, the male singer sings in **falsetto**, a "false" voice that allows men, and women, to sing in a register above their normal, speaking vocal range. The singers of the two highest parts sing in this manner and are called **countertenors** rather than sopranos or altos, as female singers are. They sing without vibrato at a very fast tempo.

Listen to the recording for the monophonic and polyphonic textures.

Listen to the entire recording following this timed listening guide.

TIME	FORM	TEXT	DESCRIPTION
0:00	A	Fair Phyllis I saw sitting all alone	It is sung monophonically by a single voice in duple meter.
0:04		Feeding her flock near to the mountainside	All voices sing four-part polyphony in the same rhythm, mixing triple and duple meter.
0:06	A (repeat)		
0:12	B	The shepherds knew not whither she was gone.	The first point of imitation in duple meter enters.
0:16		But after her lover Amyntas hied	The second point of imitation.
0:21	C	Up and down he wandered	A third point of imitation tosses a short melodic phrase "up and down" from soprano to bass among the four voices.
0:31		While she was missing	In a brief contrapuntal passage the basses and tenors enter together in contrary motion followed by the sopranos and altos, also in contrary motion.
0:33		When he found her	The countertenor and bass sing in parallel tenths (an octave plus a third), while the middle voices sing two different melodic lines with contrasting rhythmic durations.
0:36		O, then they fell a-kissing	Three- and four-part polyphony sung in the same rhythm in triple meter.
0:44	C (repeat)		
1:12	End		

What Does It Mean?

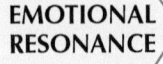

Composers during the Renaissance, like their counterparts in art and literature, sought to express individual human emotions in their work. In their vocal compositions, they created musical icons for the ideas and sentiments in the text, a technique known as **text painting**. In "Fair Phyllis," Farmer and the performers combine fast tempo and suggestive lyrics to create a jolly mood.

 Listen again to the recording, following the chart below and paying attention to the way Farmer paints the text in musical gestures.

Fair Phyllis I saw sitting alone	A single voice evokes her solitude.
Feeding her flock near to the mountainside	The polyphony of voices singing in the same rhythm suggests a unified "flock."
The shepherds knew not whither she was gone	The introduction of imitative polyphony suggests shepherds and Phyllis's lover, Amyntas, scurrying around.
But after her lover Amyntas hied	
Up and down he wandered	The short melodic phrase jumps rapidly up and down in pitch, a musical icon referencing the search over hill and dale the first time. The second time, after "O, then they fell a-kissing," it references a more intimate form of wandering up and down.
While she was missing	

When he found her

From the Renaissance on, singing in parallel thirds (in this case the countertenors and basses sing in an octave plus a third) became an icon of togetherness, love, and shared views.

O, then they fell a-kissing

Here the unified rhythm of all the voices suggests a kind of musical embrace.

What Is Its History?

The earliest European courtly secular love songs survive in manuscripts from the twelfth century. Medieval court entertainers, courtiers, and nobility from southwestern Europe known as **troubadours** (in French *trouvères*), including a few women, composed lyrics and melodies and sang them solo with or without instrumental accompaniment. Contrapuntal polyphonic styles of choral singing developed simultaneously for sacred and secular singing throughout the Medieval period. Madrigals stand out at this moment in history, the sixteenth century, because they were written in a new harmonic style based on triads, which became the harmonic foundation for later European classical music, American popular music, and jazz. As a consequence they are the oldest style of European secular vocal music widely performed today. Madrigals are also foundational for an important feature of European instrumental music: its ability to express emotions. Madrigals associated certain musical elements so tightly with textual ideas that when, in later instrumental music, the words were omitted, the idea or emotion in the musical gesture (say, a descending melodic line) retained its meaning for composers and listeners (a fall from grace, a descent into hell, or sadness, for example).

An important element of the new triadic harmony in this example is the division of voices into four categories based on the pitches they sing: from high to low, soprano, alto, tenor, and bass. To apply this harmonic style to instrumental music, instrument makers took a single type of instrument such as a fiddle, a flute, or a trumpet (a buzzed-lip aerophone made of metal) and created families of instruments of different sizes to play together in groups the four parts of this new harmonic style over this same wide range. The fiddles, like the Bulgarian *gadulka* (Chapter 3, Gateway 10), that played monophonic melodies during the Medieval period became a family of viols in sizes from soprano to bass. (A **viol** is a bowed string instrument with frets on the neck and held vertically between the knees.) During this same period a related family of bowed string instruments developed without frets on the neck. It includes, in order from low-pitched to high-pitched, the violin, viola, cello, and bass. A whistle flute common in European pastoral culture became a family of

AESTHETICS

FIGURE 4.6
The Smithsonian Consort of Viols, performing in 2009
Source: Badagnani, Wikimedia Commons.

FIGURE 4.7
The Fontanella Quintet, a recorder consort from the U.K. Left to right: great bass, tenor, alto, basset (little bass), tenor.
Source: Fontanella Quintet.

FIGURE 4.8
Painting of a consort of sackbut (early trombone) and cornets (buzz-lipped aerophone), *c.* **1545 by Giorgio Vasari (1511–1578)**
Source: Isabella Stewart Gardner Museum, Wikimedia Commons.

SOCIAL BEHAVIOR

FIGURE 4.9
Portrait of Edward de Vere, 17th Earl of Oxford
Source: Wikimedia Commons.

FIGURE 4.10
Sixteenth-century Venetian painting of a group of madrigal singers with lute
Source: Music-Images/Alamy Stock Photo.

recorders. (A **recorder** is a whistle flute with a beak that channels the player's breath over a sharp edge to produce the sound.)

These string and recorder ensembles were suitable for indoor performances and court. For outdoor occasions, louder double-reed instruments like the shawm and brass trumpets and **horns** (a buzzed-lip aerophone with a curved tube) that contributed to the pageantry of royal courts since Roman times were more effective. During the sixteenth century outdoor wind bands included these types of instruments in families from low to high pitch. These families of instruments predate today's low-pitched double-reed bassoon, high-pitched trumpets, the mid-pitched horn, and mid- and low-pitched trombones with slides for changing pitches easily. These families of instruments played madrigals and instrumental dance music at court in ensembles known as **consorts**.

The Italian madrigal caught on in England after 1560, when publications of Italian madrigals with texts translated into English began to appear there. Italian culture enthralled the English at the time. Shakespeare set a number of his plays in Italy, including *Two Gentlemen of Verona, Romeo and Juliet, The Merchant of Venice,* and *Othello, the Moor of Venice.* Singing madrigals after dinner was one of the principal forms of entertainment at courts of the nobility and in the homes of the growing class of merchants and traders enriched by Atlantic trade. Groups of all women, all men, and mixed groups sang them. Learning to sight-read from books of madrigals in musical notation was an important social grace for courtiers and wealthy, educated amateurs. King Henry VIII (*r.* 1509–1547) composed songs and played musical instruments. His daughter with Anne Boleyn, Queen Elizabeth I (*r.* 1558–1603), learned to play musical instruments and enjoyed dancing. In the *Merchant of Venice* (act V, scene 1), written about the same time as "Fair Phyllis," Shakespeare writes in a way reminiscent of Confucius and Plato about the positive effect of musical performance on the character of kings and those who serve them:

But music for the time doth change his nature.
The man that hath no music in himself,
Nor is not moved with concord of sweet sounds,
Is fit for treasons, stratagems, and spoils.
The motions of his spirit are dull as night,
And his affections dark as Erebus.
Let no such man be trusted. Mark the music.

John Farmer served as organist and choirmaster at the Anglican St. Patrick's Cathedral in Dublin, Ireland. He dedicated his one book of madrigals to Edward de Vere, Earl of Oxford, an important poet and patron of the arts. Farmer was a contemporary of William Shakespeare, most of whose highly regarded plays were published between 1589 and 1613. Although Farmer was not an especially prolific composer—he lived only thirty years after all—"Fair Phyllis" is a classic of the English madrigal genre. High school and college choirs regularly perform it today.

Although widely sung by educated amateurs, there is some record of professional entertainers singing madrigals. During the late sixteenth century northern Italian courts supported groups of professional female singers called *Concerti delle donne* (Ensembles of Women). They competed for attention with the beauty of their voices, hand gestures and meaningful looks, and the addition of all sorts of added musical devices not in the notation (ornaments, virtuoso melodic runs, sighs), all the more obviously to express the meaning of the text and charm their patrons.

WHERE DO I GO FROM HERE?

- Claudio Monteverdi (1567–1643), a master of the Italian madrigal, wrote eight books of them. The first four employ Renaissance multipart vocal polyphony. Listen to a performance of one of his most famous madrigals, "Si ch'io vorrei morire" (Yes, I want to die), published in 1601 and notice the way he paints the text in his music, including his use of chords based on the dissonant interval of a second to express a lover's yearning.

- Listen to a recording of a Renaissance chanson (song, the French equivalent of madrigal) by Clément Janequin (c. 1485–1558) called "Le chant des oyseaux" (The Song of the Birds), remarkable for its iconic text painting.

- Listen to recordings of dance music for various consorts of musical instruments by perhaps the most important composer of instrumental music of the period, Michael Praetorius (1571–1621). Notice the familiar harmonic style and identify the timbre of instruments as strings, recorders, viols, reeds, or trumpets and horns made of brass.

GATEWAY 13
RENAISSANCE LUTE MUSIC

What Is It?

The guitar, so ubiquitous in popular music today, took shape during the Renaissance. European luthiers (lute makers) reshaped the long-necked fretted *buzuq* and the short-necked, fretless *'ud* from the Arab world into a "waisted" plucked lute with a relatively long fretted neck and gave instruments of this type the names guitar and *vihuela*. Violins, viols, guitars, and *vihuela* all belong to the lute category of instruments.

Our gateway to music for Renaissance plucked lutes is a composition called "Quatro diferencias sobre Guárdame las vacas" (Four variations on [the song tune] "Take care of my cattle"). In this recording the four variations are played on a plucked lute called **vihuela**, a flat-backed waisted lute with gut frets tied around the neck and six double courses of gut strings plucked by the fingers. This composition appeared in 1538 in a collection of compositions by Spanish composer Luys de Narváez, whose birth and death dates are not known but who was active from 1526 to 1549.

FIGURE 4.11
Musician playing a *vihuela* in the Borgia Apartments (Vatican). Painting by Bernardino di Betto di Biago (c. 1454–1513).
Source: Musicarticon, Wikimedia Commons.

 Listen to the first fifteen seconds of the recording for the timbre of the vihuela.

How Does It Work?

Timbre

The timbre is bright. The double courses of strings improve the resonance of the instrument and provide a characteristic timbre slightly different from the single-string courses on the guitar.

Texture

The texture consists of two polyphonic lines, one high-pitched moving rapidly and the other a low-pitched line moving slowly.

Rhythm

The meter is a slow meter of six beats. The rhythm of the high-pitched line features short tones of equal length for the most part.

Melody

The melody, carried in the high-pitched line, mainly moves stepwise over a two-octave range. The melody of each section is organized into two phrases of four measures each.

Harmony

The harmony is based on triads. The first phrase of each melody ends on a chord on the fifth degree (V); the second phrase ends with an authentic cadence.

Form

The composition is a set of four variations on the melody of a traditional song, followed by a brief coda. It is the earliest precursor of a form commonly used in the eighteenth century called **theme and variations**, the word "theme" referring to the opening melody. Each variation uses the same chord progression in the low part.

Performance Techniques

Plucking the strings with the fingers, rather than with a plectrum as the 'ud player does in Chapter 3, Gateway 8 on music of the Middle East, is the most notable performance technique.

Listen to the recording for the six-beat meter and the two-part polyphony.

Listen to the entire performance following this timed listening guide.

LISTENING GUIDE 4.3

TIME	SECTION		DESCRIPTION
0:00	Variation #1	A	The melody descends in thirds ending on V.
0:09		A'	The melody repeats ending with an authentic cadence on the first degree.
0:18	Variation #2		A new melody moves twice as fast as the first melody, in an undulating shape.
0:34	Variation #3		Another new three-note melody is played in sequence.
0:51	Variation #4		This melody is a series of stepwise ascending melodic lines.
1:09	Coda		A descending line played in parallel thirds half as fast as the previous three variations.
1:20	End		

What Does It Mean?

AESTHETICS

Well-educated male and female courtiers in Spain played the *vihuela* alone for their own and their friends' amusement. Narváez's compositions were meant to be aesthetically pleasing rather than to express emotion. The pleasure for players and listeners derives both from the technical skill and variety of playing techniques required to play the piece and from the shifts in melodic direction and rhythm of each variation in the set of four variations. The performance may please modern listeners because of its similarity to the familiar plucked sound of the modern guitar.

Listen one more time to the performance for pleasure, paying attention to the melodic and rhythmic changes from variation to variation.

Amateur musicians at courts in Spain and all across Europe were taught to play lutes by outstanding professional court musicians and composers like Luys de Narváez. His six books of polyphonic compositions for *vihuela* contain thirty-three pieces: *diferencias*; compositions in a form called *fantasia* featuring imitative polyphony; and arrangements, with extensive ornaments and melodic embellishments, of well-known polyphonic secular songs, motets, and masses. Narváez added another skill to those of his amateur students: he was able to improvise additional melodic lines while his students played the parts he had composed for them.

In addition to the *vihuela*, two other plucked lutes, the guitar and the lute, were common in Europe during the sixteenth century. The sixteenth-century guitar was a waisted, flat-backed plucked lute with tied-on gut frets. Smaller than the modern guitar, it had five strings in single courses. It seems to have been a favored instrument in the countryside and may have been played by strumming across the strings with a plectrum or fingers.

TECHNOLOGY

The instrument with the name **lute**, as opposed to generic lutes, was a plucked pear-shaped lute with a vaulted body (that is, a rounded back rather than a flat back) made from a set of thin wooden ribs glued together. It was the most popular type of Renaissance plucked lute in most of Europe during the sixteenth century. It had six courses of strings, some single and some double, and a much shorter fretted neck than the guitar and *vihuela*. At the end of the neck the pegbox was bent back at an angle to the neck, just like the Arab *'ud* on which it was modeled. The lute, guitar, and vihuela all had a wide range suitable for playing the wide-ranging soprano-to-bass polyphonic music of the period. Players of the European lute, guitar, and *vihuela* perform polyphonic music in contrast to players of the Arab *'ud*, like A. J. Racy in the gateway to music of the Middle East in Chapter 3, Gateway 8, who perform mainly monophonic melodies.

What Is Its History?

The history of lutes, whether bowed like the viol and violin or plucked like the *vihuela*, guitar, and lute, can be traced to the Middle East. The first plucked lutes entered Europe when Arabs from North Africa conquered Spanish lands in 711. Called Moors by Christians, they ruled Andalucía, the southern region of Spain, until Christians defeated and expelled them in 1492. During the ninth century a fabulous Arab *'ud* virtuoso named Ziryab appeared at the court of the Andalucian emir. Born and trained in music in Baghdad, Ziryab moved to Syria, Tunisia, and then Córdoba in Spain. By the thirteenth century Christians in northern Spain were playing its European descendant, the lute. By the sixteenth century its name had changed from *al'ud* (the *'ud*) in Arabic to *la ud* (the ud) in Spanish and to lute in English.

The waisted, plucked guitar and *vihuela* seem to have developed from the bowed viol and violin. *Vihuela* may be a Spanish-language variant of viol. During the sixteenth century the *vihuela* and guitar were more popular in Spain than was the lute. The lute seems to have passed through Spain to the rest of Europe, where amateurs and professionals used it to accompany singing and to play instrumental compositions. It appears in many sixteenth-century paintings, often accompanying singing. Queen Elizabeth I of England enjoyed playing the lute. John Dowland (1563–1626), the most prominent English lutenist of the period, composed many instrumental pieces and **lute songs** (songs with lute accompaniment), including a *galliarde* titled "The most sacred Queen Elizabeth, her Galliard."

Luys de Narváez was born in Granada. Between 1526 and 1549 he served at the court of the Spanish King Charles V (1500–1558) and gave music lessons to his son, Crown Prince Felipe, who would become King Philip II (1527–1598). Philip ruled at the same time and for nearly as long as Elizabeth I of England. Charles V and Philip II, both devout Catholics, were the most powerful European monarchs of the sixteenth century. Although understood today as kings of Spain, they controlled vastly more land than that. They also ruled territories in the present-day Netherlands, the German-speaking Catholic territories of southern Germany and Austria, a part of Italy, and most of South America. Desiring to unite Europe and defend the Catholic faith, Charles V battled a host of enemies: the King of France, whose territories he coveted; German Protestants in the name of the Catholic faith; the Muslim Ottomans, whose advance into

FIGURE 4.12
The Lute Player by Caravaggio, c. 1600
Source: Hermitage Museum, Wikimedia Commons.

AESTHETICS

FIGURE 4.13
Miniature painting of Queen Elizabeth I playing the lute. Painting by Nicholas Hilliard (1571–1610).
Source: David Van Edwards, Wikimedia Commons.

Europe he helped to stop in a decisive battle for Vienna in 1529; and the Incas and Aztecs, whose empires in Mexico and Peru his conquistadors crushed. Apparently exhausted from the bloodshed, he abdicated his many thrones in his late fifties, retreated to a monastery, and died a few years later in 1558. Philip II continued his father's imperial ambitions, sending the Spanish Armada to humiliating defeat against Protestant England in 1588 and colonizing an archipelago in the western Pacific named after him: the Philippines.

Narváez's *diferencias* are the earliest European compositions in theme-and-variations form, which became one of the common forms in later European music. Its AABBCCDD form, similar to that of the Bulgarian *kopanitsa* (Chapter 3, Gateway 10), suggests that it may have been a concert version of a Spanish dance. The eighteenth-century composers Franz Joseph Haydn (1732–1809) and Wolfgang Amadeus Mozart (1756–1791) routinely used theme-and-variations form in their symphonies, string quartets, and solo piano pieces. One of the most frequently performed examples in this form is Maurice Ravel's (1875–1937) symphonic work *Boléro*, first performed in 1928. Named for a Spanish dance type and composed for a ballet, the variations in *Boléro* are based on changing orchestral timbres rather than on melodic variations of the sort associated with Narváez, Haydn, and Mozart. A typical jazz performance, with its opening melody and a series of choruses on the chords of the melody, is another example of theme-and-variations form pioneered by Narváez and other Spanish composers during the sixteenth century.

Spanish colonists took the *vihuela* and guitar to South America, Cuba, Puerto Rico, and the Dominican Republic, where today they exist in a tremendous number of variant forms and names. The Mexican *vihuela* (different from the Renaissance instrument), *bajo sexto*, *guitarrón*, and *requinto jarocho* and the Puerto Rican *tres* (with three triple courses), *cuatro* (with not four but five double courses), and *tiple* (with five single courses) are just a few of many examples.

The modern guitar is an outgrowth of its Renaissance predecessors. Today it has metal frets inlaid in the neck rather than tied-on gut frets, and nylon or steel strings rather than gut strings. Its current size is attributed to Spanish guitar maker Antonio de Torres Jurado (1817–1892). The electric guitar, so important in popular music and jazz, emerged in the 1920s and 1930s. Since the nineteenth century, *flamenco*, a music with Moorish roots featuring the guitar, developed among Spanish Gitanos, an itinerant people with roots in India and called Roma in other parts of Europe. Today a new genre called *flamenco arabe*, a hybrid of *flamenco* and North African Arab music, links Spanish musical culture with the culture of new immigrants to Spain from North Africa.

WHERE DO I GO FROM HERE?

- Listen to recordings of John Dowland's "Queen Elizabeth's Galliard" and two of his most popular lute songs, "Flow My Tears" and "Come Again, Sweet Love Doth Now Invite." Compare the performances of these songs by, for example, the male countertenor Gérard Lesne, the opera and recital singer Dame Janet Baker, and the popular singer Sting.

- Listen to or watch performances of *flamenco* guitar and *flamenco arabe*.

- Listen to or watch performances of Puerto Rican *tres*, *cuatro*, and *tiple*.

- Listen to recordings of one of these famous compositions in theme-and-variations form: Mozart's Twelve Variations on "Ah vous dirai-je, Maman" (the tune of "Twinkle, Twinkle, Little Star") for solo piano and Ravel's *Boléro*.

GATEWAY 14
NORTH INDIAN CLASSICAL MUSIC

What Is It?

Had Columbus landed in India, his intended destination, instead of the islands of the Caribbean Sea (the West Indies) on his voyage of discovery westward across the Atlantic Ocean in 1492, he would have found an area of the world with astonishing musical variety; a tradition of writing about music dating back to antiquity; and the Hindu and Muslim religions with their Ancient and Medieval traditions of monophonic chanting. In addition to a flourishing classical music tradition at the courts of its rulers, the Indian subcontinent was awash in a spectacular mosaic of diverse religious, popular, folk, and tribal music. During the 1500s, the same century as the European Renaissance, some of the basic principles of North Indian classical music were taking shape. Many North Indian classical musicians today trace their musical ancestry to a seminal musician of the sixteenth century, a lute player, singer, composer, and contemporary of Palestrina named Tansen (*c.* 1506–1589).

Our gateway to North Indian classical music is a recording titled "Raga Bhairvi—Dadra Taal" performed by Sharmistha Sen (1942–2021) on the *sitar*. A ***raga*** (also spelled ***rag***) is an Indian melodic mode, analogous to an Arab *maqam* and the modes of early Christian chant. *Bhairvi* (usually spelled *Bhairavi*) is the name of one of the melodic modes in the Indian system of *ragas*. A ***taal*** (also spelled ***tal*** or ***tala***) is an Indian rhythmic mode, analogous to an Arab *iqa'*. *Dadra* is the name of one of the modes in the Indian system of *talas*. What the title indicates is that this is a performance in a specific melodic mode (*raga bhairavi*) in a specific rhythmic mode (*dadra tal*). What the title does not say is that this performance will consist almost entirely of improvisations within these two modal systems.

Sharmistha Sen performs the melody in *rag bhairavi* on the *sitar*. The ***sitar*** is a long-necked, fretted plucked lute with more than twenty strings. Six or seven of them run on top of the frets and are plucked. The remainder run under the frets and are **sympathetic strings**, that is, strings that vibrate in response to the plucked pitch. They help to amplify the loudness and improve the resonance of the sound. Faiyaz Khan plays the drum accompaniment in *dadra tal* on the *tabla*. The ***tabla*** is a pair of kettle drums played with the hands. An unacknowledged player, likely a student of the melodic soloist, provides a drone accompaniment on the *tambura*. The ***tambura*** is a

FIGURE 4.14
Sharmistha Sen playing the *sitar*
Source: Daniel Neuman.

FIGURE 4.15
Abhiman Kaushal plays the *tabla* while accompanying *sitar*ist Sharmistha Sen
Source: Daniel Neuman.

four-stringed, fretless plucked lute. The player plucks each open string in turn as though playing a harp.

🔊 **Listen to the first thirty seconds of the recording.**

How Does It Work?

Timbre

The timbre of the *sitar*'s plucked strings is relatively thin and metallic. The timbre of the *tabla* includes ringing pitched sounds and dull, unpitched sounds across a range from low to high.

Texture

The texture consists of melody with drone and drum accompaniment.

Rhythm

The performance begins nonmetrically and then, after about two minutes, the *tabla* enters to create a steady beat and meter.

Melody

The melody moves mainly in stepwise motion using a heptatonic scale with a few added pitches from time to time. The melodic range is about two octaves.

Harmony

The harmony consists of the intervals between the pitches of the melody and the drone. The drone has two pitches: the tonic and the perfect fifth above it.

Form

The form has two parts, a nonmetrical opening section followed by a metrical second part, very similar to the performance of Arab *maqam* music in Chapter 3, Gateway 8.

Performance Techniques

The *sitar* player sometimes pulls the string to slide from pitch to pitch and sometimes directly plucks the string.

🔊 **Listen to the first thirty seconds of the recording for the melody-and-drone texture and the sliding from pitch to pitch.**

Timed Listening Guide

AESTHETICS

Before listening in more detail to this example, some concepts specific to North Indian music need to be introduced. The nonmetrical opening section is called **alap**. During this section the player introduces each pitch of the *raga* very carefully, one after the other, as well as melodic phrases using those pitches. The scale in *rag bhairavi* has seven basic pitches in a mode called the Phrygian mode in European music theory: E F G A B C D E. *Rag bhairavi* also includes some additional pitches: the raised 7th degree (D♯ in the scale above) is heard a few times in this performance. At the beginning Sharmistha Sen plays just three pitches, but by the end of the *alap* she is playing over a range of nearly two octaves. The timed listening guide indicates when she performs each new pitch in the *raga*.

The metrical section, when the *tabla* plays, is called **gat**. The meter is based on a *tal*, that is, a repeating cycle of strokes on the *tabla*. The basic pattern of strokes for a given *tal* is called the *theka.* Associated with each stroke is a mnemonic syllable, which allows *tabla* players to speak the rhythmic pattern during lessons and even during concerts. The basic stroke names are:

Dha = low-pitched drum stroke on the low-pitched drum played together with a bright, pitched
         stroke on the rim of the high-pitched drum;

Dhin = low-pitched drum stroke on the low-pitched drum played together with a dull, damped
          stroke on the high-pitched drum;

ta   = bright pitched stroke on the rim of the high-pitched drum;

Na   = ringing stroke in the center of the high-pitched drum.

In *dadra tal*, the *theka* of six beats produced by these strokes can be heard as a pattern of low and high strokes and spoken as a series of syllable names for the player's strokes:

1	2	3	4	5	6
Dha	Dhin	na	Dha	tin	na
low	low	high	low	high	high

In addition to these basic sounds on the *tabla*, the player improvises additional filler strokes and occasionally omits the low tone on beat 4.

The *sitar* alternates between playing a fixed melody, also called *gat*, and improvised solos. The *gat* melody is one way of expressing the *tala*: while the *sitar* plays it, the *tabla* player can improvise elaborate solos. In this performance the *gat* melody is twelve beats long and covers two cycles of *dadra tala*. Like *tabla* players, melodic soloists can sing melodies, while teaching or in performance, using mnemonic syllables similar to the ones used by European musicians called solfege. Instead of do-re-mi-fa-sol-la-ti-do, Indian musicians name the pitches sa-re-ga-ma-pa-dha-ni-sa. The pattern of intervals (half steps and whole steps) in the standard Indian scale can be written as a mode with a final on C: C D E F G A B (C). Using European pitch names and scale degree numbers (first degree = 1, second degree = 2, and so forth), the standard Indian scale and its intervallic structure can be written like this:

	1	1	1/2	1	1	1	1/2	
C	D	E	F	G	A	B	C	
1	2	3	4	5	6	7	8	

In the Indian scale system the first degree (1) and the fifth degree (5) are fixed. Degrees 2, 3, 6, and 7 can be either "natural" as in the C scale or "flatted" by a half step. These flatted scale degrees are indicated with a "flat sign" (♭). The fourth degree also has two forms, either natural or "sharped," indicated with a "sharp sign" (♯). Natural scale degrees are normally taken for granted, but if necessary they are written with a "natural sign" (♮).

Four of the pitches in the scale of *raga bhairavi* are flatted by a half step. Its pattern of intervals is written, starting on C, this way:

	1/2	1	1	1	1/2	1	1	
C	D♭	E♭	F	G	A♭	B♭	C	
1	♭2	♭3	4	5	♭6	♭7	8	

The scale *raga bhairavi* is read "C D-flat E-flat F G A-flat B-flat C."

The *gat* melody begins on beat 11 of two cycles of *dadra tal* and can be rendered like this using Indian pitch names and the numbers of the scale degrees:

11	12	1	2	3	4	5	6	7	8	9	10	11	12	(1)
♭3	4	5	–	5	5	5	5	♭7	♭6	5	–	♭3	4	5
ga	ma	pa	–	pa	pa	pa	pa	ni	dha	pa	–	ga	ma	pa

The *sitar* soloist ends two of her solos with a cadential gesture called a *tihai*. A **tihai** is a highly syncopated rhythmic pattern played three times at the end of a *sitar* or *tabla* solo that ends, in this case, on the first beat of *dadra tal*.

Listen to the entire performance following this timed listening guide.

LISTENING GUIDE 4.4

TIME	SECTION	DESCRIPTION
0:00	*Alap* (nonmetrical treatment of the *raga* in which each pitch of the scale is introduced in succession)	The opening phrase moves through characteristic phrases of *rag bhairavi* starting with a descending slide to ♭3 before introducing 4 and sliding upwards to 5.
0:14		This phrase adds two more pitches ascending with a characteristic melodic phrase of *rag bhairavi*: 1 ♭3 4 5 ♭6 5.
0:28		The *sitarist* introduces the ♮7th degree of the scale below 1.
0:49		The *sitarist* introduces the ♭7 degree of the scale near the upper octave.
1:10		The *sitarist* introduces the ♮7th degree of the scale on the way to the upper octave.
1:22		The *sitarist* descends to the lower tonic (1) adding ♭2 to the scale.
1:26		The *sitarist* expands the range of the melody below the tonic, introducing ♭6 before arriving on low 5 and returning to end the *alap* on 1.
2:03	*Gat* (the *tabla* plays in a meter of 6 beats in a *tala* called *dadra tal*.)	The *sitarist* plays the 12-pulse gat melody three times while the *tabla* improvises.
2:21		The *sitarist* improvises a solo over the 6-pulse *tabla theka* played two times.
2:26		The *sitarist* plays the 12-pulse *gat* melody one time while the *tabla* improvises.
2:32		The *sitarist* improvises a solo over the 6-pulse *tabla theka* played seven times.
2:53		The *sitarist* plays the 12-pulse *gat* melody one time.
3:00		The *sitarist* improvises a solo over the 6-pulse *tabla theka* played seven times.
3:20		The *sitarist* plays the 12-pulse *gat* melody one time.
3:26		An elaborate *sitar* solo introduces chromatic pitches in addition to the basic seven pitches of *rag bhairav* over a 6-pulse *tabla theka* played fifteen times.
4:10		An elaborate *tabla* solo over the 12-pulse *gat* melody played five times by the *sitarist*.
4:32		The *sitarist* improvises a solo ending in a *tihai* over a 6-pulse *tabla theka* played four times.
4:42		The *sitarist* plays the 12-pulse *gat* one time.
4:49		The *sitarist* improvises a solo with rapid runs ending in a *tihai* over a 6-pulse *tabla theka* played six times.
5:06		The *sitarist* plays the 12-pulse *gat* melody one last time.
5:11		Nonmetrical close.
5:19	End	

What Does It Mean?

The meanings of this performance by Sharmistha Sen derive from its position within an elaborate system of *raga*s and *tala*s, audience expectations about how a performance will evolve through time, ideas about the emotional meaning of music, and the performers' social position within Indian culture.

This recorded performance is a single expression of two elaborate theoretical systems: the system of *rag*s or *raga*s and the system of *tal*s or *tala*s. A *raga* is defined by a set of intervals in a melodic mode together with characteristic melodic phrases, ornamentation, and subtle manipulations of pitch. In aural tradition and working with a master musician who is both a spiritual and musical *guru*, student musicians absorb implicit rules for how to improvise in each *raga*. Because they must learn dozens of *raga*s, their training lasts for many years. Each *raga* is associated with a time of day, a season of the year, or an emotion or mood. Aficionados of the tradition take pleasure in identifying and following the twists and turns and moods of a particular performance. The system of *tala*s consists of a dozen or so common rhythmic cycles defined by the number of beats (6, 7, 8, 10, 12, 14, and 16 are common ones) and the pattern of strokes on the *tabla*. The longer cycles are often used for longer, serious performances and the shorter ones for shorter, more lively ones.

During the nonmetrical *alap*, knowledgeable audiences focus on following the musician's improvisation as an expression of the familiar contours of the *raga*. During the *gat* section, audience members count the beats of the *tala* as they listen, noticing each time the cycle returns to beat 1. Sometimes beat 1 occurs in the middle of the solo, creating a sense of tension in listeners. When the solo ends dramatically on beat 1, sometimes after a *tihai*, it creates a sense of pleasurable release in listeners who are closely monitoring the cycle of beats. They keep track of the *tala* by clapping, waving their right hand, and touching their fingers against the thumb of their right hand in succession from little to third finger. In effect, they perform the *tala* along with the musicians. In the case of *dadra tal* the audience claps the *tala* like this:

1	2	3	4	5	6
low	low	high	low	high	high
clap	touch	touch	wave	touch	touch
	little finger	third finger		little finger	third finger

🔊 **Listen another time to the gat section of this recording, clapping the tala and paying special attention to moment at which the theka or gat melody arrives on beat 1 of the tala .**

> **EMOTIONAL RESONANCE**

The duration of a performance of North Indian classical music varies considerably. In informal settings or for recordings, performers can demonstrate the basic form of a *raga* and *tala* performance in just five or six minutes, as Sharmistha Sen does in this recording. In a formal concert, however, it has become customary for the first *raga* performance to be quite "serious," as Indian musicians and fans say. It can take an hour or longer, a half hour or so for each section (*alap* and *gat*). This is about the length of a nineteenth-century European symphony. After such a serious performance, performers may either launch into a second serious performance or play a few shorter, more easily accessible "light" pieces requiring less concentration from the audience.

> **AESTHETICS**

The length of a serious performance varies considerably as performers sense how engaged the audience is. If the audience seems tightly focused on the details of what the performer is doing, the performance can stretch out well beyond an hour. If the audience is not made up of connoisseurs, performers may hurry things along so the audience does not become bored. *Rag bhairavi* is considered a light *raga*, a favorite of audiences, and *dadra tal* is a light *tala*, shorter than the most common "serious" *tala* of sixteen beats. Performances like this one are typically played at the ends of concerts. Sharmistha Sen placed this recording at the end of an album that contained two longer, more serious performances, one of nearly twenty-five minutes and the other of nearly thirty minutes.

Even though performances of this tradition have long been held in strictly secular contexts, whether at the courts of sultans and emperors in the past or modern-day concert halls in the great Indian cities of Delhi, Mumbai, and Kolkata, the notion persists in India that musical practice and training are acts of devotion. Modern players, whether Hindu or Muslim, believe that music is a spiritual gift and that playing music is a kind of prayer spoken in a heavenly language. Musical training and practice are understood as a kind of *yoga* (pathway) to a higher, purer, more refined plane of spiritual existence. Enjoying a performance of music is only one goal. Its higher purpose, for performers and listeners, is as a path to nirvana through total concentration on the details of musical sound. Many amateurs, both men and women, take music lessons with no thought of becoming professionals, but as an act of spiritual and educational refinement, a process similar in some respects to upper-class and upwardly mobile families in Europe, America, and Asia providing their children, especially their daughters, with piano lessons.

While amateur musicians may be male or female and Hindu, Muslim, or Christian, historically the most important and prestigious professional musicians, and the teachers of amateurs, were Muslim hereditary musicians. A hereditary musician has an **ascribed status**, that is, one limited to certain musical families who were not anxious to share their trade secrets with potential competitors outside their family. The status of professional musicians in India was, in the past, not something that just anyone, by dint of hard work and talent, could achieve. In other words, the role of musician was not an **achieved status**, as it is in many parts of the world. Because the music existed only in aural tradition and was passed on only in music lessons, it was easy to keep intimate knowledge of the tradition within families of hereditary musicians. Each family and its students are called a *gharana* ("house"). A *gharana* is recognized for having a unique style and repertoire that distinguishes it from other *gharanas*. A **guru** (guide, teacher) teaches the tradition, passing on not only lessons about music but about the practical and spiritual aspects of life as well. As a consequence, the person who receives this musical and life training is given the religious designation "disciple," not simply student. The disciple, historically a relative of the *guru*, did not pay for lessons but lived for long periods in the house of the *guru*, absorbing the music whenever the *guru* practiced or performed with colleagues. He also performed daily chores to assist the household as payment for the lessons. Assisting the *guru* in concerts by playing the *tambura* was one such task, and an honor for the disciple. Nowadays North Indian classical music is also taught in music conservatories and on the internet and, as a consequence, is available to a much wider circle of people than in the past.

Traditional Muslim hereditary players of the *sitar*, other melodic instruments, and vocalists traditionally came from a higher social class or caste than *tabla* players. The musical result is exemplified in this gateway recording. Melodic soloists with higher social status than the drum accompanist command performances, as Sharmistha Sen does in this recording. They make the contract with the recording company, the concert promoter, or the host of a concert in someone's home. They give the *tabla* player a relatively small percentage of the concert fee. They take the leading role throughout the performance, relegating the *tabla* player to an accompanying role most of the time and giving him little time in the performance to show off his considerable skills.

What Is Its History?

At the end of the fifteenth century, present-day India was divided among a number of sultanates competing for power with each other. In 1526 a great warrior named Babur united the Indian sultanates into an empire that covered much of India and parts of present-day Pakistan and Afghanistan. Babur claimed descent from Genghis Khan, the Mongol warrior whose hordes had conquered much of Asia in the 1200s and from Timur (Tamerlane), a Central Asian Turkic warrior who controlled much of the same area in the 1300s. Babur founded the Mughal Empire, a name based on the Arabic word for Mongol. It lasted from 1526 to 1857, when it fell to the British Empire. The third Mughal Emperor, Akbar the Great, extended the reach of the empire and presided over a golden age of Indian culture and art from 1556 to 1605, a period that coincides almost exactly with the long reigns of Queen Elizabeth I of England (1558–1603) and King Philip II of Spain (1556–1598). Akbar and his successors supported a fabulous court life including

Growth of the Mughal Empire, 1526–1707

FIGURE 4.16
Map of the Mughal Empire
Source: Santosh.mbahrm, Wikimedia Commons.

painting, architecture (one of Babur's successors built the Taj Mahal in the mid-seventeenth century), and music. They were also noted for their religious tolerance. Both Muslims and Hindus enjoyed considerable sway at court and in the arts.

Sharmistha Sen, along with virtually all the instrumentalists in the North Indian classical music tradition today, traced her artistic lineage to the most famous musician at Akbar the Great's Mughal court of the sixteenth century. Named Tansen, he was a contemporary of Palestrina, Farmer, and Narváez. Tansen's teacher was Swami Haridas (c. 1535–1595), a fine singer and the founder of a Hindu sect that emphasized devotional singing. Worshippers sang songs in different *raga*s throughout the day, and today Indian musicians and music theorists associate each *raga* with a time of day. *Raga bhairavi* is said to be an early morning *raga*, performed at the end of a long night of music. Tansen spent most of his life at the court of a Hindu king, where he gained fame as a singer, composer, and player of the *rabab*, a long-necked plucked lute and ancestor of the modern Indian long-necked plucked lute called *sarod*. He composed in a new vocal genre in the Hindi language called *dhrupad*, which became the model for the most serious performances of North Indian instrumental music. The texts of his *dhrupad*s, one scholar has written, "could address a god or goddess, laud a king, express feelings of intimate romantic love, describe a season, transmit musicological knowledge, or deal with a metaphysical or religious concept." He is also credited with composing instrumental music, including new *raga*s.

FIGURE 4.17
An eighteenth-century painting of Emperor Akbar, on the left, and Tansen, in the middle, both enthralled by the playing of Haridas, on the right
Source: Wazir Khan Khandara, Wikimedia Commons.

FIGURE 4.18
Sharmistha Sen taking a lesson from her *guru*, Ustad Mushtaq Ali Khan
Source: Daniel Neuman.

Late in life, word of his brilliance reached the court of Akbar the Great, and in 1562 Tansen, apparently hoping to retire, reluctantly accepted an invitation to become one of the nine "jewels" of the Mughal court. By tracing their artistic lineage to Tansen, modern North Indian classical instrumentalists like Sharmistha Sen seek to enhance their credibility and prestige with audiences and students, just as some pianists today trace their artistic heritage to famous nineteenth-century virtuosos like Franz Liszt. For these Indian musicians Tansen is the father of present-day Hindustani or North Indian classical music. *Sarod*ists trace their roots to his son, who played *rabab*, and *sitar*ists trace their roots to his daughter, who played an ancestor of the *sitar*.

**SOCIAL
BEHAVIOR**

Sharmistha Sen was one of the few female instrumentalists to have attained prominence in North Indian classical music. She was a woman, a Hindu, and a musician by achieved status. She was not a male, hereditary Muslim musician, the type of musician at the center of this tradition for hundreds of years. Her main teachers were Ustad Mushtaq Ali Khan (1911–1989) and Professor D. T. Joshi (1912–1993). Mustaq Ali Khan was a prominent *sitar*ist of the early twentieth century and the scion of the *Seniya gharana*, named after Tansen and noted for its adherence to older traditions of playing. Sen was one of a few accomplished musicians in this tradition to have been trained in both the traditional master-disciple tradition and the newer university system, where she earned a doctoral degree. After making her public debut at age thirteen, she performed regularly for All-India Radio and major music festivals. During 1983 and 1984 she was an artist-in-residence at the University of Washington and was a professor of music at Delhi University.

During the second half of the twentieth century two other *gharanas* besides the *Seniya gharana* produced the most famous North Indian classical musicians of the twentieth century, including the *sitar*ist Vilayat Khan (1928–2004) and his great-grandson Shujaat Khan (b. 1960), and the famed *sarod*ist Ali Akbar Khan (1922–2009) and *sitar*ist Ravi Shankar (1920–2012), both of whom gained prominence in the United States.

**ECONOMIC
ACTIVITY**

Today professional performers in this tradition make a living by working for the radio, giving concerts, giving lessons to private students, often Hindu and female, for pay, and moving abroad to western Europe and the United States, where their artistry is highly appreciated. As a consequence of these changes in patronage, this music is heard much more widely in India today than in the past, and the *gharanas* of particular Muslim hereditary musicians now include professionals and amateurs from far beyond their narrow circle of kin.

During the 1960s North Indian classical music became popular among young Americans seeking relief from the value system and political structures that led the United States into war in

Vietnam. Alienated from the mainstream, they took refuge not only in "sex, drugs, and rock and roll" but also in world religions and music from around the world. They studied Buddhism and Hinduism as alternatives to Christianity and Judaism and flocked to concerts by Ravi Shankar, a Hindu *sitar* player who became a spiritual and musical guru to a generation of young people hungering for alternative styles of life and music. Non-Indian listeners today, like those in the 1960s, may find the sliding pitches, drones, and nonmetrical melodies of North Indian music icons of a dreamy, perhaps intoxicated, world unbounded by social conventions. And the rapid melodic runs and fast *tabla* solos may have an attractive similarity to the virtuosity of classical, popular, and jazz musicians.

Unlike many other musical traditions in India and elsewhere, North Indian classical music never absorbed much in the way of foreign influence during the last century. On the other hand, European and American jazz, popular, and classical artists have incorporated Indian musical instruments in their music since the 1960s. George Harrison, guitarist with the Beatles, studied *sitar* with Ravi Shankar and played it on a number of recordings. In his song titled "Within You Without You" for the Beatles' 1967 album *Sgt. Pepper's Lonely Hearts Club Band*, the instrumental prelude begins with Harrison strumming across all of the *sitar*'s sympathetic strings, a characteristic gesture at the beginning of a *sitar* performance. He plays a short, nonmetrical *alap* before the Indian bowed fiddle called *sarangi* enters and continues the *alap*. After a minute of this introduction the *tabla* enters playing a familiar *tala*. The long durations of many of the song's tones and the sliding between the pitches, relatively rare qualities for European and American melodies, are striking elements of the song linking it to North Indian classical music. While George Harrison may be the most famous foreign champion of North Indian classical music, the important classical violinist Yehudi Menuhin also devoted many years of study to it and recorded an album of improvised duets with Ravi Shankar.

Of all the Indian instruments, however, it is the *tabla* that has become a fixture in the contemporary world music scene. Its jittery, dry sound has become a cliché of fusion and hybrid musical forms all over the world. Zakir Hussain (b. 1951), the son of one of Ravi Shankar's favorite accompanists and a teacher at Ali Akbar Khan's school of Indian music in the San Francisco Bay Area, is perhaps the most highly regarded *tabla* player of his generation. He lives in California, accompanies the greatest Indian melodic soloists, and participates in concerts with some of the great artists of jazz and popular music. Many of these fusions seem to be searching for some middle ground between Indian music, jazz, and popular music with a lot of attention to rhythm. Such searches are sometimes commercially driven. Sometimes they are the result of new musical inspiration in an interconnected world. And sometimes they express a complex social identity in a multicultural society.

WHERE DO I GO FROM HERE?

- Watch a video of one or more of the artists mentioned in this chapter: Ravi Shankar, Ali Akbar Khan, Vilayat Khan, and Shujaat Khan.
- Watch a video of Zakir Hussain showing off his *tabla* technique in a solo performance.
- Watch or listen to a performance of Zakir Hussain playing with such musicians as guitarist John McLaughlin, banjo player Béla Fleck, bassist Edgar Meyer, and saxophonist Jan Garbarek.

CLOSING

Many of the basic features of European and American music today can trace their roots to the sixteenth century, the European age of discovery, including:

- harmony based on triads with phrases ending in V-I cadences;
- families of instruments with ranges from low bass parts to high soprano parts;
- imitative polyphony as a way to organize sections of pieces;
- theme-and-variations form;

- the expression of emotion in instrumental and vocal music through its association with texts and its similarity to sounds in nature; and
- the invention of the violin and guitar.

These innovations reflect the humanistic and scientific spirit of the time. Similar things can be said of Indian classical music: important *raga*s and vocal and instrumental forms appear in this century.

In both Europe and India the powerful courts of Queen Elizabeth I of England, King Philip II of Spain, and Akbar the Great of the Mughal Empire, and the chapels and cathedrals of the Catholic Church, each made unimaginably rich from trade and conquest of new territories, energized and supported musicians and their art in ways that have continued to reverberate through history to the present.

THINGS TO THINK ABOUT

- Consider the features of European and American music listed above and think of some examples of music you already know that exhibit one or more of those features. Does your conception of the music you already know shift when you realize that these features are products of the Age of European Discovery? Why, or why not?
- The sixteenth-century imperial courts of England, Spain, and India are no longer important patrons of music, even if the music they patronized lives on in various forms. What institutions or people are the most important patrons of music today?

NEW TERMS

a cappella	*gharana*	*sitar*
achieved status	*guru*	soprano
alap	horn	sympathetic string
alto	imitative polyphony	*tabla*
ascribed status	lute	*tal, taal, tala*
authentic cadence	madrigal	*tambura*
bass	major third	tenor
cadence	minor third	text painting
cantus firmus	motet	*theka*
consort	oblique motion	theme and variations
contrapuntal texture	parallel motion	*tihai*
contrary motion	perspective	tonic
counterpoint	plagal cadence, amen cadence	triads
Counter-Reformation		trombone
countertenor	point of imitation	troubadour
cyclical mass	*rag, raag, raga*	trumpet
falsetto	recorder	*vihuela*
gat	Renaissance	viol

MUSIC FROM THE AGE OF GLOBAL COMMERCE (1600–1750)

DURING THE SIXTEENTH CENTURY the European seagoing expeditions of Christopher Columbus, John Cabot, Vasco da Gama, Ferdinand Magellan, Jacques Cartier, and many others set in motion dynamic new patterns of trade and forged new connections between continents and cultures. Between 1600 and 1750 European colonists, enslaved Africans, valuable commodities, culture, and musical styles began to circulate within a global economy, not just within small regions or along overland trade routes like the Silk Road. Globalization shaped new understandings not only of cultural differences but also of the place of one's own culture in the world. Europeans' command of the sea extended their power and influence around the world. For the first time in human history, one region of the world began to seem at the center, and everyone else had to react to it in some way.

> ECONOMIC
> ACTIVITY

Trade played a major role in making connections between cultures and shaping new habits of everyday life. Cotton from India and silk from China changed European styles of dress. Coffee from the Ottoman Empire and the Arabian Peninsula, tea from China, and cocoa and tobacco from the Americas were consumed in new public coffee houses, as well as at home. The Dutch gradually conquered the islands that today constitute Indonesia and grew rich from control of trade in cardamom and cloves from what was called the Dutch East Indies. Russia expanded east and south to control Siberia and the Caucasus, becoming the largest country in the world. The Ottomans attempted to extend the reach of their empire beyond the Balkans and farther into Europe, even besieging Vienna before they were finally defeated in 1683.

FIGURE 5.1
The Palace at Versailles built by French King Louis XIV
Source: Wandernder Weltreisender, Wikimedia Commons.

DOI: 10.4324/9781003269304-8

Trade enabled rulers around the world to expand their powers. The French King Louis XIV, who reigned from 1643 to 1715, proclaimed the "divine right of kings" to rule over their subjects. He established the most lavish court in Europe, and his palace outside of Paris, Versailles, became famous for its elaborate ballets and plays accompanied by music. Louis himself was an avid dancer and often participated in these productions. Other aristocratic courts around Europe envied and copied the French court as best they could, and the aristocracy competed with both Catholic and Protestant Churches for the services of the best composers and musicians and the largest orchestras.

Because European composers in this period could make a good living answering the demands for new music from the plethora of wealthy kings, princes, and religious congregations in Europe, there were a lot of them. Craftsmen working on demand, they produced vast amounts of music, which audiences for classical music today enjoy because of their clear triadic harmonies and engaging, pulsating rhythms. This chapter focuses on the music of just four of these composers as stand-ins for the music of many other prolific composers in this period:

- the operas of Claudio Monteverdi;
- the orchestral music of Antonio Vivaldi;
- the Protestant religious music of George Frideric Handel; and
- the keyboard music of Johann Sebastian Bach.

The Dutch engaged in negotiation and diplomacy with the rulers of Java, an island in present-day Indonesia. At that time Javanese court musicians were playing on a large orchestra of gongs and metallophones called gamelan. Music for the Javanese gamelan, the largest orchestra in the world outside Europe, is also presented in this chapter.

Many of the foundational elements of European classical music today have their roots in the period from 1600 to 1750.

- The string orchestra, with a few wind instruments and timpani, became a common instrumental ensemble.

FIGURE 5.2

Map of Southeast Asia and the Dutch East Indies (Indonesia)

- The genre called opera was invented.
- Compositions for keyboard instruments (organ and harpsichord) reached their first apex.
- The very idea of instrumental music (the sonata) as an equal to vocal music (the cantata) is rooted in this period.
- The modal scales and harmonic system of the Medieval and Renaissance periods gave way to a new system of major and minor keys.

This period in European music history is often called the Baroque period. The word Baroque is believed to come from a Portuguese expression for a misshapen pearl. Nineteenth-century music critics used the term **Baroque** to label what they considered, in retrospect, the exaggeratedly "misshapen" music of this period, especially its long, florid, twisting, ornamented melodic lines. Today, in domains beyond music and art, the term "baroque" is applied to anything that seems elaborate and exaggerated.

Baroque is also a term art historians use to describe the art of this period. Perhaps the most important representatives of Baroque (elaborate) style in art are the works of Italian sculptor and architect Gian Lorenzo Bernini (1598–1680). He created fountains and the interiors of many churches still visible today all over Rome. His Baroque style influenced the interiors and exteriors of Catholic Churches in Latin America and throughout the world. The church may have fostered his Baroque artistic style for its ability to express religious emotions in an impassioned way. In turn, the aristocracy adopted it as a symbol of secular wealth and opulence.

GATEWAY 15
BAROQUE OPERA

What Is It?

Opera is a theatrical musical genre that tells stories through a form of sung or heightened speech called **recitative** (melodic and rhythmic text recitation), songs with clear melodies (called **arias** in opera), choral singing (choruses), instrumental music, acting, and dancing. Invented at the end of the sixteenth century in Florence in Northern Italy, the new genre of opera marks the beginning of a new period in European music history, the Baroque. Claudio Monteverdi (1547–1643) was the first great exponent of opera and the Baroque style. Our gateway to Baroque opera is act I, scene 4 of his *L'incoronazione di Poppea* (The Coronation of Poppea). It was first performed in December of 1642 at the beginning of the Venice Carnival season, less than a year before Monteverdi's death in November of 1643. Concerto Vocale, a vocal and instrumental ensemble from Belgium conducted by René Jacobs, performs in this recording.

L'incoronazione di Poppea tells the story of Roman Emperor Nero and his mistress Poppea, who has replaced Empress Octavia in his affections. It begins with a prologue in which the Ancient Roman and Greek gods Fortune, Virtue, and Love argue about which one has more influence in human affairs, a reflection of the renaissance of Greek and Roman myths and characters in the intellectual and artistic life of the sixteenth and seventeenth centuries. As the story develops, Love protects Poppea from Octavia's attempt to have Poppea's suitor Ottone

FIGURE 5.3
Gian Lorenzo Bernini's *Ecstasy of St. Teresa* (1647–1652) in a Roman church
Source: Joaquim Alves Gaspar, Wikimedia Commons.

FIGURE 5.4
Claudio Monteverdi. Painting by Bernardo Strozzi (1581–1644).
Source: Tiroler Landesmuseum Ferdinandeum, Wikimedia Commons.

assassinate her. When Nero learns of the plot, he banishes Octavia and Ottone from Rome and crowns Poppea his new empress, a seeming victory of Love over Virtue (adultery over fidelity). The opera ends with a touching love duet between Nero and Poppea, a harbinger of three centuries of florid love duets in the operatic tradition. In this scene Poppea reveals her hope that Nero will favor her over Octavia and that Fortune and Love will protect her from the resulting troubles. Her old nurse Arnalta is worried, however, and tries to dissuade her from her plan, expressing no trust in the powers of these imaginary gods to protect her "daughter" if her ambitions become known.

 Listen to the first minute of the recording.

How Does It Work?

Timbre

A female and male singer, a recorder, and bowed and plucked stringed instruments create the timbres of this performance. A typical opera ensemble of the time might have employed one or two keyboard instruments called harpsichords, two violins, a cello, and a variety of plucked string instruments, including a lute and a **theorbo**, a bass lute with an enormously long neck and fourteen courses of strings capable of playing low-pitched bass pitches.

Texture

The singers and the recorder perform melodies to the accompaniment of the bowed and plucked strings. They play chords and a bass line.

Rhythm

The rhythm varies from nonmetrical declamation of the text (recitative) by the male singer (Arnalta) to metrical dance and song melodies by the recorder and the female singer (Poppea).

Melody

The melodies use both stepwise motion and **arpeggios**, that is, leaps through the pitches of a triad.

Harmony

The harmony moves clearly from a triad on the tonic to authentic cadences (V–I) at the end of each phrase.

Form

The form consists of alternations between three different styles: (1) repeated instrumental interludes, called *ritornellos* (returns); (2) Poppea's aria, which consists of three short metrical tunes, each of which repeats a number of times; and (3) the recitatives of Arnalta.

FIGURE 5.5
Map of Italy with the cities of Venice, Florence, and Rome

Performance Techniques

The female singer trills on a few notes, showing off her vocal technique, and both male and female singers manipulate the loudness and tempo of their singing to express their thoughts.

 Listen to the first thirty seconds of this recording for its timbre and texture.

What Does It Mean?

One aspect of the meaning of this music emerges in the way Monteverdi continues the Renaissance principle of text painting to express, in musical gestures, important words and ideas in the text. The singers amplify this connection between text and music as well, singing loudly or softly, forcefully or gently, slowly or quickly, to express the text and convey their character's inner thoughts and emotions, which might reflect the text or be slightly at odds with it.

Listen to the entire recording. Follow this timed listening guide to understand the link between the lyrics and the music.

FIGURE 5.6
Lady with a theorbo c. 1680. Painting by John Michael Wright (1617–1694).
Source: Columbus Museum of Art, Wikimedia Commons.

EMOTIONAL RESONANCE

LISTENING GUIDE 5.1

TIME	SECTIONS	LYRICS	TRANSLATION	DESCRIPTION
0:00	*Ritornello*			A small ensemble of bowed strings, harpsichord, and recorder plays three short melodic phrases in duple meter.
0:12	Poppea:	*Speranza, tu mi vai il cor accarezzando*	Hope, you caress my heart	A female vocalist sings two phrases at a middle loudness (mezzo forte), ending with a ritard, an expression perhaps of her wistful emotional state. She is accompanied by cello and harpsichord in this section and throughout.
0:20	*Ritornello*			The instrumental melody returns.
0:32	Poppea:	*Speranza, tu mi vai*	Hope, you come to me	The singer repeats the first phrase, this time loudly (forte) as if reassuring herself.
		il genio lusingando	like an alluring gift	
		e mi circondi intanto	and envelope me	
		di regio sì, ma immaginario manto.	in a royal but imaginary cloak	
0:52		*No, non temo, no, di noia alcuna* (2x)	No, I am not afraid of any trouble	She sings loudly with a steady beat in short, arc-shaped phrases that rise in sequence, all these elements expressing her confidence and affirming her lack of fear at what may befall her.

continued

TIME	SECTIONS	LYRICS	TRANSLATION	DESCRIPTION
1:06		*per me guerreggia Amor, e la Fortuna.*	Because fighting for me are Love and Fortune.	She shifts to triple meter to explain why she is so confident. The short melody repeats with slight variants in something like AAAAB form, but she ends on the second degree of the scale rather than the tonic, as if her reverie is interrupted. (It is, by the entrance of Arnalta, her old nurse.)
1:30	*Ritornello*			The instrumental melody returns.
1:45	Arnalta:	*Ahi figlia, voglia il cielo, che questi abbracciamenti non sian un giorno i precipizi tuoi.*	Ah, daughter, I wish to heaven that these embraces do not one day cause your downfall	Arnalta, a female role sung by a male tenor, sings in a nonmetrical declamatory style accompanied by just the harpsichord playing chords. The style allows her to express her ideas at almost the same rate as ordinary speech.
1:56	Poppea:	*No, non temo, no, di noia alcuna,*	No, I am not afraid of any trouble.	Poppea repeats her words and melody rather loudly, suggesting her optimism.
2:06	Arnalta:	*L'imperatrice Ottavia ha penetrati di Neron gli amori,*	The Empress Octavia has discovered Nero's loves	Arnalta resumes her recitative with a melody that rises in pitch and words that go faster and faster as a way to express her rising concern and fear for Poppea's Fortune.
		ond'io pavento e temo	and I am terribly afraid	
		ch'ogni giorno, ogni punto	that someday, some moment	
		sia di tua vita il giorno, il punto estremo.	Will bring your life to an extreme end.	
2:24	Poppea:	*per me guerreggia Amor, e la Fortuna.*	But fighting for me are Love and Fortune.	Poppea repeats her melody and words, this time a little softer, as if Arnalta's worries have given her pause.
2:46	Arnalta:	*La pratica coi regi è perigliosa, l'amor e l'odio non han forza in essi,*	The company of kings is perilous Love and hate have no strength against them.	Arnalta argues that Love and Fortune do not have the power Poppea hopes they have, singing "for-" of *forza* (strength) on a loud, singing high-pitched tone that mirrors in music the idea of strength.
		sono gli affetti lor puri interessi.	Love and hate have no strength against them.	
3:06	*Ritornello*			A new instrumental tune is introduced.
3:14	Arnalta:	*Se Neron t'ama, è mera cortesia,*	If Nero loves you, it is merely a courtesy	Arnalta's recitative continues, slowing briefly on three held, descending pitches that emphasize and express the meaning of the three syllables of "do-le-re" (regret).
		s'ei t'abbandona, non te n' puoi dolere.	If he abandons you, it should not make you regret it.	
		Per minor mal ti converrà tacere.	It would be better for you to remain silent.	
3:33	*Ritornello*			The new instrumental tune returns.
3:40	Arnalta:	*Con lui tu non puoi mai trattar del pari,*	You are not his equal,	Arnalta continues her recitative, ending with a descent over more than an octave to a very low pitch, an icon of Poppea's impending fall from the heights of her ambitions to the depths of ruin if she continues in her hope to marry Nero.
		se le nozze hai per oggetto e fine,	and if your goal is to marry him,	
		mendicando tu vai le tue ruine.	it will be your ruin.	

TIME	SECTIONS	LYRICS	TRANSLATION	DESCRIPTION
3:59	Poppea:	*No, non temo, no, di noia alcuna.*	No, I am not afraid of any trouble.	Poppea repeats her melody, this time loudly and quickly as if her resolve has returned and she is unpersuaded by Arnalta's arguments.
4:05	Arnalta:	*Mira, mira Poppea.*	Be careful Poppea.	Arnalta abandons her recitative in favor of an aria in triple meter. The cello enters to accompany her.
4:09		*dove il prato è più più ameno e dilettoso,*	Where the grass is most pleasant and delightful	Arnalta sings the words *ameno i dilettoso* (pleasant and delightful) with light melismas on some of the syllables, a musical gesture that mirrors the meaning of the words.
		stassi il serpente ascoso.	there the snakes hide.	
4:22		*Dei casi le vicende son funeste.*	Some choices can be deadly.	On the word *funeste* (deadly), Arnalta moves suddenly down a half step, a move that expresses the word's meaning but, in its surprising abruptness, might have earned the epithet "baroque" from critics of the period.
4:32		*la calma è profezia delle tempeste.*	The calm comes before the storm.	To paint the text, Arnalta sings the word "calm" quietly and the repeated word "storm" (*tempeste*) very loudly.
4:42	Poppea:	*No, non temo, no, di noia alcuna,*	No, I am not afraid of any trouble,	Poppea repeats her position loudly, still unconvinced by Arnalta's arguments.
4:50		*per me guerreggia Amor, e la Fortuna.*	because Love and Fortune defend me.	
5:02	Arnalta:	*Ben sei pazza, se credi*	You are crazy if you think	Arnalta expresses her frustration with a melody containing a series of equal-length, staccato tones jumping around in disjunct motion. She then exits the stage abruptly, defeated by Poppea's continuing expressions of hope and confidence in Love and Fortune.
		che ti possano far contenta e salva	you can be made contented and safe	
		un garzon cieco ed una donna calva.	by a blind boy and a bald woman.	
		Ben sei pazza, se credi.	You are crazy if you think so.	

At first listening, the lack of a regular beat and repeating melody in Arnalta's recitatives might sound a bit strange to newcomers to opera. The timed listening guide above links the music and the text as a way to explain the logic and expressive possibilities of recitative. The singers cultivate a vocal technique that is loud enough to be heard without amplification in large opera houses. In doing so, they produce vocal qualities that some listeners new to the genre may find off-putting because they are so different from the sound of popular singers today and what some consider "natural." Opera fans, on the other hand, revel in the vocal quality of the singers. They listen for subtle differences in tone quality among them, and they have their favorite singers.

AESTHETICS

One of the striking features of this performance is that a man sings the role of Arnalta, Poppea's aging female nurse. This reflects conventions of the seventeenth and eighteenth centuries, when men often sang female roles. Opera directors today sometimes exploit this seeming contradiction for its humorous potential, giving Arnalta large breasts or having her act out exaggerated behaviors in the manner of a contemporary drag queen. Conversely, during the seventeenth and eighteenth centuries, lead male roles, like those of Nero and Ottone, were often sung by male sopranos and altos. Today these roles are sung by countertenors, men who sing in a high-pitched, head-resonated falsetto voice. In the seventeenth century they were sung by *castrati*, male singers castrated before puberty to prevent their voices from changing from soprano

SOCIAL BEHAVIOR

to tenor or bass. In Baroque opera, castrati were much prized for their spectacularly powerful voices, and no opera could attract an audience without at least one in a lead role. Louder than female sopranos or a countertenor's falsetto, the sound of a *castrato* was interpreted as an icon of masculine power and associated with heroic male roles. Changing social and artistic values contributed to the decline in the popularity of *castrati* by the end of the eighteenth century. Italian law and papal orders put an end to the practice by the late nineteenth century, although some *castrati* lived into the early twentieth century. When male countertenors sing these roles today, the timbre of their voices sounds more feminine than heroic, inviting the audience to reconcile male and female stereotypes in new ways.

What Is Its History?

EMOTIONAL RESONANCE ⟩

Opera was a harbinger of enormous changes in musical practice during the period from 1600 to 1750. Some of these changes responded to the implications for music of "reborn" (Renaissance) texts about music by Plato and other Greek philosophers. New thinking about vocal music began in Italy, first in Florence and later in Venice, cities full of wealthy bankers and merchants who had enriched themselves through trade with the Ottoman Empire and along the shores of the Mediterranean Sea. In Florence during the late sixteenth century a group of composers and intellectuals called the Florentine camerata ("the club of Florence") began debating Greek ideas about the expressive power of music. As they read about the powerful effects on the emotions and on ethics of Ancient Greek monophonic music, they began to doubt whether the polyphonic, contrapuntal motets and madrigals of their own time were capable of achieving the same effects as the Ancient Greeks had claimed for their monophonic music.

They theorized that the reported power of Ancient Greek melody must have lain in its ability to express the emotional meanings inherent in sung lyrics and wondered whether polyphonic music obscured the meaning of the text and limited the possibilities for expressing the full extent of the meaning and emotion in it. Perhaps if a single line of melody hewed closely to the contours and rhythms of speech and emotion in the text, perhaps it could replicate the powerful expressive quality of music that the Greeks had written about. They experimented with creating melodies in a nonmetrical, declamatory rhythm that mimicked the rhythm of speech, in the process creating the style called recitative. If someone, while speaking during an emotional moment, would likely stutter or stop and start again, then music, they argued, should do so as well. If the text changed dramatically in emotion, then the melody should as well. But the Florentines could not seriously advocate for the abandonment of harmony and counterpoint in favor of Ancient Greek monophony. What to do? Their solution is called monody. This is a confusing term because it sounds like monophony and might seem to be another label for a texture with only one voice. Instead, monody reduces the texture of Renaissance-period polyphony with four equal vocal parts for soprano, alto, tenor, and bass to a texture that emphasizes the melody and places harmony in a purely accompanying role. **Monody** has a three-part texture consisting of a vocal melody (or sometimes a duet) accompanied by an instrumental bass line and chords improvised by a keyboard or lute player. The combination of bass line and chords is called *basso continuo*. While emphasizing single melodic lines gave Monteverdi and other Baroque composers new tools to express the emotion and meaning of sung texts, they continued to use familiar musical conventions developed in Renaissance and Italian polyphonic madrigals to paint the meaning of texts. In Arnalta's recitatives, for example, Monteverdi combines Renaissance expressive conventions with the new monodic style to underline the meaning of the words *forza* (strength), *funeste* (deadly), *ruine* (ruin), and *dolere* (regret).

AESTHETICS ⟩

Although the composers of the Florentine camerata tried their hand at writing opera, their first works in this new genre have been largely forgotten today. Claudio Monteverdi is considered opera's first master. He was an outstanding madrigalist before turning his hand to the new style of monody advocated by the Florentine camerata. He wrote four books of Renaissance-style polyphonic madrigals at the end of the sixteenth century while working at the court of the Duke of Mantua, a region west of Venice. Book Four, published in 1603, contains one of his most frequently performed polyphonic madrigals, "Sì, ch'io vorrei morire" (Yes, I would welcome death), notable for its exquisite painting of the text. In his fifth book of madrigals (he wrote a total of eight), published in 1605, he introduced the new style of monodic vocal composition. In one of his most performed madrigals in this new style, "Zefiro torna e di soavi accenti" (Return, O Zephyr [a breeze] with gentle motion), published in 1632, Monteverdi set two voices, a duet, against the *basso continuo*. This new style enabled virtuosic singing in the form of fast runs, trills, and other ornaments because the voices are not tethered to contrapuntal relations among the parts. In opera, this style of metrical, melodic singing was given a new genre name: aria.

Monteverdi's first opera, *Orfeo* (1607), produced at the court of Mantua, is regarded as the first successful opera, and it and *Poppea* are still performed occasionally today, especially by musicians dedicated to the revival of so-called early music. **Early music** refers to European church, court, and concert music composed before 1750,

FIGURE 5.7

***Piazza San Marco by Canaletto* (1697–1768) in 1720, with Saint Mark's Cathedral in the background**

Source: Metropolitan Museum of Art, Wikimedia Commons.

music that some modern performers believe requires "historically informed" performances because they are so different from modern practice. *Orfeo* tells the famous story of the Greek mythical musician Orpheus, who used music to save his beloved Euridice from death in the underworld. Later in his career Monteverdi moved from Mantua to Venice, where he became the music director at St. Mark's Cathedral. Opera, aimed at public audiences of wealthy merchants rather than at courtly or religious ones, combined humor, sexuality, and overwrought emotional scenes. It appealed to a broad public, and by 1700 Venice, a city of 140,000 people at the time, had sixteen opera houses. Today Santa Monica, California, a city of about the same size, has about the same number of movie theaters. Venetian opera productions, in other words, were forms of entertainment similar in their cultural impact to films today.

ECONOMIC ACTIVITY

Operas in this period were performed once or perhaps a few times and then disappeared from the repertoire in favor of new operas, a bit like movies do today. The score of *Poppea* was lost for nearly 250 years, until it was rediscovered at the end of the nineteenth century. Baroque operas, and indeed a lot of Baroque music, were forgotten for a time as European musical style changed over the next two centuries. It was revived during the nineteenth century when European intellectuals and musicians became interested for the first time in the history of their musical traditions. Modern performers have to reconstruct *Poppea* from fragmentary evidence, and performances can differ significantly. Early revivals used a modern orchestra. Later ones, based on musicological research, used small ensembles typical of the period. Directors, too, have a great deal of freedom in how they stage the opera and which sexes and voices sing the roles. Baroque operas are today rare flowers on the fringes of the modern opera repertoire.

WHERE DO I GO FROM HERE?

- Watch a video performance or two of "Speranza, tu mi vai." Note the costuming and stage action, particularly the way men dress and act the role of Arnalta.
- Compare the effects of three videos of the final love duet from *L'incoronazione di Poppea*: "Pur ti miro, pur ti godo" (I gaze at you, I possess you), one with a countertenor singing the role of Nero, one with a bass singing the role, and one with a woman singing the role.
- Listen to a performance of Monteverdi's monodic madrigal, "Zefiro torna e di soavi accenti" (Return, O Zephyr [a breeze] with gentle motion), published in 1632. Note the florid, melismatic singing style.

GATEWAY 16
BAROQUE ORCHESTRAL MUSIC

What Is It?

Today's symphony orchestra has its roots in the seventeenth century and may have been an outgrowth of the instrumental *ritornello* of opera. At first operas were accompanied by small string ensembles with the harpsichordist improvising a chordal accompaniment. By the first half of the 1700s the increasingly rich and powerful European monarchies of France, Britain (formed in 1707 by the union of England and Scotland), Austria, and Prussia (formed in northern Germany in 1701) could afford to hire large numbers of musicians for elaborate court ceremonies, concerts, and opera productions. The most famous, admired, and imitated early orchestra was the "24 Violins of the King," an orchestra that played for Louis XIV of France, who reigned from 1643 to 1715. By the end of the seventeenth century, large churches, which had long trained priests and clerics as composers and choristers, hired musicians to accompany services in the new style of monody. St. Mark's Cathedral in Venice, where Monteverdi had worked toward the end of his life, had perhaps the largest church orchestra in Europe. Court and church orchestral musicians included not only string players, who doubled the soprano, alto, tenor, and bass parts, but also players of recorders, transverse flutes, oboes, bassoons, "natural" (valveless) horns and trumpets, and timpani. Neither the number nor the kinds of instruments in an orchestra were standardized during this period, and composers were skilled in creating, and rewriting, music to suit the size and instruments of the orchestras they had at their disposal for a particular occasion.

Our gateway to Baroque orchestral music is the first movement of Antonio Vivaldi's (1678–1741) Violin Concerto in E Major, RV 269, "Spring." Like Monteverdi, Vivaldi lived and worked in Venice, Italy, and was one of the most prolific and influential composers of the Baroque period. A **concerto** is a composition that pits an orchestra, called the *ripieno* from Italian for "full" or "stuffed," against a soloist or a small group of soloists, in the case of this concerto, one or two violinists. Concertos typically have three movements: fast tempo, slow tempo, fast tempo. The term "concerto" to designate these orchestral compositions is a cognate of the term "consort," used during the Renaissance for small instrumental ensembles. *Concerto* in Italian refers to playing "in concert," that is, playing together, retained in the English expression "let's work in concert on this problem." RV 269 is a recent catalog number assigned to this piece by a scholar making a complete list of Vivaldi's compositions. "Spring" is a name Vivaldi gave the piece, one of four concertos in a set that came to be called "The Four Seasons."

The term "E Major" in the title requires some explanation. It is shorthand for a longer phrase: "in the key based on an E major scale." During the Baroque period the old system of Medieval church modes (Dorian, Phrygian, Lydian, and Mixolydian) was replaced by the major scale and the minor scale. A **major scale** can be represented by the seven pitch names with a tonic on C (C D E F G A B). A **minor scale** can be represented by the seven pitch names with a tonic on A (A B C D E F G). The system of **tonal harmony**, which Vivaldi worked in, contains twelve major and twelve minor keys with finals on any of the twelve pitches of the twelve-tone scale (C C♯ D D♯ and so on). When a major scale is played with C as the tonic, it is said to be "in the key of C major." When a major scale is played with E as the tonic, as in this concerto, it is said to

FIGURE 5.8
Antonio Vivaldi
Source: Museo internazionale e biblioteca della musica di Bologna, Wikimedia Commons.

be "in the key of E major" or simply in E major. When minor scales are played on A or G, they are called the key of A minor and the key of G minor, respectively. When a **major key** and a **minor key** share the same set of pitches, as C major and A minor do for example, they are said to be relatives of one another: the **relative major** and the **relative minor**. Triads can also be major or minor. The three pitches of a **major triad** are: the root (another word for the lowest pitch in a chord built on thirds, the pitch that gives the chord its name); a pitch a major third above the root; and a pitch a perfect fifth above the root. (C-E-G, for example, is a C major triad.) The three pitches of a **minor triad** are: the root, a pitch a minor third above the root, and a pitch a perfect fifth above the root. (A-C-E, for example, is an A minor triad). Triads in **tonal harmony** are built on each pitch of a key. Tonal harmony, sometimes also called **tonality**, is based on major and minor triads and other chords in a particular key that have cadences that move from the chord on the fifth scale degree called the **dominant** (V), to the tonic (I).

An aside: In this system of major and minor keys, the terms "major" and "minor" are also applied to the intervals between scale degrees. The interval of a half step is called a **minor second** and the interval of a whole step is called a **major second**. Each of the other intervals in a diatonic scale, except the perfect fourth and the perfect fifth, also have two sizes: major and minor thirds, major and minor sixths, and major and minor sevenths.

This performance is by the Venice Baroque Orchestra, conducted by its founder and violinist Andrea Marcon, with violinist Giuliano Carmignola in the lead solo role.

🔊 **Listen to the first thirty seconds of the recording and note the contrast between the full orchestra and the solo violins.**

How Does It Work?

Timbre

The timbre contrasts a small string orchestra plus harpsichord with the sound of solo violins, sometimes just one and sometimes two in duet.

Texture

The texture features a melodic line accompanied by bass and chords. Sometimes the violins play alone in counterpoint.

Rhythm

The meter is duple. The rhythm of the orchestra employs a constant pulse, sometimes at two levels: a fast pulse subdivides a slower constant beat. This type of pulsating rhythm is one of the hallmarks of Baroque musical style. During some of the violin solos the pulse seems to disappear and the music sounds nonmetrical.

Melody

The melodies are diatonic and move in stepwise motion, but some of the solo violin passages are chromatic.

Harmony

The movement starts in E major, shifts to the relative minor (C♯ minor), and returns to E major.

Form

The form alternates a *ritornello*, a returning melody played by the *ripieno* (the full orchestra), with passages for solo violin. The *ritornello* has the form AABB. Most times the *ritornello* consists only of the B part, played one time.

Performance Techniques

The solo violin part features many melodic ornaments and trills.

Listen to the first thirty seconds of the recording for the AABB form of the *ritornello.*

What Does It Mean?

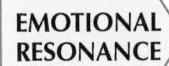

The concerto, and its cousin the sonata, join opera as the most important and long-lasting contributions of the Baroque period to European classical music genres. A **sonata**, from the Latin word for sound, is an instrumental composition for a soloist or a small group of soloists. Concertos and sonatas were the first instrumental compositions in the history of European music meant for listening in concert or church settings rather than for dancing, the amusement of amateur players, or as instrumental versions of vocal works. The question of what instrumental compositions for listening could mean, that is, how listeners are meant to understand and interpret them if they do not dance to them and if they have no lyrics, was vexing to some listeners in the seventeenth and eighteenth centuries and remains so today. One interpretation is that instrumental music is meant for purely musical enjoyment, a type of pleasure explainable through description and analysis of their musical elements. Many, perhaps most, Baroque concertos and sonatas, can be understood this way. Certainly the musical names "concerto" and "sonata" seem to focus on their musical sound and its properties.

The timed listening guide below indicates the way the first movement of the concerto modulates (changes keys) from its "home key" of E major to other keys for a significant time, in particular to the major key on the fifth degree of the scale (B major), called the **dominant key**, and the relative minor key on the sixth degree of the scale (C♯ minor, the relative minor of E major). These movements to closely related keys, often achieved through melodic sequences, allowed composers to expand the length of their works beyond the confines of relatively short dance tunes.

Another interpretation of these purely instrumental works argues that they carry with them associations and iconic musical gestures developed in sixteenth-century vocal polyphony and early seventeenth-century opera, with echoes going back even earlier to Hildegard's religious chants. In this interpretation, the long history of associations between happy texts, fast tempos, rising melodies, and the major mode and between sad texts, slow tempos, falling melodies, and the minor mode carries over into instrumental music. Thus, the moods and emotions in particular instrumental compositions can be explained in terms of their musical elements, without any direct references to a text. Those associations are implicit in purely instrumental music and give it its expressive power. Similarly, ornamentation and other instrumental devices may be icons of sounds in nature, such as birdsong, because musical icons of textual meaning, emotion, and references to natural sounds were developed in Renaissance vocal music.

Concertos and sonatas and other forms of purely instrumental European music can be enjoyed in both ways: as abstract music and as expressions of mood and emotion. Vivaldi's Violin Concerto in E major is a good example. Its title bears its strictly musical meaning and suggests listening to it for its musical properties: in this case a featured solo instrument (violin), a genre (concerto, implying a contrast between soloists and a string orchestra), and a key (E major).

Vivaldi, however, added to this concerto an additional name, "Spring." Each concerto in "The Four Seasons" has a name like this, taken from a poem Vivaldi may have written and printed in the score. This suggests that the concertos of "The Four Seasons" may be interpreted to express, or to paint, the words and moods of the poem. This link between Vivaldi's poem and his composition is an early instance of what came to be called, during the nineteenth century, **program music**: music composed to express the emotions, moods, and meanings of an unperformed verbal narrative.

Listen to the entire first movement of Vivaldi's Violin Concerto in E major, "Spring," and follow the timed listening guide to understand the link between Vivaldi's poem about spring and the way his music expresses the poem's text. The guide is preceded by the poem.

Giunt' è la Primavera e festosetti La Salutan gl' Augei con lieto canto, E i fonti allo Spirar de' Zeffiretti Con dolce mormorio Scorrono intanto: Vengon' coprendo l' aer di nero amanto E Lampi, e tuoni ad annuntiarla eletti Indi tacendo questi, gl' Augelletti; Tornan' di nuovo al lor canoro incanto.

Springtime is upon us and the birds celebrate their return with festive song, and murmuring streams are softly caressed by the breezes. Thunderstorms, those heralds of Spring, roar, casting their dark mantle over heaven, and then they die away to silence, and the birds take up their charming songs once more.

TIME	SECTION	DESCRIPTION
0:00	*Ritornello*	"Springtime is upon us." The *ripieno* plays the *ritornello* (AABB). The major key and the spritely dance tempo in a meter of four suggest the optimism of spring.
0:32	Solo violins & *ritornello*	Two solo violins play "songs of the birds," a phrase in the score, using a wide variety of iconic articulations including trills and melodic gestures followed, at 1:03, by the B melody of the *ritornello*.
1:10	Solo violins & *ritornello*	The violins play constant rapid pulses and then longer tones softly in parallel thirds to paint the poem's reference to "murmuring breezes," followed, at 1:30, by the B melody of the *ritornello*.
1:37	Solo violins & *ritornello*	Loud, low-pitched tremolos in the violins alternate with rapid ascending runs and arpeggios to paint the poem's reference to "thunderstorms roaring." The passage modulates to the relative minor key, now associated with the darkness of a storm, followed, at 2:00, by the return of the *ritornello* in the relative minor key.
2:09	Solo violins	"The birds take up their charming songs once more." Now their songs are in a minor key and use ascending chromatic melodic lines as icons of an unsettled state.
2:27	*Ritornello*	A variant of the A melody returns softly, beginning in the minor key. It starts to modulate to the major key from the beginning of the piece.
2:40	Solo violins & *ritornello*	The solo violin plays an ascending melody with a few references to birdsong and completes the modulation back to the major key, followed, at 2:53, by the BB part of the *ritornello*, ending with a ritard.
3:13	End	

The slow second movement of this concerto paints this text: "And then, on the flower-strewn meadow, with leafy branches rustling overhead, the goatherd sleeps, his faithful dog beside him." Low-pitched droning strings suggest the rustling branches, a slow melody with long tones suggests the sleeping goatherd, and two tones played over and over "very loudly" imitate, humorously, the bark of a dog. The third movement text, "Led by the festive sound of bagpipes, nymphs and shepherds lightly dance beneath the brilliant canopy of spring," is painted with imitations of the drone of a village bagpiper and a set of fast, danceable melodies in a dance form similar to the Bulgarian kopanitsa in Chapter 3, Gateway 10: AABBCCDD.

The sound of a string orchestra is well known in many parts of the world today. Coupled with the dance tempos, the constant pulse of the music, the clear and familiar tonal harmony, the repeating *ritornello* melodies, and the virtuosic violin playing, many listeners today find this and other examples of Baroque orchestral music quite pleasing.

What Is Its History?

During the Renaissance two families of bowed string instruments competed for the affection of professional and amateur musicians. The violin family, with fretless necks, seems to have been a favorite of professional musicians. The viol family, whose fretted necks made it easier to play, was favored by wealthy amateurs. By the seventeenth century the violin family was flourishing in the hands of master musicians and craftsmen, and the viol family disappeared from common use

TECHNOLOGY

until it was revived during the twentieth century as part of the early music movement. During the sixteenth century, the small northern Italian town of Cremona, Monteverdi's birthplace about 150 miles west of Venice, was home to the best violin makers (luthiers), among them members of the Amati and Guarneri families. Today professional violinists greatly admire and seek out violins made in Cremona during the late seventeenth century and early eighteenth century by contemporaries of Monteverdi and Vivaldi: Nicolò Amati (1596–1684), his apprentice Giuseppe Guarneri (1698–1744), and another possible apprentice Antonio Stradivari (1644–1737), whose Latinized name, Stradivarius, is a metaphor for excellence in all fields and whose violins are valued today in the millions of dollars.

AESTHETICS ▷

Two Italian composers are credited with developing some of the structural principles that Vivaldi used in his concertos. Arcangelo Corelli (1653–1713), a noted violin virtuoso, wrote many sonatas that allowed soloists, including himself, to show off their technique. His formal excursions into related keys, such as the relative minor and the dominant key, were also models that Vivaldi followed. Jean-Philippe Rameau (1683–1764), an important French composer of operas and keyboard sonatas and the most important music theorist of the time, used Corelli's works as models for his explanations of the new system of tonal harmony in his 1722 book *Traité de l'harmonie réduite à ses principes naturels* (Treatise on Harmony Reduced to Its Natural Principles), an explanation still influential today. Another Venetian composer, Tomaso Albinoni (1671–1750), gave the concerto its three-movement form. Vivaldi's consistent use of this form, coupled with his renown around Europe, ensured that the concerto (and the sonata) would have this form for centuries to come.

CULTURAL LINKAGES ▷

Antonio Vivaldi, a priest and virtuoso violinist, composed around 500 concertos during his lifetime, most of them at a school in Venice for young girls, some of them orphans. Judging by the demands of the music, they were exceptionally well trained. In Venice during the fourteenth century, the Catholic Church had established four "hospitals" for orphans, the children of indigent parents, and those with incurable illnesses. One, the Pio Ospedale della Pietà, functioned as a conservatory of music for girls, who were trained as singers and instrumentalists in an early form of music therapy. From 1703 to 1740, Vivaldi supervised their teaching and composed sacred and secular music for them to play and sing. Not allowed to play outside the *ospedale*, even if they left it for marriage, they gave public concerts for admiring visitors from all over Europe, including the pope. A French visitor around 1740 described a concert performed by "about forty girls" who "sing like angels," dress like nuns, have a leader with "a bouquet of pomegranate flowers over her ear," and play with a precision rivaling the famous professional orchestras of Paris.

Vivaldi's father taught him to play violin, and they concertized together throughout much of his life. The younger Vivaldi's violin technique, reflected in the virtuoso violin solos of his concertos, awed contemporary admirers. The *ospedale* contracted with him to produce two masses a year and two motets and two concertos each month. In 1717 he obtained the prestigious post of *maestro di cappella* at the court of the Duke of Mantua, where Monteverdi had worked more than a century earlier. There he wrote "The Four Seasons," whose references to nature were perhaps inspired by the countryside around this small town. The European aristocracy of the time was particularly enamored of nature and the countryside, which painters, novelists, and Vivaldi idealized in their creations. Of course peasants who lived close to nature suffered no such illusions. They endured great poverty and misery. For local theaters Vivaldi wrote and produced more than forty operas, the most popular genre of the day. At least one was performed in Prague, and they enjoyed enough success for him to dream of a commission from the Austrian Emperor Charles VI. He failed in his quest, however, and died in poverty in Vienna at the age of sixty-three after an extraordinarily successful and prolific career.

Vivaldi's instrumental concertos were published during his lifetime, and in that form they spread around Europe. They proved enormously influential among German composers including Johann Sebastian Bach, who taught himself to compose in Vivaldi's "Italian style" and transcribed some of Vivaldi's concertos for keyboard. After his death, his music manuscripts fell into the hands of private collectors and disappeared. In the 1920s some of them were discovered in a monastery in Turin, Italy. It was only during the late twentieth century that his concertos became an admired part of the classical music repertoire. His operas, like most Baroque operas, are rarely performed today, but his energetic, virtuosic concertos retain their charm, and many modern players and listeners are devoted to them.

WHERE DO I GO FROM HERE?

- Listen to a performance of another concerto ("Fall," "Winter," or "Summer") from Vivaldi's "The Four Seasons." Find the accompanying poem and listen for the way Vivaldi "paints" the text in that concerto.
- Listen to a solo concerto by Vivaldi for an instrument besides the violin: the recorder, oboe, bassoon, or mandolin.
- Listen to Johann Sebastian Bach's Brandenburg Concerto No. 5 in D Major. Instead of a solo instrument, it features a *concertino* section of violin, transverse flute, and harpsichord and is called a *concerto grosso*.
- Listen to George Frideric Handel's Organ Concerto, Op. 4, No. 5, IV: Presto, as another example of a solo concerto.

GATEWAY 17
BAROQUE SACRED MUSIC

What Is It?

Religious music during the Baroque period adopted many of the stylistic features of operatic monody and the solo concerto, including orchestral accompaniments for solo singers and for choruses singing in four-part harmony. Our gateway to Baroque sacred music is the "Hallelujah" chorus from George Frideric Handel's oratorio, *Messiah*, first performed in Dublin, Ireland, in 1742 and London, England, in 1743. An **oratorio** is a multi-movement composition that tells a biblical story in the vernacular (local) language rather than in the Latin of the Catholic liturgy. To do so, it uses many of the conventions of opera (recitatives, arias with orchestral and *basso continuo* accompaniments, and choruses), but it is performed in concert settings minus the acting, costumes, and scenery of opera. *Messiah* contains more than fifty sections, including recitatives, arias (called "airs" in English), choruses, and two instrumental *sinfonias*. It takes about two and a half hours to perform and has three parts: (1) the Christmas story, including Old Testament prophecies of the coming of a Messiah; (2) the Easter story of Christ's suffering, death, and resurrection; and (3) the resurrection of the dead and the glorification of Christ in heaven. The "Hallelujah" chorus, from the Hebrew word for "Praise God," ends Part 2. The English text was created by Charles Jennens, a gentleman farmer and friend of Handel's, who cobbled the text together from passages in the King James Bible and the Anglican *Book of Common Prayer*. In this performance John Eliot Gardiner, the conductor and a noted specialist in Baroque performance practice, the Monteverdi Choir, and the English Baroque Soloists try to recreate the choral sound of the first performance of *Messiah*, which had a choir of thirty men and boys from Dublin's two cathedrals as well as two women as soloists.

 Listen to the first thirty seconds of the recording.

How Does It Work?

Timbre

The sound is created by a small string orchestra with the addition of valveless trumpets and timpani and a chorus of men and boys.

Texture

Handel used all the textures available to him: monophony, monody, polyphony of voices singing rhythmically independent parts and parts in the same rhythm, and imitative polyphony.

FIGURE 5.9
George Frideric Handel. Painting by Balthasar Denner (1685–1749).
Source: National Portrait Gallery, London, Wikimedia Commons.

Rhythm

The meter is in four and moves along with a strong pulse and short, crisp rhythmic devices, for example, on the many repetitions of the word "Hallelujah."

Melody

The melody is in a major key, employing many leaps through the pitches of major triads, including ascending leaps of an octave.

Harmony

The harmony is tonal, in a major key.

Form

The form consists of four sections based on the text and features the repetition and return of many short melodic ideas.

Section 1:	Hallelujah (repeated)
Section 2:	For the Lord God omnipotent reigneth. Hallelujah (repeated)
Section 3:	The kingdom of this world is become the kingdom of our Lord and of his Christ.
Section 4:	And he shall reign forever and ever, King of kings and Lord of lords. Hallelujah (repeated)

Performance Techniques

The performers change dynamics from soft to loud at important moments.

Listen to the entire performance following this timed listening guide, which explains the way the musical elements change as the text changes.

LISTENING GUIDE 5.3

TIME	SECTION	TEXT	DESCRIPTION
0:00	Instrumental overture		The string orchestra begins softly, its rhythm anticipating the rhythm of the word "Hallelujah."
0:07	1	Hallelujah (repeated)	The chorus, singing in four-part harmony, repeats "Hallelujah" five times softly on the tonic chord (I) and then five more times loudly on the dominant chord (V).
0:26	2a	For the Lord God omnipotent reigneth. Hallelujah	The chorus sings in octaves on the V chord until "Hallelujah" returns in harmony, this time joined by the trumpets and timpani.
0:38	2b	For the Lord God omnipotent reigneth. Hallelujah	The chorus repeats the words, this time on the tonic chord.
0:49	2c	For the Lord God omnipotent reigneth. Hallelujah	The melody of "for the Lord . . ." and the chorus on "Hallelujah" are sung by rhythmically independent parts, with the melody passing from the sopranos to the basses to the tenors.
1:16	3a	The kingdom of this world is become	The chorus sings softly in four-part harmony to the accompaniment of the string orchestra.
1:27	3b	the kingdom of our Lord and of his Christ.	The chorus sings a variant of the melody, this time loudly and with trumpet and timpani accompaniment, the contrast a musical icon of the difference between the plain earthly world (soft) and the glorious heavenly kingdom (loud).

TIME	SECTION	TEXT	DESCRIPTION
1:36	4a	And he shall reign forever and ever,	This section features imitative polyphony, with the basses, tenors, altos, and sopranos each entering in turn on the melody.
1:59	4b	King of kings, and Lord of lords.	One part declaims the words on a single pitch while the chorus responds with "forever and ever, Hallelujah, Hallelujah" in harmony. The pitch rises with each repetition, an icon of the growing intensity of faith, joy, and praise.
2:40	4c	And he shall reign forever and ever,	The chorus sings in counterpoint.
2:51	4d	King of kings, and Lord of lords.	The chorus sings a varied repeat of 4b.
3:00	4e	And he shall reign forever and ever, King of kings, and Lord of lords. Hallelujah (repeated)	The chorus, accompanied by the trumpet and timpani, concludes loudly and triumphantly in four-part harmony.
3:44	End		

What Does It Mean?

In this chorus Handel has absorbed the text painting possibilities of Italian opera, sonically illuminating the text with signs of association and similarity. He uses rising pitch to express the intensification of faith. Trumpets and timpani, associated for centuries with royal and aristocratic festivities, create a feeling of majesty in the revelation of Christ as Lord and king. Softness reflects the ordinariness of secular life, while loudness conveys the glories of a religious life. The major key, long associated with positive and joyous moods, and short, punchy melodic phrases reinforce the brightness of the message. Doubt, which could have been expressed in an excursion to the relative minor key, is banished from this movement.

EMOTIONAL RESONANCE

What Is Its History?

George Frideric Handel was born Georg Friederich Händel in 1685 in the prosperous German trading city of Halle, about 100 miles southwest of Berlin, where his father worked at the court of a local duke. His musical talent was evident at a young age, and he was sent to study organ and counterpoint with the organist at the town church. There he learned to play and compose in all the genres of music required in the Lutheran liturgy of the time, including elaborate contrapuntal organ compositions, four-part hymn accompaniments, and performances of recitatives and arias on sacred texts, styles and techniques he eventually put to use in his English oratorios.

CULTURAL LINKAGES

The Lutheran musical traditions he learned in Halle have their roots two centuries earlier in the Protestant Reformation of the sixteenth century. Martin Luther, a trained musician, ignited the Protestant Reformation in 1517. To make religious lessons and worship more accessible to local congregations, he translated many Latin liturgical texts into German and wrote his own hymn melodies to new German texts he also composed. Lutheran services encouraged congregational singing of hymns, with organists supplying organ accompaniments in the four-part harmony of the Renaissance. As musical styles changed, so did the harmonies of these hymns.

During the seventeenth century, the new style of opera was also introduced into Lutheran religious services in a multi-movement genre called **cantata** (from Italian for "to sing") to distinguish them from the new instrumental genre sonata. By the eighteenth century the church cantata had become a set of pieces that might include an instrumental overture, an opening contrapuntal chorus, two recitative-and-aria sets, and a concluding chorale with all four parts moving in the same rhythm and suitable for congregational singing. Taken together, the cantata told a story or expressed a religious sentiment suitable for the day in the church calendar for which it was composed. Handel's contemporary Johann Sebastian Bach—born in the same year as Handel, 1685, and who lived nearly as long, to 1750—composed more than 200 cantatas for the Lutheran St. Thomas Church in Leipzig, about twenty-five miles southeast of Halle. Among Bach's most famous cantatas are "Ein feste Burg," "Wachet auf," and "Ich habe genug." Handel, who was living in England by the time Bach moved to Leipzig, never met Bach or heard his cantatas.

After a year at the University of Halle, Handel moved to Hamburg, where the first opera house in Germany had been established in 1678. There, in 1705 at the age of twenty, he composed and produced his first two operas. These works caught the attention of the wealthy Medici family, who, in 1706, invited him to Florence. As his renown spread, a group of cardinals and a wealthy patron close to the church invited him to Rome to compose oratorios. Oratorios, concert pieces in local languages based on biblical stories, were named after the church halls, the oratorios, where they were performed. Responding to the Protestant challenge to educate believers in biblical teaching, wealthy Catholic parish churches had built these church halls as places for the education of the faithful through classes, lectures (orations), and concerts in the local language, Italian. For Easter Sunday, 1708, Handel composed an oratorio titled *La Resurrezione* (The Resurrection).

Handel's operas and oratorios were much loved in Italy, attracting the notice of the German Prince Georg, Elector of Hanover; an elector was a prince with voting rights in a council of princes who ruled over lands in present-day Germany, the Czech Republic, Hungary, and Austria. In 1711 Prince Georg invited Handel to become the director of his court musicians and singers. However, Handel's reputation as an opera composer had also reached London, where in 1711 his new opera *Rinaldo*, about a knight during the First Crusade against Muslims in Jerusalem in 1099, was a huge hit with the British. In 1712 Handel left his German prince in the lurch and decamped permanently for London.

In London Handel quickly became a favorite of the nobility, including Queen Anne, who gave him a royal stipend in 1713 after he composed an *Ode for the Birthday of Queen Anne*, a setting of a long poem in her honor for soloists, chorus, and orchestra. When she died without a male heir in 1714, an act of the British Parliament designed to ensure successions to the throne only by Protestants led to the enthronement of her second cousin, Prince Georg, Elector of Hanover. Handel's former patron became King George I of Great Britain. He apparently bore Handel no grudge for leaving his previous court and increased his royal stipend.

ECONOMIC
ACTIVITY

In 1720 Handel founded an opera company called the Royal Academy of Music with the financial aid of aristocrats who were obsessed with Italian operas. Importing excellent singers from Italy, he wrote and produced more than thirty operas in Italian, one or two each year, for the next twenty-one years. In 1741, in the face of growing disinterest among the nobility in his operas, he sought to attract the growing London middle-class audience to paid performances of his music by abandoning opera and devoting himself with equal energy to oratorios in English. This middle-class audience had not studied Ancient Greek and Latin mythology and history, the stuff of opera. They did read the Bible, however, and knew biblical stories intimately, the stuff of oratorios. Before 1741, Handel had already composed English oratorios based on Old Testament stories: *Esther, Deborah, Saul*, and *Israel in Egypt*. *Messiah*, written in 1741, was his only oratorio with material from the New Testament. Its 1742 premier in Dublin was a benefit concert for the city's hospitals and debtor's prisons. After that success he returned to Old Testament stories, writing fifteen more oratorios between 1742 and 1752, a pace of one or two each year. His oratorios exploited the musical conventions of Italian operas, especially solo recitatives and arias, but they included masterful choruses, perhaps a legacy of his upbringing in the German Lutheran Church.

Oratorios in Italy and in England were performed during the Lenten season, the forty days before Easter, a time of religious contemplation when the performance of Italian opera, with its sensual, hedonistic themes, was either expressly forbidden or considered inappropriate. During Lent each year, Handel typically supervised the performance of ten or so of his oratorios, sometimes playing an organ concerto during intermission. He ended the season with *Messiah*. Often his concerts were benefits for charitable institutions. This link between his oratorios and charities turned them into much-admired civic events. In 1759 he collapsed while attending a performance of *Messiah* and died a few days later, on the day before Easter.

Most Baroque operas, sonatas, concertos, and religious works fell into disuse shortly after their first performances, especially when new styles made them sound musty and obsolete. But not *Messiah*. It is one of the few compositions from the Baroque period that has been continuously performed since Handel's day. Indeed, it is one of the most beloved and often performed compositions in the entire European classical tradition. In 1859 a *Messiah* performance celebrated the centenary of his death with a choir of nearly 3000, an orchestra of more than 400, and an audience of 10,000 in the Crystal Palace, a gigantic hall built from wood, iron, and newly invented plate glass for the Great Exhibition of 1851, one of the earliest World's Fairs. During the nineteenth century Messiah came to be associated with the Christmas season, particularly in the United States. Today, during the Advent season, the weeks leading up to Christmas Day, hundreds of choruses and orchestras all perform *Messiah*, some in concert halls, some in churches, and some in sing-along versions with the audience singing the choruses with professional soloists and an orchestra.

FIGURE 5.10
A nineteenth-century painting imagining George Frideric Handel, right arm outstretched, with King George I during a performance of his composition *Water Music* in 1717; in fact, Handel was probably on the barge directing the musicians! Painting by Edouard Jean Conrad Hamman (1819–1888).
Source: Wikimedia Commons.

The "Hallelujah" chorus, as a stand-alone movement, has long infused popular culture. Its short, repeated melodies, straightforward harmonies, constant rhythmic pulses, and repeated statements of "Hallelujah," have made it instantly recognizable—and useful, often as a musical joke. In a TV commercial or a movie, when something unexpected or wonderful happens, the opening measures of the "Hallelujah" chorus might pop up right on cue; for example, when a customer gets a great deal on a car loan or when, in the 1989 comedy *National Lampoon's Christmas Vacation*, suburban dad Clark Griswold—after much frustration—finally manages to illuminate his massive lighting display of 25,000 twinkle lights that blinds the neighbors and causes a blackout for the rest of his town.

> CULTURAL
> LINKAGES

WHERE DO I GO FROM HERE?

- Listen to other movements of *Messiah*.

- Powerful choruses in the vein of "Hallelujah" include:

    Part I, 3: "And the glory of the Lord"; and

    Part I, 12: "For unto us a child is born."

- Virtuosic arias written to showcase the skills of the singers give some idea of the florid, melismatic singing style of early eighteenth-century Baroque opera:

    Part I, 2: "Ev'ry valley shall be exalted" for tenor;

    Part I, 5: "But who shall abide" for countertenor;

    Part I, 16: "Rejoice greatly, O daughter of Zion" for soprano; and

    Part II, 38: "Why do the nations so furiously rage together" for bass.

- Listen to soprano Kathleen Battle and the trumpeter Wynton Marsalis perform the final chorale of Johann Sebastian Bach's Cantata BMV 51, "Jauchzet Gott in allen Landen" (Shout for joy to God from all lands). Listen for its unornamented hymn melody "Sei Lob und Preis mit Ehren" (Glory, and praise with honor) followed by the contrasting aria "Alleluia," with its highly ornamented melody typical of the Baroque period and an aural icon of religious ecstasy.

GATEWAY 18
BAROQUE KEYBOARD MUSIC

What Is It?

Keyboard is a generic term used today for all types of instruments that employ the layout of long white keys for the seven-pitch diatonic scale and short black keys for the five additional chromatic pitches of European music. Modern keyboard instruments include the piano and electronic synthesizer. During the Baroque period, the principal keyboard instruments were organ (a type of panpipe) and two string **zithers** called harpsichord and clavichord.

Our gateway to Baroque keyboard music is Prelude and Fugue in C major from *The Well-Tempered Clavier*, Book I, by Johann Sebastian Bach (1685–1750). The word "prelude" suggests a piece before another piece. Bach's **preludes** are short, free-form pieces often spun out from a single melodic or rhythmic idea. A **fugue**, from Latin for "flight" or "fleeing from," is a tightly organized piece featuring imitative counterpoint. *The Well-Tempered Clavier*, published in 1722, is a collection of twenty-four preludes and fugues in each of the twelve major and twelve minor keys of the tonal system. **Clavier** means keyboard in German. Bach probably performed his preludes and fugues on all the keyboard types available to him. **Well-tempered** means well tuned, that is, tuned in a way that allows pieces to sound reasonably good in all keys of the tonal system. It is played on the harpsichord by American harpsichordist and church organist John Paul.

 Listen to the first thirty seconds of the recording.

How Does It Work?

Timbre

The timbre of the harpsichord is created by a quill attached to the end of a lever on a key. The quill plucks a single string. Each tone has a metallic quality that decays rather quickly, although the low-pitch bass tones sustain a bit longer than do the high-pitched ones.

Texture

The texture of the prelude is monophonic. The fugue, starting at 2:11, begins with imitative counterpoint and continues with four rhythmically independent voices throughout.

Rhythm

The meter of both pieces is quadruple and features constant pulsation without pauses.

Melody

The melody of the prelude is based on ascending arpeggiated chords and moves mainly through leaps of a third. The opening melody of the fugue begins in ascending stepwise motion before adding leaps that curve up and down.

Harmony

The harmony is tonal, but with the addition of occasional chromatic pitches.

Form

Overall the form contrasts two movements, the first monophonic and free-flowing, the second contrapuntal and tightly wound. Both are based

FIGURE 5.11
Johann Sebastian Bach. Painting by Elias Gottlob Haussmann (1695–1774).
Source: Bach-Archiv Leipzig, Wikimedia Commons.

on the continuous repetition of a short musical idea: in the prelude, ascending arpeggios; in the fugue, a short melody repeated over and over in different polyphonic contexts.

Performance Techniques

The performer plays with a steady pulse, neither speeding up nor slowing down, except at the ends of sections, and with no pauses in the phrases. There are no crescendos or decrescendos, because harpsichords cannot produce them even if players vary the force with which they hit the keys.

🔊 **Listen to this recording and notice the contrast between the monophonic texture of the prelude and the imitative polyphony of the fugue, which begins at 2:11.**

What Does It Mean?

Bach worked his entire life in the towns, churches, and courts of what is today central Germany. He published *The Well-Tempered Clavier* while in service to a prince who was an amateur musician. These preludes and fugues had, and continue to have, a pedagogical function, as Bach wrote on the title page of *The Well-Tempered Clavier*: "for the benefit and use of studious musical youth, and also for those in this studio already well skilled in this special pastime." Bach had four goals in mind for the preludes and fugues in *The Well-Tempered Clavier*. First, as he indicated on the title page, they were exercises for beginning students and the amusement of more advanced players. They were not meant for public performance though musicians today perform them in concert. Second, by composing a pair in each of tonal harmony's major and minor keys, he demonstrated a musical solution to some problems of pitch and key that had bedeviled the tonal system, problems not evident in the older system of melodic modes but one that Chinese and Arab theorists had discovered centuries earlier. Third, modulating to different key areas within a prelude or fugue, he illustrated some of the chromatic complexities of tonal harmony. Fourth, he demonstrated his unsurpassed skill at counterpoint, especially imitative counterpoint, a technique basic to Baroque musical style and required of all church organists of the time. Although Bach, like Monteverdi, Vivaldi, and Handel, was a master of text painting and its uses in vocal and instrumental music for evoking scenes and sentiments, such expression is not at issue in these keyboard pieces. They are purely musical creations at a level of complexity that delights players and listeners today and leads many classical music critics to regard Bach as one of the greatest composers in the history of European music.

> AESTHETICS

In this C major prelude, and in others in *The Well-Tempered Clavier*, Bach creates a sense of unity by repeating the same melodic and rhythmic device in every single measure. He provides internal structure in short sections that move away from and return to the tonic chord via the dominant chord (I-V-I). Along these chordal pathways he introduces dissonant-sounding chords that enrich the palette of tonal harmony.

> AESTHETICS

The fugue is a Baroque-period instrumental extension of imitative vocal polyphony developed during the Renaissance. As a genre, the common defining feature of a fugue is the opening **exposition** of a single musical melody, called the **subject**, in imitation. The texture may have three, four, or five parts, called "voices," a term borrowed from vocal polyphony. The voices may enter in any order. In Bach's Fugue in C Major, they enter in this order: alto, tenor, bass, soprano. The first entry is called the statement, and the second entry is called the answer. The resulting four-part texture can be graphed like this, with the passage of time from top to bottom and left to right:

alto voice subject and continuation _____

tenor voice subject and continuation_____

bass voice subject and continuation_____

soprano voice subject and continuation

After all the voices have entered in imitation, the exposition ends. Bach exercised quite a bit of freedom in what he did next in the development or restatement of the subject and its movement through related key areas. He might reintroduce the subject somewhat veiled in a thick contrapuntal texture, as he does here, or he could continue with counterpoint without the subject in sections called **episodes**. Bach's Fugue in C major has no lengthy episodes; the subject continues to enter in different voices throughout the fugue, creating a strong sense of unity with little of the subject—episode contrast that characterizes some fugues. These developments after the exposition modulate to other key areas such as the dominant and the relative minor.

Listen another time to Bach's Prelude and Fugue in C Major, following this timed listening guide, which describes the formal principles outlined above.

LISTENING GUIDE 5.4

TIME	TITLE	SECTION	DESCRIPTION
0:04	**Prelude** The prelude repeats an ascending arpeggio on different chords throughout. The occasional V-I cadences create an internal sense of closure or arrival from time to time.	Section 1	The lowest pitch in each arpeggio can be heard as a bass line, creating an inherent polyphony within a monophonic texture, something heard in Shona *mbira* music. In this section the bass line descends through an octave plus a fourth, arriving at a low C, an octave below the starting pitch.
1:08		Section 2	The bass line descends again, eventually settling on low G on the fifth degree of the C scale, where it stays, creating a drone texture called a "pedal point," a reference to an organist holding down a foot pedal to create a continuous low pitch.
1:47		Section 3	The pedal point on G, which has created a dominant effect and anticipation of resolution on the tonic, resolves to low C, two octaves below the starting pitch, establishing another pedal point to the end. The chord on G just before C is a dominant seventh chord. While a triad has three pitches, a **seventh chord** adds a fourth pitch to a triad, a major or minor third above the fifth degree of the scale. A **dominant seventh chord** adds the flatted seventh degree to the triad on the fifth scaled degrees (V): in C major, G-B-D-F.
2:09		End	
2:11	**Fugue** A contrapuntal texture of rhythmically independent voices throughout with the almost continuous presence of a short melody, the fugue subject.	Section 1	The exposition: Each voice (alto, soprano, tenor, bass) enters in turn in imitative polyphony. The alto starts on C, but the soprano and tenor enter on G, creating a modest sense of movement from tonic to dominant. The bass enters on C, returning to the tonic.
2:43		Section 2	The exposition complete, the subject returns in the soprano voice within the four-part texture, followed almost immediately by the tenor, and then the alto and bass. Bach introduces chromatic pitches for two additional statements of the subject in the alto and then the tenor, as the voices modulate to the relative minor key, which the player marks with a slight ritard to end this section with a V-i (E major to A minor) cadence. (Lowercase Roman numerals [i, iv, v] are used to indicate minor chords on their respective scale degrees.)
3:20		Section 3	Returning to C major, each voice enters before the previous voice finishes the subject, a speeding or tightening up of the imitative polyphony, a technique called *stretto*, from Italian for "close," "tight," or "fast." Attention shifts quickly from voice to voice as each enters in turn with the subject. Sometimes the subject is hard to hear in the thick four-voice texture. The player ends the section with a slight pause on a cadence on the tonic.

TIME	TITLE	SECTION	DESCRIPTION
4:13		Section 4	A pedal tone on the tonic in the bass supports one last point of imitation with tenor, alto, and soprano voices entering in *stretto*.
4:34		End	

For centuries the intellectual complexity of Bach's fugal counterpoint has amazed composers and music students learning to compose in this style. It is even more amazing to think that Bach and other church organists of the period could improvise fugues. Most listeners find the constant pulsation of the prelude and fugue, and indeed of Baroque musical style, attractive. Taking the genre name "fugue" literally, a listener can hear a fugue as a musical game of tag in which the first voice to enter is "it" and tags the next voice, while all the other voices are "flying around" and "fleeing from" it.

The musical terms used to describe the elements of a fugue also provide clues to its meaning. They are borrowed from language and literature: subject, statement, answer, exposition, episode, and development all suggest that musical form can be explained as a metaphor for literary form. The familiar expression "musical phrase" is another example in this vein. When music seems abstract and not expressive of the content and emotions of an associated lyric or painting or natural scene, musical theorists since the Baroque period made sense of it using the forms rather than the thematic content of literature. Such metaphors are a common feature of human thought. Humans tend to explain most things in the world metaphorically, as if they were something else, a process that links different elements of the world together and makes them feel coherent and "natural."

> **CULTURAL LINKAGES**

What Is Its History?

The idea of using keys (levers) to activate a musical vibration in a tube or on a string originated in the third century BCE, when Greeks used keys to activate water pressure to force air over the edge of pipes in what were, in effect, panpipes. They called the instrument a *hydraulis*. Beginning in the early Medieval period, portable organs employing a bellows instead of water pressure to force air over pipe edges figured prominently in the secular musical life of the Byzantine Empire,

> **TECHNOLOGY**

with its capital in Constantinople. In 812 Charlemagne, whose father had received an organ from the Byzantine emperor, placed the first church organ in his chapel in Aachen. In 1361 a church in Halberstadt, Germany, not far from Handel's birthplace of Halle, installed the first permanent church organ. By the seventeenth century, nearly every Lutheran and Catholic Church in Europe had a permanently installed organ with most of the features of modern organs, including elaborately decorated cases in Baroque style for the pipes.

An enormously complex instrument, the Baroque organ consists of hundreds, even thousands, of flute and reed pipes of different lengths (and therefore different pitches) into which air is forced by a bellows. The pipes are organized into sets called ranks, each covering different octaves and having different timbres. The movement of the air into the pipes and ranks is controlled from a console containing two or more keyboards, called manuals; a pedalboard played with the feet; and a set of knobs called stops. A stop opens and closes the passage of air to one of the ranks of pipes. The player pulls out a stop to play a particular rank and pushes it in to stop the flow of air

FIGURE 5.12

Byzantine pipe organ, tuned bells, *aulos* (reed pipe), and *kithara* (lyre) in a Byzantine mosaic from Syria from *c.* fifth century CE

Source: Hellenic Society for Near Eastern Studies, Wikimedia Commons.

FIGURE 5.13
Baroque organ in a Catholic Church in Wuppertal-Beyenburg, Germany
Source: Beckstet, Wikimedia Commons.

SOCIAL
BEHAVIOR

to the pipes in the rank. By changing the stops and the manual, the player can alter the timbre, loudness, and octave of the organ's sound. "Pulling out all the stops" means every rank sounds, creating a huge, loud sound. The phrase has become a metaphor for a grand gesture in any human endeavor. Lutheran organists accompanied congregational singing on the organ with harmonic accompaniments. They also composed more elaborate polyphonic chorale preludes built around the melody of the hymn tune. Today these are played before and after the service, during the collection of offerings, and sometimes toward the end of a hymn—and at organ concerts.

The **harpsichord** is a plucked zither. Its shape is anticipated by the Arab *qanun* (Chapter 3, Gateway 8). It may have been invented during the Medieval period, but the oldest surviving example is from the early seventeenth century, when harpsichords provided chordal *basso continuo* parts for solo recitatives and arias. Composers directed their own orchestral compositions often while playing the harpsichord. By the eighteenth century harpsichords had one or two manuals (keyboards) covering five octaves (sixty keys or so) of multi-string courses. The timbre could be altered with stops that selected all the strings or a single string of the course to be played. In this recording, the player chose to play just a single course. Domenico Scarlatti (1685–1757), an Italian composer who worked in royal courts in Spain and Portugal and composed more than 500 solo sonatas for the instrument, launched the harpsichord and its descendant, the piano, as a solo instrument.

The **clavichord**, from Latin meaning "key," was invented about the same time as the harpsichord. The keys raise and lower metal blades to stop the strings, producing a very quiet sound not suitable for concert performances. It was used primarily at home for the amusement of the player, something like the Chinese *qin* in that regard, and as a composer's tool.

In 1685 Johann Sebastian Bach was born 100 miles southwest of Halle, in the town of Eisenach, where Martin Luther had attended school. His father worked there as a professional musician. The region was a hotbed of Protestant organ music. His forefathers going back four generations were the most numerous and famous professional town and church musicians in the area. Taught by his father and brother as a boy, he was sent to a prestigious Latin school in northern Germany, where he studied organ with leading musicians and established himself as a virtuoso organist. In contrast to Handel, the cosmopolitan life and international fame of an itinerant opera composer was not for the young Bach, and he never composed operas, the most popular genre of the age. Instead, at seventeen this devout young man returned home to take up the family craft: musical composition, performance, and teaching for towns, courts, and churches.

FIGURE 5.14
A modern organ console with four manuals, pedalboard, and stops
Source: Wikimedia Commons.

FIGURE 5.15
A single-manual harpsichord
Source: Tomwsulcer, Wikimedia Commons.

FIGURE 5.16
Clavichord from *c.* sixteenth century
Source: Gérad Janot, Wikimedia Commons.

Compared to Handel, who traveled from Germany to Italy to England during his career, Bach worked his entire life in a relatively small, forested area of Germany about the size of the state of Vermont. He held positions in local churches and courts and was relatively unknown outside that region:

- Arnstadt (1703–1707) as a church organist;
- Mühlhausen (1707–1708) as a church organist;
- Weimar (1708–1717) as an organist and court composer;
- Köthen (1717–1723) as a court composer; and
- Leipzig (1723–1750) as a church composer and town musician.

In each of these places he composed what was required of him by contract. As a church composer in Arnstadt and Muhlhausen, he improvised and composed chorale preludes and hymn harmonizations. As a court composer in Weimar and Köthen he composed concertos, dance suites for orchestras, and the preludes and fugues in Book I of *The Well-Tempered Clavier*. In Leipzig he was in charge of music for the town's four Lutheran churches and an ensemble of university students called the *collegium musicum*. For the largest church, St. Thomas Church, he was required to produce a multi-movement cantata for soloists, choir, and string orchestra for each Sunday of the liturgical calendar. He wrote more than 200 of them. He also wrote more ambitious religious works too long for a Sunday service. His *Christmas Oratorio* (1734) combines six cantatas, each performed on a different Sunday during Advent. Today it is sometimes performed in a concert lasting about three hours. He also wrote a number of Passions based on the Easter story as told in the Gospels; the *St. Matthew Passion* (1727) and the *St. John Passion* (1724) survive and are still performed today in concert. Perhaps surprisingly for a Protestant, at the end of his life, in 1749, he wrote a complete mass, his Mass in B Minor. The work is massive, and today it is regarded as one of his grandest and most moving achievements.

> **ECONOMIC ACTIVITY**

FIGURE 5.17
Map of Germany

CULTURAL LINKAGES

In these modest circumstances Bach lived a dutiful domestic life, especially compared to Handel, who never married, and Vivaldi, who was a priest. In 1707, after moving to Mühlhausen, he married his second cousin, Maria Barbara Bach, who gave birth to six children, only three of whom lived beyond their first birthday. While he was working in Köthen, she fell ill and died suddenly in 1720. The following year he married a young court singer, Anna Magdalena Wilcke. She gave birth to thirteen children, only six of whom survived. Bach continued his family's tradition, teaching all his sons to play keyboard music and compose. Four of them became distinguished composers of the next generation, continuing their father's craft and contributing to the development of the new musical styles of the mid-to-late eighteenth century.

Bach's compositions were composed for church and court, rather than the concert and opera stages, and so during his lifetime his renown was quite limited compared to Handel's or Vivaldi's. As a consequence, and as musical styles changed, his work ceased to be performed for many decades, his legacy living on mainly in the skills he bequeathed to his sons and in musical manuscripts that the next generation of composers studied. Mozart, Beethoven, and other composers of the late eighteenth and early nineteenth centuries studied his scores to learn tonal harmony and fugal and contrapuntal technique. Although they rarely wrote fugues, they inserted fugal passages within some of their compositions as icons of seriousness.

Bach's music lay mostly unperformed for nearly eighty years, except occasionally in Leipzig, until 1829, when the composer and organist Felix Mendelssohn (1809–1847), at the age of twenty, produced and conducted an abridged version of the *St. Matthew Passion* in Berlin. From an early age Mendelssohn found Bach's music inspiring. He eventually took Bach's old position at the St. Thomas Church in Leipzig and directed the town's leading civic musical organizations, as Bach had done. Mendelssohn, the scion of a prominent Jewish family that had renounced Judaism, secured the Protestant Bach's position as one of the most admired composers of the European classical musical tradition, a position he has held to the present day.

WHERE DO I GO FROM HERE?

- Listen to recordings of Bach's Prelude and Fugue in C Major played on piano and on organ and compare them to the harpsichord performance in this gateway. Which do you prefer and why?
- Listen to a recording of Bach's Prelude and Fugue in C Minor, the second one in *The Well-Tempered Clavier*. How are its elements similar to and different from those in the C Major Prelude and Fugue?
- Listen to one or more of the keyboard sonatas of Domenico Scarlatti and compare them to Bach's keyboard style in the Prelude and Fugue in C Major.

GATEWAY 19
JAVANESE COURT MUSIC

What Is It?

Java is one of many islands in an archipelago that makes up the country of Indonesia. Located between the Indian and Pacific Oceans, Java has a population of nearly 150 million people, most of whom are Muslims. Its court music dates from seventeenth and early eighteenth centuries, when powerful kings ruled most of the island before ceding power to the Dutch East India company in 1749. Entertainment at court included elaborate dances and theatrical presentations accompanied by a gamelan. A **gamelan** is a large orchestra of around forty instruments made of bronze gongs or metal keys, plus drums, a bowed fiddle, xylophone, zither, flute, and sometimes vocals. Indonesia became a nation independent of colonial rule in 1949. The majority of Javanese are Muslims, but Hinduism and Buddhism, which Islam had superseded by the sixteenth century, still resonate in Javanese cultures, including in its musical theater accompanied by the gamelan.

Our gateway to Javanese court music is a composition for gamelan called "Ketawang Puspawarna Laras Slendro Patet Manyura." In this recording women soloists and a chorus of men perform with the gamelan. The composition is played at the opening of concerts at two Javanese princely courts, successors to the royal court of the seventeenth and eighteenth centuries. Its long name places it within a well-developed musical system and includes the name of the piece, its form, its tuning system, and its melodic mode.

FIGURE 5.18
Javanese gamelan with two women soloists
Source: Gunawan Kartapranata, Wikimedia Commons.

- *Ketawang* is a musical form based on a rhythmic cycle of sixteen beats.
- *Puspawarna* is the name of this composition in the *ketawang* form: it means "kinds of flowers."
- *Laras* means tuning system.
- *Slendro* is one of two tuning systems in Javanese music: it has five approximately equidistant pitches in an octave.
- *Patet*, also *pathet*, means melodic mode.
- *Manyura* is one of three melodic modes in the *slendro* tuning system.

The composition is called "Puspawarna" for short.

"Puspawarna" in the title is a poem with nine stanzas or **verses** (groups of lines in a poem). Each stanza describes a flower in a way that makes a metaphorical connection between floral beauty and attractive qualities of women:

> Flower of the *kencur* plant, always spoken of with admiration, her body is well-shaped and her movements graceful, she is so charming in speech that one feels carried away.
> Flower of the starfruit tree, when picked soon comes back; she shines sweetly indeed like a precious jewel, she is the queen of flowers and the essence of women.
> Flower of the durian tree, one stops to look at it amazed at her shape; her sweet smiles and her elegant speech embrace the senses.
> Flower of the sugar palm bends over the durian branches; whenever I am looking at you and thinking of the flower, I become wistful.
> Flower of the banana tree hangs down over a pond; it is fitting for those of noble descent to have a demure expression and unaffected manners.
> Flower of the teak tree, scattered around the house, I stand and look out, waiting for you endlessly, not knowing if I will match.
> Flower of the betel palm opens fragrantly in the evening; I am overwhelmed to receive your visit, hoping that you will grant your favor.
> Flower of the cotton plant, constantly cut, I strongly desire to adore you, to fulfill your wishes unresistingly.
> Flower of the pandanus plant, scattered on the floor, when you come down to my place do not be anxious, I will surrender.

The liner notes to this recording say, "the mood it evokes is of ripeness or fulfillment. The text refers to different kinds of flowers, each symbolizing a different *rasa* (mood)." The mood of ripeness is presumably created by the association between the lyrical references to many fruit-bearing plants and the music. This performance contains two of the nine stanzas.

Listen to the first thirty seconds of the recording.

How Does It Work?

Timbre

The piece employs a variety of timbres. At the core is the sound of bronze gongs and metal bars, a metallic sound very rich in overtones. Drums, a bowed lute called *rebab*, xylophone, bamboo flute, plucked zither, women soloists, and a chorus of men add to the timbral opulence.

Texture

The texture is a complex weave of many melodic lines produced by the gongs, a bowed lute, the women's voices, and the men's voices, with drum accompaniment. Sets of low-, mid-, and high-pitched gongs mark the rhythmic structure. Keyed metallophones, gongs, xylophone, and zithers play heterophonic elaborations of the melody at higher pitches.

Rhythm

Three kinds of rhythm interact in this performance. Forming the foundation are the gongs, each of which plays tones of a single duration in a steady pulse. Over this steady pulse, the soloists sing nonmetrically, the male singers sing a metrical melody with a variety of long and short tones, and the flute and bowed fiddle play a mix of metrical and nonmetrical phrases.

Melody

The men's vocal melody is broken up into a series of descending phrases with a variety of steps and leaps in a pentatonic scale of approximately equidistant intervals.

Harmony

The piece is a polyphonic, heterophonic weave of many melodic lines, but harmony in the European sense is not present.

Form

Every verse of the poem "Puspawarna" is performed to the same melody, and so the form could be written AAA and so forth. In Ancient Greece this unit of a poetic verse with its music was called a **strophe**. Today, songs with the same music for each verse of the lyrics are said to be in **strophic form** and are called **strophic songs**. They are perhaps the most common song form in the world. In this recording the gamelan performs two strophes. A *rebab* solo begins the piece, and an instrumental section precedes each of the two strophes.

Performance Techniques

The drummers control the tempo and tempo changes. The chorus of men supplies vocal calls that add to the excitement during the instrumental sections.

 Listen to the first thirty seconds of the recording focusing on its layered texture and rich timbre.

Timed Listening Guide

The form of this piece is supported by a series of ten rhythmic cycles whose beginnings and ends are marked audibly by the sounding of the gamelan's lowest-pitched knobbed gong. This lowest-pitched gong is named *gong ageng* (the word "gong" comes into English from Indonesia). Each rhythmic cycle, called a *gongan*, consists of sixteen beats, many marked by the sounding of knobbed gongs at different pitches. In the chart below, pitch is represented vertically, time horizontally. The names of the gongs sounding on each beat, from low to high, are: G = gong, N = *kenong*, P = *kempul*, T = *ketuk*, p = *kempyang*.

16	1	2	3	4	5	6	7	8	9	10	11	12	13	14	15	16
	p		p		p		p		p		p		p		p	
		T				T				T				T		
				–								P				
								N								
G N																G N

This elaborate cyclical rhythmic structure, called *bentuk* in Javanese, sounds beneath the melody, marking its phrase structure. In English it is called the **colotomic structure**, from Latin meaning "to cut." These gongs cut up time into beats or pulses. The gamelan's texture consists of three layers: (1) a rhythmic, cyclical (colotomic) structure played on knobbed gongs; (2) a mid-pitched, mid-tempo melody played on metallophones; and (3) high-pitched, fast-tempo elaborating parts.

Listen to the entire recording following this timed listening guide, which describes the formal principles outlined above. Count the beats and notice the sounding of the gong and *kenong* on beat 16 and the *kenong* on beat 8. Each one marks the end of the men's melodic phrases.

LISTENING GUIDE 5.5

TIME	DESCRIPTION
0:00	The piece begins with an eight-beat introduction, first on the *rebab,* followed by the drums.
	Instrumental interlude:
0:07	*Gongan* 1: The full orchestra enters on the low gong in a fast tempo with the women soloists singing and calls by the male chorus. The tempo gradually slows.
0:22	*Gongan* 2: The tempo is established with the melody and elaborating instruments marking, in a clock-like manner, each of the sixteen pulses of the cyclical structure. Notice the vocal calls. The soloists sing, somewhat buried in the texture. In another recording they might sound quite prominently.
	First strophe:
0:46	*Gongan* 3: The male chorus enters two and a half beats before the *kenong* sounds, the halfway point in the *gongan*. Their melody cadences on the *gong ageng* at the end of the cycle. The soloists continue to sing.
1:13	*Gongan* 4: The male chorus enters with the second phrase of the melody, which cadences halfway through the cycle on the *kenong*. The third phrase enters and cadences on the *gong ageng* at the end of the cycle.
1:40	*Gongan* 5: The male chorus continues with the fourth and fifth phrases of the song, the fourth phrase cadencing on the *kenong* and the fifth on the *gong ageng*, as in *gongan* 4.
	Instrumental interlude:
2:08	*Gongan* 6: Instrumental interlude with male vocal calls.
2:37	*Gongan* 7: Instrumental interlude with vocal calls by the men and the women singing in the background.
	Second strophe:
3:04	*Gongan* 8: Men begin the second strophe of the song with the first phrase as in *gongan* 3. Women continue to sing in the background.
3:37	*Gongan* 9: Men sing the second and third phrases of the song melody as in *gongan* 4. The tempo speeds up slightly toward the end of the *gongan*.
3:58	*Gongan* 10: Men sing the fourth and fifth phrases of the song as in *gongan* 5. Note the dramatic ritard before the final *gong ageng* sounds.
4:33	End: The *gong ageng* sounds. Notice how long the low gong continues to ring, taking ten seconds to decay into silence at 4:44.

What Does It Mean?

Gamelan music is played in one of two tuning systems. To play in these two different scales, some gamelans have two sets of instruments, one for each of the pitch systems. Both are arranged together on the floor, each set at a ninety-degree angle to the other set. The musicians, seated on the floor, shift their positions to play in the tuning system appropriate to each composition. One tuning system is called *slendro*, the five-tone equidistant pentatonic scale heard in "Puspawarna." It has intervals about halfway between a major second and a minor third. The other tuning system, called *pelog*, is a seven-tone heptatonic system from which five (but sometimes six or seven) main pitches are chosen. The distance between the five main pitches in *pelog* varies from roughly a half step to about a major third. Unlike European music, in which the pitches and intervals are standardized, there is no external standard against which to measure pitches and intervals in this tradition. Although every gamelan adheres to the principles of the two tuning systems, each gamelan possesses its own unique set of pitches and intervals and thus a unique sound.

The forty or so bronze instruments of a gamelan are not owned by individuals, as most instruments of the European orchestra are. Rather, the entire orchestra is owned by a prince, a wealthy individual, a broadcasting company, or a music conservatory. New owners commission the making of all the instruments as a set and place them in their palace, home, or institution. The largest gongs, gong, *kenong* and *kempul*, hang on wooden frames. The melody instruments consist of two rows of tuned, knobbed gongs that are set on strings within a wooden frame; metal keys arranged over individual bamboo resonators within a wooden frame; and xylophone, zithers, flute, and *rebab*. Musicians come empty-handed to rehearsals and performances to play on the set of instruments the patron provides.

The master blacksmiths who forge these beautiful bronze instruments are held in extraordinarily high regard not least because, through their mastery of fire, they infuse each instrument of the gamelan, and the gamelan itself, with a living spirit. Because they believe the gamelan contains a living being, some musicians approaching the gamelan to take their seats do not step over any of the instruments, believing that to be disrespectful. Instead they may bow and say "excuse me" to the spirit of the gamelan as they pass between the instruments to reach their position. At the time of its making, the maker, the owner, or the leader of the orchestra may give the gamelan a name that captures its particular sound quality. During the eighteenth century, a female poet at a Javanese prince's court mentioned gamelans with the names "Swept Away," "Smile," and "Misty Rain." Gamelans in the United States at UCLA, the University of Michigan, and Oberlin College are named "Venerable Dark Cloud," "Venerable Lake of Honey," and "Venerable Diamond," respectively.

Compositions like "Puspawarna" reflect Hindu/Buddhist culture. The cyclical rhythmic structure of Javanese gamelan music can be understood as an icon of Hindu/Buddhist beliefs in the cyclical nature of life. In contrast, Christianity emphasizes the progression of life from birth to adulthood to death to a life after death, for which the Baroque concept of fugal development may be an icon.

FIGURE 5.19

A 2018 Javanese *wayang kulit* performance in Wellington, New Zealand. The Javanese *dhalang* (puppeteer) Budi Surasa Putra controls the puppets with attached rods.

Source: Dave Wilson.

Although "Puspawarna" is a concert piece, gamelan accompanies the many forms of musical theater in Java. The characters in these plays may be humans, three-dimensional rod puppets, paintings on a scroll, or two-dimensional shadow puppets made from water buffalo hide.

Shadow-puppet theater accompanied the spread of Hinduism to Java. Performances tell romantic stories from the Ancient Hindu Sanskrit epics, the *Ramayana* and the *Mahabharata*. The *Ramayana* tells the story of Prince Rama, whose wife, Sita, is kidnapped, and who he rescues with the help of the monkey king Hanuman and his army. The *Mahabharata*, the longest epic poem ever created at nearly two million words, is nearly ten times longer than Homer's *Iliad*. It tells the story of a conflict between two families competing for power after the death of the king. Both feature ideal representatives of fidelity, filial loyalty, evil, greed, and other human qualities. They teach Hindu philosophy and values and suffuse Javanese culture in ways analogous to the Bible stories in Christian cultures. The association of gamelan with these stories gives its sounds some of its meaning.

FIGURE 5.20
The same *wayang kulit* performance from the audience's perspective
Source: Dave Wilson.

What Is Its History?

The history of the gamelan begins in the Bronze Age, a period from around 3000 BCE to 1200 BCE, when bronze, an alloy of copper and tin, was the hardest and most useful human-made material. During the Bronze Age humans learned to make tools and decorative items by melting (smelting) and combining copper and tin ores and pouring the hot liquid mixture into wax casts. Even after 1200 BCE, when humans learned to smelt iron to make an even harder metal for tools, bronze remained a favorite material for sculptures and musical instruments. Working with bronze was known to all the ancient civilizations from Mesopotamia, Egypt, and Greece to India, Southeast Asia (Indonesia and Thailand), East Asia, and Africa. Beautiful items from these cultures have been preserved to the present. In these areas, gongs and bells made of bronze have long been associated with religious rituals. Gongs and bells are classified as struck idiophones. A **gong** is a metallic idiophone with a surface diameter greater than its depth, a **bell** is an idiophone with a depth greater than its surface diameter, and a **cymbal** is an idiophone with a flat plate and no depth.

TECHNOLOGY

Tuned Chinese bell chimes date from between 3000 and 2000 BCE. In Europe church bells, once believed to exorcize demons and keep the devil at bay, have been used since the Medieval period for signaling calls to worship and funerals (the death knell). Indonesian bronze gongs date from around the first century BCE. These were flat gongs like the gongs called tam-tams played today in symphony orchestras. They produce a shimmery white noise rather than a specific pitch. The gongs of the gamelan have a central raised "boss," a raised area that produces a specific pitch when struck.

Java is an extraordinarily fertile land, and the cooperation required to grow rice has been a part of the culture since ancient times. Accumulated wealth from rice cultivation led to the formation of regional kingdoms from the fourth century CE onward. Hinduism was the main religion of these kingdoms, and *wayang kulit* performances were accompanied by small ensembles, some containing bronze bossed gongs. In the sixteenth century Islam became the dominant religion, and a powerful kingdom controlled most of central Java. The kings believed themselves to rule

CULTURAL
LINKAGES

with divine authority at the same time their contemporary, King Louis XIV of France, was proclaiming the divine right of kings. The first large gamelans became aural symbols of royal power. But at just about the same time, the Dutch East India Company arrived in western Java in search of expensive spices to send back to Europe. The company, acting on behalf of the Dutch crown, was able to extend its influence to the central Javanese kingdom by the early eighteenth century. Two princely courts survived as regional administrators in the towns of Surakarta and Yogyakarta.

"Puspawarna" is part of the legacy of this seventeenth- and eighteenth-century tradition. Again, from the liner notes: "The piece is performed for the entrance of the prince. . . . The text and melody are attributed to Prince Mangkunegara IV of Surakarta (reigned 1853–1881), to commemorate his favorite wives and concubines." Perhaps there were nine of them, each one honored by a stanza of the poem. This piece is introduced in this chapter because it is played in an orchestral tradition that developed about the same time as the European Baroque orchestra was formed, and for largely the same reasons: the patronage of kings and princes made rich by a new European-initiated system of world trade across the vast oceans of the world. After Indonesia became an independent country in 1949, only Yogyakarta managed to retain its status as a kingdom within the Republic of Indonesia. Today wealthy businesses, state broadcasting companies, and educational institutions in Java have joined the Yogyakarta prince in the patronage of this musical tradition.

"Puspawarna" seems to float along without any dramatic changes. It does not get louder or softer, although it slows down and speeds up gradually. It doesn't modulate to other scales or modes. It goes in a circle rhythmically. Its equidistant intervals don't seem to move toward cadences on a tonic, giving it a floating quality that impressed the French composer Claude Debussy (1862–1918) when he heard a Javanese gamelan at a World's Fair in Paris in 1889 (Chapter 9, Gateway 32). At the end of the nineteenth century and the beginning of the twentieth century European composers were seeking alternatives to the very directed nature of European tonal music, which moves through a series of chord progressions and key areas from the tonic key to other keys to the dominant key and back to the tonic key. Some composers in the early twentieth century chose to abandon tonal harmony altogether. Debussy was so impressed with gamelan music that he wrote at one point that "Javanese music obeys laws of counterpoint which make Palestrina seem like child's play." Without abandoning tonal harmony completely, he experimented in some of his compositions with mimicking what sounded to him like the gamelan's floating sound. In a solo piano sonata entitled *Pagodes* (Pagodas), composed in 1903, Debussy created a musical icon of Javanese gamelan music on the piano by employing a pentatonic scale rather than the usual European heptatonic scale. Low pitches mimic the deep gongs, and very high pitches suggest the metallic timbre of the gongs and metallophones. In many sections of the piece, the music moves along in constant pulsating rhythm as the gamelan does. Like "Puspawarna," Debussy's composition sits in one tonal place, created in this case by long-held drone tones as the melodies move up and down in stepwise runs, essentially going nowhere. The effect, like the sound of the gamelan, can be transfixing.

During the 1960s, when programs in ethnomusicology in the United States began to invite visiting artists from abroad to teach their musical traditions, American universities became patrons of the Javanese gamelan tradition. A UCLA professor, Mantle Hood, who had written his doctoral dissertation on *patet* in Javanese music, brought the first university gamelan to the United States. (A Western Javanese gamelan was played at the Chicago World's Fair of 1893. It is exhibited at Chicago's Field Museum, and in the late 1970s it helped spawn a still-active gamelan ensemble tradition in that city.) Robert Brown, an ethnomusicology Ph.D. from UCLA, made this recording of "Puspawarna"' in Java and wrote the liner notes. In 1977 it was included on a "golden record" that NASA sent into space on the Voyager 1 space probe. The golden record was intended for any extraterrestrial beings that might find it in the distant future. It contained greetings in fifty-five human languages, a whale "greeting," environmental sounds, and a sampling of some of what the producers regarded as the greatest music in the world, including "Ketawang Puspawarna," Bach's Prelude and Fugue in C Major, Bulgarian bagpiping with a singer, the Chinese *qin*, Mbuti hunter gatherers from Central Africa, North Indian classical music in *rag bhairavi*, and recordings of Beethoven, Chuck Berry, Louis Armstrong, and others.

WHERE DO I GO FROM HERE?

- Watch a video performance of Javanese gamelan in Java (many of the available videos are of American and European gamelan ensembles) and listen for the complex structure of colotomic instruments marking time, melodic instruments, and elaborating instruments. Does watching the ensemble in action affect the way that you understand how the music works?

- Watch part of a performance of Javanese *wayang kulit* with gamelan accompaniment. To what extent does your understanding of gamelan shift when hearing it in this setting?

- Listen to a performance of Claude Debussy's *Pagodes*. In what ways does it resemble a gamelan performance? In what ways is it different?

- Listen to the sound recordings on NASA's "golden record" and comment on the choices.

CLOSING

The period from 1600 to 1750 represents an important turning point in the history of European court and church music. Some of the most important new developments include:

- the use of dissonance to express sorrow and anguish;
- the showcasing of vocal and instrumental virtuosity and improvisation;
- the cultivation of music to express affects in the text, and of instrumental music that used those devices to express emotions or pastoral scenes;
- the emergence of the practice of playing bass and chords to accompany melodies, alongside the older practice of multipart polyphony;
- the invention of a new vocal style called recitative that allowed for the creation of a new genre of theatrical storytelling with music called opera;
- a shift from having the harmony follow from counterpoint to the writing of chordal harmony, which the counterpoint needed to reflect;
- the development of instrumental music, specifically the orchestra and the keyboard solo, as the rival of vocal music;
- the development of system of tonal harmony including a set of twenty-four keys (twelve in each of the major and minor modes) to replace the modal system of Medieval and Renaissance music;
- the use of tonal harmony and its directional movement from tonic (I) to dominant (V) and back to the tonic (I); and
- the development of musical notation in its present form.

All of these musical devices, ensembles, and genres are part of the European classical music tradition today. For that reason, the Baroque period is considered to be the start of what is called the "common practice period." What is common between Baroque music and European classical music that came later is the underlying principle of tonality, the concerto, the string orchestra, solo keyboard works, and opera. Otherwise, little of the vast repertoire of Baroque music is performed today by major orchestras and soloists. Its performance has been championed by specialized groups and individuals dedicated to its "authentic," "historically informed" performance and to piano students and composers-in-training interested in learning compositional techniques that represent one of the high points of European contrapuntal practice.

Although many of today's musical practices have their roots in the Baroque period, not all the features of today's musical culture were present in the music of the Baroque period. Composers were not considered artists who create unique works of art as they are today. Baroque composers were, instead, artisans and craftsmen who wrote music to satisfy the demands of their patrons. That is why Vivaldi wrote hundreds of concertos, Handel dozens of operas and oratorios, and Bach hundreds of cantatas and keyboard pieces. They were paid to produce them, and to do so quickly.

FIGURE 5.21

Barbara Strozzi holding a bowed viol. Painting by Bernardo Strozzi (1581–1644).

Source: Gemäldegalerie Alte Meister, Wikimedia Commons.

This chapter focused on only four composers of the Baroque period: Monteverdi, Vivaldi, Handel, and J. S. Bach. The increase in the financial power of churches and courts created a patronage system that supported dozens of excellent and productive musical craftsmen during this period. (In Indonesia the wealth of the king during this period created the large gamelan orchestra and the ability to hire a large coterie of musicians to play it.) All of these composers were men, which surely reflects the mores of the time. It would have been almost impossible for a woman during this period to hold sway at court or in the church. One woman who did manage to carve out a composing and performing career for herself was Barbara Strozzi (1619–1677). She did so in the confines of the homes of wealthy merchants in Venice, where Monteverdi was living and working early in her life. Under the patronage of her father, she composed many madrigals and cantatas and had them published.

Even though today we regard the prodigious output of these men and women as works of art, their art was the by-product of a cultural system with an insatiable demand for new, quickly produced works. Composers did not have the time to worry about making great art, and, as a consequence, they often copied tunes and other devices from their own earlier work and from other composers. Similarly, today we assume that, in their performances, musical performers are expressing emotions that they actually feel. This is true, for example, of popular songs. Audiences often interpret them as reflecting the autobiographical experiences of the writer or singer. And in classical music performers close their eyes and sway as they play, as if they themselves are in the throes of the emotions they are expressing. During the Baroque period, the affects were in the music and the musical gestures—it was the sound of the music itself that stirred emotions in listeners and not the biographies of the composers or the antics of the performers. Musical composition as art and performance as the expression of internal emotions would have to wait for later periods of European music history.

THINGS TO THINK ABOUT

- Compare the way different societies and institutions (courts in Europe and Java, and the Catholic and Protestant Churches) during this period directed their patronage of music and of related traditions and rituals. Who benefited from these systems of patronage? Who was left out of this system?

- Given the global circulation of goods and resources during this period, what are some of the ways that music circulated from its place of origin to other places? Give specific examples if you can.

NEW TERMS

aria	cantata	concerto
arpeggio	*castrato*	cymbal
Baroque	clavichord	dominant key
basso continuo	clavier	dominant seventh
bell	colotomic structure	early music

episode
exposition
fugue
gamelan
gong
harpsichord
keyboard
major scale, major key,
  major triad, major second

minor scale, minor key,
  minor triad, minor second
modulate, modulation
monody
opera
oratorio
prelude
program music
recitative
relative major and minor keys

ritornello
seventh chord
sonata
strophic form, strophic song
subject
theorbo
tonal harmony
verse
well-tempered

MUSIC FROM THE AGE OF ENLIGHTENMENT AND REVOLUTION (1750–1815)

THE EUROPEAN MUSIC FEATURED in this chapter has its roots in the musical life of Vienna, a city somewhat removed from many of the major social, political, and intellectual currents of the day. These included political revolutions in the United States in 1776, France in 1789, and Haiti in 1791. These revolutions were inspired, in part, by a philosophical movement known as the Enlightenment. Philosophers of the **Enlightenment** advocated for reason over adherence to tradition and opposed both religious dogma and monarchical rule like those in France and England. Intellectuals of the period engaged in spirited debates while consuming new drinks made possible by global trade (coffee, tea, and cocoa) served in a new institution: the coffeehouse. By around 1710 London had nearly 500 of them. Over a favorite drink and a smoke, the leisured and literate classes all over Europe gathered in coffeehouses to talk politics and discuss the exciting new developments in science, philosophy, and literature, gatherings that fueled open-minded and reasoned discussions. Coffeehouses even hosted occasional musical performances as they do today. Against this backdrop of teeming new political ideas, aristocratic musical patronage entered its last stage in the Austrian Empire, which included present-day Austria and Hungary and parts of the neighboring Slavic-speaking nations of Slovenia, Croatia, Slovakia, the Czech Republic, and Ukraine.

FIGURE 6.1
An English tavern or coffee house, mid-eighteenth century. Painting by Joseph Highmore (1692–1780).
Source: Yale Center for British Art, Wikimedia Commons.

DOI: 10.4324/9781003269304-9

The social and political drivers of these revolutions were dissatisfaction with the status quo, whether taxation without representation in the American colonies, food scarcity in France, or slavery in Haiti. The institution of slavery was in turn driven, to some extent, by Europeans' newfound love of tea, coffee, and cocoa. These bitter drinks created an enormous demand in Europe for sugar to sweeten them. Sugar plantations in the New World required vast numbers of fieldhands to satisfy this need. Since Europeans and their germs had killed as much as 90 percent of the Native population in the Americas, plantation owners turned to Africa as a source of slave labor. Between the sixteenth and nineteenth centuries, millions of Africans were kidnapped, shipped across the Atlantic, and enslaved to work on the sugar and tobacco plantations of the Caribbean and Brazil and the rice fields of the North American colonies. Under brutal and horrific conditions, at least five million people died either on the way to ships after being kidnapped, on the ships during the passage across the Atlantic, or within the first year of their arrival in the Americas. The fruits of their labors were shipped from the New World to England and the European continent. By the eighteenth century there were twice as many Africans in the Americas as Europeans. By the time the slave trade ended in the middle of the nineteenth century, an estimated twelve million Africans had been shipped in bondage to supply labor in the New World and millions more had died en route. More than 50 percent of all enslaved Africans came to the Americas during the 1700s, which coincides with what has been called the Classical period of European music history, one of the subjects of this chapter. In this chapter we will also look at the new religions that enslaved Africans created in the Americas, religions that combined African traditional and Roman Catholic beliefs and practices: Candomblé in Brazil, Santería in Cuba, and Vodou in Haiti. The drum music of these religions is one of the inspirations for the rhythms of Latin popular music today. Many devotees of Vodou participated in the revolt of self-liberated slaves against the French in Haiti in 1791, a revolt that led to national independence in 1804.

European intellectuals in this period, especially in France, argued for the power of reason and logic as keys to understanding human and physical nature. By the eighteenth century many Europeans understood themselves to be living in an "enlightened" age free of the dictates of religious dogma. In newspapers and books and at cafés, coffeehouses, salons in wealthy homes, and even in public theaters, churchmen, aristocrats, and newly rich merchants discussed universal human rights and disputed Louis XIV's assertion of the divine right of kings. This sense of a new world order based on republicanism, that is, the rule of the people rather than of a monarchy, undercut the power of the aristocracy and enabled revolutionary ambitions.

The Enlightenment gave birth to a new age of science and scholarship. Isaac Newton (1643–1727) created the scientific method to help distinguish fact from fiction in the natural world. Beginning in 1712, Jean-Jacques Rousseau (1712–1778) wrote a *Dictionnaire de musique*, which covered not only European classical music but also music from many parts of the world. It is intellectual activity like this that characterized the Enlightenment.

Although the power of reason and the scientific method and the new discoveries in physics, biology, and astronomy are often celebrated as a scientific revolution, religion retained tremendous power over people's thinking. Influenced by Enlightenment thinking, religious tolerance seems to have improved during the eighteenth century. Women's position in society also improved somewhat during this period, and a number of women

FIGURE 6.2
University of Virginia Rotunda
Source: Aaron Josephson, Wikimedia Commons.

became well-educated and productive writers, composers, thinkers, and leaders of salon culture, especially in Paris.

The politics of the Enlightenment, its championing of the rights of "man," and the political revolutions that followed in its wake had the effect, in the musical domain, of encouraging composers to regard themselves as autonomous artists with some independence from wealthy patrons. The lives of Haydn, Mozart, and Beethoven, in sequence, read like a parable of the transition in European music from aristocratic and church patronage of musical craftsmen to the emergence of the independent, self-employed musical artist. Mozart and Beethoven, in particular, began to think of themselves not so much as artisans, as Baroque composers had, but as artists who could legitimately seek the freedom to compose as they wished. Of course, practicing these ideals, that is, not having the support of wealthy patrons, put them in grave economic jeopardy. It meant that they had to rely on other sources of income such as giving instrumental and composition lessons, receiving royalties on their published works, and producing and selling tickets to their own public concerts at which they played or conducted their new compositions.

One Enlightenment idea, that the natural, rather than the supernatural, world is the controlling force in people's lives, led to aesthetic changes in music as well. Some composers after 1750 regarded the ornamentation, elaborations, and imitative counterpoint of the Baroque period as excessive, "artificial," and "unnatural." As a consequence, some patrons and musicians of the late eighteenth century favored artistic styles that they thought of as simple, balanced, and "natural." This can be seen clearly in the domain of architecture, where the elaborate filigree and wavy lines of Baroque buildings, fountains, and sculptures were replaced by the regular "rhythm" of columns and unadorned facades characteristic of Greek architecture. This borrowing of architectural style from Classical Greece is what gives the music and art of this period its name: the Classical style. Thomas Jefferson (1742–1826) was the leading exponent of this style in the new United States. His designs of buildings at the University of Virginia set the style for government buildings in Washington, D.C. and in state capitals for years to come.

Some composers turned away from the expression of emotion and affect in the Baroque manner to what they considered a more elegant style. They stripped their music of excessive dissonance, elaborate counterpoint, and virtuosic ornamental display. They favored, instead, shorter musical phrases in balanced, "periodic" four- or eight-measure lengths; clear melodies in the top voice with subservient polyphonic accompaniments in the lower voices; new instrumental forms with repeats of a small amount of melodic material; and the inclusion within a single movement of contrasting, even rapidly changing, affects. Composers and critics during this period regarded these new practices as less artificial than Baroque styles and thus truer in spirit to the simplicity and balance of nature.

Musicians today still regularly perform the compositions of the three composers featured in this chapter: Franz Joseph Haydn (1732–1809), Wolfgang Amadeus Mozart (1756–1791), and Ludwig van Beethoven (1770–1827). All lived and worked in or near Vienna, the capital of the Austrian Empire, which controlled much of central Europe until its defeat by Napoleon in 1806. As a thriving imperial capital, Vienna provided ample opportunity for patronage by the emperor, the nobility, wealthy merchants, and foreign embassies. At the time, many other composers besides these three were famous, particularly in the genre of Italian opera, which continued to be an extraordinarily popular entertainment. But only the operas of Mozart are still frequently

FIGURE 6.3
The U.S. Capitol Building in 1846
Source: John Plumbe, Wikimedia Commons.

FIGURE 6.4
Map of central Europe with the cities of Vienna, Prague, Bonn, and Salzburg

performed in the repertoire of modern opera companies.

Haydn, Mozart, and Beethoven composed far less religious music (masses, oratorios, and cantatas) than their Baroque predecessors had. Instrumental music dominated vocal music for the first time in European music history, although opera remained extraordinarily popular and influenced the aesthetics of instrumental music. The principal instrumental musical genres of the Classical period were the symphony, the solo concerto, the string quartet, and the solo sonata, especially the piano sonata. The symphony and the concerto were continuations of Baroque practices. The piano sonata was an outgrowth of Baroque solo harpsichord compositions but in new forms. The string quartet (two violins, viola, and cello) was a new genre of chamber music. The gateways of this chapter are a string quartet by Haydn, an opera by Mozart, and a symphony by Beethoven. All were created at the height of the transatlantic slave trade, and so we include an example of music from Brazil, a genre called Candomblé, which took shape during this period.

GATEWAY 20
CLASSICAL-PERIOD CHAMBER MUSIC

What Is It?

Chamber music is a term that refers to small ensembles that, during the eighteenth century, played in the chambers, the rooms, of noble and wealthy palaces and homes. Our gateway to chamber music of the Classical period is Austrian composer Franz Joseph Haydn's (1732–1809) String Quartet No. 62 in C Major, Op. 76, No. 3, "Emperor," Movement IV. He composed it around 1797. A **string quartet** consists of four players performing on instruments of the violin family: two violins, viola, and cello. **Op.** is short for **opus** ("work" in Latin). Some composers (or their publishers) used opus numbers to identify their compositions in chronological order. No. 3 refers to this string quartet's placement in a set of six string quartets in Opus 76. Movement IV is the fourth movement of a typical Classical-period string quartet in four movements or sections. "Emperor" is an epithet that musicians and publishers have assigned to this quartet. It refers to the theme of the third movement, an anthem Haydn composed to honor the Habsburg Emperor, Franz II. This performance is by the Kodály Quartet from Hungary, where Haydn spent much of his career.

 Listen to the first thirty seconds of the recording.

How Does It Work?

Timbre

Two violins, a viola, and a cello playing over about a four-octave range create a rather warm sound.

Texture

The texture has mainly four lines that sometimes move in block chords and at other times interweave contrapuntally.

Rhythm

This movement is in a meter of four beats to the measure. In some parts of the movement, each beat is subdivided into three pulses called **triplets**.

Melody

The melodies mainly move in conjunct motion.

Harmony

The tonal harmony of the movement begins in the key of C minor and ends in the key of C major, the key at the start of the quartet's first movement.

Form

This movement is in **sonata form**. Sonata form consists of three sections: the **exposition** (the presentation of the **themes** [often two contrasting melodies]), the **development** (the variation and mixture of the themes in various ways), and the **recapitulation** (the return of the themes in an altered manner). This example features themes made of motives. A **motive** is a short melodic, rhythmic, or harmonic idea.

Performance Techniques

The playing features sudden contrasts of loud and soft.

FIGURE 6.5
Franz Joseph Haydn looking a bit like his contemporary, George Washington (1732–1799). Painting by Thomas Hardy (c. 1757–1805).
Source: Royal College of Music Museum of Instruments, Wikimedia Commons.

FIGURE 6.6
Map of the lands ruled by the Habsburg family from 1282 to 1815
Source: Andrein, Wikimedia Commons.

Listen to the first thirty seconds of the recording for three different textures: (1) block chords; (2) a melody presented in imitative counterpoint; and (3) fast scalar runs in triplet rhythm.

Listen to the entire recording following the timed listening guide.

LISTENING GUIDE 6.1

TIME	SECTION	DESCRIPTION
0:00	Exposition	Three block chords in C minor (motive 1) played loudly alternate with a six-note conjunct melody with the rhythm short-long-short, short-long-short (motive 2) played softly.
0:14		Three block chords (motive 1) followed by fast running notes in triplets (motive 3) ends on G major, the dominant chord (V) of C minor.
0:24		Omitting the three block chords, the six-note conjunct motive (motive 2) begins in imitative counterpoint and then continues in counterpoint cadencing in E♭ major, the relative major of C minor.
0:56		The fast scalar runs (motive 3) return in E♭ major and the three block chords move to an accompanying role with the occasional three-note melodic motive (motive 2).
1:27	Exposition	The exposition repeats exactly.
2:53	Development	The conjunct melody (motive 2) begins in imitative counterpoint and is joined in counterpoint by the fast scalar triplet runs (motive 3).
3:31		The fast scalar triplet runs take over and are passed among the four instruments.
3:42		A new melodic phrase based on the scalar runs is played by the first violin. The recapitulation modulates through a number of key areas from E♭ major back to C minor for the recapitulation.
3:49	Recapitulation	As above, but the melody ends with a pause on G, the dominant seventh chord of C minor.
4:03		A transitional melody leads into the fast-running scalar triplets (motive 3) tossed among the four instruments ending in another pause on G major.
4:30		This time, instead of returning to C minor as in the exposition, the conjunct melody (motive 2) is played in C major, the parallel major of C minor.
4:59		The piece closes with iterations of all three motives. The fast-running scalar triplets (motive 3) return not in E♭ major as they did at this point in the exposition but in C major. Toward the end the conjunct melody (motive 2) returns in counterpoint, and the movement ends with a final cadence of block chords (motive 1) on C major, the opening key of this quartet's first movement.
5:16	End	

What Does It Mean?

AESTHETICS

The meaning of this string quartet movement can be thought of from three perspectives: its aesthetics, that is, how it is constructed and meant to be listened to; the emotional or expressive ideas and feelings it invokes; and its relationship to the cultural, social, and economic systems that produced it.

Understanding the aesthetic meaning of string quartets and their close relatives, symphonies, at the end of the eighteenth century requires a return to the problem posed by Baroque instrumental sonatas and concertos of the early eighteenth century. What does purely instrumental music mean? As a French commentator of the time asked, in a somewhat complaining voice, "Sonata, what do you ask of me?" In other words, how are we to understand purely instrumental music without lyrics? Each movement of a string quartet or symphony is an instrumental sonata in the sense of an instrumental composition without words.

One way to understand an instrumental sonata, in this case one movement of a Haydn string quartet, is to follow its formal organization closely as we did in the previous section on "how does it work." Mozart, Haydn, Beethoven, and other composers of the Classical period developed a new way of composing instrumental music that music critics in the nineteenth century called **sonata form**. Sonata form developed first as a practice without a theory. It became the most common musical form for the opening movements of string quartets, symphonies, and solo sonatas in the late eighteenth century, and it was sometimes used in other movements as well, as Haydn used it for Movement IV of this string quartet.

Composers using this form constructed compositions based on two or three contrasting melodic ideas. Sometimes these ideas were complete melodies, and sometimes, as in this string quartet movement, they were musical motives of various kinds (block chords, a short melodic fragment, scalar runs). In sonata form, these melodic ideas are first presented, then "developed" in a variety of ways, and then presented again or "recapitulated." Composers of this period "developed" these musical motives by repeating them in sequence, using them to modulate or transition to other keys, giving them to different instruments to play, and setting them in different forms of counterpoint. These techniques enabled Classical-period composers to extend the length and internal coherence of instrumental music in logical, coherent, and "economical" ways.

The expectations created by these formal procedures gave the music a predictability that audiences appreciated then and now. Late eighteenth-century listeners, and experienced listeners today, could expect that, after the first theme, they would hear a second, contrasting theme. After these two themes repeated, their motives would "develop," and then the movement would conclude with a return of the two themes in slightly altered form. This alternation of expectation and the satisfaction of expectation generates a certain kind of aesthetic pleasure, a meaning distinct from the iconic meaning church and court music in Europe had gained for many centuries through similarities between musical elements and ideas expressed in poetry and painting and imagined pastoral scenes and sounds.

The labels that nineteenth-century music critics gave to the sections of sonata form (exposition, development, and recapitulation) suggest that they thought Haydn, Mozart, and Beethoven were "saying something" in these otherwise abstract musical works. These terms are borrowed from the art of rhetoric, that is, the art of creating arguments in essays and speeches designed to persuade readers and listeners. This terminology metaphorically links the meaning of sonata form to a three-part literary argument: the exposition of a couple of ideas or themes, their development and logical relationship, and their recapitulation or restatement in conclusions.

> CULTURAL
> LINKAGES

But what were these composers telling their listeners? What was their argument? Because of the long history of association between musical gestures and the lyrics they accompanied in vocal compositions from Hildegard to Handel, many musical gestures in European music had acquired emotional and expressive resonance. Classical-period composers exploited these indexical connections between music and mood and ideas in their instrumental music—and music aficionados understood them at the time, as do keen listeners today.

> AESTHETICS

The three musical motives in this Haydn string quartet can be understood in this way. The three block chords played loudly on the main beats at the beginning have long associations with "themes" of strength, seriousness, anger, concern, and so forth. The narrow-range, six-note conjunct melodic fragment, which consists of off-beat pick-up notes and emphasizes pitches a half step away from their neighbors, is associated with themes along the lines of yearning, pleading, sadness, weakness, fragility, and tenderness. The fast running triplet scales could be icons of youthfulness, energy, a journey, and so on. Given these long-standing associations between mood and music, some listeners may understand this string quartet movement as a conversation or an argument between these three contrasting themes, ideas, emotions, or moods.

The lyrics of vocal music in songs, oratorios, and operas create more clear-cut and less ambiguous iconic connections between particular musical ideas and the themes, moods, emotions, and characters they represent. Mozart wrote operas that made just these kinds of associations between mood and character, as we will discuss in the following gateway.

🔊 Listen again to this recording with the themes, moods, and emotions. Does thinking about these themes, moods, and emotions help you to understand this performance better? Or do you prefer to hear it in more abstract, aesthetic, and formal terms?

This string quartet movement can also be understood in terms of the cultural, social, and economic conditions that produced it. Beginning in 1761 and for most of his career, Haydn worked as a liveried servant in the courts of the Hungarian Princes Paul Anton and Nikolaus Esterházy, scions of one of the richest noble families in the Austrian Empire. Esterháza, their country estate a hundred miles or so east of Vienna, had 126 rooms and featured two concert halls, an opera house, and a marionette theater. Hundreds of people attended events there. Each morning and afternoon Haydn had to inquire of the princes whether any musical entertainment was required that day for their and their guests' amusement. To serve the princes' musical enthusiasms, Haydn produced a stunning quantity and range of compositions. A catalog created in the twentieth century lists more than 700 works in thirty-two genres. To fulfill his obligations, Haydn wrote ninety symphonies. **Symphonies** are multi-movement compositions for string orchestra with the addition of wind instruments and percussion; they lack the contrast between soloist and orchestra of a concerto. For some years Haydn produced more than a hundred opera performances a year for them, including a dozen or so of his own composition. For less grand occasions the princes had an insatiable appetite for chamber music performances and for chamber-music compositions that they enjoyed playing as amateur musicians with Haydn. To satisfy this demand, Haydn wrote string quartets, duos, and trios; keyboard sonatas; trios for violin, cello, and keyboard; and songs. For the prince's chapel he wrote religious music.

After some experimentation, Haydn settled on a four-movement form (fast—slow—minuet—fast) for his symphonies and string quartets, the standard form for compositions in these genres ever since. He wrote most of his string quartets in sets of six, a practice that Mozart and Beethoven and some later composers adopted. Listeners in the late eighteenth century understood the musical style that Haydn was developing as an elegant reflection of their courtly lifestyle and the new style of architecture in the buildings going up around them. The relatively simple melodies and the absence of the elaborate ornamentation that characterized Baroque musical style seemed to mimic the spare, clean look of the colonnaded buildings of late eighteenth-century neoclassical architecture, which contrasted with the ornate, sinuous style of Baroque exteriors and interiors (Figures 6.2 and 6.3). Some called the resulting elegant and graceful musical style *galant*, a French word used to describe a stylish, fashionable man (*galant homme*) or, in German, *empfindsamer stil* (sensitive style). To audiences of the time, this musical style seemed particularly pleasing, its elegance a mirror of the powdered wigs, silver shoe buckles, brocaded jackets, ruffled collars, and tight leggings worn during this period by men of fashion all over Europe and in the American colonies. Its relative simplicity, compared to Baroque style, fit well with the carefree courtly life of central Europe during the late eighteenth century. And it was attractive to a growing audience of wealthy merchants, bankers, and tradespeople who sought the trappings of aristocratic life.

What Is Its History?

Haydn lived and worked in the Austrian Empire (also named the Habsburg Empire after its ruling family), a large multinational territory in central Europe. He was born in 1732 about thirty miles southeast of Vienna in a small town where his father and grandfather had been mayors. When he was eight, the choir director at St. Stephen's Cathedral in Vienna heard his beautiful singing voice and invited him to join the cathedral choir, where he remained until his voice changed and he was dismissed at age seventeen. Haydn became a freelance musician, playing violin in local bands hired by serenaders and in the Emperor's court orchestra as an extra player when needed. "I barely managed to stay alive by giving music lessons to children for about eight years," he told an early biographer. After he left the cathedral choir school, he taught himself to compose by studying the compositions of J. S. Bach's son, C.P.E. Bach, one of the most popular composers of the time, and a treatise on counterpoint, mentioned in the previous chapter, written by the Viennese composer and theorist Johann Joseph Fux (c. 1660–1741) and titled *Gradus ad Parnassum*.

In his late twenties his success as a freelancer finally landed him his first paying job as *Kapellmeister* for a Czech nobleman with a small orchestra for whom he composed his first symphony. In 1761, at age twenty-nine, his work caught the attention of Hungarian Prince Paul Anton Esterházy, who hired Haydn as his assistant musical director. Both Paul Anton and Nikolaus were keen musicians. They gave Haydn the money to hire fine virtuoso instrumentalists and singers for musical productions at the family's palace in the city of Eisenstadt and at Esterháza, their country estate. With his own orchestra at his disposal and constant demand for new music from his patrons, he experimented with new ways of composing symphonies and string quartets. One of his experiments led to the addition of the minuet to what had been the three-movement concerto form. The **minuet**, a graceful and stately dance in triple meter, was a popular social and court dance during the eighteenth century. Alexander Hamilton's wife Eliza reported that the slow minuet was the favorite dance of the rather formal George Washington at the balls he reluctantly had to host and attend after his inauguration in 1789 as the first U.S. president.

In his own time, and today, Haydn was much admired in Vienna and around Europe for his string quartets and symphonies. Visitors to Esterháza from all over Europe reported on his music, and the prince gave him permission to publish some of it, spreading his fame around the continent. Prince Nikolaus died in 1791, ending thirty years of intense demands on Haydn's compositional skills. Nikolaus's son and grandson were much less interested in music and disbanded the palace orchestra, keeping Haydn on the payroll with a sinecure and the sole duty to write a Mass each year. Having achieved an international reputation as an outstanding composer, he

FIGURE 6.7
Minuet danced at a ball given by French King Louis XV in 1755
Source: Lebrecht Music and Arts Photo Library/Alamy Stock Photo.

accepted invitations for two lengthy sojourns in England, where he wrote and performed the last twelve of his symphonies (the so-called London Symphonies, nos. 93–104). Regarded in England as a musical genius, Haydn was able for the first time to mingle socially with high society. He even received an honorary degree from Oxford University. Thus, Haydn experienced in his own lifetime a transformation from musical servant to treasured artist, a transition in patronage of, and attitudes toward, composers that echoed through the late eighteenth and nineteenth centuries and continues today.

When Haydn returned to Austria from his London successes, he visited his birthplace and was touched to find a statue in his honor placed there. After writing his six Opus 76 string quartets around 1797, he turned his attention to the composition of Masses and two oratorios, *The Creation* (1798) and *The Seasons* (1801), before ill health stopped him. He died in 1809.

Haydn's legacy in European classical music is vast. He made fundamental contributions to the symphony, the string quartet, and the creation of sonata form. These three musical innovations of the Classical period have resonated in European classical music ever since. The young Wolfgang Amadeus Mozart admired Haydn's string quartets and wrote his own in sets of six, as Haydn had. He dedicated his Op. 10 string quartets of 1785 to Haydn. Ludwig van Beethoven studied with Haydn for a brief time after he arrived in Vienna in 1792 at the age of twenty-two. His eighteen string quartets are among the most admired in the repertoire. Because of these Classical-period composers' interest in the genre, the string quartet joined the symphony as one of the most important genres of European classical music. From the nineteenth century to the present, many composers have written substantial numbers of string quartets, including Franz Schubert, Antonín Dvořák, Béla Bartók, and Dmitri Shostakovich.

Haydn's string quartets began as small-scale entertainment in the palaces of the aristocracy and for the self-amusement of professional and amateur musicians. Haydn and Mozart enjoyed playing them, and some stories suggest they may have played together on at least one occasion. String players today enjoy playing them not least because, unlike in an orchestra where they must bow to the demands of the conductor, they work together in a sensitive musical conversation among equals. Toward the end of the eighteenth century and during the early nineteenth

AESTHETICS

century, something like modern-day professional string quartets were forming and performing sometimes in concert halls, as they do today. Recently some string quartets, like the Kronos Quartet and Harlem Quartet in the United States, and the Soweto String Quartet in South Africa, have taken the genre into new areas of fusion with world music, popular music, and jazz.

WHERE DO I GO FROM HERE?

- Listen to the other three movements of Haydn's String Quartet, Op. 76, No. 3, "Emperor," and try to follow their formal organizations. Movement I is fast and in sonata form. Movement II is a minuet and uses the European dance form AABB. Movement III consists of a theme and variations on an anthem melody he composed for Austrian Emperor Franz II after hearing "God Save the King" during his time in London, and a number of variations.
- Listen to the first movement of Haydn's last symphony, Symphony No. 104 in D major "London": I. Adagio—Allegro. All but one of Haydn's twelve London symphonies begin with a slow (adagio) introduction before the fast section of the first movement in sonata form. Once the slow introduction ends, try to follow the "story" of the movement by listening for its two contrasting themes and following their exposition, development, and recapitulation.
- To understand how modern string quartets are engaging with music beyond the classical tradition, listen to the Kronos Quartet's recording of "El Llorar," a traditional Mexican *son* (song) from the Huasteca region along the gulf coast of Mexico from their album *Nuevo*; the Harlem Quartet's rendition of "A Night in Tunisia" by bebop jazz trumpeter Dizzy Gillespie from their album *Cross Pollination*; and the Soweto String Quartet from South Africa playing "Kwela," a traditional song on their album *Zebra Crossing*.

GATEWAY 21
CLASSICAL-PERIOD OPERA

What Is It?

Our gateway to Classical-period opera is act I, scene 1 from the Austrian composer Wolfgang Amadeus Mozart's (1756–1791) opera *Le Nozze di Figaro* (The Marriage of Figaro) composed in 1786 in Vienna. Called "Cinque . . . dieci" (Five . . . ten) after the first sung words, it is a "little duet" (*duettino*) between Figaro, valet to Spanish Count Almaviva, and Susanna, maid to Countess Almaviva. The scene begins with Figaro and his fiancée Susanna each distracted by preparations for their wedding. Figaro is measuring their new apartment in the palace, presumably thinking of what delights are in the offing, while Susanna is going on about her pretty new wedding cap (in modern terms, her veil).

FIGARO
misurando
Cinque . . . dieci . . . venti . . . trenta . . . trentasei . . . quarantatre

SUSANNA
specchiandosi
Ora sì ch'io son contenta;
sembra fatto inver per me.
Guarda un po', mio caro Figaro,
guarda adesso il mio cappello.

FIGARO
Sì mio core, or è più bello,
sembra fatto inver per te.

SUSANNA e FIGARO
Ah, il mattino alle nozze vicino
quanto è dolce al mio/tuo tenero sposo
questo bel cappellino vezzoso
che Susanna ella stessa si fe'.

FIGARO
measuring [the wedding bed]
Five . . . ten . . . twenty . . . thirty . . .
Thirty-six . . . forty-three

SUSANNA
gazing into a mirror
Yes, I'm very pleased with that;
It seems just made for me.
Take a look, dear Figaro,
Just look at this cap of mine.

FIGARO
Yes, my dearest, it's very pretty;
It looks just made for you.

SUSANNA and FIGARO
On this morning of our wedding
How delightful to my (your) dear one
Is this pretty little cap
Which Susanna made herself.

In this recording the English bass Thomas Allen plays Figaro, the American soprano Kathleen Battle sings the Susanna role, and the Italian conductor Riccardo Muti leads the Vienna Philharmonic, an international cast typical of opera performances today.

🔊 Listen to the first thirty seconds of the recording.

How Does It Work?

Timbre

A full Classical-period orchestra accompanies a hardy operatic bass voice and a light soprano voice.

Texture

The texture combines the orchestra with vocal parts that vary from solos to singing independent melodic lines to parallel thirds.

Rhythm

The meter is in four. The rhythm is varied and changeable, including constant pulsation in the bassoon accompaniment at one point.

Melody

The scene contrasts Figaro's melody, built from a two-pitch descending motive, with Susanna's, which consists of longer phrases in stepwise motion.

Harmony

The harmony is tonal in a major key.

Form

The scene begins with an orchestral introduction followed by Figaro's solo and then Susanna's. The two then sing independent melodic lines until joining together in parallel thirds.

Performance Techniques

The most striking technique is the operatic vocal sound, one capable of filling a large opera house without amplification.

🔊 Listen to the first thirty seconds of this recording again, this time paying attention to the timbre and texture of the two singing voices.

What Does It Mean?

This scene is filled with musical gestures suggestive of the text and of the characters' thoughts and their genders. In this scene Mozart links the unspecified emotional contrast of the two themes in sonata form to the particular emotions of the two characters' words, thoughts, and actions. Whereas in the Classical-period symphony and string quartet the two themes of sonata form engage in a metaphorical dialogue through close proximity and counterpoint, in opera the combination of words and themes creates a theatrical dialogue between two characters. The scene can also be understood formally to work out a truncated version of the three parts of sonata form:

1. Exposition: the first theme sung by Figaro and the second theme sung by Susanna;
2. Development: Figaro's theme is broken into motives for Figaro and Susanna to sing in counterpoint as they converse;
3. Recapitulation: Susanna's theme is heard twice, but the first theme is omitted since Figaro adopts Susanna's melody and her point of view and abandons his preoccupations and his melody.

FIGURE 6.8
Figaro and Susanna in a performance of *The Marriage of Figaro* in St. Petersburg
Source: ITAR-TASS News Agency/Alamy Stock Photo.

FIGURE 6.9
Soprano Kathleen Battle as Susanna in *The Marriage of Figaro* at the Metropolitan Opera
Source: Johan Elbers, The LIFE Images Collection/Getty Images.

Listen to the entire recording following this timed listening guide, which examines the iconic links between music, text, action, and the thinking of Figaro and Susanna.

LISTENING GUIDE 6.2

TIME	FORM	SECTION	TEXT	TRANSLATION	DESCRIPTION
0:00	Exposition (orchestral prelude)	first theme			The strings play short phrases beginning with repeated pitches and ending with a descending, disjunct leap.
0:16		second theme			The oboes play a contrasting narrow-range, undulating, stepwise melody with bassoon on the bass part.
0:32	Exposition (repeat, with vocalists)	Figaro (first theme)	*Cinque . . . dieci . . . venti . . . trenta . . . trentasei . . . quarantatre*	Five . . . ten . . . twenty . . . thirty . . . thirty-six . . . forty-three	The strings play the first part of the first-theme phrase and Figaro sings the numbers on the descending leaps at the ends of phrases, the punchy, short motive an expression of his masculinity in this case. The rising pitch over the course of his solo represents his increasing excitement at the prospect of marriage.
0:53		Susanna (second theme)	*Ora sì ch'io son contenta;* *sembra fatto inver per me. Guarda un po', mio caro Figaro, guarda adesso il mio cappello.*	Yes, I'm very pleased with that; It seems just made for me. Take a look, dear Figaro, Just look at this cap of mine.	Susanna sings her solo to the second-theme melody, its undulating, stepwise motion now an expression of her femininity.
1:03	**Development**	Susanna and Figaro	They repeat their words		The A theme is broken apart and set in counterpoint: Figaro repeats his descending leaps, while Susanna sings the repeated pitches of the first half of the first theme. In this case, the counterpoint, with each character repeating what they sang before, suggests that the two of them are not listening to one another. They are preoccupied with their own thoughts.
1:26	**Recapitu-lation**	Figaro (second theme)	*Sì mio core or è più bello sembra fatto inver per te.*	Yes, my love, it is very pretty. It seems just made for you.	Figaro finally hears Susanna, expressed literally by echoing her words and metaphorically by singing her theme.
1:37		Susanna and Figaro (transition)	They sing previous text		They sing back and forth in conversation briefly until finally they sing, in parallel thirds, an icon of their love, and a melodic sequence that rises in pitch, an icon of their increasing passion.
2:03		Susanna and Figaro (second theme)	*Ah, il mattino alle nozze vicino quanto è dolce al mio/tuo tenero sposo questo bel cappellino vezzoso che Susanna ella stessa si fe'.*	On this morning of our wedding How delightful to my (your) dear one Is this pretty little cap Which Susanna made herself.	Figaro and Susanna sing her theme in parallel thirds, a musical portrayal of Figaro's devoted attention to Susanna's delight in her wedding cap.
2:42	End				

This opera scene illustrates the way the conventions of vocal music lend meaning to instrumental music and vice versa. In instrumental music a punchy, loud two-note motive had, over the years, come to represent some sort of strength as we saw in the string quartet movement in the previous gateway. Once Figaro or some other masculine character in opera sings such a motive, the general representation of strength becomes the particular representation of the character's masculinity. After this connection is made often enough in vocal music, then similar gestures in instrumental music might, as a consequence, be interpreted as masculine, rather than as vaguely strong. A soft undulating melody in instrumental music had come to represent a lilting, delicate feeling. Once sung by Susanna or another attractive female character in opera, similar instrumental melodies might be interpreted as representing the character's femininity as well. This back-and-forth between instrumental and vocal music allowed the specific emotions of musical gestures in opera to be interpreted as general emotions in instrumental music and vice versa.

> EMOTIONAL RESONANCE

Although act I, scene 1 establishes the sincere love of Figaro and Susanna for one another, audiences can predict that there may be some trouble in their future, since the opera lasts three hours. The problems begin in the next scene, when Susanna confides in Figaro that she has heard that Count Almaviva, who "scours the countryside for fresh beauties," hopes to exercise the privilege supposedly accorded Medieval lords to bed their servants, a *droit du seigneur* (right of the lord). Figaro, outraged, hatches a plot to expose and embarrass the count with the aid of Susanna, the countess, and the count's young page, Cherubino, played by a woman in what is called a "trousers role." Structured as a classic French farce, characters enter rooms as others hide in closets or jump out of windows to escape detection. Mistaken identities abound, many of them playing with Cherubino's male/female character, creating continual confusion and mirth. At play's end, the count's lechery is exposed for all to see. He begs the countess to forgive him and she agrees, all promise to be happy, and they set out "to the sound of a gay march" to celebrate the wedding of Figaro and Susanna.

Although modern audiences enjoy Mozart's music and the farcical elements of the opera, at the time the opera was understood as an indictment of the nobility and its exploitation of the lower classes. The opera's source was a popular French play composed in 1778 by Pierre Beaumarchais (1732–1799), a remarkable figure whose activities included the invention of a reliable mechanism for pocket watches, music instructor at the French court, playwright, spy, diplomat, and arms dealer. In the latter three capacities he advocated for the entry of France on the side of the colonists in the American Revolution and supplied the revolutionary army with weapons, uniforms, and other provisions. King Louis XVI immediately understood the play as an indictment of the aristocracy and his government, and he refused to allow its public performance, even over the objections of his queen, Marie Antoinette. The play finally premiered to enormous success in 1784 at an important public theatre in Paris.

> POLITICAL ACTIVITY

The Austrian Emperor Joseph II also objected to the public performance of the play, but his court librettist for Italian operas, Lorenzo da Ponte (1749–1838), working with Mozart, omitted Figaro's angry denunciation of the count and the nobility at the end of the play and turned it into a comparatively harmless comedic romp about jealousy and male arrogance. Their version passed the censors and entered public performance in Vienna just two years after the play's public debut in Paris. The opera was so successful that Mozart and da Ponte received a commission for a second opera, which premiered in Prague the next year, 1787, just a month after the signing of the new U.S. Constitution. Titled *Don Giovanni* and based on a seventeenth-century Spanish story about Don Juan, a shameless womanizer, this lord commits murder, refuses to repent, and goes to hell, a much darker, more devastating critique of aristocratic privilege than *The Marriage of Figaro*.

In 1789, just five years after the premiere of Beaumarchais's play, desperately poor peasants, urban laborers, and women ignited the French Revolution against the wealth and privilege of the aristocracy. Perhaps Louis XVI was right to worry about the play's potential effect. Georges Danton, a leading figure in the revolution, said the play "killed off the nobility," and Napoleon, who came to power in the wake of the revolution, thought the play had "already put [the Revolution] into action." Evidently, Louis XVI, Danton, and Napoleon believed in the power of art to alter social and political conditions.

CULTURAL
LINKAGES

The play and the two operas by Mozart and da Ponte also captured the libertine spirit of the time. Catherine the Great, Empress of Russia from 1762 to 1796, and the Venetian roué Giacomo Casanova (1725–1798) were just two of the most notorious avatars of eighteenth-century libidinous license. Reflecting the spirit of the age, wealthy slave-owning landowners of the southern American colonies also took advantage of their own version of the *droit du seigneur*. In 1787, the year of *Don Giovanni*'s premiere, Sally Hemmings, a fourteen-year-old enslaved to Thomas Jefferson, joined him in Paris, where he had been the American minister to the French court since 1784. They returned to the new United States in 1789, she having borne him a child.

What Is Its History?

ECONOMIC
ACTIVITY

Mozart, an astonishing child prodigy, set the European music scene ablaze during a brief thirty-five-year lifetime before illness doused his spirit and his unparalleled musical gifts in 1791. His father, Leopold, a violinist and court musician for the prince-archbishop of the Salzburg region 200 miles west of Vienna, taught music to Wolfgang and his older sister Maria Anna (nicknamed "Nannerl"), his two surviving children. Both proved to be enormously talented. He called Wolfgang a "gift from God." He was a keyboard virtuoso by the age of five, when he began dictating solo keyboard pieces and violin sonatas to his father. In 1762 Leopold took leave of his court responsibilities and led his children on a tour of the royal courts of Europe, including those of Maria Theresa, Empress of Austria, and her daughter Marie Antoinette and of King George III in London. Not only did this trio create a sensation, with Nannerl often receiving top billing as a keyboard virtuoso, but young Wolfgang absorbed like a sponge the latest musical styles around western Europe. Once Nannerl reached her teens and marriageable age, Leopold no longer allowed her to tour and perform, and she was forced to live the domestic life typical of women of the time. Father and son continued to travel for more than a decade in search of fame and a suitable position for the youthful phenom as a court *Kapellmeister* like the one Haydn enjoyed. In 1770 they traveled to Italy, where, at the age of fourteen, Wolfgang composed his first opera and then two others in the next three years. His Italian successes did not lead to the hoped-for position at Maria Theresa's imperial court in Vienna. She lumped Mozart and other composers into a category of "useless people" who would "degrade" the court by "go[ing] around the world like beggars." Evidently, aristocratic support for musicians was not universal.

Wolfgang's fame, including the composition of some twenty symphonies by the age of seventeen, earned him only a relatively low-paying position at the court of Salzburg's archbishop. He was especially frustrated that the archbishop did not support opera, which he loved. He continued to compose symphonies, keyboard works, and religious music, but yearned for a more suitable position. In 1781 he had a final falling out with the archbishop on a visit they made to Vienna for the coronation of Maria Theresa's son, Emperor Joseph II. There the archbishop treated him like a lowly servant rather than like the musical celebrity he had become in the rest of Europe. He quit the archbishop's service in a huff and stayed in Vienna, determined to make it on his own as a freelance musician with thirty-four symphonies to his credit.

For the next eleven years, from 1781 until his death in 1791, Mozart tested the limits of an independent artist in a European musical culture where most outstanding composers, including Haydn, J. S. Bach, C.P.E. Bach, and Vivaldi, had depended on employment at aristocratic courts or in wealthy churches and religious institutions. The one genre where a composer might make it on his own was opera, the most popular genre of music among the moneyed bourgeoisie and the aristocracy. Handel had made a similar decision seventy years earlier when he left the employ of the Elector of Hannover in 1712 for the world of Italian opera in London.

FIGURE 6.10

The Mozart family with a portrait of Mozart's mother, Anna Maria, in the background. Painting by Johann Nepomuk della Croce, c. 1780.

Source: Artexperts, Mozarteum, Salzburg, Wikimedia Commons.

Unlike Handel, who shared in the production and profits of his London operas, Mozart was paid a very modest flat fee for his operas, not enough to sustain him and his new wife, Constanze, a singer. (They had six children, two of whom survived to adulthood.) To support himself, Mozart turned to the production of his own public concerts. A virtuoso keyboard player, he organized well-attended subscription concerts to show off his and his students' skills. They performed his keyboard sonatas and concertos on the new instrument, the fortepiano, an early version of the modern piano, which was replacing the harpsichord in popularity. **Fortepiano** means "loud-soft" and refers to a precursor of the modern piano with a narrower range (five or six octaves) and a lighter, thinner sound than the modern piano. During his eleven years in Vienna he wrote some sixteen piano concertos, nine piano sonatas, seven symphonies, and many string quartets, six of them published as Opus 10 and named in honor of Haydn. He also received commissions to write five more operas during these years, including two in the year of his death. In September of 1791 he fell ill from an unknown infection while in Prague for the premiere of one of them. Although well enough to conduct the premiere of the other, *The Magic Flute*, in October in Vienna, his condition soon worsened, and he died on December 5, 1791.

By the early eighteenth century, opera had conquered all of Europe. In the Baroque period it had developed into a highly structured form featuring a contrast between recited speech (recitative) accompanied by the harpsichord and an often florid aria accompanied by the full

CULTURAL
LINKAGES

orchestra. Composers wrote arias to show off the skills of the singers, especially the *castrati* playing the lead male roles. The action proceeded in a rather artificial way (the term "baroque" is practically synonymous with artifice), each character impressively declaiming their position and then, after showing off their vocal skills, exiting the stage to wild applause. Opera was especially beloved by the aristocracy, not least because the plots of Baroque-period operas told the stories of Ancient Greek gods and Roman emperors, who, when they acted benevolently, were exemplars of noble virtue.

By the late eighteenth century this type of opera was declining in popularity, and composers began to write in a new style, de-emphasizing the virtuosity of arias and writing more duets and choruses. The plots shifted from tales of ancient times to stories about contemporary ordinary people, often caught in comic situations. *Castrati* ceded popularity to a new kind of character, the *basso buffo* (the bass buffoon). People began to distinguish between two types of Italian opera: *opera seria* (serious opera), the older style; and *opera buffa* (comic opera), the newer style. *Le Nozze di Figaro* is an *opera buffa*.

Yet a third type of musical drama competed with Italian opera for the public's attention. Called *ballad operas* in English and **Singspiel** in German, these productions were sung in the local language and dispensed with recitative in favor of spoken dialogue, features appealing to audiences with little or no knowledge of Italian. Mozart's first success as a freelancer in Vienna was a *Singspiel*, composed in 1782, called *Die Ent führung aus dem Serail* (The Abduction from the Seraglio), and his *The Magic Flute*, a *Singspiel*, has long been an audience favorite.

Mozart's *opera buffa*s and *Singspiel*s are the oldest operas in the standard repertoire, although Monteverdi's *Orfeo*, Handel's *Rinaldo*, and a few others are heard occasionally. Mozart's two *opera seria*s have been less performed, their old-fashioned style militating against their popularity with modern audiences attuned to the "natural" style of musical dialogue and emotional expression that Mozart perfected in *Le Nozze di Figaro*.

FIGURE 6.11

Teatro La Fenice ("The Phoenix"), built in the 1790s in Venice and restored in 2004 to a mid-nineteenth-century style after a fire

Source: Youflavio, Wikimedia Commons.

FIGURE 6.12

Soprano Diana Damrau singing "The Queen of the Night" from *The Magic Flute* in Salzburg in 2006

Source: AFP/Stringer/Getty Images

WHERE DO I GO FROM HERE?

- Watch three different video performances of *Le Nozze di Figaro*, act I, scene 1, the *duettino* between Figaro and Susanna, and compare the variety of ways modern opera directors stage the scene.
- Listen to performances of three arias from *Le Nozze di Figaro* to get some idea of their lyrical quality, which contrasts with the virtuosity of Baroque opera: Figaro's "Non piu andrai"; Countess Almaviva's "Porgi, Amor"; and Cherubino's "Voi, che sapete che cosa e amor."
- Listen to "Der Hölle Rache kocht in meinem Herzen" (Hell's Vengeance Boils in My Heart), also known as The Queen of the Night aria, from *The Magic Flute* and written in the florid, virtuosic style of Baroque *opera seria*.
- Listen to "Là si darem la mano," a *duettino* from *Don Giovanni* between the don and Zerlina, a peasant girl. Structured much like "Cinque . . . dieci," notice the way its musical gestures signal first her resistance to his advances and then her acquiescence.

GATEWAY 22
CLASSICAL-PERIOD SYMPHONIES

What Is It?

The symphony orchestra is a large ensemble of bowed strings (violins, violas, cellos, and basses), woodwinds (flute, clarinet, oboe, bassoon), brasses (horns, trumpets, trombones, tubas) and percussion (timpani, bass drum, snare drum, cymbals, and others). Its core repertoire consists of concertos, opera overtures, and symphonies. The most well-known symbol of classical music today, the symphony orchestra took something like its modern form in the late eighteenth century in the hands of Haydn and Mozart. The symphonies they composed for orchestra set the standard for the number of movements (four), the types of movements (sonata form, minuet, theme and variations, rondo), and the sound of the orchestra with the addition of a standard set of woodwind, brass, and percussion instruments to the Baroque-period string orchestra.

Our gateway to Classical-period symphonies is the first movement of Ludwig van Beethoven's (1770–1827) Symphony No. 5 in C Minor, Op. 67. Premiered in 1808 at a concert he produced in Vienna to showcase his compositions and piano skills, it is the most famous composition in all of European classical music. His nine symphonies are considered both the apotheosis of the Classical-period symphony and early expressions of an artistic sensibility known as Romanticism. Hungarian-born conductor Sir Georg Solti (1912–1997) conducts the Vienna Philharmonic in this recording.

FIGURE 6.13

The Dublin Philharmonic Orchestra in a form typical of the nineteenth century. First row, from left to right: first violins, second violins, cellos, violas, and basses. Second and third row risers, from left to right: four horns, piccolo, two flutes and two clarinets, two oboes and two bassoons, and three trumpets. Back row, from left to right: four percussionists including bass drum and timpani, three trombones, and one tuba.

Source: Derek Gleeson, Wikimedia Commons.

How Does It Work?

Timbre

The sound is created by an orchestra. In addition to the strings, the clarinet, horn (sometimes called the French horn), bassoon, flute, and oboe sound prominently in brief solo roles, and trumpet and timpani create excitement at various points.

Texture

The textures are rich and varied and feature important unison and solo passages.

Rhythm

The meter is duple. A striking four-note rhythmic motive (short—short—short—long), marked by a pause, opens the movement and is heard throughout, creating a strong sense of unity.

Melody

The opening melody is built up from the opening motive. The second theme is longer and dissolves into its constituent motives, at one point to a single tone.

Harmony

The harmony is tonal, starting and ending in C minor with excursions to other keys.

Form

Sonata form organizes the work at the macro level. At the micro level the opening rhythmic motive, heard throughout as melody and accompaniment, is also an important formal element.

Performance Techniques

Dynamics provide perhaps the most striking performance element. Long crescendos build excitement, as do sudden changes from loud to soft and soft to loud.

Listen to the first fifty seconds of the recording and notice the different treatments of the opening four-note motive.

Listen to the entire recording following this timed listening guide, which outlines the form and some of the features of the piece.

LISTENING GUIDE 6.3

TIME	FORM	SECTION	DESCRIPTION
0:03	**Exposition**	First theme	The movement opens with two forte statements by the strings of a short—short—short—long motive in sequence followed by a soft melody built on that motive. After a dramatic crescendo, the theme ends with a long-held tone played by the violins.
0:22		First theme (slightly varied)	A varied repeat of the first theme with another long crescendo ending in two loud chords. The short—short—short—long motive is introduced as an accompaniment figure in the basses.
0:47		Second theme	A horn call announces the second theme, a soft, lyrical melody played first by the orchestra, then the clarinet, then the orchestra, finally ending with another long crescendo and some transitional material.
1:09		Third theme	A new melody in pulsatile rhythm is introduced ending with a loud cadence based on the short—short—short—long rhythmic motive, followed by a pause.

TIME	FORM	SECTION	DESCRIPTION
1:28	**Exposition repeats**		
2:55	**Development**	Section 1	A solo horn plays the opening motive answered by the orchestra. The opening motive is then traded, like a conversation, among the instruments of the orchestra ending in a long crescendo.
3:31		Section 2	The strings enter with the same melody from the second theme horn call, which during this section is reduced to two tones and then to one tone with a decrescendo to piano.
4:04		Section 3	The opening motive re-enters suddenly and loudly and alternates with the soft horn motive followed by another long crescendo.
4:17	**Recapitulation**		The opening motive returns, this time very loudly and played by the full orchestra including trumpets and timpani. At the end of the first statement of the first theme, instead of the violins' held tone, an oboe holds the tone and plays a short unaccompanied melody. The second theme horn call is played by the bassoon instead of the horn. The recapitulation ends with a rush to the now familiar cadence introduced in the exposition.
5:56	**Coda**		Instead of stopping at the cadence as expected, the full orchestra continues loudly playing what amounts to a second development section.
		Section 1	The full orchestra plays the opening motive loudly in different ways until some new melodic material is introduced.
6:26		Section 2	A new, ascending theme is introduced and varied.
7:00		Section 3	The recapitulation, with full orchestra, seems to begin again but is abruptly cut short with three forte playings of the opening motive and ten loud cadential block chords.
7:24		End	

What Does It Mean?

AESTHETICS

Part of the meaning of this piece resides in its relationship to the expectations of early nine-teenth-century audiences steeped in the music of Haydn and Mozart and the elegant style they had developed. It fulfills those expectations by working within the conventions of sonata form and the fast-tempo opening movement of a Classical-period symphony. But Beethoven stretched those conventions in new ways, deepening the expressive possibilities of the style. He expanded the ending of the movement in a coda (a tail at the end of the movement) with a lengthy second development, even introducing a new theme almost halfway through the coda. His cadences at the end of the movement, and at the end of the entire symphony, are loud and long, as if he felt that the excursions to other keys in the development section created such insta-bility that they required the insistent reiteration of the tonic key. His long crescendos from piano to forte add drama, as do the sudden pauses and abrupt shifts from loud to soft. Finally, Bee-thoven took Haydn's and Mozart's practice of building movements from short musical ideas or breaking melodies into their constituent motives to a new extreme in this movement. He started with a motive and built not only a melody, but many melodies, accompaniments, and the entire movement from a single tiny melodic and rhythmic cell (short-short-short-long).

EMOTIONAL RESONANCE

In addition to understanding this symphony in terms of its roots in the conventions of Clas-sical-period symphonies, it can also be understood as an example of the early flowering of a new intellectual movement in European society: Romanticism, a theory of art developed during Beethoven's lifetime. **Romanticism** claimed that literature, painting, and music was at its best when it expressed an artist's interior emotions. Music critics have interpreted Beethoven's compositions, including his Fifth Symphony, as an expression of his emotional life. This kind of interpretation was something new for European music, something that made Beethoven an early exemplar of Romanticism in music. In that vein, the symphony can be interpreted as a representation of the internal personal anguish and loneliness he was feeling at this time in his life. In 1798, at the age of twenty-seven, he noticed that he was having hearing problems, which worsened significantly between 1798 and 1808. In 1801 his letters to a friend describe his anguish and his reluctance to engage others socially lest they discover his growing deafness. In 1802 his doctors recommended that he retreat to the countryside for the sake of his mental and physical health. He sought refuge from his troubles by walking and working outside Vienna from time to time. One common interpretation of the opening short—short—short—long motive is as an icon of knocking at the door, specifically fate knocking at the door. Whose fate? Beethoven's, presumably. The roiling character of the movement created by the changes in dynamics and its minor key seem to suggest a fate beset with personal problems. The horn call and second theme may represent one hoped-for solution to the problem. Horn calls in European classical music had long referenced rural hunting horns, and the lyrical second theme suggests a hoped-for respite in the outdoors from inner turmoil. The overall arc of the movement, in which the first theme dominates throughout and at the end, suggests that the cure was only temporary. On the other hand, the symphony, which begins in C minor, ends with a fourth movement in C major rather than the more conventional C minor of the first movement. Beethoven, referencing centuries of associations between mode and mood (major = happiness, minor = sadness), fended off any criticism of his choice of key by saying, "joy follows sorrow, sunshine [follows] rain."

🔊 **Listen one more time to this performance for pleasure, paying attention to the shifting drama in the music and the possibility of its expression of Beethoven's inner life.**

Beethoven occasionally wrote in his scores that a movement should be played "innermost feeling," an indication that he understood his music as the expression of those feelings. In fact, Beethoven's music is often interpreted as an early example of music as an externalization of the inner emotional life of the composer or musician. Dating back many centuries, European classical music had developed the ability to represent exterior natural scenes and sounds, the contents of a painting, and the emotions and ideas of a poem, song lyric, or opera libretto. But it wasn't until the advent of Romanticism that these emotions and ideas were believed to originate in the inner, emotional life of the composer.

If composers were expressing their "innermost feelings" in their compositions, it follows that the musicians who played these works must access their own innermost feelings to produce them in sound. This idea gave rise to the sorts of performance mannerisms typical of solo and chamber recitals today: closed eyes, furrowed brows, serious faces, and swaying bodies. Audiences are supposed to understand these as external signs of internal emotions. And they probably help musicians and their audience feel those emotions.

Although Beethoven may have sought some solace during pleasant strolls outside Vienna, the Romantics prized the complexity, irregularity, volatility, and fierceness of nature as a mirror

FIGURE 6.14
Bell Rock Lighthouse. Painting by J.M.W. Turner (1818).
Source: Scottish National Gallery, Wikimedia Commons.

> **CULTURAL LINKAGES**

of inner human turmoil, and they valued an artist's ability to represent those qualities in art. For example, paintings of country scenes and sunsets were called Romantic. The turbulent, brooding landscapes and seascapes of the English painter J.M.W. Turner (1775–1851) exemplified Romanticism in visual art. Beethoven was to do something similar in his Sixth Symphony, which also premiered in 1808.

In German literature, one of the progenitors of Romanticism was Johann Wolfgang von Goethe (1749–1832), a polymath famous today as the author of the epic two-part "closet play" (meant to be read rather than staged) *Faust*, about a doctor who made a tragic deal, "a Faustian bargain," with the devil. (A performance takes about fifteen hours to read!) The first part was published in 1808, the year Beethoven's Symphony No. 5 debuted in concert. His earlier novel *The Sorrows of Young Werther* (1774) helped to launch Romanticism as a literary movement. In it, a passionate young man's unrequited love for a woman who marries another man (something that happened to Beethoven) leads him to suicide. The book seems to have emerged from Goethe's own emotional turmoil at the age of twenty-four: as an old man, he wrote of it, "That was a creation which I, like the pelican, fed with the blood of my own heart." This link between inner passion and outer creativity was one of the hallmarks of Romanticism. The English poet laureate William Wordsworth (1770–1850), born the same year as Beethoven, argued that poetry should spring from "the spontaneous overflow of powerful feelings." He and other Romantic poets fed the idea that poetry, and by extension music and painting, were expressing the poet's, composer's, or painter's emotions. In this intellectual environment, the works of Beethoven were interpreted in much the same way. In 1810, just two years after the premier of Beethoven's Symphony No. 5, the German writer and composer E.T.A. Hoffmann (1776–1822) wrote that "Beethoven's music stirs the mists of fear, of horror, of terror, of grief and awakens that endless longing which is the very essence of romanticism."

Many of the ideas about music that people take for granted today have their origins in the Romantic view that works of literature, music, and painting express the inner world of the artist. At least four ideas associated with the Romanticism of this period continue to resonate in European classical music to this day: (1) the concept of the genius; (2) reverence for the work of art; (3) the notion that musicians are expressing their "innermost feelings" when they perform; and (4) musicians' obligation to perform composers' music just as they intended them to. In Romantic terms, a genius was an artist who could create a completely original work not indebted to previous work. Until the end of the eighteenth century, composers were considered skilled craftsmen. Under the unceasing demands of secular and religious patrons, they routinely borrowed from their own previous work, and that of other composers, and fit their compositions into well-established stylistic norms if only to meet their deadlines. Haydn, Mozart, and Beethoven were probably the first composers accorded the exalted status of "genius."

In addition to interpreting Beethoven's compositions as highly personal expressions of his own inner states rather than as mere text painting or entertainment, early nineteenth-century music critics began to regard his work as art, a concept given new meaning during this period by Enlightenment philosophers. For most of their history, Europeans regarded art as the skillful making of something. Art was synonymous with mastery of a craft, whether painting, cabinet making, or playing and composing music. Today, these master makers of things are called craftspeople and artisans, and their work is called artisanal. This definition puts a great deal of emphasis on the makers of art and their ability to create something useful and well made. This equation of art and craft was challenged during the Enlightenment, when the German philosopher Immanuel Kant (1724–1804), in his *Critique of Judgment* (1790), linked art to aesthetic judgments of the beautiful, the sublime, the good, and the agreeable. Kant was interested less in the making of art and more in art's supposed ability to generate sensory experiences that could be judged aesthetically as beautiful or ugly, tasteful or crude, good or bad. Such aesthetic verdicts, he suggested, could be based on substantive qualities in the work of art itself, qualities such as elegance, balance, complexity, and the like. Written during

Beethoven's lifetime, this Enlightenment view of art affected the reception of Beethoven's work as art in this new sense.

If the composed work was an example of art, it followed that the performer's principal obligation was to render it as accurately as possible according to the composer's artistic intentions. This was a new idea in the history of European music. Up to this point, some solo instrumentalists and opera singers had treated the composer's written music as a template on which to add their own interpretations through ornamentation, variation, and other kinds of improvisation. Kant's ideas suggested that the composer was the true artist, and performers were reduced to artisanal servants of the composer's art. E.T.A. Hoffman argued that musicians had a "sacred" duty to perform the compositions of Beethoven with reverence, as if Beethoven were a musical god. This view of the obligation of performers to the compositions of composers is now a standard feature of much thinking about European classical music performance practice, but it was not always so.

What Is Its History?

Beethoven, like J. S. Bach and his sons, was born into a multi-generational musical family. His grandfather, born in Flanders (the Dutch-speaking area of Belgium), became the *Kapellmeister* to the Elector of Cologne, whose palace was in Bonn. His father Johann, a court singer, keyboardist, and Ludwig's first music teacher, recognized his son's prodigious talent and organized his first public concert at the age of seven. At ten Ludwig began studying with the court organist, and at fourteen he was employed as assistant organist in the court chapel. At seventeen he traveled to Vienna hoping to study with Mozart, but stayed only two weeks before returning to Bonn. In 1791 he met Haydn when the famous composer passed through Bonn to and from his first trip to London. In 1792, at the age of twenty-two and with the financial support of the Elector, he headed once more to Vienna, this time to study with the old master. He remained there for the rest of his life.

SOCIAL BEHAVIOR

In Vienna, his letter of introduction from the Elector of Cologne gave him access to the salons of the aristocracy. They invited him to display his keyboard skills, especially his ability to improvise, at their salons, and they commissioned compositions from him. Over the next five years he published mainly chamber music for piano and various combinations of instruments for the amusement of professional and amateur players in the elite Viennese social scene. He gave piano lessons to the aristocratic young ladies of marriageable age, but any romantic interest in them he may have had, including one he addressed in a letter as "Immortal Beloved," went unrequited. Their families would not allow them to marry a commoner and a musician of modest financial means. If those refusals were not galling enough, Beethoven, although he depended on wealthy nobles for financial support, regarded himself as their equal as a human being. Inspired by the French Revolution's ideals of *liberté*, *egalité*, and *fraternité*, he deeply resented any demands or interference his patrons made on his art, a position that Haydn was not free to take with his patron, Prince Nikolaus Esterházy.

By 1800 the Viennese public had recognized the thirty-year-old Beethoven as the city's finest piano virtuoso and improviser (improvisation contests were popular in Vienna) and a worthy successor to the compositional legacy of Haydn and Mozart, whose style he had absorbed. In 1800 he debuted his Symphony No. 1 in concert, launching an artistic trajectory that would establish his own legacy as one of the greatest composers in the history of European classical music.

AESTHETICS

Today, Beethoven's symphonies are among the most admired, performed, and written about compositions in the canon of European classical music. A **canon**, a word that originally meant "rule," is a collection of works that scholars, critics, performers, and audiences have judged particularly worthy, important, influential, and possessing artistic value. Within the European classical music canon, some composers are judged, at particular moments in history, more worthy than others, and some of their compositions are judged more important than others. Among

FIGURE 6.15
Beethoven in 1804.
Painting by Josef
Willibrord Mähler
(1778–1860).
Source: Museen
der Stadt Wien,
Wikimedia
Commons.

CULTURAL
LINKAGES

FIGURE 6.16
Beethoven in
1823. Painting by
Ferdinand Georg
Waldmüller
(1793–1865).
Source: Kunst
Historisches
Museum, Wien,
Collection of
Ancient Instruments.

Beethoven's nine symphonies conductors and audiences have responded most positively to his third, fifth, sixth, seventh, and ninth symphonies. Musical canons and their subdivisions are not immutable, however, and they change as taste in music and other cultural values change.

European classical music enthusiasts routinely refer to this canon of compositions as "Great Music." Important works of European literature and philosophy are called "Great Books." These two canons, plus the European canon of Great Art, form the "Western canon," a phrase that puts these works at odds with music, literature, and art from non-European traditions and new work by women, minorities, and people living outside the European "high" cultural orbit. Thus, the making of canons has implications for cultural politics, for example, when teachers and professors argue over which works of literature, art, and music, especially those outside the Western canon, deserve to be included in school and college curricula.

During Beethoven's life and for the rest of the nineteenth century and into the twentieth century, Beethoven's symphonies echoed in the consciousness of many classical composers, including Johannes Brahms, Anton Bruckner, and Gustav Mahler working in Vienna; Hector Berlioz in Paris; and Pyotr Ilyich Tchaikovsky and Dmitri Shostakovich in Russia. Beethoven's Fifth Symphony has assumed a prominent place in popular culture since its premier in 1808. The New York Philharmonic included it in its first concert in 1842. When Morse code, a combination of dots and dashes representing letters, was developed in the 1840s to send telegraphic signals, the pattern short—short—short—long was assigned to the letter V. During World War II the Allies began using the V sign, made with the fingers, to signal the hoped-for victory over the Germans. The British Broadcasting Company (BBC) started its wartime broadcasts with the four-note opening of Beethoven's Fifth Symphony played on the timpani, turning that motive into an iconic sign of victory (V is also the Roman numeral for five). Nowadays the organist at Los Angeles Dodgers baseball games plays the two statements of the opening motive of Beethoven's Fifth Symphony whenever a Dodger pitcher achieves victory by striking out a batter. In the 1970s the first movement of this symphony was included on the Voyager Golden Record sent into outer space as an example, along with recordings of Bulgarian music and rocker Chuck Berry, for extraterrestrials to hear a selection of earthlings' finest music making.

WHERE DO I GO FROM HERE?

- Compare the first movement of Beethoven's Symphony No. 5 to the first movement of Haydn's Symphony No. 101 in D major, "The Clock," one of his London Symphonies composed about fifteen years before Beethoven's. How does their treatment of melody differ in these two movements? How would you describe the general emotional quality of these two symphonic movements and what elements of music are contributing to those qualities?
- Listen to the other three movements of Beethoven's Symphony No. 5. Notice the way the opening motive of the first movement returns in various forms in movements III and IV, creating a sense of unity across the entire symphony.
- Listen to Beethoven's Symphony No. 6 "Pastoral," premiered in 1808 along with his Symphony No. 5, and notice the way he "paints" or represents scenes from nature in it.

GATEWAY 23
MUSIC OF THE ATLANTIC SLAVE TRADE

What Is It?

The transatlantic slave trade reached its height during the eighteenth century. In Latin America, the Roman Catholic church converted enslaved Africans to Christianity by allowing them to map their traditional pantheon of gods onto Catholic saints and to continue to use traditional forms of drumming, singing, and dancing in religious rituals honoring both traditions. These new syncretic religions are particularly strong in Cuba, Haiti, and Brazil. Our gateway to music of the Atlantic slave trade is a recording of a song for an African-derived Brazilian religion called **Candomblé** (pronounced kahn-dom-BLEH). Candomblé focuses on a pantheon of male and female deities called *orixás* (pronounced o-ri-SHAZ). Each *orixá* controls a domain of nature or human life (water, war, thunder and lightning, disease, and so forth) and has favorite colors, foods, songs, percussion rhythms, and dances. This recording is titled "Ijexá for Oxum." *Ijexá* (pronounced ee-zhe-SHA) is a dance and percussion rhythm named for a town in Nigeria where the Yoruba people live. Oxum (pronounced oh-SHOON) is a female *orixá* associated with water, fertility, beauty, and vanity. Her color is yellow. Jorge Alabê (ZHOR-gee a-la-BEH), a well-known master drummer and Candomblé initiate from Brazil who lives in San Francisco, leads a small ensemble with a two-pitch bell player and three drummers, who also sing. Alabê is an honorific name for a master of the tradition. He plays and improvises on the lead, low-pitched drum and sings the lead solo vocal part.

FIGURE 6.17
Modern oil painting by Joseph Nunes of Oxum portraying her personality (vanity), color (yellow), and the water she controls
Source: Wikimedia Commons.

 Listen to the first thirty seconds of the recording.

How Does It Work?

Timbre

The sound consists of three barrel-shaped drums (*atabaque*, pronounced a-ta-BA-kee) of different sizes (low-, medium-, and high-pitched), a two-pitch (low and high) iron bell (*agogô*), solo male voice, and male chorus.

Texture

The texture consists of a soloist and unison chorus singing over an accompaniment of four interlocking percussion parts.

Rhythm

An eight-beat meter is expressed in **polyrhythm** (a texture made of multiple, different, simultaneous rhythms, also called cross-rhythm) on the bell and three drums. The singers sing syllabically without a lot of rhythmic variety. The rhythm of the bell can be written like this, where H = the high pitch; L = the low pitch; and = rest:

1 &	2 &	3 &	4 &	5 &	6 &	7 &	8 &
H H	- L	- L	L -	H -	H -	L -	L -

Melody

The melodies consist of short descending phrases moving stepwise through a narrow-range, four-pitch or five-pitch (pentatonic) scale.

FIGURE 6.18
Jorge Alabê playing a drum (*atabaque*)

Harmony

The singers sing solo and in unison.

Form

The drummers play repeating rhythmic patterns with variations by the lead drummer, who plays the lowest-pitched drum. The singers sing a set of six slightly different songs, each based on one line of text. Each song has a solo-and-chorus, call-and-response structure.

Performance Techniques

The drums are played with the hands using damped and ringing sounds in the center and edge of the drumhead.

 Listen to the first thirty seconds of this performance with attention to the call-and-response structure of the performance and polyrhythmic drum part.

Timed Listening Guide

The six songs in this recording are in a language called Anago, which is descended from a dialect of the Yoruba language in Nigeria. Using a rich set of metaphors and allusions within a complicated theology, the songs evoke ideas and stories about Oxum and the town, spelled Ijesha, and the Ogun region of Nigeria where these practices are believed to have originated. After the bell and drums enter one at a time, the lead singer salutes Oxum, calling her "mother" (*ye ye*). The songs call her mother of the river and a princess from the town of Ijexá (Ijesha) in the Ogun region, and they ask the devotees to behold her beauty.

Listen again to the performance following this timed listening guide.

LISTENING GUIDE 6.4

TIME	SECTION	DESCRIPTION	WORDS
0:00	Instrumental intro	The bell enters followed by the three drums in turn from highest to lowest pitch.	
0:13	Salutation to Oxum	The lead singer enters with a short descending phrase of two pitches a minor third apart (G-E).	*Ye ye O*
0:17	Song 1	The lead singer sings a four-pitch solo melody (B-A-G-E) followed by chorus. They sing the song four times.	*Ye ye o ye ye xolodo*
1:06	Song 2	The solo singer introduces a new melody, adding new pitches higher in the range to create a descending pentatonic scale (E-D-B-A-G-E). The chorus responds, and they sing the song five times.	*A da ba o umafe*
1:38	Song 3	The singer starts a new song with a choral response, sung four times.	*[I]jexa moro bogum*
2:04	Song 4	A new melody with choral response, sung six times.	*Ojo ma tindo lara ojo*
2:43	Song 5	After a brief pause a new melody is introduced a half step higher with choral response, sung six times.	*A oro um maleixe are orô mimoriô*
3:26	Song 6	A final new melody is introduced a half step lower on the original pitch. The chorus responds, and the song is sung three times.	*Orixalá coma kenké*
4:01	End		

What Does It Mean?

This recording takes on meaning in a number of ways: in relation to an elaborate religious system, Candomblé; in relation to the religious rituals in which this song, and others like it, might be performed; and in relation to the history of the tradition, which devotees trace to similar religions along the west coast of Africa, home to the present-day countries of Nigeria, Ghana, Benin, and Angola.

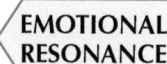

Candomblé is concentrated in the cities of Salvador and Recife along the northeastern shore of Brazil. Candomblé devotees undergo years of spiritual training, after which they may be able to go into trance and be possessed by the *orixá* who has become their spiritual "mother" or "father." Performances of songs like "Ijexá for Oxum" occur during ceremonies called *festas* held in ceremonial houses (*casas*) or yards (*terreiros*), each controlled by a spiritual "family." There may be a hundred or more of those in a large city like Recife. *Festas* begin in the early evening and last into the morning hours. Forty or more participants wear white clothing, some with colored accessories associated with their deity. During the ceremony the drummers perform a variety of songs and rhythms, each one associated with a particular *orixá*. While the lead drummer sings and the drummers drum, the participants dance and sing the choral responses, sometimes in improvised harmony. If conditions are right, some devotees may become visibly emotional while dancing to and singing the songs of their *orixá*. At that point the drummers and lead singer intensify their performance, hoping that the devotee will quickly become possessed. Those possessed typically cry out and fall to the ground, at which point caretakers surround them, wipe off sweat, hold them, and stand them up so they may dance while possessed. For devotees, possession is a hoped-for result of participation

FIGURE 6.19
Map of Brazil with the cities of Recife and Salvador

FIGURE 6.20
Map of the slave-trading regions of Africa

FIGURE 6.21
Candomblé possession
Source: Sylvia McIntyre-Crook.

in the ceremony. Emotional attachment to their spiritual father or mother functions as a psychological and emotional release from the tensions of everyday life, in a safe place surrounded by other devotees.

Lyrics, melodies, drum rhythms, and dances are associated with the potential presence of a particular *orixá*. Some of the rhythms are iconic signs: a slow tempo may represent the movements of an *orixá* in the form of an old man. Normally only those devotees who have pledged themselves to a particular *orixá* become possessed when they hear, sing, and dance to that *orixá*'s song. Occasionally an uninitiated person will go into trance, but musicians never do while performing.

What Is Its History?

CULTURAL LINKAGES

The Portuguese initiated the transatlantic slave trade in 1526, and over the next three centuries nearly five million enslaved Africans were brought to Brazil, the most of any country in the Americas. Brazil abolished slavery in 1888, the last country in the Americas to do so. Of the estimated twelve million Africans shipped to the Americas, 50 percent arrived during the eighteenth century. Many worked on the Caribbean islands in present-day Cuba, Puerto Rico, the Dominican Republic, Jamaica, and Trinidad and Tobago. Around 450,000 ended up in the United States. Enslaved Africans were brought to Brazil to work on sugar and tobacco plantations during the seventeenth and eighteenth centuries.

Enslaved Africans brought with them knowledge, skills, aesthetic preferences, and religious beliefs learned in Africa and, to the extent possible, kept them alive in the New World. African-derived religious practices similar to Candomblé, including call-and-response singing with African words accompanied by polyrhythmic drum ensembles in honor of deities, survive in Cuba under the name Santería (the worship of saints) and in Haiti with the name Vodou (from the name of a similar West African religion, Vodun). The Catholic Church condemned these African religious practices as witchcraft and at various times banned them, but the enslaved Africans kept them alive. One way to gain the acceptance of the church was to

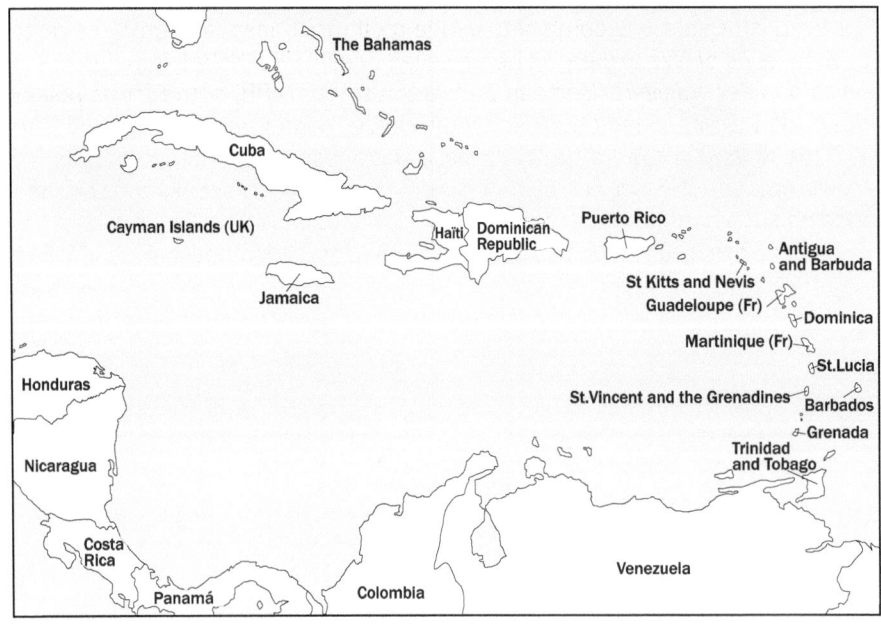

FIGURE 6.22
Map of the Caribbean

link the Africans' pantheon of deities to the names and symbolism of Catholic saints. For example, Oxum (Ochún in Santería) is linked to the Virgin Mary and shares some of her symbology; Oxóssi, the deity of the hunt, is linked to St. George, who slayed a dragon in return for a kingdom's conversion to Christianity; and Omolu, the deity of disease and medicine, is linked to St. Lazarus, whom Jesus raised from the dead. The historical record contains references to these practices, including one observer in 1790 who wrote, "the blacks divided by Nations dance with the instruments unique to each one." The word "Nations" refers to African ethnic groups brought to Brazil. Today those nations are preserved not as ethnic groups but as slightly different religious practices under the umbrella of Candomblé, a term that appeared in print in 1807. Although the songs, rhythms, dances, and beliefs of Candomblé clearly have their roots in Africa, all these elements have surely changed over the nearly five centuries since enslaved Africans were first brought to Brazil.

FIGURE 6.23
Dancing Ogun, the *orixá* of iron, blacksmiths, warriors, and drivers
Source: Toluaye, Wikimedia Commons.

Devotees and most Brazilians understand Candomblé as having its roots in West African religious practices, which have an analogous set of deities, many with similar names. The language of "Ijexá for Oxum" contains words and phrases transmitted from a dialect of the Yoruba language of Nigeria. Devotees, called *povo de santo* (people of the saint), originally were of African descent, but today they may be of any race. Many Brazilians interpret these religious practices as symbols of Brazilian national identity.

The African musical legacy in Brazilian culture, especially the polyrhythmic drum rhythms, continues to resonate in various forms of popular music up to the present. The most ubiquitous genre, samba, permeates Brazilian musical life. **Samba** emerged as a genre of popular music and dance in the early twentieth century. It is performed at the pre-Lenten Carnival and at patron saint festivities, marches, birthday parties, and soccer matches. In the 1920s and 1930s popular dance bands modeled on U.S. jazz bands referred to their music, some based on samba rhythms, as *samba-canção* (samba-song). One of the most famous of these samba singers, Carmen Miranda (1909–1955), "the ambassador of samba," starred in American movies in the 1940s. In the 1950s Brazilian musicians combined samba rhythms, transposed onto the guitar, with a soft, smooth vocal style of jazz to create a genre called *bossa nova* (new thing). Successor genres include *música popular brasileira* (Brazilian popular music) or MPB, noted for its political lyrics, and *samba/pagode* (samba/celebration), a contemporary commercial music. Under the rubric "Latin music," the legacy of the transatlantic slave trade, especially its rhythms, permeates the popular music not just of Brazil but also of Spanish- and French-speaking Central and South America, including such genres as *son cubano* from Cuba, *cumbia* from Colombia, *merengue* and *bachata* from the Dominican Republic, *zouk* from Haiti, and cosmopolitan genres such as Latin jazz, salsa, and *música tropical*.

WHERE DO I GO FROM HERE?

- Watch a video of a Candomblé ceremony.
- Listen to famous samba singer Clara Nunes (1942–1983) sing the song "Ijexá (Filhos de Ghandi)," a song that uses the *ijexá* rhythm. Filhos de Ghandi (Sons of Gandhi) is a famous "street Candomblé" group (*afoxé*) from Salvador.
- Listen to the song "Beleza pura" (Pure Beauty), written and sung by composer and guitarist Caetano Veloso (b. 1942), noted for his contributions to *bossa nova* and MPB.

CLOSING

During the second half of the eighteenth century, European composers elevated tunefulness, straightforward homophonic accompaniments, and the expression of multiple affects in a single movement over such elements of Baroque musical style as imitative counterpoint, elaborate figuration, and the expression of a single affect in a single movement. Instrumental music competed with vocal music, especially opera, for the favor of audiences by absorbing many of opera's expressive conventions. Secular music surpassed religious music as the principal medium of compositional practice. And public concerts, music lessons for the wealthy merchant and bourgeois classes, and royalties from published compositions began to supplant courtly patronage as the means of support for composers, who began to regard themselves, and were regarded by their audiences and critics, as artists and not merely as servants and craftsmen.

During the nineteenth century the compositions of Haydn, Mozart, and Beethoven came to be viewed as the finest representatives of the European musical tradition. They became the "classics" for nineteenth-century listeners and the masterpieces against which all future composers and their works would be measured. The African-derived religious music of Catholic countries in Latin America and the Caribbean provided the roots of the proliferation of Latin popular music styles beginning in the nineteenth century and continuing to the present. Both the European music and the African-derived music of this period might be said to represent triumphs of human creativity, one supported by unimaginable wealth and the other in response to unimaginable degradation.

THINGS TO THINK ABOUT

- Nearly all cultures have used music to connect humans to the supernatural world. Compare the way Candomblé devotees use music in their religious ceremonies to the way Medieval Christians, Muslims, Tibetan Buddhists, and the Shona people have used it. Are there any patterns in the use of music in these different religious traditions?

- Some of the music of this period is meant to be pleasurable in an abstract way that depends on the attractive combination of its musical elements, and some of it is meant to express emotions in some way. Do you favor one or the other of these approaches in the music you listen to? If so, which one, and why do you favor it? If not, why not?

NEW TERMS

Candomblé	motive	*Singspiel*
canon	opus (Op.)	sonata form
development	*orixás*	string quartet
Enlightenment	polyrhythm	symphony
exposition	recapitulation	theme
fortepiano	Romanticism	triplets
minuet	samba	

MUSIC FROM THE EARLY NINETEENTH CENTURY (1815–1850)

EUROPEANS SPENT MUCH of the nineteenth century working through the political and social aftermath of the American, French, and Haitian Revolutions. These revolutions had opened the Pandora's box of freedom and the right of the public to rule itself free of monarchical tyranny. The early nineteenth century, however, saw the rise of a new form of tyranny when French dictator Napoleon attempted to impose the ideals of the French Revolution on all of Europe. Napoleon Bonaparte (1769–1821) was a French military leader who supported the French Revolution of 1789. In 1799, after successful military campaigns on behalf of the new republic, he engineered a military coup ostensibly to bring order to the chaotic conditions in post-revolutionary France. In 1804 he crowned himself Emperor of France. For the next decade he fought eighteen major battles, from Spain and the island of Malta in the southwest to Russia in the northeast, to extend his power across most of the continent. In 1815 he was finally defeated and removed from power by a coalition of European forces at the Battle of Waterloo in Belgium.

Napoleon's maniacal personal ambition was paired with a desire to improve the workings of government on behalf of the people in something of the spirit of the French Revolution. In the territories he conquered, he introduced many reforms that live in the present, including rewarding merit, a system of laws known as the Napoleonic code, religious tolerance, and secular education. His most significant political legacy was the unification of the mosaic of small principalities and duchies in German-speaking central Europe and the city-states and small kingdoms on the Italian peninsula.

At the Congress of Vienna following Napoleon's defeat at Waterloo, the victorious European "great powers" attempted to restore the old order and recreate the political conditions that existed before the French Revolution and the Napoleonic wars. The Bourbon royal family was restored to the French throne in the person of Louis XVIII, whose brother, Louis XVI, and sister-in-law, Marie Antoinette, died at the guillotine during the revolution. Napoleon's unification of Italy was undone and reorganized into its previous political structure with states ruled by the Austrian Empire, by a Bourbon king in Naples, and by a Papal State.

Although his European aggressions were unwelcome, Napoleon had shown German and Italian military men and intellectuals the possibility of unified German and Italian states, which they achieved in 1861 in Italy and 1871 in Germany. During the first half of the nineteenth century, political discussions and revolutionary organizing occurred mostly behind the scenes. Musical life across Europe was largely disconnected from

FIGURE 7.1

Napoleon Bonaparte portrayed as Napoleon I, King of Italy, in 1805. Painting by Andrea Appiani (1754–1817).

Source: Wikimedia Commons.

DOI: 10.4324/9781003269304-10

politics, as if people needed a rest from the previous decade of war and tumult. Paris became the capital of music, art, and culture during this period, taking Vienna's place. Intellectuals, artists, and aristocrats from all over Europe, and from the French countryside, moved to Paris. This chapter contains gateways looking at three composers who flourished in Paris: the Italian Gioachino Rossini, the Frenchman Hector Berlioz, and the Pole Frédéric Chopin.

Another revolution, the **Industrial Revolution**, also impacted the cultural and musical life of Europe during this period. Its innovations in manufacturing, transportation, and communication had many practical and musical consequences. The invention of the steam engine, in 1775, powered looms that wove textiles much more quickly than before and enriched producers who sold vast quantities of material for clothing. By mid-century locomotives for trains had lessened travel times between, and knitted together, far-flung communities. The installation of gas lighting indoors and outdoors allowed factories to stay open after dark and be even more productive. And nightlife developed along gas-lit city streets. More efficient and precise methods of casting iron led to a stronger metal and to the building of massive structures including iron bridges, the first in 1778 in England, and the Eiffel Tower in 1889. Cast iron and steel frames for pianos allowed more strings to be held under greater tension, which increased the piano's range, enriched its tone quality, and lengthened the decay of each tone.

The deployment of these production aids allowed large numbers of workers to gather in one factory and for factory owners to accumulate great wealth through manufacturing. Factory workers' wages inspired people to move from the countryside to the city in search of wage labor. Cities became the home to three new urban social classes: (1) the **bourgeoisie** (a French word denoting a city dweller), consisting of lawyers, insurance agents, accountants, bankers, and financiers, to serve (2) **capitalists**, the new class of factory-owning manufacturers who needed the management skills of the bourgeoisie to run their businesses, who hired (3) the **proletariat**, the laborers who produced the goods manufactured in newly efficient factories. Capitalists seeking to make cities more livable for themselves and the bourgeoisie formed civic symphonic societies, built concert halls, and patronized opera concerts. The bourgeoisie had the money to buy tickets, fill the halls, and hire professional musicians as music teachers for their daughters, for whom playing the piano became a sign of good breeding. In the United States the bourgeoisie and the proletariat constituted the audience for a new form of popular entertainment, the minstrel show. Improved manufacturing techniques and advanced engineering led to the addition of valves to brass instruments, which increased their versatility for performing in all the keys of tonal music and led to their integration into large orchestras, which filled the grand concert halls built in the nineteenth century with sound.

Early nineteenth-century music was also influenced by a new worldview and theory of art called Romanticism, which developed toward the end of the eighteenth century and flourished during the first half of the nineteenth century (Chapter 6, Gateway 22). Today the word "romantic" has two common meanings: expressions and displays of affection for another person and proposals and ideas that are unrealistic or too idealistic. During the early nineteenth century, the terms **Romantic** and **Romanticism** referred to expressions in literature, music, and painting of an artist's interior expe-

FIGURE 7.2
Steam locomotive *Hibernia*, built in 1834
Source: Wikimedia Commons.

riences of passion, restlessness, longing, and striving. Romanticism in music is represented in two gateways: a symphony by the Frenchman Hector Berlioz and a short piano piece by Polish émigré to Paris Frédéric Chopin. The chapter concludes with a first look at American popular music and the way it responded to the institution of slavery during the first half of the nineteenth century.

GATEWAY 24
EARLY NINETEENTH-CENTURY OPERA

What Is It?

Our gateway to European opera composed during the early nineteenth century is the *cavatina* "Una voce poco fa" (A voice a while ago [resonated here in my heart]) from the *opera buffa* (comic opera) *Il barbiere di Siviglia* (The Barber of Seville) by Gioachino Rossini (1792–1868). A *cavatina* is a character's introductory aria in early nineteenth-century opera. Based on a play by Pierre Beaumarchais, the author of *The Marriage of Figaro* (Chapter 6, Gateway 21), it premiered in Rome in 1816. In this opera Count Almaviva appears not as the womanizing scoundrel he is in Mozart's *The Marriage of Figaro*, but as a charming and respectful (and wealthy) young suitor. Figaro acts not as his servant but as a clever factotum (a jack-of-all-trades) in the guise of a freelance barber able to make people look good and to solve their social problems. Count Almaviva approaches Figaro for advice on how to attract the young and beautiful Rosina to marry him for love, not money. Rosina, who has her own large dowry, lives with her ward, the pompous Dr. Bartolo, who hopes to marry her for her money when she comes of age. Typical of French farces, Figaro advises Almaviva to disguise himself as a poor student named Lindoro and to serenade Rosina from the street below her window. Hearing his song, Rosina muses in "Una voce poco fa" about her future with the attractive Lindoro, implicitly rejecting Dr. Bartolo and Count Almaviva as spouses. From this setup all manner of silliness ensues (more disguises, hiding in closets, unexpected knocks at the door, mistaken identities) through two acts and nearly three hours until, at last and inevitably, love prevails. Rosina and Almaviva marry, and she, in a gesture of goodwill, leaves her dowry to Dr. Bartolo—a happy ending reminiscent of Mozart's *The Marriage of Figaro*. In this 1957 recording the role of Rosina is sung by Maria Callas, accompanied by the Philharmonia Orchestra (London) directed by Alceo Galliera.

FIGURE 7.3
Gioachino Rossini in 1815. Portrait by Vincenzo Camuccini (1771–1844).
Source: Collection of Museo del Teatro alla Scala in Milan, Wikimedia Commons.

 Listen to the first minute of the recording, the orchestral introduction and the first phrase of Rosina's aria, for a general sense of the style.

How Does It Work?

Timbre

The sound of a full orchestra combines with the sound of a soprano, an operatic female voice with a very wide range whose quality ranges from smooth and rich in the low register to bright and vibrant in the upper register.

Texture

The texture consists of clear instrumental and vocal melodies accompanied by chords played by the orchestra.

Rhythm

The meter is in three at first and then changes to four in the second half. The vocal rhythms are quite varied and feature fast melodic runs and ornaments, the alternation of short and long notes, tempo changes, and holds (*fermata*) on high-pitched climactic notes to show off the voice.

Melody

The melody is in a major key and features scalar runs and occasional leaps of a fourth or fifth or more.

Harmony

The harmony is tonal in a major key without modulations to other keys.

Form

After an orchestral introduction, the singer performs an aria in two parts, a **double aria**. The first part, called *cantabile*, sets the text syllabically (mostly). After a brief orchestral *ritornello*, the second part, called *cabaletta*, sets the text melismatically and is filled with dramatic pauses and flashy ornamentation.

Performance Techniques

Rossini composed this aria with technically demanding runs and ornaments. The singer is also free to slow down and speed up, pause the melody, and add her own ornaments during the repetitions of the melody, at the ends of phrases, and on long-held notes. Audiences listen for the singer's displays of ornamental creativity and virtuosity in a style known as *coloratura* (coloring) and watch her acting for clues to the thoughts and feelings of her character at that moment. In this performance by Maria Callas, notice her gradual dynamic changes on individual notes and phrases.

Listen to the entire recording following this timed listening guide.

LISTENING GUIDE 7.1

TIME	SECTION	FORM	TEXT	TRANSLATION	DESCRIPTION
0:00	**Orchestral Introduction**				In a slow triple meter, the strings are featured. The repeated short-long, short-long rhythm in the first phrase changes to a pulsating rhythm in the second phrase.
0:37	**Cantabile**	A	*Una voce poco fa/qui nel cor mi risuonò*	A voice a while ago/resonated here in my heart	The vocal melody, also in triple meter, echoes the short-long rhythm of the Introduction but at a slower tempo.
0:47		A′	*Il mio cor ferito è già/e Lindor fu che il piagò*	My heart has been pierced/And Lindoro inflicted the wound	The second phrase (line of text) echoes the first on different pitches.
1:00		BB′	*Si, Lindoro mio sarà/lo giurai, la vincerò*	Yes, Lindoro will be mine/I swear it, I will win	The two melodic lines are sung twice to a melody that starts with an excited upward leap on Lindoro's name and descends in ornamented stepwise motion suggestive of her delight. The repeat of the melody has more ornaments than the first. As the singer focuses on the ornamented melody, the sense of a beat is almost lost.
1:28		C	*Il tutor ricuserà/ io l'ingegno aguzzerò.*	My guardian will refuse me/I shall sharpen my wits.	She predicts her future in a speech-like melody.
1:35		C	*All fin s'acceterà/e contenta io resterò*	In the end he will accede/and I will rest content.	

TIME	SECTION	FORM	TEXT	TRANSLATION	DESCRIPTION
1:41		BB′	*Sì, Lindoro mio sarà/lo giurai, la vincerò*	Yes, Lindoro will be mine/I swear it, I will win	She repeats her expression of delight with even more ornaments. At the cadences, the singer adds many ornaments not in the score.
2:33	**Orchestral** *ritornello*	AA′			The meter changes to four beats to the measure. Featuring the flute, the four-measure melody (A) repeats on different pitches (A′) and ends with a four-measure concluding phrase.
3:02	**Cabaletta**	A	*Io sono docile, son rispettosa*	I am docile, I am respectful.	The vocal repeats the *ritornello* melody.
3:12		A′	*Sono obbediente, dolce, amorosa*	I am obedient, sweet, loving.	
3:20		BB′B″	*Mi lascio reggere, mi lascio reggere, mi fo guidar, mi fo guidar (Ma!)*	I let myself be ruled (2x), I let myself be guided (2x). (But!)	The repetitions in the text are set on three short phrases.
3:36		CC′	*Ma se mi toccano/ dov'è il mio debole/ sarò una vipera, serà E cento trappole/ prima di cedere/ farò giocar, giocar.*	But if they touch me/where I am weak/I will be a viper. And a hundred tricks/before giving up/I would play.	The melody becomes more rhythmic and "spritely," mirroring the defiant spirit of the words.
3:54		DD′	*E cento trappole/ prima di cedere/ farò giocar, giocar.*	And a hundred tricks/before giving up/I would play.	The words are repeated twice more on a new, slow melody, the second time through with much more ornamentation. The slowing and the repetition serve to emphasize her scheming.
4:20		E	*Io sono docile, son rispettosa/ Mi lascio reggere, mi fo guidar (Ma!)*	I am docile, I am respectful/I am obedient,/I let myself be guided (But!)	The orchestra enters with a pulsing melody and crescendos through this section drowning out Rosina's repetition of her opening words on a new melody. She finally arrives on a loud, long-held high note to conclude the section.
4:41		CC′	*Ma se mi toccano/ dov'è il mio debole/ sarò una vipera, serà/ E cento trappole/ prima di cedere/ farò giocar, giocar.*	But if they touch me/where I am weak/I will be a viper/And a hundred tricks/before giving up/I would play.	The melodies repeat.
5:02		DD′	*E cento trappole/ prima di cedere/ farò giocar, giocar.*	And a hundred tricks/before giving up/I would play.	
5:36		F	*E cento trappole farò giocar*	And hundred tricks I'll play	A coda in which the words are repeated many times and the orchestra gets louder. The singer ends on a scalar run up to a high note followed by an ornamented descent to the tonic, and the orchestra finishes energetically and loudly.
6:16	End				

What Does It Mean?

Gioachino Rossini [Joh-a-KEE-no Ro-SEE-nee] was, along with Beethoven, one of the two most admired European composers of the early nineteenth century. Most of his operas were written in Italian for major Italian opera houses in Venice, Naples, Milan, and Rome. But they were quickly adopted in the repertoires of opera companies in Paris, Vienna, London, Berlin, and other European capitals. Asking why his operas were so popular is a good place to start in assessing the meaning of "Una voce poco fa."

Italian opera had been the most popular musical genre in European cities since the seventeenth century, when aristocrats from all over Europe began vacationing in Venice during the pre-Lenten Carnival season to attend the newest productions by Monteverdi and his contemporaries (Chapter 5, Gateway 15). During the early eighteenth century the German composer George Frideric Handel learned to compose operas in Italy and found fame creating them for aristocrats in London (Chapter 5, Gateway 17). During the late eighteenth century Mozart's Italian operas were popular among the Austrian nobility (Chapter 6, Gateway 21). During Rossini's time, dozens of Italian composers were writing new operas for some eighty opera companies in towns and cities in Italy. Opera in this period had qualities similar to movies today. Both tell stories about human events and emotions, require large investments of money to produce, last two to three hours, are shown in theaters designed for the purpose, and feature star performers. Rossini achieved his fame against this backdrop of opera's popularity and its central importance in the urban cultural and social life of Europe.

Rossini's popularity can be measured by the sheer number of operas he wrote. During the twenty years from 1810 to 1829, between the ages of eighteen and thirty-eight, he composed thirty-nine operas—about two per year. In 1823, twenty-three of his operas were performed in opera houses around Europe. Opera house managers invited him to write operas at such a furious pace because audiences enjoyed them and would buy tickets to them. But why did audiences find them so enjoyable?

The musical features of "Una voce poco fa" provide part of the answer. Audiences then and now love to hear the sound of the human voice, in Rossini's case the wide vocal range, the singer's voice quality (timbre), her technical skill at ornamentation and rapid scalar runs, and the voice's capacity for expressing human emotions. Rossini, who had trained as a singer, was particularly sensitive to a singer's abilities and often composed arias to show off the vocal range and the skills of the singers who debuted the roles in his operas. Among their skills, singers of this period were expected to embellish the written score with their own ornamentation or *coloratura*. Some of the ornaments in Callas's recording of "Una voce poco fa" are her own or part of singers' oral tradition. Rossini and his audiences loved the way his singers sang, a manner that came to be called *bel canto* (beautiful singing).

All opera composers of the eighteenth and early nineteenth centuries, including Handel and Mozart, were writing arias that gave singers plenty of opportunities to shine. What seems to have distinguished Rossini from his many Italian contemporaries was the rhythmic energy of his melodies, his vivid orchestral accompaniments, and his use of repetition. Repetition, especially of melody, helps audiences understand any music at first hearing. The German and Austrian composers Bach, Haydn, Mozart, and Beethoven took one or two melodies or short melodic motives and subjected them to melodic, harmonic, and rhythmic "development" (Chapters 5 and 6). But this compositional practice requires a great deal of careful attention to follow the "journey" of a melody or motive through many keys, contrapuntal lines, and instruments. Rossini took a vastly different tack. His arias, including "Una voce poco fa," consist of many melodies repeated at least once and often many times. They don't split into motives, and they don't move through many different keys as the music of Bach, Haydn, Mozart, and Beethoven does. They remain intact and repeat in varied form the second time, usually with more ornamentation on what is already a highly ornamented melody. Coupled with the aria's dance-like rhythmic energy, the occasional orchestral crescendos, and the skillful singing, the melodic repetition in "Una voce poco fa" creates an enjoyable listening experience for opera audiences then and now.

Rossini extended his fondness for melodic repetition within an aria to the repetition of the double aria form throughout an entire opera. Most of his operas consist of the formulaic repetition of this form through a series of "numbers," each number consisting of a recitative that outlines the situation and the plot followed by an aria or double aria for a soloist or a duet and a finale to end the act with the cast gathered on stage to sum up what has just transpired. These compositional formulas enabled him to compose very quickly. Sometimes he churned out an opera in as little as two or three weeks. But these formulas meant that the audiences of the time knew exactly what to expect. After the musically uninteresting recitative that advanced the plot, they knew to expect some vocal fireworks, often in two parts, ending in a grand conclusion. In *Il barbiere di Siviglia*, for example, Rosina sings one other solo "number" in the second act, "Contro un cor." It is structured almost exactly like "Una voce poco fa," and its final cadence repeats the one in "Una voce poco fa."

Rossini's operas were all about listening pleasure. Wanting to make going to the opera a pleasure rather than a drag (with long recitatives), he created a style of opera that pleased listeners by the brilliance of its surface effects, neither challenging them to think more deeply about the meaning of the music nor making great demands on their attention. Audiences in those days sat in lighted auditoriums, where they ate and drank and chatted as the singers sang recitatives to outline the often implausible plot. They only paid attention when one of the characters launched into a virtuosic solo. Rossini, not wanting to bore his audiences, kept things moving along musically in ways that delighted audiences.

Although audiences loved Rossini's operas during his active years, critics and intellectuals of the day differed in their interpretation of their meaning and value. His work raised three significant general issues for critics of the day. One concerned how to value compositional creativity. Negative reviews criticized him for reusing material from an earlier opera in a later one. The melody of "Una voce poco fa" had already been used in an earlier opera in a kind of self-plagiarism. Many other prolific composers working to deadlines, like Johann Sebastian Bach, for example, had done this in the past, but by the early nineteenth century the idea that creativity was defined by completely original work was emerging (Chapter 6, Gateway 22).

CULTURAL LINKAGES

Another criticism focused on the richness of his orchestral accompaniments, something he had learned from studying Haydn and Mozart in school. He used these techniques to create entertaining instrumental overtures and *ritornello*s in the middle of his arias, *cavatina*s, duets, and finales. Some Italian critics reacted negatively. They thought his importation of "German" instrumental "noise" interfered with, and sometimes even covered up, the beauty of "Italian" vocal melody. Some German critics, on the other hand, thought that Rossini's emphasis on melody lacked the contrapuntal and harmonic richness of Mozart's Italian operas (Chapter 6, Gateway 21).

Another debate centered on the relationship between words and music. For more than 300 years Italian madrigal and opera composers of the Renaissance and Baroque eras, respectively, had mastered the art of creating melodies that amplified the emotional resonance of a particular text through iconic word painting. Rossini seemed to shun this tradition, asking the audience to focus on melodic abundance and virtuoso singing unrelated to the specific emotions (happy, sad, anxious) of the characters singing them. Critics noted unhappily that he sometimes used a *cavatina* from a sad scene in one opera for a happy scene in a later one.

This disconnect between musical style and textual meaning in Rossini's operas led philosophers to reconsider their aesthetic theories of the nature and value of music. For some philosophers, music was an art inferior to literature, painting, sculpture, and dance because, unlike those arts, they believed that music could not represent emotions and scenes from the real world without the aid of the texts associated with it. In response, Georg Wilhelm Friedrich Hegel (1770–1831), an important founder of modern European philosophy, wrote approvingly after hearing a Rossini opera in Vienna that "We no longer need or want any text; nothing at all is left beyond the musical note of feeling." He understood that music could create general emotions in listeners independent of iconic representation. Arthur Schopenhauer (1788–1860),

Hegel's rival, concluded, partly influenced by Rossini's operas, that music, because it could be unlinked from representation of the observable world and still be expressive, was the purest artistic expression of the human will and hence it occupied the highest, not the lowest, position among the arts. Schopenhauer believed that Rossini's melodies, in their independence from the text, had the ability to reach deeper into the human soul and spirit and inner essence than did the more representational art forms.

What Is Its History?

Rossini achieved fame in this period by writing in both of the two principal styles of Italian opera current during his youth: *opera seria* (serious opera), historical dramas about tragic figures from ancient or "classical" Greece and Rome; and *opera buffa* (comic opera), stories of human folly and indiscretion, set in the present—something like a TV sitcom, but with virtuosic singing. His parents, both musicians, introduced him to these forms as a child growing up in Pesaro, an Italian town on Italy's northeastern Adriatic coast. Opera, once the domain of the aristocracy, had become popular among the growing class of bourgeois patrons of the arts, a growth fueled by the beginnings of the Industrial Revolution and the French revolutionary idea of *egalité* (equality). Public opera houses were built throughout Italy, providing many opportunities for untrained singers, including women like Rossini's mother Anna, to become paid performers. She took her son to her performances at local opera companies, and she and his father provided early instruction in singing, piano, and composition. By the age of twelve he was singing in recitals of operatic arias with his mother and composing his first sonatas for a string quartet of two violins, cello, and bass. At fourteen his parents moved to the large city of Bologna, where he enrolled in the city's prestigious music academy and studied the vivid orchestral writing of Haydn and Mozart.

In his youth Rossini was especially impressed with the coloratura singing of *castrati*, male opera singers who performed both male and female leading roles. Later in life Rossini wrote:

> I have never forgotten them. The purity, the miraculous flexibility of those voices and, above all, their profoundly penetrating accent—all that moved and fascinated me more than I can tell.

FIGURE 7.4

The opera house *La Fenice*. In the early nineteenth century, patrons arrived by gondola.

Source: Wikimedia Commons.

Rossini's voice as a child was so sweet that an uncle suggested to his family that he become a *castrato*. His mother opposed this, and the practice was soon outlawed. Even as the *castrato* tradition was ending, they remained among the most important teachers of *coloratura* singing to both male and female singers. Since he could no longer write for *castrati*, Rossini transferred his love of that voice to contraltos, women whose rich lower registers he thought most resembled the sound produced by *castrati*. The role of Rosina was originally written for a contralto, a rare vocal type today.

Rossini graduated from the music academy in 1810 at the age of eighteen and was lucky enough to receive a commission to write an opera for a small theater in Venice. Its unexpected local success led to an invitation from Venice's most prestigious opera house, *La Fenice*. They gave him the libretto for an *opera seria* called *Tancredi* based on a novel by Voltaire (1760) and set in medieval Sicily. It premiered in 1813. His first international success, it was performed all over Italy and Europe for the next twenty years. Meanwhile, he began to receive commission after commission from the best opera houses in Italy and abroad.

The richest of these opera houses was the enormous 2400-seat Teatro San Carlo in Naples, then the third-largest city in Europe. This public opera company supported itself with a casino in the lobby. The casino's reliable infusion of money meant that the Naples opera company could hire the best singers, have the best orchestra, and put Rossini, the emerging most popular composer in Europe, under contract. The audience's interest in the singers of opera meant that famous male and female singers were sometimes paid two or three times what Rossini was for the first run of one of his operas. In Naples he composed quite a few operas with roles for his future wife Isabella Colbran (1785–1845), one of the most celebrated contraltos of the period and a composer of many songs. She had an enormous range of nearly three octaves, with a rich, velvety sound in the low register and a bright sound in the high register. Some writers have suggested that Maria Callas's voice is similar to descriptions of Colbran's voice. Coincidentally, both she and Callas retired from opera performance at the same age, forty-two. While under contract in Naples, Rossini was invited to Rome, where in 1816 he premiered *Il barbiere di Siviglia*. As his fame spread, he visited Vienna, London, and Paris, always with an eye on long-term contracts that would guarantee him a stable income.

FIGURE 7.5
Isabella Colbran at the keyboard c. 1835. Painting by Johann Baptist Reiter (1813–1890).
Source: Wikimedia Commons.

From 1824 to 1829 Rossini lived in Paris, where Italian opera was more popular than those in French. He became director of the Théâtre Italien, which gave him the opportunity to champion the works of even younger composers (he was only in his thirties at this point), especially two whose fame came to rival his own, Gaetano Donizetti (1797–1848) and Vincenzo Bellini (1801–1835), both of whom he outlived by many decades. While in Paris, he learned French and wrote four operas in that language. The overture to his last opera, *Guillaume Tell* (1829), became a pre-internet meme in American popular culture from the 1930s through the 1950s when it was parodied in Disney cartoons and used as the theme music for the enormously popular radio and TV show *The Lone Ranger*. Because of its association with *The Lone Ranger*, for many listeners today the last section functions as a sonic icon of a galloping horse. Both this overture and the overture to *Il barbiere di Siviglia* are frequently performed today on symphony programs, which commonly include an opera overture or a modern composition, a symphony, and a concerto.

> **CULTURAL LINKAGES**

Enormously productive for twenty years, by 1830, at the age of thirty-eight, Rossini no longer possessed the physical and mental energy necessary to maintain his career as an opera composer. He did retain his enthusiasm for composing and continued to write songs, chamber music, and a few religious works until his death in 1868. Later in life he had to endure the declining popularity of his operas. The style and the aesthetics of opera were changing. Unlike Monteverdi and Mozart, Rossini had not tried to "express" or "represent" the emotions of particular characters and texts in his music. He loved, and wanted to feature, elaborately ornamented singing, no matter the specific emotion of the character at that moment in the opera. The composer's "chief duty," he said, "is to offer musical delight." By mid-century a new melodic style was developing. Composers and singers were abandoning *coloratura* ornamentation in favor of long-held notes that showcased singers' vocal timbre and power in the service of their character's emotional expression. In 1851 the German opera conductor and composer Richard Wagner (1813–1883) wrote a long treatise called *Opera and Drama* criticizing Rossini's operas for the way his musical "numbers" stopped the forward movement and dramatic impact of the plot. He argued for a new style that placed music in service of the characters' emotions and the plot, precisely what Rossini

> **AESTHETICS**

FIGURE 7.6
Maria Callas performing in Giacomo Puccini's *Madame Butterfly*
Source: Getty Images/Bettmann.

opposed (Chapter 8, Gateway 28). The Italian composers Giuseppe Verdi (1831–1901) and Giacomo Puccini (1858–1924) followed suit, becoming the new lions of Italian opera and pushing Rossini's operas out of the repertory, with one exception. *Il barbiere di Siviglia* has remained popular with opera audiences for more than 200 years.

Rossini lamented the loss, in this new style, of *bel canto* (beautiful singing), which was no longer necessary, desired, or even possible. This loss persisted until the middle of the twentieth century when a few singers, including Maria Callas, began to revive *coloratura* singing. The interest of singers, coupled with new editions of his operas by historical musicologists, has meant that Rossini's operas, neglected for a century and a half, are today performed by major opera companies along with operas in this style by his contemporaries Donizetti and Bellini. Among the American-born singers admired for their *coloratura* portrayals of Rosina, in addition to Callas, are the mezzo-sopranos Marilyn Horne (b. 1934) and Frederica von Stade (b. 1945) and the soprano Beverly Sills (1929–2007). Later in life Sills enjoyed a distinguished career as an opera administrator, acting as general manager of the New York City Opera and chairwoman of the Metropolitan Opera. These and other modern singers love the opportunity Rossini provides for showing off their *coloratura* vocal technique, if they have it. Von Stade, for example, told interviewers, "I really believe so much in *bel canto*, and particularly Rossini's music. It does everything that can be accomplished through the voice. . . . 'This is hard, but I am fantastic because I can do this.' . . . That's what Rossini is."

WHERE DO I GO FROM HERE?

- Watch a video of the soprano Beverly Sills singing "Una voce poco fa" in an opera performance. Notice the joy she takes in her singing and compare her vocal quality and *coloratura* to those of Maria Callas.

- Watch a concert video of the other famous *cavatina* from *Il barbiere di Siviglia*, Figaro's "Largo al Factotum," performed by the American baritone Thomas Hampson. His acting and the rapid-fire lyrics give some idea of the humor in this *opera buffa*.

- Watch a video of *Il barbiere di Siviglia* under the direction of the conductor Claudio Abbado with the Spanish mezzo-soprano Teresa Berganza in the role of Rosina. Notice the stage business and acting as you follow the plot (turn on subtitles).

GATEWAY 25
PROGRAMMATIC ORCHESTRAL WORKS

What Is It?

The influence of Beethoven's symphonies resonated throughout the nineteenth century and beyond. Viennese composers Johannes Brahms (1833–1897) and Gustav Mahler (1860–1911), for example, used the symphony orchestra to express generalized dramatic, roiling feelings and emotions in the Romantic tradition, as Beethoven had in his Symphony No. 5. Other composers employed musical icons to depict more specific stories and characters, in the manner of Beethoven's Symphony No. 6 "Pastoral." In some cases, they used written texts or programs to link their music to particular ideas, emotions, and narratives, in the manner of Vivaldi's Violin Concerto in E minor ("Spring") (Chapter 5, Gateway 16), substituting an unheard text for the words of a character in opera. Such compositions are called **programmatic** (or **program music**), that is, they tell a story.

Our gateways to programmatic symphonic writing are the first and fourth movements of Hector Berlioz's (1803–1869) *Symphonie Fantastique: Épisode de la vie d'un artiste . . . en cinq parties* (Fantastical Symphony: An Episode in the Life of an Artist, in Five Parts). Berlioz composed and first performed *Symphonie Fantastique* in 1830, just three years after Beethoven's death. A symphony in five movements, it combines the Romantic idea of art as an outward expression of inner passions with the idea, exemplified in Beethoven's Symphony No. 6 ("Pastoral"), that music can describe scenes and tell stories, in this case the composer's fantasies about the fate of his love for a famous English actress named Harriet Smithson.

 Listen to the first thirty seconds of the fourth movement.

How Does It Work?

Timbre

Berlioz expanded the Classical-period orchestra to include a larger string section, four instead of two bassoons, four timpani, and instruments rarely used before in symphonic music: the ophicleide (a low-pitched, keyed brass instrument invented in 1817 and replaced later in the century by the tuba), two harps, and the **English horn** (a low-pitched relative of the oboe). He also created new timbral effects, such as having the violinists strike the strings with the wood of their bows (*col legno*, with wood) to create a rustling sound.

FIGURE 7.7
Hector Berlioz in 1832. Painting by Emile Signol (1804–1892).
Source: Villa Medici, Rome, Wikimedia Commons.

Texture

The polyphonic texture varies greatly, but Berlioz uses monophonic unisons and octaves to great effect.

Rhythm

The tempo and meter of the movements follow the conventions of the Classical-period symphony for the most part.

Melody

Each movement of the symphony has its own melodies, but one melody appears in varying forms in all five movements. That melody, played first in Mvt. I, represents the beloved, the English actress Harriet Smithson. Berlioz calls the melody his *idée fixe*, his obsession or mania. It is a long melody with an ever-rising pitch contour that seems to express his yearning for her love.

Harmony

The harmony is tonal with occasional loud dissonances to express the composer's troubled emotional life and fantasies.

Form

The first movement has some of the features of sonata form. The fourth movement march has some features of European dance form (AABB) and some of theme and variations.

Performance Techniques

In addition to the *col legno* technique, Berlioz requires very high-pitched and low-pitched playing from the musicians and **glissandos** (slides between two pitches) from the wind instruments, among other techniques. In the score he provides very detailed signs for crescendos and decrescendos for individual notes and phrases, all designed to increase the emotional impact of the music. His long crescendos and sudden changes from loud to soft are reminders of Beethoven's use of these techniques for expressive purposes.

FIGURE 7.8
An ophicleide
Source: Crosby Brown Collection of Musical Instruments. Metropolitan Museum of Art, Wikimedia Commons.

What Does It Mean?

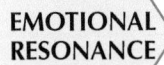

How Berlioz's *Symphonie Fantastique* works is inextricably tied to what it means. What it means is in turn linked to the shape of the entire symphony and its relationship to an "episode" in Berlioz's life. As a music student in Paris, Berlioz attended performances in 1827 of Shakespeare's *Hamlet* and *Romeo and Juliet* by a traveling English theater company. He fell in love with Shakespeare, eventually learning English to be able to read the plays. He also fell in love with Harriet Smithson, who played Ophelia and Juliet. He bombarded her with love letters to no avail. In 1830 he composed his *Symphonie Fantastique* as an expression of his love sickness. For the symphony he wrote a program, a narrative describing the internal passions and thoughts represented in the music. In the timed listening guides for each movement, his program is given before the description of each movement, beginning with this preface:

The composer's intention has been to develop, insofar as they contain musical possibilities, various situations in the life of an artist. The outline of the instrumental drama, which lacks the help of words, needs to be explained in advance. The following program should thus be considered as the spoken text of an opera, serving to introduce the musical movements, whose character and expression it motivates.

The timed listening guides that follow are for the first and fourth movements, with some descriptions of the way the *idée fixe* appears in the other movements.

Mvt. I: Reveries. Passions (Largo, Allegro)

The author imagines that a young musician, afflicted by the sickness of spirit which a famous writer (François-René de Chateaubriand, 1768–1848) has called vague passions (le vague des passions), sees for the first time a woman who unites all the charms of the ideal person his imagination was dreaming of, and falls desperately in love with her. By a strange anomaly, the beloved image never presents itself to the artist's mind without being associated with a musical idea, in which he recognizes a certain quality of passion, but endowed with the nobility and shyness which he credits to the object of his love.

FIGURE 7.9
Harriet Smithson
Source: George Clint,
Wikimedia Commons.

This melodic image and its model keep haunting him ceaselessly like a double *idée fixe* (a musical and a psychological obsession). This explains the constant recurrence in all the movements of the symphony of this melody, which launches the first allegro. The transitions from this state of dreamy melancholy, interrupted by occasional upsurges of aimless joy, to delirious passion, with its outbursts of fury and jealousy, its returns of tenderness, its tears, its religious consolations—all this forms the subject of the first movement.

Listen to the first 5:30 of Mvt. I, until the second theme is introduced, following this timed listening guide, which indicates the link between musical gestures and the composer's program.

LISTENING GUIDE 7.2

TIME	PART	SECTION	DESCRIPTION
0:00	Slow Introduction	Section 1	The opening is very quiet.
1:38		Section 2	A very fast melody enters and the music continues with a long crescendo followed by rising and falling melodies, pauses, and sudden changes in dynamics, all reminiscent of Beethoven's dramatic style.
4:53	Allegro in quasi sonata form Exposition	Theme 1	A long melody with long phrases, each higher than the first. This is the *idée fixe*, whose rising pitches suggest increasing yearning for the beloved.
5:30		Theme 2	New melodic ideas and thicker textures are introduced.

The second movement, "A Ball," is a waltz, a popular triple-meter couple dance during the nineteenth century. Two sprightly melodies convey a carefree scene, but then the third melody, the *idée fixe*, enters quietly in the flute and oboe. They are accompanied by the strings playing motives from the waltz theme to suggest that his obsession with his beloved cannot be erased even on such a lighthearted occasion. The third movement, "Scene in the Countryside," uses the oboe and English horn, long symbols of the outdoors in European orchestral music, to evoke a peaceful pastoral scene. The *idée fixe* returns even in a setting where the artist has sought relief from his obsession.

Mvt. IV. Marche au Supplice (March to the Scaffold) (Allegretto Non Troppo)

Convinced that his love is unappreciated, the artist poisons himself with opium. The dose of the narcotic, too weak to kill him, plunges him into a sleep accompanied by the most horrible visions. He dreams that he has killed his beloved, that he is condemned and led to the scaffold, and that he is witnessing his own execution. The procession moves forward to the sound of a march that is now somber and fierce, now brilliant and solemn, in which the muffled noise of heavy steps gives way without transition to the noisiest clamor. At the end of the march the first four measures of the idée fixe *reappear, like a last thought of love interrupted by the fatal blow.*

Listen to the entire fourth movement following this timed listening guide.

LISTENING GUIDE 7.3

TIME	SECTION	DESCRIPTION
0:05	Introduction	Timpani open the movement, with punctuations in the low strings and muted horns.
0:31	A	The low strings leap up an octave and then play a descending stepwise minor-scale melody over nearly two octaves to create a musical picture of the composer's descent into hell and his slow steps to the gallows.
0:44	A'	The violas join the cellos and basses for a repeat of the theme, accompanied by a countermelody in four unison bassoons.
0:57	A''	The violins take the theme, now in major, while the lower strings play a countermelody of their own.
1:09	A'''	This treatment of the melody repeats.
1:21	A''''	Accompanied by the bassoon countermelody, the low strings play the descending theme in its original form, while the upper strings play it in inversion, that is, ascending. All the strings play pizzicato (plucking rather than bowing the strings).
1:41	BB	The brasses, including the very low tuba, erupt with a syncopated marching tune in major, representing the triumph of justice for the artist's imagined evil deed. The section ends on a dissonant chord, suggesting the composer's disturbed emotional state.
2:05	Repeats from the beginning	
4:08	A	The A theme returns, this time with each note of the melody (or small groups of notes) assigned to a different group of instruments—including the bass drum and cymbals! This technique is called "tone color melody." Its use here is one of the earliest examples in orchestral music.
4:19	BB	The marching tune returns, slightly re-orchestrated in the winds, and with an active accompaniment in the strings.
4:50	A	Berlioz repeats the tone color melody, but continues on with a driving statement of the A theme in the brass. The theme continues, gradually rising in both pitch and tension.
6:12	C	Just as the movement seems about to end, the orchestra abruptly stops as the clarinet sounds the *idée fixe*, the artist's final thought. It is interrupted by a loud attack from the full orchestra, representing the fall of the guillotine, followed by descending pizzicato pitches that depict the bouncing of the artist's severed head after its fall. The movement ends with triumphant chords signaling the delivery of justice and relief from the nightmare.
6:39	End	

The fifth movement, called "Dreams of a Witch's Sabbath," is full of unusual timbral and expressive effects that place the artist in a hell full "of a frightful troop of ghosts, sorcerers, monsters of every kind, come together for his funeral." The *idée fixe* is heard one final time, this time played by a clarinet in a high-pitched manner with glissandos that seems to mock the artist and his obsession.

What Is Its History?

CULTURAL
LINKAGES

Berlioz was born near the southeastern French town of Grenoble to a well-educated doctor. At twelve—relatively late in life for a future composer—he began studying guitar, but he never learned to play piano or violin, the standard tools of most composers. The orchestra became his instrument. Sent by his father to study medicine in Paris but repulsed by the dissection table, he soon abandoned his medical studies in favor of long hours studying musical scores in the library of the Paris Conservatoire. Largely self-taught in counterpoint, he began private study of composition and was admitted to the conservatory in 1826 at the age of twenty-three. In 1828 he first heard Beethoven's symphonies, whose expressive range he expanded in his *Symphonie Fantastique*. In his memoirs he wrote, "I saw the giant form of Beethoven rear up. The shock was almost as great as that of Shakespeare had been. Beethoven opened before me a new world of music, as Shakespeare had revealed a new universe of poetry."

In 1830, as a revolution broke out that deposed the French king (the monarchy had been restored after Napoleon's demise in 1815), he won the conservatory's prestigious composition prize, the Prix de Rome, which gave him a five-year stipend and the opportunity to study in Italy for two years. In 1833 Harriet Smithson finally agreed to marry him. They had a son the next year, but the marriage did not fulfill his Romantic dreams. They separated after a few years, but he continued to provide for her until she died in 1854.

Berlioz supported himself by organizing concerts of his works, much as Mozart and Beethoven had. But because he desired such large performing forces, these efforts were expensive and exhausting. To earn money, he turned to writing musical criticism and to conducting. He was very good at both. He traveled around Europe, to England, Germany, and Russia, conducting his own work and those of others to great acclaim. Today he is regarded as one of the first star orchestral conductors. Although he enjoyed successes in Paris and around Europe, he seems to have felt underappreciated by the French public. Illness brought his composing to a halt in 1862, and he died, embittered, in 1869.

AESTHETICS

FIGURE 7.10

"Cajetan," a caricature by Anton Elfinger lampooning Berlioz's grandiose effects and noisy instrumentation. Its title: "Fortunately the hall is solid . . . it can stand the strain!"

Source: Wikimedia Commons.

Composers outside France greatly admired Berlioz's compositions for the depth of their emotional expression and their innovative treatment of the orchestra. The Hungarian Franz Liszt (1811–1886), the German Richard Wagner (1813–1883), and Russians Pyotr Ilyich Tchaikovsky (1840–1893) and Nikolai Rimsky-Korsakov (1844–1908) all heard him conduct his works in concert. They carried his Romantic ideas and orchestral techniques into the second half of the nineteenth century. Liszt, for example, composed more than a dozen one-movement orchestral pieces called **symphonic poems** or **tone poems**, instrumental compositions that express emotions and tell stories. These in turn inspired a generation of late nineteenth-century composers to write similar one-movement programmatic tone poems.

In 1844 Berlioz, having created all manner of new orchestral sounds in his compositions, published his *Grand traité d'instrumentation et d'orchestration modernes* (General Treatise on Instrumentation and Modern Orchestration), an influential book on **orchestration**, the art of composing for orchestral instruments singly and in combination. Composers studied it for decades. Like his compositions, the book contributed mightily to the flowering of orchestral tone color in the late nineteenth century.

Until the first half of the nineteenth century, orchestras as permanent performing organizations existed mainly in commercial opera houses and the courts of wealthy aristocrats. Beethoven and Berlioz had to draw on those resources and freelance musicians to produce public concerts of their orchestral music. The collapse of aristocratic patronage and the growing interest in instrumental music for orchestra during the first half of the nineteenth century led wealthy citizens in many cities in Europe and the United States to form civic organizations to support orchestras dedicated to instrumental music. The Philharmonic Society of London, formed in 1813, commissioned Beethoven's Ninth Symphony, which premiered in 1824. They also invited the German composer Felix Mendelssohn (1809–1847) to visit many times. He wrote his Scottish Symphony and Hebrides Overture for performances there. The Vienna and New York Philharmonic Orchestras were created in 1842. Today many orchestras in the United States carry the name "civic" to indicate their origins as organizations founded and supported by a city's community leaders.

Conservatories of music were another new source of patronage for orchestral music. The first was the Paris Conservatoire, founded in 1795 in the wake of

ECONOMIC ACTIVITY

FIGURE 7.11
An unhappy Hector Berlioz in 1863 at age sixty. Photograph by Pierre Petit (1832–1909).
Source: Bibliothèque national de France, Wikimedia Commons.

the French Revolution. The Vienna Conservatory was founded in 1819 and England's Royal Academy of Music in 1822. In 1828 The Concert Society of the Paris Conservatory was founded to support performances of symphonies by Beethoven, Mozart, and Haydn. Conservatories spread widely in the second half of the nineteenth century, and in the 1860s conservatories were established in St. Petersburg and Moscow, as well as the first in the United States at Oberlin College in 1865.

WHERE DO I GO FROM HERE?

- Find a program for, and listen to a recording of, Modest Mussorgsky's (1839–1881) *Night on Bald Mountain* (1867), a tone poem.
- Find a program for, and listen to a recording of, Nikolai Rimsky-Korsakov's (1844–1908) *Scheherazade* (1888), a four-movement programmatic orchestral suite.
- Find a program for, and listen to a recording of, Richard Strauss's (1864–1949) *Till Eulenspiegel's Merry Pranks* (1895), a tone poem.

GATEWAY 26
ROMANTIC-PERIOD PIANO MUSIC

What Is It?

The **piano** is a stringed zither on which eighty-eight keys are attached to hammers, which strike the strings. It is a successor to the harpsichord, on which plectra attached to the keys pluck the strings. Invented around 1700, it largely had replaced the harpsichord by the end of the eighteenth century. An early version of the piano, called fortepiano, was the preferred keyboard instrument of Mozart and Beethoven, both of whom wrote solo concertos and sonatas for it and were concertizing virtuoso performers on it. Our gateway to Romantic piano music of the early nineteenth century is Frédéric Chopin's (1810–1849) Waltz in C-sharp Minor, Op. 64, No. 2 composed in 1847. Born in Poland, Chopin lived his adult life in Paris. A **waltz** is a ballroom dance for couples in triple meter. This waltz is performed by Artur Rubinstein (1887–1982), who, like Chopin, was born in Poland. He was one of the most famous pianists of the mid-twentieth century.

Listen to the first thirty seconds of the recording.

How Does It Work?

Timbre

A solo modern grand piano, with its relatively pure tone quality, plays throughout.

Texture

The texture consists of a high-pitched melody accompanied by alternating bass tone and chords.

FIGURE 7.12
This photograph of Frédéric Chopin in 1849, the year of his death, by Louis-Auguste Bisson (1814–1876) may be the oldest photograph, using a technology called daguerreotype, of a European composer
Source: Music-Images/Alamy Stock Photo.

Rhythm

The meter is triple. Artur Rubinstein plays some sections with a steady beat and some with **rubato** ("robbed time" in Italian), that is, a slight lengthening of certain beats and a slight shortening of others. In this performance the second of the three beats is sometimes slightly held and the third beat is sometimes slightly rushed. The melodic rhythms are quite varied: one melody uses long and short tones; another is pulsatile; and a third features syncopation.

Melody

The melodies consist of long, undulating phrases in minor and major keys with some chromaticism.

Harmony

The harmony is tonal with two sections in a minor key and one in a major key.

Form

The form is a version of European dance form: AABBCCBBAABB.

Performance Techniques

Rubinstein uses rubato in some sections but not others, and occasionally employs **accelerandos** (speeding up the tempo) and ritardandos or ritards (slowing down the tempo). The playing is legato throughout.

Listen to the first thirty seconds of this recording for the triple meter played with rubato. Listen to the entire recording following this timed listening guide.

TIME	FORM	DESCRIPTION
0:00	AA	The first melody features ascending leaps and descending scalar passages. Rubinstein plays the waltz meter relatively slowly. The triple meter is clear from the alternation of bass note and chords (bass—chord—chord), but the beat is not steady. He plays it with rubato.
0:46	BB	A new pulsatile melody alternating arpeggios with chromatic scales is introduced at a faster tempo with no rubato. The beat is steady. At the end of this section, Rubinstein slows the tempo, that is, he plays a ritardando or ritard, to signal the end of the section.
1:14	CC	A third melody is introduced at a slower tempo than the second section. The melody, which contains many tiny subdivisions of the beat, is syncopated against the triple meter in the left hand. Quite often an accented melody tone occurs on the third, weak beat of the triple-meter pattern. Try counting the 1-2-3 meter performed with rubato and hearing the accented note from time to time on beat 3.

TIME	FORM	DESCRIPTION
1:54	BB	
2:18	AA	
3:06	BB	Rubinstein starts through the second (B) melody at a slower tempo than he did previous times and employs accelerando to speed up and then ends the performance with a ritard to a very high pitch.
3:40	End	

What Does It Mean?

Chopin, who arrived in Paris from Poland in 1831, the year after the premiere of Berlioz's *Symphonie Fantastique*, was in some sense Berlioz's opposite. Whereas Berlioz did not play the piano and wrote lengthy works for large orchestras, Chopin, a virtuoso child prodigy on the piano in the mold of Mozart and Beethoven, wrote exclusively for the piano in very short forms,

<AESTHETICS

some pieces less than a minute long. Like Mozart and Beethoven, he used his piano compositions to show off his prodigious keyboard skills. But unlike them, he felt out of his element in public concerts and composed only two piano concertos, one set of variations for piano and orchestra, and three piano sonatas. He preferred the intimate atmosphere of Parisian salons, gatherings of the wealthy elite of Paris for performances and discussions of the arts and politics. For these occasions, he composed dozens of very short, single-movement works.

One of the meanings Chopin's listeners might have attributed to such salon performances was indebted to the Romantic theory that the performer, in this case also the composer, was expressing his inner feelings in the music. In the Romantic atmosphere of the time, his performances, filled with fluctuating tempos, rubato, and melodic twists and turns both sweeping and subtle, may have been interpreted as the sensitive expressions of Chopin's inner life, including the suffering of a refugee from wars in Poland, nostalgia for his homeland, and perhaps more intimate desires. Young women were reported to have been so overcome with emotion while hearing him play that they fainted.

FIGURE 7.13

Nine positions of the waltz from Thomas Wilson's *Correct Method of German and French Waltzing* (1816)

Source: Wikimedia Commons.

<EMOTIONAL
RESONANCE

FIGURE 7.14

Frédéric Chopin playing for the Radziwiłłs, an aristocratic Polish family, at a Berlin house party in 1829. Painting by Henryk Siemiradzki, 1887.

CULTURAL
LINKAGES

Chopin eschewed sonata form in favor of a multitude of solo piano genres, some of them in dance meters (waltzes and Polish *mazurka*s and *polonaise*s); some suggesting a mood (ballades, nocturnes, impromptus, scherzos); and some implying abstract musical content (études, preludes). Each of these genres had its own associated meanings. The waltz, for example, has its roots in the Austrian countryside. By the early nineteenth century it had replaced the courtly minuet as the most fashionable ballroom dance among the upper classes of Europe. Young people were drawn to it because it was faster than the staid minuet. They could dance facing one another, their arms around one another's shoulders and waists, while spinning rapidly around the dance floor. Dancing face to face, as opposed to holding hands side by side as in the minuet and other Baroque dances, shocked the sensibilities of the older generation, even though one dance tutor published in 1816 shows dancers at arm's length in rather dignified poses. In the same year the *Times of London* described an aristocratic ball with a rather less modest dancing style, apparently not at arm's length but with bodies "compressed":

> We remarked with pain that the indecent foreign dance called the Waltz was introduced (we believe for the first time) at the English court on Friday last . . . it is quite sufficient to cast one's eyes on the voluptuous intertwining of the limbs and close compressure on the bodies in their dance, to see that it is indeed far from the modest reserve which has hitherto been considered distinctive of English females. So long as this obscene display was confined to prostitutes and adulteresses, we did not think it deserving of notice; but now that it is attempted to be forced on the respectable classes of society by the civil examples of their superiors, we feel it our duty to warn every parent against exposing his daughter to so fatal a contagion.

Chopin composed more than a dozen waltzes, but they were not intended to accompany dances. He played them in the salons of Paris high society, where he was a fixture at their soirées. If he had played his waltzes for dancers, he would have had to maintain the beat very strictly. But Chopin's waltzes were meant for listeners not dancers, and so Rubinstein, following Chopin, uses contrasting tempos, accelerando and ritardando, rubato, and syncopation to evoke the sentimental possibilities in what otherwise is a dance genre.

What Is Its History?

TECHNOLOGY

The invention of the piano, with its hammering rather than plucking mechanism, was the work of Bartolomeo Cristofori (1655–1731). Born near Venice in the same region where the violin was perfected, he was hired in 1688 by the wealthy Medici family in Florence to care for its large collection of musical instruments. In their workshops he made important contributions to harpsichord design before creating what he called his fortepiano, "which makes soft and loud [sounds]," in 1700. It drew relatively little interest until it entered public performance around 1760, just in time for Mozart, who made it his favorite instrument. Mozart's fortepianos had about five octaves of keys with the hammers striking two strings tuned in unison. During Beethoven's life the sustaining power of the piano's tones was improved considerably and its range extended to six and then seven octaves. In 1843 the Chickering & Mackays company of Boston patented a piano with an iron frame, which supported thicker and tenser strings and thus a richer and more sustained sound. The modern grand piano was born. During the 1860s a German immigrant to New York founded the Steinway & Sons piano company, which today accounts for a huge percentage of fine piano sales.

SOCIAL
BEHAVIOR

Chopin was born Fryderyk Franciszek Chopin in a small town west of Warsaw, Poland. He spent his youth in Warsaw studying music. His father, a French émigré, played flute and violin and tutored the children of local nobles in French. His Polish mother played and taught piano. He gave his first public concert and composed his first piece, a Polish dance called *polonaise*, at age seven. During his teenage years he studied piano, composition, and counterpoint at the Warsaw music conservatory, founded in 1810 and now named in his honor *Uniwersytet Muzyczny*

Fryderyka Chopina. His teachers proclaimed him a genius. In 1829, after attending a concert in Warsaw by the most famous violin virtuoso of the day, Niccolò Paganini (1782–1840), Chopin dedicated a set of piano variations titled *Souvenirs de Paganini* to him. Paganini's 24 Caprices for Solo Violin, Op. 1, a set of short studies exploring the technical demands of the violin, inspired Chopin to begin composing a similar set of twenty-four études for the piano, Op. 10 (12 études) and Op. 25 (12 études) between 1829 and 1836.

After graduating from the Warsaw conservatory in 1829, he spent the next two years traveling around Europe giving concerts that included his only works for piano and orchestra: a set of variations on the theme of the *duettino* "Là ci darem la mano" from Mozart's *Don Giovanni* (mentioned in Chapter 6, Gateway 21) and two piano concertos. While traveling abroad in 1831, Chopin learned that an uprising to depose Tsar Nicholas I of Russia as king of Poland had failed. Warsaw had been reduced to a military outpost of the Russian Empire. Chopin decided to remain with other members of the Polish upper classes in exile in Paris, where he lived for the rest of his life.

By the time Chopin arrived in Paris at the age of twenty-one, he had learned that performing concertos and sonatas before large audiences in concert halls was not for him. He was physically slight and had been a sickly child, and his delicate piano style did not seem suitable for those large venues and genres. He preferred the intimate surroundings of evening parties in the homes of the wealthy, where he often improvised new work. Among his first patrons was Jakob Mayer Rothschild, one of five brothers with banks in Paris, London, Frankfurt, Vienna, and Naples. The family had accumulated the largest fortune in history to that point. Chopin, grateful for Rothschild's early and continued patronage, dedicated his Waltz in C-sharp Minor, Op. 64, No. 2 to Rothschild's daughter Charlotte. Other than these small events, he gave very few public concerts, and, when he did, they were often in the small recital hall of the Pleyel piano company, which supplied his pianos. Otherwise, he supported himself by giving piano lessons to the children of the wealthy and with royalties from his published works.

> ECONOMIC ACTIVITY

His nostalgia for Poland was given voice in compositions in two Polish dance rhythms. The *polonaise* is a dance in a slow triple meter with sharp staccato rhythms. Chopin wrote ten of these. The *mazurka* is a dance in a fast triple meter, and he wrote more than forty of these. In 1836 Chopin's contemporary, the important German composer and music critic Robert Schumann (1810–1856), wrote about Chopin's *mazurka*s in a manner recalling Confucius's and Plato's beliefs in the power of music:

> EMOTIONAL RESONANCE

> If the mighty autocrat in the north [Tsar Nicholas I of Russia and Poland's nemesis] could know that in Chopin's works, in the simple strains of his *mazurka*s, there lurks a dangerous enemy, he would place a ban on his music. Chopin's works are cannon buried in flowers!

Like the waltz, the *mazurka* spread across Europe and to the Americas. Today in Sweden, the folk dance genre *polska* (Polish dance) is based on the meter and rhythm of the *mazurka*.

Chopin wrote in many other genres as well. Among them are a set of twenty-four miniature preludes in each of the twelve major and minor keys, an homage to J. S. Bach's *Well-tempered Clavier*, which he admired (Chapter 5, Gateway 18). He also composed some twenty **nocturnes** (evening serenades). The invention of the genre called "nocturne" is credited to John Field (c. 1782–1837), a composer born in Ireland but active in Russia later in his life. Unlike the generally cheery dance pieces, nocturnes evoke sad moods of lonely nights and a sense of foreboding in the face of unconquerable natural forces, ideas pervading early nineteenth-century Romanticism. Field's eighteen nocturnes feature slow-tempo, song-like melodies played with rubato in the right hand over arpeggiated chords in the left hand but with none of the technical brilliance Chopin would bring to them. Field used the sustain pedal on the newly resonant piano to allow the tones to ring without being dampened. These techniques combine to create icons of watery, dream-like experiences and a rather somber mood popular in the early nineteenth century. His nocturnes influenced similar ones by many more famous composers of the nineteenth century, including Chopin.

FIGURE 7.15
**Frédéric Chopin in 1836. Watercolor by
Maria Wodzińska (1819–1896).**
Source: National Museum, Warsaw, Wikimedia
Commons.

Chopin's health, weak since childhood, grew worse after 1842. His compositional productivity diminished though he occasionally rallied to perform. In February 1848 he gave his last concert in Paris. Later in the year, during a visit to England, he played for Queen Victoria and her consort, Prince Albert. At his last concert, in London in November 1848, he reportedly weighed less than 100 pounds. A year later, some 3000 people from all over Europe attended his funeral in Paris.

During his lifetime, Chopin met and knew personally many of the leading figures of European music, including Hector Berlioz, who was seven years his senior. Most were men famous at the time and part of the canon of "great composers" today. Two were women: brilliant musicians whose possibilities for inclusion in the canon were limited by their gender. Among the men was Franz Liszt (1811–1896). He and Chopin lived near one another and were close friends during the 1830s. Liszt was a more flamboyant personality than Chopin, and he, unlike Chopin, concertized widely throughout Europe for many years. During his theatrical performances he embellished the compositions he was performing, including Chopin's, with ornaments and new chords. His concerts created a sensation, especially among young women, and made him, in twenty-first-century terms, a rock star. Liszt's piano compositions were partly inspired by Chopin's and are even more virtuosic.

Before Chopin left Warsaw he met another young contemporary, also a child prodigy, Felix Mendelssohn (1809–1847), in Berlin. The child of a wealthy Jewish family that had converted to Christianity, Mendelssohn's piano miniatures, a set of forty-eight *Songs without Words* written from 1832 to 1845, are much admired today. Unlike Chopin, Mendelssohn composed in all the major genres of the day, including five symphonies, concertos for piano and for violin, string quartets, oratorios, cantatas, and one opera. His most famous work is probably an orchestral overture and suite of pieces composed as incidental music for a production of Shakespeare's *Midsummer Night's Dream*. The most famous of them is the ubiquitous "Wedding March."

Felix's older sister Fanny Mendelssohn (1805–1847) was also a prodigious, if less well-known, musical talent. She composed more than 600 pieces, most of them songs and short piano pieces, many with associated poems. One impressive collection, called *Das Jahr* (The Year), is a set of twelve pieces, each named for a month of the year. Because of prevailing views of women's roles in those days, her family tolerated but did not encourage her composing. Her father wrote to her in 1820, when she was just fifteen and Felix was eleven, "Music will perhaps become his [Felix's] profession, while for you it can and must be only an ornament." Because of the limitations placed on her as a woman composer, she wrote only one orchestral work, an overture, and only began publishing her works in 1846, the year before her death. Her reputation as a composer languished until recently, when modern scholars and performers have discovered and championed her work.

Robert Schumann (1810–1856) was yet another famous pianist/composer and Chopin contemporary. Born in Germany to a father who was a writer and publisher, Schumann was enthralled both with literature and writing and with playing and composing music. His teacher, Friedrich Wieck (1785–1873) of Leipzig, believed he could become the greatest pianist of the age.

During his twenties, from 1830 to 1838, he composed only piano works, including programmatic suites of short pieces with evocative titles like *Papillons* (Butterflies), *Carnaval*, *Kinderszenen* (Children's Scenes), *Novelletten* (Novellas), and *Nachtstücke* (Night Pieces). In 1834 he indulged his literary side by creating a musical magazine, *Neue Zeitschrift für Musik* (New Journal for Music), in which he joined Berlioz to become one of the most important music critics of the day. A generous soul, in an 1836 essay, he declared Chopin a genius. When an injury to his left hand ended his performing ambitions, he turned in 1839 and 1840 to composing songs, and in 1841 he composed the first of four symphonies. In 1852 he wrote the last work published during his lifetime—like Mozart, a Requiem mass. In 1854, after suffering mental health problems for years, he attempted to take his own life, after which he asked to be committed to an insane asylum, where he died in 1856 at the age of forty-six.

While Schumann was studying with Friedrich Wieck, he fell in love with his teacher's daughter, Clara Wieck (1819–1896). A piano prodigy, she started touring Europe with her father in 1830 at the age of eleven. Even the redoubtable Paganini was taken with her virtuosity, and Liszt and Chopin praised her performances. Robert and Clara married in 1840 over the strenuous objections of her father. They had eight children, yet through it all, as Clara Schumann, she continued her career as one of the most celebrated piano virtuosos of the nineteenth century, performing more than 2000 concerts in a sixty-year career that ended in 1891. In her concerts, she championed the work of her husband and played compositions by Bach, Beethoven, Mozart, Chopin, and others. In that way she was a model for a new kind of piano virtuoso, not the composer/performer but one who was principally a vessel for the faithful performance of other composers' works. But because it was still expected of soloists that they would play some of their own works for solo piano in concert, something not expected of modern pianists, Clara composed many solo piano pieces, including, in 1853, *Variations on a Theme by Robert Schumann*. Today she is recognized, along with Fanny Mendelssohn, as an important composer of the nineteenth century.

WHERE DO I GO FROM HERE?

- Listen to these short piano pieces by Frédéric Chopin: Nocturne No. 8 in D-flat Major, Op. 27, No. 2; Mazurka No. 5 in B-flat Major, Op. 7, No. 1; and Polonaise No. 3 in A Major, Op. 40, No. 1 ("Military").
- Listen to Franz Liszt's *Grande études de Paganini*, S141: No. 3 in G-sharp Minor ("La Campanella," The Little Bell) and compare its style to an étude by Chopin.
- Listen to Fanny Mendelssohn's *Das Jahr*: No. 2. February.
- Listen to Clara Schumann's *Variations on a Theme by Robert Schumann*.

GATEWAY 27
EARLY AMERICAN POPULAR MUSIC

What Is It?

Enslaved Africans brought the concept of the banjo to North America during the seventeenth century and re-created it there. During the early nineteenth century the banjo became a ubiquitous presence in American popular culture when white musicians adopted it for use in minstrel shows, where they parodied the music, behavior, and speech of the enslaved population. The modern **banjo** is a fretted, long-necked plucked lute with four strings running the length of the neck and a fifth, shorter string running halfway up the neck. The resonator consists of a circular hoop with a membrane of animal skin or plastic stretched over it.

FIGURE 7.16
Rhiannon Giddens plays the fretless banjo
Source: Wikimedia Commons.

Our gateway to American music of the early nineteenth century is a modern song that evokes, and opens a door to, this era of American music. Singer/songwriter and multi-instrumentalist Rhiannon Giddens (b. 1977) composed and sang the song, titled "Julie," on her 2017 album *Freedom Highway*. In this recording she also plays the banjo and is accompanied by fiddle and bass. Giddens composed "Julie" using the old-time style of rural Appalachian music in an old European genre called the **ballad**, a short song that tells a story. In this recording Giddens plays a fretless banjo, an older construction style from the nineteenth century. Giddens composed "Julie" after reading Andrew Ward's 2008 book, *The Slaves' War: The Civil War in the Words of Former Slaves*. The lyrics are cast in the form of a dialogue between Julie, an enslaved servant, and her owner, her "mistress."

 Listen to the first thirty seconds of the recording.

How Does It Work?

Timbre

A relaxed female solo voice sings in her mid-range with the muted sound of the plucked, fretless banjo, fiddle, and bass.

Texture

The texture is heterophonic, as the voice, banjo, and fiddle all perform slightly different versions of the melody. The banjo's short fifth string sounds a syncopated, high-pitched drone, and the bass adds an intermittent, plucked drone tone.

Rhythm

The meter is duple with occasional syncopations as in the short-long-short rhythm on the opening syllables, "Ju-lie oh."

Melody

The melody is based on a pentatonic scale with flat third and flat seventh, the same scale as the Candomblé example in Chapter 6, Gateway 23, sometimes called the minor pentatonic scale. It consists of four phrases each with a slightly different shape.

Harmony

The harmony is drone-like on the pitches of the pentatonic scale.

Form

This is a strophic song with seven strophes. Musicians and listeners today often refer to strophes as **verses**. In "Julie," each verse consists of four lines of poetry and four melodic phrases in the musical form abca. Each verse repeats a textual refrain, either "Julie, oh Julie" or "Mistress, oh mistress." An instrumental introduction precedes the first strophe. A short instrumental interlude based on the first melodic phrase breaks up each exchange between Julie and her mistress. Between each pair of exchanges, Giddens and the fiddle player play the complete verse melody. The performance ends with two instrumental renditions of the tune. The performance increases subtly in intensity as it moves from no bass accompaniment to a bass tone every four beats, then every two beats, then every beat.

Performance Techniques

Slides from pitch to pitch are heard in the singing and in the banjo playing. She plucks the banjo's string using an old technique called clawhammer style, which comes from West Africa.

Listen to the entire performance following this timed listening guide.

LISTENING GUIDE 7.5

TIME	SECTION	DESCRIPTION	SENSE OF THE LYRICS
0:00	Instrumental introduction	The banjo plucks the rhythm, and then the banjo and fiddle play the four-phrase verse melody heterophonically. Just before the verse the bass enters with a long bowed drone on the tonic pitch that continues almost uninterrupted until the beginning of the third verse.	
0:25	Verse 1	The singer enters and sings the first verse accompanied heterophonically by banjo and fiddle.	Julie, oh Julie, see the [Union] soldiers have come to free you.
0:43	Short interlude	The banjo and fiddle play the first (a) phrase of the verse melody.	
0:47	Verse 2	Same as Verse 1	Mistress, oh mistress, I see the soldiers and I am waiting until they come for me.
1:04	Long interlude	The banjo and fiddle play all four phrases (abca) of the verse melody.	
1:25	Verse 3	The bass joins the voice, banjo, and fiddle with a plucked tone every four beats.	Julie, oh Julie, don't leave this house and everything you have ever known.
1:43	Short interlude	The bass becomes slightly more active, almost outlining the melody with its own addition to the heterophony.	
1:46	Verse 4	The bass adds a "pick-up note" before the first beat of each measure.	Mistress, oh mistress, I will leave with what remains of my family.
2:04	Long interlude	The bass plays an ostinato that oscillates between the lower tonic pitch, the fifth, and the tonic an octave higher. This continues through Verse 5.	
2:24	Verse 5		Julie, oh Julie, please tell them the money belongs to you.
2:41	Short interlude		
2:48	Verse 6	The bass plays the pick-up note and main note every two beats, all on the tonic. The singer ends with a decrescendo on a long-held tone and the bass transitions back to playing one tone every four beats.	Mistress, oh mistress, I will not lie, because you got that money by selling my children.
3:14	Verse 7	The singer sings more softly and slowly than before. She ends on a long-held tone and then crescendos on it until the instrumental postlude starts.	Mistress, oh mistress, best wishes but "I'm leavin' hell."
3:47	Postlude	The instruments play the verse melody, this time with bass plucking a drone tone on the tonic on every beat.	
4:04	Postlude	The instruments play a repeat of the verse melody.	
4:22	End		

What Does It Mean?

Beyond the meaning of the lyrics, which capture one of the horrors of slavery, the tearing of children from their parents to be sold for profit, part of the meaning of this song is Rhiannon Giddens's reclaiming of the string band tradition of the Appalachian Mountains as her own. Fiddle and banjo music and the singing of songs in this style were, for most of the twentieth century, associated almost exclusively with those mountains and the rural white musicians who have kept it alive into the present. In this recording Rhiannon Giddens makes the point that enslaved African American musicians contributed to this tradition as soon as they arrived in North America during the seventeenth century. From Africa they brought with them memories of three-stringed, long-necked, fretless plucked lutes with a skin-covered gourd or wooden body. One such instrument, called *ekonting*, is played today by the Jola people of the West African countries of Senegal, The Gambia, and Guinea-Bissau. Each of the *ekonting*'s three strings is a different length.

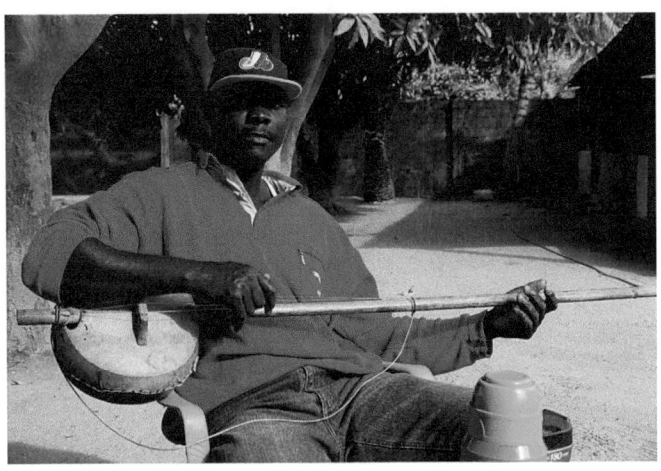

FIGURE 7.17
Musa Diatta plays ekonting in Bijilo, The Gambia
Source: Scott V. Linford.

By the eighteenth century enslaved African Americans had reconstructed a modified fretless version of the *ekonting* in the United States and the Caribbean. Contemporary accounts refer to it as banjer and banjo, which almost surely are African-derived names. The number of strings on these early American gourd banjos varied widely and was eventually standardized at five. Frets were added to the neck in the late 1800s. Giddens's fretless banjo is a nod to the older style of fretless banjo played by enslaved African Americans in the early nineteenth century, and its wooden hoop body is typical of banjos of the late nineteenth century.

The playing style Giddens employs also has its roots in Africa. It is called **clawhammer style**. She curls the four fingers of her right hand into a claw shape and strikes the strings with the fingernail of her index finger in a downward motion. She plucks the short fifth string (and sometimes the other strings) with her thumb. This technique is similar to one observed today among players of the *ekonting*. Her playing technique differs from the modern three-finger picking style most white banjo players use today. This performance gains its meaning in part from the fact that a Black woman is playing the banjo in a style that contrasts with the way many rural white musicians have played it since the 1940s. By doing so, she affirms the multifaceted roots of American rural music in Africa.

Enslaved populations in the United States were also exposed to the violin. They took to the instrument quickly because it was similar to bowed, gourd-bodied lutes in West Africa. On it they played with a raspy timbre favored in African music (Chapter 3, Gateway 9). By the eighteenth century, artwork depicted fiddlers playing at the dances of their white masters. Runaway slave notices mentioned that some of them could play "remarkably well on the violin." Some rural white fiddlers have reported that they learned from Black fiddlers.

The song style and storytelling form of "Julie" are rooted in American versions of old Scottish, Irish, and English songs that European settlers brought with them to the Appalachian Mountains in the eighteenth and early nineteenth centuries. Many of their songs employ pentatonic scales and feature dialogue between characters, usually a man and a woman. In writing "Julie," Giddens adopted these stylistic elements to create a new song that sounds as old as the hills and valleys of Appalachia in a manner that Black and white singers of the region have shared for three centuries.

During the first half of the nineteenth century, the banjo emerged from the Appalachian Mountains and the rural countryside to become the featured instrument of the most popular form of public entertainment in the period, the minstrel show. **Minstrel shows** presented white entertainers, mainly from the north, masked in "blackface" makeup. They imitated and ridiculed both free and enslaved African Americans in ostensibly Black styles of speech, dance, and music: "stump speeches," humorous dialogues, skits about life under slavery on the plantation, step dancing, cakewalking (an exaggerated high-stepping dance), and songs and instrumental tunes on the fiddle and banjo, tambourine, and bones (two pairs of animal bones or wooden sticks held in each hand and rattled together in rhythm). Stereotypical characters in minstrel shows included "Jim Crow," who moved and danced in an exaggerated style and who would eventually give his name to repressive segregationist laws in the South after Reconstruction in the late nineteenth century; "Mammy" or "Auntie," an older woman who raised and loved the children of her mistress; and "Uncle," the elder of a happy enslaved family and friend of his master. The minstrel show is arguably the source of negative stereotypes about African Americans that persist to this day.

A common theme of the songs and skits of minstrel shows was the happy lives of enslaved workers on the plantation, a gross misrepresentation that helped to justify the mandatory return of runaway slaves discovered in northern states under the draconian Fugitive Slave Act of 1850. "Julie," whose lyrics are borrowed from the oral narrative of a freedwoman after the Civil War, reveals the kind of painful experiences that minstrel shows suppressed. Rhiannon Giddens's playing of the banjo restores the instrument's dignity within African American culture after the ignominy it suffered in minstrel shows.

Despite the racist stereotypes they created, minstrel shows launched the careers of many African American performers, who initially were forced to wear blackface makeup so that audiences would believe they were white performers pretending to be Black—a cruel irony. The Rabbit's Foot Company, a minstrel troupe of Black performers founded by a Black entrepreneur, toured in the South during the first half of the twentieth century and launched the careers of Ma Rainey, Bessie Smith, Ida Cox, Brownie McGhee, Big Joe Williams, and other later stars of the classic blues (Chapter 9, Gateway 33).

Minstrel shows also provided a venue for the composition and performance of some of the earliest American popular songs. The most prominent composer of these songs was Stephen Foster (1826–1864). He wrote more than 200 songs, some which achieved anthem-like status: "Oh, Susanna" for the California Gold Rush of 1848; "Old Folks at Home" ("Swanee River," 1851) for the South as a whole; and "My Old Kentucky Home" (1853) for the state of Kentucky in particular. Other well-known songs of his include "Jeannie with the Light Brown Hair" (1854); and "Beautiful Dreamer," published posthumously in 1864. In line with the practices of minstrelsy, some lyrics to his songs included racist epithets for African Americans and parodied African American dialects in the lyrics, as in "Camptown races, sing dis song, do dah do dah." Even though they served to degrade many Americans, his songs were taught in schools throughout the twentieth century, becoming something like American folk songs. Some still are taught with the lyrics stripped of their faux Black dialect and some with only their melodies in elementary school instrumental classes, though their connection to the legacy of minstrelsy continues.

FIGURE 7.18
The cover of a Christy's Minstrels songbook
Source: Boston Public Library, Wikimedia Commons.

FIGURE 7.19
Stephen Foster
Source: Three Lions/Stringer/Getty Images.

The banjo also inspired at least one American composer of classical music during the early nineteenth century. Louis Moreau Gottschalk (1829–1869) was born in New Orleans to a Jewish father and a Creole (the French- and Spanish-speaking communities of Louisiana) mother. He had five half-siblings (the children of his father's mistress) of mixed Black and white descent. From them and from the musical scene in New Orleans he gained an appreciation of African American musical styles and incorporated them into his short, Chopinesque piano character pieces. He toured widely as a piano virtuoso throughout North and South America, often playing his own compositions based on the African American tunes he heard growing up in Louisiana. He was widely admired in Europe as well as in the United States. He gave a sensational concert in Paris in April of 1849, a few months before Chopin died in the same city. At the concert he debuted a composition named "Bamboula: Danse des Nègres," dedicated to an admirer, the Queen of Spain. In 1853 he published another popular showpiece called "The Banjo," which imitates the plucking style and ostinato rhythmic patterns of banjo players.

What Is Its History?

The Appalachian fiddle and banjo tradition was a prominent feature of African American musical life during the eighteenth century. The minstrel show spread the popularity of this tradition among urban white musicians. By the twentieth century, the tradition had become an index of rural white communities in the southeastern United States. Later additions to white rural musical ensembles were plucked zithers, guitar, mandolin, and bass. In 1939 Bill Monroe (1911–1996), a mandolinist from Kentucky, formed a group called the Blue Grass Boys, consisting of mandolin, banjo, fiddle, guitar, and bass and featuring singing in tight three- and four-part vocal harmonies. When other southern groups began to imitate their lineup and sound, a new genre was born, taking its name from the name of Monroe's group: **bluegrass**. Bluegrass added to rural styles a great deal of syncopation, improvisation, and fast tempos—elements borrowed from jazz and popular music. Bluegrass began alongside other styles at the roots of country music (Chapter 11, Gateway 42), but since the 1940s it has had a history of its own that, while always intertwined with country music, has produced its own stars and generated its own audiences.

In 1954 Elvis Presley recorded one of the well-known songs of the Blue Grass Boys, "Blue Moon of Kentucky," as the B side of his first successful 45 rpm recording, an up-tempo rhythm & blues number called "That's All Right" first recorded by Mississippi blues singer Arthur "Big Boy" Crudup (1905–1974). During the 1960s, folk music revivalists, including Bob Dylan, Joan Baez, and Judy Collins, were steeped in the Appalachian song, fiddle, and banjo tradition. Among its most famous regional exponents were Jean Ritchie (1922–2015), a singer and zither player from Kentucky, and Doc Watson (1923–2012),

CULTURAL LINKAGES

FIGURE 7.20
Louis Moreau Gottschalk
Source: Brady-Handy Photograph Collection. Library of Congress, Wikimedia Commons.

FIGURE 7.21
Ben and Lew Snowden of The Snowden Family Band from Clinton, Ohio, playing from the gable of their home. They played professionally from 1850 to 1920.
Source: Ohio Historical Society, Wikimedia Commons.

a blind singer and guitarist from North Carolina. Many singers of commercial country music have roots in this tradition as well (Chapter 11, Gateway 42). Mainly an amateur form of music making today, as it was in its heyday, summer festivals of "string band music" or "ole time (or old-time) music" take place across the country.

Rhiannon Giddens was born in North Carolina and received her bachelor's degree in opera performance from the Oberlin Conservatory, founded in 1865 and the first college and conservatory to welcome Black students. In 2005 she formed the Carolina Chocolate Drops with three other musicians. Their 2010 album *Genuine Negro Jig* won the Grammy for Best Traditional Folk Album. They learned some of their repertoire from Joe Thompson (1918–2012), one of the oldest of the old-time Black fiddlers, who played with his cousin, the banjo player Odell Thompson. In 2015 Giddens released her first full-length solo album, *Tomorrow Is My Turn*. She received a MacArthur "Genius" Fellowship in 2017, the same year she released "Julie" on the album *Freedom Highway*.

One of Giddens's inspirations was Elizabeth Cotten (1893–1987), a Black singer, guitarist, and banjo player born in Chapel Hill, North Carolina. She became famous during the folk music revival of the 1960s, when, in her sixties, folk singers Peggy and Mike Seeger, half siblings of Pete Seeger, discovered her and brought her to public attention. Her most famous song, "Freight Train," was recorded by many artists, including Bob Dylan, Joan Baez, and Peter, Paul, and Mary. Giddens has recorded Cotten's song "Shake Sugaree" in tribute.

The racist imagery of minstrel shows has remained remarkably persistent in American culture to the present. In 1927 the famous Jewish American entertainer Al Jolson (1886–1950) sang in blackface a song called "Mammy" in the first "talking picture," *The Jazz Singer*. From 1928 to 1960 the radio show "Amos 'n' Andy" featured white actors voicing the roles of Black characters in dialogues similar to those of minstrel show characters. Musical films from the 1930s through the 1950s featured historical evocations of minstrel shows, with such famous stars as Fred Astaire, Bing Crosby, and Judy Garland performing in blackface. Two recent TV series, *The Office* and *30 Rock*, included white characters in blackface, ostensibly to critique the continuing presence of blackface in popular entertainment. In 2020, within a month of the killing of George Floyd at the hands of Minneapolis police officers and the subsequent Black Lives Matter protests, one producer apologized for "the pain these have caused," and the blackface episodes of these shows were pulled from streaming services. In a similar vein, the well-known brand images for Aunt Jemima's syrup and Uncle Ben's rice, remnants of minstrel shows' racist stereotypes, were finally "retired."

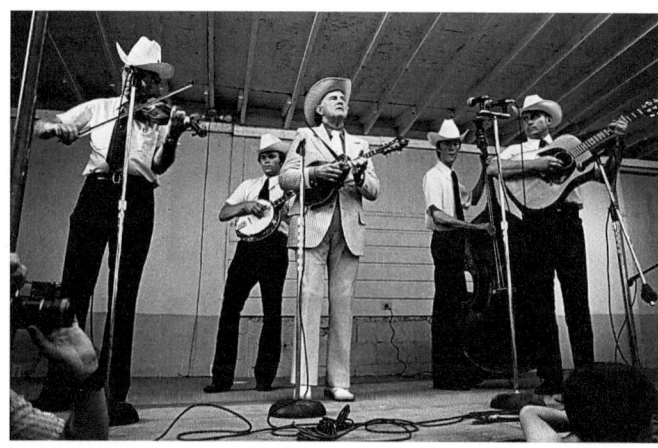

FIGURE 7.22
Bill Monroe and his Blue Grass Boys in 1973
Source: Tom Hill/Contributor/Getty Images.

FIGURE 7.23
Elizabeth Cotten, who plays the guitar left-handed without changing the order of strings, with her guitar "Stella" in 1977
Source: Glasshouse Images/Alamy Stock Photo.

WHERE DO I GO FROM HERE?

- Listen to "Old Corn Liquor" by fiddler Joe Thompson (1918–2012) and banjo player Odell Thompson (1912–1994), cousins who were among the last musicians of their generation to continue Black fiddle and banjo traditions.
- Listen to the Carolina Chocolate Drops' recording of "Snowden's Jig (Genuine Negro Jig)."
- Listen to a recording of "The Banjo" by Louis Moreau Gottschalk. What elements of this piano music convey the sound of a banjo?

CLOSING

Among the principal economic and intellectual factors shaping European music of nineteenth-century Europe and the United States were the Industrial Revolution and a literary and philosophical movement known as Romanticism. Because of this last factor, music historians have commonly referred to the early nineteenth century as the **Romantic period** of European music history. It could, to equally good effect, also be called the Industrial period. In the domain of European classical music today, a number of practices and ideas have their roots in the first half of the nineteenth century:

- The modern piano, with its steel frame and taut strings, starts to take shape.
- The celebration of virtuoso performers and of the musical interpretations of commanding symphony and opera conductors originate in this period.
- The notion that some composers are geniuses and that performers must honor their compositional intentions is also a product of the early nineteenth century.
- The idea that instrumental music could have a narrative thrust and convey a verbal story became a taken-for-granted feature of European classical music.
- In the United States, African American music entered the mainstream of white popular culture for the first time, not in the bodies of Black musicians, singers, and dancers, but in the imaginations of white performers with little but a stereotypical and deeply racist understanding of African American culture. These stereotypes have persisted in popular entertainment and product branding.

THINGS TO THINK ABOUT

- Compare the effects of the Industrial Revolution on each of the worlds of music opened up by the gateways in this chapter.
- Given what you now know about Romanticism, how do those ideas about music compare to your own beliefs about the nature of music and what music is capable of expressing?

NEW TERMS

accelerando	clawhammer style	pizzicato
ballad	*coloratura*	program
banjo	double aria	programmatic music, program music
bel canto	English horn	
bluegrass	glissando	proletariat
bourgeoisie	*idée fixe*	Romanticism, Romantic
cabaletta	Industrial Revolution	rubato
cantabile	minstrel show	symphonic poem
capitalist	nocturne	tone poem
cavatina	orchestration	waltz

MUSIC FROM THE LATE NINETEENTH CENTURY (1850–1890)

DURING THE SECOND HALF of the nineteenth century the Industrial Revolution produced a parade of new inventions that changed the way people lived and communicated, including the sewing machine (1850s), telephone (1876), incandescent light bulb (1879), and, most importantly for music, the phonograph (1877). The Industrial Revolution and the continuing domination in the European political sphere of aristocratic families led to two radical responses. First, the doctrines of socialism and communism, elaborated most famously by the German philosopher and economist Karl Marx (1818–1883), sought solutions to the growing disparity between rich and poor and the degraded conditions of workers (the proletariat) in the new factories of Europe. Second, **ethnic nationalism**, the notion that each European ethnic group had the right to its own nation-state, challenged the imperial regimes of central and eastern Europe: the Russian, Austro-Hungarian, and Ottoman Empires.

The contribution of socialism and communism to nineteenth-century musical life seems to have been limited to a few marching songs for laborers to use in their protests and to the institution of brass bands, which represented labor unions, factories, and both left and right political parties in mass demonstrations (Chapter 9, Gateway 34). The other radical response to the political status quo in Europe, nationalism, was, on the other hand, an important driver of creativity in classical music. At the end of the eighteenth century German writers brought a radical new concept to the idea of the nation. Previously, the revolutions in the United States and France had posited the notion that all those defined as "men" living in a nation had "certain unalienable rights," including the right to govern themselves and to be full-fledged "citizens" of a republic rather than subjects of a king ruling by divine right. In the United States and France, for example, all citizens are meant to have these rights, regardless of their ethnic origins or when they or their families arrived in those countries, though in reality, these rights are typically not enjoyed equally by all. This type of nationalism is today known as **civic nationalism**, "civic" referring to a society and its citizens.

FIGURE 8.1
**South Australia
(Adelaide) Police Band
in 1907**
Source: Wikimedia
Commons.

DOI: 10.4324/9781003269304-11

The German writers of the late eighteenth century rejected citizenship and residency as the basis for political participation and argued instead that each ethnicity (groups that share a language and many cultural practices like music and dance) was a "nationality" with a right to its own nation-state. Under this doctrine an ethnic group becomes a nationality. This philosophy arose in a geopolitical environment in which there were very few nation-states defined by nationality. Many of the nation-states in Europe today (Germany, Italy, Greece, Poland, and so on) did not exist at the beginning of the nineteenth century. Instead, many Europeans lived either in a small duchy, principality, or city-state, or they lived in a large empire that contained many nationalities. The map of Europe around 1815 illustrates this point. Russia was a huge empire that included the present-day countries of Poland, Ukraine, Finland, Latvia, and many others. The Ottoman Empire included present-day Turkey, Greece, Bulgaria, Romania, and others. The Austro-Hungarian Empire included present-day Austria, Hungary, Croatia, Slovakia, the Czech Republic, Ukraine, and the northern part of Italy. Great Britain comprised four "nationalities": the English, Scottish, Welsh, and Irish. Sweden and Norway were governed by a common king, and Iceland was a colony of Denmark. At the other extreme, present-day Germany and Italy were a jumble of small territories. In 1815 only a few countries resembled modern nation-states, among them France, Spain, Portugal, and the Netherlands. Much of the political history of Europe in the nineteenth century can be understood as a battle, led by writers, philosophers, and political activists with the aid of some military men, for the sovereignty of particular nationalities within the boundaries of nation-states. Among these intellectuals were composers and performers, who used instrumental music, plus songs and operas with words in "national languages," to rouse national sentiments and encourage these political movements.

In this chapter the German composer Richard Wagner and the Czech composer Bedřich Smetana represent nationalism in music. Neither Germans nor Czechs lived in nation-states in

FIGURE 8.2
Map of European nations today

FIGURE 8.3
Map of Europe around 1815
Source: Alexander Altenhof, Wikimedia Commons.

1850. During the second half of the nineteenth century, both composers' compositions contributed to the intellectual and artistic agitation for German and Czech national status. Nationalism as part of the spirit of the times also had a life in the United States, as those under the sway of nationalism wondered what form the national music of this relatively new nation would take. When formerly enslaved African Americans from the South began appearing in the North performing classical concerts of "Negro spirituals," the nationalist Czech composer Antonín Dvořák, who lived in the United States for a few years in the 1890s, argued that their music, as well as that of Native Americans, could provide the basis for an American national music.

Early in the nineteenth century, the U.S. government regarded Native societies as nations and entered into treaties with them. During the late nineteenth century, after pushing Native groups off their lands onto reservations and fighting them in a series of wars on the Great Plains, the U.S. government stripped them of their status as sovereign nations; banned performances of religious rituals with drumming, singing, and dancing; and placed children in "Native schools" with the goal of erasing their culture and language. Our gateway to the modern intertribal pow-wow examines the way it keeps Indigenous cultures, values, and community life alive in the wake of these depredations.

Though slavery had been abolished in 1865 in the United States, many African Americans in the following years continued to work as sharecroppers under conditions similar to slavery. Gruesome acts of violence continued as well, and lynchings of African Americans became frequent in the South as a way of intimidating Black communities and promoting the notion of white supremacy. After the Reconstruction Era (1865–1877), white lawmakers began to pass "Jim Crow" laws mostly (but not only) in the American South, the name Jim Crow borrowed from the name of a character type in blackface minstrelsy. For nearly a hundred years, until the passage of the 1964 Civil Rights Act, Jim Crow laws legalized racial segregation in public facilities, relegating African Americans to separate facilities for education, public transportation, and other public spaces such as restaurants, hotels, bathrooms, and drinking fountains. These facilities were inferior and poorly funded in comparison to those for whites, and in many instances they were not available at all. Until the passage of the 1965 Voting Rights Act, Jim Crow laws also suppressed the voting rights of African Americans and disenfranchised Black citizens through poll taxes and literacy tests. In this late nineteenth-century culture of segregation, violence, and oppression, African American spirituals entered the mainstream of American culture. In this chapter we look at their origins under slavery and their legacy in this period and beyond.

GATEWAY 28
LATE NINETEENTH-CENTURY OPERA

What Is It?

Since its invention around 1600, opera in the Italian language, even when composed by an Austrian like Mozart or a German like Handel, had been the most popular musical genre in Europe. Even Beethoven, whose creations were in an entirely different style and spirit, is said to have admired the operas of his younger contemporary Gioachino Rossini, the most popular opera composer of the early nineteenth century (Chapter 7, Gateway 24). During the second half of the nineteenth century German composer Richard Wagner (1813–1883) reacted strongly against Italian opera. He believed that the emphasis on virtuosic arias and the contrast between recitative and aria broke up the dramatic flow to deleterious effect. Writing in a more flowing style that obliterated the distinction between recitative and aria, he wrote his librettos in German and ceased to call his creations operas. He called his works **music dramas**. Today some critics consider them among the most important artistic creations, not just musical creations, of the late nineteenth century.

Our gateway to Wagner's music dramas and late nineteenth-century Italian opera is the orchestral Prelude and final aria, *Liebestod*, from his music drama titled *Tristan und Isolde*, composed between 1857 and 1859. Unlike most opera composers, who relied on librettists for the story and lyrics, Wagner wrote both the libretto and the music for his music dramas. The story of Tristan and Isolde originates in twelfth-century Medieval **romances**, written stories about mythical and legendary figures and the source of the term "Romanticism." The most famous in English are the stories of King Arthur, Sir Lancelot, and Guinevere and the Knights of the Round Table. Wagner knew the story of Tristan and Isolde through its retelling by German poet Gottfried von Strassburg (d. *c.* 1210).

Isolde was an Irish princess engaged to be married, but Tristan, a young knight from Cornwall on the southwest coast of England, killed her lover in battle. In act I Tristan travels to Ireland to convince Isolde to marry his uncle, King Marke of Cornwall. On the sail from Ireland to Cornwall, Isolde, a master of magic potions, tries to poison Tristan to avenge his killing of her fiancé and attempts to take her own life with the poison as well. Her handmaid, realizing her intent, substitutes Isolde's love potion for the poison, and Tristan and Isolde fall madly in love. In act II, while King Marke leads an evening hunting party, Tristan sings to Isolde that their passion can flourish only at night (remember the nocturne), not in the light of day and of reason and responsibility, which they are flouting under the potion's spell. Upon his return King Marke discovers Tristan's betrayal of their friendship, and one of his

FIGURE 8.4
Richard Wagner composing at the piano, 1843
Source: AF Archive/Alamy Stock Photo.

knights mortally wounds Tristan. In act III Tristan has been taken to Brittany in northern France to die, but he longs for Isolde to arrive and comfort him. She does, just in time. He dies in her arms. She faints and, after awakening, sings this final aria recounting her vision of the two of them in the other world, a transfiguration that will, through death, allow their love to live forever.

How Does It Work?

Timbre

Wagner required a very large orchestra and then wrote for its entire range from very low to very high pitches. Flutes and horns are prominent.

Texture

The texture is a wash of chords in the background with melodies emerging out of the mass of sound. Sometimes orchestral and vocal melodies sound in counterpoint.

Rhythm

The melodic rhythms often consist of very long notes, so the tempo seems slow, an expression of languorous, deep emotion. If the duration of the entire work is considered an aspect of rhythm, then *Tristan und Isolde* is very long by operatic standards, running to nearly four hours compared to the more usual three.

Melody

The Prelude, like Classical-period sonata form, has two recurring themes. Wagner called such recurring themes **Leitmotifs** (guiding or leading motives). Unlike a Classical-period symphony, the *Leitmotifs* of the Prelude do not represent contrasts between strong (possibly masculine) and weak (possibly feminine) themes. Rather, both have similar yearning qualities, the first created by chromaticism and the second through a sequence of rising pitches. If they represent the yearning of Tristan and Isolde, then that yearning is not gendered. The *Liebestod* aria also has two *Leitmotifs*, the first one referred to as the "*Liebestod* [Love-Death] *Leitmotif*" and the second one the "bliss *Leitmotif*" in the timed listening guide.

Harmony

The harmony is tonal but highly chromatic, moving continuously through many keys and thus sounding rather unstable, as if expressing shifting emotions. Occasional dominant seventh chords suggest an imminent release of tension to the tonic chord, a characteristic of tonal music. But Wagner avoids their resolution throughout the opera until the very end, maintaining their tension and creating a sense of yearning through what he called "endless melody."

Form

The form of both the Prelude and *Liebestod* aria features frequent repeats and returns of the *Leitmotifs*, but not in a predictable or regular pattern.

Performance Techniques

Frequent crescendos and decrescendos of varying length are the most striking performance techniques. In the *Liebestod* aria, the orchestra, at certain points, becomes so loud that it is no longer simply an accompaniment to the voice. It becomes something like a character in the drama and almost drowns out the singer.

What Does It Mean?

As in Berlioz's *Symphonie Fantastique*, how this opera works and what it means are inextricably interwoven. The Prelude has an implicit program or meaning as it anticipates the love story of the opera: the uncontrollable amorous yearning of Tristan and Isolde for one another.

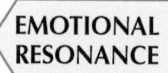

EMOTIONAL
RESONANCE

Timed Listening Guide: Prelude

Listen to the entire recording of the Prelude following this timed listening guide. It is performed by the Vienna Philharmonic conducted by Georg Solti.

LISTENING GUIDE 8.1

TIME	DESCRIPTION
0:00	The cellos open quietly in unison on a melodic motive designed to create a sense of unfulfilled yearning: an upward leap followed by a chromatic descent and chromatic ascent. The woodwinds enter on the fourth tone with a chord not belonging to traditional tonal harmony. It is made up a perfect fourth (D#–G#) and an augmented fourth (F–B) and has been called "the Tristan chord." The phrase ends, unresolved, on a dominant seventh chord and is followed by a long pause.
0:28	The phrase repeats in sequence at higher and higher pitches, creating a musical image of rising passion. The melody is reduced to two pitches a half step apart, creating a sense of "leading" somewhere until the full orchestra enters loudly but inconclusively.
1:51	A new yearning theme is introduced in the cellos: three phrases rising in sequence to a final large ascending leap followed by orchestral crescendos and diminuendos as the melody "develops," creating a sense of churning emotions.
3:26	The second yearning theme returns and develops rather quietly for a while until it gradually increases in loudness.
5:25	The second yearning theme returns a third time loudly followed by the churning orchestra and a fourth time in the brasses. The violins begin playing an ever higher set of scales, and then reintroduce the second theme again. The orchestra crescendos to an almost unbearable level of intensity.
7:31	The climax ends, and the orchestra gradually descends in pitch and loudness. The first yearning theme returns in the cellos and the two themes interweave in counterpoint through louder and softer passages.
9:17	The timpani plays a roll, and the English horn plays the first yearning theme. The roll continues and the bass clarinet plays the theme very softly, ending with the double basses in unison to silence, followed by two soft plucked tones, the lovers' yearning apparently exhausted, yet still unsatisfied.
10:32	End

The combination of the contrapuntal interweaving of the yearning quality of the two melodies, the continuous surging of the music through degrees of loudness and softness, and the crescendo to the loudest possible sound and gradual decrescendo creates probably the most intense musical expression of passionate sexual love in the history of European music. Critics in the late nineteenth century noticed this, and some seemed embarrassed by it. A critic for the *Allgemeine musikalische Zeitung* (General Musical Journal) reported in 1865 of *Tristan und Isolde*:

> Not to mince words, it is the glorification of sensual pleasure, tricked out with every titillating device. . . . We think that the stage presentation of the poem *Tristan und Isolde* amounts to an act of indecency.

After a performance in 1882 in London a critic in *The Era*, a weekly magazine, wrote:

> We cannot refrain from making a protest against the worship of animal passion which is so striking a feature in the late works of Wagner. . . . The passion is unholy in itself and its representation is impure, and for those reasons we rejoice in believing that such works will not become popular. . . . Wagner's music, in spite of all its wondrous skill and power, repels a greater number than it fascinates.

Clara Schumann wrote that *Tristan und Isolde* was "the most repugnant thing I have ever seen or heard in all my life."

There are many duets in *Tristan und Isolde*, but *Liebestod* is the only section resembling an aria. The music paints the lyrics in a European musical tradition that is hundreds of years old. The orchestra represents Isolde's emotions as she sings, at times overwhelming the sense of her words with the intensity of her feelings of love and joy at her vision of their radiant transfiguration into an eternal spiritual state of love after death.

Timed Listening Guide: Liebestod

Listen to the entire recording of the *Liebestod* following this timed listening guide, which explains the meaning of the music in relation to its musical elements and the text. It is sung by Leontyne Price (b. 1927) with the Philadelphia Orchestra conducted by Henry Lewis (1932–1996).

FIGURE 8.5
Tristan and Isolde in the first 1865 production, photo by Joseph Albert (1825–1886)
Source: Wikimedia Commons.

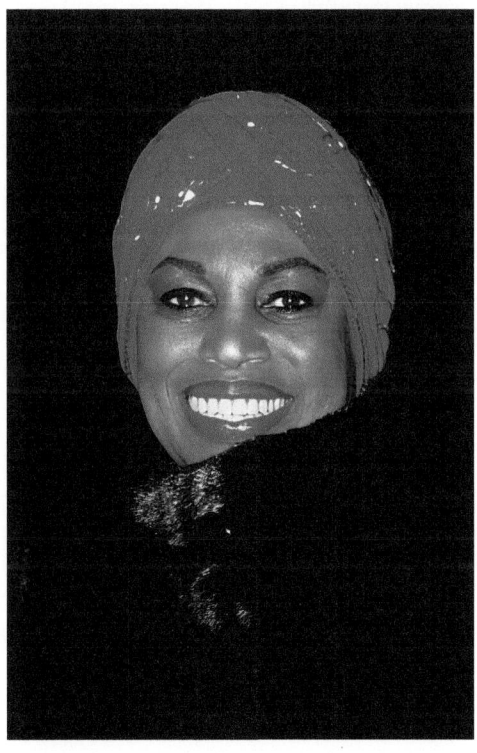

FIGURE 8.6
Leontyne Price, the first African American opera singer to perform leading roles at the Metropolitan Opera and the leading opera houses of Europe, at the Meyerhoff Concert Hall in Baltimore, Maryland, 1995
Source: John Mathew Smith and www.celebrity-photos.com, Wikimedia Commons.

FIGURE 8.7
Henry Lewis, the first African American to regularly conduct American symphony orchestras, with his wife, the notable Rossini mezzo-soprano Marilyn Horne, 1961
Source: Carl van Vechten, Library of Congress Prints and Photographs Division, Wikimedia Commons.

TIME	GERMAN TEXT	ENGLISH TRANSLATION	DESCRIPTION
0:00	*Mild und leise wie er lächelt*	How mild and tenderly he smiles	The *Liebestod Leitmotif*, sung very softly and slowly, consists of two short, four-tone, arch-shaped phrases, the second one slightly higher than the first.
0:14	*wie das Auge hold er öffnet,*	How sweetly he opens his eyes.	The *Liebestod Leitmotif* repeats on the second line of text, getting slightly louder.
0:26	*seht, ihr's, Freunde? Seht ihr's nicht?*	Do you see, friends? Do you not see?	Isolde sings new material as the *Liebestod Leitmotif* is taken up by the orchestra.
0:36	*Immer lichter, wie er leuchtet,*	How brightly he shines,	The melody rises to near the top of Isolde's vocal range, painting the words "shines" and "soars high among the stars."
	stern-umstrahlet hoch sich hebt?	How high he soars among the stars?	
1:03	*Seht ihr's nicht?*	Do you not see?	The *Liebestod Leitmotif* is heard in the orchestra.
1:09	*Wie das Herz ihm mutig schwillt,*	How valiantly his heart swells,	Isolde sings the *Liebestod Leitmotif* again.
	voll und hehr im Busen ihm quillt?	Beats fully and sublimely in his breast?	
1:33	*Wie den Lippen, wonnig mild,*	How lips, soft and gentle	The orchestra brings the *Liebestod Leitmotif* into the foreground before Isolde enters with another melodic line.
1:49	*süsser Atem sanft entweht?*	softly exhale sweet breath?	Isolde sings the *Liebestod Leitmotif*, and the flutes enter in counterpoint with a new motive signifying bliss: an upward leap followed by a rapid scalar descent.
2:04	*Freunde! Seht! Fühlt und seht ihr's nicht?*	Friends! Look! Do you not feel it and see it?	The music becomes louder and more agitated.
2:22	*Höre ich nur diese Weise,*	Do I alone hear this melody,	Isolde sings again the Liebestod *leitmotif* as the orchestra interjects the bliss motive from time to time.
	die so wundervoll und leise,	which so wonderfully and tenderly	
	Wonne klagend, alles sagend,	Softly mourning, saying all,	
	mild versöhnend aus ihm tönend,	gently forgiving sounds from him,	
3:12	*in mich dringet, auf sich schwinget,*	penetrates within me, rising up,	Isolde's singing "rises up" louder and higher in a scalar ascent.
	hold erhallend um mich klinget?	Sweetly echoes and rings around me?	
3:36	*Heller schallend, mich umwallend,*	Sounding clearly, surrounding me	The orchestra rises higher and higher in sequence, burying Isolde's singing as she "dives" into its "roaring . . . surging swell" and "ringing sounds."
	sind es Wellen sanfter Lüfte?	Are they waves of soft breezes?	
	Sind es Wogen wonniger Düfte?	Are they clouds of wondrous fragrance?	
	Wie sie schwellen, mich umrauschen,	As they swell and roar around me,	
	soll ich atmen, soll ich lauschen?	Shall I inhale them, shall I listen to them?	
	Soll ich schlürfen, untertauchen?	Shall I sip them, dive into them?	
	Süss in Düften mich verhauchen?	Sweet scents shall I exhale?	

TIME	GERMAN TEXT	ENGLISH TRANSLATION	DESCRIPTION
	In dem wogenden Schwall	In the surging swell	
	in dem tönenden Schall	in the ringing sounds,	
4:45	*in des Welt-Atems wehendem All*	In the world's breath encompassing all	The music begins to "sink" in pitch and loudness, and the "bliss" motive returns.
	ertrinken, versinken	To drown, to sink	
	unbewusst höchste Lust!	Unconscious, what utter bliss!	
6:21			A crescendo returns to the Prelude's opening, "yearning" *Leitmotif*, which ends on the dominant seventh chord.
6:35			This time, four hours after the Prelude, the dominant seventh chord at the end of the first phrase of the Prelude resolves to the tonic for the first time in the opera, the release from love's yearning in death. The music drama ends on a long crescendo and diminuendo to silence.
7:05	End		

Wagner's musical style in *Tristan und Isolde* stands in marked contrast to the style of Italian opera popularized by Gioachino Rossini, Gaetano Donizetti and Vincenzo Bellini during the first half of the nineteenth century and to a lesser extent the late nineteenth-century successors, Giuseppe Verdi (1813–1901), born the same year as Wagner, and Giacomo Puccini (1858–1924). These five composers boast at least forty operas in the modern standard operatic repertoire, with Verdi alone having written about twenty of them. Although Verdi and Puccini followed Wagner to some extent in moving away from Rossini's florid vocal style (*bel canto*), Wagner found Verdi's treatment of the orchestra stunted, once commenting sarcastically that Verdi used the orchestra like a guitar. Indeed, to showcase the vocalists, Verdi often wrote orchestral accompaniments consisting of little more than bass and block chords in alternation—like a guitarist might play. If in Italian opera the music seems to serve the singers, Wagner wanted the music to serve the drama. To this end he composed in a musical style without a strong distinction between recitative and aria. He developed the orchestra not as an accompaniment to the singing but as a character capable of conveying the psychological reality behind the singers' words.

AESTHETICS

What Is Its History?

The romance of Tristan and Isolde, two people whose love violates social conventions (Tristan's loyalty to King Marke) in a way that can only be resolved in death, is a Medieval love story that reverberates through the history of European literature and music. At the end of the sixteenth century Shakespeare retold a version of it in *Romeo and Juliet*, even including a magic potion that the Friar gives to Juliet to mimic death. Goethe's *The Sorrows of the Young Werther* (1774) is another version, resolved by the death of the male lover, who shoots himself. In 1827 Hector Berlioz, under the spell of Shakespeare and Harriet Smithson, wrote *Symphonie Fantastique*, whose male protagonist, like young Werther agonizing over unrequited love, dies from an overdose of another magic potion, opium. Thirty years later Wagner brings the story full circle in his music drama *Tristan und Isolde*. The Romeo-and-Juliet version of the story continues to reverberate in American popular culture, including Leonard Bernstein's Broadway show *West Side Story* (1957), which was revived as a 2021 film, and even Disney's *High School Musical* (2006).

CULTURAL LINKAGES

Richard Wagner was born in 1813 in Leipzig, where Bach lived and worked during the last twenty-seven years of his life. He was raised by a family of thespians and imagined that he would

SOCIAL BEHAVIOR

become a writer and poet until he heard the music of Beethoven. He studied composition for a few years but never developed great skill as a performer. Like Berlioz, his instrument was the orchestra. After numerous disappointments, Wagner's first success was an opera called *Rienzi* written in German in the Italian opera style on an Italian historical theme of the people of Rome rising up against the nobility. Produced in 1842, its success led to his appointment as director of the opera there, his first job and one that gave him the security to write and produce his next three operas, all with his own poetry and all on Germanic themes. One of them, *Lohengrin* (1850), was based on a Medieval romance about the son of Percival, a knight at King Arthur's Round Table charged with finding and keeping the Holy Grail.

In his Dresden operas after *Rienzi*, Wagner abandoned the style and stories of Italian opera and began to develop the hallmarks of his personal style: his own poetic librettos based on Medieval Germanic myths, legends, and romances; a vocal writing style called ***arioso*** between the florid, melodic arias and the recitatives of Italian opera; *Leitmotifs* as indexes of characters, thoughts, emotions, objects, and places; chromaticism and unresolved harmonies played over long stretches of "endless melody" as expressions of rising and falling emotional states; and the orchestra and its palette of colors as a character in the drama equal to the vocalists.

POLITICAL ACTION

Wagner was not able to attend the premiere of *Lohengrin* in 1850 because in 1849 he had fled Dresden under threat of arrest for his participation in an uprising in 1848 against the tyranny of German princes and dukes and in favor of the unification of Germany's many principalities into a German nation. In 1848 Europeans of all classes, including the nobility, urban workers, and rural peasants, were suffering economic hardships and chafing against autocratic rule, whose end was the promise of the French Revolution. The Irish potato famine was causing a million deaths and another million to emigrate. Karl Marx and Friedrich Engels published their *Communist Manifesto* in February of that year. Revolutions began in January in Sicily against Spanish rule. In February the French toppled their constitutional monarch. In March German students and intellectuals, including Wagner, engaged in mass demonstrations in favor of national unity and freedom of the press. The authorities issued a warrant for Wagner's arrest, and he escaped to Zurich, Switzerland, where he lived for a decade.

CULTURAL LINKAGES

In Switzerland, cut off from support for his musical compositions, he wrote essays on his views of music and art, including *The Artwork of the Future* (1849), in which he outlined his ideas for the way a ***Gesamtkunstwerk*** (total artwork) could unite all the elements of drama (poetry, music, stage design, and acting); *Judaism in Music* (1850), an anti-Semitic screed in which he claimed that Jews like Felix Mendelssohn, born and working in Germany, could not express the German national spirit but could only produce entertainment for money rather than great art, as ethnic Germans could; and *Opera and Drama* (1851), in which he outlined the methods he was using to create what would become his magnum opus: a set of four operas called *The Ring of the Nibelung*, also known as the Ring cycle or simply The Ring. Based on old Viking sagas written down from oral tradition in Old Norse, a Germanic language, and on a Medieval German romance, Wagner began writing it during the 1850s, when he had no hope of its being produced. It tells a multigenerational story of a world inhabited by humans, gods, and underworld creatures (Nibelungs [dwarves] and mermaids), all greedily seeking power and wealth symbolized by a golden ring. In the end, their avarice comes to nothing, and everything is destroyed. With no hope of having these operas produced, he turned to *Tristan und Isolde*, inspired in part by his own extramarital affair.

Wagner's interest in Germanic myths, legends, and romances, his desire for a unified German state, and his anti-Semitism had its origins in a new philosophy, ethnic nationalism, created by German writers at the end of the eighteenth century and developed by Wagner and others during the nineteenth century. In its virulent form, advocates of ethnic nationalism believed that the nation-state should contain only members of the nationality that defined it and that other nationalities and ethnicities resident in the nation should be expelled from its territory.

When the arrest warrant for Wagner was lifted in 1862, he returned to Germany. In 1864 the eccentric eighteen-year-old King Ludwig II of Bavaria invited him to Munich. The eighteen-year-old king's patronage allowed Wagner to produce *Tristan und Isolde* in 1865, his first premiere since *Lohengrin* in 1850. Ludwig also supported the production of the first two operas of the Ring cycle, *Das Rheingold* (The Rhine Gold) in 1869 and *Die Walküre* (The Valkyries) in 1870.

In 1871 Wagner and his family moved to the small town of Bayreuth near Munich, where they began building an opera house suitable for the production of his Ring cycle. With the help of King Ludwig, as well as "Wagner societies" formed in Berlin, Vienna, Leipzig, and London, The Ring premiered in its entirety in 1876 at a music festival at the new Bayreuth opera house, including the last two operas of the cycle: *Siegfried* and *Götterdämmerung* (The Twilight of the Gods). One of the great cultural events of the nineteenth century, Wagner's festival was attended by kings and many of the most famous composers of the day. After Wagner's death from a heart attack in 1883, the annual or biannual festival at Bayreuth became a pilgrimage site for Wagner's legions of fans, and the Wagner family has continued to manage it to the present. Wagner's music dramas have entered the standard repertoire of opera houses around the world. *Tristan und Isolde* is especially popular, and performances of individual operas from the Ring Cycle are regularly performed. Mounting the entire cycle is an enormously costly, ambitious, and rare undertaking. Productions of it are treated by the press as major, newsworthy cultural events.

FIGURE 8.8

Bavarian King Ludwig II's *Schloss Neuschwanstein* (New Swanstone Castle), the inspiration for Disneyland's Sleeping Beauty Castle

Source: Library of Congress, Wikimedia Commons.

Wagner's musical style, with its "endless melodies," chromaticism, harmonies liberated from the need to cadence regularly, and its rich orchestration, was enormously influential. Austrian and German composers Gustav Mahler, Richard Strauss (1864–1949), and Arnold Schoenberg (1874–1951) adopted many of its elements, while Frenchmen Claude Debussy (1862–1918) and Maurice Ravel (1875–1937) and Russian Igor Stravinsky (1882–1971), working in France, reacted against it in their compositions. It became the basis for American movie music, which is full of Wagnerian orchestral evocations of the emotions the characters are experiencing. And it set the stage for the eventual dissolution, during the first half of the twentieth century, of tonal harmony in European classical music.

The artistic impact of Wagner's music has always stood in relief against his deplorable personal life: his unpaid debts to his many benefactors, his infidelities, and his anti-Semitism, which lost him friends and admirers during his lifetime. Wagner's anti-Semitism continues to present a dilemma for some performers and audiences and raises the question of whether art can or should be separated from the artist. His music, a favorite of Adolf Hitler, became associated with an even more appalling form of anti-Semitism than he espoused. Even so, a number of important Jewish musicians, during his lifetime and since, have loved and championed his music. His operas have never been produced in Israel, although in 1981 conductor Zubin Mehta led a selection from *Tristan und Isolde* in Tel Aviv as an encore after announcing that audience members and musicians who objected to its performance could leave. A few left, but most stayed. Wagner's "Wedding March" (aka "Here Comes the Bride") from *Lohengrin* is probably more used today than Mendelssohn's, and "The Ride of the Valkyries" from *Die Walküre* enlivened a scene of attacking helicopters in Francis Ford Coppola's Vietnam War film *Apocalypse Now* (1979).

WHERE DO I GO FROM HERE?

- Watch a few videos of the *Liebestod* and compare the ways it has been staged. Does the staging affect your perception of the music? Do you prefer one of the stagings over the others and, if so, why?

- Listen to "The Ride of the Valkyries" from Wagner's *Die Walküre*. Other than its appearance in *Apocalypse Now*, can you find other appearances of this composition in popular culture? How have those added to or changed its meaning, from your perspective?

- Listen to Vincenzo Bellini's "Casta diva" (Chaste Goddess) from *Norma* (1831) and compare its musical elements and representations of emotions to Wagner's *Liebestod*.

GATEWAY 29
EUROPEAN MUSICAL NATIONALISM

What Is It?

During the late nineteenth century ethnic nationalism was arguably the most powerful political current and one of the most important sources of musical inspiration in Europe. At a time when large

FIGURE 8.9
Bedřich Smetana around 1880, by Jan Vilímek (1860–1938)
Source: Wikimedia Commons.

parts of Europe were either controlled by large, multi-ethnic empires or divided into small principalities and city-states, ethnic nationalists argued that every ethnic group had a right to its own nation-state. After lengthy struggles for national unity, Italy was formed in 1861 and Germany in 1871. The Slavic, Hungarian, and German ethnic groups of the Austro-Hungarian Empire fought for their independence, as did the people of the Balkans, who sought independence from the Ottoman Empire. In this inflamed political environment many composers wrote music expressing nationalist sentiments in the hope of inspiring their people.

Our gateway to European **musical nationalism**, the expression of nationalist sentiment in music, is a symphonic tone poem called *Vltava*, premiered in 1875 by the Czech composer Bedřich Smetana (pronounced BED-reekh SME-ta-na) (1824–1888). Vltava is the name of a river running through Czech lands in central Europe. The river's name in German is Moldau, and in English this work is commonly known as *The Moldau*. It is one of a collection of six symphonic poems titled *Má Vlast* (My Homeland) that Smetana wrote to represent Czech history, culture, and landscape. Of these, *The Moldau* is the most frequently performed today. Conductor Jiří Bělohlávek (1946–2017) and the Czech Philharmonic Orchestra perform it.

 Listen to the first thirty seconds of the recording.

How Does It Work?

Timbre

A variety of orchestral colors, featuring flutes and horns, express each moment in the story of the river's flow through Czech lands.

Texture

The textures are contrapuntal throughout with occasional block chords, especially at cadences.

Rhythm

A variety of duple, triple, and compound meters are deployed. Compound meters are meters where each beat divides into three pulses of equal duration. **Compound duple meter**, for example, has two pulses per measure, each of which divides into three quicker pulses for a total of six pulses per measure.

Melody

Melodies feature stepwise motion. The main theme, representing the Moldau, has an arch shape and a recurring long—short—long—short rhythm; a contrasting "water" theme features rapid runs with an undulating, "wavy" shape.

Harmony

The harmony is tonal in both major and minor keys.

Form

The piece employs something like rondo form, with the Moldau and water themes returning after contrasting excursions to other material.

Performance Techniques

The performance features long crescendos and decrescendos and sudden contrasts of loud and soft in a manner reminiscent of Beethoven's symphonic style.

 Listen to the first 1:30 of this performance for the way the opening "rippling" melodies come together in the "broad" Moldau theme.

What Does It Mean?

The meaning of the performance derives partly from the way the music expresses the program that Smetana wrote for it and inserted into each section of the score. Here is an excerpt of his program:

FIGURE 8.10
Prague's Vyŝehrad Castle on the Moldau River (Vltava). Smetana and another famous Czech composer Antonín Dvořák (1841–1904) are buried in the Vyŝehrad cemetery next to the church. Photo by Stanislav Jelen.
Source: Wikimedia Commons.

The musical poem reflects the pride, oppression, and hope of the Bohemian people. Two springs pour forth in the shade of the Bohemian Forest, one warm and gushing, the other cold and peaceful. Their waves, gaily flowing over rocky beds, join and glisten in the rays of the morning sun. The forest brook, hastening on, becomes the river Vltava. Coursing through Bohemia's valleys, it grows into a mighty stream. Through thick woods it flows, as the gay sounds of the hunt and the notes of the hunter's horn are heard ever nearer. It flows through grass-grown pastures and lowlands where a wedding feast is being celebrated with song and dance. At night wood water nymphs revel in its sparkling waves. Reflected on its surface are fortresses and castles—witnesses of bygone days of knightly splendor and the vanished glory of fighting times. At the St. John Rapids the stream races ahead, winding through the cataracts, heaving on a path with its foaming waves through the rocky chasm into the broad river bed—finally. Flowing on in majestic peace toward Prague—finally. Flowing on in majestic peace toward Prague and welcomed by time-honored Vysehrad [castle]. *Then it vanishes far beyond the poet's gaze.*

Listen to the entire performance following this timed listening guide with quotes from the score suggesting the meaning of the music.

TIME	FORM AND PROGRAM	DESCRIPTION
0:00	Introduction: "The source of the Vltava"	Two solo flutes, accompanied by pizzicato strings, play undulating phrases representing the flowing and turning streams that will join to form the great Moldau River. The tension gradually increases until the flutes in parallel thirds form an icon of the sources of the Moldau coming together. The arrival of the streams at the Moldau is signaled by a sudden drop in register, with the undulating melody played by the strings.
1:00	AABC	The Moldau theme (A) in E minor, triple meter, and three stepwise phrases is played by the violins, with the undulating, rolling river gesture continuing below it as accompaniment. The undulating accompaniment transitions back to a repeat of the Moldau theme.
1:54	ABCA	A varied repeat of the Moldau theme. A third playing of the Moldau theme is abruptly interrupted after the A phrase by the brass section, playing loudly.

LISTENING GUIDE 8.3

continued

TIME	FORM AND PROGRAM	DESCRIPTION
2:44	"Hunt in the Woods"	A brass fanfare begins, played by horns and trumpets. Fanfares based on the overtone series of a natural, valveless horn are common musical icons of a hunt in symphonic music. The fanfare eventually breaks down into a single, repeated pitch and decrescendo, which serve to predict a transition to the next section.
3:49	"Country Wedding"	A village dance melody, with narrow range, frequent short, repeated notes, drone-like accompaniment, and steady pulsatile rhythm. The music gets louder, and then quickly fades away, as if passengers on a boat sailing along the Moldau are moving out of earshot of the village dancing scene.
5:10	"Moonlight Dance of the Nymphs"	The bassoons announce a new section with long-held notes before the flutes, harp, and strings, muted to suggest a distant, eerie sound, enter quietly with the undulating water theme. A new melody with long-held notes enters, punctuated by the horns. The music grows louder in anticipation of a new section, and the undulating water theme returns in the flutes and strings.
7:58	ABCA	The Moldau theme returns, mostly unchanged.
8:48	"St. John's Rapids"	Loud brasses, accompanied by running lines in the strings and woodwinds, portray the winding, churning rapids. Beyond its pastoral iconicity, it may represent the challenging struggle for national recognition. A scalar descent to a sudden pianissimo is followed by an ascending scalar passage presaging a new section.
10:03	A': "The broad flow of the Vltava"	A variant, faster rendition of the first (A) phrase of the "Moldau" theme returns in the parallel major key with quick arpeggiated accompaniment figures in the strings. The challenge has been met; the nation will prevail against the forces arrayed against it.
10:31	Coda	Fortissimo block chords segue into a Beethoven-style extended set of V-I cadences to emphasize the triumph of the nation ending in a decrescendo return to soft references to the undulating river theme. The piece ends abruptly with a very loud two-chord V-I cadence.
12:06	End	

In *The Moldau* Smetana, like Beethoven in his Sixth Symphony and Berlioz in the third movement of *Symphonie Fantastique*, paints a pastoral scene in music. But in this case it is not a generalized rural scene, as in those works, but a specific place in the territory where Smetana was born, a province of the Austrian Empire called Bohemia and today part of the Czech Republic. Using the techniques of programmatic music and evoking the spirit of Romanticism, Smetana was expressing in *The Moldau* his love of his homeland (*vlast*).

Two interrelated phenomena awakened his patriotism: nationalism as a political philosophy and an uprising in 1848 in Prague by Czech nationalists against the Austrian Empire. Smetana and many other composers living in empires and in small principalities used programmatic instrumental music like *The Moldau*, plus songs and operas with texts in their "national language" about the "nation's" historical events, rural legends, and tales, to rouse national sentiments and encourage these political movements. Programmatic music proved exceptionally useful, since the program could specify references to particular places like "St. John's Rapids" and the Vltava River. Rural peasant song and dance tunes, as in the section of *The Moldau* labeled "country wedding," also provided icons of the national culture and soundscape. Smetana's *The Moldau* has long captivated Czech listeners and those beyond the Czech lands.

What Is Its History?

POLITICAL
ACTIVITY

Bedřich Smetana was born in 1824 in a provincial Bohemian town. His father, a beer brewer and amateur musician, spoke mainly German, the language of the Austrian Empire. A gifted pianist,

Smetana gave his first public performance at age six. Throughout his youth he was a popular figure at salons of the wealthy German-speaking elite. He moved to Prague in 1843 and began his study of composition there. His early works were mainly for solo piano until 1848, when nationalistic revolutions broke out across Europe. Beginning in March 1848, nationalists in Bohemia and Hungary, seeking cultural autonomy or independence, rose up against the conservative, repressive government of the Austrian Empire. The revolutionary activities in Prague galvanized the twenty-four-year-old Smetana, who joined his comrades on the barricades in June and composed his first patriotic works, a *National Guard March* for piano and *Song of Freedom* for chorus. The Bohemian revolution, along with most of the others around Europe, was crushed. Luckily, Smetana was neither killed nor jailed.

The 1850s were an unhappy decade for Smetana. Locals interpreted his compositions as too progressive, too influenced by those of Berlioz, Liszt, and Wagner, and so he found a conducting job in Gothenburg, Sweden, something of a backwater. In 1862 he returned to Prague when the imperial government in Vienna loosened its policies concerning the Czech language. A Czech-language newspaper and a theater producing plays and operas in Czech were allowed to start up. Over the next twenty years Smetana enjoyed considerable success as he established the Czech nationalist style of composition in eight Czech-language operas based on Czech stories, the most famous of which is *The Bartered Bride* (1870). Between 1872 and 1879 he composed his *Má Vlast* cycle of six tone poems.

> CULTURAL
> LINKAGES

Smetana was only one of many European composers inspired by nationalist ideology and political activity during the nineteenth century. Some even turned to the collection of rural peasant songs in the national language. The songs and dances of these rural farmers, along with tales in oral tradition like those collected in Germany by the Brothers Grimm, were idealized as the perfect, ancient, unadulterated expression of the nation, *das Volk* (the folk, the people) in German. Their songs came to be called folk songs in English. Some collectors were particularly interested in the lyrics of the **folk songs** as expressions of the "national soul" of a particular nationality, but composers were mainly interested in their melodies and rhythms. They adopted folk tunes as themes for their symphonies, tone poems, and operas. They abstracted modal, metrical, rhythmic, and textural features (like bagpipe drones) from folk tunes to write their own themes. And they used flutes, oboes and English horns, clarinets, and horns, all associated with the outdoors and the countryside, to "paint" pastoral village scenes in music.

Some European nationalist composers, like Smetana, sought to arouse national sentiment in favor of national identity and nation-state status in opposition to a dominating political regime. Among them were:

Country	Composer	Composition
Hungary vs. Austria	Franz Liszt (1811–1886)	*Hungarian Rhapsody* No. 2 in C Sharp Minor (1847)
Bohemia/Czech vs. Austria	Antonín Dvořák (1841–1904)	*Slavonic Dances* (1878, 1886)
Norway vs. Sweden	Edvard Grieg (1843–1907)	*Peer Gynt Suite* No. 1 (1875)
Finland vs. Russia	Jean Sibelius (1865–1957)	*Finlandia* (1899)

Another group of composers, working in already established nations, used folk tunes and their elements to create "national sentiment" in contrast to the prevailing "international" style coming mainly from Vienna and Paris. The second group includes composers from Russia, which had an empire that subsumed many national groups, and from Spain, which for centuries had been a kingdom. In Russia and Spain composers attempted to create a sense of national identity different from that of neighboring nations.

Nation	Composer	Composition
Russia	Alexander Borodin (1833–1887)	*In the Steppes of Central Asia* (1880), tone poem
Russia	Modest Mussorgsky (1839–1881)	*Boris Godunov* (1874), opera
Russia	Pyotr Ilyich Tchaikovsky (1840–1893)	*Marche Slave* (1876), tone poem
Russia	Nikolai Rimsky-Korsakov (1844–1908)	*Russian Easter Festival Overture* (1888)
Spain	Isaac Albéniz (1860–1909)	*Suite Española* No. 1, Op. 47 (1886), piano solo

While ethnic nationalism was a central aspect of the political, cultural, and musical life of Europe during the late nineteenth century, its application in the United States was not obvious. The population of an idealized, nationalist European nation-state consisted of a single nationality, which could be represented and evoked in music by the rural "folk music" of that nationality. The music of the multiethnic United States, however, could not, and cannot, be reduced to the sounds of a single ethnicity. What music could a classical composer use to represent the supposed national soul of the United States? In the 1890s Czech nationalist composer Antonín Dvořák supplied one possible answer after he accepted an invitation to become the director of the National Conservatory of Music in New York City. New York philanthropists had founded the National Conservatory in 1885 with the goal of providing a low-cost music education to the needy, including women, minorities, and the disabled. In 1893 their offer of a substantial salary attracted Dvořák, one of the most admired composers in Europe at that time. Once in America, he set about to discover the basis for an American national style. One of his African American students, Harry Burleigh (1866–1949), introduced him to "Negro spirituals," which Dvořák championed, along with Native American music, as the musical sources of American classical music. Burleigh, a baritone who went on to compose classical arrangements of spirituals, became one of the first important African American composers. In 1893 Dvořák employed pentatonic scales characteristic of both African American and Native American music for some of the themes of his Symphony No. 9 in E Minor, "From the New World," Op. 95. It was an immediate hit with orchestras all over the world and is still regularly performed. Neil Armstrong took a recording of it to the moon in 1969.

In 1895 homesickness took Dvořák back to Prague. In his wake two Jewish composers born in Brooklyn kept the flame of American musical nationalism alive in the twentieth century: George Gershwin (1898–1937) with his orchestral one-movement composition *Rhapsody in Blue* (1924) and opera *Porgy and Bess* (1935), based on African American and Jewish melodic elements; and Aaron Copland (1900–1990), whose scores for ballets *Billy the Kid* (1938), *Rodeo* (1942), and *Appalachian Spring* (1944) evoke the landscape and culture of rural white America (Chapter 10, Gateway 40). For nearly thirty years, from the 1970s to early 2000s, numerous bills were introduced in Congress to designate the Appalachian square dance the national dance of the United States. They all failed, an illustration of the difficulty of applying European notions of musical and ethnic nationalism in a nation defined by civic nationalism and multiculturalism.

HARRY T. BURLEIGH

FIGURE 8.11
Harry Burleigh
Source: Wikimedia Commons.

WHERE DO I GO FROM HERE?

- Listen to *Eight Slavonic Dances*, Op. 46, No. 1 by Antonín Dvořák. Note similarities to the melody of Smetana's "country wedding" in *The Moldau*.

- Listen to one of the pieces listed above by a Russian musical nationalist composer. What musical elements suggest that this composition is in a national style?

- Listen to Symphony No. 9 in E minor, "From the New World," Op. 95, Mvt. II by Antonín Dvořák. Where else have you heard these themes?

GATEWAY 30
AFRICAN AMERICAN RELIGIOUS MUSIC

What Is It?

After the Civil War ended in 1865, a number of social activists began to record in musical notation the songs of newly freed African Americans. Among these "slave songs" were many religious songs called **spirituals**. Another group of activists, members of the American Missionary Association, an antebellum Protestant abolitionist organization, founded Fisk University in Nashville in 1866, just a year after the end of war, with the stated purpose to educate "the most helpless and neglected class [freed slaves]" on the model of northeastern universities like Harvard and Yale. The founders believed that "the reign of equal educational privileges and equal rights . . . if successful, would revolutionize the state" of Tennessee. They argued that education, modeled on the private colleges of New England, was indispensable if the South in general, and newly freed African Americans in particular, were to flourish after the Civil War.

FIGURE 8.12
The Fisk Jubilee Singers in 1882, with Ella Sheppard at the keyboard
Source: Deep Roots Magazine, Wikimedia Commons.

One of those northern college traditions was the glee club. Glees, descendants of the English madrigal (Chapter 4, Gateway 12), were popular a cappella songs in three- and four-part harmony sung by gentlemen members of English social clubs (glee clubs) between 1750 and 1850. In the United States during the second half of the nineteenth century, glee clubs morphed into all-male collegiate choirs, starting with the Harvard Glee Club in 1858, the University of Michigan Men's Glee Club in 1859, and the Yale Glee Club in 1861. They performed a wide repertoire of classical and popular music. Among these collegiate choirs was a vocal ensemble of men and women at Fisk University called the Fisk Jubilee Singers. They formed in 1871. Nearly forty years later, in 1909, another incarnation of the ensemble, a male quartet, recorded "Swing Low, Sweet Chariot," the first spiritual ever recorded. Our gateway to African American religious music of the late nineteenth century is a recording of "Swing Low, Sweet Chariot" by the Fisk Jubilee Singers from the early 1980s.

 Listen to the first minute of the song, the first verse and chorus.

How Does It Work?

Timbre

A female soloist sings in the falsetto manner of a classically trained singer alternating with a choir of male and female voices.

Texture

The texture alternates solo singing with a chorus singing block chords.

Rhythm

The meter is duple with some syncopation, as in the opening short—long—short rhythm on the words "swing—LOW—sweet."

Melody

The melody has an undulating shape in a pentatonic scale.

Harmony

The harmony is triadic with a V-I cadence at the end of each phrase.

Form

This is a strophic song. It begins with a refrain. Each strophe alternates a verse and a refrain. Each verse and each refrain is performed in solo-chorus, call-and-response form.

Refrain:
Swing low, sweet chariot (solo)
Coming for to carry me home (chorus)
Swing low, sweet chariot (solo)
Coming for to carry me home (chorus)

Verse 1:
I looked over Jordan and what did I see (solo)
Coming for to carry me home (chorus)
A band of angels coming after me (solo)
Coming for to carry me home (chorus)

Verse 2:
If you get there before I do (solo)
Coming for to carry me home (chorus)
Tell all my friends I'm coming too (solo)
Coming for to carry me home (chorus)

Verse 3:
I'm sometimes up and sometimes down (solo)
Coming for to carry me home (chorus)
But still my soul seems heavenly bound (solo)
Coming for to carry me home (chorus)

Performance Techniques

The female soloist sings with vibrato in a classical style with almost no variation from strophe to strophe.

Listen to this recording with these elements in mind, following this timed listening guide.

LISTENING GUIDE 8.4

TIME	SECTION	DESCRIPTION
0:00	Chorus	Soloist and chorus sing the refrain "Swing low . . ." in tonal harmony.
0:32	Verse 1	"I looked over Jordan" sung to the same melody as the refrain. In the second line of text, "A band of angels . . .," the choir hums the choral harmony.
1:02	Chorus	"Swing low . . .," the second time through with the choir humming the chords.
1:36	Verse 2	"If you get there . . ."
2:08	Chorus	"Swing low . . .," the second time through with the choir humming the chords.
2:40	Verse 3	"I'm sometimes up . . ."
3:13	Chorus	"Swing low . . .," sung a little more softly and slowly than before, ending with a ritard.
4:02	End	

What Does It Mean?

Many meanings have been associated with "Swing Low, Sweet Chariot" and other spirituals. Some of the meanings derive from the words, some from the style of performance, some from the performers, some from the sources of the spiritual songs, and some from their unique position in American society.

Spirituals entered the repertoire of college choirs like the Fisk Jubilee Singers after the Civil War from transcriptions (notations) of the singing of formerly enslaved Africans, including some of the original members of the choir. Created by the enslaved, spirituals registered, in a highly distilled fashion, the cruelty and suffering they endured and their hope for freedom either in this world or the next. The lyrics borrow their imagery from biblical stories they heard at outdoor religious services called camp meetings, some of which were about the exodus of the Israelites from Egypt and their crossing the Jordan River to Canaan, the promised land. From readings of Deuteronomy 12:10, they heard, "But when ye go over Jordan, and dwell in the land which the Lord your God giveth you to inherit, and when he giveth you rest from all your enemies round about, so that ye dwell in safety . . ." These enslaved men and women created spiritual songs based on this biblical imagery as coded messages of encouragement and resistance: the chariot that took the prophet Elijah to heaven (from 2 Kings chapter 2) as their mode of transportation to the promised land of freedom, "over Jordan," where other runaways had gone before, but "I'm coming too." Other spirituals evoke a trip to freedom on a boat ("Michael, row the boat ashore") or a metaphorical train ("I hear the gospel train is coming . . . get on board, children") on the underground railroad; reference the biblical story of a plea to the Egyptian Pharaoh to release the enslaved Israelites ("Tell old Pharaoh . . . let my people go"); convey hope of salvation from the misery of slavery ("Children, we shall all be free," "Steal away, steal away to Jesus, I ain't got long to stay here," and "Didn't my Lord deliver Daniel"); and express their sorrows and woes under the master's lash ("Nobody knows the trouble I seen," "I'm troubled in mind," and "I've been buked and I been scorned").

Enslaved African Americans originally sang spirituals in a call-and-response style with hand-clapping, stamping, and dancing. They sang in unison and in parallel harmonies typical of some African singing styles. But the Fisk Jubilee Singers followed a different performance model, one consistent with the mission of the university.

> **AESTHETICS**

The Fisk University treasurer George L. White (1838–1895) had a modest music education and believed that choral concerts by a group of Fisk singers might be able to raise money for the college, which was in dire need of financial support. He and his students adapted the unison, improvised tradition of slave songs to the contemporary, notated, classical style and harmonies of university glee clubs. Adding choral arrangements of Stephen Foster's popular songs to their repertoire, a group of eleven male and female students, along with White and a white female principal of a Black school in Alabama, set out in October of 1871 on what they thought would be a month-long tour of the northern states to give concerts and raise $20,000 for the university.

> **ECONOMIC ACTIVITY**

The project was beset with difficulties, not least the resistance and prejudice they endured. Maggie Porter, a singer with the group, reported that "There were many times when we didn't have a place to sleep or anything to eat. Mr. White went out and brought us some sandwiches and tried to find some place to put us up." White hoped that churches would sponsor his students' concerts, filled as they were with sacred songs. But northern audiences knew African American culture mainly through the distorting lens of minstrelsy (Chapter 7, Gateway 27). White's hoped-for sponsors, members of polite, religious society, viewed such performances dimly and sometimes refused to sponsor their concerts. When they did sponsor one, they were poorly attended until word of mouth and favorable newspaper reviews attracted larger audiences. A contemporary account of their trip includes these descriptions of the reception and the meaning northern listeners attached to their singing of spirituals:

> **EMOTIONAL RESONANCE**

> Was there not so much odium attached to negro concerts, as represented by burnt cork minstrels, that people of taste and character did not think it becoming to rush in crowds to a paid concert by negroes? . . . People came to despise, to ridicule, to wonder, but remained to admire, and to bury their foolish prejudices. . . . Once under the magnetism of their music, prejudice melted away, and praise of their performance was upon every tongue. . . . The music carried the people with ecstasies of sympathy and pleasure. . . . Gray-haired men

wept like little children. . . . Our people can now listen to the genuine soul music of the slave cabins [sung by] living representatives of the only true, native school of American music.

In this period of segregation, racial violence, and Jim Crow laws, the weeping of these northern concert audiences may reveal a complex mix of emotions: sympathy and compassion for the experiences of these singers; pleasure at their musical skill; grief for the hundreds of thousands of lives lost in the civil war that ended slavery; and perhaps guilt and repentance for their attitudes towards Black Americans.

Because of the difficulties in attracting an audience to their concerts, the Fisk Jubilee Singers' first tour lasted five months rather than the planned one month. They returned to Fisk University in March of 1872 to a warm welcome, having, at great personal sacrifice, met their goal of raising $20,000. "The permanency of the university was assured," a chronicler of their trip wrote. The first building on the Fisk campus was named Jubilee Hall.

These old songs in their new form, coupled with the positive reception of northerners, led the Fisk singers to change their own understandings of the songs. Many of the student singers had been freed before the war and only after their emancipation had "learned their letters," some self-taught. Those who hadn't been enslaved knew about life under slavery from parents and grandparents. The father of Ella Sheppard (1851–1914), the group's pianist and the best educated among them, lived in Nashville and "had bought himself for $1800," meaning that he had purchased his own freedom. He then bought his daughter Ella from her mother's owner in Mississippi and moved to Ohio to escape slavery. There Ella was able to study voice and piano. She wrote that the spirituals

were sacred to our parents, who used them in their religious worship and shouted over them. . . . It was only after many months that gradually our hearts were opened to the influence of these friends and we began to appreciate the wonderful beauty and power of our songs.

Her ambivalence toward the songs was anticipated in *My Bondage and My Freedom*, a book written in 1855 by Frederick Douglass (1818–1895), freed from slavery before the Civil War and an ardent and influential abolitionist and social reformer:

I did not, when a slave, understand the deep meanings of those rude, and apparently incoherent songs. I was myself within the circle, so that I neither saw or heard as those without might see and hear. They told a tale which was then altogether beyond my feeble comprehension; they were tones, loud, long and deep, breathing the prayer and complaint of souls boiling over with the bitterest anguish. Every tone was a testimony against slavery, and a prayer to God for deliverance from chains. The hearing of those wild notes always depressed my spirits, and filled my heart with ineffable sadness. The mere recurrence, even now, afflicts my spirit, and while I am writing these lines, my tears are falling. To those songs I trace my first glimmering conceptions of the dehumanizing character of slavery. I can never get rid of that conception. Those songs still follow me, to deepen my hatred of slavery, and quicken my sympathies for my brethren in bonds.

What Is Its History?

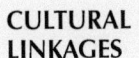

The term "spiritual" for a religious song dates to the early 1700s during a Protestant religious movement called the Great Awakening. Some Protestants advocated for a new kind of personal religious experience based on redemption from sin and personal salvation. Preachers traveling in the South sought both Black and white converts, and some white ministers invited Blacks into their congregations. New religious and social movements almost always require new songs, and so, in 1707, Dr. Isaac Watts (1674–1748), a minister in England, published a collection of new *Hymns and Spiritual Songs* with tuneful melodies and rhyming poetry in a contemporary language designed to be appealing and easily understood. Among Watts's hymns were "Joy to the world, the Lord is come" and "When Isra'l, freed from Pharaoh's hand/left the proud tyrant and his land," which resonates in the spiritual "Go Down, Moses": "When Israel was in Egypt's land/Let my people go/Oppressed so hard they could not stand/Let my people go." Other composers added more hymns to this tradition later in the eighteenth century, including "Amazing Grace (how sweet the sound)" and "On Jordan's stormy banks I stand/and cast a wishful eye on Canaan's fair and happy land/I am bound for the promised land." In Black spirituals Canaan stands for Canada, the northernmost stop on the underground railroad.

During the first half of the nineteenth century a Second Great Awakening among Baptists and Methodists in the south spread Christianity to the "unchurched," both whites and Blacks, at camp meetings and revival meetings where the enslaved heard these hymns and spiritual songs and transformed them in aural tradition into their own language and musical style. The style echoes African elements also preserved in Candomblé (Chapter 6, Gateway 23), such as pentatonic scales with a minor third and a minor seventh and improvised call-and-response singing. Watts's lyrics about sin and personal salvation were remade to reference salvation from the harsh reality of slavery.

Something close to the original performance style of African American spiritual songs is preserved today by performers from the Georgia and South Carolina Sea Islands. During the eighteenth century these mosquito-infested, malaria-infected places sent plantation owners scurrying to higher, healthier ground on the mainland. Enslaved Africans were left in charge of growing rice using tidal flows of water. They had brought knowledge of these skills with them from the west coast of Africa. Left to their own devices, Blacks living on or near the islands preserved musical styles closer to their African roots than did mainland Black populations in contact with white culture. Recent recordings by Bessie Jones and the Georgia Sea Island Singers and The McIntosh County (Georgia coast) Shouters give some idea of the antebellum style of singing by Blacks. These groups perform **ring shouts**, which originated among enslaved African Americans as religious rituals featuring dancing in a circle, hand claps, and call-and-response singing. A modified, subdued version of this style is conveyed in a performance of the spiritual "Roll, Jordan, Roll" in the 2013 movie *12 Years a Slave*, which won the Academy Award for Best Picture.

The first printed collection of African American songs, titled *Slave Songs of the United States*, was published in 1867 by three white abolitionists from the north who had worked in South Carolina to aid the enslaved during the Civil War. The Fisk Jubilee Singers took some of their songs from that collection but also learned from other sources. After a white minister heard them sing in Nashville, he taught them "Swing low, sweet chariot," which he had heard sung by workers at his school in Mississippi and which he attributed to a recently freed African American named Wallis Willis.

Choirs at other Black colleges founded by missionaries in the 1860s and 1870s took up this glee-club style of spiritual singing and have enjoyed considerable fame since then, including choirs from Morehouse College, a men's college founded in Atlanta in 1867; Hampton University, founded in 1868 in Virginia; and Tuskegee University, founded in 1881 in Alabama (freed slave Booker T. Washington [1856–1915] was its first president). Choral conductors at these schools, including R. Nathaniel Dett (1882–1943), a composer and director of the Hampton Singers, and William L. Dawson (1899–1956), a choral conductor and composer at Tuskegee, have over the years produced sophisticated arrangements of spirituals. These "concert spirituals" have long been a point of pride in the Black community and a staple of the music programs in Black colleges and universities. In the twentieth century they entered the repertoire of white college and high-school choirs and became an important genre in the pantheon of American classical music.

The movement of spirituals into the mainstream of American music was aided in no small part by Henry T. ("Harry") Burleigh, whose grandfather had bought his own freedom in 1835. Raised in Erie, Pennsylvania, his grandfather taught him to sing spirituals. Burleigh studied voice and gained some fame locally as a classical singer before he was accepted at the National Conservatory of Music in New York in 1892, just in time to meet its new director, Antonín Dvořák, and introduce him to spirituals. Burleigh arranged spiritual songs for voice and piano and toured the country as a concert artist, spreading the popularity of spirituals. Since then, under his influence, many African American classical singers have included spirituals, along with European opera, in their repertoire. Among them were Roland Hayes (1887–1977), who had studied at Fisk and had sung in the Fisk Jubilee Singers; Marian Anderson (1897–1993), who in 1939 sang a famous concert for 75,000 people at the Lincoln Memorial after being denied access to segregated concert halls in Washington, D.C.; and Paul Robeson (1898–1976), a famous Broadway actor and singer. More recently African American opera singers Kathleen Battle, Jessye Norman, and Leontyne Price have included spirituals in their recitals.

In 1874, just as the Fisk Jubilee Singers were spreading excitement about African American spirituals at home and abroad, American composer Philip Bliss (1838–1876) published *Gospel Songs: A Choice Collection of Hymns and Tunes*, with the goal of updating the style and language of Protestant religious music, including Dr. Watts's spirituals. White and Black composers linked to the Pentecostal movement have created **gospel songs** ever since. In the 1930s Black **gospel quartets**, in some sense descendants of the Fisk Jubilee Singers, gained fame on the radio, including such groups as the Dixie Hummingbirds, the Five Blind Boys of Alabama, and the Soul Stirrers. In the same decade a blues singer from Georgia named Thomas A. Dorsey (1899–1993), the so-called father of Black gospel music, composed "Take My Hand, Precious Lord," made famous by Mahalia Jackson (1911–1972), the most important mid-twentieth-century gospel singer. The favorite gospel song of Dr. Martin Luther King Jr., she sang it at his funeral in 1968.

WHERE DO I GO FROM HERE?

- Listen to the 1909 recording of "Swing Low, Sweet Chariot" and some of the other early recordings of the Fisk Jubilee Singers. What similarities and differences do you notice among them?
- Watch a video of Bessie Jones and the Georgia Sea Island Singers or the McIntosh County Shouters singing songs of slavery and performing ring shouts. Which musical elements connect to spirituals, and which musical elements are reminiscent of examples of African music and Candomblé?
- Listen to a performance of the gospel song "Precious Lord, Take My Hand" by Mahalia Jackson.

GATEWAY 31
NATIVE AMERICAN POW-WOW DRUMMING, SINGING, AND DANCING

What Is It?

Pow-wows are intertribal gatherings of the Indigenous people of the United States and Canada. They feature drumming and singing for social, contest, and exhibition dancing. Two styles of drumming, singing, and dancing are prominent at pow-wows today: Northern Plains Style, which extends from Kansas into Canada, and Southern Plains Style, from Oklahoma and the Southwest. Socializing, trading (buying and selling Native products and food), and sharing and learning about Native ways are also important elements of a pow-wow. Our gateway to Native American pow-wow drumming, singing, and dancing is a recording in the Northern Plains Style of a song for a contest dance, a Men's Traditional Dance called "Old Sioux Warrior Dance Song" performed by the Ironwood Singers at the 106th Rosebud Sioux Fair during the summer of 1982. As the reference to the 106th iteration of this fair suggests, American Indian fairs with rodeos, parades, carnivals, circuses, and drumming, singing, and dancing have their roots in the late nineteenth century.

Men's Traditional Dance, along with Grass Dance and Fancy Dance, are three categories of contest dancing for men at pow-wows. Women's contest categories are Women's Traditional Dance, Fancy Shawl (or Women's Fancy) Dance, and Jingle Dress Dance. "Sioux" in the song title is a name Europeans gave to the Očhéthi Šakówiŋ, a large confederation of tribes who live on the northern Great Plains of the United States; they refer to themselves by such names as Lakȟóta and Dakȟóta. Rosebud is one of five Sioux reservations in South Dakota. For this recording the Ironwood Singers consisted of eight men and one woman. The men sit around a large bass drum with the head facing up. Together, they all sing and hit the drumhead in unison, each holding a single drumstick. The woman stands behind the circle of men and sings. Together, they constitute an ensemble called a **Drum**.

 Listen to the first thirty seconds of the recording.

How Does It Work?

Timbre

The men's voices are high-pitched, loud, and full-voiced at the beginning of some phrases and remain loud and strong as they descend in pitch. The drum creates a deep, resonant sound.

Texture

The texture features the low-pitched pulsating beats of the drum accompanied by the singers' melody. The MC's comments and the sound of the dancer's bells, which can be heard in the powwow arena, also contribute to the texture.

FIGURE 8.13

The Ironwood Singers at the 106th Rosebud Sioux Fair in 1982. Left to right: Harold Condon, Kenny Haukaas, Robert Kim King, Harvey Larvie, Stan Pretty Paint, Ernie Ray Running, George Whirlwind Soldier, Dave White, Sandra Black Bear White.

Source: Tony Isaacs, Indian House.

Rhythm

The rhythm is based on the steady beating of the drum. The beats are mostly unaccented and not in a particular meter. The vocalists fit their melody in between the beats of the drum as much as possible.

Melody

The melody has a wide range of nearly two octaves. Built on a pentatonic scale, melodic phrases have either a descending or a flat contour.

Harmony

Native Americans describe harmony in terms of a good relationship between the singing and the drumming and the footwork of the dancers, who wear jingling ankle bells or other sounding items on their regalia. Performers try to bring these relationships into what they call "harmony."

Form

This song, like all pow-wow songs, is strophic. It consists of four verses, called **push-ups**. The beginning of each push-up is marked by the lead singer singing solo on a very high-pitched phrase, after which the rest of the singers join him and repeat the opening phrase. Push-up refers to the extraordinary vocal effort the singers must make to hit these very high pitches at the beginning of each push-up.

Performance Practice

The singers sing very loudly with a pulsating quality but still try to blend their voices so that no one sticks out. The drummers increase the tempo and loudness after the second push-up. At the end of the fourth push-up they return to a softer sound.

Listen for the high-pitched solo voice at the beginning of the first push-up and continue listening until you hear the lead singer begin the second push-up.

Listen to the entire recording following this timed listening guide.

LISTENING GUIDE 8.5

TIME	SECTION	FORM	DESCRIPTION	SONG TEXT
0:00	MC announcement		Drum beats softly as the MC says, "Hau. OK Ironwood, song number two" [of the Men's Traditional Dance contest].	
0:08	Push-up 1	A	Solo lead singer sings a melody consisting of three very high pitches on the five syllables of the text sung twice.	*Kȟolá mánipe* (2x) (My friends are marching)
0:12		A	All the singers repeat the lead singer's phrase.	*Kȟolá mánipe* (2x)
0:18		B	The singers begin on a lower pitch than they did in A and descend on a pentatonic scale to the tonal center. At the end of the phrase, the drummers play four "hard beats." The next phrase (section C) begins slightly before the fourth hard beat.	*Kȟolá mánipe, mánipe*
0:22		C	The singers begin on a lower pitch than they did in B and descend below the tonal center, echoing the A phrase an octave lower and ending with three vocables (e, e, e) on the tonal center.	*Kȟolá mánipe* (2x) *e e e*
0:29		A'	The singers sing the first half of the A phrase	*Kȟolá mánipe* (1x)
0:33		BC	As above	As above
0:43	Push-up 2	AA'BC A'BC	As above	As above
1:16	Push-up 3	AA'BC A'BC	The drummers increase the tempo and beat the drum louder.	As above
1:46	Push-up 4	AA'BC A'BC	The drummers keep the faster tempo but on the second time through the A'BC section they play a little quieter toward the end and reintroduce the hard beats.	As above
2:20	MC Announcement		"Hau! How about a big round of applause for the dancers and singers. . . . Thank you very much. . . ."	
2:29	End			

What Does It Mean?

This recording was made during a performance for contest dancing at an outdoor social event, a pow-wow. The meaning of this song arises not only from the aesthetics of performance but from the relationships among the Drum, the dancers, the Lakȟóta who live at Rosebud, the members of other tribes attending the pow-wow, the larger community of Native North Americans, the non-Indian spectators, and the tragic history of conflict between Indigenous people and European settlers, homesteaders, and the U.S. and Canadian governments.

Pow-wows typically last two days over a weekend. They are widely advertised on the internet, and Drums, dancers, traders, and Indian and non-Indian spectators are invited to attend. Participants come from miles around, typically within a day's drive of the venue. Pow-wows take place outdoors in grassy fields and indoors in arenas, gymnasiums, and hotel ballrooms.

Pow-wows may be organized and sponsored by tribes at a particular reservation; Indian-owned casinos; Native American student groups at universities; and Native-run organizations in cities with large Native American populations. Different sponsors may have slightly different motivations for doing so, but they all seek to serve the well-being of intertribal

SOCIAL BEHAVIOR

communities in the United States and Canada. The organizers sometimes offer substantial cash prizes for the best Drum and the best dancers in each contest category. Some participants count on their winnings as a source of income or at least to pay their travel expenses, in effect becoming professional singers and dancers. Organizers hold "blanket dances" for spectators and dancers to offer donations to pay the expenses of traveling Drums and community members in need.

Typically, the pow-wow dance space is defined by a circle of many Drums, together with the MC's table. The organizers select a host Drum and invite other Drums from the area. Traditionally Drums consisted exclusively of men, but today a pow-wow may include all-female, mixed gender, and Two-spirit (LGBTQ+) Drums. Beyond the circle of Drums sit the spectators. The traders set up their tables and cooking stands behind them.

This physical circular organization has a conceptual counterpart, which Tara Browner (Oklahoma Choctaw) calls a "Sacred Hoop." The center circle is the circular drum itself. It is a living being with a spirit that must be carefully looked after and respected. When the Drum is not performing, the drum may be covered with a blanket, and someone will remain nearby to look after it. The next circle consists of men sitting around the drum. Their drumming produces "the heartbeat of the people." It provides the spiritual energy that brings the community together and inspires the dancers to dance well. Outside the men's circle, the women stand and sing. The drum beats are fundamental, and the singers and dancers accompany the drum beats, not the other way around. The dancers form the next circle. They refer to each of the Drum's push-ups as a **round**. They step on the beat and move their legs and upper bodies in subtle and sometimes athletic ways. Some dance for entertainment, some for money, some for pride in their family and tribal traditions, and all dance to honor ancestors, relatives who have fought in past wars, and future generations who they hope to inspire to take up these traditions. When the drummers play their "hard" beats, the dancers hear them as "honor" beats, and make a gesture such as raising a fan in their hand to honor those they are thinking about as they dance. The circle of dancers is surrounded by spectators and traders. The Great Spirit, manifest in all creation, encircles all the participants, making what may appear to be a secular event into a sacred one, a Sacred Hoop.

Pow-wows have a somewhat predictable agenda with variations that depend on the region of the country, the organizers, and the input of the MC. Commonly they begin with a Grand Entry, a parade of all the participants into the arena with a Grand Entry Song provided by the host Drum. At the head of the Grand Entry an elder often carries a staff with eagle feathers, a highly valued symbol of bravery and spiritual power. After him men and women military veterans, often in uniform, bear national, state or provincial, and military-branch flags. Veterans are held in high esteem for their service to the nation and the community, and they link the modern pow-wow to tribal warrior societies of the past. As the flags are posted by the MC's table, a Drum sings a Flag Song and a Victory Song. Following the flag bearers, the designated Head Dancers lead the dancers into the circle in the regalia of their contest dances, in age-graded order from oldest to youngest. Separate contests may be held in each dance category for "golden agers," adults, youths, and "tiny tots." After the Grand Entry the dance contests begin. An MC keeps everything running on time,

> CULTURAL
> LINKAGES

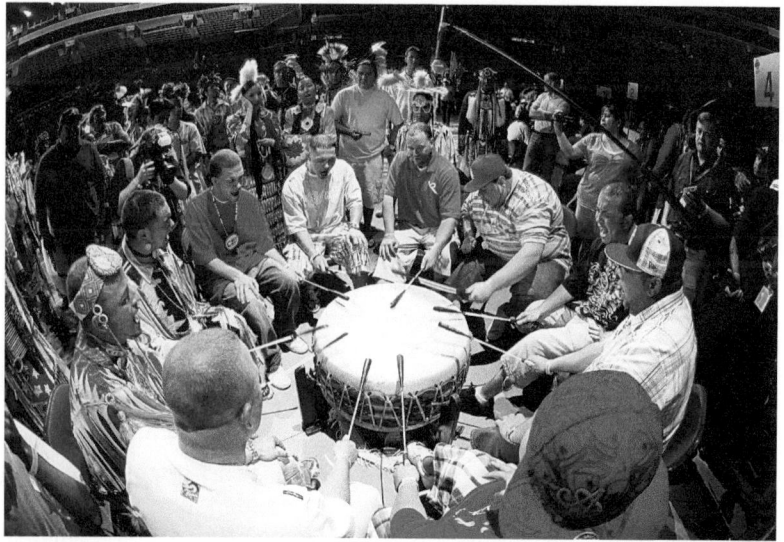

FIGURE 8.14

Drum with men seated around the drum and two women singers standing outside the circle

Source: Walter Larrimore/National Museum of the American Indian, Wikimedia Commons.

FIGURE 8.15
Grand Entry led by elders and bearers of the U.S. and Canadian flags
Source: Katherine Fogden/National Museum of the American Indian, Wikimedia Commons.

telling the next group of dancers when they need to be ready for their contest and cueing one of the Drums to perform a song for the next dance. Between contests there are a variety of "social" or "intertribal" dances for all participants and spectators, whether in regalia or street clothes; "honor dances" requested to remember someone in the community or a historical event; "blanket dances" to collect money for a group or person in need; and exhibition dances from outside the pow-wow tradition, such as Aztec dances and the dances of local tribes. At the end of the pow-wow, awards are given out for first, second, and third place in each dance category. Each day concludes with a Retreat Song for "retiring the colors" (the removal of the flags).

Pow-wows mirror the social life of Native communities in the United States and Canada on many levels. On reservations dancers and drummers often learn from older family members who take them under their wing and teach them these traditions along with other aspects of Indigenous life such as cooking, the sewing of regalia, and the spiritual nature of all things in the world. In cities, learning may begin among a group of friends who decide to use these traditions as a way to express an identity alongside other identities typical in mainstream urban life. Dancers and singers often speak of their performances as acts of respect for the elders who taught them. They also speak of their participation in the pow-wow as a means to keep Native ways alive and to inspire young people to take them up in a context where Indigenous lifeways have been under continuous threat since the first European colonists arrived in North America.

The transmission of dance traditions depends on young people learning to properly assemble and wear the regalia for the dances they choose to perform. This might include learning how to sew a dress or make a moccasin, how to assemble the elaborate bustles some dancers wear on their backs and arms, and how to decorate the regalia with handcrafted and purchased items. Elders may give young dancers items to include on their regalia as a sign of the continuity of tradition and teach them how to attach eagle feathers properly so they won't fall off and dishonor the dancer and the symbolic meaning of the feather. The careful attention to the tiniest details of dance regalia is an outward sign of respect for these traditions and, in addition to dance moves and stepping on the Drum's beat, one of the important criteria in judging dance contests.

Pow-wow singing, drumming, and dancing also express tribal identity. The words of some songs, for example, are in Native languages and unique to a tribe. Although pow-wows contain many shared elements, people notice differences indicative of tribal identity, from the organization and protocols of the event to details in regalia, dance movements, and songs. One noticeable musical difference is between the high-pitched singing of Northern pow-wow Drums (from Canada to the southern Kansas border) and the lower-pitched singing of Southern pow-wow Drums from Oklahoma and the Southwest. Beyond these tribal and regional differences, intertribal pow-wows are an expression of Indigenous identities, worldviews, and solidarities. They provide a much-needed form of resistance to the external threats to Native societies and sovereignty posed by the policies of the national governments of the United States and Canada. In spite of this tragic history of betrayal and genocide, since World War I Indigenous people have volunteered in large numbers to serve in the militaries and foreign wars of the United States and Canada. The pow-wow color guards, Flag Song, Victory Song, Retreat Song, and the honors paid to veterans celebrate Native Americans' valor in service to all the people of the United States and Canada.

The cultural meanings attached to elements of the pow-wow are just as varied as its social meanings. Each tribe, each family, and even each person may give unique meaning to these elements based on their life experiences. For example, younger Native people who regard the tradition of women standing behind the seated male drummers as an expression of gender hierarchy may try to change the tradition by having women sit with the men or by creating all-women groups seated at the drum. Others have argued that when women stand, their singing can be better heard and not be absorbed acoustically by the bodies of male singers. Ethnomusicologist John-Carlos Perea (Mescalero Apache, Irish, German, Chicano) reports that he was taught by an elder that standing women represent mothers encircling the male singers just as a pregnant woman encircles her baby. The high-pitched singing at the opening of each push-up is then said to represent "the cry of a newborn baby," an interpretation that gives women a central role in Drum performances and places men and women in a complementary rather than hierarchical relationship.

Although the pow-wow may appear to an outsider as a fun secular event full of jokes from the MC, social dancing, vibrant contest performances with extraordinarily elaborate dress and athletic movements, and good food and shopping, in many if not most cases Native people assign a spiritual or sacred meaning to these activities. In doing so, they do not divide the world into sacred and secular domains as European-derived culture often does. Rather, they understand all the world as suffused with sacred elements. Since they learn these spiritual beliefs from family and friends in oral tradition rather than from widely read sacred scripture and shared liturgies, some of the interpretations vary from person to person. For example, Jingle Dress dancer Michelle Maas (Anishinaabe-kwe), a mental health advocate for the Native community in San Francisco, was told that the Jingle Dress Dance originated in the 1920s in the Great Lakes region of Canada when a man had a vision in a dream that a dress with jingles could heal his ailing daughter. Women made such a garment for her, dressed her in it, and helped her around the dance circle. By the fourth round, she could make it on her own and was cured. Maas concludes, "The Jingle Dress is also called a medicine dress for this reason. . . . The sound the jingles make when dancing is a prayer that someone is healed." This story may also suggest that performing a song four times for four dancing rounds has a healing or spiritual power and reflects Native divisions of the world in four colors (races) and four directions (north, east, south, west). Eddie Madril

EMOTIONAL RESONANCE

FIGURE 8.16
Jingle Dress Dancer
Source: Katherine Fogden/National Museum of the American Indian, Wikimedia Commons.

FIGURE 8.17
Men's Fancy Dancer
Source: Katherine Fogden/National Museum of the American Indian, Wikimedia Commons.

(Pasqua Yaqui) from the central valley of California specializes in Fancy Dance, the most physically demanding of the contest dances. He frames his relationship to the tradition in terms of responsibility:

> My responsibility is not to dance really good and win competitions. My responsibility is not to dance really good and make people like me. My responsibility as a dancer is that dance is prayer. Pow-wow should be prayer, pow-wow should be church.

These examples illustrate the many ways individual participants in pow-wow dancing and singing construct a sacred meaning for themselves based on the stories they have been told, their own experiences as participants, and their hopes for the future of their people and traditions.

What Is Its History?

Something like the modern pow-wow began to emerge in the United States during the late nineteenth century against a backdrop of a century of U.S. government false promises, broken treaties, expropriation of lands, forced migrations, and cultural assimilation. Indigenous people today are still dealing with the consequences of these traumas, and the pow-wow, with its songs and dances, is a form of resistance against assimilation, a balm that soothes social and psychological wounds, a source of pride in Native American culture, and an expression of hope for the future.

The conditions for the development of the pow-wow as an expression of peaceful and productive intertribal communication were created when the U.S. Congress passed the Indian Removal Act of 1830. For many years white settlers had been moving from the Atlantic coast west and south beyond the Appalachians toward the Great Lakes and into Florida and the Southeast, where they came into conflict with local Native tribes and pushed them off their lands. On behalf of the settlers, the U.S. government entered into treaties with these nations, incentivizing them to move west of the Mississippi River to "Indian Territory," where the government promised they could have free land and govern themselves as independent nations. Some refused to leave and stayed behind. But during the 1830s, prodded by the administrations of Presidents Andrew Jackson and Martin Van Buren, an estimated 60,000 members of the Creek, Cherokee, Chickasaw, Choctaw, and Seminole nations in the Southeast traveled to a large Indian Territory reduced today to the state of Oklahoma. Thousands died along the way in an exodus that one tribal leader called a "trail of tears."

In Indian Territory they reconstituted themselves as sovereign nations with their own constitutions and laws as did the many tribal groups they encountered there. Among them were the Wichita, who were native to the region; tribes that had been removed from the Great Lakes region, including members of a union of Ojibwe, Odawa, and Potawatomi nations called the "Three Council Fires"; and Plains Indians who had entered the area from the north in the eighteenth century, including Apaches, Kiowa, and Comanches. In 1851 Congress created the Indian reservation system, and in 1871 they stripped American Indians of the right to negotiate with the U.S. government as sovereign nations. White settlers followed the Natives westward, and soon the conflict over land in Indian Territory resulted in the reduction of the size of Indian reservations. The Apache Nation of Oklahoma, for example, had been given about three million acres for its reservation, but after the government allotted land to individual resident whites and some Natives, the Apache reservation was reduced to less than 30,000 acres. In 2010 Native Americans made up 9.4 percent of the state's population, and today Oklahoma lists thirty-nine American Indian nations within its borders. This phenomenon of many distinct Native tribes living in close proximity on small reservations was an important factor in the development of the modern intertribal pow-wow.

After the Civil War ended in 1865, the Lakȟóta and other tribes on the northern Great Plains continued to resist white expansion in a series of battles, the most famous of which was their annihilation of a U.S. cavalry unit at the Battle of Little Bighorn in the Montana Territory in 1876. The Indian Wars came to an end in 1890 after the notorious massacre of nearly 300 men, women, and children at Wounded Knee on the Pine Ridge Reservation in South Dakota. Ever since, Lakȟóta, and all Native people, have continued to struggle for their autonomy and rights. During the late nineteenth century, the government changed its policy from removal to assimilation. It created "Indian schools" with the goal of erasing Indigenous language and culture and encouraging the adoption of white patterns of land ownership, farming, and work in cities. Expressions of Native religions were banned, including singing and dancing at sacred ceremonies.

Beginning in the 1870s, one outlet for Native dancing was the "wild west show." These shows, which continued into the early twentieth century, romanticized life in the American West and made famous a host of performers including Buffalo Bill Cody, Will Rogers (Cherokee), Tom Mix, Annie Oakley, and Calamity Jane. In 1885 the Lakȟóta visionary and chief Sitting Bull joined Buffalo Bill's Wild West Show for a year. Other Native participants in such shows over the years included Red Cloud (Lakȟóta), Chief Joseph (Nez Perce), and Geronimo (Apache). The cast of the shows could be over 1000 people and included Native people in enactments of religious dancing for entertainment and reenactments of battles and raids between "cowboys and Indians," rodeos, races, sharpshooting exhibitions, and parades. Some believe that the pow-wow Grand Entry may be a legacy of the wild west show parades and that Fancy Dance stems from Indian dancers being encouraged to "fancy up" their dances to make them more entertaining for non-Native spectators.

CULTURAL LINKAGES

Entertainments for non-Native people allowed Native singing and dancing to continue despite the ban on Native religious expression. They became prominent features of fairs, rodeos, circuses, and carnivals. Pow-wows as independent events for drumming, singing, and dancing seem to have emerged in the 1920s, the name possibly borrowed from a Narragansett language term for spiritual leader. In the 1930s and 1940s pow-wows were held to honor soldiers going off to and returning from war, establishing a link between pre-contact warrior societies and modern military service, expressed in this gateway recording and in the respectful treatment of military veterans and national flags during the pow-wow. Today pow-wows and pow-wow singing continue to change to fit the times. New songs in English comment on social media and other aspects of modern life, and the participation of women and the inclusion of non-binary people is keeping pace with changes in the larger society in which Native Americans live today. While pow-wow songs have deep roots in tribal culture, today they are also an expression of the modern experiences of Native Americans.

Modern life in the United States and Canada has taken some Native Americans into other forms of music making besides pow-wow drumming, singing, and dancing. One is new music composed for an intertribal handmade, end-blown wooden whistle flute. Among its most famous exponents are R. Carlos Nakai (Navajo, Ute), Kevin Locke (Lakȟóta), and Doc Tate Nevaquaya (Comanche). Since the early twentieth century Native people have participated actively in the shared culture of North America by contributing to many genres of music. Examples include the swing jazz singer Mildred Bailey (Coeur d'Alene), jazz bassist Oscar Pettiford (Oklahoma Choctaw, Cherokee), rock singer and guitarist Robbie Robertson (Cayuga, Mohawk), folk singer Buffy Sainte-Marie (Piapot Cree), classical composer and conductor John Kim Bell (Mohawk), electronic group The Halluci Nation (Tim "2oolman" Hill [Mohawk], and Ehren "Bear Witness" Thomas [Cayuga]), Black Eyed

FIGURE 8.18

Canadian-born Piapot Cree folk singer Buffy Sainte-Marie (b. 1941), the first Native individual to win an Oscar for Best Song in a Motion Picture, performing at the Riddu Riđđu Festival of Indigenous Arts in Norway

Source: Marius Fiskum, www.mariusfiskum.no. Wikimedia Commons.

Peas rapper Jaime Luis "Taboo" Gomez (Shoshone), and innumerable country music bands, among them Billy ThunderKloud (Gitksan) and the Chieftones from Edmonton, Alberta.

WHERE DO I GO FROM HERE?

- Find and listen to a recording of a pow-wow song in the Southern Plains style. Using the elements of music, describe the similarities and differences in style between it and the Northern Plains style described in this gateway.

- Find and watch a video of a pow-wow and look for the Grand Entry, a men's Fancy Dance, and a women's Jingle Dress Dance. Pow-wow.com is a good source for such videos. Examples of a Two-spirit (LGBTQ+) pow-wow can be found at the website of the Bay Area American Indian Two-Spirits, host of one of the largest Two-spirit pow-wows (www.baaits.org).

- Read about and listen to recordings by one of the Native musicians or groups mentioned in this gateway performing in a genre of music other than pow-wow drumming and singing.

- Today, Indigenous people all over the world are engaged in sustaining musical traditions in worlds that have been transformed by land dispossession and other traumas at the hands of settlers, mainly from Europe. Read about and listen to music from the Aotearoa New Zealand Māori group Tararua and their participation in the revival of traditional Māori musical instruments (*taonga pūoro*), whose use nearly died out completely after European settlement.

CLOSING

During the late nineteenth century composers kept alive the Romantic spirit of the early years of the century by writing tone poems and other instrumental music designed to express in music the emotions inherent in poetic images, philosophical ideas, fictional narratives, and works of art. Their orchestral and piano music took on a fuller sound due to changes in the manufacture of metals and musical instruments and to the willingness of wealthy patrons to take the place of the aristocracy in support of extravagant and expensive forms of music making. Nationalism unleashed a new *raison d'être* for composers: serving the aspirations of their national community for a sovereign, independent nation-state. The musical legacy of this period includes:

- school and military brass bands;
- the modern piano;
- the current size of the large symphony orchestra;
- the public concert in a large concert hall; and
- music conservatories (and university schools of music).

African American music continued to enter the mainstream of American musical life beyond minstrelsy and the parodied banjo in the form of spirituals created by enslaved African Americans and arranged in a European manner for college choirs. Native Americans joined in intertribal entertainments at fairs, carnivals, and "wild west shows" as one way to keep their traditions in the face of official government suppression of them.

THINGS TO THINK ABOUT

- Compare the way the musical worlds opened by the four gateways in the chapter respond to the ambitions of ethnic nationalism.
- All the types of music in the four gateway recordings in this chapter are performed today. Compare their meaning and impact in the late nineteenth century with their meaning and impact today.

NEW TERMS

arioso	*Gesamtkunstwerk*	nationalism
civic nationalism	gospel quartets	pow-wow
compound meter	gospel songs	push-up
Drum	*Leitmotifs*	ring shout
ethnic nationalism	music drama	romances
folk songs	musical nationalism	spirituals

Music History in the Age of Recordings

THE AGE OF RECORDINGS begins around 1890, with the sale of the first musical recordings. It continues to the present. The use of electricity and electronics to record, produce, and transmit music, which began in the 1920s, is the defining feature of this era of music history. People all over the world now enjoy the ability to hear music whenever they want and in the absence of the musicians who perform it. Recordings have revealed a vast repository of human music making that previously was largely unknown to people who could not hear it live. Recordings have captured virtually the entire history of twentieth-century and twenty-first-century musical life. They have been indispensable for understanding those traditions that, before the advent of recording technology, were transmitted in aural rather than written tradition. Recordings have helped to knit together people and societies around the world who are able to hear and see each other sing, play, and dance and imagine worlds far beyond their own.

During the twentieth century the United States replaced Europe as the dominant force in world affairs, its military and economic muscle matched by its influence in music, movies, and fashion. As a consequence, Part III shifts focus to American music. Two categories of music become prominent in this part of the book: American popular music and jazz. **American popular music** is the most heard music in the United States for obvious reasons. First, by definition the term "popular" is an adjective for anything that is widespread among the people (the populous). Second, its primary mode of transmission is through recordings, so it can be heard everywhere, not only in formal concerts. Third, young people use popular music as a resource for courting, for socializing, and for establishing new and emerging identities. Fourth, the popular music of the United States has spread around the world in the wake of its symbolic, economic, and military power during the age of recordings. The principal form of popular music is the song, a piece of music with poetic lyrics. Since teenagers and young adults are the primary audience for popular music, the main themes of its song lyrics concern newfound and hoped-for love and romance set in danceable rhythms. Beyond romantic love, popular songs have also registered the values of youth, and the populace, in every period of history and in every society.

Jazz originated at the beginning of the twentieth century among the descendants of enslaved Africans in the United States. Throughout its history jazz has been played all over the world by musicians of all racial and ethnic backgrounds. It occupies a space between American popular music and classical music, and it overlaps with both. Like popular music, it is transmitted in recordings, and, like classical music, in written form as well. Like popular music, its principal form historically has been the song or other relatively short composed structure. But like classical music it sometimes features intricate long-form compositions, especially those written for large jazz bands. It is carried on in both instrumental and sung traditions. While recordings are important in jazz, it lives in live performances, where musicians show off their improvisatory and technical skills. Like popular music, jazz flourishes in small bars, restaurants, and nightclubs, but, like classical and popular music, the most famous jazz artists fill large concert halls and outdoor music festivals.

Each of the six chapters in Part III contains gateways representing popular music, jazz, classical music, and at least one other musical tradition that emerged during the time period covered in the chapter.Source: Christian Bertrand/Shutterstock.

DOI: 10.4324/9781003269304-12

MUSIC FROM THE TURN OF THE TWENTIETH CENTURY (1890–1918)

IN 1877 THOMAS EDISON invented the phonograph, making recording and playback of sound possible for the first time. Though early phonographs were recorded to fragile tinfoil and later wax cylinders, by the 1890s recordings were being made on flat discs that could be used to make many duplicates. The self-playing player piano was also invented at the end of the nineteenth century. Player pianos read long rolls of paper with piano performances recorded on them via perforations and mechanically re-played those piano performances. For the first time, it became possible to reproduce a musical performance and to hear it in a time and place distant from where it was originally performed. These technologies ushered in an era that transformed the ways that people experienced music. Musical performances could be preserved, musical sounds could be distributed widely, and recordings (including piano rolls) could be bought, sold, and owned. Edison and his contemporaries surely could not have imagined the multibillion-dollar music industry that developed after recordings and radio replaced sheet music as the main way people consumed popular music in the 1920s. Thanks to recordings it is possible to construct detailed histories of jazz, all kinds of popular music, and rural, court, and religious traditions from North America and around the world dating back to around 1900. This chapter traces the beginning of these histories in the age of recordings during the period between 1890 and the end of World War I in 1918.

Technological innovations in sound recording were just one aspect of changes in social, economic, and cultural life in many parts of the world. During this period many people moved to cities, where the availability of electricity transformed many aspects of daily life. Industrialization accelerated rapidly, especially in the United States. European power in world affairs continued to decline, a process begun in the nineteenth century as European imperial powers lost colony after colony to independence movements in the Americas.

In 1890 traditional European monarchies were firmly in place in much of the continent, but after a devastating world war from 1914 to 1918 Europe lay in economic ruin, with many of its imperial rulers, who had been the source of so much musical patronage for centuries, deposed. The United States, in contrast, had enjoyed extraordinary industrial and economic growth in the 1890s. In 1917 it intervened decisively in what Americans at the time called the European War on the side of Britain, France, and the Russian Empire against Germany, the Austro-Hungarian Empire, the Ottoman Empire, and Bulgaria. World War I was the first war

FIGURE 9.1

Thomas Edison in 1878 with an early model of his phonograph. Photo by Levin C. Handy.
Source: Bardy-Handy Collection. Library of Congress, Wikimedia Commons.

DOI: 10.4324/9781003269304-13

conducted with weaponry produced on an industrial scale, including newly invented tanks and airplanes. It resulted in more than nine million dead and countless millions wounded. During and immediately after the war, the Russian Empire had become the Soviet Union, and the Austro-Hungarian and Ottoman Empires had dissolved into a plethora of small nation-states. At the end of the war in 1918, the United States had emerged as the most economically powerful country in the world. The twentieth century has been called the "American century" for the scope of the United States' global reach and influence in politics, economics, and culture, including music.

Between 1890 and 1918, European stability was challenged not only by political strife among nations and empires but by social and economic unrest as well. Misery among working-class industrial workers coupled with poverty in rural villages caused a flood of emigrants from Europe to the United States, Argentina, and Australia (some six million people immigrated to the United States from Europe between 1901 and 1910, and American cities grew enormously in size). There was growing resistance to European colonialism and imperialism in the Americas, Africa, India, and Southeast Asia. This political and economic malaise stimulated new thinking and creativity among European artists and intellectuals, who began to question the inevitability of European progress and cultural superiority. Their work contained radical departures from the cultural, intellectual, and artistic traditions of the nineteenth century.

Intellectuals began to question the nature of human psychology and the physical world. Sigmund Freud (1856–1939) theorized that unlocking the unconscious was the key to understanding human behavior, and he developed a process of therapeutic interventions for psychologically troubled individuals that he called psychoanalysis. Albert Einstein (1879–1955) undermined the previously taken-for-granted dichotomy between energy and matter, arguing that matter could be transformed into energy in his famous equation $E = mc^2$. As scientists showed that the psychological and the material worlds were more complex than initially thought, movements in the visual arts like impressionism, surrealism, and cubism shifted away from realistic representations of the world and towards capturing sensory experiences and psychological states. In his cubist works Pablo Picasso showed ways to do that, beginning with early paintings like his 1907 *Les Demoiselles d'Avignon* (The Damsels [young women] of Avignon). The content of the painting, five nude prostitutes (the Avignon in the title is a reference to a street in Barcelona known for its brothels) facing unabashedly toward the viewer, was scandalous in its time. Its form was equally surprising for its elimination of three-dimensional perspective in favor of two dimensions; its treatment of the human body as a set of geometrical shapes; and its drawing of the two faces on the right to resemble African masks he had seen in a French ethnographic museum. This last move captured the turn-of-the-century fascination with Asian, African, and Middle Eastern cultures, whose works of art were on display in museums and in world's fairs in major cities in Europe and the United States.

Collectively these artists came to be called modernists and their work examples of modernism. Modernists wanted to liberate themselves from traditional artistic norms in ways analogous to revolutionaries trying to bring down the old economic and political order in Europe. The notion of modernism in music also arises at this time. Like visual artists, modernist European composers began to move away from musical sounds that were considered pleasing and easily understood and towards music that called those values into question and demanded deeper engagement from listeners. Tonal harmony, the basis for European classical music for the previous two centuries, began to fade among European composers. Modernist musical aesthetics changed the course of classical music in the age of recordings.

The period from 1890 to 1918 is also a time when popular culture emerged as a significant force in the world's cultural life. The term "popular" is used to reference the taste of the general public (the populace) and refers both to large numbers of people (popularity) and to the lower and middle classes. The idea of popular culture for large masses of people became possible only with the late nineteenth-century growth of cities and the expansion of education to nearly all segments of the general population. Until this time, cultural production (books, folklore, art, music) in Europe was not widespread, that is, popular. Rather, each class or stratum of society (the church, the courts of the aristocracy, the urban bourgeoisie, and the rural peasantry) had its own kind of music. Universal education and masses of people living and earning wages in towns and cities created a new literate audience with modest amounts of money and leisure time to spend on cultural activities such as reading, visiting museums to view art, acquiring copies of paintings rather than originals, attending sports events, buying tickets to vaudeville shows and motion pictures, and purchasing newly invented phonographs to play music at home. Many also purchased pianos for their homes and, in the United States, purchased sheet music produced by a popular music industry of publishers and songwriters known as Tin Pan Alley. Dominating the printing and distribution of sheet music in the late nineteenth and early twentieth century, this industry was centered on a single block on 28th Street in New York City. The street was known as Tin Pan Alley for the cacophonous street sound of dozens of pianos simultaneously playing different songs from the publishers' offices as songwriters promoted their songs to publishers and professional singers looking for new material.

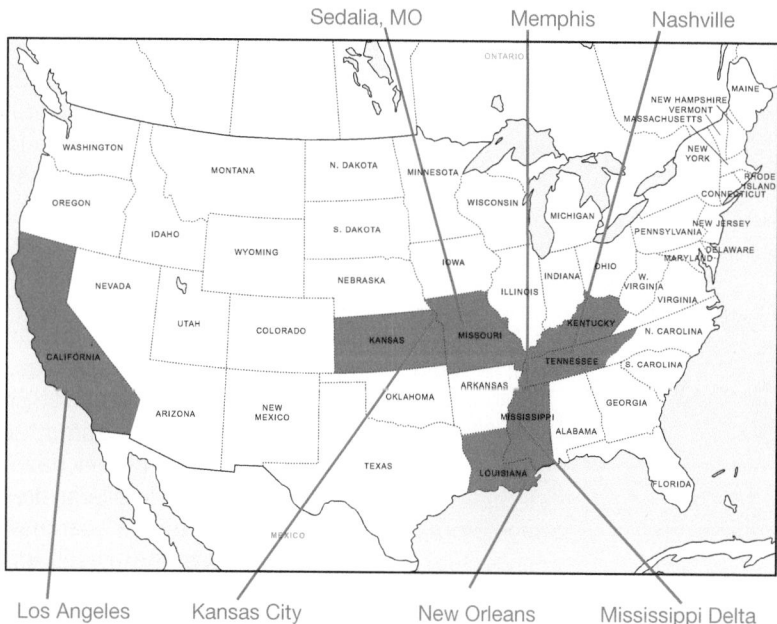

FIGURE 9.2
Map of the continental United States

Not everyone lived in cities, of course. Some people in the United States still lived in the countryside. They farmed the land in conditions that demanded hard work and barely met their needs for daily subsistence. Arguably the most significant musical genre that emerged under these conditions was the blues, a genre created by African American communities in rural areas of the South, where Jim Crow laws institutionalized the suppression of Black voting rights, and lynchings and other violent legacies of slavery persisted. The blues, along with vaudeville songs, outdoor band concerts, and the new genre of ragtime, were all part of the dynamic popular musical culture in the United States during this period.

This chapter includes several gateways to types of music that were products of these changing times:

- the blues, one of the precursors to jazz and a genre that has enjoyed a rich history in its own right;
- American band music, which proliferated in this period as a popular music;
- American popular piano music, through the example of ragtime, a genre showing influence from a number of musical traditions;
- early modernism in European classical music in the compositions of Claude Debussy and Igor Stravinsky; and
- a genre of Balinese gamelan that emerged in the wake of Dutch conquest of the island of Bali.

 ## GATEWAY 32
CLASSICAL MUSIC AT CENTURY'S END

What Is It?

At the end of the nineteenth century, German and Austrian composers were still absorbing the lessons of Beethoven and Wagner. In Paris, however, artists and writers were creating a

FIGURE 9.3
Claude Debussy
Source: Nadar. Paris, Wikimedia
Commons.

FIGURE 9.4
**A faun in the form of the Greek
god Pan teaches young Daphnis,
the son of Hermes and a nymph,
to play the panpipes**
Source: Virtus Incertus, Wikimedia
Commons.

new movement, one that came to be called modernism. **Modernism** refers to the rejection of traditional boundaries and rules in art. In this vein, some late nineteenth-century French artists were imagining new ways to paint the natural world. They were literally blurring their images and figuratively blurring the "rules" that painters had followed since the Renaissance, and their movement was called **impressionism**. Some French writers, known as **symbolist poets**, were abandoning logic and narrative in favor of evocation and suggestion. Our gateway to music that participated in this French modernist movement at the end of the nineteenth century is a one-movement orchestral work by French composer Claude Debussy (1862–1918) titled *Prélude à l'après-midi d'un faune* (Prelude to the Afternoon of a Faun), first performed in 1894. This work renders in music the poem *L'après-midi d'un faune*, written by the important symbolist poet Stéphane Mallarmé (1842–1898).

Mallarmé's poem relates the thoughts of a faun awakening from a dream. A faun is not a young deer (fawn) but the Roman analog of the Greek god Pan, a horned half-man-half-goat creature (*satyr* in Greek) who roamed the forests playing his panpipes in search of pleasure with wine and young female deities (nymphs). The poetry is full of evocative, surprising, and contradictory poetic images of the sights and sounds of the forest: "stifling with heat the cool morning struggles"; "an arid rain"; "scintillating flowers"; "frivolous shade." Against this sylvan backdrop, in language that is direct but elusive, the faun tries to remember his lovemaking with two nymphs—or, as he says, "Did I love a dream?" His flute-playing, from which rain and breezes flow, provides a "prelude" to his amorous adventures. But the effort proves too much and, addressing the nymphs, he concludes, "With no more ado . . . I must sleep . . . and . . . open my mouth to wine's true constellation! Farewell to you, both: I go to see the shadow I have become."

 Listen to the first thirty seconds of the recording.

How Does It Work?

Timbre

Debussy uses timbre, for which tone color is an apt synonym, to paint in music Mallarmé's depiction of the changing sensations of the forest scene and the faun's desultory mood. A flute solo represents Pan's flute, and horn calls suggest the outdoors. The sound of woodwinds, long associated with the outdoors in European classical music, is featured prominently. The strings play **tremolos** (on strings, short, rapid, back-and-forth bowing) softly to suggest the rustling of breezes through the forest leaves and the changing, dappled light. The timbres change continuously but gradually to suggest the faun's flow of memory and sensation.

Texture

The piece begins with an unaccompanied flute solo. Often the strings play soft murmuring sounds in the background to woodwind and horn solos.

Rhythm

A sense of pulse is almost completely absent. The music flows along, like a breeze or a brook, unconstrained by a beat or meter.

Melody

The opening flute melody has an inverted arch shape and uses a mainly chromatic scale.

Harmony

The harmony is tonal, but cadences are spaced far apart, and so the feeling of tonality is considerably weakened.

Form

The piece has an ABA form. The A sections are based on the inverted arch-shaped, chromatic flute melody. In the B section a new melody is introduced.

Performance Techniques

The most striking performance techniques involve the use of mutes to quiet the horns and the strings and create a muffled sound. In one section the strings bow over the fingerboard rather than near the bridge, as usual, to create a new tone color. The score directs the flute player to play "sweetly and expressively."

Listen to the first minute of this performance for the melodic shape of the solo flute melody and the shimmering timbre of the orchestra when it enters.

Listen to the entire recording following this timed listening guide.

TIME	SECTION	FORM	DESCRIPTION
0:00	A	a	A solo flute enters with a chromatic, inverted arch-shaped melody in its low register.
0:25		b	The orchestra enters with a harp arpeggio suggesting shimmering forest light followed by horn calls.
0:57		a	The flute melody returns, this time accompanied by soft, long tones in the orchestra.
1:36		c	The orchestra enters on a dominant seventh chord. It seems to suggest light rather than tension, followed by a new melody based on thirds which "develops" into a three-tone motive.
2:04		a'	The orchestra enters quietly on a sustained chord and then the flute plays its melody. It continues to play variants of the melody in a way that sounds improvised.
2:43		a"	The flute plays a faster version of the melody over the shimmering sound of harp arpeggios. The section resolves on a major chord and a slight pause, suggesting a new section is coming.
3:22	B	Melodic runs	The tone color (timbre) of the orchestra changes, followed by rapid runs by different instruments.
3:51		d	A new melody is introduced by the oboe followed by a series of gentle crescendos and decrescendos and changing tone colors in the orchestra, the first time the traditional timbre of a string orchestra asserts itself.
5:10		ee'e"	The orchestra plays a new melody with a series of descending phrases, followed by a varied repeat, and then a short motive from the melody.
6:57	A' (a variation of the A section)	a'a"a''' a''''	The flute plays the opening melody but more slowly than at the beginning, followed by suggestions in the oboe and flute of forest sounds. The oboe plays a repeat of the melody followed by the flute playing it twice more. The oboe plays the very end of the melody.
9:27		cadence	A cadence on a major triad followed by the horns playing the opening melody in parallel thirds to a soft ending on a major triad.
10:07		End	

LISTENING GUIDE 9.1

What Does It Mean?

For the French musical public in 1894, *Prélude à l'après-midi d'un faune* meant something in relation to nearly a century of expressive Romantic music by Beethoven, Berlioz, Chopin, Wagner, and Smetana and in relation to the current artistic climate in France. Just as Debussy did in *Prelude to the Afternoon of a Faun*, Beethoven, Berlioz, and Smetana had painted rural scenes in their music, one indicator of the Romantic fascination with the wildness and restorative qualities of nature as opposed to the regulated intensity of urban life. Chopin had modeled a dreamy, rhythmically fluid expressivity. And Wagner's *Tristan und Isolde* was just one example of the Romantic interest in Ancient and Medieval myths and legends like the story of Pan. At one level, Debussy's prelude could be interpreted as following in that long Romantic tradition.

At another level, Debussy's dreamy, gauzy, gentle music matches the artistic and literary milieu of France during the late nineteenth century and represents an important break from the dramatic, surging, emotional compositions of Beethoven, Berlioz, Wagner, and Smetana. In *Prelude to the Afternoon of a Faun*, Debussy appears to be trying to match Mallarmé's elusive, free-form, illogical ("arid rain") poetry by blurring the logic of tonality and using fluid rhythms to create a free-flowing musical style devoid of traditional meters.

French painters of the period were also challenging the conventions of their art. In 1874, while Debussy was a student at the Paris Conservatory, Camille Pissarro (1830–1903), Claude Monet (1840–1926), and Auguste Renoir (1841–1919) mounted an exhibition that scandalized the artistic establishment. Although their paintings of rural landscapes and seascapes continued the Romantic fascination with nature, they did so in a new style that erased the formality and energy of traditional representations in favor of suggestions of the shapes they were viewing, the colors they were seeing, and the way light illuminates an ever-changing, fluid natural world. One critic, responding negatively to the exhibit, seized on a painting by Monet called *Impression: Sunrise* and sarcastically dubbed the style impressionism. The name stuck. Debussy's *Prélude à l'après-midi d'un faune* represents the sonic expression of the late nineteenth-century French literary and artistic world, and his style is often called musical impressionism, although Debussy disliked the epithet, probably because of its negative connotation at the time.

As a young musician Debussy was fascinated by Wagner's music, which was all the rage in the Paris of his youth. In 1888 and 1889 he attended the Bayreuth festival and absorbed Wagner's new approach to "endless melody." The opening phrase of Wagner's *Tristan* Prelude echoes eerily in the opening of Debussy's *Prelude*, each with their solo opening lines, shared chromatic, inverted arch-shaped melodies (much extended in Debussy), and opening, unstable, non-tonic chords. In the B section the strings enter and play subdued echoes of the sweeping crescendos and decrescendos so prominent in the *Tristan* Prelude. On the other hand, in *Prelude to the Afternoon of a Faun*, Debussy rejects the dramatic, emotional character of Wagner's music. Rather than expressing the surging passions of characters in a drama or the composer's unrequited love as in *Symphonie Fantastique*, Debussy paints, following Mallarmé's text, a gentle picture of an idyllic forest afternoon.

FIGURE 9.5
***Impression: Sunrise* by Claude Monet**
Source: Musée Marmottan Monet, Wikimedia Commons.

Listen one more time to *Prélude à l'après-midi d'un faune* for the pleasure of Debussy's "impressionistic" painting of a dreamy, wine-soaked summer day.

What Is Its History?

Debussy was born in 1862 to a family of shopkeepers in a small town a few miles west of Paris. He began studying piano at seven years old and, at age ten, entered the Paris Conservatoire, where he studied for the next eleven years. In 1884 Debussy won the Conservatory's prestigious Prix de Rome for composition. In 1889 he attended the Paris *Exhibition Universelle*, a world's fair for which the Eiffel Tower was built. Cultural exhibits and shows from various parts of the world included a "Negro village," which displayed people as if in a zoo; Buffalo Bill's "Wild West Show" with sharp-shooter Annie Oakley (Chapter 8, Gateway 31); and performances by a Javanese gamelan (Chapter 5, Gateway 19). The sound of the gamelan, with its approximately equidistant pentatonic scale, made a profound impression on Debussy. He began using equidistant chromatic scales and equidistant six-pitch (hexatonic) **whole-tone scales** (e.g., C-D-E-F -G -A), instead of the minor scales and chords typical in European classical music. His short piano composition "Pagodes" (1903) uses a pentatonic scale and extreme high and low pitches to suggest the sound world of the Javanese gamelan.

Debussy was not especially productive. In addition to *Prelude to the Afternoon of a Faun*, his most famous symphonic work, other highly regarded works include a ballet premiered in 1912 in Paris by the Ballets Russes called *Jeux* (Games); an often-played string quartet (1893); numerous short pieces for solo piano, the most famous of which are "Clair de lune" (1905), based on a symbolist poem by Paul Verlaine (1844–1896), and *Children's Corner*, a suite of six pieces (1908); and one opera, titled *Pelléas et Mélisande*, which eschews arias in favor of a speech-like recitative style that would become the norm of twentieth-century operas.

Debussy's innovations were enormously influential in France and the United States in the early twentieth century. He knew all the most important composers in the French musical scene, all of whom had to react in one way or another to his work. Among the champions of his innovative musical style were French composers Erik Satie (1866–1925) and Maurice Ravel (1875–1937) and three foreign composers residing in Paris: Manuel de Falla (1876–1946) from Spain; Igor Stravinsky (1882–1971) from Russia; and Arthur Honegger (1892–1955) from Switzerland. In the United States, composers Duke Ellington (1899–1974) and George Gershwin (1898–1937) studied Debussy's orchestrations and harmonies, which included, for example, ninth chords (chords built in thirds that include scale degrees 1, 3, 5, 7, and 9) moving in parallel motion. This type of chord movement is not technically allowed in traditional classical tonal harmony, but it became a common feature of jazz. Later in the century German composers adopted some of his innovations, and the dreamy, fluid quality of his music resonates in New Age music, which first came to prominence in the 1960s and 1970s.

FIGURE 9.6

Debussy and Igor Stravinsky in Paris
Source: Bettmann/Getty Images.

WHERE DO I GO FROM HERE?

- Compare the elements of Debussy's *Estampes*: 1. "Pagodes," which imitates the Javanese gamelan, to the elements of the Javanese gamelan performance heard in Chapter 5, Gateway 19.
- Listen to a piano roll recording of Debussy playing "Clair de lune" on YouTube.
- Listen to *Jeux d'eau* (Play of Water) (1901) for piano by Maurice Ravel. How does this music resemble and differ from the piano music of Debussy and Satie?

GATEWAY 33
THE BLUES

What Is It?

The musical genre known as the blues provides the foundation for much of American popular music and jazz during the age of recordings. Historians trace its roots to African American culture at the turn of the twentieth century. Our gateway to the blues is "Backwater Blues" by the vocalist Bessie Smith (1892–1937). Even though it was recorded in 1927, in some of its musical elements and lyrical themes it is an example of a blues with roots in the period from 1890–1918. The blues came to prominence during this period and was widely performed in rural and urban African American communities, though rarely recorded. A **blues** is a strophic song most typically in a repeating AAB form of twelve bars. The blues were (and are) an entertainment music for enjoyment, dancing, and partying. They also were (and remain) a way for performers and audiences to deal with hardships of economic oppression, racism, sexism, infidelity, domestic abuse, and other perils of daily life. As a genre name, it derives from phrases like "I've got the blues" used when people are feeling down.

FIGURE 9.7
Bessie Smith in 1936
Source: Everett Historical, Shutterstock.

One of the defining features of the blues is what has come to be called **blue notes**. These are pitches that fall in between the pitches of the twelve equal-tempered pitches of the piano. Often they are up to a half step lower than a scale degree of the major scale, usually the third, fifth, or seventh. Sometimes the resulting blues scale sounds like a minor mode, even if the underlying harmony is major. These blue notes can give the blues a characteristic sad quality. Many recordings of the blues, including this one, have a swing feel. In a **swing feel**, beats are subdivided unequally with the first note longer than the second note, sometimes suggesting an underlying triple subdivision of the beat. The relative length of notes in swing often depends on the tempo of the music. A uniform swing feel in a group is best achieved when musicians listen to one another and synchronize the ways that they are swinging the rhythmic durations.

 Listen to the first thirty seconds for the overall sound and the swing feel.

How Does It Work?

Timbre

This recording features a female vocalist with a particularly bright tone along with a piano. The recording technology of 1927 results in the timbre of both the voice and the piano sounding slightly muffled.

Texture

The texture can be described as melody with accompaniment, where the vocalist carries the melody most of the time and piano provides the accompaniment.

Rhythm

The song has a steady beat in a duple meter maintained by the piano. The vocalist and the pianist incorporate a swing feel throughout the performance. They also incorporate a good deal of syncopation.

Melody

The melody is based on a major mode with a great deal of microtonality as the vocalist slides between pitches. It also relies heavily on blue notes.

Harmony

The piano establishes the harmonic structure, which features triads and dominant seventh chords, each one with a duration of either two or four bars.

Form

After a two-bar piano introduction, the song takes the form of a strophic song where each verse lasts twelve measures. The lyrics of each of the seven verses have an internal form of AAB, where one line of text (A) is repeated with different underlying harmony and usually a different melody, followed by a new line of text (B) and a new melody.

Performance Techniques

In addition to sliding between pitches, Bessie Smith is very flexible with her phrasing, one of the markers of a master of the blues style. In some phrases, she seems to rush slightly and sings slightly ahead of the beat. For others, she seems to slightly delay and sings the lyrics slightly late or behind the beat. Sometimes she sings the phrases directly on the beat. In addition, after each line of text the piano plays a short improvised phrase, which means each line of text is a call and response between the vocalist and the pianist.

Listen to the first thirty seconds, the first verse, for the way Bessie Smith slides into pitches and anticipates or delays beats.

Listen to the entire example following this timed listening guide.

LISTENING GUIDE 9.2

TIME	FORM	INTERNAL FORM	LYRICS	DESCRIPTION
0:00	Instrumental introduction			A piano plays a rolling repeated pattern in the low register of the piano, setting up a swing feel and a steady pulse maintained throughout the recording.
0:04	Verse 1	A	When it rains . . .	The vocalist sings the opening verse. She
0:13		A	When it rains . . .	slides upwards to the pitch on the "five"
0:23		B	Then trouble's . . .	and "skies" in the first line and "rains" in the second line. She slides downwards at the end of the pitch when she sings "night" in both of the first two lines. The piano remains in the background while she is singing, but responds to each line with an improvisation. The improvisation after the first "B" line is a good example of syncopation.
0:32	Verse 2	A	I woke up . . .	
		A	I woke up . . .	
		B	That's enough trouble . . .	
1:00	Verse 3	A	Then they rowed . . .	
		A	Then they rowed . . .	
		B	I packed . . .	
1:28	Verse 4	A	When it thunders . . .	In verse 4, between the first and third lines,
		A	When it thunders . . .	the left hand of the piano shifts from its rolling
		B	There's thousands . . .	repeated pattern to a more active, descending low-register line emphasizing a swing feel, which is featured in place of the high register improvisations that have been happening so far. This perhaps serves as an icon of the low sound of thunder referenced in the lyrics.

TIME	FORM	INTERNAL FORM	LYRICS	DESCRIPTION
1:54	Verse 5	A	Then I went . . .	Verses 5, 6, and 7 feature a new style in the piano accompaniment where the left hand plays only on the beat in punchy, accented notes that resemble a march.
		A	Then I went . . .	
		B	Then looked . . .	
2:21	Verse 6	A	Backwater blues . . .	The improvised piano responses in Verses 6 and 7 are generally in a lower register and less active than in previous verses, perhaps reflecting the mood of the lyrics that conclude the vocalist's story of hardship without resolution of that hardship. At the same time, they continue an upbeat, swinging, danceable rhythm.
		A	Backwater blues . . .	
		B	Cause my house . . .	
2:49	Verse 7	A	Mmmmmmmm . . .	
		A	Mmmmmmmm . . .	
		B	There ain't no . . .	
3:11				The piano plays its final response and ends the song on an accented major chord.
3:16	End			

What Does It Mean?

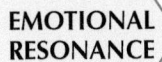
EMOTIONAL RESONANCE

The lyrics of this blues tell the story of a flood that destroys the home of the song's protagonist and the homes of many others. Each verse tells part of the story, which includes a five-day rainstorm (verse 1), the protagonist getting trapped in her house by the flood waters and evacuated in a rowboat (verses 2 and 3), the displacement of many other people (verse 4), a reflection by the protagonist on her now-destroyed house (verse 5), and a lament on having nowhere to live (verses 6 and 7). These devastating lyrics are set to a bouncy, rhythmic feel on the piano. While these musical elements seem contradictory, they demonstrate some of the nuances of the blues. For Black communities subject to segregation, discrimination, and violence under Jim Crow laws, the blues was music for coping with racial oppression and music for dancing and having a good time. "Backwater Blues" embodies both purposes with its danceable rhythms and lyrics that comment on the suffering of a community after a natural disaster and, more subtly, the way that racism and economic oppression exacerbated that suffering.

The AAB form of each strophe of the blues is an important part of what makes the blues both an effective means of catharsis amidst adversity and a vehicle for fun and entertainment. It can be understood as a pattern of tension-release-resolution. The first line of each strophe of a blues introduces a situation or problem (tension) and is typically sung over a harmony based on the tonic chord (I) for the full four measures of the line. The second line restates the lyrics of the first, but it is not simply a repeat of the text, as it shifts the emphasis of the first line through harmonic, melodic, and expressive changes. When the first line of each strophe's lyrics is restated in the second line, the underlying harmony moves to the IV chord for two measures before returning to the I chord for the next two measures. Bessie Smith also alters her performance of the melody, sliding on different words, modifying the duration of particular notes and the rhythm of the line, or changing pitches microtonally to create blue notes in the melody. For example, in verse 5 when she sings "then I went and stood upon a high and lonesome hill" the first time, she ascends to a high sustained pitch on the word "went." When she repeats the line over the IV chord, she remains in a lower, relaxed register and stretches out the pitch on the word "I." With its emphasis on "went," the first line could be interpreted as expressing the strain and anxiety in the act of going. The second line's lower register perhaps makes it sound more "blue," and by stretching out the word "I," Smith might be accentuating the loneliness of leaving a destroyed home, and in a sense releasing the tension of the first line.

These repeated lines in the typical form of the blues set up the resolution that the third (B) line of text brings. This part of the blues form typically occurs over a V chord for the first two bars, which, as a dominant, leads strongly back to the I chord for the final two bars, giving the harmony a sense of resolution. The B line in verse 5, "then looked down on the house where I used to live," answers the question of why the protagonist went to the top of the lonesome hill, an answer that brings this blues to an even darker image of the results of the flood, the image of homelessness. Blues singers employ a number of narrative strategies connecting the B lyrics of the blues to the preceding repeated A lyrics. They move the storyline along, interpret the A lyrics in a surprising way, introduce humor, or make the struggle of the story even heavier. The harmony and lyrics work together to bring a brief moment of resolution to each strophe of the blues. The resolution in the lyrics is often not a happy one, and the cyclical, strophic nature of the blues prevents the resolution from being too final, providing an immediate opportunity to continue dealing with the issue at hand in the next strophe.

 Listen again to the first strophe of "Backwater Blues." Listen for the changes in harmony, the ways that Smith alters her performance of the melody, and the way these musical gestures enhance the emotional qualities in the text.

"Backwater Blues" was recorded and released in 1927 in response to a flood in Nashville that forced nearly 10,000 people, mostly African Americans, from their homes. Flooding in areas of the American South near the Mississippi River and other waterways has long been an inevitable consequence of weather patterns. After heavy rains, lowlands are often flooded with backwater, stagnant water that is not part of the main flow of the river. These less desirable (and less valuable) floodplains were typically the home of Blacks and lower-class whites.

CULTURAL
LINKAGES

The recording became popular in the aftermath of a catastrophic Mississippi flood later that year, where over 90 percent of the flood victims were African Americans. Although white flood victims were entitled to receive relief services for free, Black flood victims were forced to pay for food and other services and in some cases take loans from landowners that they had to "pay back" through unpaid work in the fields in a version of slavery. This was one of a number of ways that the practices of slavery continued long after the end of the Civil War. The blues provided one way to deal with this oppression at an individual and collective level.

Since the lyrics do not mention these issues directly, finding the meanings of "Backwater Blues" involves interpreting the lyrics as a coded reference to oppression and shared adversity. In her study of Bessie Smith and other blues singers, scholar and activist Angela Davis has argued that the blues is not merely a series of complaints about life's challenges, but a way of strengthening a collectivity and offering glimpses of the possibility of moving beyond oppression.

A number of musical elements of the blues have their roots in African music and the music of African slaves in the American South, including microtonality and call and response. The microtonality that we hear in Bessie Smith's performance can be traced through the transatlantic slave trade to many musical traditions of the Americas (Chapter 6, Gateway 23). Though many other musical traditions around the world share this trait, in the case of the blues it is a marker of an African American aesthetic that appears alongside musical elements drawing on European roots such as harmony based on thirds and the fixed equal temperament of the piano. The call and response in "Backwater Blues" involves Bessie Smith presenting each line as a "call" characterized by her expressive use of pitch and rhythmic flexibility and the pianist, James P. Johnson, offering "responses" as short, improvised phrases. With its roots in a number of musical traditions of Africa, call and response requires collective interaction. Call and response among musicians and between musicians and audience members is common in the blues, as well as in forms of music making that became common during and after the time of slavery in the United States, such as work songs, ring shouts, field hollers, and spirituals (Chapter 8, Gateway 30). The call-and-response elements of these genres offer a communal, shared experience where many participants interact in musical ways. These forms of collective participation fostered community, communication, and solidarity among African Americans in the time of slavery and during Reconstruction and Jim Crow.

Listen again to several strophes of "Backwater Blues" for the way the vocal and piano perform call and respond with one another.

What Is Its History?

The blues emerged in impoverished African American communities of the American South, mostly likely in the period after the Civil War at the beginning of the Jim Crow era. Documentation of the blues from the turn of the twentieth century is scarce because the blues was not originally written down and recording technology was not yet prevalent. Blues songs were first published as sheet music in 1912. "Backwater Blues" and many of Bessie Smith's songs were not recorded until the 1920s.

"Backwater Blues" is an example of what is known as the classic blues. **Classic blues** were usually sung by Black female singers accompanied by a band or a pianist. Because there were at least two people performing together, forms, meters, and harmonies had to be established or more or less agreed upon in advance. Bessie Smith was a protégé of Gertrude "Ma" Rainey (1886–1939), who was known as "The Mother of the Blues" since she was one of the first African American women to perform blues music professionally. Rainey became well known through her tours, beginning in 1906, with a Black-produced minstrel show (Chapter 7, Gateway 27); she and her husband, William "Pa" Rainey, were billed as "Assassinators of the Blues." Mamie Smith (1883–1946), no relation to Bessie, was the first to record the blues in 1920.

FIGURE 9.8
Gertrude "Ma" Rainey
Source: Wikimedia Commons.

The classic blues was usually performed in theaters, tents, and "juke joints" (informal entertainment houses that were a big part of African American social life) where audiences paid to attend organized performances. These settings created a space for Black female singers and their audiences to engage with topics that were considered off limits in public, topics such as domestic violence, marital infidelity, and homosexuality intertwined with the struggles of racial discrimination and economic oppression. Rainey's "Prove It on Me Blues" (1928), for example, deals with female homosexuality. In Bessie Smith's graphic "Send Me to the 'Lectric Chair" (1927), she sings as a protagonist who catches her man with another woman, kills him in retribution by cutting his throat, and remorselessly asks a judge to give her the death penalty. Blues like these gave voice, sometimes in the form of exaggerated fantasies, to the lived experiences of their audiences, especially those of Black women. When recording technology became more readily available in the early 1920s, recordings of the classic blues were popular among Black audiences on what were known as **race records**: phonograph recordings of African American musicians produced between the 1920s and 1940s and marketed to African American consumers.

Bessie Smith, known as "The Empress of the Blues," was born in Chattanooga, Tennessee. Her rise to prominence began in 1909 when she began performing in Black theater and tent shows in the South, Midwest, and East Coast. Along with Rainey, she enjoyed widespread popularity starting in the early and mid-1920s with the advent of race records and their promotion of classic blues. Smith sold over four million records between 1924 and 1929, starred in the short film *St. Louis Blues* (1929), performed on Broadway, and became an international symbol of the classic blues singer. The 1920s also witnessed the rise in popularity of jazz, and Smith recorded and performed with some of the most well-known jazz musicians of her time such as Louis Armstrong, Coleman Hawkins, and James P. Johnson (the pianist on "Backwater Blues"). These collaborations demonstrate that, though the blues was in many ways a precursor to the development of jazz, there was a great deal of exchange among musicians of these genres as each contributed to the development of the other.

In the late 1920s and 1930s, the popularity of classic blues records inspired the recording of the country blues or rural blues, which had developed at the end of the nineteenth century. The **country blues**, as its name suggests, emerged in rural areas. It typically involved a male

FIGURES 9.9A AND 9.9B

An advertisement for Ma Rainey's "Prove It on Me Blues" in the September 22, 1928, national edition of the African American newspaper *The Chicago Defender*

Source: Alex van der Tuuk.

singer accompanying himself on the guitar, fiddle, or banjo. The performer could adjust the form, tuning, and harmonies of a given song to better suit the lyrics of the song, the vocal range of the singer, or his mood or whims, since he did not have to depend on coordinating with other instrumentalists or the preset tuning of a piano. The country blues was not always divided neatly into three four-bar phrases per strophe, but sometimes varied by strophe depending on the lyrics. W. C. Handy (1873–1958), the composer of the popular "St. Louis Blues" (published as sheet music in 1914), said that he was inspired by a country blues singer that he witnessed in 1903 performing at a train station in Tutwiler, Mississippi, in the Mississippi Delta region. Though no one can say for certain where or when the blues first developed, this region is today considered the birthplace of the blues. In the late 1920s a number of country blues musicians began to release race records, including Blind Lemon Jefferson (1893–1929), Charley Patton (1891–1934), and Eddie "Son" House (1902–1988).

One of the best-known country blues musicians is Robert Johnson (1911–1938), whose recordings from 1936 and 1937 inspired innovations in guitar performance by countless performers including Jimi Hendrix, Stevie Ray Vaughan, Eric Clapton, and the Rolling Stones. His most influential songs include "Sweet Home Chicago" (1936), "Love in Vain" (1937), and "I Believe I'll Dust My Broom" (1937). Like other country blues musicians, a robust mythology arose around Robert Johnson both during and after his life. The central story about Johnson

FIGURE 9.10
Robert Johnson, with guitar, and blues musician Johnny Shines (1915–1992) c. 1935
Source: Getty Images/Robert Johnson Estate.

is that he met the devil at a crossroads at midnight and sold his soul in exchange for an incredible ability to play the guitar. Though many have sought to attribute this legend to the fantasies of passionate fans, Johnson recorded several songs that propagated this myth, including "Me and the Devil Blues" (1937) and "Cross Road Blues" (1936). Myths about great musicians can be found in musical traditions almost everywhere. These myths serve to explain the seemingly unbelievable virtuosity of a musician or elevate a musician to a god-like status and great renown. Johnson died one year after his final recordings, but they continue to inspire blues musicians and those exploring the roots of guitar-based popular music genres.

The blues has continued to develop as a genre in its own right alongside jazz. Blues musicians like Muddy Waters, B. B. King, and Taj Mahal have continued the legacy of Robert Johnson and others as guitarist-singers of the blues. There are blues clubs and blues festivals all over the world. Chattanooga has dedicated both a museum and a performance venue to Bessie Smith. The film director Martin Scorsese directed a seven-part documentary series *The Blues* (2003), which traces the history of the blues. In 2015 actor-rapper-singer Queen Latifah starred as Bessie Smith in a biographical film titled *Bessie*. In 1982 the distinguished playwright August Wilson (1945–2005) wrote a biographical play titled *Ma Rainey's Black Bottom*. A film adaptation starring award-winning actors Viola Davis and Chadwick Boseman was released to great acclaim in 2020. For more than a century, the blues has served people everywhere as a vehicle for entertainment, dance, the expression of emotion, and the experience of collective solidarity in the face of struggle.

WHERE DO I GO FROM HERE?

- Listen to a Robert Johnson recording and explore its sound and meaning. What issues do the lyrics approach? What aspects of form or meter vary in each strophe, if any? Are there any more recent recordings of the song you chose that you could compare with Johnson's recording?

- Listen to some 1920s or 1930s recordings from the blues singers Mamie Smith, Gertrude "Ma" Rainey, Blind Lemon Jefferson, or Eddie "Son" House. Compare the musical elements of these recordings with those of "Backwater Blues."

- Watch the film *Ma Rainey's Black Bottom*. How does the film depict Ma Rainey and the social world of blues performance? What does it suggest about the economics of the recording industry with regard to race?

GATEWAY 34
AMERICAN BAND MUSIC

What Is It?

During the nineteenth century, municipal bands, large ensembles of wind instruments and percussion, played an important role in the popular culture of the United States and Europe. At the turn of the twentieth century, recording and radio technology had not yet transformed the way people listened to music (that happened about twenty years later). Bands in the United States thrived because they provided popular entertainment across the country. The most prominent composer of band music was John Philip Sousa (1854–1932). Our gateway to American band music is his composition "The Stars and Stripes Forever" (1896). Sousa composed more than a hundred marches, many of which are still played today. "The Stars and Stripes Forever" is his best-known march. By an act of Congress in 1987, it was declared the National March of the United States of America.

FIGURE 9.11
John Philip Sousa
Source: Elmer Chickering, Wikimedia Commons.

Bands are sometimes called wind ensembles, symphonic bands, concert bands, or, when the musicians play while marching or performing coordinated movements, marching bands. In the United States today band music is performed most often in high schools, college and university music programs, military ensembles, and competitive drum and bugle corps. This recording of "The Stars and Stripes Forever" is by "The President's Own" United States Marine Band, which Sousa raised to national prominence during his time as its conductor (1880–1892). Today the U.S. Marine Band is considered one of the premier bands in the United States.

 Listen to the first twenty seconds of this recording.

How Does It Work?

Timbre

A variety of timbres are produced by the ensemble of brasses, woodwinds, and percussion in different combinations.

Texture

Several versions of melody with accompaniment appear throughout the piece, with the final section of the piece adding an **obbligato**, which in band music means a second melody played simultaneously and in counterpoint with the main melody. Sections of homophonic rhythm are interspersed throughout.

Rhythm

Duple meter, characteristic of marches, is heard throughout, with prominent syncopations in the melody and "oom-pah" (low–high) accompaniments.

Melody

The melodies are generally in a major mode with some chromaticism.

Harmony

The piece uses tonal harmony throughout, plus quickly shifting chromatic harmonies in several sections.

Form

The form is a version of the typical American march form, which Sousa helped to standardize. It follows a variation of the European dance form, IAABBCC'DCC'DCC'. The melody of each section in a march is called a **strain**.

FIGURE 9.12
"The President's Own" United States Marine Band in 2017
Source: GySgt Rachel Ghadiali.

- Introduction (I): a fanfare (4 bars).
- First strain, or section (A): the first melody (16 bars), with balanced four-bar phrases (repeated once).
- Second strain (B): the second melody (16 bars). It is common for the second strain to be played softly once, and then repeated loudly, a performance practice tradition often not notated on the score.
- Trio (C): the third melody, played legato (16 bars). March trios are often in a secondary key: the subdominant for major-key marches (like in this example), and the relative major for minor-key marches. The trio here is repeated with some variation in the harmony and melody (C').
- Break strain, or "dogfight" (D): the fourth strain is often the most exciting music of a march and contrasts sharply with the more reserved trio melodies (24 bars).
- Repeat of the trio: the repetition of the trio features an added obbligato, played by a solo piccolo (CC').
- Repeat of the break strain (D).
- Grandioso: the final repetition of the trio melody (CC'), played at a loud dynamic, a fuller texture, with the obbligato (this time with all of the piccolos playing together), and with an additional countermelody in the trombones.

Performance Techniques

This performance by "The President's Own" United States Marine Band features great dynamic contrast among the various strains of the form. It also demonstrates the way that musicians in large wind ensembles precisely match articulations so that a given note played by multiple musicians is played uniformly in both accent and length.

Listen to the first minute or so and notice the slightly contrasting timbre between the first and second time through the first strain (A) and the contrast between the relatively strong quality of the first strain and the more lyrical second strain (B).

Listen to the entire recording following this timed listening guide.

LISTENING GUIDE 9.3

TIME	SECTION	FORM	DESCRIPTION
0:00	Introduction		A four-bar fanfare in octaves, with the full ensemble playing. Notice the syncopation in the second measure and the ascending chromatic line in the third measure.
0:04	First Strain	A	The major-key melody, in E-flat major, features a rhythm where a beat is divided into a long note followed by one or two short notes. This is typical of American march style and is less used in, for example, British marches.
0:19	Repeat of First Strain	A	
0:34	Second Strain	B	A more lyrical melody, with long held notes, is played softly the first time. Notice the playful, off-beat octave displacements in the upper winds.
0:50	Repeat of Second Strain	B	Second strain repeat, played loudly the second time, with the addition of full brass and percussion. Such changes provide variety to music that is otherwise notated as an exact repeat.
1:06	Trio	C	The trio modulates to the key of the IV chord (A-flat in this case) and presents a stately melody of long-held tones played by the saxophones and clarinets. This phrase ends on the dominant of the new key in what is called a half-cadence.
1:24		C′	The melody repeats in the second half of the trio with some variation, and the harmony ventures into more distant territory before ending with a full authentic cadence.
1:39	Break Strain	D	Lasting twenty-four bars, the "dogfight" has the first uneven phrase structure in the march (three eight-bar phrases), the only real departure from the archetypal American march form. This is also the most chromatic and exciting music in the march, the purpose of which is to contrast with the majestic trio melody. The downward chromatic lines seem to reference and invert the upward chromatic line from the introduction.
2:04	Repeat of Trio	C	The solo piccolo obbligato is added to the trio.
2:22		C′	Second half of the trio.
2:37	Repeat of Break Strain	D	The break strain is repeated exactly.
3:03	Final Trio ("grandioso")	C	The trio is played with full brass and percussion, including a new countermelody in the trombones and the obbligato played by the entire piccolo section.
3:18		C′	Second half of the final trio.
3:34	End		

What Does It Mean?

"The Stars and Stripes Forever" has its roots in one of the main activities for military and community bands of the nineteenth century—marching—though bands played both on parade and in concert performances. The typical form for earlier marches was more repetitive than the form Sousa later used for "The Stars and Stripes" and many of his other marches. This earlier march form would proceed through an introduction (I) and two repeated strains (IAABB) and a trio with two repeated strains (CCDD) before returning to the introduction and first two strains again (IAABB). When nineteenth-century bands played earlier marches in parades, an audience member might

CULTURAL
LINKAGES

hear the first two strains first at a distance, and again minutes later when the band was much nearer. In this context a march full of repeats would not sound repetitive to audience members, since they would be experiencing a shift in dynamics and perhaps the overall sound because of the shifting location of the band. The American modernist composer Charles Ives (1874–1954) was inspired by this kind of listening experience. He includes a version of it in "Putnam's Camp," the second movement of *Three Places in New England* (1911–1914), a composition for symphony orchestra. The orchestra is divided into multiple groups, each performing its own tune in its own key and meter, mimicking the sound of multiple community bands in a parade.

AESTHETICS

Sousa, in his marches written for the U.S. Marine Band and for his own professional touring band towards the end of the nineteenth century, changed the form of the march to better suit concert performances. The form for "The Stars and Stripes Forever" does not return to the beginning and repeat the first two strains. Instead, it proceeds sequentially from the first two repeated strains (AA, BB) to the trio (CC'), and then to a final section where the break strain alternates with the trio, with one repetition (DCC DCC'). For concert music, it was more compelling to bring the composition to a climax, creating the effect of a general crescendo from the beginning of the piece to the end. Sousa's march form concludes with the exciting break strain and the thick texture of the final trio featuring a melody and two countermelodies. These techniques created a sense of linear, forward momentum (as opposed to a repeating, cyclical motion) and gave marches a welcome variety.

 Listen again to "The Stars and Stripes Forever" and try to identify the sections of the form without relying on the timecodes given in the listening guide.

What Is Its History?

CULTURAL LINKAGES

Europeans first learned about military bands in their battles with the Ottoman Empire during the seventeenth century. Ottoman armies were accompanied into battle by a *mehter*, a band of valveless trumpets, **shawms** (loud, double-reed aerophones), drums, and cymbals and other idiophones. Early European and American military bands employed **fifes** (high-pitched, side-blown flutes), bagpipes (in Scotland), and drums. By the mid-nineteenth century, brass instruments had added valves, which made it possible for them to play chromatic melodies in all keys rather than being confined to the pitches of the overtone series. Bands began to feature the brass and sometimes eliminate woodwinds, and most towns in Europe, the United States, and Latin America had their own municipal bands. From the first half of the nineteenth century through World War I, bands of brass, woodwinds, and percussion were an important part of popular culture in Europe, the United States, and Latin America. Manufacturers, labor unions, high schools, and universities sponsored marching and concert bands to represent them on various occasions. In all these contexts, bands were used to create an emotional bond to the group they represented, whether the military unit (morale), the country (patriotism), the labor union (solidarity), or the school (pride).

Although the repertoire of brass bands is rooted in military marches, bands of the late nineteenth and early twentieth centuries played a wide variety of music, including popular dance music of the period (waltzes, polkas, and the cakewalk) and arrangements of classical music. During the nineteenth century, melodies from classical operas entered Italian popular culture when municipal brass bands played them for outdoor festivities. The Union Army in the American Civil War is said to have had 500 bands. By 1890 virtually every town in the United States had a band and a park or town square with a bandstand for bands to play on. The total number of bands likely exceeded 10,000. As America prospered and began pursuing its own imperial ambitions in the Philippines and Latin America in the 1890s, the patriotism indexed by brass bands playing military marches and the national anthem became an important feature of American musical life. That tradition continues today at sporting events where school bands promote enthusiasm for country and team before, during, and after games.

John Philip Sousa was born in Washington, D.C. His father, a Marine band musician, enlisted him in an apprentice program run by the U.S. Marine Band at age thirteen. After serving as its conductor, Sousa formed his own band in 1892 and concertized around the world for nearly forty years, becoming known as "The March King." Sousa also helped to design the **sousaphone**, a version of the tuba that marching players support on their shoulders and that sounds over the rest of the band.

One of the other well-known bandleaders of the period was James Reese Europe (1880–1919), a leading musician in the African American music scene of New York City in the 1910s. His large ensembles of African American musicians performed arrangements of marches, popular songs, spirituals, and blues songs in many settings, including Carnegie Hall, where he performed a number of times between 1912 and 1915. During World War I, he served as a lieutenant and led the band of the 369th Infantry Regiment of the New York National Guard (an all-Black regiment known as the "Harlem Hellfighters"). When the Hellfighters were deployed to France in 1918, Reese and the Infantry Band performed extensively for military and public audiences and became famous throughout Europe. One of the main features of the music of all of his ensembles was the prominence of a syncopated style and repertoire drawn from a genre of piano music called ragtime, which African Americans had pioneered at the end of the nineteenth century. A forerunner to jazz, ragtime and its history are the subject of the next gateway.

Bands have continued to be an important part of musical life of the United States throughout the age of recordings. Most high schools and universities have both concert bands that perform concerts and marching bands that perform in parades and in support of sports teams. Each U.S. high school and university has a "fight song," a song that is closely associated with the school team and played as a way to encourage fans to cheer for their team. The marching band halftime show has become a standard feature at high school and university football games. In many cases these shows involve elaborate displays of musicianship and field marching. Some high school bands work on one show per year and enter competitions against other high school bands throughout the school year. Independent non-profit musical organizations called drum and bugle corps have also developed annual elaborate field performances for a competition season that occurs in the summer.

Music for marching bands now includes a broad number of styles and a large repertoire in addition to the marches of Sousa and others. In the elaborate field performances by competitive high school bands and competitive drum and bugle corps, compound and additive meters of great complexity serve to inspire intricate movements of musicians as they march through complicated formations on the field. Musical compositions for concert bands since Sousa's time also employ twentieth- and twenty-first-century classical musical styles.

FIGURE 9.13
Ottoman-era Turkish military band called *mehter*. Painting by Arif Pasha 1939.
Source: National Library, Ankara. Wikimedia Commons.

FIGURE 9.14
Three sousaphones of the UCLA Marching Band
Source: UCLA Marching Band.

WHERE DO I GO FROM HERE?

- John Philip Sousa composed 136 marches during his lifetime. Find a recording of a march other than "The Stars and Stripes Forever" and figure out the form of that march. How is it similar to and different from the form of "Stars and Stripes"?

- Did your high school have a fight song? Research that fight song, or the fight song of another high school, college, or university, and find out when it was written, who composed it, and whether it has undergone any changes in its history. What is the form of the fight song?

- Find some recordings of James Reese Europe's band and compare them to recordings of a band playing Sousa marches.

GATEWAY 35
RAGTIME

What Is It?

Nearly a half century after Louis Moreau Gottschalk became the first important American classical composer and performer by sometimes borrowing from African American traditions, African American musicians began to develop a new approach to composing for and performing on the piano. Called ragtime, this new style was all the rage at the turn of the century. The most famous of these compositions, "Maple Leaf Rag" (1898) by Scott Joplin (c. 1868–1917), is our gateway to ragtime and American popular piano music at the turn of the twentieth century. **Ragtime** features a "ragged" or syncopated rhythm accompanied by a steady bass line with regular accents in duple meter. The texture, meter, and form of this and many other **rags** (the name for compositions in the ragtime style) mirror those same musical elements in the popular marches of the nineteenth century. This recording is by Richard (Dick) Zimmerman (b. 1937), a ragtime historian and performer who is one of the key figures associated with a revival of ragtime that began in the second half of the twentieth century.

 Listen to the first thirty seconds of "Maple Leaf Rag."

How Does It Work?

Timbre

The timbre is the sound of a solo piano.

Texture

The piano performs a number of textures, including a melody in the right hand with an accompaniment of the left hand alternating between a bass note and a chord; arpeggios through both hands; and block chords in both hands. The alternating bass note-chord in the left hand mimics the "oom-pah" accompaniment style of a march.

Rhythm

The piece is in a duple meter with highly syncopated rhythms throughout.

Melody

The melody includes stepwise motion as well as motion through arpeggiated chords in a major key.

Harmony

The harmony is tonal throughout. As in a Sousa march, after the first two strains in one key (A-flat), the trio modulates to the key of the IV chord (D-flat). Unlike a Sousa march, the final strain returns to the original key.

Form

"Maple Leaf Rag" is a multi-strain ragtime march, with related repeating sections whose form follows almost exactly the common form of Sousa's and other classic American marches. Here the form is AABBACCDD, a variant of European dance form similar to the form of "The Stars and Stripes Forever" (Chapter 9, Gateway 34).

Performance Techniques

This recording by Dick Zimmerman deviates quite a bit from the notated score of "Maple Leaf Rag" in terms of rhythm and pitch. Zimmerman adds syncopation where none is notated in some cases, plays an octave higher in the right hand in two different strains, and adds arpeggios and other ornamentation in a number of instances. In the trio Zimmerman plays with a slight swing feel at a few brief moments, but most of the performance is played "straight," a term used by musicians to describe equal subdivisions of the beat in contrast to a "swing feel." Such variations on the notated version of the piece were typical of the performers of the early twentieth century.

Listen to the first thirty seconds of "Maple Leaf Rag" and notice the three contrasting textures and the syncopated melody.

Listen to the entire piece following this timed listening guide.

FIGURE 9.15
Scott Joplin
Source: Pictorial Press Ltd/Alamy Stock Photo.

TIME	SECTION	FORM	DESCRIPTION
0:00	First Strain	A	The melody of the first strain includes arpeggiated chords and some stepwise motion in a syncopated, "ragged" rhythm. The texture varies quite a bit during the strain, including bass note-chord alternation, block chords, and arpeggios.
0:20	Repeat of First Strain	A	The first strain is repeated with slight ornamentations and variations introduced by the performer that do not appear in the notation.
0:40	Second Strain	B	The second strain introduces a different arpeggiated melody accompanied by a regular "oom-pah" gesture that alternates between a bass note and a chord. This became a common pattern for a jazz style known as "stride piano," as the left hand "strides" between the low bass note and the higher chord. In this performance the right hand is played one octave higher than written, and the performer introduces more variations and syncopations that do not appear in the notation. This mimics what participants in the stride piano scene and historians have reported about the performance practice of the time, in which skilled players would compete in what were called "cutting contests" to show off their improvisatory and technical skills while playing a composed rag or other popular song.
1:01	Repeat of Second Strain	B	The second strain repeats, this time with the right hand in the written octave, but again with a number of variations on the notation introduced by the performer.
1:21	Return of First Strain	A	A repeat of the opening strain, but with some changes added by the performer. One change can be heard at the end of the first two phrases, where the performer adds an ascending arpeggio in the right hand (1:23–1:26).
1:42	Trio	C	The stride piano pattern continues in the trio, with one interruption for an arpeggiated pattern. Similar to the second strain, the right hand is played an octave higher than written for most of this first statement of the trio. For the trio, the key moves to the key on IV (D-flat major).
2:02	Repeat of Trio	C	The trio is repeated with the right hand playing in the notated octave.

LISTENING GUIDE 9.4

TIME	SECTION	FORM	DESCRIPTION
2:23	Fourth Strain	D	The fourth strain for the most part abandons the alternating bass-chord stride piano pattern in favor of a pattern where the bass note on the downbeat in each measure is generally followed by two chords and then another bass note. It also returns to the original key (A-flat).
2:43	Repeat of Fourth Strain	D	The fourth strain repeats, with a slight ritardando in the final few bars.

What Does It Mean?

The hallmark of the ragtime style is its rhythmic syncopation. In "Maple Leaf Rag" the melodies in the right hand accent various offbeats while the left hand plays a constant stream of single notes and chords on the beat. The "oom-pah" pattern in much of the left hand derives from the popular marches of the nineteenth century and a popular ballroom dance called the two-step. The syncopation in the right hand, however, is a departure from these influences.

The name ragtime comes from a practice known as "ragging," where a performer would take a known melody and add syncopated, "ragged" rhythms. When ragtime was first popular between the mid-1890s and around 1918, this kind of syncopation was heard as a feature of African American music, perhaps because it was related to the rhythmic patterns typically played on the banjo, the most common instrument used in minstrel shows (Chapter 7, Gateway 27). The syncopated ragtime melodies interlocking with the regular, on-the-beat bass rhythm is a trace of the African practice of superimposing multiple rhythms on top of one another. Another rhythmic influence is the Cuban **habanera rhythm**, a syncopated rhythm that, in a bar of four beats, accents the first beat, the offbeat after beat two, and the fourth beat. It appeared in George Bizet's opera *Carmen* in 1875 and later in the tango, a popular dance from Argentina that swept through Europe and the United States at the turn of the twentieth century. This rhythm, along with other musical elements with roots in Latin America, was part of what the ragtime and early jazz pianist Ferdinand "Jelly Roll" Morton (1890–1941) called the "Spanish tinge" in jazz. He considered the Spanish tinge an integral part of the jazz sound, as is evident in his performances and published compositions, the first of which, "Jelly Roll Blues" (1915), is arguably the earliest published jazz composition. The melody in the trio of "Maple Leaf Rag" begins with two repetitions of the habanera rhythm.

 Listen to the Trio (C) of "Maple Leaf Rag" at 1:42 to identify the habanera rhythm.

Many types of ensembles played ragtime during its heyday, including dance bands, brass bands, banjo and mandolin ensembles, and symphony orchestras (the ensembles of James Reese Europe from the previous gateway are some of the most famous instances). In many cases, ragtime was music for dancing in settings like juke joints. The moderate tempo of "Maple Leaf Rag" certainly lends itself to dance. Publishing ragtime compositions as sheet music for solo piano meant that ragtime could also be played at home. Pieces like "Maple Leaf Rag" sold thousands of copies. "Maple Leaf Rag" can be performed exactly as notated in the 1899 sheet music, but its melodies, rhythms, and harmonies can also be embellished and adapted, as they are in this recording.

Embellishing existing popular songs was a common practice among ragtime and early jazz pianists such as Jelly Roll Morton, James P. Johnson, and Willie "the Lion" Smith (1897–1973). They elaborated on well-known songs to showcase their virtuosity and musical creativity for audiences and fellow musicians. Each had his own style, which was sometimes associated with a geographical region (e.g., Morton in New Orleans style, Johnson and Smith in East Coast style, and Scott Joplin in Midwestern style).

In the 1910s Johnson, Smith, Fats Waller (1904–1943), and others developed a piano style known as **stride piano**. It featured the left hand "striding" between bass notes and chords, along with heavy syncopation and many other virtuosic techniques. In many cases the stride pianists performed "Maple Leaf Rag" and other compositions at blistering tempos, which either led to extremely fast technical dancing or settings where audiences did not dance but instead listened to and appreciated the skills of the performer. In this recording of "Maple Leaf Rag," the pianist Dick Zimmerman embellishes the melody, rhythm, and harmony of "Maple Leaf Rag" to give some idea of what a live performance of this composition might have sounded like in the early years of the twentieth century.

FIGURE 9.16
Front cover of the sheet music to "Maple Leaf Rag"
Source: Scott Joplin (public domain), Wikimedia Commons.

 Listen to both repetitions of the second strain (B) of "Maple Leaf Rag" (0:40–1:21) for the shift in octave in the first repetition and the arpeggio ornamentation at the beginning of the second repetition.

What Is Its History?

Ragtime became a popular style during the mid-1890s. By the time Scott Joplin published "Maple Leaf Rag" in 1899 (it was composed in 1898), over 100 rags had already been published. The word "rag" first appeared in published sheet music in 1896, and the first instrumental song with "rag" in the title, *The Mississippi Rag* by bandleader William H. Krell, was published in 1897. "Maple Leaf Rag" was and remains the most famous rag. It started the craze for amateurs to learn to play composed rags from sheet music. During the heyday of ragtime, American marches and ragtime borrowed ideas from one another, so that marches often sound like rags and rags often sound like marches.

> **CULTURAL LINKAGES**

Scott Joplin was born in Texas, began playing piano as a teenager, and was educated by a German teacher in classical music theory. He traveled as a musician throughout the South and Midwest before settling in 1895 in Sedalia, Missouri, where he earned a living teaching piano. Like other Black pianists of his time, he developed a style of piano playing where he would "rag" popular songs and marches by improvising and adding syncopation. While in Sedalia, he composed the "Maple Leaf Rag," named after the town's "Maple Leaf Club," a social club where he often played. He wrote more than forty rags as well as other compositions, including two operas, *A Guest of Honor* (1903, now lost) and *Treemonisha* (1911). In 1916 Joplin's playing was registered on seven piano rolls. Joplin died in 1917 and, by the early 1920s, ragtime had begun to fade in popularity as a new popular music, jazz, was gaining favor among dancers and listeners. In reality, early jazz, with its syncopations and dance-friendly tempos and styles, sounded very similar to ragtime, so this change was at first one of terminology rather than of style.

Joplin's music and the ragtime style enjoyed several revivals during the twentieth century, the most significant in the 1970s, as the result of increased attention from classical musicians and

FIGURE 9.17
James P. Johnson
Source: Granamour Weems Collection/Alamy Stock Photo.

scholars. The pianist and musicologist Joshua Rifkin released an album of Joplin rags in 1970. He performed them exactly as they were notated on the sheet music without embellishment, treating them, in other words, like classical music. Arrangements of Joplin rags constituted the score to the popular 1973 film *The Sting*. Several collected editions of piano rags also appeared in the 1970s, making the sheet music broadly available to the public (most rags had fallen out of print). Dick Zimmerman recorded a five-LP set titled *Scott Joplin: His Complete Works* in 1974. *Treemonisha* was performed for the first time in 1972 by the Atlanta Symphony and fully staged by the Houston Grand Opera in 1976. A novel named *Ragtime* was published in 1975. It served as the inspiration years later for a Broadway musical of the same name, premiered in 1996. These and other revivalist activities brought Joplin's music and ragtime to broader public attention. Joplin was awarded a Special Citation by the Pulitzer Prize board in 1976, nearly sixty years after his death at age 49. Since then ragtime has continued to inspire musicians and composers in jazz and classical music as well as in many other musical scenes and genres.

WHERE DO I GO FROM HERE?

- Find a recording of Joshua Rifkin performing "Maple Leaf Rag" and a piano roll rendition of it played by Scott Joplin on a player piano. Notice the differences between Rifkin's precise performance of the notated score and Dick Zimmerman's performance filled with embellishments and adaptations. Is Scott Joplin's piano roll performance closer to Rifkin's or to Zimmerman's?

- Choose one of the stride pianists, either James P. Johnson, Willie "the Lion" Smith, or Fats Waller, and investigate his musical and personal biography and the context for the development of the stride piano style.

- The Broadway musical *Ragtime* (1996) and its subsequent revivals feature ragtime as a musical style along with a number of other styles. Look into the storyline of the musical and its soundtrack. How does the use of ragtime serve the storyline? What musical elements of ragtime do you hear in the soundtrack?

GATEWAY 36
CLASSICAL MUSIC IN THE NEW CENTURY

What Is It?

During the 1890s Claude Debussy tested the limits of tonal music. During the first two decades of the twentieth century, Igor Stravinsky (1882–1971) from Russia and Arnold Schoenberg (1874–1951) and his students Anton Webern (1883–1945) and Alban Berg (1885–1935), working in Vienna, pushed tonality aside in favor of new approaches to musical harmony and melody. Our gateway to the music of these early twentieth-century European modernists is *The Rite of Spring* (*Le Sacre du Printemps*), a 1913 composition by Igor Stravinsky. Originally including the subtitle *Scenes from Pagan Russia*, it was composed as a ballet for the Ballets Russes, a company of Russian dancers, choreographers, and visual artists in Paris. Today it is commonly performed as an orchestral concert piece. Since its debut this composition has been frequently performed by symphony orchestras the world over, and there are over 100 recorded versions of it. This recording, by the London Symphony Orchestra conducted by Claudio Abbado, was released in 1997.

 Listen to the first thirty seconds of the recording.

How Does It Work?

Timbre

The Rite of Spring features a wide palette of timbres from the instruments of a large symphony orchestra. In the opening section woodwinds play in a number of combinations, and an astounding twenty woodwind players are required to perform the piece.

Texture

This piece includes a variety of textures from solos to thickly layered contrapuntal parts.

Rhythm

The rhythmic elements are varied, including nonmetrical sections, sections with steady duple meter, and sections with changing and irregular meters. There are also many instances of polyrhythm, especially where beats are divided into two equal subdivisions by some members of the orchestra and into three equal subdivisions by others at the same time.

Melody

The melody is mainly in a minor mode.

Harmony

The harmony has many dissonant, modern-sounding **chord clusters** based on seconds and thirds.

Form

The form is based on solos and small groups alternating with contrasting dynamics.

Performance Techniques

Ornamentations such as trills are played throughout the piece by many of the instruments. Some of the musicians, such as the bassoonist who plays the opening solo, are required to play pitches that are extremely high or low for their particular instruments.

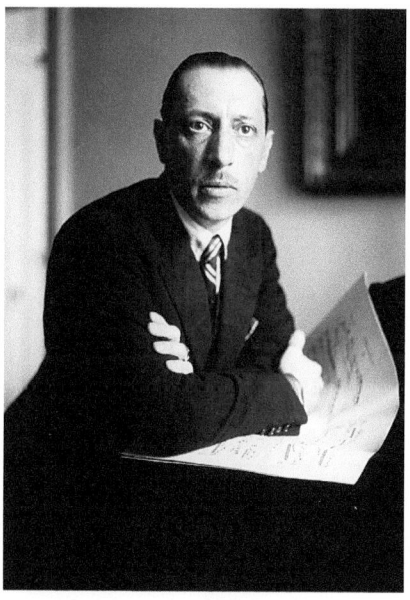

FIGURE 9.18
Igor Stravinsky
Source: George Grantham Bain Collection at the Library of Congress. Wikimedia Commons.

 Listen to the recording of *The Rite of Spring* with these elements in mind.

The Rite of Spring has two parts: Part I, titled "The Adoration of the Earth"; and Part II, titled "The Sacrifice." This timed listening guide includes the first two sections of Part I: the orchestral introduction and "The Augurs of Spring."

Listen another time and follow along with the timed listening guide.

TIME	SECTION	DESCRIPTION
Track 1:		
0:00	Introduction	The piece begins with an unaccompanied bassoon playing at the upper limit of its range. This is a Russian folk melody in a minor mode.
0:10		Other wind instruments gradually enter with non-triadic chordal harmony. Stravinsky's use here of wind instruments continues their centuries-long use as signifying the outdoors.
0:54		The melody disappears, replaced by a multi-layered texture featuring undulating chromatic lines in the winds as well as a number of sustained pitches. Solo lines, characterized by fast-moving notes, emerge from this texture. Some moments of a steady pulse appear periodically and then disappear.
2:08		The thickness of the layering and the loudness of the orchestra builds, accompanied by a steady pulse in the low strings.

LISTENING GUIDE 9.5

TIME	SECTION	DESCRIPTION
2:39		The orchestra suddenly stops and the solo bassoon restates the opening melody, transposed down a half step.
2:48		Other winds enter with trills and triplet flourishes. The violins begin softly playing a four-note pizzicato ostinato.
Track 2:		
0:00	The Augurs of Spring: Dances of the Young Girls	The strings, accented by the horns, play a repeating pattern of pulsating chords. The violin, violas, and four of the horns play a dominant seventh chord and the cellos, basses, and other four horns play a major chord based on a tonic one half step higher than that of the dominant seventh chord. This creates a new kind of chord made of adjacent pitches called a **chord cluster**. These chord clusters are played loudly and in a driving rhythm, providing some of the piece's most memorable material, which was perhaps shocking to the ears of its first listeners.
0:08		The English horn plays the four-note ostinato originally played in the pizzicato violins as a solo, accompanied by bassoons playing staccato repeating figures and cellos playing a pizzicato eight-pitch repeating figure.
0:13		The string ostinato accented by the horns returns. It continues to alternate with sections featuring the eight-pitch repeating figure from the low strings and the four-note ostinato originally played by the pizzicato violins and then the English horn. The trumpets introduce triplet rhythm, creating a polyrhythm with the duple-meter strings ostinato. The trumpets play a short melody that descends chromatically. This motive and others are introduced and developed as they are played by different instruments and in different permutations and variations throughout the orchestra.
1:38		A solo horn introduces a folk melody in a major mode. This melody is then taken up by a flute soloist as it is combined with variations on earlier motifs and ostinatos.
2:11		The trumpets and cellos present a chant-like theme in a minor mode.
2:27		The music becomes suddenly softer, and the texture builds again, thickening and adding layers as the folk melody introduced by the horn is developed across the orchestra and a climax of loudness and thick texture is reached to introduce the next section of the piece, titled "Ritual of Abduction."
2:54	End	

What Does It Mean?

EMOTIONAL RESONANCE

As an orchestral ballet, the storyline of *The Rite of Spring: Scenes of Pagan Russia* depicts a series of imaginary ancient Slavic rituals, beginning innocently with traditional line dancing but culminating in the sacrificial death of a young girl, ordered by a tribal elder. Each of its scenes, with titles like "Ritual of Abduction," "Spring Round Dances," "Mystic Circles of the Young Girls," and "Ritual of the Ancestors," is meant to evoke a part of the storyline, emphasizing ideas of the "primitive," something old, ancient, and mystical imagined to be connected to rural village or "folk" culture. The recordings of the orchestral introduction and "The Augurs of Spring" present some of the musical sounds connected to notions of rural life. The bassoon opens the introduction with a Russian folk melody at the top of its range in a minor mode, performing a timbre that sounds unfamiliar and perhaps strange to those who have not heard the extreme high range of the bassoon or Russian rural folk melodies. When the horn plays another folk melody during "The Augurs of Spring" section (this one in a major mode), it continues the horn's association with the pastoral in European classical music. This relatively simple folk

FIGURE 9.19
An example of costumes and sets from the original production of *The Rite of Spring*
Source: Public domain, Wikimedia Commons.

melody is later heard in the flute and a number of other instruments, played in contrast to the many rhythmic and harmonic complexities occurring throughout the piece. Stravinsky took these melodies from published collections of folk music. The opening bassoon melody, for example, came from a song in an anthology of Lithuanian folk songs published in 1900.

🔊 Listen again to the opening to Track 1 of *The Rite of Spring* as well as Track 2 at 1:38 to identify these melodies.

Polyrhythms, asymmetrical patterns of accents, and frequently changing meters occur throughout the piece. These techniques create instability, tension, and excitement, as their irregularity and unpredictability would not have been something audiences were accustomed to hearing. In addition, they would have opened up new possibilities for choreography that did not depend on movements grouped in regular patterns of two, three, or four.

> AESTHETICS

For harmony, Stravinsky stacks layers of pitches and melodies, often in multiple keys, to create dense, dissonant musical textures. An example of this is the opening to "The Augurs of Spring" where two different chords are played simultaneously in the strings and horns, a harmonic technique called **polytonality**. Polytonality provides particular sets of dissonances and consonances depending on which keys are sounding at the same time. They may share some pitches in common, some of the pitches of one of the keys may be in consonant intervals with pitches of the other key, or the pitches of one key may be in dissonant intervals with those of another. These simultaneities form new types of harmonies that may be built not only on intervals of thirds, but also on intervals of seconds, fourths, or any number of others. This is one example of how modernist composers of this period sought to move away from the traditional tonal harmony of European classical music. Another composer who did so was Arnold Schoenberg, who, after the turn of the century, turned away from the expansive Romantic style he had composed in during the late nineteenth century and began to espouse **atonality**, the refusal of a tonal center and the predictable key relationships that had been the guiding principle in music composition since the eighteenth century.

🔊 Listen to the opening of Track 2 of *The Rite of Spring* again for these features of harmony and rhythm.

In *The Rite of Spring*, Stravinsky's modernist explorations of polytonality draw on material from musical folklore for inspiration, just as nationalist composers of the nineteenth century did. Since he extended the harmonic vocabulary of many Russian nationalist composers (Chapter 8, Gateway 29), some critics consider his folklore-inspired works "neonationalist." Even folk melodies, such as the bassoon solo or the pastoral horn melody, are enmeshed in modernist harmonic structures that may have been inspired by additional folk music sources as well, which music historians have traced to anthologies of folk music that would have been available to Stravinsky. These additional folk sources are masked by harmonies that push the boundaries of tonality while modernist harmonies are masked by the diatonic folk motifs that appear throughout the composition. This "fusion" of the modern and the folkloristic is one of the features that has made *The Rite of Spring* a perennial favorite for orchestras and audiences long after its debut in Paris with the Ballets Russes.

The departure from tonality in *The Rite of Spring* (and other modernist works of this period) was, in some ways, a response to broader shifts in European society. The political order dominated by European empires and monarchs was declining, revolutions were springing up in soon-to-be former European colonies, and new understandings of the complexities of the psychological and material worlds were emerging in the work of intellectuals like Sigmund Freud and Albert Einstein. In European classical music, this broader crisis of confidence in older ways of thinking can be heard in the music of composers who questioned the value of tonal music that was meant to express or induce emotion and to be relatively easily understood. One way to interpret the modernist shift away from tonality in *The Rite of Spring* is that it reveals a questioning of the philosophical and social underpinnings of nineteenth-century European society and an exploration of new, ostensibly more complex musical terrain.

> CULTURAL LINKAGES

What Is Its History?

The Rite of Spring, and its reliance on Russian folklore, demonstrates the lasting impact of the musical nationalism that had emerged in Europe in the nineteenth century (Chapter 8, Gateway 29). Stravinsky's mentor was the Russian composer Nikolai Rimsky-Korsakov (1844–1908). Rimsky-Korsakov had advocated for the development of a national Russian style of composition in the last decades of the nineteenth century and had published two collections of Russian folk songs to that end.

In 1909, Stravinsky's composition *Fireworks* was heard at a concert in St. Petersburg by Sergei Diaghilev (1872–1929), a Russian impresario who, starting in 1907, was presenting the best Russian concert music, operas, and ballets in Paris. Diaghilev was impressed and commissioned the young Stravinsky to compose for his company three works of ballet music: *The Firebird* (1910), *Petrushka* (1911) and *The Rite of Spring*, all of which drew on elements of musical folklore. Diaghilev's company, the Ballets Russes, spotlighted the most famous Russian dancers of the period including Anna Pavlova and Vaslav Nijinsky. The company was a locus of modernist innovation. Diaghilev commissioned new scores from the leading French composers of the period, including Claude Debussy (*Jeux*, 1913), Maurice Ravel (*Daphnis et Chloé*, 1912), and Erik Satie (*Parade*, 1917). His set designers included leading modernists Pablo Picasso (1881–1973) and Henri Matisse (1869–1954), as well as the fashion designer Coco Chanel (1883–1971). Many of the ballets, including *The Rite of Spring*, played to the fascination at the time with the exotic, the folkloric, and the primitive. For *The Rite of Spring*, Nijinsky invented an entirely novel choreography focused on stomping and lurching movements, which imagined an ancient pagan way of life. He attempted to capture a sense of village dance traditions and the ways that peasants are rooted to the earth. The Russian designer, painter, and writer Nicholas Roerich (1874–1947) designed the sets and costumes. In the context of a broader revival affirming Russian national identity through folk arts, Roerich was an avid student of folk culture. He was particularly interested in archeology as a way to understand the look and sound of ancient Slavic culture. He worked closely with Stravinsky and introduced him to a good deal of folk music, some of which formed the basis for the musical material of *The Rite of Spring*. Roerich's costumes and sets conjured an imagined "primitive," ancient Russia along with Nijinsky's choreography and Stravinsky's score, all reflections of a "neoprimitive" movement in the visual and performing arts.

The premiere of *The Rite of Spring* on May 29, 1913, incited one of the most famous riots in the history of European music. In the full house of the Théâtre des Champs-Élysées in Paris, what began as boos and hisses in the opening measures soon devolved into shouting, fistfights, and people throwing vegetables and other objects at the stage. Accounts vary as to whether the police were called in, but, in any event, forty people were removed from the theater and order was largely maintained through the rest of the evening. While Stravinsky later boasted that it was his music that had driven the audience into hysterics, others have claimed that Nijinsky's controversial choreography provoked the violent response, with its stomping and rootedness in the ground perhaps offending the sensibilities of a Parisian crowd accustomed to balletic elegance and a seeming ability to defy gravity. Musicologist Richard Taruskin has even speculated that the riot may have been pre-arranged by Diaghilev in order to generate publicity.

Regardless of the cause of the riot, *The Rite of Spring* was only performed as a complete ballet and orchestral work seven times before the outbreak of World War I in 1914. It was performed as a concert piece (without a ballet) for the first time just before the war and received positive reviews. In 1940 it was included in the Disney animated film *Fantasia*, the only work by a living composer to appear in a score full of well-known classical orchestral compositions. In the decades that followed, *The Rite of Spring* became a standard part of the orchestral concert repertoire, even though Stravinsky for the most part left behind this particular style of Russian neonationalist-modernist composition after 1920. There have been a wide variety of choreographic interpretations over the years. In 1987 the choreographer Millicent Hodson worked with Chicago's Joffrey Ballet to reconstruct Nijinsky's choreography, and the Joffrey performers danced in replicas of Roerich's costumes.

Like Stravinsky, other composers from the turn of the twentieth century were also exploring ways to extend and depart from tonality. In Vienna Arnold Schoenberg extended the expressionism and emotion of Wagner and other German and Austrian composers of the late nineteenth century. He explored atonality and the boundaries between speech and singing in his work *Pierrot Lunaire* (1912). In the early 1920s, Schoenberg pioneered a practice of composition based on the organization of the twelve chromatic pitches into ordered non-repeating sequences known as **tone rows**. This approach, which became the basis for **serialism**, was explored by Schoenberg and his students Alban Berg, Anton Webern, and Hanns Eisler (1898–1962). After 1920 Stravinsky entered what some have called his "neoclassical period" (*c.* 1920–1951), followed by his "serial period" (*c.* 1952–1968). After living in Russia, Switzerland, and France in the 1920s and 1930s, he moved to the United States at the outbreak of World War II in 1939, where he became a citizen and lived until his death in 1971.

Modernism only goes so far in explaining European classical music in the period from 1890 to 1918. Many European composers continued to compose using the lush chromatic harmonies, programmatic content, and large operatic, symphonic, and concerto forms of the nineteenth century, including Gustav Mahler, Richard Strauss, Jean Sibelius, Sergei Rachmaninoff (1873–1943), and many others. Their tonal compositions, more than Schoenberg's atonal and twelve-tone ones, are still frequently performed for contemporary concert audiences, along with Stravinsky's *Rite of Spring*.

WHERE DO I GO FROM HERE?

- Listen to Schoenberg's *Pierrot Lunaire*. How does it challenge conventions of melody, harmony, and timbre prevalent in classical music of the late nineteenth century?

- Find an orchestral work from 1890–1918 by Mahler, Richard Strauss, Sibelius, or Rachmaninoff, and compare that work to *The Rite of Spring*. What are some of the similarities and differences between their musical elements?

- *The Rite of Spring* and other compositions by Stravinsky have inspired the musical soundscape of many twentieth- and twenty-first-century orchestral Hollywood film scores. Bernard Herrmann (1911–1975), a frequent collaborator of Alfred Hitchcock, seems to have drawn on some elements of *The Rite of Spring* for his iconic score to the Hitchcock film *Psycho* (1960). Watch the film and identify similarities between *The Rite of Spring* and Herrmann's score. What effect does the music have on the mood of the film?

GATEWAY 37
BALINESE GAMELAN

What Is It?

In 1908 the Dutch conquered the Hindu island of Bali in present-day Indonesia after having first invaded the island with their military in 1846. In the wake of the collapse of traditional Balinese political structures, music for gamelan orchestras similar to those of Java (Chapter 5, Gateway 19) changed dramatically, beginning around 1915. Our gateway to this new kind of twentieth-century Balinese gamelan music is a piece from later in the century titled "Tabuh Sekar Jepun" (1968) arranged by the Balinese composer I Wayan Gandera (1945?–2002). It is an example of a performance of a **gamelan** *gong kebyar*, the most popular type of Balinese gamelan orchestra for much of the twentieth century. Like Javanese gamelans, gamelan *gong kebyar* is composed mainly of bronze percussion instruments and is played by several dozen musicians. "Tabuh" is the word for an individual composition and "Sekar Jepun" means "Japanese flower," a reference to a West Indian jasmine flower said to have been brought to Bali by the Japanese and commonly used both for ceremonial offerings and for decoration on headdresses for dance and other performances. It is common in Bali to name a composition after a flower.

🔊 **Listen to the first thirty seconds of this recording to get some idea of this type of gamelan sound.**

FIGURE 9.20
Map of Bali

How Does It Work?

Timbre

A Balinese gamelan *gong kebyar* orchestra consists of hanging knobbed gongs, rows of knobbed gongs set in wooden boxes called *reyong*, and a number of slab-key metallophones, called *gangsa*, struck with hammers. Each individual *gangsa* instrument has a two-octave range, and together the *gangsa* instruments cover a range of four octaves. Altogether, the gamelan *gong kebyar* collection of idiophones spans a five-octave range. Gamelan *gong kebyar* also includes a pair of *kendang* (two-headed, barrel-shaped drums), *ceng-ceng* (cymbals), a *suling* (bamboo flute), and a *kempli*, a knobbed, kettle-shaped gong used to keep the pulse. These timbres can be heard in various combinations during the recording of "Tabuh Sekar Jepun."

The gongs and metallophones of gamelan *gong kebyar* are made in pairs to have a slight difference in pitch between the gongs or keys of the two instruments in each pair. Each pair of instruments is thought of as male and female, with female instruments having a slightly lower pitch. This difference in pitch causes a beating effect that is called *ombak*, which means "waves." The speed of the beating is designed to be absolutely consistent over the entire range of the orchestra. Without *ombak*, the sound is considered dead. Each gamelan orchestra is tuned to itself, not to match other gamelans. There is no standard tuning. Instead, each orchestra is a unique entity.

Texture

Although played by several dozen musicians, a Balinese gamelan acoustically pulsates as if a single instrument. The texture of a Balinese gamelan has been called "stratified polyphony." In this texture, the lowest-pitched instruments move slowly and provide the foundations for the faster, more complex ornamentation of the higher-pitched instruments. In this modern composition, however, I Wayan Gandera highlights several instruments and instrumental sections of the gamelan, either by featuring them unaccompanied or by assigning them a pattern that stands out in relation to the other instruments.

Rhythm

This piece is composed in sections. Some phrases have even numbers of beats (2, 4, 8, or 16) and some are nonmetrical. In the second half of the piece, these phrases are expressed as regular, repeating cycles. The use of repeating cycles is one of the most recognizable elements of gamelan performance. The largest gong marks the *last* beat of each cycle, not the first, and coincides with the last note of the melody. Sometimes, however, melodies can span multiple gong cycles. "Tabuh Sekar Jepun" features several examples of multiple-cycle melodies.

Melody

Balinese melodies (*pokok*) are played by *gangsa* metallophones with a lower pitch range and elaborated upon by those with a higher pitch range. Like the gong cycles, they are regular and repetitive. The melody that ends the piece, which is based on a popular Javanese song, is sixteen beats long. It is ornamented in three different ways (by the *gangsa*, *reyong*, and *kendang*) at various times in the piece, and played in two different speeds, each of which provides different opportunities for musical expression.

This piece uses a five-note subset of the seven-note scale system known as *pelog*. The gamelan can only play these five pitches, which are irregularly spaced: three notes close together, then a large gap, then two more closely spaced notes.

FIGURE 9.21

Balinese gamelan, with musicians playing an instrument called *reyong* **in the foreground**

Source: travelib Indonesia/Alamy Stock Photo.

Harmony

Groups of different notes sounding at the same time often occur in Balinese music, but these are usually not intended to be heard as chords. One of the only times something analogous to chords happens is during *gangsa* parts, when a player who usually would play an interlocking part stops playing that part and instead plays the melody line three notes higher than usual. This yields an interval that sounds something like a fifth.

Form

Traditional Balinese pieces follow a three-part form often described as head (exposition), body (the central movement, often played at a slow tempo), and feet (the exciting conclusion). This piece only roughly follows this model. The main melody is in fact the last movement, not the middle, which is instead occupied by an extended section showcasing the sounds of the *reyong* and the *kendang*. This final section has its own internal form of fast, slow, fast.

Performance Techniques

One of the more striking techniques heard in this piece is called *kotekan*, in which two parts interlock while playing figures too fast to be played alone. Instead, they are divided between two partners in a variety of configurations, sometimes involving a pattern where partners alternate playing every other note. Players dampen the ringing of each note so that it does not overlap with the notes of their partners. On the *gangsa*, this is accomplished by striking a key with a mallet in one hand and then quickly grabbing the key with the other hand to stop the vibration. On the *reyong*, however, a cylindrical mallet must be held in each hand. The dampening, then, must be done by the same hand that has just struck the note, at lightning-fast speeds.

Listen to the first thirty seconds of this performance with these timbral and textural elements in mind.

Listen to the entire recording following this timed listening guide, which gives the Balinese name of each section.

TIME	SECTION	GONG CYCLE	DESCRIPTION
0:00	*kebyar*	N/A	The entire ensemble plays short phrases in unison, with no clear meter or steady tempo. The last note of each phrase is marked with a stroke of the largest gong.
0:08	*reyongan*	N/A	*Reyong* "solo." This one instrument is played by four musicians. In this section, the *reyong* plays *kilitan*: melodic patterns each consisting of four adjacent tones divided between a pair of interlocking players, and doubled an octave higher by the second pair. Several times in this section, the "harmonization" of two pitches simultaneously sounding at an interval of a "fifth" can be heard. Around 0:41 the largest gong can also be heard, marking the end of this section.
0:43	genderan	N/A	This section showcases the *gangsa* (metallophone) instruments and features a combination of interlocking and unison phrases. At 0:56 the *kempli* is heard for the first time, dictating a pulse. At 1:08 the largest gong clearly resounds, marking the end of the phrase. After the striking of the gong, the *ombak* beating effect from the tuning of the instruments can be heard clearly.
1:10	*reyongan*	N/A	Similar to the previous *reyongan* section.
1:26		*bapang* (8 beats)	The *reyongan* continues, but now a steady gong cycle is introduced and the pulse implied in the earlier *reyongan* is made explicit. The *reyong* phrases are interposed with short unison phrases from the *gangsa* section.
2:52	*kendangan*	*bapang*	*Kendang* (drum) duet. The gong cycle is reinforced with an eight-beat *pokok* (base melody). The *reyong* and *ceng-ceng* (cymbals) mirror the drums' patterns and variations which unfold over numerous iterations of the cycle. The end of this section exits the gong cycle with a group solo by the *gangsa*, which is concluded with a sounding of the largest gong.
4:02	*genderan*	N/A	Similar to *genderan* section above.
4:34	A (3x)	*lelonggoran* (16 beats)	This melody, played together by the full ensemble here, is derived from the popular Javanese song "Suwe Ora Jamu."
4:49	A' (*genderan*, 3x)	*lelonggoran* (16 beats)	The *pokok* continues while the *gangsa* elaborate it with an interlocking ornamentation called a *kotekan*.
5:06	A (2x)	*lelonggoran* (16 beats)	Repeat of A.
5:17	A" (9x)	*lelonggoran* (16 beats)	The *pokok* is the same as the previous section although it is played twice as slow. The *reyong* plays a melodic elaboration of the melody, while the *kendang* (accompanied by the *ceng-ceng*) play a pattern that repeats every three gong cycles (a total of three times). In this section the *suling* (bamboo flute) is heard clearly for the first time. It plays the *pokok* and adds some ornamentation to the melody.
6:32	A''' (3x)	*lelonggoran* (16 beats)	The same *pokok* is played at the faster original tempo from A. The *gangsa* plays the *kotekan* from A' in addition to the rhythmic elements from A.
6:49	End		

What Does It Mean?

On the island of Bali the performing arts have long been an important part of everyday life. Many Balinese learn and perform gamelan as part of their normal lives, and there are more than twenty-five varieties of gamelan in Bali that perform regularly, of which six or seven are common throughout the island. Gamelan *gong kebyar* is one of the most frequently performed types of gamelan in Bali. The meanings of gamelan *gong kebyar* can be as complex as its musical organization, and this gateway focuses on just two of its many facets of meaning: (1) the way that gamelan performance in general is an emblematic and experiential example of the value for collectivity in Bali; and (2) the ways that gamelan *gong kebyar* is meaningful as a modern, twentieth-century form of gamelan performance.

Today, the main settings for gamelan performance are rituals that mark either the life cycle (e.g., marriages, birthdays, cremations) or temple festivals. Gamelan performances also occur on national holidays, for village events like fundraisers, and for tourists. Gamelans of all types perform on these occasions. In many cases they are intertwined with dance, theater, and other performing arts such as shadow puppetry. With the dozens of musicians required to perform gamelan, often in cooperation with dancers and puppeteers, the performing arts in Bali are almost always communal efforts. This is an expression of the value Balinese society places on cooperation and community spirit.

CULTURAL LINKAGES

Balinese villages are divided into sections, each one called a *banjar*. Community organizations called *sekaha* are formed within the *banjar* to execute integral tasks, including organizing religious rituals, managing the cultivation of rice, and playing gamelan for temple ceremonies. When a community has a need, the appropriate *sekaha* gathers and finds a way to meet that need to sustain the life of the community. Gamelan musicians organize themselves into these collective groups, and they perform for celebrations and other occasions that require gamelan performance. Their goal in participating in rituals, ceremonies, and other performances is not to showcase individual musicians, but rather to create a sense of oneness within the group. Certainly some individuals are more proficient than others in gamelan performances, but these qualities serve to elevate the overall quality of the ensemble rather than showcase the skills of one person over the others.

SOCIAL BEHAVIOR

The communal aspect of gamelan *gong kebyar* performance in "Tabuh Sekar Jepun" is evident throughout the piece as the musicians remain coordinated with one another through many different tempos, several elaborations of the *pokok* melody, and the *kotekan* technique where players' parts precisely interlock to form fast melodic and rhythmic passages. The very opening *kebyar* section of the piece features a few short nonmetrical unison phrases played with precision by the entire ensemble, without the guide of a steady beat. The final section of the piece contains a clear example of the *kotekan* technique in the first elaboration of "Suwe Ora Jamu" in the *gangsa* (A'). The extremely fast line is played through close coordination of multiple musicians as they interlock their parts with one another. These challenging and virtuosic performance techniques are part of the reason that gamelan *gong kebyar* is one of the most popular styles of gamelan for musicians and audiences. In order for these techniques to be performed properly, they require extensive training and practice.

AESTHETICS

Devoting so much time to music (as well as dance and other arts) is made possible by an environment perfectly suited to agriculture. People need to spend only about half of their time working in the fields to produce enough food to sustain themselves. There is also a great demand in Bali for the arts, artistic production, and artists. The arts are vibrant in Bali as highly respected and valued elements of society because they are integral to religious practice, sources of popular entertainment, and the basis of a great deal of cultural tourism. Gamelan is a pervasive aspect of the arts in Bali, and though most Balinese people do not regularly produce art as adults, those who participate in gamelan find themselves among communities, organizations, and audiences that are supportive of their work.

CULTURAL LINKAGES

Listen to the kebyar section at the beginning of the piece as well as the A' section featuring the kotekan technique (beginning at 4:49), keeping in mind that this level of precision is accomplished by a number of musicians working together.

The word *kebyar* means "to burst open" or "to flare up suddenly." It refers to the explosive sound of the gamelan when all of the metallophones, gongs, and drums are struck together at once. This sound, encompassing a range of more than five octaves, produces piercing high frequencies, rich pulsating metallic timbres in the mid-range, and booming low frequencies from the larger gongs. *Kebyar* passages that feature this sound may occur throughout a piece, and often appear at the beginning (heard in this example from 0:00 to 0:08). Gamelan *gong kebyar* is best known

AESTHETICS

for repertoire featuring these types of explosive moments that highlight the dynamic qualities of its component instruments, often involving sudden shifts in tempo, dynamic, texture, or pitch material.

This so-called *kebyar* style differentiates it from much of the ritual ceremonial gamelan music from before the emergence of gamelan *gong kebyar* in the early twentieth century. This earlier ritual repertoire could be considered "continuous," meaning that the music continues in a steady flow of tempo, texture, and dynamics without abrupt or sudden changes. Pieces used for rituals and ceremonies are typically not attributed to individual composers. Soon after the emergence of gamelan *gong kebyar*, individual composers began to be recognized as the composers of new compositions. These pieces are termed *kreasi baru* or "new creations," a term used for gamelan *gong kebyar* compositions since the early twentieth century. Composers today continue to produce *kreasi baru* for gamelan *gong kebyar*, exploring new possibilities for the *kebyar* style.

> **CULTURAL LINKAGES**

The virtuosity, dramatic contrast, and other features of gamelan *gong kebyar* have fascinated Balinese musicians and composers, as well as tourists, researchers, and composers from outside of Bali. While gamelan *gong kebyar* performances continue to serve ritual functions and remain an integral part of community life, they also serve as entertainment for tourists as tourism has become an integral part of the Balinese culture and economy over the last 100 years. Today, over four million tourists typically visit Bali per year, and many of them are interested in experiencing aspects of Balinese culture such as its music. Many gamelan *sekaha* perform for tourist groups regularly in villages, outside temples, on stages at hotels, at restaurants, or at festivals. Tourism has generated more revenue and interest in all forms of gamelan, inspired the composition of even more new repertoire, stimulated the creation of new ensembles, and encouraged the revival of pieces that had become nearly obsolete. In tandem with the rise of tourism, festivals and competitions between gamelan *sekaha*, as well as a robust conservatory system for music and the performing arts, have also risen to prominence in Bali. These institutions actively promote gamelan throughout Bali and beyond, and their activities and devotion to gamelan result in the continuation of existing repertoires, excellence in performance, many new compositions that explore the sonic possibilities in gamelan, and high levels of virtuosity that are especially notable in gamelan *gong kebyar* performances like "Tabuh Sekar Japun."

What Is Its History?

> **CULTURAL LINKAGES**

Hinduism has been the predominant religion in Bali since around 500 CE, when the religion came to Southeast Asia from India and fused with the local animist religion. Islam spread to the islands of Southeast Asia beginning in the thirteenth century or earlier. By the sixteenth century some Javanese Hindu aristocrats began relocating to the neighboring island of Bali, taking their courts and their court gamelan orchestras with them. From this time until the beginning of the twentieth century, eight courtly centers in Bali served as patrons of a flourishing arts tradition perhaps unparalleled anywhere in the world. Gamelans played for Hindu temple ceremonies and court functions and accompanied shadow puppet theater and court dancing, all in elegant, slow-tempo music, as they once did in Java.

The imperial ambitions of European powers between the sixteenth and early twentieth centuries had enormous impact in areas of the world they sought to colonize and on the lives of people who lived in those places. By the nineteenth century the Netherlands controlled much of this part of Asia, but they had not completely conquered the southern part of the island of Bali. In 1906 and 1908 the Dutch mounted decisive military campaigns that succeeded in deposing the remaining traditional kings (*rajas*) of southern Bali and imposing colonial control over the whole island. Both of these battles had horrifying ends. Unable to defend themselves against European rifles and cannons with their swords and knives, the Balinese faced certain defeat. To preserve their honor, they met the Dutch army passively, with a ritual suicide, called *puputan*. Here is an account of the first of these battles:

> On September 14, 1906, an overwhelming Dutch force landed at Sanur beach; there was no significant resistance and the force marched to Denpasar, Bali, as if in a dress parade. They passed through a seemingly deserted town and approached the royal palace, noting smoke

rising from the *puri* [palace] and, most disquietingly, they heard a wild beating of drums coming from within the palace walls. Upon reaching the palace, a silent procession emerged, led by the Raja, borne by four bearers on a palanquin. The Raja was dressed in traditional white cremation garments, wore magnificent jewelry, and was armed with a ceremonial *kris* [dagger]. The other people in the procession consisted of the Raja's officials, guards, priests, wives, children and retainers, all of whom were similarly attired. When the procession was a hundred paces from the Dutch force, they halted and the Raja stepped down from the palanquin and signaled a priest who plunged his dagger into the Raja's breast. The rest of the procession began killing themselves and others. A "stray gunshot" and an "attack by lance and spear" prompted the Dutch to open fire with rifles and artillery. Women mockingly threw jewelry and gold coins at the troops. As more people emerged from the palace, the mounds of corpses rose higher and higher. Approximately 1,000 Balinese died. The soldiers stripped the corpses of the valuables and sacked the ruins of the burned palace.

Balinese traditional religion sanctions such ritual suicides, which have their analogs in village rituals accompanied by gamelan music. In these rituals the evil witch Rangda, with her hideous tongue, threatens the villages. The villagers, in trance, rush to attack her in defense of the village, but she turns their daggers against them and they try to stab themselves in the chest with their own weapons. Fortunately the benevolent *barong*, a shaggy, friendly, ox-like beast, prevents the suicides, defeats Rangda, and the village is saved. In the *puputans* of 1906 and 1908, the power of the *barong* was no match for the Dutch army. The suicides were carried out and the Balinese went down to a staggering defeat that, in its mass, self-inflicted violence, shocked the world, the Dutch public, and the Balinese themselves.

In the area of culture and music the *puputans* had three important consequences. First, the Dutch government decided to support the arts in Bali and turn the island into a tourist destination, which it remains today. Second, gamelan orchestras moved from the now-defunct courts into village social life, where *sekaha* devoted to music, theater, and dance became the sources of patronage. Third, a new genre of music emerged—gamelan *gong kebyar*.

The origins of gamelan *gong kebyar* can be traced to the northern coastal town of Singaraja, the Dutch colonial capital in the mid-nineteenth century. It was a locale with much contact with broader Southeast Asian and European culture. In the first decade of the twentieth century at the time of the complete Dutch takeover of the island, a literary revival was underway in the north of Bali centered on a new awareness of Hindu texts. People formed *sekaha pepaosan* (reading clubs), and groups from different *banjar* began to compete against one another, singing Hindu poetry in front of audiences at temple ceremonies and night markets. The excitement of audiences for these kinds of competitions led *sekaha* to explore new formats. Gamelan *gong kebyar* came about as these competitions began to experiment with the addition of gamelan accompaniment. The poetry performances in these settings alternated with gamelan music, which resulted in the abrupt and rapid shifts in the music that have come to characterize gamelan *gong kebyar*. By this time music, dance, and drama were already frequently integrated in Balinese performing arts, but this juxtaposition of discontinuous and different musical sounds one after the other was something new. There is evidence that some of the exciting techniques of gamelan *gong kebyar* may have had antecedents in earlier styles of gamelan, but this was the first time they had been used in a competitive display of virtuosity, creating

FIGURE 9.22
The Balinese witch Rangda as dramatized today
Source: Niradj, Shutterstock.

FIGURE 9.23
The *barong* protects the entranced villagers, who are attempting ritual suicide
Source: theskaman306, Shutterstock.

what must have been an exhilarating effect for performers and audiences alike. *Sekaha* soon began to cultivate the *gong kebyar* style and to invent new techniques of musical surprise and ingenuity, and competitions between groups became popular, even at times sponsored by the Dutch.

In the 1920s and 1930s, tourism began to develop in Bali, and its reputation for being a hot-bed for traditional culture and performing arts spread, with some gamelans performing regularly at hotels and one being sent to perform at the 1931 Paris Colonial Exhibition. Musicians became aware of how they were contributing to perceptions of the island because of the enthusiastic responses of international audiences. Gamelan ensembles of older genres began to absorb some of the stylistic traits of *gong kebyar*, though some Balinese were critical of this challenge to older traditions. Balinese society was undergoing drastic changes under Dutch colonial rule, and the musical changes embodied in gamelan *gong kebyar* and other genres it affected reflect these changes.

Since Indonesia declared its independence at the end of World War II in 1945, gamelan *gong kebyar* has continued to develop both in Bali and around the world. Conservatories, competitions, and festivals have fostered performance and innovation, and tourism has become a significant source of patronage for many *sekaha*, especially after the opening in 1969 of an international airport on the island. Universities, museums, and community groups in the United States, Europe, and Australasia have purchased complete Balinese gamelans. There are over 100 gamelans in the United States alone. Universities offer courses that teach students how to perform gamelan *gong kebyar* and other styles. Gamelan ensembles outside Indonesia are also often connected to the community life of Indonesian people living abroad or to Indonesian embassies, consulates, and cultural institutions, and outside attention has contributed to the preservation and valuing of these traditions by the Balinese. Today both inside and outside Bali, gamelan *gong kebyar* continues to thrive as it captivates performers and audiences in a multitude of settings.

WHERE DO I GO FROM HERE?

- Find a gamelan on your college or university campus or one near you. What kind of gamelan is it? Is it Balinese? Is there an active ensemble learning gamelan *gong kebyar*? Attend a concert and experience the sounds of gamelan in person. Or, even better, see if you can get permission to attend a rehearsal of this ensemble to see how a group of people learns and rehearses gamelan performance techniques.

- Locate a video online of the *koketan* technique. Do the performers make it look easy, or does its complexity and technicality seem evident?

- Have you encountered musical performance as a tourist anywhere before? What are some of the ways that you think tourism may have affected the genre of music you encountered as a tourist?

CLOSING

The gateways to music between 1890 and 1918 in this chapter include three examples from music for popular audiences in the United States, two examples of European classical music, and one example of music under European colonial rule. All these examples illustrate the increasing interconnectedness of the world, which was in part related to the ways that European powers had colonized much of the world over the preceding four centuries. The blues arose as African Americans suffered during Reconstruction and the Jim Crow era, when new forms of oppression continued the legacy of slavery. American band music grew out of industrial-era instrument technologies and European dance forms, with even deeper roots in Ottoman military music. Ragtime drew on the form of marches and on African American and Latin American rhythmic sensibilities to inspire a widely popular music and dance phenomenon. Debussy and Stravinsky reacted against the confines of European tonal harmony and pursued new forms of musical modernism. Balinese gamelan *gong kebyar* sprang up almost immediately after the Dutch conquered Bali, drawing on new sources of patronage, new audiences, and new forms of social organization as it became a world-renowned genre.

All of these forms of music making could also be called modern in the sense that they are to some extent breaking with traditions of the past as they engage with changes occurring in the world. At the same time, however, each of these gateways remains to some extent grounded in the traditions of the past. This struggle between remaining connected to tradition on the one hand and innovation free from the constraints of the past on the other is a hallmark of the music of this period, and indeed of most forms of music making since then. Musical continuity and transformation is evident in the meanings and histories of the music explored in this chapter, and these themes will continue through the rest of the chapters in Part III as they explore the music of the age of recordings.

THINGS TO THINK ABOUT

- The blues, ragtime, and gamelan *gong kebyar* all emerged among communities who had been oppressed, exploited, or conquered by European colonial powers. Compare the various ways that these communities grappled musically with, contested, and negotiated the challenges they faced.

- The musical styles and genres in this chapter all represent either something new or something old that changed to something new. Compare the social and cultural factors that stimulated change in these cases.

NEW TERMS

atonality	impressionism	shawm
blue notes	*kotekan*	sousaphone
blues	*mehter*	strain
chord cluster	modernism	stride piano
classic blues	obbligato	swing feel
country blues	polytonality	symbolist poets
fife	race records	tone row
gamelan *gong kebyar*	ragtime	tremolo
habanera rhythm	serialism	whole-tone scales

MUSIC FROM THE INTERWAR PERIOD (1918–1939)

THE PERIOD BETWEEN THE end of World War I in 1918 and the beginning of World War II in 1939 can be divided into two decades. The first, sometimes called the Roaring Twenties, featured unprecedented economic growth in the United States and among the victorious European nations in World War I. An epic stock market crash on October 24, 1929, ushered in the second decade of the interwar period, the Great Depression.

While the economic prosperity of the Roaring Twenties is often celebrated in contrast to the widespread despair of the Great Depression, it was enjoyed by a minority, as at least 60 percent of American families lived on an income below the standard of what could provide for the basic necessities of life. A growing middle class and wealthy elite in North America and Europe could afford the new inventions of the pre-war generation, such previously unheard-of luxuries as an automobile, a telephone, and new electricity-powered radios and phonographs. This sector of the population could now hear music of all kinds at home, not just in a concert hall or the salons of the wealthy. To sell to this market, record companies recorded classical music, jazz, popular music, and music targeted at particular ethnic or regional communities.

The Roaring Twenties also coincides with the first Great Migration, the movement of roughly 1.6 million African Americans from the rural American South to cities of the Northeast, Midwest, and to a lesser extent, the West, between 1916 and 1930. They relocated to pursue economic opportunities and to seek escape from segregation, rural poverty, and lynching. In New York City the first Great Migration contributed to the "Harlem Renaissance," a national flourishing of African American arts and literature named for an African American neighborhood north of Central Park in New York City. It included the work of writers like Langston Hughes and Zora Neale Hurston, musicians like Duke Ellington, and other Black intellectuals.

The press, along with writers such as F. Scott Fitzgerald (1896–1940), dubbed The Roaring Twenties "The Jazz Age." Jazz was a slang word that had a number of meanings before it became the name of a musical genre. In print it was first used on the West Coast in writing about baseball, meaning "lively" or "energetic," with its first known published appearance describing a baseball pitch (a curveball called a "jazz ball") in the *Los Angeles Times* in 1912. By 1915 it was being used in Chicago newspapers to describe a new lively kind of music, and by the end of World War I it was being used to refer to sex. In the 1920s, jazz was used to describe these things and more, including virtually all dance music, a great deal of which would probably not be categorized as "jazz" today. With all that the word jazz encapsulated at the time, calling the 1920s "The Jazz Age" seemed an apt way to describe an American society energized by the end of war and moving on from a deadly influenza pandemic in 1918 that had killed as many as 100 million people worldwide. By the end of the interwar period, the word jazz was being used around the world as a name for a musical genre that enjoyed mass popularity. Two gateway recordings are devoted to jazz in this chapter: one by Louis Armstrong (1901–1971) and His Hot Five that demonstrates musical innovations of Black migrants from the South in urban settings such as Chicago and New York City, and one by the big band of Duke Ellington (1899–1974), one of the great American composers of the twentieth century.

DOI: 10.4324/9781003269304-14

Victory in World War I also inspired a new American confidence in the role of the United States in the world. President Woodrow Wilson claimed that the United States had fought a just "war to end all wars." Patriotism spread through the population, not least among the children of Jewish immigrants who had fled economic and political oppression in eastern Europe before the war. Some of them became the most prominent composers of popular songs, including Irving Berlin (1888–1989), who wrote "God Bless America" in 1918. Another one, George Gershwin (1898–1937), a popular songwriter influenced by Jewish traditions and emerging jazz styles, also wrote a classical tone poem called *Rhapsody in Blue* in the nationalist vein, which is the subject of a gateway in this chapter.

The victory over war and disease gave many something to celebrate. One more victory also got the party started. In 1918, after a long struggle, women in the United States were given the right to vote. They felt a new confidence, and some of them, called flappers, adopted unconventional behaviors, including wearing daring, uncorseted, knee-length dresses, cutting their hair in short bobs, and drinking and smoking in public. These women, from the class of white middle-class and wealthy elites, felt free to participate on their own terms in the jazz-soaked social life of the times.

Disposable income was spent not only at clubs with live music and on home entertainment like radio and phonographs, but on spectator sports. Sports heroes became part of the cultural landscape for the first time, including boxer Jack Dempsey, college football player Red Grange, and the "wonder horses" Man o' War and Seabiscuit. Baseball became the national sport (though the "jazz ball" never caught on), and huge new stadiums were built for fans to follow their favorites, like the New York Yankees' slugger Babe Ruth.

All this entertainment flourished in spite of the passage in 1920 of the Eighteenth Amendment to the U.S. Constitution banning the sale of alcoholic beverages. This unleashed a wave of smuggling from Canada, Mexico, and the Caribbean run by gangsters whose internecine rivalries raised the noise level of the Roaring Twenties. Prohibition finally ended with the passage of the Twenty-First Amendment in 1933.

After the 1929 stock market crash, for most of the second decade of the interwar period the Great Depression brought on suffering for the bulk of the population of the United States and most of the world. A drought wiped out farmers in the Midwest, another source of misery. Poverty and inflation in Germany made the demagoguery of Adolf Hitler appealing to the masses. After he came to power in 1933, the specter of war hung over Europe. Threatened by Hitler, many Jews emigrated to the United States, invigorating musical life in classical music circles. Most prominent among them was the Austrian composer Arnold Schoenberg.

In spite of economic hardship during the Depression of the 1930s, the United States and Mexico enjoyed a "golden age" of cinema. In 1927 the first "talking picture," tellingly titled *The Jazz Singer*, continued the blackface minstrel tradition and anticipated vast numbers of "musicals," films in the 1930s that featured the popular singing and dancing stars of the day, including Bing Crosby, Fred Astaire, Ginger Rogers, and Judy Garland. In Mexico, mariachi music figured prominently in films with singing stars like Jorge Negrete and Pedro Infante. A gateway in this chapter is devoted to this genre. People also flocked to large ballrooms to listen and dance to the music of big bands led by Duke Ellington and other bandleaders, whose recordings they also bought to listen to at home and heard on the radio. This escapist fare in movies, Broadway shows, big band dance music, and sound recordings was eagerly consumed by audiences seeking relief from economic desperation.

GATEWAY 38
EARLY JAZZ

What Is It?

The word "jazz" had a number of meanings in the inter-war period, referring to dancing, sex, and music of many styles. As the genre of music known as jazz today developed in the course of the age of recordings, musicians and historians have looked back to the 1910s and 1920s, when the word jazz was first associated with music, and have called some styles of music in this period "early jazz." Our gateway to early jazz is "Struttin' with Some Barbecue" (1927) composed by Lillian (Lil) Hardin Armstrong (1898–1971) and performed by Louis Armstrong and His Hot Five. In a style of what is known today as **New Orleans jazz**, a rhythm section (in this case piano and banjo) backs up three melodic instrumentalists (usually playing trumpet or cornet, clarinet, and trombone) who play together in polyphony and call and response, and also as improvising soloists. Louis Armstrong (1901–1971) grew up in New Orleans, performing on the cornet (similar to the trumpet) as a teenager. This and other recordings of Louis Armstrong and His Hot Five from the late 1920s were recorded in Chicago, a destination for Armstrong and many other Black musicians from the South and Southwest during the first Great Migration. The recording's emphasis on single soloists improvising with a rhythm section accompaniment is an example of the innovations of Black musicians who had migrated from the south to urban centers like Chicago, New York, and Los Angeles.

FIGURE 10.3

Louis Armstrong and His Hot Five. From left to right: Louis Armstrong (trumpet), Johnny St. Cyr (banjo), Johnny Dodds (clarinet), Kid Ory (trombone), and Lil Hardin Armstrong (piano).
Source: Getty Images/Gilles Petard.

This gateway is also an early example of one of the most common forms in jazz performance, in which a **head** (melody) is played, followed by a number of improvised solos over the internal form and underlying harmony of the head and ending with a repeat of the head. A series of chords in a piece of music is called a **chord progression**, since the chords progress in time from one to the next. The improvised solos are based on the underlying harmony, the chord progression, of the head. Each improvisation based on the chord progression of the head is called a **chorus**. So, if an improvised solo lasts for two repetitions of the basic form, it lasts for two choruses.

 Listen to the first thirty seconds of the recording.

How Does It Work?

Timbre

The timbres of the cornet, clarinet, trombone, banjo, and piano can all be heard clearly.

Texture

The texture includes both individual and collective improvisations by the cornet, clarinet, and trombone over a chordal accompaniment played by the banjo and piano.

Rhythm

The song is in a duple meter, with a swing feel. The banjo and piano for the most part play steady pulsatile chords, while the other instruments add syncopated and swung rhythms.

Melody

The melody is generally in a major mode, and tends to arpeggiate through chord tones rather than move stepwise through a scale.

Harmony

The harmony is based on a series of major and minor triads as well as some dominant seventh chords. Some chromaticism can be heard from time to time.

Form

After a 12-measure intro, a repeating 32-bar form is introduced, which has an internal form of ABA'C, with each section lasting eight bars. The first time through, that is, during the first chorus, this 32-bar form is a statement of the melody. The second chorus features a clarinet and then a trombone solo, and the third chorus features a cornet solo. The final chorus is a restatement of the head.

Performance Techniques

During each statement of the melody by the cornet, the trombone and clarinet can be heard simultaneously improvising with the cornet. After the head, however, the clarinet, trombone, and cornet each perform solo improvisations over the form. Each of these three instruments performs microtonally, bends the start or end of pitches, and adds various types of ornamentation as they imitate the sound of a human voice singing the blues.

Listen to the introduction and the head (to about 0:32) and pay attention to the polyphonic, simultaneous lines of the trumpet, trombone, and clarinet.

Listen to the entire performance, following this listening guide, which describes each chorus.

LISTENING GUIDE 10.1

TIME	SECTION	FORM	DESCRIPTION
0:00	Introduction		The song starts with a twelve-bar introduction, featuring a prominent melody in the cornet and improvisation in the clarinet and trombone. Bars 1–4 and 9–12 feature an accompaniment with a steady beat, while in bars 5–8, the banjo, piano, clarinet, and trombone play sustained chords on beat one of each measure while the cornet plays eighth notes and syncopated figures.
0:14	Head (first chorus)	A	The cornet begins the melody or "head." This melody generally ascends up an arpeggio and then partially descends along the same or a similar arpeggio. The clarinet and trombone improvise while the cornet plays the head, and their parts are more active in between the cornet phrases, in a call and response of sorts. The banjo provides a steady pulse on every downbeat. The piano performs a bass line on beats one and three, reminiscent of the "oom-pah" bass line of marches and the bass line as performed in ragtime solo piano.
0:24		B	The harmony in the second eight bars of the head shifts to a series of chords that tend to be minor, but are still in the original key. The texture remains constant here and throughout the head.
0:34		A'	The first four bars of A' are about the same as the first four bars of A. In the second four bars, the harmony and melody are different from A.
0:44		C	At the end of these last eight bars of the head, the banjo plays two bars solo, ascending chromatically on a series of chords, one on each downbeat.

TIME	SECTION	FORM	DESCRIPTION
0:54	Clarinet solo (second chorus)	A	The clarinet improvises over the first sixteen bars of the form, accompanied by a new texture in the piano and banjo where the piano abandons its "oom-pah" bass line and joins the banjo in playing a chord on each downbeat. The accompaniment stops for the last two bars and the clarinet plays on its own.
1:04		B	The clarinet continues improvising with the accompaniment, though the accompaniment stops for the last two bars and the clarinet plays on its own in a brief section called a **break**, since it is a break in the continuity of the chugging rhythmic playing of the rhythm section.
1:13	Trombone solo (second chorus continues)	A′	The trombone begins its improvised solo, taking advantage of the instrument's slide mechanism to perform ornamentation that slides between pitches. The accompaniment also shifts again. The banjo continues to play chords on every beat, but the piano is now playing chords only on every other beat, beats two and four. This emphasis on beats two and four is a typical feature of the swing feel.
1:23		C	The solo continues, and again the last two bars occur with no accompaniment and the trombone plays the end of the solo on its own.
1:33	Cornet solo (third chorus)	A	The full-chorus cornet solo begins. The improvised melody Armstrong plays draws not only on the major mode, but also on the blues, especially the lowered third blue note. His playing is highly syncopated throughout. The accompaniment changes once again; now the banjo and piano only play chords on beats two and four.
1:43		B	The solo continues, and again the last two bars occur with no accompaniment as the cornet plays a break.
1:53		A′	The solo continues over the harmony of A′.
2:03		C	In this section, the final solo before the return of the head, the final two bars of the form are replaced with four bars of an unaccompanied, syncopated rhythm played in harmony by the cornet, clarinet, and trombone.
2:15	Head (final chorus)	A	The head returns, this time with the cornet adding some improvised flourishes that distinguish this statement of the head from the one at the beginning. The texture is the same as in the initial statement of the head.
2:26		B	The clarinet takes a particularly active role in the improvisation in this B section. The last two bars break once again for a solo banjo rhythmic figure.
2:36		A′	A′ is similar to its appearance in the initial statement of the head, with more active clarinet and trombone improvisations.
2:46		C	For the last C section, the accompaniment drops out, and the clarinet, cornet, and trombone play in homophonic rhythm. They repeat the final two bars of this figure and hold a sustained chord to finish the performance.
3:02	End		

What Does It Mean?

Louis Armstrong and His Hot Five play "Struttin' with Some Barbecue" with some elements of music rooted in the entertainment scene in New Orleans before 1918, music that came to be called jazz. They also hint at some of the directions that jazz would take in the years following this recording. The ensemble of three wind instruments (cornet, clarinet, and trombone) and a rhythm section (in this case banjo and piano) plays the head in a polyphonic texture that was

AESTHETICS

common for this kind of group. The cornet plays the main melody, adding some embellishment and ornamentation. The clarinet plays a countermelody that is much more active than the cornet part and fills in the gaps in the cornet melody. In the initial head the clarinet is generally playing lower than the cornet, while in the final head the clarinet frequently plays in a range that is higher than the cornet melody. The trombone plays a less active countermelody than the clarinet, emphasizing the important pitches in the harmony and often using the slide of the trombone to slide from one note to the next in a technique sometimes called "tailgating," a reference to bands playing on the backs of trucks during Mardi Gras and other festive parades.

Several musicians improvising together in polyphony is called **collective improvisation**. In some forms of New Orleans jazz dating back to this period and earlier, the texture is primarily heterophonic, as all of the musicians improvise by simultaneously embellishing pre-composed melodies in different ways. One of the effects of this texture is that listeners' attention is not necessarily focused on the primary melody alone, but can be drawn to other elements such as the countermelodies, the rhythmic breaks at the end of some of the choruses, and the syncopated rhythms.

This texture, common in New Orleans jazz and other jazz styles, is also an enactment of collectivity, a way of making music where the focus is on the group as a whole, as musicians play embellished or improvised individual parts simultaneously. Collective interaction of this kind has its roots in several older forms of African American music and dance from the United States including spirituals, ring shouts, and work songs (Chapter 8, Gateway 30). Many scholars suggest that it is also a legacy of polyphonic practices from a number of African musical traditions, such as the polyphony of Central African foragers (Chapter 1, Gateway 1) or the inherent polyphony created by the interlocking parts of *mbira* players (Chapter 3, Gateway 9). Though this kind of polyphony is based on harmonies rooted in the tonality of European classical music, the collectivity heard in this polyphonic texture is also a thread that can be traced through several African and African American musical practices. The collectivity in the improvisation of the musicians and the social collectivity in the places the music was played reinforced one another; the polyphonic musical texture is in many ways an icon of the communal dance and social interaction that goes along with it.

TECHNOLOGY ▷ Lil Hardin Armstrong composed "Struttin' with Some Barbecue" with the intention that it would be recorded. Technological limitations in recording at the time meant that the maximum duration of one side of a record was around three minutes, and so the composition and the number of choruses had to fit within that time constraint. New Orleans jazz, however, was often music for dancing, and single songs would often last much longer than three minutes. The polyphonic or heterophonic texture of the style developed in New Orleans and other cities would continue for longer periods of time, engaging with dancers at social and other community events such as funeral processions that typically involved dance. When Black musicians from New Orleans and other areas of the South moved to places like Chicago, they adapted their musical styles and created new ones to work with new technology like recordings. Their records allowed listeners to hear their performances in places far distant from where they were recorded.

Though the recording of "Struttin' with Some Barbecue"—especially the head—provides some clues into what this kind of entertainment music in New Orleans and elsewhere might have sounded like before this period, it also demonstrates the emergence of the improvised solo as a key element of jazz performance that was happening as musicians migrated to northern urban centers. The clarinet and trombone solos, each lasting half of a chorus, mainly outline the underlying chords played by the piano and the banjo. By contrast, Louis Armstrong plays a longer cornet solo lasting a full chorus, demonstrating his virtuosity as a soloist. His solo includes extensive syncopation and microtonal blue notes like the lowered third over major harmonies, revealing influences of the blues and ragtime in his improvisation. This texture of an improvising soloist with rhythm section accompaniment was a new development in jazz during this period. Even in the context of the head, Armstrong's cornet features more prominently than the other instruments, whose polyphonic lines seem to be in supporting roles of his melody. Louis Armstrong's recordings of this era helped set the stage for jazz to become a setting for soloists to demonstrate their skill in improvising, usually with a rhythm section accompaniment in musical dialogue with the soloist. This focus on solo improvisation became one of the hallmarks of jazz, and is one of the main characteristics today in most types of jazz.

Listen again to the solos in "Struttin' with Some Barbecue." Identify where the soloists use syncopation and listen for the blue notes in the cornet solos.

What Is Its History?

The word jazz was first used to describe music in 1915 in Chicago newspapers. The first record-ing to use a form of the word jazz was "That Funny Jas Band from Dixieland" (1916) by a white duo named Collins and Harlan. They recorded in the style of minstrelsy, singing in an exagger-ated stereotype of what was considered a "Black dialect." In 1917 a group of white musicians from New Orleans with the name "The Original Dixieland Jass Band" (ODJB) recorded the song "Livery Stable Blues" in New York, and it became a hit. Some of the members of ODJB had previously played in white brass marching bands in New Orleans, bands whose repertoire included popular minstrel and ragtime songs. As a result, elements of ragtime and minstrelsy were featured in the music of ODJB, as were blues and other popular songs of the day. In part because of their name and the popularity of their recording, audiences began to refer to these kinds of music as jazz, and they associated it with New Orleans. Although the band tried to take credit for inventing jazz as a new style of popular dance music, the roots of jazz had been grow-ing deeply among African American and Creole (mixed-race, French- and Spanish-descended) musicians from the blues and ragtime music scenes of New Orleans and throughout the South during the decades before 1917.

CULTURAL LINKAGES

Although no recordings exist of New Orleans bands before 1917, photographs suggest that these bands featured lineups similar to that of the ODJB. The ODJB performed with a "front line" of cornet or trumpet, clarinet, and trombone accompanied by a rhythm section of piano and a drum set. Similar to the head of "Struttin' with Some Barbecue," the frontline musicians in ODJB recordings improvised simultaneously, creating a polyphonic texture of independent musical lines. The piano and drum set provided a constant pulse and the oom-pah, bass-chord accompaniment of a marching band. African American and Creole musicians were playing some-thing like this style of dance music in New Orleans, throughout the South, and in the northern and midwestern cities they were moving to as part of the first Great Migration, and recording technology enabled the spread of this music even farther. It must have sounded incredibly fresh to dancers in New York clubs and elsewhere in 1917. They were familiar with dance bands play-ing conventional arrangements that featured the melody plus harmonic accompaniment on piano and bass. Chances are the simultaneously improvised three-part polyphony of this New Orleans style, coupled with the rhythmic drive of a drum set, would have knocked them off their feet.

Early New Orleans jazz musicians have said that "jazz" was not used to describe their music, which they viewed as a version of ragtime that included improvisation. But the well-documented musical life of New Orleans before the explosion of jazz as a musical genre helps in understanding some of the music that developed later in places like Chicago among musicians like Louis Armstrong, Lil Hardin Armstrong, and the rest of the Hot Five. New Orleans had a lively outdoor brass-band music scene tied to Carnival (Mardi Gras) cele-brations and funerals in the African American community. In Africa, funerals are in many cases a time to celebrate the life of the deceased, and this tradition endured in New Orleans. Street bands played, and still play, a mournful tune on the way to the cemetery, but a joyful one on the way home. These street brass bands feature both bass drum and snare drum

FIGURE 10.4

A promotional postcard for the Original Dixieland Jazz Band

Source: Getty Images/GAB Archive.

FIGURE 10.5
The front page of an 1890 edition of *The Mascot*, a New Orleans newspaper, depicting a caricature of well-to-do white passersby reacting negatively to the sounds of an African American band, perhaps playing a precursor to jazz
Source: F. Bildestein (public domain), Wikimedia Commons.

FIGURE 10.6
The modern drum set
Source: Dave Wilson.

along with sousaphone and other wind instruments. The Rebirth Brass Band, the Dirty Dozen Brass Band, Hot 8 Brass Band, and many other brass bands are still a lively part of the New Orleans music scene today.

New Orleans also boasted an indoor musical culture. Bands played for dances in all the ethnic communities of the city (including Black, Creole, and white) plus, to some extent, in the many brothels that served sailors and others in this port city. When the brass bands came indoors and musicians sat down on stage to play for dancers, the string bass substituted for the sousaphone in some cases. Piano, guitar, and banjo were added to provide chordal accompaniment. And, in perhaps the most important innovation, a drummer for one of the New Orleans dance bands named Dee Dee Chandler invented a contraption (a pedal he could "kick" with his foot to play the bass drum) that allowed him to play both bass and snare drums simultaneously while sitting down. Musicians called this combination trap set (short for contraption), a drum kit, or drum set and the bass drum a "kick drum" after the way it was played. An important later addition to the drum set, common in the 1930s, was the **hi-hat**, a pair of similar cymbals mounted on a stand with a foot lever that, when depressed, crashed the cymbals together. Drum sets may include one or more mid-sized "tomtom drums" or "toms" attached to the bass drum or standing on the ground, as well as a number of single cymbals mounted on stands.

The Creole musicians who played this early kind of dance music belonged to the middle class in the integrated French quarter of the city. They had music educations and could read the music of John Philip Sousa, Scott Joplin, and other composers of band music and ragtime. They maintained and developed the syncopations of ragtime and the polyphonic principles of band music, applying them to their performances. They also continued the ragtime performance tradition of improvisation, a legacy of African and other musical traditions from the time of slavery. These traditions had overlapped with one another for centuries in places like New Orleans, with its rich multiplicity of cultures and its ties to the Caribbean and Latin America. In this setting, musicians, as a matter of course, improvised over popular dance music, rags, and blues.

By the time World War I had ended, Black and Creole musicians were already leaving New Orleans and other parts of the South for New York, Chicago, California, and Paris, bringing their ragtime- and blues-inflected music to the already vibrant music scenes in those cities and planting the seeds of what would become known as the "Jazz Age" in the cultural life of the United States, Europe, and Asia. New Orleans-born Jelly Roll Morton relocated to Los Angeles in 1917 before moving to Chicago in 1923 and then New York in 1928. While in L.A., he performed there and on tour up and down the West Coast with other Black musicians who had migrated from Texas, Mississippi, and other parts of Louisiana. In these urban environments, and as bands began to travel around the country and the world and record their music using new recording technologies, musical styles began to change in a number of ways. One of the notable changes was the greater focus on solo improvisation, the development of which was significantly influenced by Louis Armstrong.

Armstrong was born to a poor family in New Orleans. He received formal musical training in school and real-world musical experience playing in the bands of Joe "King" Oliver (1881–1938), one of the leading cornet players and bandleaders of the period and his mentor. In 1922 Armstrong followed Oliver to Chicago to play in Oliver's Creole Jazz Band, leaving the South for a northern city like so many other African Americans had at the time. Armstrong's technique was stronger than the other trumpeters in Chicago, and Oliver began to give him space in the band's arrangements to expand solo breaks into longer solos, as he does in "Struttin' with Some Barbeque." Encouraged by his future wife, the pianist Lil Hardin, who played in Oliver's band, Armstrong began to form his own bands. In 1927 he recorded Hardin's "Struttin' with Some Barbecue" with his Hot Five, a recording that illustrates this new version of New Orleans jazz with collective improvisation and Armstrong's brilliant solo playing. Between 1925 and 1928, Armstrong completed several dozen recordings with his Hot Five and his Hot Seven, which added a drum set and a tuba to the Hot Five instrumentation. Like "Struttin' with Some Barbecue," other recordings from these sessions such as "West End Blues" (1928) and "Potato Head Blues" (1927) showcase the groundbreaking melodic, rhythmic, and timbral elements of Armstrong's soloing, along with ensemble playing characteristic of New Orleans jazz.

Armstrong's long career after the 1920s departed from the New Orleans jazz style as he performed in many settings as an instrumentalist and as a vocalist. As a vocalist he was highly influential in the development and popularity of **scat singing**, vocal improvisations using vocables to imitate the sounds of musical instruments. In the 1930s and early 1940s, he performed almost exclusively as a soloist with big bands, both on trumpet and as a singer. During and after this time, he became well known for recording and performing popular Broadway and other songs that became known as the Great American Songbook, though he also returned to a New Orleans-style format beginning in the late 1940s. For much of his life, he was one of the most famous individuals in the United States and served as a cultural ambassador of the United States in government-sponsored performances abroad. His 1964 release of the song "Hello Dolly" (from the Broadway musical of the same name) was his last recording to hit number one on the charts. When it reached number one on

FIGURE 10.7
Photo of King Oliver's Creole Jazz Band. From left to right: Johnny Dodds (clarinet), Baby Dodds (drum set), Honoré Dutrey (trombone), Louis Armstrong (second trumpet), King Oliver (first trumpet), Lil Hardin (piano), William Johnson (bass, also holding banjo).
Source: Getty Images/Bettmann.

FIGURE 10.8
Louis Armstrong (right) appearing on a television program with trumpet player and music executive Herb Alpert in 1967
Source: Getty Images/David Redfern.

the *Billboard* charts, it unseated the Beatles' unprecedented three-month run in the number one position with their string of three hits: "I Want to Hold Your Hand," "She Loves You," and "Can't Buy Me Love." In 1967, Armstrong released "What a Wonderful World." Included in popular films such as the 1987 film *Good Morning Vietnam*, it has become a standard for events like first dances at wedding receptions and has been re-recorded in new arrangements by such artists as Nick Cave, Sarah Brightman, and Rod Stewart, who recorded the song in a duet with Stevie Wonder.

Louis Armstrong's influence in jazz and popular music during his life (and after his death) cannot be underestimated. Though in the 1930s he first departed from his performance of the styles categorized today as New Orleans jazz, these styles have had a history of their own since then, independent of Armstrong. During the 1930s, styles of New Orleans jazz became

FIGURE 10.9
The Preservation Hall Jazz Band in action, 2010
Source: Philip Scalia/Alamy Stock Photo.

less popular and gave way to big bands, the subject of our next gateway. Since then, however, New Orleans jazz has enjoyed several revivals in the United States and around the world, the first of which gained a broad audience in the 1940s and 1950s in the United States and Europe. In New Orleans today, New Orleans jazz caters to both tourists and locals. The Preservation Hall Jazz Band has been performing in New Orleans and on tour around the world since its inception in the early 1960s. The band has collaborated with popular bands such as The Foo Fighters and Arcade Fire. They seem to be continuing, in a different form, the mixing of musical influences and cultures that characterized New Orleans in the first half of the twentieth century, when jazz first became a national and international musical phenomenon.

WHERE DO I GO FROM HERE?

- Listen to "West End Blues," "Potato Head Blues," or another recording from the Hot Five or Hot Seven sessions. How are the musicians interacting in their collaborative improvisation? Compare the musical elements in these recordings with examples of the blues and ragtime discussed in Chapter 9, Gateways 33 and 35.

- Listen to "Livery Stable Blues" by the Original Dixieland Jazz Band. What elements does this recording share with minstrelsy? What elements of ragtime and the blues does it contain?

- Select three or four recordings made by Louis Armstrong in different stages of his life. To what extent are they connected to jazz of this early period?

GATEWAY 39
SWING

FIGURE 10.10
Duke Ellington in 1946
Source: William Morris Agency (management), Wikimedia Commons.

What Is It?

Swing was one of the most popular styles of music during the 1920s and 1930s. It was played by large jazz ensembles called **big bands** (sometimes called dance bands). They filled large ballrooms with their sound, entertaining dancers in energetic dance styles such as the Lindy Hop, the Charleston, and dozens more. Both swing music and the dances that emerged along with it were part of a craze that took the United States and much of the world by storm. By 1935, "swing" was being used consistently by the music industry as a musical genre name, marking the beginning of what is known as the "swing era." Big bands of the swing era had a typical instrumentation of five saxophones, four or five trombones, four or five trumpets, and a rhythm section typically including drums, bass, piano, and guitar. One of the most influential musicians and composers in the development and popularity of swing was Edward Kennedy "Duke" Ellington (1899–1974), whose big band, beginning in the late 1920s, was one of the most well known. Our gateway to swing is a composition by Ellington and trumpet player Bubber Miley (1903–1932) called "Black and Tan Fantasy." Composed and recorded in 1927 during the period leading up to the swing era, "Black and Tan Fantasy" demonstrates some of the classic sounds and cultural meanings that characterize Ellington's music and the music of big band swing.

 Listen to the first thirty seconds of this recording.

How Does It Work?

Timbre

This composition features the big band timbres of saxophones, trombones, and trumpets, along with piano, banjo, bass, and drums. In addition, trumpet and trombone timbres are frequently altered with the addition of mutes.

Texture

Several textures can be heard, including several versions of melody with block-chord accompaniment, solo piano, and some brief moments of contrapuntal texture.

Rhythm

The meter is a quadruple meter, and a swing feel is heard throughout. The tempo of the pulse ranges between about 108 and 112 beats per minute, which makes it suitable for dancing.

Melody

The melody begins in a minor mode, then shifts into a major mode. In both minor and major modes, blue notes are emphasized from time to time. Sometimes the melody is improvised by soloists.

Harmony

The harmony follows minor and major tonal chord progressions, usually in triads and seventh chords.

Form

The form begins with a 12-bar blues in a minor key, followed by a 16-bar section in the parallel major key. **Parallel major and minor keys** have the same tonic pitch. (For example, C minor and C major are parallel keys.) The recording continues with five choruses of a 12-bar blues in the same major key, the last one with a two-bar extension.

Performance Techniques

Performers frequently play microtonally. The brass instruments bend pitches and use mutes in a way that helps them mimic the sounds of a human voice. In the final chorus we also hear call and response between the trumpet and the full band.

Listen to the first thirty seconds again and pay attention to the muted trumpet sound, pitch bends, and the underlying, accompanying pulse.

Listen to the entire recording following this timed listening guide.

TIME	SECTION	DESCRIPTION
0:00	1st Chorus	The piece begins with a muted trumpet playing a minor melody along with a muted trombone playing in harmony. The trumpet and trombone are accompanied by pulsing block chords in the rhythm section. The end of this 12-bar minor blues section and the beginning of the next section is marked with a cymbal crash played by the drummer.
0:27	16-bar interlude	An alto saxophone plays a 16-bar composed solo that is two repetitions of an eight-bar phrase in an AA form reminiscent of a European dance form. The saxophone is accompanied by the pulsing banjo and piano as well as sustained chords played by the other wind players and the bass player playing with a bow. The harmony in this section is characterized by chromaticism, especially in the two bars at the end of the first eight-bar phrase where the harmony changes on every beat.
1:02	2nd Chorus	The trumpet plays an improvised solo over a 12-bar major blues form, beginning with a sustained high-pitched tone on the tonic for the first four bars. The trumpet player, Bubber Miley, is playing through a straight mute and is using a "plunger mute," which he moves with his hand to adjust the timbre and pitch as he plays. A prominent growling effect in the trumpet can be heard in the second half of this chorus.
1:29	3rd Chorus	The trumpet timbre shifts again as it improvises over another chorus of a major blues, emphasizing pitch bends and the lowered-third blue note.
1:55	4th Chorus	The piano plays a solo, drawing on characteristics of stride piano such as the "oom-pah" figure where the left hand alternates between low bass notes and a higher-pitched chord.
2:21	5th Chorus	The trombone plays an improvised solo, again with a muted sound that affects the timbre. About halfway through, the trombone performs an effect that sounds like laughter or the imitation of a horse's whinny.
2:48	6th Chorus	The trumpet returns, beginning with two bluesy two-bar phrases that are answered by accented chords played by the full band in a call-and-response style. This chorus begins as a major blues, but on the eleventh bar, the harmony returns to the minor key from the beginning of the piece. This final phrase is a quotation from the "Funeral March" theme of Frédéric Chopin's Piano Sonata No. 2, Op. 35 in B-flat minor (1839), and extends the length of the blues form by two bars to a total of fourteen bars.
3:23	End	

FIGURE 10.11
Duke Ellington (in front of piano) and his orchestra pose for a portrait c. 1935
Source: Getty Images/Michael Ochs Archives.

What Does It Mean?

The musical elements of "Black and Tan Fantasy," reveal much about the experience of big band music and swing in the 1920s and 1930s as well as about its roots in the blues, early jazz, and music of Africa and the African diaspora.

"Black and Tan Fantasy," like much big band music of this period, features a swing feel in a moderate tempo with an emphasis on beats two and four of a four-beat measure. Its rhythmic elements point to how big bands like Duke Ellington's orchestra functioned primarily as live entertainment for dancing. The label on the initial recording of "Black and Tan Fantasy" lists

"Duke Ellington and His Orchestra" as the performing ensemble along with the name "Fox Trot," a well-known couple dance. Dancing to the swinging rhythms of big bands in large ballrooms full of dancers as well as smaller dance clubs became wildly popular in the 1920s and 1930s in New York, throughout the United States, and around the world. Beginning in 1927, Ellington's band performed regularly at New York's Cotton Club, a venue in Harlem that catered almost exclusively to white patrons and relied on the legacy of minstrelsy, setting Black musicians on a stage that replicated a mansion on a southern plantation, complete with a backdrop that depicted weeping willows and quarters for the enslaved. Other clubs in Harlem were frequented predominantly by African Americans, excluded from white venues like the Cotton Club. "Black and tan" clubs, a third type, were small cabarets, usually in Black neighborhoods, that attracted both Black and white patrons, though they were sometimes segregated inside. As one of the few public spaces where whites and African Americans could socialize in close proximity, Black and tan clubs were expe-

FIGURE 10.12
Cab Calloway leading his big band and an audience of dancers at the Cotton Club in 1937
Source: Getty Images/Bettmann.

rienced by many white patrons as erotic, dangerous, and playful places where they could go "slumming," living out their fantasies of pushing against the boundaries of segregation. Ellington's "Black and Tan Fantasy" plays on the sexual anxieties and desires of his white audiences, musically placing "Black" and "tan" elements in close proximity to one another and featuring sounds of the blues and timbral effects that would be titillating for much of his paying public at the time.

The form of "Black and Tan Fantasy" juxtaposes the 12-bar blues of each chorus and the 16-bar interlude that appears after the first chorus. The blues sections draw on microtonality, blue notes, timbral effects added by mutes, and other musical elements that mark the music as distinctly African American. These musical elements—especially the growling timbres of muted brass instruments—were distinctive aspects of Ellington's music and led to his style being called "jungle music." While this term reinforced racist stereotypes about African Americans likely held by the Cotton Club's white patrons, Ellington himself also used the term, recognizing that it served to promote and advertise his unique style as a composer and arranger. The 16-bar interlude departs from the "jungle" sound, drawing instead on some of the conventions of ragtime such as the syncopated melody with an "oom-pah" accompaniment and the use of a European dance form (AA) as its internal form. It also adopts the chromatic harmonies of the late nineteenth-century European classical tradition. Ellington seems to be creating a musical icon of the Black and tan ideal by situating the formal, timbral, and melodic elements of the African American roots of the blues in close proximity to the 16-bar interlude and its European musical roots in texture, form, and harmony.

< **AESTHETICS**

🔊 Listen again to "Black and Tan Fantasy" and pay attention to the contrasts between the 12-bar blues sections and the 16-bar interlude.

Ellington's musical commentary in "Black and Tan Fantasy" also has a few more layers adding to its rich and complex meaning. The melody in the first chorus is a modification of a spiritual titled "The Holy City," a composition that co-composer and trumpet player Bubber Miley said he learned from his mother. This spiritual was commonly sung in both Black and white Christian churches at the beginning of the twentieth century. The original melody of "The Holy City" is in a major mode, and the lyrics state: "Jerusalem, Jerusalem; lift up your gates and sing." This is a tribute to the holy city of Jerusalem, often used in Christianity as a metaphor for heaven, where

< **CULTURAL LINKAGES**

unity with God is achieved and the perils of life on earth—such as Jim Crow and other racial discrimination—have disappeared (see Chapter 8, Gateway 30). In "Black and Tan Fantasy," there are no lyrics and the melody is transformed into a minor mode and into a blues. Ellington's transformation of a Christian hymn tune into a blues symbolically unites African Americans' religious and worldly experiences, as if their Christian belief in life after death is reaching into their daily experiences of racial injustice and suffering as a danceable blues that can offer a moment of entertainment and pleasure and, perhaps, a Black and tan fantasy that imagines a future without racial injustice.

The final phrase of "Black and Tan Fantasy" references Frédéric Chopin's Piano Sonata No. 2 in B-flat minor, Op. 35, known as the "Funeral March." By including this musical quotation, Ellington draws a strong connection to the European classical tradition, which he studied. At the same time, he closes his "Black and Tan Fantasy" with a signifier of death—a funeral march—indicating with a playful dash of humor that the fantasies of the Black and tan clubs, whatever they are, certainly have not been realized in any satisfactory way.

What Is Its History?

CULTURAL LINKAGES

The history of "Black and Tan Fantasy" can be connected to both the emergence of big bands and swing music in the interwar period and the personal biography of Duke Ellington. The development of many swing dance styles can be traced to Harlem's Savoy Ballroom, which opened in 1926. This enormous space filled an entire city block and had a 4000-person capacity. It boasted a lavishly adorned interior and provided a high-class experience for a relatively low entrance fee. It was open to both white and Black guests but, unlike the Cotton Club, its primary patrons were from the surrounding Black neighborhoods.

The stock market crash of 1929 and the ensuing Great Depression left many people struggling to make ends meet as the 1920s came to a close. Most Americans certainly did not have the means to purchase records, and record sales plummeted. As a live experience of music and dance, big bands and swing provided an escape and a distraction from the anxieties of the Great Depression rather than a way to engage with or reflect on those anxieties. If they couldn't afford to attend live performances, fans could hear the music on the radio, and restaurants and nightclubs played it on **jukeboxes** (coin-operated record players) that later on ended up playing a role in rejuvenating the recording industry.

FIGURE 10.13
The Savoy Ballroom in 1942
Source: Getty Images/Weegee (Arthur Fellig)/International Center of Photography.

Big bands and styles of swing dancing were widespread by the late 1920s. When the music industry adopted swing as a genre label during the mid-1930s, the swing era began. Big band swing music and dancing to it dominated the popular culture of the United States until the mid-1940s. Hundreds of bands toured the country, some with Black band leaders like Fletcher Henderson (1897–1952), Jimmie Lunceford (1902–1947), Cab Calloway (1907–1994), and Chick Webb (1909–1939), and some with white leaders like Benny Goodman (1909–1986) and Glenn Miller (1904–1944).

During the swing era, jazz vocalists such as Ella Fitzgerald (1917–1996) and Billie Holiday (1915–1959) became important contributors to big bands and their popularity. Carrying on Armstrong's legacy as a jazz vocalist, their recordings were often creative interpretations of well-known songs, some of which became massively popular hits. In 1935 Fitzgerald began performing with a big band led by Chick Webb (1905–1939) on recordings and at venues like the Savoy Ballroom. She later became known for masterful scat singing that incorporated elements of bebop, a style of jazz that emerged in the 1940s. Holiday, known for her original and expressive interpretation of song melodies and the distinct timbre of her voice, first recorded with the Benny Goodman big band in 1933. Her 1939 recording of "Strange Fruit" was an emotional and graphic account of a lynching in the American South. It remains one of the most striking examples of jazz musicians directly engaging with racial injustice.

While many sophisticated whites in New York enjoyed traveling uptown to hear and see what they viewed as exotic shows at the Cotton Club and other venues in Harlem, prevailing racist attitudes meant that white audiences in much of the rest of the country did not hire Black bands to play for their dances. Instead of dancing to the style of "hot" big bands coming out of Harlem, they danced to "sweet" bands, like Paul Whiteman's, who were known for playing popular songs in styles that featured slower tempos and less improvisation. Many white musicians, however, loved the "hot" jazz they were hearing in clubs and on recordings and taught themselves to play it. The first of these white musicians to break into the national consciousness playing hot jazz was Benny Goodman. Born in Chicago to a Jewish immigrant family from eastern Europe, he studied classical clarinet as a child and continued to play it throughout his life. But he found New Orleans clarinet players who he heard in Chicago nightclubs in the early 1920s equally fascinating. A prodigy, Goodman was playing professionally by the age of thirteen. When he was still a teenager, he moved to New York in the late 1920s and played in bands and small groups and recording sessions with many of the outstanding musicians of the day, including Black musicians.

FIGURE 10.14
Billie Holiday studio portrait in 1939
Source: Getty Images/Gilles Petard.

By the early 1930s Goodman was leading his own big band. John Hammond, a music producer for Columbia Records who was tuned in to the music of the African American community, heard Goodman and suggested that he purchase and perform the "hot" arrangements of Black bandleader Fletcher Henderson (1897–1952), who was having trouble keeping his band together during the Depression. The Goodman band's new arrangements, featuring improvisation and the driving rhythms of Black bands, became a sensation in the first half of 1935 when Goodman's band was regularly featured in a national radio broadcast. White youth flocked to hear and dance to Goodman's band. Other white jazz musicians quickly followed suit, forming their own popular bands, among them Glenn Miller, Tommy Dorsey, Woody Herman, and Artie Shaw.

While Goodman's big bands made him a household name at the time, he also made contributions to the history of jazz and American popular music that were quieter but just as profound. Goodman is usually credited with being the first white bandleader to perform on stage with African American musicians, a radical move in the midst of the harsh racial segregation of the time. He did so in small combos (trios, quartets, and sextets) that would become the model for jazz for generations to come. These **combos** (short for "combination," a small jazz ensemble) featured much more improvisation than his and other big bands did. They included, in addition to Italian American drummer Gene Krupa (1909–1973), three of the most important Black jazz musicians of the day: the pianist Teddy Wilson (1912–1986), the vibraphonist Lionel Hampton (1908–2002), and the guitarist Charlie Christian (1916–1942). Goodman and his integrated combos were performing an imagined future without the legal racial segregation that characterized American society at this time.

FIGURE 10.15
Benny Goodman and his big band
Source: Getty Images/Bettmann.

Two bandleaders, Count Basie (1904–1984) and Duke Ellington, transcended the swing era. They continued performing long after the 1930s and 1940s as their music influenced the development of jazz far beyond the dance hall. Basie's band came from Kansas City, which, like many cities throughout the United States, played host to **territory bands**, dance bands that performed in a geographic area within a day trip of their home city. As an active center for several such bands, Kansas City served as a home base in the 1920s and 1930s for other influential musicians such as bandleader Bennie Moten (1894–1935) and Mary Lou Williams (1910–1981), a pianist, arranger, and prolific composer. Basie and his band relocated to New York and enjoyed great popularity there and nationally. But as the popularity of swing waned after World War II, he and other bandleaders struggled to keep their groups working, and Basie had to break up his band. In the 1950s he re-formed the band, touring the country and accompanying popular vocalists like Frank Sinatra, Tony Bennett, and Sarah Vaughan until his death in 1984.

Many music historians and critics regard Duke Ellington as one of the most significant American musicians of the twentieth century. He was born in Washington, D.C., where he was raised in a middle-class family. He formed his first dance band as a teenager in the 1910s, drawing on the formal musical training he had received as a child as well as on music he had heard in his younger years, in particular the Harlem stride piano style he heard from pianists James P. Johnson and Willie "the Lion" Smith when they performed in D.C. on tour. The stride style significantly shaped Ellington's compositions and arrangements for big band from his first composition at age fourteen, "Soda Fountain Rag" (based on James P. Johnson's "Carolina Shout") to the stride piano fourth chorus in "Black and Tan Fantasy" to his 1964 recording "Second Portrait of the Lion," dedicated to Willie "the Lion" Smith.

After moving to New York in 1923, he formed his band, the Washingtonians. By 1926, he had begun to develop his own style in compositions such as a ragtime dance called "East St. Louis Toodle-O" (1926), also co-composed with Bubber Miley, and "Black and Tan Fantasy." His renown as a composer beyond the world of big band swing was recognized at his debut at Carnegie Hall in 1943. There, he and his band premiered his three-movement composition *Black, Brown, and Beige*, an instrumental work that Ellington said was a musical parallel to the history of African Americans. A three-part "tone parallel" (Ellington's gesture to the tone poem of European symphonic music), the piece depicts the time of slavery through references to work songs and spirituals; the blood Black Americans shed building of the United States (including as members of the military) through references to the blues and emulations of train whistles and other sounds of modernization; and the vibrant entertainment and intellectual life of urban Black communities like Harlem since World War I through the use of a collection of dance music and other styles, including a waltz, meant to signal "sophistication."

In the course of his life, Ellington composed music both alone and collaboratively with other musicians. He was known for carrying a pencil and paper with him on the road, composing music as it came to him on trains, on buses, in hotels, or wherever he found himself. His body of work includes not only popular songs and compositions for big band, but also ballets, scores for film and television, and symphonic works for orchestra. All of his music contains elements of jazz, though Ellington himself was ambivalent about the word "jazz," finding the label confining. He was known to say that the music he composes is instead "the music of humankind" or "Negro folk music." Under any label, Ellington's work is interrelated with the history of Black Americans. It expresses struggles against racial injustice, provides sounds for celebration and entertainment, and embodies Black contributions to the fabric of American life.

FIGURE 10.16
From left to right: Lionel Hampton, Teddy Wilson, Benny Goodman, and Gene Krupa
Source: United Archives GmbH/Alamy Stock Photo.

Duke Ellington's most significant collaborator, Billy Strayhorn (1915–1967), joined him in 1938 as a fellow composer and arranger. Strayhorn contributed significant works of his own to the Ellington band repertoire, most notably "Take the 'A' Train" (1939), which became one of the theme songs for the band. Another one of Strayhorn's best-known compositions is "Lush Life," most of which was written when Strayhorn was a teenager, though its first performance was not until 1948 with the Ellington band. "Lush Life," with music and lyrics by Strayhorn, features complex chromatic harmony and an angular melody, both of which pushed the limits of conventional practices in jazz at the time. These unconventional practices were welcomed by Ellington as he explored the boundaries between European classical composition, jazz, blues, other African American musical traditions, and music cultures he encountered as he traveled the world. The lyrics of "Lush Life" speak of isolation, romantic loss, and loneliness, and they gesture to Strayhorn's experience as a Black gay man.

In the 1950s and 1960s, many compositions from this period bear both of their names. In the mid-1960s, Strayhorn developed esophageal cancer and his health declined steadily until his death in 1967. One of his last compositions was titled "Blood Count" (1967), a piece whose title refers to

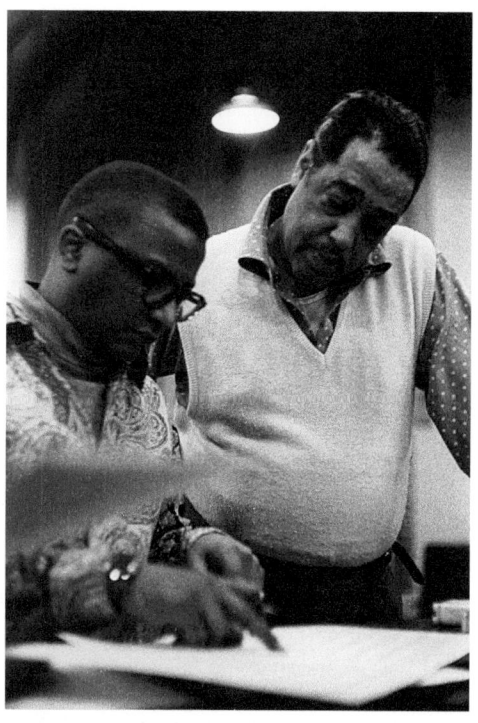

FIGURE 10.17

Billy Strayhorn (left) and Duke Ellington at work in 1956

Source: Getty Images/Ben Martin

blood tests he was receiving in the hospital. It features passionate and emotional solo playing by alto saxophone player Johnny Hodges. This piece and other Strayhorn compositions and arrangements were featured on the Ellington album . . . *And His Mother Called Him Bill* (1968), an homage from Ellington to his compositional partner of nearly thirty years.

Duke Ellington's renown stretched beyond the boundaries of the United States for much of his career. Between 1963 and 1973, the U.S. State Department sponsored tours abroad. Through "jazz diplomacy" the U.S. government hoped that live performances by American jazz musicians would produce in audiences abroad warmer affinities for the United States and for its foreign policy. Many jazz musicians participated in these tours, but none more frequently than Ellington, who performed throughout the Middle East, Africa, Asia, the Soviet Union, eastern Europe, and Latin America. He often composed music specifically about the city or country he was visiting. The results were albums with titles like *Far East Suite* (released in 1967, inspired by a 1963 tour and co-composed with Strayhorn) and *Latin American Suite* (released in 1972, inspired by a 1968 tour). He met and collaborated with local musicians, many of whom were national (or international) stars in their own right. On his final tour in 1973, he performed with the Ethiopian jazz composer and vibraphonist Mulatu Astatke in a concert with Astatke's ensemble sharing the stage with Ellington's big band. At this time Ellington was already suffering from lung cancer, which would take his life months later in the spring of 1974. Since his death, he has been memorialized in countless ways including streets, bridges, and parks named after him, three posthumous Grammy awards (he received nine during his life), and a posthumous "Special Citation" by the Pulitzer Prize board for his lifetime of work in 1999. Stevie Wonder's hit song "Sir Duke" (1976) was a tribute to Ellington, and hundreds of other artists have composed homages to him and his work with Billy Strayhorn.

WHERE DO I GO FROM HERE?

- Listen to *Black, Brown and Beige* and identify the musical elements that it shares with "Black and Tan Fantasy," or with the blues, ragtime, or other music that you know.
- Listen to "Blood Count" and other Billy Strayhorn compositions on the album . . . *And His Mother Called Him Bill* and compare them to pieces where Ellington is the sole composer.
- Listen to one or two pieces from *Far East Suite* or *Latin American Suite* and describe the way Ellington engages with musical traditions from those parts of the world.

GATEWAY 40
AMERICAN SYMPHONIC NATIONALISM

What Is It?

One of the trends in classical music in interwar America was the development of a repertoire that had a particularly "American" sound. One of the most-performed symphonic compositions in this American nationalist vein is *Rhapsody in Blue* by George Gershwin (1898–1937), our gateway to American symphonic nationalism and a work written originally for piano and jazz band in 1924. It was later scored for piano and symphony orchestra. A **rhapsody** is a one-movement composition that has a free-flowing, improvisatory character and that many European composers employed to evoke national sentiment with folk or newly composed folk-like melodies. This performance is by the Columbia Symphony Orchestra conducted by Leonard Bernstein.

 Listen to the first thirty seconds of the recording and notice the bent notes and timbre of a jazz orchestra at the beginning of this piece of classical music.

How Does It Work?

Timbre

The piece alternates solo piano with full orchestra, with episodes for solo clarinet, horns, and muted solo trumpet playing "wah-wah" sounds reminiscent of Bubber Miley's playing in "Black and Tan Fantasy" by Duke Ellington and His Orchestra.

Texture

The texture is chordal and contrapuntal, although the opening unaccompanied clarinet solo is a striking and memorable feature of the piece.

Rhythm

The meter is in four with syncopated rhythms, rubato, and varied tempos.

Melody

Many of the themes are based on a blues scale, in alternation with major-mode melodies.

FIGURE 10.18
"A Portrait of George Gershwin at a Piano" (in concert attire) by Edward Steichen
Source: Getty Images/Edward Steichen.

Harmony

Traditional tonal harmony with jazz-inspired chords.

Form

The piece presents six main themes, each played by the orchestra in alternation with piano solos that show off the pianist's virtuosity in both classical and jazz styles.

Performance Techniques

The upward clarinet glissando over nearly two octaves and other "bent notes" characteristic of jazz and blues are featured in what is otherwise a composition in the classical tradition.

Listen to the entire recording following this timed listening guide.

TIME	SECTION	DESCRIPTION
0:00	Introduction	The work opens with an arresting solo clarinet playing an upward glissando, a signature element of the piece, and one suggested by the first clarinetist to play the piece and later adopted by Gershwin.
0:07	A (orch)	The clarinet, joined by the orchestra, continues with the first theme, which descends through a scale that includes chromatic tones and blue notes (flat 7th, flat 6th, flat 5th, and flat 3rd) with jazz-like slides into pitches.
0:41	B (orch)	The horns introduce a second melody built on a motive of a single pitch played four times and repeated on blue notes (1111 ♭7 ♭7 ♭7 ♭7 1111 ♭3 ♭3 ♭3 ♭3) before descending through a scale that features blue notes mixed in with some tones of a major scale.
0:55	A (orch)	Muted trumpets play the first theme creating "wah-wah" effects evocative of early jazz.
1:05	C (piano) A (orch)	The piano enters with a short third theme before the full orchestra returns to the first theme.
1:29	C (piano)	The piano plays a solo beginning with the third theme followed by arpeggiations and chords in a style derived from nineteenth-century classical pianism followed by a series of sequential modulations to new keys.
2:16	A (piano) C (orch)	The piano plays the A theme in a rubato tempo, and sections of the orchestra play aspects of the C theme in response, featuring a bass clarinet. More nineteenth-century-style arpeggiations, chords, and modulations in the piano follow.
3:44	A (orch)	The orchestra enters grandly and loudly with the first theme.
4:13	D (orch)	A long growl in the brass (created by a self-explanatory technique called "flutter-tongue") signals a transition to something new: the growling brass introduces a short, up-tempo, arc-shaped, major-mode melody accompanied by flourishes on the piano.
4:40	B (orch)	The solo clarinet plays parts of the B melody, interspersed with grand arpeggiated gestures on the piano.
4:56	B (orch)	The second theme returns grandly and loudly in the full orchestra before fading into soft melodic fragments ending in four syncopated chords and a pause.
5:42	B + A (piano)	A second piano solo returns to the second theme, accompanied at one point by the horns holding long tones. The piano introduces a swing rhythm and continues with the first theme played fortissimo.
7:56	E (piano)	The piano solo continues by introducing a fifth theme featuring many blue notes softly in a slow, rubato tempo. Soon the melody in the right hand is syncopated against pulses in the left hand, creating a jazz feel. Plenty of nineteenth-century piano flourishes follow.

LISTENING GUIDE 10.3

continued

TIME	SECTION	DESCRIPTION
10:14	F (orch)	The sixth theme, in a major mode, features longer-held tones than the previous themes. Combined with a medium tempo and medium dynamic level and played by the full orchestra with brief responses from the horns, the effect is broad, romantic, and occasionally majestic.
12:13	F + C (piano)	A fourth piano solo features the sixth theme with mainly classical piano gestures. The C theme briefly returns.
14:15	F (orch)	The brass section enters with the sixth theme, this time with rapid dynamic changes on individual pitches, while the piano continues its flourishes. The orchestra increases in loudness and slows down to signal a change.
15:14	B + A (orch)	The second theme in full orchestra and piano (played with a swing feel!) are followed by the first theme crescendoing to a grand finale with a brief reference to the third theme.
16:25	End	

What Does It Mean?

EMOTIONAL RESONANCE

Much of the meaning of *Rhapsody in Blue* comes from its combination of jazz and classical styles. The swing rhythms, syncopation, melodies using blue notes, and jazz harmonies are performed by a classical symphony orchestra, with its wide timbral palette, and pianistic techniques borrowed from classical music. The result is a musical icon of the union of European and American, specifically African American, musical sensibilities. Czech nationalist composer Antonín Dvořák, during his sojourn in the United States in the 1890s, suggested that African American music, specifically spirituals, could provide the basis for a unique American national style of classical music (Chapter 8, Gateway 29). By 1924 other African American genres, especially ragtime, blues, and jazz, had exploded into the national consciousness. Gershwin, the son of Russian-Jewish immigrant parents, used jazz to fulfill Dvořák's prediction that African American music could provide the basis for an American national style, creating in *Rhapsody in Blue* a composition that responded to the tradition of nineteenth-century European nationalist classical music but that sounded uniquely American.

Another important American nationalist composer of the period, Aaron Copland (1900–1990), worked in a similar vein but turned to various rural traditions for inspiration. Copland grew up, like Gershwin, in New York City and was exposed to jazz even as he studied European classical music. His early work combined jazz with the gnarly dissonances of modernist compositions such as those of Igor Stravinsky's *Rite of Spring*. However, the Depression of the 1930s strengthened Copland's commitment to leftist causes and ideas. That commitment, along with an increased interest in ballet, film, and children's music, motivated him to develop a simplified style for many of his compositions beginning in the 1930s and 1940s. These compositions reached a wide audience, including not just aficionados of modernist music or the bourgeois audience for traditional classical music but

FIGURE 10.19
Aaron Copland conducting
Source: Pictorial Press Ltd/Alamy Stock Photo.

the "common man" as well. His style in these compositions employed the same technique as nationalist composers in Europe had. He borrowed folk tunes or created folk-like melodies, maintained the tonality of traditional classical compositions, and introduced modern harmonies and techniques judiciously in a manner guaranteed to be accessible to many people. As a result, his compositions in this more accessible style, like those of Gershwin, retain their appeal today. Often played on patriotic occasions, they have become icons and indexes of American national identity and sentiment. Among his most famous compositions are *El Salón México* (1936), *Billy the Kid* (1938), *Rodeo* (1942), *Fanfare for the Common Man* (1942), *Appalachian Spring* (1944), and *Clarinet Concerto* (1948), a classical work commissioned by jazz clarinetist Benny Goodman.

Part of the social meaning of the music of Gershwin and Copland is related to their ethnicity. Both were the children of Jewish immigrants from eastern Europe (Russia, Ukraine, and Lithuania). During the interwar period, they and other American Jews were at the center of American musical life in classical and popular music. The prolific songwriter Irving Berlin (1888–1989), for example, immigrated as a child with his family to New York. His love for his new country inspired his song "God Bless America" (1918) and numerous others that have entered the so-called Great American Songbook. With the exception of Cole Porter (1891–1964) and Hoagy Carmichael (1899–1981), virtually all the popular song writers of the interwar period were Jewish.

SOCIAL
BEHAVIOR

During the interwar period, music composed for music theater in New York (Broadway shows) and the new "talking pictures" were at the center of American musical life. The first successful feature-length "talkie" was *The Jazz Singer* (1927), starring Al Jolson, featured a story about a Jewish performer who continues the harmful legacy of blackface minstrelsy on stage. Movie "musicals" were filled with the popular songs of the day. At age fifteen Gershwin left school to play piano for a music publisher in Manhattan's Tin Pan Alley. In addition to "plugging" other people's songs to performers, he began writing his own songs for Broadway musicals and for Tin Pan Alley. In 1919, his song "Swanee" was picked up by Al Jolson and became his first big hit. Over the course of his short life—he died of brain cancer at the age of thirty-eight—Gershwin, with his brother Ira as his lyricist, wrote many of the most popular and enduring songs of the interwar period, mainly for Broadway shows. Many of his compositions have become common vehicles for jazz performance and improvisation called **jazz standards** and are still performed frequently by jazz musicians today, including songs like "Someone to Watch Over Me" (1926), "I Got Rhythm" (1930), and "Love Is Here To Stay" (1937).

Classical composers also provided background music to bring out the dramatic, romantic, or comedic character of scenes. One of the pioneer composers of movie music in this interwar period was another Jewish immigrant, originally from Hungary, Max Steiner (1888–1971). A child prodigy born to a well-to-do theater impresario and inventor, Steiner was invited to London at the age of eighteen to conduct musical shows and operettas. Stranded as an enemy alien in London at the beginning of World War I, he immigrated to the United States, where he continued his work as a conductor and arranger for Broadway shows. In 1929 he moved to Hollywood to do the same for the new talking pictures.

During the silent film era, pianists and organists improvised musical accompaniment to underscore the emotional quality and action of the scene. They applied the programmatic clichés of nineteenth-century orchestral music to match the character of the images on the screen. In the early years of talking films, producers and directors eschewed this kind of background music in favor of something they could not have in silent films, diegetic sound only. **Diegetic sound and music**, from a Greek word meaning narration, is the sound that the characters in a

FIGURE 10.20

Max Steiner conducting a film score in a recording studio for large orchestras, called a "scoring stage"

Source: RGR Collection/Alamy Stock Photo.

play or film actually perform or hear: a lullaby sung to a child, a dance band playing on screen, or the sound of a news broadcast coming from the radio. Diegetic sound is an integral part of the narrative structure of plays and movies. Diegetic songs defined the movie musicals of the interwar period, performed by such stars as Fred Astaire, Ginger Rogers, and Bing Crosby. In 1932, when a film producer unhappy with a sequence in a new film complained to Steiner, the composer suggested that he could add an **underscore** (music accompanying the action in a film) to the sequence to see whether it would improve its impact. Steiner did, the producer was happy, and a new era in film composition was born. Steiner, who has been called "the father of film music," went on to compose more than 300 film scores including for three of the classic films of the period: *King Kong* (1933), *Gone with the Wind* (1939), and *Casablanca* (1942). Since then the emotional impact and success of films has depended as much on an indispensable musical underscore (or "score") as on the cinematography, plot, action, acting, dialogue, and visual effects. Much film scoring today still uses the iconic, expressive conventions of nineteenth-century orchestral music, pioneered by classical composers like Max Steiner. Today we can add another "c" to one definition of European classical music: music for church, court, concerts, and cinema. Thanks to George Gershwin and others, it is also common for film composers to use jazz and popular-music styles in their film scores.

What Is Its History?

The word "rhapsody" in the title of *Rhapsody in Blue* comes from the Greek word for a reciter of epic poetry, the most famous of whom was Homer in his *Iliad* and *Odyssey*. The word eventually became associated with literary expressions of emotion. Under the spell of Romanticism during the early nineteenth century, the term was used in the titles of compositions, especially for piano, that expressed musical emotions. During the late nineteenth century, nationalist composers began writing one-movement symphonic works intended to evoke national sentiment. Some were tone poems, like Smetana's *The Moldau*, but many were called rhapsodies. Among the most famous are Franz Liszt's nineteen *Hungarian Rhapsodies* for solo piano, Maurice Ravel's *Rapsodie Espagnole* (1908) for orchestra, Ralph Vaughan Williams's three *Norfolk Rhapsodies* for orchestra (1906), and Pancho Vladigerov's (1899–1978) *Bulgarian Rhapsody "Vardar,"* for violin and piano (1928). Gershwin's *Rhapsody in Blue* falls squarely in this tradition of these evocative nationalist compositions. Gershwin loved classical music.

Figure 10.21 Paul Whiteman and his orchestra, c. 1925
Source: Getty Images/Chicago History Museum.

He regularly attended concerts of new compositions by his contemporaries. He studied with various piano and composition teachers in his youth and, after becoming well established as a composer of both popular songs and classical music, traveled to Paris in 1926 and 1928 hoping to study with Maurice Ravel. Ravel much admired jazz, and Gershwin's treatment of it, but he refused to take him as a student, famously writing to his American admirer, "Why become a second-rate Ravel when you're already a first-rate Gershwin?" *Rhapsody in Blue* was his first and most popular classical orchestral composition, but his Concerto in F (1925) and a tone poem called *American in Paris* (1928), written after his first stay in Paris, are still frequently performed, as is his opera *Porgy and Bess* (1935), based on a novel by DuBose Heyward (1885–1940) about Black life on Catfish Row, a tenement on the waterfront in Charleston, South Carolina.

Rhapsody in Blue was the result of a commission from Paul Whiteman (1890–1967) to write a "jazz concerto" for his jazz orchestra. Born in Denver, Whiteman believed that jazz, with its roots in Black communities, could be made "respectable" for white audiences if it were classicized. In 1924 he organized a famous concert in New York in which he contrasted his version of what he regarded as the undisciplined, free-wheeling style of nightclub jazz with what he called symphonic jazz. Among other pieces played that evening, *Rhapsody in Blue* debuted with Gershwin as piano soloist and a jazz band augmented with a string section. The audience included many contemporary stars of the classical music scene including Russian composer and piano virtuoso Sergei Rachmaninoff. The concert created a stir, and Whiteman became known for a time as "the king of jazz." Whiteman was a friend of many Black musicians in New York, some of whom he hired to write arrangements for his band. Given the racial segregation of the times, however, he did not hire them to play in his bands. Eventually his brand of "symphonic jazz" lost favor, and by the 1930s bands of a different sort, such as those of Fletcher Henderson, Duke Ellington, and Benny Goodman had achieved a different kind of synthesis between improvisatory jazz and the compositional tradition of European classical music, though Henderson and Ellington saw Whiteman's music as an important precursor to their compositional styles.

After Gershwin's death, the composer Ferde Grofé (1892–1972), who had arranged *Rhapsody in Blue* for Whiteman's jazz orchestra, rearranged it for symphony orchestra in 1942. *Rhapsody in Blue* is structured episodically in the manner of nineteenth-century tone poems, and, though it lacks the careful motivic development of eighteenth- and nineteenth-century European classical music, it became an enduring, popular, and respected addition to the classical music repertoire, one with a distinctly American flavor. At the opening ceremonies of the 1984 Olympic Games in Los Angeles, eighty-four pianists played *Rhapsody in Blue*, creating an indexical relationship between the work and American culture for all the world to hear. In 1987 United Airlines started using *Rhapsody in Blue* in its advertising, onboard safety announcements, and its terminal at Chicago's O'Hare Airport. This commercial use has been so ubiquitous that it may have altered the way people understand the piece today, perhaps erasing for them its meaning as a musical symbol of American national identity.

WHERE DO I GO FROM HERE?

- Listen to George Gershwin's *American in Paris* and compare its musical elements and form to *Rhapsody in Blue*.
- Listen to Aaron Copland's *Appalachian Spring*, "Doppio Movimento." What about it sounds "American"?
- Listen to some of the most well-known songs (arias) from Gershwin's opera *Porgy and Bess*, including "Summertime," "I Got Plenty O'Nuttin'," "It Ain't Necessarily So," and "I Loves You, Porgy" in versions from the opera itself and performances of them by singers in popular music styles. What about these arias do you think makes them appealing as stand-alone songs independent of the original opera?

GATEWAY 41
MEXICAN AND MEXICAN AMERICAN MARIACHI MUSIC

What Is It?

Mexican mariachi music is one of the best-known musical traditions in the world, a sonic symbol (or index) of Mexico everywhere and of Mexican American culture and identity in the United States. Mariachi music today, played by musicians who call themselves mariachis (the origin and literal meaning of the term is obscure), varies from one or two musicians singing and accompanying themselves on guitar while serenading diners in a restaurant to a large ensemble of two trumpets, three or more violins, guitar, *vihuela* (a small guitar-shaped instrument), *guitarrón* (a large guitar-shaped instrument), and harp, with the musicians wearing sombreros and decorative

FIGURE 10.22
Mariachi Sol de México performs with Espinoza Paz (center) at the 2015 Latin Grammy Awards. From right to left, the instruments are guitar, *vihuela*, *guitarrón*, harp, trumpets, and violins.
Source: Getty Images/Kevin Winter.

FIGURE 10.23
A map of the state of Jalisco in Mexico
Source: Wikimedia Commons.

trajes de charro, suits that were the traditional attire of wealthy nineteenth-century Mexican landowners. Mariachi music emerged at the end of the nineteenth century, but it assumed something like its present sound when it was included in Mexican movie musicals of the 1930s and 1940s. Today the repertoire of mariachi ensembles includes a diverse collection of old regional, rural songs in a genre called *son* (literally "sound" or "style"), songs composed for musical films of the 1930s and 1940s in a genre called *canción ranchera* (ranch songs), popular songs in a genre with roots in Cuba called *bolero ranchero* (ranch boleros), regional folk genres like *huapango* from eastern Mexico, polkas, and arrangements of classical pieces and the latest popular songs. Our gateway to mariachi music is "La Negra," the best-known song in the rhythmically active style known as *son jalisciense* (*son* from the Mexican state of Jalisco), performed by Mariachi Vargas de Tecalitlán.

 Listen to the first thirty seconds of this recording.

How Does It Work?

Timbre

Bowed violins, trumpets, plucked and strummed accompanying instruments (*vihuela*, *guitarrón*, guitar, and harp), and male vocals in an almost operatic style contribute to the timbre.

Texture

The rhythmically active accompaniment by the *guitarrón*, *vihuela*, harp, and guitar (together they are called the *armonía* or "rhythm section") supports the melody on violins and trumpets (which together form the *melodía* or "melody section"), and vocals.

Rhythm

Triple meter (2+2+2) alternates with, or is played at the same time as, compound duple meter (3+3). Much of the underlying rhythm of mariachi is created by the *armonía*. The various rhythmic patterns of the *guitarrón*, *vihuela*, harp, and guitar interlock with one another. They function as a single unit that provides the rhythmic foundation for the group. In mariachi music, the rhythmic patterns played by the *armonía* distinguish one regional style from another. The rhythmic patterns played by the *armonía* in "La Negra" indicate that it is in the *son jalisciense* style.

Melody

The melody is in a major mode throughout, with one exception in the D section where the beginning of the vocal line lowers the seventh scale degree of the major mode.

Harmony

Most of the melodies are performed in parallel thirds and are played and sung over a harmony that includes I, IV, and V chords, sometimes in a repeating chordal ostinato. Mariachi musicians today refer to the I chord as *primera* (first), the V chord as *secunda* (second), and the IV chord as *tercera* (third), perhaps a ranking of their importance or the frequency of their occurrence. When teaching a new song to musicians, sometimes leaders of a group will hold up one, two, or three fingers to indicate which chord comes next. Just as it provides the rhythmic foundation, the *armonía* also provides the harmonic foundation for the group.

Form

"La Negra" has five distinct sections that alternate between verses with vocals and instrumental-only interludes: A (instrumental), B (with vocals), C (instrumental), D (vocal), and E (instrumental). Each section is made up of a series of several short repeating melodic phrases (labeled a, b, c, and so forth).

Performance Techniques

Prominent in this recording are *gritos*, high-pitched shouts in the falsetto range, from members of the ensemble. In live performances musicians and audience members often perform *gritos* to express their excitement and increase the intensity and enthusiasm of the performance. Mariachi Vargas de Tecalitlán includes *gritos* in this recording to emulate the live experience of mariachi music and to feature all of the sonic elements that make songs like "La Negra" exciting for listeners.

Listen to the first thirty seconds of this recording and pay attention to the texture of the melody over a bass line, the parallel thirds in the *melodía* (trumpets and violins), and the *gritos* .

Listen to the entire recording following this timed listening guide.

LISTENING GUIDE 10.4

TIME	SECTION	PHRASES	DESCRIPTION	LYRICS
0:00	Instrumental Prelude		The trumpets and violins begin in a slow rubato tempo, but are soon joined by the *guitarrón, vihuelas,* guitars, and harp, though the harp may be difficult to hear. Together they establish a triple meter (2+2+2) and gradually perform an accelerando, repeating the I chord over and over before switching to the V chord. As they switch to the V chord, the first of many *gritos* (shouts) from ensemble members adds to the building excitement of the music.	
0:13			The group begins a pattern of two measures in triple meter followed by one measure in compound duple meter (3+3) and another in triple meter. This pattern happens twice and is outlined by strong accents, especially in the trumpets and violins, at the start of each measure in triple meter, and on beats one and four of the measures in compound duple meter.	
0:21		aa	The violins play a major-key melody (a) in thirds, and the trumpets respond with the same melody in thirds.	
0:25		bbb	The violins and trumpets play a new major-key melody (b) together, repeating it three times.	
0:32		c	Another new major-key melody (c) in thirds begins, with the first half played by the violins and the second half by the trumpets.	

TIME	SECTION	PHRASES	DESCRIPTION	LYRICS
0:36		c'	The phrase repeats, this time with the second half played by the violins and trumpets together with an extended ending that sets up the entrance of the vocals. The bright plucking of the high-pitched strings of the harp may be faintly audible in the background.	
0:42	Song Verse	d	The male vocals enter, singing a new two-phrase major melody (d) in thirds. They repeat this melody four times, which emphasizes the compound duple meter, while the accompaniment in the plucked and strummed strings continues with a triple meter. The lyrics sing of a beautiful woman that causes sorrows (*pesares*) for the singer because she seems to show romantic interest in him, but she hasn't told him when she'll want to be with him. The trumpets and violins respond to the singers' phrases, almost as if to agree with their sentiment.	*Negrita de mis pesares . . .*
		d		*Negrita . . .*
		d		*A todos . . .*
		d		*Así me . . .*
0:59	Instrumental Interlude		The violins return to the repetition of the I chord in a similar fashion to the opening of the recording, but maintaining the fast tempo that has been established.	
1:03		eee	The violins play yet another new melody (e) that repeats three times and maintains a strong triple meter. On the second time, the harp can be heard faintly playing in between beats one and two in a syncopated rhythm. On the third time, the rhythm shifts to emphasize the compound duple meter.	
1:14		fff	Another new melody appears (f) that repeats three times. The first half is played by the violins, and the second half by the trumpets. In each second half of the melody, the *armonía* strongly accents every note of the melody. For the last repetition of f, the violins join the trumpets in the second half. They are joined by some *gritos* that raise the excitement going into the next section.	
1:27		g	The violins play long sustained tones (one per measure) that follow the chordal ostinato of IV-I-V-I for a new melody (g) that includes two repetitions of the pattern.	
1:35		g'	The trumpets join the violins on the chordal ostinato and together they emphasize a compound duple meter while the rest of the band plays the triple meter. Some high-pitched *gritos* help build the intensity.	
1:43		g"	The entire ensemble plays the chordal ostinato together on an accented triple meter, ending with an accent on beat two of the final measure, which sets up the entrance of the vocals in the next section.	
1:51	Song Verse	h	The vocals enter with a new, two phrase melody (h). This time the melody ascends to a pitch that is not in the major mode ($\flat$7). The lyrics here ask when the beautiful woman will be brought to the singer, and the brief change in mode suggests the uncertainty, stress, and longing behind the question.	*¿Cuándo me traes . . .?*
1:59		h	The melody repeats with the same lyrics.	*¿Cuándo me traes . . .?*

TIME	SECTION	PHRASES	DESCRIPTION	LYRICS
2:06	Instrumental Closing	fff	The call-and-response melody f returns and repeats three times.	
2:18		i	One last new melody (i) enters, where the violins and trumpets outline two repetitions of the chordal ostinato (IV-I-V-I) in a triple meter.	
2:27		i′	The same melody repeats, but this time the entire ensemble plays only accents on the beats.	
2:35		i″	The ensemble plays the same melody once again, playing two accented pitches for every beat. The chordal ostinato repeats two and a half times before the pulse stops. The violins and trumpets play an unaccompanied, slower, three-note ascending melody, and the recording ends with the ensemble playing two final accented I chords all together.	
2:50	End			

What Does It Mean?

Of the hundreds of songs in the mariachi repertoire, "La Negra" is considered the unofficial anthem of mariachi. Most groups begin or end performances with "La Negra," and they are often asked to begin with this song to set the tone for an event. One of the most striking elements of "La Negra" and music in the *son jalisciense* and other *son* subgenres is its fast tempo and energetic rhythm suitable for dancing. "La Negra," the best-known *son jalisciense* in the mariachi repertoire, showcases this spirited rhythmic aspect of the genre with its fast tempo, shifting accents in the interlocking patterns of the *armonía*, and alternating and layered combinations of triple and compound duple meters.

> AESTHETICS

This kind of high-energy rhythm is important in mariachi music, which is often used for celebrations and festive occasions, such as weddings, fifteenth-birthday celebrations called *quinceañeras* (in the United States) or *quince años* (in Mexico), baptisms, company parties, and more. Not all mariachi music is fast, but the rhythmic energy of songs like "La Negra" helps to create a celebratory atmosphere at these kinds of events. It is quite the challenge for musicians to successfully perform the various syncopated interlocking patterns by the *armonía* and the quickly shifting and overlapping meters by the entire ensemble. If these are not executed well, the performance loses its rhythmic drive and the appropriate atmosphere is more difficult to achieve. If they are performed excellently by master musicians like Mariachi Vargas, they can help induce the positive emotions of celebration that audiences are looking for.

> EMOTIONAL RESONANCE

Other sounds that make "La Negra" perfectly suited for celebratory events are the major mode, which is understood to be a "happy" sound, and the *gritos* that occur throughout the recording. The musicians utter *gritos* in the instrumental sections of the recording, often when one repeated phrase is transitioning to another (e.g., the transition from phrase f to phrase g between 1:24 and 1:27). They help ramp up the energy through the transition. When mariachi is performed at celebrations, ensemble members and audience members alike shout out *gritos* as they express their pleasure in the music and the festivities, and they inspire others to feel the same way. Even when mariachi music is performed on stage at large concerts or at formal events, *gritos* shouted out by members of the group and the audience are part of making the performance more exciting.

🔊 Listen to "La Negra" and follow the musical elements that add to the celebratory nature of the music, such as meter shifts from triple to compound duple, changes in the *armonía* pattern, and *gritos* .

The lyrics of "La Negra" are also full of meaning connected to emotion. The lyrics sing of longing for a particular woman who in the first line is called "Negrita," an endearing diminutive version of "La Negra," which means simply "the beautiful woman," or "the dark-haired one." The poetic lines are arranged in *coplas*, poetic stanzas of four lines that rhyme in a pattern of a-b-a-b. In "La Negra," each of these lines has precisely eight syllables. Many of the lines are repeated in the course of the song, a feature common to mariachi lyrics.

At certain points, the vocalists seem to express the meaning of the lyrics in the ways they perform the melody. For example, the second line metaphorically describes how this beautiful woman flirtatiously bats her eyes by describing them as "flying paper" (*papel volando*). When they sing the word *volando*, they slide up into the pitch of the second syllable and seem to slightly stretch out that syllable (*vo-LAN-do*) in a way that almost mimics what might be the rhythm of the batting of the eyes. As the first section continues, they perform the same slide-up and sustained pitch on the rhyming words *cuando* (when) and *penando* (suffering). The singer laments that, even though the woman has agreed to be with him, no one knows *when* this will happen, and, as a result of his longing, he is *suffering*. Many mariachi songs also have double meanings. "La Negra" is also understood to refer to locomotives (and their black color) that took young soldiers off to battlefields during the Mexican Revolution in the early twentieth century, inducing sorrow and suffering for different reasons. As "La Negra" pairs these lyrical and musical expressions of sadness, longing, and suffering with the major key, driving rhythm, and celebratory atmosphere, the song's performance may suggest that it is best to deal with the perils of love, heartbreak, and war by coming together with friends to celebrate, rather than wallowing in despair. Then again, many audience members might not think much about the lyrics at all, but instead simply enjoy hearing a familiar song sung in an emotive style by a talented group.

Like all mariachi music, "La Negra" is also a symbol of Mexican and Mexican American identity. The combination of timbres, the textures of the mariachi trumpets and violins, the vocal style of singing in thirds, and the rhythmic patterns of the *armonía* combine to create the mariachi sound, a sound that is identified as distinctly Mexican. Wearing sombreros and *charro* suits, singing lyrics in Spanish, and performing known repertoires associated with certain regions and life-cycle events, mariachi ensembles are recognized in Mexico, the United States, and all over the world as musical and visual expressions of Mexico and Mexican and Mexican American identity.

What Is Its History?

CULTURAL
LINKAGES

Some of the mariachi repertoire and some of the instruments used in mariachi date to the earliest decades of the Spanish conquests of the Americas and the Caribbean in the sixteenth century. Conquistadors, missionaries, and colonists brought Spanish singing styles, musical rhythms, and musical instruments to what they called New Spain, which is today's Mexico. Among the instruments were the violin, the harp, and plucked lutes with waisted bodies like the guitar and the *vihuela* (Chapter 4, Gateway 13). The Spaniards of New Spain played their songs on these instruments and taught the local native population to play them as well. For centuries fiestas and dances in the Mexican countryside have resounded with the timbres of these instruments in various combinations, together with the sharp vocal quality of southern Spain and rhythms switching between triple (2+2+2) and compound duple (3+3) meters common in Spanish folk songs. Those rhythmic sensibilities continue to play a prominent role in mariachi music.

The modern sound of mariachi as a large ensemble, and of mariachi music as both an urban and a rural phenomenon, began in the very early twentieth century when small four- and five-piece groups calling themselves mariachis came from the countryside of Jalisco to Mexico City to perform on special occasions for Mexican president Porfirio Díaz (1830–1915), who ruled as a virtual dictator from 1876 to 1911. President Díaz boosted the Mexican economy for the wealthy but not for the poor, many of whom began to migrate to Mexico City in search of a better life. They brought their rural mariachi music with them and transformed it over time into popular urban music. From 1910 to 1917 Emiliano Zapata (1879–1919) and Pancho Villa (1878–1923) led a peasant revolution, forcing President Díaz to resign in 1911. When a new group of populist leaders and intellectuals came to power in 1917, their version of nationalism celebrated the music and culture of the rural folk as symbols of national identity, just as Europeans had done in the late nineteenth century (Chapter 8, Gateway 29). As a popular urban music with roots in rural Mexico, mariachi music by this time was perfectly situated to take on this role as a symbol of Mexican national identity.

Beginning in the 1930s, Mexican motion pictures, with diegetic music that was performed with sound on screen, portrayed rural life and music in a positive light. Actors and singers in the mariachi tradition became huge media stars. The movie-music version of mariachi music, controlled by music producers and arrangers more than the musicians themselves, began to change. Through the new media of gramophone records and talking pictures, jazz and American popular music had spread to many corners of the world, and the instruments of jazz, especially the trumpet and clarinet, influenced the modernizing sounds of many folk traditions, including mariachi music. Trumpets, clarinets, and more violins were added to the ensemble to increase the dramatic impact of the music on screen. Although some of its rhythms and other musical elements have deep historical roots, the modern mariachi sound, born out of the film music of the 1930s and 1940s, is a far cry from the regional, rural music that inspired it.

There are a number of mariachi ensembles based in Mexico and the United States that boast their own long histories. The story of Mariachi Vargas de Tecalitlán provides an example of the changes to mariachi music since the beginning of the twentieth century. Its history began in 1897 in a town in the southern part of Jalisco called Tecalitlán where Gaspar Vargas (1880?–1969) formed the group. Until 1931 when Gaspar's son Silvestre took over the group, the instrumentation included harp, a five-string guitar called *guitarra de golpe*, and two or three violins. Silvestre Vargas expanded the group to include *guitarrón*, guitar, and more violins, and under his leadership the group moved to Mexico City where they were featured in many films in the 1930s and 1940s. In the early 1940s they also added a trumpet player to the group, Miguel Martínez Domínguez (1921–2014), who established many of the stylistic conventions for mariachi trumpet playing.

FIGURE 10.24
Mariachi Vargas in the early 1930s
Source: Silvestre Vargas Museum, Wikimedia Commons.

FIGURE 10.25
Mariachi Vargas around 1950
Source: Iván Lenovy, Wikimedia Commons.

The group also added classically trained violinist Rubén Fuentes (b. 1926) to the group. He became musical director in 1950 and continued to transform the mariachi sound to better suit stage performance and mainstream consumption. For example, performances of *sones* like "La Negra" previously might have lasted twenty or thirty minutes. After they were recorded in short three-minute commercial versions during this period, shorter versions based on recordings became standard. Since the 1950s Mariachi Vargas has influenced mariachi performance styles around the world, releasing dozens of albums and performing extensively in Mexico and the United States, sometimes with symphony orchestras in formal settings. In 1987 they famously collaborated with the pop singer Linda Ronstadt (b. 1946) on the Grammy-winning double-platinum album *Canciones de mi Padre*, a tribute to Ronstadt's Mexican heritage. Today Mariachi Vargas promotes mariachi through educational initiatives, festivals, and competitions. While rooted in the traditions of mariachi music they helped establish, they are—as they have

FIGURE 10.26
Mariachi Los Camperos de Nati Cano from Los Angeles. Nati Cano is holding a *vihuela* in the center of the group.
Source: Courtesy of Smithsonian Folkways Recordings.

been throughout their history—constantly adapting their music in dialogue with developments in technology, the emergence of new audiences, and ways of passing along the music of mariachi to younger generations.

In the United States mariachi music has become an important marker of Mexican American identity. One of the groundbreaking groups in this regard has been Mariachi Los Camperos de Nati Cano from Los Angeles, another group with a long history. Natividad (Nati) Cano (1933–2014), the founder of the group, was born in the small town of Ahuisculco, Jalisco, the son of a mariachi musician. As a young musician he made his way to Guadalajara, the capital city of Jalisco, where as a teenager he played violin in the Guadalajara Symphony. He eventually settled in Los Angeles and became one of the central figures in Mexican American mariachi music. After World War II, immigration to the United States from Mexico greatly increased, and audiences were hungry for entertainment that connected them to their Mexican identity. In the late 1960s and 1970s the Chicano movement had followed the civil rights movement in advocating for the rights of Mexican Americans. By then mariachi had already become a cultural symbol and served as a point of pride for the community. Beginning in 1961, Mariachi Los Camperos de Nati Cano captivated this new generation of Mexican Americans and helped transform mariachi into a widely respected form of artistic performance. Tens of thousands

FIGURE 10.27
Mariachi Las Alteñas from San Antonio, Texas. Las Alteñas refers to women who work in the highlands of Jalisco and the musicians' goal to reach the highest artistic standard.
Source: Mariachi Las Alteñas.

of people have heard Mariachi Los Camperos in concert in the nearly six decades of its existence. The group has performed at concert venues such as the Kennedy Center in Washington, D.C., and Lincoln Center in New York City, as well as at the White House. Other mariachi groups from the United States have their own histories and fans, including Mariachi Sol de México, Mariachi Reyna de Los Angeles, Mariachi Los Galleros, Mariachi Divas de Cindy Shea, and many more.

While mariachi was originally a predominantly male tradition, women have a long history performing it, and women's participation in mariachi has increased in recent decades. In the 1970s women began to perform in some of the leading mariachi ensembles for the first time, including the violinist and singer Rebecca Gonzales in Mariachi Los Camperos de Nati Cano. She set the stage for other prominent female mariachi musicians, including the award-winning all-women groups Mariachi Divas de Cindy Shea, Mariachi Reyna de Los Angeles, and Mariachi Las Alteñas from San Antonio, Texas.

> **SOCIAL BEHAVIOR**

As mariachi ensembles perform on some of the most prestigious stages of the world today, many mariachi musicians continue to perform in restaurants, at private parties, and at other celebratory events. The music is now taught in many high schools throughout the American Southwest from California to Texas. School mariachi ensembles compete in festivals modeled on the music competitions of high school concert and marching bands, symphony orchestras, and choirs. In Chicago, César Maldonado, the son of Mexican immigrants, started a non-profit in 2013 called the Mariachi Heritage Foundation. This organization partners with local public schools to teach mariachi to low-income youth, many of whom come from immigrant families. In 2017, eighteen of these students (nine boys and nine girls) aged eleven to eighteen released the album *Nuestra Herencia* (Our Heritage) under the ensemble name Mariachi Herencia de México. *Nuestra Herencia* became one of the best-selling mariachi albums of all time, reaching #2 on the iTunes Top Latin Album charts and garnering a Latin Grammy nomination for Best Ranchero/ Mariachi Album.

WHERE DO I GO FROM HERE?

- Find a video of Mariachi Los Camperos de Nati Cano performing "La Negra" and compare it to the version of "La Negra" by Mariachi Vargas.
- Find some videos of Mariachi Divas de Cindy Shea. In what types of live settings do they perform?
- Find a video of an American high school or university mariachi group performing at a competition. Identify similar rhythmic patterns to those heard in "La Negra" and explain why there are such similarities.

CLOSING

The interwar years from 1918 to 1939 were a time of great change in the world's music. Jazz became a central element of popular music alongside popular songs from Broadway and Tin Pan Alley. America's European-derived classical music made its mark on the European classical tradition with compositions that sounded distinctly American. Finally, aurally transmitted rural musical traditions, like Mexican mariachi music, became widely known in "talking" motion pictures. The film and record industries spread music of all kinds to millions of listeners near and far. The history of music was forever changed by these new developments, which continue to play a prominent part in music today.

THINGS TO THINK ABOUT

- Compare the way new technologies of this period (records, radio, and movies) affected the musical sound and meaning of the genres in the chapter.
- Compare the way immigration from abroad and internal migration within the United States affected the musical worlds introduced in this chapter.

NEW TERMS

big band
break
chord progression
chorus
collective improvisation
combo
diegetic sound and music

guitarrón
head
hi-hat
jazz standard
jukebox
New Orleans jazz

parallel major and parallel
  minor keys
rhapsody
scat singing
territory bands
underscore
vihuela

MUSIC DURING WORLD WAR II AND ITS AFTERMATH (1939–1950)

WORLD WAR II WAS one of the darkest periods of the twentieth century. In spite of the devastating loss of life, a remarkable amount of the music listened to and performed today has its roots in this period. One of the leading symphonists of the twentieth century, Dmitri Shostakovich, wrote four of his fifteen symphonies during this time. Today orchestras all over the world regularly perform them. The compositions of the Frenchman Olivier Messiaen for organ, orchestra, and chamber ensembles are still much admired and performed. Jewish composers of this period suffered greatly, some losing their lives in Nazi death camps and others forced to emigrate from central Europe to the Americas. Much of their music was neglected until recently, when some performers began to champion their works. Among them, James Conlon, conductor of the Los Angeles Opera, has been performing operas and symphonic and choral works of World War II-era Jewish composers under the rubric "Recovered Voices." In jazz this period saw the emergence of a new style, bebop, which was the first of a plethora of new styles sometimes called, collectively, modern jazz. Jazz musicians and fans still learn from and enjoy the recordings made in this period by musicians like trumpeter Dizzy Gillespie, alto saxophone player Charlie Parker, vocalist Ella Fitzgerald, drummer Kenny Clarke, and pianist Bud Powell. The harmonic principles developed in this era by musicians playing bebop are arguably the basis of so-called straight-ahead jazz today.

The earliest recordings of rhythm & blues, the precursor of rock and contemporary R&B, come from this period, and country music emerged from its regional home in the southern United States to enter the mainstream of American popular music. Finally, today many tropical-themed restaurants, vacation resorts, and cruise ships employ a steel pan player as an index of fun in the sun. Transcending its roots in the society and culture of wartime Trinidad, steelband music has become an important local art form, a global party music, and a national symbol for Trinidadians both at home and abroad.

Even before Adolf Hitler usurped power in Germany in 1933, he had developed a racist theory in which the German people and others of Nordic descent were superior to all other races, including the Slavs, Jews, and Roma (pejoratively called Gypsies). Based on earlier theories of white supremacy, Hitler's theory was implemented by his Nazi Party in the form of a policy called *Lebensraum* (living

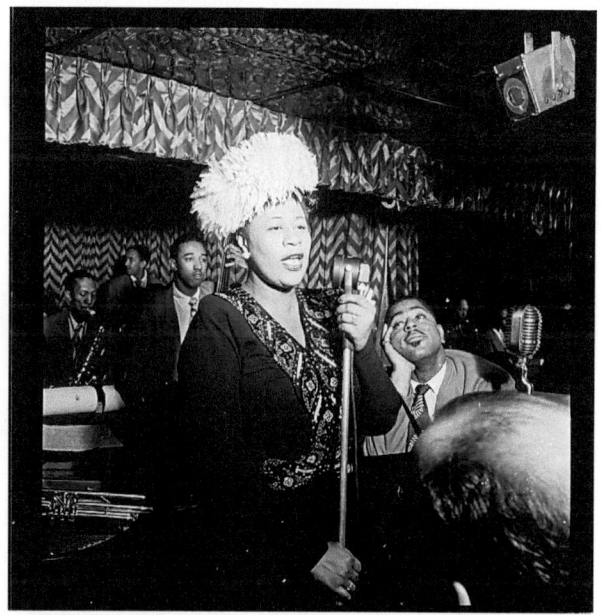

FIGURE 11.1

Ella Fitzgerald performing in 1947, with Dizzy Gillespie (right) admiring her performance
Source: William P. Gottlieb Collection. Library of Congress.

DOI: 10.4324/9781003269304-15

space). It argued that if a supposedly superior race like the Germans were suffering from over-crowding and a shortage of food, it had the right to extend its territory by conquering the land of a neighboring inferior people. Using that pretext, on September 1, 1939, Hitler ordered his army to invade Poland, a land of Slavic people across Germany's eastern border. Britain and France declared war on Germany a few days later.

Japan had already invaded China in 1937, ostensibly to end European imperialism in East Asia, an invasion the Chinese resisted bitterly. The United States, at the time reluctant to enter other people's wars, waited to declare war on Japan and Germany until a few days after the Japanese attacked the U.S. naval base at Pearl Harbor in Hawaii on December 7, 1941. The world, not just Europe, was now engulfed in a global war that lasted until the middle of 1945. The scale of death and destruction during World War II is beyond comprehension. The total of military and civilian deaths linked to combat, disease, and famine was between sixty and eighty-five million people, including six million Jews exterminated in a Holocaust administered by Hitler's Nazi regime. After the war, a new geopolitical "three-world order" developed. The United States and its capitalist allies in western Europe, Canada, Australia, and Japan constituted the "first world"; the Soviet Union, its eastern European communist client states, China, Vietnam, and North Korea became known as the "second world." Countries that possessed neither communist nor well-developed capitalist economies were labeled the "third world."

Soon the United States and the Soviet Union, the two "superpowers," were pitted against each other in a nuclear arms race called the Cold War because it never erupted into open conflict. When the Soviets tested their first atomic bomb in 1949 to match the ones the United States developed and used during World War II, the tension of the Cold War escalated dramatically. With ballistic missiles to deliver their nuclear weapons, both superpowers had the means to destroy the other, and fear of nuclear annihilation gripped the people of the world, affecting popular culture for years to come.

By 1945 third-world countries had had enough of European and American imperialism, and strong anti-colonial movements developed in Latin America, Africa, and Asia. Although a hot war never destroyed the United States and the Soviet Union and their allies, each began to support internal conflicts in countries of the third world in "proxy wars," arming and sometimes intervening on one side or the other in a bid to gain the sympathy of the communist or non-communist side in local, anti-colonial revolutions. In 1946 Vietnam, led by the French-educated communist Ho Chi Minh (1890–1969), declared its independence from France. The Vietnamese fought a bloody war until 1954 to drive the French out and then another war to rid themselves of the Americans from 1955 to 1975. In 1947 Pakistan and India declared their independence from British rule. After Britain withdrew from its occupation of Palestine in the eastern Mediterranean in 1947, Israel declared its independence in 1948, engaging in subsequent violent conflicts with Arab countries over their right to a state on land also claimed as a homeland by Palestinians. The Chinese communists won their anti-colonial battle against nationalist forces in 1949, inspiring many in the third world. Ghana, the first of the African countries to declare its independence, did so peacefully in 1957, and many parts of Africa followed suit in the 1960s. A communist revolution was successful in Cuba in 1959.

Such an all-encompassing world war, and the ensuing anti-colonial struggles, severely disrupted musical life all over the world. But the need to create and enjoy music is unstoppable, and musical life endured throughout this period. Soldiers and their supporters on the home front still needed

FIGURE 11.2
Glenn Miller directs his Army Air Force Band in a performance for U.S. and Allied troops in England, 1944
Source: U.S. Air Force, Public Domain.

entertainment, and popular, mass culture continued in service to the morale of the troops and their families during the war. In the United States, the USO (United Service Organization) was formed in 1941 to provide a "home away from home" for soldiers. If they were not already serving in the military themselves, stars of the music and movie industries volunteered to provide shows for soldiers stationed at home and abroad. The camp shows were held well behind the frontlines, but the service was dangerous. Glenn Miller, the leader of one of the most popular swing-era big bands of the 1930s, was too old to engage in combat, so he enlisted to lead military marching bands and dance orchestras. On a flight from Britain to France across the English Channel in 1944, six months after the Allied invasion of Normandy, he and his plane disappeared, never to be found. Jewish composers and musicians who had not left central Europe in the 1930s were sent to Nazi death camps, where they were exterminated or died from starvation, cold, or psychological distress. Many Jewish and non-Jewish composers during and after the war wrote deeply moving compositions expressing their, and their compatriots', experience of this horrible conflagration. Around the world new genres and styles of music emerged to reflect the economic and political life of the postwar period. This chapter deals with key developments in several worlds of music during a period torn by war, ideological differences, and nationalist, anti-colonial aspirations.

GATEWAY 42
COUNTRY MUSIC

What Is It?

During and after World War II, popular music started to shift. The popularity of swing was declining, the economy had recovered from the Great Depression, and young people, labeled "teenagers" for the first time in 1941, began to purchase records. A new genre called "country and western," today called "country," gained great popularity after the war. Its most significant figure at the time was guitarist and singer/songwriter Hank Williams (1923–1953), whose 1949 song "I'm So Lonesome I Could Cry" is our gateway to country music.

 Listen to the first thirty sections of the recording to get an idea of the sound.

Country music is a commercial genre of popular music rooted in early twentieth-century rural music, mostly from white communities of the American South. Definitions of country can vary widely even among country fans, but it historically has been associated with the image of the cowboy, sung narratives about working-class life, and an underlying (or overt) Christian theology and values. Country often draws on references to symbols of work in rural settings (trucks, farms, ranches, horses), family relationships of many kinds, heterosexual love relationships and struggles, and collectivities like churches and small towns. Country singers often perform with a Southern accent or other vocal techniques like yodeling associated with locations in the rural South. It is also associated with instruments such as fiddles, banjos, and steel guitars, even though some country music doesn't include any of those timbres. "I'm So Lonesome I Could Cry" features a fiddle and a steel guitar. Alongside Hank Williams, the musicians appearing on this recording are Jerry Byrd (1920–2005) on lap steel guitar, Louis Innis (1919–1982) on rhythm guitar, Tommy Jackson (1926–1979) on fiddle, Ernie Newton (1908–1976) on bass, and Zeke Turner (1923–2003) on lead guitar. About a year before recording "I'm So Lonesome Could Cry," they began playing together as a unit they called "The Pleasant Valley Boys." These musicians all had active careers as country performers on stage and on

FIGURE 11.3
Hank Williams
Source: WSM radio (public domain), Wikimedia Commons.

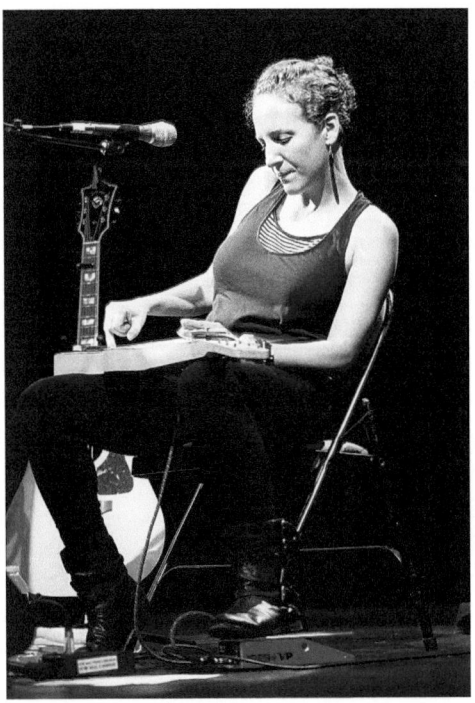

FIGURE 11.4
**Natalia Zukerman playing lap steel guitar
at a festival in Brooklyn, New York, in 2012**
Source: Getty Images/Al Pereira.

FIGURE 11.5
**Steve Fishell playing the pedal steel guitar
in 2013**
Source: Getty Images/Guitarist Magazine.

hundreds of recordings. Most of these songs were recorded in Nashville, which has been the center of the country music industry throughout most of its existence.

How Does It Work?

Timbre

The timbres of the recording include Hank Williams's voice, a strummed acoustic guitar, an electric lap steel guitar, an upright bass, a lead electric guitar, and a fiddle.

Texture

The texture features Williams's solo voice over an accompaniment of the other instruments. The bass plays on beat one of every measure (and sometimes other beats), the acoustic guitar strums percussively on every beat, and the lap steel guitar and the lead guitar complement the melody with background riffs and lines played in between phrases. The fiddle enters only for its solo, which is accompanied by the bass, acoustic guitar, and lead guitar.

Rhythm

Each beat of the waltz-like triple meter is subdivided into three, which give the song a rhythmic feel similar to swing. The tempo is anchored by the rhythmic strumming of the acoustic guitar on each beat. It continues slowly and steadily until the very end of the song, when it slows down even more.

Melody

Williams's melody is in a major mode and outlines chord tones of the underlying harmony. While many of the phrases start with Williams ascending and sliding into a long note, each phrase ends with a descending interval, sometimes a large leap.

Harmony

Each strophe follows the same harmonic structure based on a major key. The harmony remains mostly on the I chord, with the IV chord making an appearance at the start of each strophe's third phrase. Each strophe ends on a cadence that moves from V to I.

Form

After a short introduction, the form is strophic. Two verses are followed by a strophe for a steel guitar solo, a third verse, a fiddle solo, and a final fourth verse. Each verse has four phrases (AA'BC), the last one sung to the refrain "I'm so lonesome I could cry" in all cases except for the second verse.

Performance Techniques

Williams's voice, the lap steel guitar, and to a lesser extent, the fiddle, can be heard sliding into and out of pitches. Vocalists in country (and many other genres) use this kind of microtonality to express a variety of emotions, similar to the ways that Bessie Smith and other early blues singers had (Chapter 9, Gateway 33). On the **lap steel guitar**, musicians lay the instrument on their laps, pluck the strings with metal picks attached to the fingers of the right hand, and use a steel bar in the left hand to adjust the pitch (the steel bar is where the steel guitar gets its name). The sliding of the steel bar up and down the strings produces the characteristic "twangy" sliding sound of the lap steel guitar so common in country music. A related instrument is the pedal steel guitar, which produces a similar sound, but with many more possibilities for melody and harmony. The **pedal steel guitar** today typically has two necks of ten strings each that rest on a frame, like a table. Attached to each neck is a set of pedals and knee levers that adjust the pitches of strings to make even more glissandos and pitch bends possible than with the steel bar alone.

Listen to the introduction and first two verses with these elements in mind.

LISTENING GUIDE 11.1

TIME	FORM	DESCRIPTION	LYRICS
0:00	Introduction	The electric guitar leads into the introduction with a few pickup notes on the guitar's lower strings. These few notes set up the tempo, the triple meter, and the subdivision of the beat into three. On beat one, the bass, the strummed acoustic guitar, and the lap steel guitar enter together to play four bars that set the stage for the first verse.	
0:06	Verse 1	Williams sings the first verse, which has an internal form of AA'BC. Williams stretches out and slides into the long notes of the melody on "hear," "*lone*some," and others, which tend to be the highest pitches in each phrase.	Hear that lonesome . . .
0:32	Verse 2	Williams sings the second verse in a similar manner to the first. In this verse the lead guitar can be heard clearly responding to the vocal lines with short improvised phrases in a call-and-response manner.	I've never seen . . .
0:58	Lap steel guitar solo	The steel guitar plays a solo, a relatively simple improvisation that paraphrases the melody. This solo showcases the way the steel guitar can perform large and small glissandos, sliding up to and between pitches.	
1:24	Verse 3	The third verse continues the style of the first two verses, with more call and response from the lead guitar.	Did you ever hear . . .
1:50	Fiddle solo	The fiddle plays an improvised solo that is a variation on the melody. Throughout the solo, Tommy Jackson plays on two strings at once with his bow, a technique called a double stop. He also occasionally slides between pitches by sliding his left finger along the string on the fingerboard of the fiddle to ornament his melody in a way characteristic of fiddle playing in country music.	
2:16	Verse 4	In the final verse the lap steel guitar is more prominent, playing in a higher register as it complements the vocal line along with the lead guitar. The last lines of the lyrics address an absent lover, revealing the source of loneliness expressed by the song. The tempo gradually slows down on the last phrase and the band plays the final major chord together.	The silence . . .
2:45	End		

What Does It Mean?

"I'm So Lonesome I Could Cry" is one of country music's best-known songs, and its sound reveals some of the broader historical conventions of country music, as well as the ways that lyrics help create personas that audiences can connect with.

The most obvious markers of country music in this recording are the fiddle and the steel guitar. The fiddle, which is just another name for a violin, has been associated with forms of rural music and country since long before Williams's time. Its sound and the ways that Tommy Jackson plays double stops and adds ornamentation connect this recording to fiddle playing of earlier types of rural American music. The steel guitar provides a specific "twang" with its "crying" glissandos and slightly nasal timbre that characterizes it as country. The strophe where the

AESTHETICS

steel guitar plays a solo enriches the meaning of the recording, as Jerry Byrd avoids virtuosic or intricate improvisation in favor of a simple adapted version of the melody. It seems as if the crying sound of steel guitar is too lonely and depressed to play anything but a simple line whose notes stretch out for long durations without showcasing any of the technical capabilities of the instrument that a more lively and happy emotion might inspire.

Listen again to "I'm So Lonesome I Could Cry" for the sounds of the fiddle and the steel guitar in both solo sections and during the verses.

EMOTIONAL RESONANCE

Like many country songs and most popular music, the lyrics of "I'm So Lonesome I Could Cry" are at the center of the song's meaning. The poetic lyrics gesture towards rural life with their references to nature, but they relate those references to loneliness and isolation. Birds—and even the moon—are crying, time moves slowly through a night that is long and dark, leaves are dying in autumn, and stars are, like tears, silently falling out of the sky. Through these evocations of a shared rural life, the song invites the audience to join the vocalist in his (or her, if a woman sings this song) despondence. The first three verses address the audience directly, telling them to listen to lonesome birds and asking rhetorical questions that suggest that this experience of loneliness is one that can be understood and shared. Not until the end of the last verse does Williams turn to address his lover, whose absence reveals the reason for his loneliness. Unlike many of Williams's other songs, which express emotions in a straightforward way, the song doesn't describe feelings about a breakup or tension in a relationship, but rather draws the audience into solidarity with the singer through extended metaphors. It provides the possibility for listeners to experience loneliness along with someone else who understands. The lyrics also construct an image of Williams as a person experiencing hardship, living in a world of loneliness that extends beyond his personal heartbreak to an experience shared even with animals, the moon, and the stars.

When a singer in popular music is thought to be genuinely experiencing and expressing the meanings of his or her lyrics, that singer is often said to be "authentic." Personal authenticity is often a desired value in a performance of country and other popular music genres, especially when a vocalist is also the songwriter, as in the case of Hank Williams. The audience interprets the lyrics as an expression of feelings actually felt or events truly experienced by the performer, regardless of whether that is the case or not. In fact, Hank Williams did come from a life of poverty, hardship, and adversity, and his songs deal with those themes. In some cases, though, a singer-songwriter might write a song about a broken relationship and later, even if she is single or happily in a relationship, she will sing the song as if she is experiencing the pain and sorrow of a broken relationship all over again. This kind of personal authenticity is particularly intriguing in cases where, for example, a wealthy, successful performer might sing about economic hardship and challenges like struggling to pay the bills, or a star known to live in a big city sings about life working on a farm and living in a small town.

In addition to song lyrics, other elements of vocal performance can help construct a persona that is perceived to be authentic. In "I'm So Lonesome I Could Cry," for example, at the end of the first and third verses, Williams's voice breaks into a higher register when he sings the word "lonesome" (around 0:27 and 1:44). These vocal breaks (and others like it throughout the song) resemble the sound of crying itself, which helps listeners perceive that Williams actually is feeling sad and lonely. The sound of the vocal break is also reminiscent of a yodel, a vocal technique common in rural musical traditions that predate country music. In combination with Williams's southern drawl, heard in the way he stretches out the long notes of each phrase, vocal breaks add to the perception of Williams as an "authentic" country singer, singing honestly—and in an old, traditional way—about a rural experience of loneliness.

CULTURAL LINKAGES

In country music, authenticity is also grounded in the notion of tradition, that is, a perception of "the old way." Country music perceived as authentic relies on timbres and performance styles of the fiddle, steel guitar, and acoustic guitar to sound old, paradoxically rejecting commercial trends and borrowings from pop music even as artists seek commercial success. Performers can also help build audience perceptions of authenticity through what they wear (for example, cowboy hats and boots) and other aspects of their appearance, how they visually market their albums, and, for the more famous, how they manage their public image.

 Listen once more to "I'm So Lonesome I Could Cry," noticing the breaking of Williams's voice at various points of the song and other ways that his interpretation of the melody expresses the emotion described by the poetic lyrics.

What Is Its History?

As the gateway to the blues in Chapter 9 described, during the 1920s record companies began marketing recordings of Black artists performing the blues and other genres as "race records," targeting an audience of African Americans. During the 1920s and 1930s record companies were also making records that targeted a niche market of rural whites. They called them **hillbilly records**. These recordings initially featured white musicians playing ballads, folk songs, and fiddle and banjo tunes that had developed in rural areas of Appalachia and the South among immigrants from the British Isles. Early hillbilly records often played up stereotypes of rural life, especially in their visual marketing, which might feature the performers dressed with floppy hats and worn-out, rolled-up overalls. But the influence of urban music like Tin Pan Alley songs was quite present in the hillbilly repertoire, and many fans of hillbilly music were people who had migrated to cities from rural areas. One of the first successful musicians to record hillbilly records was Fiddlin' John Carson (1874–1949), a fiddle player who had moved with his family to Atlanta in 1900 to work at Exposition Cotton Mills. He became well known in the Atlanta area by winning a number of fiddle competitions, and his 1923 recordings became the first commercially successful hillbilly records. Early hillbilly musicians like Carson and the banjo player Uncle Dave Macon (1870–1952) were seasoned musicians by the time recording technology became widespread, and their commercial records played a role in what would later become country music.

Younger musicians recording hillbilly records in the late 1920s were even more influential in the styles of country that Hank Williams and other country artists later performed, and they were part of a shift in hillbilly records from a focus on instrumental music to one on vocals. Hailing from Clinch Mountain in western Virginia, Sara Carter (1898–1979), her husband Alvin Pleasant (A. P.) Carter (1891–1960), and her cousin Maybelle Carter (1909–1978), began recording hillbilly records as the Carter Family in 1927, with Sara on lead vocals and autoharp (a strummed zither), Maybelle on supporting harmony vocals and guitar, and A. P. on bass vocals. Their 1928 hits "Wildwood Flower" and "Keep on the Sunnyside" and other recordings established the guitar in hillbilly and later country music. Also setting standards for the style were Sara and Maybelle's style of vocal harmony and Maybelle's guitar-picking style, later called "The Carter Scratch," which alternated between a melody in the bass strings and rhythmic strumming in the higher strings. They performed together through the early 1940s and began an ongoing four-generation legacy of hit-making Carter family members including Maybelle's daughter June Carter (1929–2003) and June's husband Johnny Cash (1932–2003).

In 1927 Mississippi-born Jimmie Rodgers (1897–1933) recorded his first hit song, "Blue Yodel," which borrowed from Black blues singers a variation on the AAB blues form in which the first two lines repeated the same text over two different harmonies (Chapter 9, Gateway 33). He also added

FIGURE 11.6
Fiddlin' John Carson in the 1920s
Source: Wilbur Smith, Wikimedia Commons.

CULTURAL LINKAGES

FIGURE 11.7
The Carter Family c. 1931. From left to right:
Maybelle, Sara (with autoharp), and A. P.
Source: Getty Images/Michael Ochs Archives/Stringer.

a phrase of yodeling on vocables inspired by vaudeville acts that imitated Austrian yodelers. His 114 recordings and the Carter Family's nearly 300 recordings and years of radio performances established much of the early repertoire and singing and guitar playing styles that would have a lasting influence on country music for years to come.

Beyond hillbilly records, other media also played a role in the spread of the roots of country music in the United States. In 1925 WSM radio in Nashville, Tennessee, began broadcasting a regular "barn dance" featuring live performances of rural white popular songs, comedy, and storytelling. Uncle Dave Macon was one of its first stars, appreciated for both his songs and his humorous banter. This program was later renamed the Grand Ole Opry, a show that continues today as a legendary institution attracting the best established and aspiring country performers. Hollywood "westerns" featured singing cowboys, like Gene Autry (1907–1998) and Roy Rogers (1911–1998), in the 1930s and 1940s, bringing rural music to a mass audience.

After the war, in 1949, *Billboard* magazine changed the name of the chart that kept track of record sales for hillbilly records from "hillbilly" to "country" or "country and western." In the meantime, a more raw version of country music had been brewing in bars called "honky tonks" frequented by the working-class in the Southwest, especially in Texas, Oklahoma, and California. Featuring fiddle, acoustic rhythm guitar, bass, electric lead guitar, and lap steel guitar, it was clearly absorbing the influence of jazz and another genre emerging among African American musicians and audiences by the 1950s, called rhythm & blues. This music became known as **honky-tonk music**, and the lyrics of its songs focused on personal relationships and heartbreak in laments like "I'm So Lonesome I Could Cry."

The most important songwriter and performer of honky-tonk country music was Hank Williams. Born in Alabama, he began his professional career on the radio in 1937 at the age of fourteen. He was plagued by alcoholism, prescription drug abuse, and instability in his personal life. He died at the age of twenty-nine, officially of heart failure, though details of his death remain mysterious and are the stuff of myth among country music fans. The hard times and heartache that he sang about may have been so intense that they led to Williams's death. In his short life he wrote more than 160 songs, thirty-five of which made the *Billboard* country and western chart's top ten, with eleven of them climbing to number one.

Country music is defined as a genre of popular music because it is music produced commercially and meant to be enjoyed by people in their everyday lives—to be, well, popular. "Pop music," another genre of popular music that arose around this time, is usually used to describe music and performers who have been embraced by a large, young, mainstream audience. Since the 1950s, the relationship between pop and country is something that fans, artists, managers, and others involved in the country music industry have debated and experimented with in many ways.

In country music the "Nashville sound" emerged at the end of the 1950s. Vocalists such as Patsy Cline (1932–1963) and Jim Reeves (1923–1964) recorded with textures created in the recording studio and borrowed from pop recordings of the time. These textures included a drum set, piano, orchestral string sections, and sweet-sounding "oohs" and "aahs" in background vocals. It eliminated instruments traditionally associated with country such as the solo fiddle and the banjo. The steel guitar was still present, but more as a supporting timbre blending into the texture of the recording and without the distinctive "crying" sound heard in "I'm So Lonesome I Could Cry." During the 1950s and 1960s a contrasting style, the "Bakersfield sound," developed in honky-tonks in and around Bakersfield, California, a hundred miles north of Los Angeles. Bakersfield sound recordings featured a shuffle rhythm derived from rhythm & blues and an instrumentation of electric guitar, electric bass, steel guitar, rhythm guitar, and drums, creating the same sound on recordings that would be heard in a honky-tonk rather than one dreamed up in the studio like the

"Nashville sound." Merle Haggard (1937–2016) emerged from the Bakersfield scene and is now regarded as a legend of country music.

During the 1970s Dolly Parton (b. 1946), Tammy Wynette (1942–1998), Loretta Lynn (b. 1932) and others performed in a style known as "classic country," which combined the Nashville sound with a return to instruments like the crying slide guitar and the fiddle associated with twang and honky-tonk. These musicians are known for their superb vocal skills, successful songwriting, business acumen, and songs that resonated with the day-to-day concerns of working-class and middle-class white women in America.

Over the last thirty or forty years, the tension in country music between staying close to the signs of its "authentic" past and engaging with pop music has persisted. Since the 1980s George Strait (b. 1952) has emulated Hank Williams in his honky-tonk musical style and appearance. He appeals to audiences drawn to country artists they perceive as authentically connected to country music's traditions. Strait's neotraditional style was one inspiration for the biggest country star in history, and one of the best-selling musicians of all time, Garth Brooks (b. 1962). Brooks became the face of modern country in the 1990s by combining honky-tonk styles with the high-tech entertainment showmanship of pop and rock stadium concerts. He attracted a large and loyal fan base, even though many country fans have condemned him for what they see as an abandonment of tradition and selling out for commercial gain. In 2005, Carrie Underwood (b. 1983) won the second season of the reality singing competition *American Idol* by performing in a variety of pop styles. She was embraced by country fans to become one of today's most successful country singers. One of the world's biggest pop stars today, Taylor Swift (b. 1989), began her career as a teenage country singer-songwriter. In the years after her 2010 country album *Fearless* won the Grammy for Album of the Year, she left the sounds of country behind to team up with pop producers and released some of the best-selling pop hits of the 2010s.

FIGURE 11.8

Taylor Swift performs onstage during the 42nd Annual Academy of Country Music Awards in 2007

Source: Getty Images/Ethan Miller.

In addition to negotiating the relationship of country music to pop, country artists, fans, and the broader country music industry have been dealing for many years with questions surrounding the genre's complex relationship to racial identity. In the first half of the twentieth century hillbilly music was defined by its white performers (as opposed to the Black performers of race records), though many hillbilly fiddle and guitar styles were drawn from Black performance styles made popular through minstrelsy (Chapter 7, Gateway 27). Racism played a role in early country music in, for example, the prevalence of blackface minstrelsy performances at the Grand Ole Opry into the 1950s. During the 1920s and 1930s, when segregation was the norm in the United States, Black and white musicians performing these styles sometimes worked together. Harmonica player DeFord Bailey (1899–1982) performed at the Grand Ole Opry from 1927 to 1941 and was country's first Black star. A. P. Carter collected Appalachian folk songs on trips together with a Black neighbor, and Jimmie Rodgers performed on stage and recorded with Black artists.

In 1967 Charley Pride (1934–2020) became the second African American to perform at the Grand Ole Opry. He became a star and a country legend, but only after his management concealed his racial identity until his career was well established on records and radio to avoid potential racial discrimination from the genre's mostly (but not exclusively) white audience. Pride showed that, for him, country music connected to something other than racial identity, and he captivated country fans everywhere with his songs grounded in the genre's conventions. Pride was an anomaly in a genre long associated primarily with white musicians and fans. Country music's connections to rural life, the South, and working-class experience have made room over many years for the

FIGURE 11.9
Mickey Guyton performs with her band at Christmas in Rockefeller Center in 2021
Source: Ralph Bavaro/NBC/NBCU Photo Bank via Getty Images.

participation of Black artists and fans, even though until recently country radio stations have been reticent to play the music of Black country artists.

Today a number of Black country artists have risen to prominence as the country music industry has begun to celebrate Black country musicians and fans. Jimmie Allen (b. 1985) was the first Black artist to have his debut single hit number one on the country radio charts, and he has won several awards as a new artist in country music. In 2015 Mickey Guyton (b. 1983) became the only Black female country artist signed to a major label, and her 2021 album *Remember Her Name* was nominated for three Grammys including Best Country Album. Other artists like Yola, Brittney Spencer, and Willie Jones have achieved success in country with their skilled songwriting, inspiring performances, and cross-genre experimentation as they build on country music's sounds and meanings and contribute their own.

WHERE DO I GO FROM HERE?

- Find a recording by Uncle Dave Macon from the 1920s and compare it to either "Keep on the Sunnyside" (1928) by the Carter family or "Blue Yodel" (1927) by Jimmie Rodgers. How are they similar and different? What elements in each one may have influenced later country musicians like Hank Williams?

- Listen to some other Hank Williams recordings such as "Your Cheatin' Heart" and "Lovesick Blues." How do they compare to "I'm So Lonesome I Could Cry"? Can you identify the form and connect it to Tin Pan Alley songs or the blues? How do these or other Hank Williams recordings support the narrative of authenticity that arose about him and his life?

- Look into the roots of the steel guitar, some of which go through Hawaiian music, and trace them through to the embrace of the instrument by country music. Can you find recordings of steel guitar playing earlier than the 1940s? In what genres and styles was it prominent? How is it used today outside country music?

- Listen to Kasey Musgraves's album *Golden Hour* (2018), the most recent country album to win the Grammy for Album of the Year. How does the album blend country with other musical styles and genres, and negotiate the relationship between pop and country?

- Take a look at the book *Country Music: A Cultural and Stylistic History* by Jocelyn Neal, upon which much of this gateway is based. Are there other artists, styles, or eras of country music that interest you? Which ones and why?

GATEWAY 43
BEBOP

What Is It?

During the 1940s a new style of jazz challenged the musical conventions of swing and big band jazz. Called **bebop**, it featured solo improvisation and harmonic complexity, at often very fast tempos. "Ko Ko" (1945) by Charlie Parker's Re-Boppers is our gateway to bebop. Alto saxophonist Charlie Parker (1920–1955) was one of the most virtuosic and innovative bebop musicians, and "Ko Ko" gives a taste of his sensational skills in improvisation. He worked closely with trumpet player Dizzy Gillespie (1917–1993), also heard on this recording. Parker (known as "Bird"), Gillespie (known as "Diz"), and other bebop musicians shifted the focus of jazz to the solo improviser, a legacy of the brilliant solos of Louis Armstrong and others. This recording features a typical bebop ensemble, known as a jazz combo. **Jazz combos** usually consist of one or two instrumental soloists with a **rhythm section** of drums, bass, and piano or guitar. In this case, the combo includes an alto saxophone and a trumpet accompanied by a rhythm section of piano, bass, and drums. The rhythm section musicians here include Curley Russell (1917–1986) on bass, Argonne "Dense" Thornton (1919–1983) on piano, and Max Roach (1924–2007) on drums. There is some dispute about whether Dizzy Gillespie actually played piano *and* trumpet on this recording, or whether Gillespie played the piano part and Miles Davis (1926–1991) played the trumpet part. Regardless of who actually appears on the recording, it is a classic example of many of the characteristics of bebop, features virtuosic performance, and provides a window into the history of bebop and jazz since the 1940s.

How Does It Work?

Timbre

This recording features Parker's bright alto saxophone and Gillespie's muted trumpet. Also heard is the rhythm section of upright bass, piano, and drum set, featuring the sound of a nearly constant shimmering cymbal called the "ride cymbal."

FIGURE 11.10
Charlie Parker in 1947
Source: William P. Gottlieb Collection. Library of Congress.

Texture

The main texture consists of solo saxophone with rhythm section, but there is also a drum solo and a few moments where the trumpet and saxophone play solos and duets accompanied only by the drums.

Rhythm

"Ko Ko" has a blistering tempo of around 300 beats per minute (a march, for example, is around 120 beats per minute). Because of this fast tempo, the steady bass drum beat often heard in swing is impractical in the bebop style. Instead, the beat is kept in the ride cymbal with the drummer playing almost constantly in a stream of pulses and swung subdivisions of the pulse that lay the foundation for the fast swing feel. Max Roach also adds syncopated hits on the snare drum and the bass drum to complement the soloist and the other members of the rhythm section. The bass plays steady pulsatile notes that move mostly stepwise in what is called a **walking bass line**. The piano plays sparingly, adding mostly sustained chords that fill out the harmonic structure of the song in support of the soloist and other members of the rhythm section. On top of this rhythm the pre-composed and improvised melodies in the saxophone and the trumpet consist of many lines of quick notes in a swing feel, interspersed with accents and rhythmic variations that are highly syncopated.

FIGURE 11.11
Dizzy Gillespie in 1947
Source: William P. Gottlieb Collection. Library of Congress.

Melody

The melodies played in the introduction seem to imply a minor mode, but the improvised melodies played by Parker are generally based on major modes and follow along with the harmony of the underlying chord progression. The melodies move by steps, by leaps, and often chromatically as they move in and out of consonance and dissonance with the harmony.

Harmony

After the harmonically ambiguous introduction, the harmony follows the chord progression of the jazz standard "Cherokee," an instrumental song with an AABA form composed by Ray

Noble in 1938. The harmony of the A section remains closely related to the key of the tonic, but the harmony of the B section (called the **bridge** because it connects the second and final A sections) moves in more adventurous directions to some distant keys. A **jazz standard** is a song that is frequently used as a vehicle for jazz performance, commonly in a form where a performance of the melody is followed by improvisations over the harmony of the song. Many jazz standards were originally popular songs in the interwar period having been performed on Broadway or having been written as Tin Pan Alley songs, whose "golden age" was in the 1920s and 1930s. Many jazz standards, and many Broadway and Tin Pan Alley songs of this era, have an AABA form.

Form

"Ko Ko" begins with a pre-composed introduction. There are then two choruses of saxophone improvisation over an AABA form, followed by a drum solo that lasts for a shorter duration than the full AABA form and a repeat of the introduction.

Performance Techniques

Virtuosic improvisation is one of the main features of this recording. In the course of his improvised solo, Parker plays characteristic blues phrases and melodic lines that vary greatly in length and rhythm. He even quotes a well-known melody from a New Orleans march. He and Dizzy Gillespie also at times play certain notes in a line so softly that these notes can hardly be heard at all, but are implied. These notes are said to be "ghosted," and "ghosted notes" play a crucial role in creating exciting, dynamic, and rhythmic complexity within long strings of quick notes in a swing feel.

Listen to the first thirty seconds of the recording with these elements in mind.

Listen to the entire recording following this timed listening guide. Feel free to pause and repeat sections as you read and listen if they seem to be going by quickly.

LISTENING GUIDE 11.2

TIME	SECTION	INTERNAL FORM	DESCRIPTION
0:00	Introduction		Parker and Gillespie play a pre-composed line in octaves, accompanied by drums. This line is fast and syncopated, and it ends with a sudden octave drop by both musicians, accented by the drums.
0:06			Gillespie's trumpet, accompanied by the drums, plays a solo improvised line of nearly all quick notes, some of which are ghosted.
0:12			Parker takes a turn with a solo improvisation on saxophone, playing three phrases of running quick notes that are broken up with longer notes.
0:19			The introduction closes with the trumpet and saxophone playing a line in harmony with one another before the drums drop out and they play one last phrase in octaves.
0:25	Chorus 1	A	A crack on the snare drum launches Parker's improvised solo. He plays a steady stream of quick tones for much of the solo. At 0:28 he plays two short phrases and then plays them again with some of the pitches modified to suit the changing harmony. In a sense he is performing call and response with himself as an improviser.
0:38		A	In this A section, we hear Max Roach responding and interacting with Parker's solo more actively, mostly through accents he is playing on the snare drum. Here and throughout the saxophone's dizzying lines, Parker varies the way that he accents some notes and ghosts others, creating the effect of a rhythm that is constantly shifting on and off the beat.

TIME	SECTION	INTERNAL FORM	DESCRIPTION
0:50		B	The harmony of the bridge moves to its more distant key, and Parker's first two phrases outline the harmony while including some slight microtonal sliding of the pitch at the end of each phrase. His last phrase here continues into the beginning of the next A section.
1:03		A	Parker continues to play in long streams of quick tones with syncopated accents, before ending this chorus with a long sustained pitch that is picked up by the piano and accents in the bass drum.
1:16	Chorus 2	A	The first phrase of this chorus is a quotation from the New Orleans march "High Society," a demonstration of Parker's familiarity with the roots of jazz.
1:28		A	The fast chromatic gesture in the high register of the saxophone that starts this A section is one that Parker uses in many improvisations, and is one of a number of his signature phrases.
1:41		B	Parker plays a dance-like repeating syncopated rhythm that interlocks with the sustained on-the-beat chords of the piano, the walking bass, and the constant swing feel of the drums.
1:54		A	The phrase begun at the end of the B section again continues through to the start of this final A section. The most clear reference to the blues can be heard in one of Parker's last phrases at 2:05, where he quickly slides up to the flatted third, a blue note.
2:07	Drum solo		Roach plays an improvised drum solo that starts out as a sort of syncopated, accented conversation between the bass drum and the snare before the bass and snare gradually begin playing together. The drum solo is shorter than a full AABA chorus.
2:29	Introduction (restated)		The introduction from the beginning of the recording repeats, with a greater emphasis on the cymbals from Roach. The recording ends after the harmonized line between Parker and Gillespie, concluding with an octave drop and punctuated with a hit on the bass drum.
2:53	End		

What Does It Mean?

Bebop musicians built on the musical foundations of jazz built by musicians like Bessie Smith, Louis Armstrong, and Duke Ellington, but they also forged new musical pathways that were exciting for them as players and for the audiences they were attracting. Those audiences were focused on listening rather than dancing, and they were smaller than the large audiences that enjoyed dancing to the music of big bands in large ballrooms. Some musical elements of bebop heard in "Ko Ko" are familiar from earlier styles of jazz such as an emphasis on syncopation, solo improvisation, a swing feel, and the microtonality and call and response characteristic of the blues. But bebop musicians like Charlie Parker put even more focus on solo improvisation, pushed tempos to extreme speeds, and favored complex harmonies and small combos of four or five musicians.

> AESTHETICS

"Ko Ko" showcases many of the musical features of bebop, even though it is limited by the recording technology to about three minutes. Perhaps the most striking element is that the majority of the recording is devoted to Parker's solo improvisation. Parker's solo takes place over a 32-bar AABA form featuring the chord changes to an existing song, "Cherokee." Bebop musicians took well-known songs of their time and turned them into vehicles for exploring ideas in improvisation, a practice still common in jazz today. In this case, the melody of "Cherokee" is absent, either because the musicians did not want to pay royalties to the song's composer or so that there could be more time in the recording dedicated to Parker's improvisation. Instead, the recording starts with an introduction that includes both pre-composed and improvised lines in the saxophone and the trumpet that returns at the end of the recording. This is an example of the melody-improvisation-melody (or head-solos-head) form that characterizes the vast number of small group jazz recordings and performances not only in 1940s and 1950s bebop, but in the decades since.

Another striking feature of this recording is its extraordinarily fast tempo, which is much too fast for dancing. This music is meant for listening and to be appreciated as art, especially the art of improvisation over complex harmonic progressions. Musicians playing in a bebop style listen to one another improvise, they respond to each other musically in a kind of musical conversation, and they sometimes even verbally encourage one another. When bebop was emerging in the 1940s, its audiences were fascinated by musicians' displays of virtuosity and musical interaction as they enjoyed the music in small, intimate clubs and bars that did not always have room for dancing.

Interaction among the musicians can be heard at several points in the recording. For example, at the end of Parker's first chorus, he concludes the final A section with a sustained pitch—a stark contrast to the flurry of notes that have preceded it. The piano echoes Parker by performing the same pitch, sustaining it and repeating it several times into the beginning of the second chorus. The drummer plays three consecutive accents in the bass drum, almost to punctuate the way Parker decisively ends his first chorus. This accent pattern outlines the habanera rhythm heard in Scott Joplin's "Maple Leaf Rag" (Chapter 9, Gateway 35), a rhythm that comes up throughout this recording of "Ko Ko" and pervades bebop and other styles of jazz. The "Spanish tinge" of jazz continues in bebop even as musicians take it and other existing jazz styles in new directions.

Parker's improvisation also points to how bebop got its name. He plays a number of long phrases that abruptly end with two eighth notes that descend by a leap—one example is the opening phrase of Chorus 1, around 0:26. When singers like Ella Fitzgerald improvised bebop solos while scat singing, they might have sung those two-note descending leaps on the syllables "re-bop" or "be-bop," which gave the style (and Parker's Re-Boppers) its name.

Listen again to "Ko Ko," paying attention to the end of the first chorus and the interaction among the piano, saxophone, and drums and the habanera rhythm played in the bass drum.

Bebop musicians were particularly interested in exploring harmony through their virtuosic improvisations. The melodic lines that Parker plays in his "Ko Ko" improvisations could be said to be outlining or implying the underlying harmony, even though his melodic lines often move in a stepwise motion. For example, at the beginning of the bridge of the first chorus (0:50), he plays two phrases one after another that are basically identical, but the second one is lower in pitch than the first by a whole step. The underlying harmony for the second phrase is one whole step lower than that of the first, and Parker is clearly following that harmonic motion in his improvised solo. The pitches he chooses to emphasize in this phrase also demonstrate how bebop musicians tended to explore more adventurous harmony. The simplest harmonies consist of triads, which include the first, third, and fifth degrees of a scale or mode. Dominant seventh chords, which add the flatted seventh degree of the scale to the triad, represent the next level of complexity. Here, on Parker's repeated phrases a whole step apart, he gives weight to the final pitch of each of these two phrases, which in both cases happens to be the ninth degree of a major chord. When jazz musicians talk about chord tones like the ninth, the eleventh, or the thirteenth, they call them the **upper extensions** of the chord, because they do just that—they extend the chord upwards. Sometimes these pitches can be altered by being raised or lowered a half step, which results in upper extensions called **altered extensions** like the flat nine, the sharp eleven, and the flat thirteen. These upper and altered extensions add complexity to the harmony, create dissonance in a given chord, and open up possibilities for improvisations that can melodically explore these dissonances and complexities in new ways. In this example, when Parker lands on "the nine" of a major chord, he is essentially a whole step away from both the tonic pitch and the third of the chord. This results in three simultaneous pitches a step apart from one another, producing a brief dissonance that is desirable in this setting and indicates mastery of improvising over quickly changing harmonies.

Complex harmonies based on intervals of both seconds and thirds were not new contributions of bebop musicians to jazz. Composers and musicians in the jazz of the 1920s and 1930s, Duke Ellington in particular, relied heavily on these kinds of modernist harmonies in their compositions and improvisations. With bebop and its focus on virtuosic improvisation, however, modernist explorations of harmonic complexity became the norm in jazz composition and improvisation.

Listen one more time to "Ko Ko" for pleasure, and see if you can enjoy the ways that Parker's solos express the chord changes. Pay attention to moments of harmonic dissonance. Do you find them pleasant or unpleasant?

Beyond its aesthetic meaning, bebop was embedded in the social life of the times. The innovators of bebop were, for the most part, Black musicians. Most big bands were still segregated at this time, and during the early 1940s more high-profile jobs were going to white musicians and bands. This segregation of bands and the shared experience of Black musicians brought these musicians together as they developed new ways of making music. As a result of jobs going to whites and young male musicians being drafted to fight in World War II, some African American bandleaders reduced the size of their bands, and musicians found it more difficult to find work performing. At the same time, racial tensions in Harlem were growing. In 1943 a policeman shot a young Black soldier, which resulted in a night of rioting along 125th Street and the death of six people. As Black and white soldiers fought abroad on the side of the United States in World War II, African Americans grew increasingly frustrated with a world at home where they were still experiencing segregation, inequality, and injustice. There seemed to be a dissonance between the freedoms soldiers were fighting for and the conditions of everyday life for African Americans in the United States. Bebop can be understood as a way for Black musicians to consciously—but non-verbally—express something revolutionary in response to the racial, economic, and political issues permeating African American communities during and after World War II. By showcasing virtuosity, creativity, and innovation in a modern bebop style drawing on the blues, swing, and other music with roots in the African American experience, Black musicians made a strong musical statement about their place in the broader American artistic landscape.

> SOCIAL
> BEHAVIOR

What Is Its History?

The new approaches to harmony, melody, and rhythm in bebop have their roots in the music and lives of musicians playing in swing bands. In addition to Charlie Parker and Dizzy Gillespie, some of the main musicians involved in the development of the bebop style were pianists Thelonious Monk (1917–1982) and Bud Powell (1924–1966), bassists Ray Brown (1926–2002) and Oscar Pettiford (1922–1960), and drummers Max Roach and Kenny Clarke (1914–1985). These musicians were all actively playing either in territory bands or in New York swing bands and became accomplished instrumentalists by performing night after night in these groups. Historians have a few different interpretations of how bebop developed among these skilled musicians. One of the most common interpretations is that it developed in after-hours jam sessions in New York, where big-band musicians gathered after their evening performances to play together in small Harlem nightclubs such as Monroe's Uptown House and Minton's Playhouse. These kinds of informal jam sessions had been part of what jazz musicians and their predecessors had been doing for decades. Competitive "cutting contests" were part of this scene just as they were for stride pianists years earlier. These competitive exchanges were often displays of masculine one-upmanship as much as they were demonstrations of musical prowess. At places like Minton's, musicians would challenge each other to higher levels of speed, virtuosity, and harmonic complexity as they improvised over the chord changes to well-known standards like "I Got Rhythm" and "Cherokee," as well as the 12-bar blues. In this interpretation, bebop emerged almost organically from these kinds of spontaneous musical interactions in the early 1940s.

> SOCIAL
> BEHAVIOR

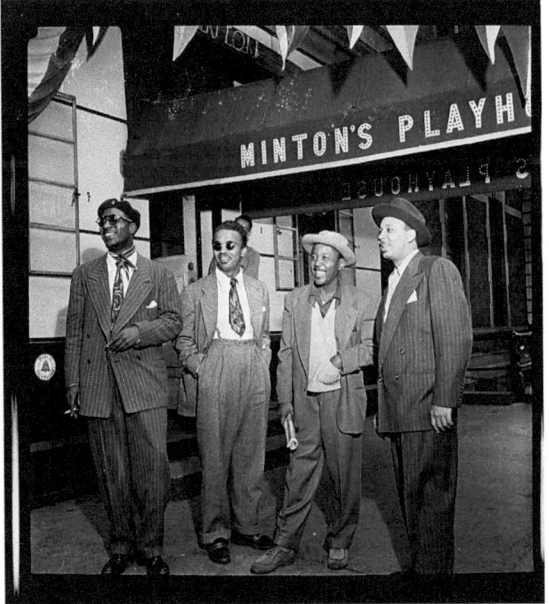

FIGURE 11.12

From left to right: pianist Thelonious Monk, trumpet player Howard McGhee, trumpet player Roy Eldridge, and bandleader and Minton's Playhouse manager Teddy Hill, outside Minton's in 1947

Source: William P. Gottlieb Collection. Library of Congress.

ECONOMIC
ACTIVITY

CULTURAL
LINKAGES

Another interpretation is that these musicians were intentionally developing the new approaches of bebop as they actively toured with big bands. In these contexts, musicians would play the same music multiple times a day, often with only short solos and little room for experimentation or extended improvisation. In between shows, musicians would spend time in dressing rooms to practice, hang out, write letters, and kill time. On tour with Cab Calloway's band in the early 1940s, Dizzy Gillespie avoided the monotony of this routine by either playing practical jokes on his bandmates or developing and practicing new melodic and harmonic ideas to insert into his short solos. He was known to rehearse with musicians backstage, demonstrating new ways he was hearing upper extensions and ways that more dissonant chords could substitute for existing chords of a given composition. These experiments did not always please Calloway and other band leaders accustomed to existing styles, but they were attractive to certain musicians, who also participated in the development of these new approaches. For much of 1943, Parker and Gillespie played together in the big band of the pianist Earl "Fatha" Hines (1903–1983). This sustained contact between the two has been called an "incubator" for bebop, as they worked intensely together in independent practice sessions, developed new compositions for the Hines band, and helped create an environment where interest in bebop among their bandmates would also develop.

It is likely that both after-hours jam sessions and the more intentional cultivation of new techniques on tour—by Gillespie in particular—played some role in the development of bebop. One of the reasons it is difficult to figure out how bebop emerged is related to the recording industry. From 1942 to 1944, the musicians' union (the American Federation of Musicians) imposed a ban on all recording by its members in a dispute with record labels over the dissemination of royalties. For this reason, this period in the development of bebop is not documented on recordings. In addition, the new innovations of musicians could not be circulated among musicians themselves (let alone to audiences) by way of records. Instead, the music spread through word of mouth, musicians playing together in big bands, and the exchange of musical ideas at jam sessions. "Ko Ko," recorded in 1945 shortly after the ban ended, is an example of a way of making music that evolved over several years of musical interaction for which there is no recorded evidence.

The history of bebop is also rooted in the lives of its innovators, in particular Charlie Parker and Dizzy Gillespie. Charlie Parker was born in Kansas and grew up in Kansas City, first playing in local bands as a teenager before relocating to New York. He was well known for practicing for more than ten hours a day to improve his playing (what is known in jazz as "woodshedding," maybe because a person went out to a woodshed to practice). Before he was twenty years old he was widely revered for his incredible facility on the saxophone and his lightning-fast improvisations with all of their harmonic and rhythmic complexity. His many recordings with Gillespie and others are full of examples of his technical and creative prowess as a saxophonist and improviser. Though bebop was not a mass popular music like big band swing had been, Parker's music was able to reach large audiences in some cases. Jazz record producer Norman Granz put together two recording sessions, one in 1949 and one in 1950, where Parker performed standards in his distinctive style with a small orchestra. These sessions resulted in two albums, each titled *Charlie Parker with Strings*, that were the most commercially successful albums of Parker's career. The familiar sounds of a symphonic orchestra playing well known standards were more broadly appealing than the modernist and experimental sounds of bebop, which could be shocking and hard to grasp for audiences used to the danceable music of swing.

Parker, from a young age, struggled with addiction to both heroin and alcohol, which led to his untimely death at age thirty-four.

Dizzy Gillespie, born in South Carolina, taught himself how to play the trumpet, studied music formally in North Carolina, and made his way north to Philadelphia and then New York, where he played in swing big bands by the age of twenty. Gillespie rejected hard drugs and enjoyed a long career as a musician, composer, and bandleader. During the 1940s he held bebop together, hosting gatherings of musicians at his apartment in Harlem and spreading to others the harmonic and musical ideas developed by pianist-composers like Mary Lou Williams and Thelonious Monk. He later formed a big band, reworking bebop and other later jazz styles for the now-standard big band instrumentation.

Gillespie helped cultivate jazz as music for listening— sometimes incorporating humor and other banter for the sake of entertainment. His openness to new and different styles of music had an enormous influence on the development of Latin jazz, evident on a recording titled "Manteca," his 1947 collaboration with Cuban percussionist and composer Chano Pozo. He nurtured the careers of many musicians in his bands, including trombonist and arranger Melba Liston, saxophonist John Coltrane, pianist John Lewis, trumpeter Lee Morgan, and trumpeter Quincy Jones. Jones would go on to great success as a record producer (he produced Michael Jackson's hit 1982 album *Thriller*, for example) and enjoy a career spanning six decades and all areas of the entertainment industry. Like Duke Ellington, Gillespie led bands on world tours sponsored by the U.S. State Department, where he was simultaneously a representative of the United States and an honest critic of the state of race relations in America. He passed away in 1993 at the age of seventy-five after a lifetime as one of the central figures of jazz.

A number of other musicians involved in bebop's early years impacted the development of jazz through the remainder of the twentieth century and beyond. The tenor saxophonist Dexter Gordon (1923–1990) was a leading musician playing

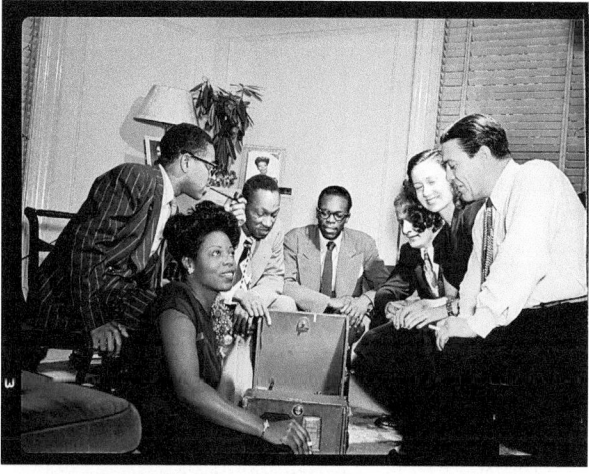

FIGURE 11.13
Mary Lou Williams (front) also hosted events at her apartment, where bebop and other music were discussed, such as this 1947 gathering, photographed for a magazine. From left to right around Williams are Dizzy Gillespie, Tadd Dameron, Hank Jones, Milt Orent, Dixie Bailey, and Jack Teagarden.
Source: William P. Gottlieb Collection. Library of Congress.

FIGURE 11.14
Dizzy Gillespie in 1991
Source: Roland Godefroy, Wikimedia Commons.

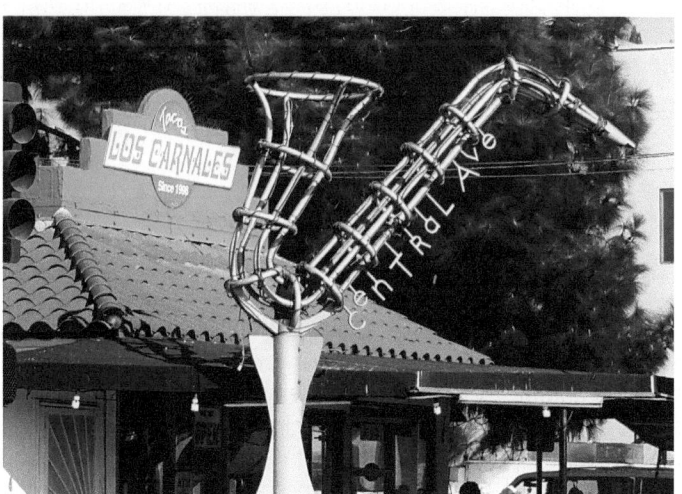

FIGURE 11.15
A sculpture celebrating Los Angeles's Central Avenue legacy in jazz
Source: Jengod, Wikimedia Commons.

FIGURE 11.16
Thelonious Monk at his home in 1963
Source: Getty Images/The Estate of David Gahr.

AESTHETICS

bebop in the 1940s Los Angeles scene along Central Avenue, an African American neighborhood that stretched south from downtown L.A. Some of the most notable jazz musicians of the past (such as Charles Mingus and Ornette Coleman) and today (such as Kamasi Washington) have emerged from Los Angeles jazz scenes, many with roots in the Central Avenue scene of the 1940s and 1950s.

The pianist Thelonious Monk, famously mentored by the pianist and composer Mary Lou Williams and known as one of the house pianists at Minton's, lived into the 1980s and left a legacy of influential compositions and recordings that continues to inspire musicians today. The pianist Jason Moran (b. 1975) has been presenting an acclaimed multimedia performance examining pianist Monk's creative process at jazz festivals and concert venues since 2007.

Students learning jazz in the United States today are typically exposed to bebop as a fundamental style of performance and improvisation. They often learn to transcribe the improvised solos of musicians like Parker and Gillespie, writing down and learning to emulate these improvisations note for note. The bebop style is thus still performed widely in educational institutions and continues to influence the development of musicians who are formally trained in jazz.

WHERE DO I GO FROM HERE?

- Listen to some other recordings by Charlie Parker such as "Now's the Time," "Ornithology," "Anthropology," and "Confirmation." How are they similar and different to one another?
- Listen to "Manteca" by Dizzy Gillespie and Chano Pozo. What musical elements of bebop can you hear clearly? What elements derive from Latin American sources?
- Find some Thelonious Monk recordings such as "Round Midnight," "Epistrophy," "Rhythm-a-Ning," and "Evidence." How do Monk's melodies differ from Parker's and Gillespie's recordings? Find a video of pianist Jason Moran's tribute to Monk, *In My Mind*. To what extent does Moran's work help you better understand or connect to Monk's music?

GATEWAY 44
CLASSICAL MUSIC AND WORLD WAR II

What Is It?

Our gateway to classical music of the World War II era is the first movement of Symphony No. 7 ("Leningrad"), Mvt. I ("War") composed in 1941 by Russian composer Dmitri Shostakovich (1906–1975). The symphony, a gargantuan work in terms of both performing forces and length, requires two separate brass sections and seventy to eighty minutes to perform. The four movements are called "War," "Recollection," "My Homeland," and "Victory." These names harken back to a tradition at least as old as the eighteenth-century symphonies and string quartets of Franz Joseph Haydn, when listeners and critics added names to his works with abstract titles like Symphony No. 101 ("The Clock) and String Quartet Op. 33, No. 3 ("The Bird"). These nicknames suggest associations or similarities between musical gestures and something outside the music. The nickname given to this Shostakovich symphony links it to the city of Leningrad, today called St. Petersburg. The "war" of the first-movement title is World War II from 1939 to 1945. This performance is by the Leningrad Symphony led by the Latvian conductor Mariss Jansons (b. 1943).

 Listen to the first thirty seconds.

How Does It Work?

Timbre

All the timbral resources of a modern symphony are present, with an emphasis on bass and snare drums.

FIGURE 11.17
Dmitri Shostakovich in 1950
Source: Roger & Renate Rössing/Deutsche Fotothek, Wikimedia Commons.

Texture

The movement begins with strings playing monophonically in octaves after which a variety of textures are used for expressive purposes.

Rhythm

The meter is in four with contrasts between march-like rhythms and more tranquil passages with long-held tones.

Melody

The melodies employ quite a bit of disjunct motion, which gives the movement its modern feel compared to eighteenth- and nineteenth-century symphonies. The melodies are based on heptatonic modes with pitches outside those modes in some places.

Harmony

The harmony is tonal but with a lot of chromaticism.

Form

The form is a variant of sonata form but with a lengthy march section in the middle. The internal form of the march section is based on theme-and-variations form.

Performance Techniques

The usual techniques of symphonic playing are on display.

 Listen to the first minute of this performance for the angular, slightly chromatic first theme.

Timed Listening Guide

As the nicknames for the symphony and first movement suggest, listeners and critics have interpreted this movement as referencing one of the most famous battles of World War II: the siege of Leningrad. Beginning in September 1941, the German army surrounded the city and blocked supplies and reinforcements from entering. The siege lasted more than two years, until January of 1944, and resulted in huge numbers of deaths. This movement can be interpreted as a programmatic representation of the events and feelings of the citizens of Leningrad during the siege.

Listen to the entire recording following this timed listening guide, which interprets the references to war in the music.

TIME	FORM	SECTION	DESCRIPTION
0:00	**Exposition**	First theme	The unison strings play the first theme in C major, perhaps an icon of the citizens of the city standing together in resistance. Punctuations from the trumpets and timpani suggest a martial atmosphere. The theme, built on a C major triad, adds non-chord tones in the first repetition of the theme to create a restless feeling (an icon) of unease and anxiety. Eventually the full orchestra enters in dense counterpoint to develop the theme somewhat.
1:31		Transition	The first transition features a quiet passage led by the flute.
2:03		Second theme	The second theme enters. It is an unadorned, lyrical melody in G major, iconic perhaps of the calm before the storm of war. It begins softly in the violins and then, after a short interlude in the winds, moves to the low strings.
4:36		Transition	The second transition features the piccolo playing a tranquil melody based on descending scales in sequence. The long drone at the end of the section creates a feeling of foreboding.
5:54		Third Theme: March	The march section begins with the soft sound of the snare drum. The march theme, in E♭ major (a favorite key of military wind bands, including for pieces such as "The Stars and Stripes Forever"), enters quietly in the strings, as if the approaching army is far away. The melody mixes conjunct scalar descents with angular disjunct leaps in the upper strings to create an awkward effect perhaps intended to mock, iconically, the approaching German forces. The theme goes through twelve variations of harmony, counterpoint, and instrumentation, growing louder and more menacing over time, an obvious icon of the approaching army. The unrelenting snare drums are particularly intense, and, by the end of the variations, crashing percussion joins them to almost drown out the melody in an iconic rendition of artillery fire.
14:52	**Development**		The development section begins when suddenly the key shifts from E♭ major to A major (the unusual interval of a tritone), and the brass section erupts with a variation on the march theme and passages based on fragments of the march. The polyphony, combined with the loud drums, creates an icon of the chaos of war. The section ends with a dramatic fortissimo ascending scale passage in octaves.
16:58	**Recapitulation**	First Theme	The primary theme returns, signaling the beginning of the recapitulation. Its phrases are in a new order, with the initial melodic line entering in the low brass around 17:12. It is also now in C minor with thundering drums and brass, the melodic mode and the instrumentation constituting musical icons of the sadness of the citizens of a city in ruins after the German attack. Later in the section the unison texture that opened the symphony also returns.
19:11		Transition	The scalar transition material first heard in the piccolo returns in the key of F♯ major, a tritone away from the tonic key of C, played by the violins and flute and later the solo flute and solo clarinet, as if representing solitary figures walking amidst the ruins.
20:16		Second Theme	The bassoon plays a transformation of the second theme accompanied by the piano and pizzicato strings. The alternation between measures in four and measures in three suggests a person staggering through the ruins of war.
22:40	**Coda**		The first theme is heard quietly in the violins in its original major key, as if a distant memory of the city before the war. It is followed by the descending melodic lines from the second transition. The march theme returns quietly, implying perhaps that, after the bombardment, these Germans are not going away.
25:50	End		

What Does It Mean?

One of the meanings of this composition is embedded in its musical style. It combines stylistic elements of the Classical period of the late eighteenth century with harmonic and melodic elements that emerge in the twentieth century. The Classical, late eighteenth-century elements include the sound of a symphony orchestra, the use of a variant of sonata form, and tonal harmony. The modern elements include the insertion into sonata form of a long set of variations on a march tune, the angular melodies with some pitches outside the tonal system, and dissonant harmonies. Combining these elements points the composition in two directions at the same time: toward something old and traditional and something new and fresh. The composer surely hoped to create a work that an audience familiar with eighteenth- and nineteenth-century music would find familiar and attractive but that acknowledged more recent changes in musical style introduced by Wagner, Debussy, Stravinsky, and others. This style, because of its references to elements of Classical-period music, has been labeled **neoclassicism**.

In 1942 the score of the symphony was smuggled out of Leningrad and performed in Moscow, London, and New York to great acclaim. It was understood as a defiant expression of Russian resistance to the German invasion, and it bolstered the morale of the Allies fighting Hitler. The nicknames for this symphony date from this period. After the war, however, and after the 1953 death of Joseph Stalin, the ruthless dictator who had ruled the Soviet Union since the death of Vladimir Lenin in 1924, a new interpretation of the work emerged in reports of interviews with Shostakovich and friends who knew him well. According to those reports, Shostakovich had begun to compose this symphony well before the war reached Leningrad. Its musical gestures referenced not the siege of Leningrad but Joseph Stalin's siege of Soviet life and mentality during the 1930s, when he was responsible for the deaths of millions of Soviet citizens in the murders or imprisonment of the intellectual and political elite of the country; a genocidal famine in Ukraine; and the forced relocation of entire ethnic groups from European Russia to Siberia and Central Asia. In this version the march in the center of the movement references not the invading German army but the slow and steady growth of an oppressive, suffocating political regime. While the "Leningrad" Symphony can be interpreted as representing Soviet resistance to the Nazi invasion, Shostakovich later claimed that it had a much broader scope and was dedicated, as he put it, to the city "that Stalin destroyed and Hitler merely finished off." This story illustrates the way musical meaning depends on context and the way it can change from person to person and time to time.

FIGURE 11.18

Dmitri Shostakovich as firefighter (right) on the roof on the Leningrad Conservatory during the siege of Leningrad

Source: Music-Images/Alamy Stock Photo.

What Is Its History?

Dmitri Shostakovich is the most important Russian composer of the Soviet era (1917–1991). Born in St. Petersburg, he was a child prodigy as both a composer and pianist. He entered the St. Petersburg Conservatory at age thirteen. His graduation piece, composed at age nineteen, was his Symphony No. 1 (1925). It was premiered to great acclaim in Berlin and Philadelphia just a few years later, and his fame as a composer in western Europe and America was assured. Shostakovich, who was paid a salary as a musical worker by the Soviet state, was astonishingly prolific. He composed fifteen symphonies, a few dozen orchestral suites and concertos, dozens of chamber works for string quartet, piano, and various other combinations, a dozen operas and ballets, and more than thirty film scores.

AESTHETICS

POLITICS

ECONOMIC ACTIVITY

Shostakovich's career provides one of the most interesting examples in music history of the collision between politics and art. After the Soviet Revolution in 1917 and his graduation from the conservatory in 1919, Shostakovich loyally served the Soviet Union in various capacities throughout his life, including for nearly thirty years as a member of the Supreme Soviet of the Russian Federation and of the Soviet Union. As with so many other prominent figures during this time, however, his loyalty to the Soviet cause could not protect him from the capricious, monstrous rule of Joseph Stalin, general secretary of the Soviet Communist Party from 1922 until his death in 1953.

In 1936 Stalin launched the Great Terror, during which he liquidated or imprisoned many influential intellectuals and political leaders, including some of Shostakovich's friends and family. Stalin attended the premier of Shostakovich's opera *Lady Macbeth of Mtsensk* in 1936. Shortly after that, the work was condemned in the party-controlled press as "formalist," that is, as music that focused on modern musical elements and not linked iconically or indexically to the tastes and needs of the proletarian masses. Although Shostakovich rehabilitated his reputation with Stalin with compositions like Symphony No. 7 written during World War II, he was again attacked as a formalist after the war in 1948. Although Stalin spared him the fate of his friends, perhaps because he recognized Shostakovich's compositional mastery, Shostakovich lived in constant fear of Stalin. Later in life, he confessed to always keeping a packed suitcase at the ready, in case he had to flee at a moment's notice.

In September 1941, Shostakovich was living in his hometown of Leningrad when Nazi forces attacked the city. During the siege of Leningrad, which lasted nearly three years and cost more than 900,000 lives by the time it ended in 1944, Shostakovich served on a fire brigade. He wrote the first three movements of his Seventh Symphony during the attack, and finished the fourth in a nearby town after he and his family were forced to evacuate. An orchestra cobbled together from the dozen or so remaining professional musicians in the city, plus as many amateurs as they could find, premiered the work during the siege in 1942.

Shostakovich was just one of many European composers who expressed their experiences of World War II in their music. Others include Olivier Messiaen from France; Viktor Ullmann, a German-Jewish composer from the area today known as the Czech Republic; and Arnold Schoenberg, an Austrian-Jewish composer who immigrated to the United States in 1934, a year after Hitler came to power in Germany.

Olivier Messiaen (1908–1992) was one of the most important and innovative composers in the history of French music. A prodigy like Shostakovich, he entered the Paris Conservatoire at the age of eleven and excelled in piano and organ performance, composition, improvisation, and music history. Messiaen's musical style, partly influenced by his having heard Javanese gamelan and other Asian traditions, avoids the narrative conventions of traditional and neoclassical European music, conventions such as harmonic cadences and passages through various key areas. Instead, he favored various mathematical devices that created static formal structures. A devout Catholic, much of his output contains theological references. Messiaen was also an expert ornithologist and traveled the world transcribing birdsong, which he then included in some of his works, including a 1953 work for piano and orchestra titled *Réveil des oiseaux* (Awakening of the Birds).

When the German military invaded France in 1940, they captured Messiaen, who was serving in a medical unit, and imprisoned him for a year in a labor camp in Poland. There he composed his *Quartet for the End of Time* for an ensemble of four professional musicians in the camp who played clarinet, violin, cello, and piano. They premiered the work for other camp prisoners in January of 1941. The eight-movement work is inspired by a passage from the book of Revelation from the New Testament. Rather than creating icons of the sounds of war or feelings of despair, as Shostakovich did in his Seventh Symphony, Messiaen uses the biblical text to express the apocalyptic sentiments spreading across Europe during the darkest years of World War II.

FIGURE 11.19
Olivier Messiaen in 1930
Source: Paul Fearn/Alamy Stock Photo.

Viktor Ullmann (1898–1944) was born in the Czech lands of the Austro-Hungarian Empire to a German-Jewish family that had converted to Catholicism. After serving in the army during World War I, he moved to Vienna and studied for a time with Arnold Schoenberg, whose techniques he absorbed and developed into his own style. During the interwar years he worked as a conductor in Prague and other European cities while composing an impressive array of orchestral and chamber-music works, song cycles, an opera, and music for plays. After the Germans invaded Czechoslovakia in 1939, Ullmann, now classified as a Jew in spite of his family's conversion to Christianity, was sent in 1942 to Theresienstadt, one of more than 300 concentration camps the Nazis established in Germany, Poland, and Czechoslovakia for political prisoners and those deemed inferior to the "master race," like Jews, Roma, gays, and the disabled. A few of these camps were classified as death camps, the most notorious of which was Auschwitz in southern Poland. Theresienstadt, in the Czech lands, was designated a "model community" and housed many educated, middle-class Jews from Germany and central Europe. Artists, composers, and musicians were encouraged to develop a cultural life in the camp, children were educated, and many musical performances of classical music and jazz were held there. Ullmann composed nearly two dozen works while at Theresienstadt, including a one-act opera in 1944 called "The Emperor of Atlantis." In June of 1944 the Nazis, trying to conceal rumors about death camps and their plan to exterminate the Jews, invited the Danish Red Cross to inspect the facility and view the cultural life and the relatively good conditions there. After their visit, Ullmann was sent in October of 1944 to Auschwitz, where he was killed in the gas chambers.

The Emperor of Atlantis, subtitled *Death's Refusal*, is Ullmann's final work. Throughout his career, he had struggled to resolve his avant-garde sensibility with his desire to communicate directly to a broad audience. In his final works, he fused the atonality of Schoenberg, the accessibility of contemporary German theater music by Kurt Weill (1900–1950) and others, and references to Bach and Beethoven. This chamber opera, composed for seven singers and thirteen instruments, is an allegorical commentary on the deep immorality of fascism and its total disregard for the value of human life. In one act with four scenes, it takes place in a world at war. The Emperor, who lives alone in a chamber without windows and rules his empire by telephone, declares total war and attempts to persuade Death to help him in his cause. Insulted, Death refuses to participate or to carry out his work at all. Soon, the Emperor begins to hear reports that no one in the war is able to die, even those with grave wounds. With the world descending into chaos and the war falling apart, Death appears to the Emperor and offers to resume his duties only if the Emperor himself volunteers to be his first victim. Realizing there is no alternative, the Emperor agrees, takes Death's hand, and is led away while the other members of the cast sing a final hymn, "Come, Death, our honored guest," set in a four-part homorhythmic harmonic style reminiscent of the German Lutheran chorale tradition. When the Nazi guards saw the opera in rehearsal, they did not fail to notice its allegorical character, and the performance was canceled. It received its first performance in 1975 in Amsterdam, and has been performed fairly frequently since, including by the Los Angeles Philharmonic in 2012 and by the Atlanta Opera in socially distanced outdoor performances staged in a circus tent in 2020.

POLITICS

FIGURE 11.20
A "stumbling block," a plaque commemorating the deportation and death of Viktor Ullmann laid in a street near the Hamburg State Opera in Germany, one of more than 60,000 such stones in honor of victims of the Holocaust
Source: Ajepbah, Wikimedia Commons.

FIGURE 11.21
Arnold Schoenberg teaching music theory and composition at UCLA in 1951
Source: INTERFOTO/Alamy Stock Photo.

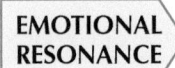

Arnold Schoenberg (1874–1951) was arguably the most influential composer of the twentieth century. In the first decade of the twentieth century he pushed Wagner's experiments with tonality beyond their limits into atonality (Chapter 9, Gateway 36). In the 1920s he and others in Vienna developed a new system for ordering music called **twelve-tone serialism**. In this system, all twelve pitches of the European scale are treated equally without regard for hierarchies like tonic and dominant. The twelve pitches are arranged in a series or "row" of pitches that become the basis for many kinds of compositional transformations, formal structures, melodies, and harmonies. He avoided Ullmann's fate when he, and many other Jewish composers, writers, and intellectuals, left Germany in the 1930s before the worst atrocities of the Holocaust began. After the war, in 1947, he wrote a cantata using twelve-tone serial techniques for narrator, male chorus, and orchestra called *A Survivor from Warsaw*, named for the Polish capital, which had a large Jewish ghetto during the war. Based on a survivor's account of wartime experiences, Schoenberg's text recounts the harrowing story of beatings at the hands of the Nazis and being marched off to the gas chambers, to which the victims respond by singing a hymn in Hebrew expressing their love for "the Lord your God." In recent years it has been performed as a prelude to pieces with related themes in the German and Austrian tradition, including Beethoven's Symphony No. 9, with its hopeful invocation of the brotherhood of man, and Mozart's Requiem.

WHERE DO I GO FROM HERE?

- Listen to the fourth movement, "Victory," of Shostakovich's Symphony No. 7. What Classical-period form does it use, and what musical devices express the sense of the "title" of the movement?
- Listen to one or more movements from Olivier Messiaen's *Quartet for the End of Time* and describe the elements of music you can hear.
- Listen to Arnold Schoenberg's *A Survivor from Warsaw* and discuss the way he uses various musical elements to express the emotional sense of the text.
- Find a recording of Viktor Ullmann's *The Emperor of Atlantis* and listen to excerpts from it. Based on what you know of the storyline of this chamber opera, how do its musical elements and references to older styles of music add to its meaning?

GATEWAY 45
TRINIDADIAN STEEL PAN MUSIC

What Is It?

Steel pan music arose in Trinidad in the 1940s as Trinidadian musicians began to make instruments out of metal cans and barrels that had previously been used for other purposes. These containers were turned into pitched percussion instruments called **steel pans** (or simply "pans") by pounding or hammering the surface in a way that subdivides it into smaller areas, each of which can be tuned. Today **steelbands** are large ensembles of various types of steel pans, usually made from fifty-five-gallon oil drums, plus a rhythm section known as the "engine room" consisting of non-pitched percussion instruments including a drum set, congas, large metal scrapers, and vehicle brake drums called irons struck with metal rods. These community-based groups, often with up to 100 members each, perform sophisticated and complex musical arrangements in many styles and genres.

The development of the steelband is closely linked with Carnival, a festival preceding the Christian observance of Lent. Steelbands also participate in competitions against one another where they showcase their creative arrangements and compositions as well as their masterful performance skills. The most prominent steelband competition is Panorama, which began in 1963 and is held most years during Carnival celebrations in Port of Spain, Trinidad's capital.

Our gateway to steel pan music is a recording of the Renegades Steel Orchestra performing their winning performance from the 1993 Panorama competition. Titled "Mystery Band," it is an arrangement of a calypso (a Caribbean song genre) composition originally by Lord Kitchener (1922–2000) and arranged for the Renegades by Jit Samaroo (1950–2016).

 Listen to the first thirty seconds of the recording to get an idea of the sound.

How Does It Work?

There are steel pans of several different sizes. The highest-pitched pans, called "tenors," have thirty or more notes in a single pan and can play a chromatic scale. The deepest-pitched pans, called "basses," have only two or three notes per pan, so musicians combine several drums in one set to form a complete chromatic scale. A set of bass pans usually includes six drums, but sometimes nine, or even twelve. Since the bodies of the instruments function as resonators, the lowest-pitched instruments use virtually the entire oil drum, while the high-pitched instruments are cut so that the size of the skirt of the drum extends down less than a foot. Pans with pitches in the middle range include "guitars" and "cellos," and their size is in between that of the tenors and that of the basses. Steel pans are played with a pair of rubber-tipped mallets. Because these instruments belong to the idiophone family of tuned gongs, their overtone structure is particularly rich, producing a shimmering, sometimes piercing timbre. One of the arts of steel pan making is to shape the sections of the pan surface not only to play a given pitch in a tempered scale but also to control the overtone structure of the pans so they sound good when played together in bands.

Timbre

Timbres in this recording include the shimmering steel pan sound of the high-pitch tenors, the mid-range cellos, and the low-pitch basses. The non-pitched percussion of the engine room can also be heard throughout.

Texture

This recording is an example of the typical four-layer steelband texture. The tenors play the lead melody, often doubled or harmonized by complementary lower-pitched pans called double tenors and double seconds. The background pans (including cellos and guitars) "strum" chords in a syncopated rhythmic pattern. The basses play a repetitive bass line. And the instruments of the engine room play an interlocking, polyrhythmic part that continues with a number of variations throughout the recording.

Rhythm

The rhythm is in a duple meter with interlocking polyrhythms among the instruments of the engine room, which produce a steady, nearly uninterrupted **groove** (a short, repeated musical pattern). The melodies, countermelodies, strumming, and bass line also include a great deal of syncopation.

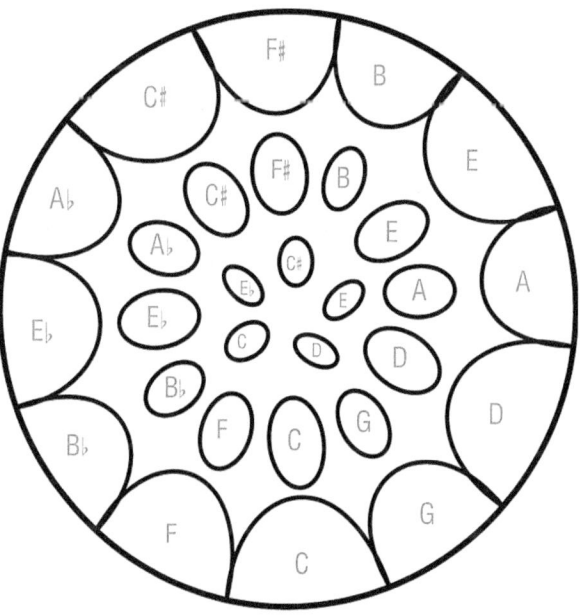

FIGURE 11.22

A drawing of the shape and pitches of the highest-pitched Trinidadian steel pan, the tenor, viewed from above

Source: Alex Sawicka-Ritchie.

FIGURE 11.23

Exodus steel orchestra members performing in downtown Port of Spain for Carnival in 2015

Source: John de la Bastide/Shutterstock.

FIGURE 11.24

Members of a steelband in London performing on basses (left), cellos (center, front), and tenors (center, rear)

Source: Getty Images/Mike Kemp.

Melody

Some melodies are in major modes and some are in minor modes. In most cases the melodies are drawn from the calypso song "Mystery Band" composed by Lord Kitchener and elaborated upon. **Calypso** is a style of song that developed in Trinidad in the early twentieth century as an Afro-Trinidadian form of social commentary on living conditions in a society under European colonial rule. In calypso, a singer is backed up by a band and draws on humor and wordplay to entertain audiences.

Harmony

The harmony moves through a number of key centers, based on the harmony of the original calypso. The variations generally follow the harmony of the original themes, but additional chromatic harmonies are introduced in some of the variations.

Form

Like many arrangements for Panorama, this piece is in a theme-and-variations form. After an introduction, the arrangement follows the original form of "Mystery Band" (ABCDE), followed by a number of variations on that form. Some newly composed material is added in between variations at some points of the recording.

Performance Techniques

This music is being played by around 100 musicians. Each section of the band must perform with extraordinary precision and coordination with the other sections. When a large group of musicians succeeds in this endeavor it can be quite impressive. There is little variation in timbre or texture throughout the recording. Perhaps the most interesting elements to follow are the changes in the melodies and harmonies, which demonstrate the skill and creativity of the arranger, especially when expertly executed by the ensemble.

Listen to the entire recording as you follow the timed listening guide.

LISTENING GUIDE 11.4

TIME	SECTION	DESCRIPTION
0:00	Introduction	After two percussion beats from the engine room, the introduction begins, which launches right into the thick four-part texture with the entire ensemble performing together. The melody of this introduction is heavily syncopated.
0:23		The band completely stops other than the drummer playing a pulse in the bass drum and hi-hat. Gradually the pans enter, playing an arpeggiated figure over a pentatonic scale in a massive crescendo along with the high-pitched white noise of the scrapers in the engine room. At the height of the crescendo, the band plays a unison syncopated figure on the V chord to set up the initial presentation of the themes of "Mystery Band."
0:39	A	The melody to the calypso "Mystery Band" begins with the first eight-bar phrase (A), which has an internal form of aa. The syncopated major melody is heard clearly in the tenors, supported by the strumming of the cellos, the simple repeating ostinato in the basses, and the intense driving polyrhythm of the engine room.

TIME	SECTION	DESCRIPTION
0:54	B	Phrase B is similarly eight bars and in a major mode, and can be distinguished by its melody, which begins with five quickly repeated pitches in succession (its internal form is bb'). The percussion group accents the rhythms of the melodic gestures, especially the syncopated phrase endings.
1:09	C	This eight-bar phrase is through-composed and, though it stays generally in a major key, begins with a chromatic harmonic progression, three slightly dissonant chords that descend by half steps.
1:24	D	Phrase D is an eight-bar phrase in a minor key with an internal form of dd'. After a large upward leap of an octave from the end of the previous phrase, the melody descends through the minor scale with a syncopated rhythm. At the end of the phrase, the chords begin to move back towards the original major key.
1:39	E	In this sixteen-bar phrase back in the major key, each of the four-bar subdivisions of the phrase begins with two statements of a short-long-short syncopated figure.
2:10	A'	The first variation on A changes the melody quite a bit, and adds a number of syncopated accents in the engine room, cellos, and basses. The harmony becomes slightly more chromatic.
2:23	B'	This variation stays close to the original B melody at first, and then continues to elaborate on the syncopated part of the first phrase of B through a number of harmonic and melodic iterations.
2:38	C'	The initial chromatic harmonic progression of C can be heard in the cellos and basses, but the tenors perform a technical and intricate new melody over that progression.
2:54	D'	The percussion slightly thins out for this variation of D, and the drums play a series of accents while the cymbals and other high-frequency sounds of the engine room play only on the beat in a "swooshing" effect.
3:08	E'	The full engine room cranks up again, and the short-long-short motive from E returns, but not as prominently as the first time. A countermelody in the cellos descends chromatically. The entire band plays a series of unison syncopated hits to end this section and change to a new major key.
3:50	A"B"C"D"E"	The melody shifts to the cellos in a new major key, while the tenors play in a supporting role. They play new variations on each section.
5:13	F	A brief section of new material brings the tenors back to the forefront of the texture and gradually moves the tonality to a new key.
5:32	A"'B"'C"' D"'E"'	The tenors assume control of the melody, transforming it to a minor key for A"' and B"'. These variations continue to demonstrate the technical abilities of the musicians and the skills of the arranger.
6:55	G	New material enters with new harmonies and melodies. This section is called a "jam." It cyclically alternates between two chords and seems to suspend the forward linear motion of the theme and variations form.
7:12	A""B"" etc. . . .	More variations continue until the end of the recording, along with some sections of new material.
10:08	End	

What Does It Mean?

Steel pan music is a cherished Carnival tradition in Trinidad. Carnival is celebrated before Lent in countries with Roman Catholic heritage all over the world (in New Orleans it is called Mardi Gras). In Trinidad, its central festivities take place on the Monday and Tuesday before Lent begins on Ash Wednesday. They include parades, dancing, elaborate masquerade costumes, and a number of music competitions. Steelbands originally functioned to provide musical accompaniment to the dancing and costumed masquerades of Carnival parades. The duple meter, moderately

CULTURAL LINKAGES

FIGURE 11.25
Carnival masqueraders in the streets of Port of Spain, Trinidad
Source: Getty Images/Sean Drakes.

FIGURE 11.26
The Mighty Sparrow performing in Amsterdam in 1989
Source: Getty Images/Frans Schellekens.

fast tempo, and complex syncopation in "Mystery Band" are all rooted in the Trinidadian style of dancing on the road at Carnival. While steelbands still participate in Carnival parades, today DJs with large (and loud) speaker systems on flatbed trucks provide most of the music for dancers and other Carnival revelers, usually in a newer popular style of beat-driven dance music called soca. Where the extraordinary music of steelbands shines is in the context of music competitions like Panorama, an annual competition associated with Carnival.

With a history stretching back over fifty years, Panorama is a competition with a number of stages (preliminary rounds, semifinals) that occur for about a month before the final competition, which typically takes place on the Saturday before Carnival begins. Bands spend up to two months (the time between New Year's and Lent) preparing their ten-minute Panorama performances, which showcase the skills of both performers and arrangers. Each Panorama performance is usually based on a well-known contemporary calypso song.

Calypso has been central to the repertoire of steelbands since they first appeared. In its sung form, calypso focuses on wordplay, humor, and showmanship, and is an effective mode of storytelling and commenting on social issues of the day. In the weeks leading up to Carnival, calypsonians (as calypso singers are called), accompanied by backup singers and a large backup band (drums, guitar, electric keyboard, bass, saxophones, trumpets) perform in theaters called "calypso tents" in Port of Spain to entertain audiences with their wit and masterful musical storytelling. As part of their performing personas, calypsonians take on fanciful names. Some of the biggest stars have been Atilla the Hun (not Attila), Singing Sandra, Lord Invader, Lord Kitchener, and Mighty Sparrow. In addition to its storytelling function, calypso has also been popular for dancing and for the Carnival parade. Before soca became the most common music in the Carnival parade, calypso music provided a steady beat for people processing down the road in a dance style that moved forward with swaying short steps. The bouncing excitement created by the interlocking rhythms of calypso and the "breaks," where the entire band stops playing momentarily, can generate great energy and stimulate enthusiasm among all participants. Calypso's historical function as a music for dancing can be clearly heard in the polyrhythms, breaks, and the overall rhythmic feel of "Mystery Band."

 Listen again to "Mystery Band" and focus on the interlocking rhythms, steady tempo, breaks, and whether you feel like it makes you want to dance or walk with a bounce in your step.

AESTHETICS ⟩ Today calypso songs deal with a wide range of topics: politics, patriotism, moral behavior, and other forms of social commentary. When steelbands perform well-known calypsos for Panorama (like Lord Kitchener's "Mystery Band"), it is important that the melody is clear, since audiences and judges will likely know the melody and the lyrics that are a big part of why the song is significant. It is also important, however, to demonstrate creativity, which is where the theme-and-variations form comes in. In the very first Panorama competition in 1963, an arranger named Tony Williams decided to experiment with theme-and-variations form, a concept that he borrowed from the symphonies of European classical music. It enabled him to maintain the familiar calypso melody and harmony while allowing creative experimentation. He also borrowed from European classical music the concept of harmonic modulation in the form of key changes. These techniques impressed audiences and judges and remain common in Panorama performances. Arrangers today add newly composed material for introductions, transitions, and "jams." Jams, like section G of "Mystery Band" starting at 6:55, usually repeat a pattern of two or four chords in a cycle, which suspends the linear forward motion established by the theme-and-variations form. On top of that pattern, the band plays an exciting and perhaps technical part. Jit Samaroo, the arranger of "Mystery Band" for the Renegades, was a master arranger known for his relatively short jams and arrangements that showcased the dexterity and high level of technical proficiency of the musicians.

🔊 **Listen once more to "Mystery Band" and focus on the form, the ways that the variations modify the original themes and the shift in the sense of forward motion during the jam at G (6:55).**

Over the past half century, Panorama has significantly shaped the music of steelbands, and not only by introducing theme and variations as the most common form. The competition also transformed steel pan music into a staged (rather than a parade) performance that emphasizes intricately pre-composed music rather than improvisation. Steelbands cover a wide repertoire beyond calypso. While Panorama has promoted the performance of calypso music, other competitions have focused on the performance of arrangements of well-known works from the history of European classical music. Steelbands also perform and record arrangements of American popular songs, adding their characteristic interlocking calypso rhythms and the rich timbres of steel pans to give the songs a new, Trinidadian sound.

What Is Its History?

The British, Dutch, Spanish, and French colonized the Caribbean islands of Trinidad and Tobago in the sixteenth and seventeenth centuries and began to bring enslaved Africans to the islands. When the British finally secured complete control of the two islands in 1797, the population was estimated at about 2000 Europeans and 10,000 enslaved people of African descent. The enslaved Africans of the French and Spanish colonists had adopted the Catholic tradition of the pre-Lenten Carnival and played African drums to accompany their celebrations. After the abolition of slavery in 1834 Afro-Trinidadians became enthusiastic participants in the public Carnival, bringing their own flavor and interpretation to the Carnival traditions of Europeans. In the period from 1845 to 1917, thousands of immigrants from India were brought to Trinidad as indentured servants to replace the labor of the enslaved. Today Indo-Trinidadians are the largest population group in Trinidad and Tobago (nearly 40 percent), with people of African descent representing a slightly smaller percentage of the population.

⬦ **CULTURAL LINKAGES**

During the 1880s the British banned the use of African-derived drums at Carnival after deadly rioting among revelers. Participants quickly turned to found objects like spoons and bottles, cookie tins, brake drums, garbage-can lids, and especially an ensemble of bamboo stamping tubes called *tamboo bamboo*. Bamboo tubes of different sizes and pitches were struck on the ground and/or struck with sticks to form interlocking polyrhythms that accompanied singing. Eventually, metal instruments began to replace bamboo tubes, first because they were louder and more durable, and, later on, because they turned out to be tunable. Steelbands emerged out of this African-derived tradition of inventing musical instruments from found objects.

⬦ **TECHNOLOGY**

Early found-object containers of choice for steel pans included the steel drums used by the Bermudez Biscuit Company, caustic soda drums, garbage cans, and paint cans. Musicians figured out how to beat the bottoms of these containers into sections, each with its own pitch. The innovators of steel pan instruments were from poor communities, and the music was first associated with lower socioeconomic classes. The first steelband ensembles emerged around 1940, but during World War II Carnival celebrations were banned. They were not heard again publicly until 1946.

POLITICS

Steelbands attracted attention from Trinidadian intellectuals who, under the influence of musical nationalism, viewed the music as a kind of "urban folk" music suitable to represent the Trinidadian nation. The cultural status of steel pan music began to rise in the late 1940s as a result of government support of a steelband association and a national steel orchestra, the Trinidad All Steel Pan Orchestra (TASPO), as well as positive responses from the press in the U.K. after a 1951 TASPO performance. TASPO was one of the early groups to use another found-object container, the larger fifty-five-gallon oil drum that spread in popularity and is still the standard drum used for making steel pans today.

CULTURAL LINKAGES

Oil was discovered in Trinidad in the nineteenth century, and from the early twentieth century Trinidad was an important oil producer. Discarded oil drums were a part of the environment and during World War II Trinidad became a major oil depot (and site of American military bases) supplying the Americans and the British with fuel for their airplanes, tanks, and ships. TASPO helped the fifty-five-gallon drum become more common, but it wasn't until the invention of stands on wheels in the late 1950s that these large instruments became fully standard because they were too heavy to carry slung around the neck on the road. When the fifty-five-gallon oil drum caught on and panmen (tuners of steel pans) in Port of Spain started to tune fifty-five-gallon drums, they had to jump the fence of the American naval base at night to steal them. These larger drums were shaped into instruments of different sizes to play melody, harmony, and bass parts that eventually became the tenors, guitars, cellos, and basses used today. Other metal objects, like brake drums, became the collection of percussion instruments that make up today's engine room rhythm section.

By the 1970s, steelband was part of the curriculum of some schools, and by the 1980s women became integrated into the previously male-dominated membership of steelbands. Today commercial sponsors, often large corporations, support the building and maintenance of instruments for large steel bands like the Renegades. When they won Panorama with "Mystery Band" in 1993, the Renegades were sponsored by the oil company Amoco (today known as BP). These corporate sponsorships continue today as a public relations opportunity for corporations to show a commitment to the community.

CULTURAL LINKAGES

"Mystery Band" is just one example of Panorama-winning performances by the Renegades, who, with their arranger Jit Samaroo, won the competition nine times in the 1980s and 1990s. Samaroo, of Indian descent, is one of the most prominent figures in the steel pan scene today not only in Trinidad, but in steelband circles around the world. The Renegades returned to the top with Panorama wins in 2018 and 2019 with the arranger Duvone Stewart (b. 1976). Other steelbands with ongoing success at Panorama include Phase II Pan Groove, the Trinidad All Stars, and the Desperadoes, each working with their own highly skilled arrangers.

FIGURE 11.27
Lord Kitchener in 1956
Source: Getty Images/Popperfoto.

From the 1960s through the 1990s, over half of the winning Panorama performances, including the Renegades' "Mystery Band," were based on calypsos by the calypsonian Lord Kitchener, born Aldwyn Roberts. Beginning in the 1940s, Lord Kitchener set the standard for calypso music and is one of the most highly revered calypsonians of all time. As steelbands gained prominence, Lord Kitchener (and others) began writing calypso songs with steelband performance in mind, including "pan tunes" like "Mystery Band" whose lyrics refer directly to steel pan music and whose musical elements lend themselves to performance by steelbands. Though Lord Kitchener was known for composing and performing in a variety of musical styles, his pan tunes remain classics in the calypso and steel pan repertoires.

During and after World War II calypso and steel pan music became well known in much of the world. The tradition of social and political commentary in calypso made it an ideal mode of critique of the negative impact of the American presence in Trinidad during the war. The calypsonian Lord Invader (b. Rupert Grant, 1914–1961), sang perhaps the most famous calypso song of the war era, "Rum and Coca-Cola." In it he sings of how the "Yankee dollar" (spent by American military personnel stationed in Trinidad) had negative consequences for the island, including an increase in prostitution. The lyrics of the first verse open with the young girls of

Trinidad giving the "Yankees" a "better price" because the Yankees "treat them nice." The chorus closes with the line "both mothers and daughters working for their Yankee dollar." In 1944 the Andrews Sisters, an American singing group noted for tight harmonies and songs about the war like "The Boogie-Woogie Bugle Boy of Company B" (1941), recorded the song with modified lyrics. Through their efforts and those of the American popular entertainer Harry Belafonte (b. 1927), who spent part of his youth in Jamaica, calypso entered the mainstream of popular music in the United States during the 1950s and 1960s.

Today steel pan music is played in cities all over the world. Panorama has inspired similar competitions in cities like New York, where Brooklyn hosts the largest and most skilled steel pan scene outside Trinidad. Many U.S. universities teach steelband ensembles, some of which were founded by well-known Trinidadian panmen. Steel pan tuner Cliff Alexis, for example, helped create the first steel pan degree program at Northern Illinois University, about a decade after he started working there in 1985. Another tuner, Ellie Mannette (b. 1926), started the University Tuning Project at West Virginia University in 1991. Arranger Ray Holman (b. 1944) started the University of Washington Steelband in 1998 during a residency there as a visiting artist. Steelband music also plays a role in tourism both in Trinidad and around the world. It has become an index of relaxing and carefree island life in the tropics, even though its emergence in Trinidad during World War II tells a different story.

WHERE DO I GO FROM HERE?

- Listen to Lord Kitchener perform "Mystery Band" with its lyrics, and compare it to the version performed by the Renegades.
- Watch a video of the Renegades' Panorama-winning performance of "Mystery Band," paying attention to not only the technical skills of the pan players, but the overall social environment of the performance at Trinidad's Carnival celebration.
- Find some examples of steelband performances that are arrangements of European classical works or American popular songs. How do the steelbands musically adapt these compositions to suit their purposes? Which musical elements remain the same?
- Take a look at the book *Carnival Music in Trinidad* by Shannon Dudley (Oxford: Oxford University Press, 2004), upon which much of this gateway is based. How do some other musical genres contribute to Trinidadian Carnival celebrations?

CLOSING

Musicians and their audiences around the world responded to and engaged with the events of World War II in countless ways. A recovering economy in the United States after the war led to a new era of business success in the music industry, and newly named genres like country attracted hordes of fans and made stars out of artists like Hank Williams. Musicians like Charlie Parker and Dizzy Gillespie created a new, modern mode of expression in jazz— bebop—expanding the harmonic and melodic structures of their music in the context of segregated all-Black big bands on the road, while other African Americans were being killed on the battlefield as they fought a war against the racist ideologies of Adolf Hitler and the Nazis. European composers wrote music that indexed and iconically represented the horrific experience of the war and offered a subtle, unspoken critique of those in power. Some, like Messiaen and Ullmann, composed music in concentration camps and death camps, defiantly commenting on their conditions as prisoners with music. The wartime operations of the United States and Britain had musical consequences in Trinidad, where musicians transformed discarded oil drums into the sounds of one of today's most distinct and vibrant musical traditions.

As the war faded into the past and a new era of economic prosperity began for many, a new generation would challenge not only racial and other injustices in American society, but also the continued involvement of the American military in wars and violent conflicts abroad.

THINGS TO THINK ABOUT

- Compare the various ways that World War II and its effects stimulated music and musicians during this period.
- National identity and nationalism appears as a theme in several of the gateways in this chapter. How and why does music become a marker of national identity in the various settings discussed in this chapter?
- Compare the ways country, bebop, and steel pan music illuminate the legacies of slavery in the Caribbean and the United States and the ways they dealt directly or indirectly with slavery in the past and discrimination and injustice in the present.

NEW TERMS

altered extensions	honky-tonk music	steel pan
bebop	jazz combo	steelbands
bridge	jazz standard	twelve-tone serialism
calypso	lap steel guitar	upper extensions
country music	neoclassicism	walking bass line
groove	pedal steel guitar	
hillbilly records	rhythm section	

MUSIC FROM AN AGE OF DISENCHANTMENT AND PROTEST (1950–1975)

TREMENDOUS UPHEAVAL in American society and culture marked the period from 1950 to 1975. Singer-songwriter Bob Dylan (b. 1941) wrote "the times they are a-changin'," and musicians responded to the turmoil with new musical styles and practices. The victory on the European and Pacific fronts in World War II, postwar economic prosperity, and a baby boom created a new confidence for many that America was the greatest and most powerful country in the world. But anxieties persisted. The United States had introduced nuclear warfare to the world and killed tens of thousands of civilians in the Japanese cities of Hiroshima and Nagasaki in the final stages of World War II. After World War II, as the Cold War intensified, the Soviet Union built its own nuclear arsenal to contend with the military power of the United States. Americans fought in proxy wars in Korea (1950–1953) and Vietnam (1955–1974) against Soviet-supported enemies in efforts to stave off the perceived threat of communist expansion.

The tension between optimism and pessimism about the future in the United States provided fertile ground for seeds of dissension and unrest to grow among three important segments of society: white youth, African Americans and other minorities, and women. During the 1960s, anti-war protests, race riots in a number of U.S. cities, and the assassinations of President John F. Kennedy (1963), his brother, Senator and presidential candidate Robert Kennedy (1968), and civil rights activist Martin Luther King Jr. (1968), created a widespread sense of despair that eclipsed the optimistic national mood of the 1950s.

By this time African Americans had long been fighting against segregation and for equal rights. In the first half of the century organizations like the NAACP, founded in 1909, initiated legal action in the courts, organized mass protests, published and publicized key statistics, and produced artistic material. Despite progress on many fronts, African Americans returning from World War II were still denied rights enjoyed by their white fellow citizens through legalized segregation, which persisted, especially in the South. They had risked their lives, and their comrades in arms had lost their lives, to protect a society that, on the one hand, had condemned an enemy that regarded certain races as inferior, and on the other hand, continued to condone unequal legal rights and violence based on race at home. In 1954 the landmark Supreme Court decision *Brown v. Board of Education* ruled that so-called separate but equal schools in the segregated South were, in fact, unequal. The next year Rosa Parks of Montgomery, Alabama, was arrested for refusing to sit in the customary place for Blacks at the back of a city bus. The bus boycott that followed her defiance helped catalyze the civil rights movement, which took the quest for integration and equality beyond the courts and into the streets. It featured repeated acts of civil disobedience, including sit-ins at whites-only lunch counters, peace marches, and freedom rides. The religious leaders of the movement, including Rev. Martin Luther King Jr., Jesse Jackson, and Ralph Abernathy, advocated non-violent resistance. But anger and

DOI: 10.4324/9781003269304-16

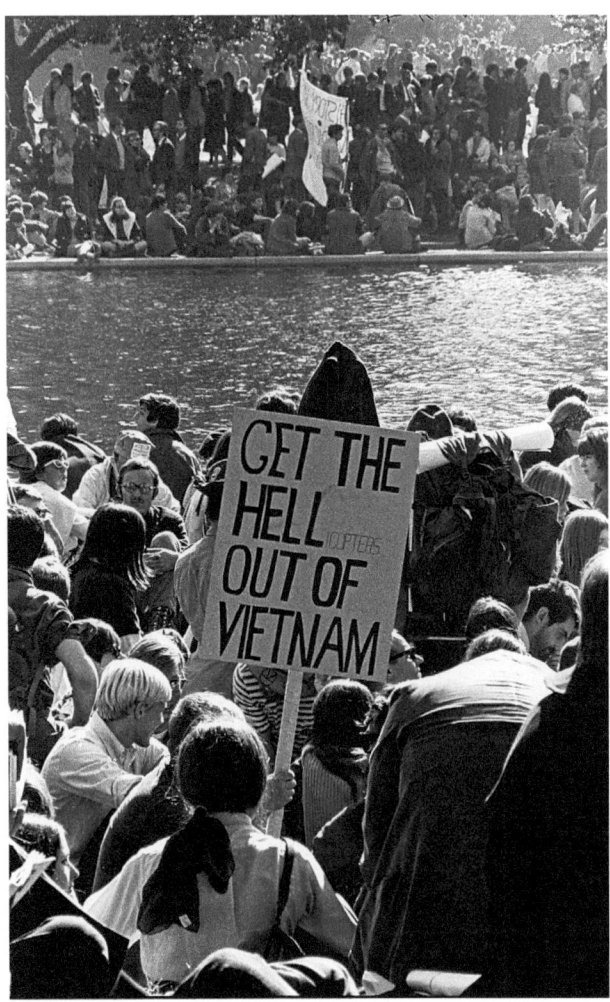

FIGURE 12.1
Vietnam War protesters, 1967
Source: Frank Wolfe. Lyndon B. Johnson Library.

frustration percolated in Black neighborhoods in cities. Growing despair and desperate economic conditions led to a bloody rebellion in the Watts neighborhood of Los Angeles in 1965, and violence erupted in many other cities after the assassination of King in 1968. The civil rights movement moved the country toward equality for all, achieved to some extent in the Civil Rights Acts of 1964 and 1968 and the Voting Rights Act of 1965. The sense in the 1950s and 1960s that the rights of African Americans were at last being legally recognized led to the development of an optimistic new genre of popular music: soul music, one of the predecessors of today's contemporary R&B.

When the large numbers of babies born right after WWII entered adolescence in the 1950s and 1960s, they developed a sense of themselves as a separate group within society, a group with a new label: teenagers. Their aggressive pursuit of their own values in music, clothing, and behavior led to a "generation gap" between them and their parents and contributed to the sense of tension and anxiety during this period. When in 1964 young men began to be conscripted in large numbers to fight in Vietnam, this group of young adults erupted into opposition to the war. Some took their anti-war arguments into the streets in massive public demonstrations, while others, called hippies, expressed their disgust with a mainstream flowing in the wrong direction by "tuning in [to music and alternative religions], turning on [to sex and drugs], and dropping out [of mainstream culture and society]." In addition to their opposition to the Vietnam War in the 1960s, a feeling of solidarity among many white youth with the civil rights movement fueled their alienation from the mainstream, and many joined African Americans in peace marches and freedom rides. The taste in music of whites in this new generation, including a love of African American musical styles, coupled with their opposition to the Vietnam War, drove a dramatic change in white popular music taste away from the swing-era music of their parents and towards rock and roll and rock from the mid-1950s to the mid-1970s.

The restiveness of white youth and African Americans inspired other liberation movements in the United States, including the women's liberation movement, the Chicano Movement, gay and LGBT rights movements, and the American Indian Movement. Each one affected music making by members of those communities. The notion of a liberation movement was taken from anti-imperialist liberation movements around the world and especially in Africa, where virtually the entire continent threw off colonial rule during this period. The gateways that follow examine major developments in popular music, jazz, European-derived classical music, and salsa. All these styles responded in one way or another to the turmoil of this period.

Two of the most important genres of American popular music today, rock and contemporary R&B, can trace their roots to the period from 1950 to 1975, a period of enormous upheaval in American society. On the other hand, much, though by no means all, of what contemporary composers in the European classical music tradition are doing today can be explained as a response to the sensibilities of this period. In jazz, new experimental and so-called free styles of composition and improvisation developed alongside explorations of how jazz could be fused with a number of popular music genres. And Puerto Ricans in New York contributed a new genre, salsa, to music scenes in the United States and elsewhere.

GATEWAY 46
RHYTHM & BLUES AND SOUL

What Is It?

Rhythm & blues developed in American cities during World War II (1939–1945) as a new form of African American dance music. The term "rhythm & blues" has come to reference a plethora of African American musical styles that distinguish it from earlier race records and from the blues. Some of the distinctive musical elements of rhythm & blues when it first emerged include a strong **backbeat** (accents on beats 2 and 4); flashy showmanship and choreography by performers; bands consisting of piano, electric guitar, bass, drums, and saxophone; and themes of love, suffering, and triumph. Soul music first emerged in the 1950s as a type of rhythm & blues. It also draws on musical elements from Black gospel music (especially vocals), blues, and jazz. Linked to the civil rights movement and the Black Power movement, its lyrics include social commentary in addition to songs about love and personal relationships.

Aretha Franklin's (1942–2018) original recording of "(You Make Me Feel Like) A Natural Woman" (1967) is our gateway to rhythm & blues and soul. Franklin, known as the "Queen of Soul," is considered both a soul and a rhythm & blues artist. "A Natural Woman," a signature song in her storied career, was written for Franklin by songwriting duo Carole King (b. 1942) and Gerry Goffin (1939–2014). Franklin's powerful vocal performance of the song has defined it as an anthem of self-love and empowerment for women.

 Listen to the first thirty seconds of the recording.

How Does It Work?

Timbre

The recording is dominated by Franklin's vocal timbre, which ranges from breathy, slightly scratchy, and relaxed to powerfully full and clear. Timbres also include background vocalists with similar timbres, piano, drums, electric bass, and orchestral strings and brass.

Texture

The texture consists mainly of vocal lines accompanied by a rhythm section, along with a vocal ensemble and additional instruments.

Rhythm

The meter is a steady duple meter with each of the two beats divided into threes in a swing feel. The snare drum consistently plays on the second of the meter's two beats, which, like the second and fourth beats of a meter of four, is considered the backbeat, a common dance-oriented rhythmic practice in rhythm & blues.

Melody

The melody in the vocal is mostly in a major mode, with considerable microtonality. The chorus melody is almost exclusively in a pentatonic mode with occasional inclusion of blue notes, and the bridge melody briefly hints at a minor mode.

Harmony

Harmonies typical of gospel music occur throughout the recording. These include frequent movements between the IV chord and the I chord in the chorus, and harmonies that follow a bass line that descends by steps.

FIGURE 12.2
Aretha Franklin performing at Madison Square Garden in 1968
Source: Getty Images/Jack Robinson.

Form

"(You Make Me Feel Like) A Natural Woman" takes a form common in pop music: verse, pre-chorus, chorus, verse, pre-chorus, chorus, bridge, repeating chorus. A **bridge** is a section common in popular music that usually occurs only once. Most bridges introduce new melodies, harmonies, and lyrics (and sometimes timbres and textures) that contrast with earlier material and form a bridge between two sections, often two repetitions of the chorus towards the end of a recording. The bridge in "Natural Woman" introduces new melodic and harmonic material, before a return to the repeating chorus.

Performance Techniques

Aretha Franklin's striking vocal techniques include a wide pitch range and an approach to rhythm that varies between strictly following the pulse and anticipating or delaying phrases in relation to the pulse. She demonstrates extraordinary control over her voice, a virtuosity that is highly valued in soul music.

Listen for these features in the first minute of the recording.

Listen to the entire recording while following this timed listening guide.

LISTENING GUIDE 12.1

TIME	SECTION	DESCRIPTION	LYRICS
0:00	Verse 1	After a brief piano introduction on some gospel harmony, the lead vocal enters with a relaxed, slightly raspy timbre, delaying some of the rhythms after the beat. The group of women background vocalists respond to the "call" of the first three lead vocal phrases by singing a strongly accented "ah-oo" in harmony with one another. All singers and instrumentalists perform in a swing feel in the meter of 6 beats, and the backbeat (beat 4) is played by the snare drum throughout the verse. Halfway through the verse, a string section enters playing staccato on each beat, and brass enters playing sustained pitches.	Lookin' out . . .
0:28	Pre-chorus 1	The rhythm of the lead vocal becomes more accented, and the strings replace the background vocalists in the response role, abandoning the swing feel to play quicker, evenly subdivided pitches.	Before the day I met you . . .
0:39	Chorus	The lead vocal begins on its highest pitch so far, with a clear timbre that continues through the chorus. Franklin is joined by the background vocalists, who sing in harmony with the lead. The brass takes on the response role in the call and response with a descending line, while the strings ascend to their highest pitches of the song so far, playing long, sustained pitches. The final phrase of the chorus, the first statement of "feel like a natural woman," features a sudden homophonic texture. The vocalists and the bass perform in harmony on a descending line with no other accompaniment. After the descending phrase, the background vocalists sing again, an emphatic, bluesy unison response on the word "woman."	You make me feel . . .
0:54	Verse 2	The second verse is similar to the first, though it features a more rhythmically energetic lead vocal. This time there are no responses from the background vocalists, and the piano responds to the lead vocal's phrases.	When my soul . . .
1:20	Pre-chorus 2	The second pre-chorus is like the first with different lyrics, and slightly more active playing in the drum set leading into the chorus.	Now I'm no longer doubtful . . .
1:31	Chorus	Franklin sings the first few words alone before the background singers join her in harmony.	You make me feel . . .
1:45	Bridge	The strings continue playing sustained pitches in the same range as the chorus. More minor harmonies are featured, and the lead vocal melody and the responses from the background vocalists follow this harmony on lines featuring blue notes like a lowered 7th and a lowered 3rd.	Oh, baby . . .

TIME	SECTION	DESCRIPTION	LYRICS
2:09	Chorus	At the end of this chorus, the "woman" response in the background vocals is at a higher pitch, with more accent and emphasis.	You make me feel . . .
2:22	Chorus	For the first two "you make me feel" phrases, Franklin slightly delays the start of the melody, making the rhythm more syncopated, but singing "feel" squarely on the downbeat.	You make me feel . . .
2:36	Fade out	The lead vocal reaches its highest pitch on the first "you," and the chorus repeats as the overall volume of the recording fades.	You make me feel . . .
2:46	End		

What Does It Mean?

"(You Make Me Feel Like) A Natural Woman" is generally interpreted as a song of empowerment for women, in part because of Aretha Franklin's powerful and expressive vocal performance of the song. Like many love songs, the song's lyrics speak about two individuals, "You" and "I." "I" conveys her thoughts, her emotions, and a sense that her past was a time of struggle or suffering. When she sings about being tired and uninspired, her vocal timbre is relaxed, breathy, and slightly hoarse, qualities that listeners may hear as an icon of fatigue. The song doesn't say much about the anonymous "You" making "I" feel good. Centering the song on the woman protagonist allows listeners to interpret the song freely, inserting the kind of person for "You" that makes the song meaningful to them. "You," in the song, plays a supporting role to "I," who overcame her suffering to achieve a new positive emotional state. The protagonist has "peace of mind," feels "good inside," has confidence about life in general, and feels "so alive" and so "natural" in her body. Though Aretha Franklin did not write "(You Make Me Feel Like) A Natural Woman," her vocal performance of the song connects it to her persona. When she sings it, she seems to be expressing something about herself.

When the chorus enters with the celebratory words "You make me feel . . .," Franklin's vocal timbre shifts from the relaxed, breathy sound of the verse to an energetic, clear timbre iconic of her more positive frame of mind. She sings in a higher part of her vocal register, with a highly resonant sound. Singing these high pitches with such power and clarity is physically difficult for any person. It requires significant air flow supported by the full body. Listening to Franklin produces not only a sense of awe at her vocal skills, but also an understanding of the powerful energy she uses to sing each chorus and to express the exultant and grateful state of mind and body at the heart of the song. Listeners to Franklin's timbre can remember, or imagine, in their own lives the intense experience of celebration and triumph that she expresses and what it might feel like to be the powerful person singing the song.

The word "woman" at the end of each chorus declares the newfound true self. Franklin sings the first pitch of "woman" squarely on the first beat of the measure, which suggests that this new confidence in the self is grounded and will last. She also sings this pitch as a blue note, slightly lower than the third scale degree of the major tonality of the song, with a microtonal slide on both pitches of "woman" to load the word with expression. These techniques echo the way Bessie Smith and other women blues singers used pitch as a way to communicate emotion and meaning (Chapter 9, Gateway 33). In the third and fourth choruses, the background vocalists' sing "woman" at an even higher pitch, increasing the intensity with which the song celebrates women who are connected to their true selves.

In addition to Franklin's vocals, the recording borrows from Black gospel music the slightly swung style of piano playing and the song's harmonies, especially the frequent I-IV-I plagal or "amen," cadences, common in church music traditions since the Renaissance. Other musical elements such as the use of blue notes and the pervasive use of call and response connect the recording to many genres of African American music. Call and response is a feature of the blues, of Black gospel music, and of the relation between a preacher and a congregation in the Black church. The practice of preaching in many African American churches often flows seamlessly

EMOTIONAL RESONANCE

CULTURAL LINKAGES

between speaking and singing. Preachers bridge talking and singing by speaking melodically with accented rhythms and by singing in a conversational manner. As preachers preach, congregations respond by speaking, shouting, singing, and applauding. Sometimes an organist or a band joins in, and everyone may join together to sing a particular song in an improvisatory call-and-response manner. Dancing and body movements are also often part of this communal church experience, a collective building of energy through preaching, singing, musical performance, and movement. Live recordings of Aretha Franklin showcase the dynamic relationship between performer and audience in soul music, akin to the relationship between preacher and congregation. Studio recordings, like this one, lack that interaction, but the call and response between the lead vocal and the rest of the musicians provide listeners with a hint of the dynamics of live performances.

In the context of the civil rights movement of the 1960s, Aretha Franklin, in this song and many others, was celebrating what it means to be Black in a context where African Americans were experiencing discrimination of all kinds. Mainstream standards of beauty tended to valorize traits associated with white women. Part of the meaning of this song is about being a Black woman who triumphantly overcomes the trials of life to proudly proclaim her confidence in herself. Her (and other performers of soul music) borrowing of so many musical elements from Black gospel music infuses secular texts with something like the religious fervor and positive feeling created in a Black church service (though the commercializing and secularizing of gospel performance style was considered controversial in some religious communities). Whereas the blues of previous decades told sad stories of failed relationships, poverty, misfortune, and a dismal, inescapable fate, soul music borrows the church's celebratory belief in a better life in the future, "in the sweet by and by, [where] we will meet on that beautiful shore," as an old hymn has it. Soul music, in contrast to the blues, proclaims a new hope for a better life in the present and the future. Franklin's performance in this song is an iconic expression of that religious optimism and enthusiasm reframed as an expression of individual personal growth.

FIGURE 12.3
Aretha Franklin performing in 1970
Source: Getty Images/Jan Persson.

What Is Its History?

Beginning in about 1940, an estimated five million African Americans joined a Second Great Migration. In contrast to those who had moved from rural areas of the South to cities mostly in the North and Midwest in the First Great Migration during and after World War I, they moved from urban areas of the South to the urban North, Midwest, and West, bringing their skills to factories producing military equipment during World War II and other products afterwards. Seeking better economic opportunities and life away from the Jim Crow laws of the South, they encountered racial oppression after they migrated as well, in such forms as discriminatory housing practices and segregation. In the segregated communities of Los Angeles, New York, Cincinnati, Detroit, and Chicago, musicians who had migrated from the South developed new styles of dance music combining jazz, blues, and gospel. During the 1940s this new kind of dance music, which often featured a lead electric guitar, was labeled "rhythm & blues."

Soul music has its roots in a new style of Black gospel music that gained popularity in the 1930s. Blues pianist Thomas A. Dorsey (1899–1993), who had served as music director for blues singer Ma Rainey in the 1920s, began to infuse gospel songs with musical elements borrowed from the blues. Dorsey's collaborator Mahalia Jackson and other gospel singers developed a style influenced by recordings of Bessie Smith and other blues singers. Beginning in the late 1930s vocalist and guitarist Sister Rosetta Tharpe (1915–1973) became one of the first commercially successful gospel artists. Her innovative guitar playing, including the use of a distorted timbre on electric guitar, pioneered techniques that later shaped rock and roll (Chapter 12, Gateway 47). She was one of the first to perform gospel in secular venues like Harlem's Cotton Club and on tours around the country. In the 1940s, a form of gospel often performed by gospel quartets (groups of four or more vocalists singing in four-part harmony) also became popular in live performances, recordings, and radio broadcasts. Gospel quartets trace their roots to "jubilee quartets" associated with university groups like the Fisk Jubilee singers (Chapter 8, Gateway 30); minstrel show quartets, themselves inspired by jubilee quartets; and barbershop quartets. Rhythm & blues dance music embraced elements of this new style of gospel music. For example, rhythm & blues a cap-pella vocal harmony groups called "doo-wop" groups (named after the vocables these groups added to songs to make them more rhythmic) became popular among both Black and white audiences. Black rhythm & blues musicians in the 1950s began rewriting the lyrics to blues-style gospel songs as love songs, the beginnings of what became soul. In 1954, the blues and jazz pianist Ray Charles (1930–2004) recorded a rhythm & blues version of a recording from earlier that year called "It Must Be Jesus" by a Black gospel quartet called The Southern Tones. Charles's song "I Got a Woman (That's Good to Me)" changed the lyrics and was a hit, setting the tone for future secular borrowings of the spirit and the style of Black gospel music.

In 1959 Berry Gordy (b. 1929) founded Motown Records, named for his hometown Detroit ("Motor Town") and grounded in the dance beats of rhythm & blues. In a move that mimicked to some extent the assembly-line approach to car-making in Detroit, Motown employed resident singers, songwriters, producers, and musicians, many of them in their teens and twenties, to churn out hit after hit for the baby boomers of the

FIGURE 12.4
Sister Rosetta Tharpe posing with a guitar in 1938
Source: James J. Kriegsmann/Blz, Wikimedia Commons.

> **ECONOMIC ACTIVITY**

1960s. The accompanying studio musicians, known collectively as the "Funk Brothers," played a significant role in establishing the sound of Motown including, for example, walking bass lines similar to bebop's chromatic style. The renowned Funk Brothers bass player James Jamerson (1936–1983) can be heard performing in this style on dozens of Motown hits such as Marvin Gaye and Tammi Terrell's "Ain't No Mountain High Enough" (1967), Gladys Knight & the Pips' version of "I Heard It through the Grapevine" (1967), and Martha and the Vandellas' "(Love Is Like a) Heatwave" (1963). With songs geared towards young people with themes of romance and relationships, along with captivating dance beats, 1960s and 1970s Motown artists like Diana Ross & the Supremes, the Temptations, the Jackson 5, and Lionel Richie attracted enor-mous audiences across barriers of race, class, and geography. Motown's marketing, promotion, and management practices worked hard to cross these boundaries by developing and controlling the public images of its artists and promoting their records and performances widely in demo-graphics beyond African American communities.

Near the end of the 1960s, soul was established as a named music genre. The word "soul" in music was initially used in the 1950s to describe a feeling in the music of African American jazz musicians. By the early 1960s, hard bop musicians such as pianist Horace Silver, drummer Max Roach, and organist Jimmy Smith had embraced the term "soul-jazz" as a signifier that their styles of jazz had a "soulful" feeling (Chapter 12, Gateway 48). A gospel-flavored blues feeling with a swing feel, the "soul" style of soul-jazz often included the distinctive sound of the Ham-mond B-3 organ popular in Black churches since the 1930s. The Hammond B-3 has the ability to change its timbre quickly when players move sliding drawbars to increase or decrease the vol-ume of different components of the sound. Brighter timbres can cut through the sound of a large congregation singer, and more mellow timbres can provide a sense of reflective calm. In a 1961

> **CULTURAL LINKAGES**

article in *Ebony* magazine about soul in jazz, the author Lerone Bennett Jr. describes soul this way: "There is in the music a new note of racial pride, a celebration of ties to Africa and a defiant embrace of . . . all that middle-class America condemns." Bennett foreshadowed meanings of the word "soul" that the Black Power movement would embrace and extend during the mid-1960s. "Soul" emphasized Black pride, self-determination, and economic empowerment. The word became a way for African Americans to signify blackness and cultural self-determination in areas such as fashion, hairstyles, cooking (soul food), slang, special recognition handshake greetings, and terms of belonging such as "soul brother" and "soul sister." By the end of the 1960s, it was well-established that anything with the label "soul" was connected to pride in African American culture and identity and a desire for equality and justice for African Americans.

FIGURE 12.5
A Hammond B-3 organ
Source: Cliff, Wikimedia Commons.

Some of the pioneers of 1960s soul music and of its links to the civil rights movement had performed in gospel quartets. Sam Cooke (1931–1964) was the lead vocalist for a gospel quartet called the Soul Stirrers (1950–1956) before releasing his first rhythm & blues hit "You Send Me" (1957) and later the civil rights anthem "A Change Is Gonna Come" in 1964, the year of his death. James Brown (1933–2006), the "Godfather of Soul," sang in gospel quartets, and his intense preacher-influenced vocals can be heard on his first hit with the Famous Flames, "Please, Please, Please" (1956). Along with his vocal aesthetic, punctuated by improvisatory shouts, hollers, and "grunts," Brown brought other elements of Black gospel to his live performances, including engaging with the audience and building intense energy through dance. Brown is also known for layering his music with dense, polyrhythmic textures. This polyrhythmic style, featuring his percussive vocal interjections, can be heard on recordings like "Papa's Got a Brand New Bag" (1965) and "I Got You (I Feel Good)" (1965). His complex, multi-layered syncopation and grooves with driving, percussive bass lines, and guitar riffs with percussive effects defined the style of a new genre called **funk** music. He became known as "Soul Brother No. 1" because of his unabashed promotion of Black pride, which can be heard in songs such as "Say It Loud—I'm Black and I'm Proud" (1968) and "Get Up, Get into It, and Get Involved" (1970).

Aretha Franklin, the Queen of Soul, also became a civil rights icon because of her commitment to equality, and a number of her songs entered the soundtrack of the movement. She grew up singing gospel and playing piano in the Detroit church of her father, the Reverend C. L. Franklin, famous nationally for his recordings of stirring sermons. She was inspired by Sister Rosetta Tharpe and by gospel singer Mahalia Jackson, and was lifelong friends with gospel-soul singer Mavis Staples (b. 1939), who, with her family group the Staples Singers, also championed the civil rights movement. Franklin's gospel vocal and piano styles can be heard on her version of Otis Redding's 1965 recording "Respect" (1967). Her vocals and her arranging skills, her use of blues and gospel inflections, and the addition of the famous "R-E-S-P-E-C-T" section transformed the song into a civil rights anthem as Black Americans demanded the respect denied them through centuries of injustice, discrimination, and violence. The feminist movement of the 1970s also took up the song, which contributed a musical dimension to the movement's advocacy of equal rights for women. Franklin

FIGURE 12.6
James Brown performing in 1964
Source: Michael Ochs Archives/Getty Images.

later reflected on her own personal experience with Black pride, what she calls "the black revolution," gesturing towards the themes of "(You Make Me Feel Like) A Natural Woman":

> Well I believe that the black revolution certainly forced me and the majority of black people to begin taking a second look at ourselves. It wasn't that we were all that ashamed of ourselves, we merely started appreciating our natural selves, . . . you know, falling in love with ourselves just as we are. We found that we had far more to be proud of.

Other songs by Franklin connected to social activism include "Think" (1968), with its memorable repetition of the word "freedom," and "Black, Gifted, and Proud" (1971), a heavily gospel-influenced **cover** (a new version of an existing song) of Nina Simone's original 1970 song, featuring Franklin's piano playing. Simone (1933–2003) was a singer, pianist, and composer whose work spanned jazz, soul, rhythm & blues, and classical music. She was called the High Priestess of Soul, and she is well known for her activism and for her numerous songs demanding social change, including "Why? (The King of Love Is Dead)" (1968), which deals with the murder of Dr. Martin Luther King Jr.

By the late 1960s, the concept of "soul" had become increasingly common in discourse about African American music and the civil rights movement, and evident in album titles such as *Dictionary of Soul* (1966) by Otis Redding, and song titles such as "Soul Man" (1967) by Sam and Dave (written by Isaac Hayes and David Porter) and "Sweet Soul Music" (1967) by Arthur Conley. From the 1960s into the 1970s artists like Curtis Mayfield, Chaka Khan, Donny Hathaway, Patti LaBelle, Gladys Knight, Marvin Gaye, Tina Turner, and Stevie Wonder sang songs about love, despair, social change, and hope. Though the sound of 1960s soul declined in popularity towards the end of the 1970s, these and other soul artists of this era have continued to provide inspiration for musicians and audiences in the decades since then.

In the 1980s rap and hip-hop became the preeminent genres for challenging the structures of racial oppression. The "soul" category on the *Billboard* charts was replaced with the category "Black Music," before "R&B" replaced it in 1990 as a separate category from rap and hip-hop. In the 1980s, Black artists such as Prince, Whitney Houston, and Michael Jackson built on rhythm & blues, gospel, soul, and funk styles in their music. These artists' presence in mainstream media on MTV and in films also helped them cross over into pop music and gain enormous popularity, record sales, and global audiences. Vocal harmony groups like Boyz II Men, En Vogue, and SWV became massively popular in the 1990s. Some musicians began to be marketed as "neo-soul" artists, notably D'Angelo for his 1995 album *Brown Sugar* and Erykah Badu, beginning with her album *Baduizm* (1997). Many R&B artists since the 1990s, instead of turning primarily to the blues and gospel like their rhythm & blues predecessors, have incorporated the increasingly popular sounds of hip-hop into their music. Artists like Mariah Carey, Usher, Aaliyah, Beyoncé, Rihanna, Alicia Keys, Mary J. Blige, Janelle Monáe, Toni Braxton, John Legend, Jill Scott, SZA, Frank Ocean, and H.E.R. have all been celebrated for their originality, for the powerful themes of their music, and for the combinations of Black styles in which their music is grounded. Meanwhile,

FIGURE 12.7
Nina Simone in 1966
Source: Getty Images/David Redfern.

FIGURE 12.8
Aretha Franklin and her backup singers performing at the Kennedy Center Honors, 2015
Source: CBS Photo Archive/Contributor, Getty Images.

the Black gospel tradition promoted by Thomas Dorsey, Mahalia Jackson, and others has been carried forward by artists such as James Cleveland, Edwin Hawkins, Andraé Crouch, Yolanda Adams, the Winans family, and Kirk Franklin, and it continues to cross over with secular genres including hip-hop and contemporary R&B.

As for Aretha Franklin, her career didn't stop when soul declined in popularity. She continued to perform for adoring audiences until her death from pancreatic cancer in 2018. Her return-to-gospel live recording *Amazing Grace* (1972) was the best-selling album of her career. After her passing, the video of her live 2015 performance of "(You Make Me Feel Like) A Natural Woman" at the Kennedy Center Honors, a tribute to songwriter Carole King, went viral. Perhaps fittingly for an artist with such a long career, those remembering Franklin's life were drawn to a performance by her as a 73-year-old. Decades after she first recorded the song, she still compelled her audiences to celebrate the power of womanhood and to appreciate their true, natural selves.

WHERE DO I GO FROM HERE?

- Find the YouTube video of Aretha Franklin performing "(You Make Me Feel Like) A Natural Woman" at the Kennedy Center Honors in 2015. Make a list of the elements of gospel music you observe in the musical style and in the overall performance practice.

- Compare Aretha Franklin's recording of "Respect" to the original recording by Otis Redding, who wrote the song. Describe the differences in her approach to melody, lyrics, form, and vocal performance. How does her re-interpretation of the song make it "her" song, a woman's, rather than a man's, song?

- View the documentary *Summer of Soul* (2021), directed by Questlove, about the 1969 Harlem Cultural Festival. Choose three artists mentioned in this gateway and analyze their performances, focusing on their interactions with the audience.

GATEWAY 47
ROCK

What Is It?

Rock music first emerged as **rock and roll** in the 1950s, when musicians like Chuck Berry (1926–2017), Elvis Presley (1935–1977), and others brought together musical elements from genres marketed to white audiences like country with those from genres marketed to Black audiences like rhythm & blues. In the early 1960s, early rock and roll declined in popularity, and Black vocal music became popular among young audiences from labels like Motown and girl groups such as the Shirelles, the Ronettes, and Martha and the Vandellas. British bands playing rock and roll like the Beatles and the Rolling Stones took the United States by storm in the mid-1960s as part of the so-called British Invasion. In the second half of the 1960s rock audiences participated in social movements that advocated for peace in the midst of the Vietnam War and stood in solidarity with the civil rights movement and desires for racial justice in the United States. Since then, rock has spawned many subgenres that are today enjoyed by people of virtually all ages around the world.

One of the key figures in the history of rock is the guitarist, vocalist, and songwriter Jimi Hendrix (1942–1970). Hendrix came to prominence in the late 1960s and pioneered innovative technologies and new techniques and sounds for the guitar that still inspire guitarists everywhere. His group, the Jimi Hendrix Experience, released three successful albums in the 1960s and, along with Hendrix, included Mitch Mitchell (1948–2008) on drums and Noel Redding (1945–2003) on electric bass. Their 1968 recording of Bob Dylan's (b. 1941) song "All along the Watchtower" from the album *Electric Ladyland* is our gateway to rock.

🔊 Listen to the first thirty seconds of the recording.

How Does It Work?

Timbre

One of the most fascinating aspects of this and other Hendrix performances is his experimentation with the timbre of the guitar. In the course of the recording there are many effects added to the guitar, which make its timbre gritty and rough at some points, smooth and clear at others, and nasal and cutting at others.

Texture

Throughout the recording the texture is a combination of drums and percussion, electric bass, and several layers of guitars, all of which support Hendrix's voice and his electric guitar.

Rhythm

The underlying rhythm is a typical rock beat. On beat one of nearly every measure, the drummer plays the bass drum, in many cases preceded by a "kick" on the second half of beat four. The bass drum also plays a variety of syncopated rhythms underlying the beat throughout the recording. The drummer plays strong accents on beats two and four (the backbeat) on the snare drum and other percussion, and driving pulses on other parts of the drum set and sometimes on the bass drum.

Melody

The melodies of the vocal lines and the guitar solos are largely based on pentatonic modes, which include the ♭3 and ♭7 as blue notes.

FIGURE 12.9

The Jimi Hendrix Experience. From left to right: Mitch Mitchell, Jimi Hendrix, and Noel Redding.
Source: Pictorial Press Ltd/Alamy Stock Photo.

Harmony

The harmony mostly repeats a cycle of four chords. It begins on a minor chord as the tonic, walks down a step to a major chord, down another step to another major chord, and up a step to the previous major chord. The cycle repeats following these chords, though sometimes, at the end of an eight-bar phrase, the last chord is replaced with a minor chord on the fourth scale degree.

Form

The form of this song is strophic, with six eight-bar verses sung in pairs by Hendrix. The verses alternate with instrumental phrases featuring guitar solos whose duration ranges from one to four eight-bar strophes.

Performance Techniques

Beyond his explorations of new timbres, Hendrix uses many innovative recording technologies in this recording, especially the ability to separate and "move" sounds between the left and right channels. Especially when listening with headphones, the guitar at times seems to move between the left and right ears.

Listen for these elements in the first thirty seconds of the recording.

Listen to the entire performance following this timed listening guide.

TIME	SECTION	DESCRIPTION	LYRICS
0:00	Introduction	The introduction begins with the rhythmic pattern that accents the second half of beat three and beat four. The first eight bars introduce a groove based on this pattern in the acoustic rhythm guitar, bass, and drums. The next eight bars feature Hendrix playing a solo on lead guitar.	
0:17	Verse 1	The drums become much less active, and Hendrix's lead vocal replaces the lead guitar, which begins to respond to his blues-inflected vocal in a call-and-response manner. This call and response continues through each verse.	There must be . . .
0:35	Verse 2	Hendrix's blues-like vocal continues in a slightly higher register.	Businessmen they drink . . .
0:52	Guitar solo	After a drum fill on the toms, the drums become much louder and more active, supporting an eight-bar lead guitar solo that includes many blues references including some microtonal bent pitches.	
1:09	Verse 3	Hendrix's vocal continues for verses 3 and 4 in a similar manner to verses 1 and 2.	No reason . . .
1:26	Verse 4	At times Hendrix's vocal blurs the line between singing and speaking, such as on the lyrics "talkin' falsely now."	But you and I . . .
1:43	Guitar solo	After Hendrix shouts "Hey," a lead guitar solo begins, starting out with similar characteristics to the previous solo.	
1:58		After eight bars, the texture thins as the drums become less active, and the guitar solo continues with a quite different timbre. The guitar plays sustained pitches and long slides like those typically heard on steel guitar, with effects such as reverb.	
2:15		After another eight bars, Hendrix shouts "Hey" again, and the volume increases with more active drums, bass, and rhythm guitars. The lead guitar solo shifts to a more cutting timbre. Hendrix is using a **wah-wah pedal**, which allows him to adjust the timbre of the guitar with a foot pedal as he is playing. Waves of sharper, more nasal timbres are heard as he solos here.	
2:32		For the final eight bars of this solo, the lead guitar playing continues without the wah-wah effect and a more rhythmic approach. The solo ends with an ascending pentatonic scale that seems to be aiming for the tonic in a high register, but the solo ends before the guitar reaches that climax.	
2:49	Verse 5	Hendrix sings "All along the watchtower" in a high register, launching verses 5 and 6, which continue the texture and sensibilities of the first four verses.	All along the watchtower . . .
3:06	Verse 6	The snare drum plays a constant pulse on all four beats at many points during these verses.	Outside in the cold . . .
3:23	Guitar solo	After a final shout of "Hey" from Hendrix, this guitar solo starts with three long pitches, the first and third on the tonic, and the second one step higher. It ends with the same ascending pentatonic scale as the previous solo.	
3:39		The pentatonic lead up, this time, reaches the tonic in the high register for the climactic moment of the recording. Hendrix holds this pitch for the remainder of the recording by repeating it over and over, mostly playing a constant stream of quickly moving notes. The pitch is also sustained by effects like reverb. In the course of these last eight or nine bars, the high sustained guitar sound shifts between the left and right channels, sometimes sounding as if it is traveling back and forth between the two. After eight bars, the overall volume begins to fade out, providing the illusion that the band continues to play as their sound gradually disappears.	
3:58	End		

What Does It Mean?

The musical elements of "All along the Watchtower" reveal much about both Jimi Hendrix and about rock in general. One of the striking elements of this recording is that guitar solos take up more than half of the time of the recording, making the lead guitar at least as important as the vocal and its lyrics. The changes in timbre, range, texture, and dynamics among the eight-bar guitar solo sections shape the overall progression of the song to a much greater extent than the lyrics do. In a sense, the verses of this song form a framework for showcasing Hendrix's guitar playing and his innovations in the sound of the guitar.

Hendrix is well known for his groundbreaking use of technology for the electric guitar, particularly his use of a pedal known as a wah-wah pedal. The **wah-wah pedal** manipulates the timbre of the guitar to sound like a human voice pronouncing the words "wah-wah." The wah-wah pedal is connected by a cable to both the electric guitar and the amplifier (sometimes in combination with other pedals), and takes the electronic signal from the electric guitar, modifies it, and

FIGURE 12.10

A wah-wah pedal (right) connected to a number of other guitar effects pedals
Source: Dave Wilson.

sends that modified sound to the amplifier. Some pedals have only on-off switches or knobs that can be turned to adjust various effects. The wah-wah pedal, however, has a foot pedal that rocks forwards and backwards. As the pedal is depressed, higher frequencies in the tone are emphasized and the "wah" sound is produced as a result. The wah-wah pedal can be heard clearly at 2:15 during the third eight-bar section of Hendrix's longest guitar solo on this recording. The first wah-wah pedal was invented in 1966 just two years before this recording. Though Hendrix was not the first to use this particular pedal, he made the sound of the wah-wah pedal famous through his use of it here and in other examples, such as the opening of "Voodoo Child (Slight Return)" (1968) from *Electric Ladyland*. This kind of manipulation of timbre is reminiscent of the ways brass players use plunger mutes to produce a similar wah-wah effect, as in Duke Ellington's "Black and Tan Fantasy" (Chapter 10, Gateway 39). The wah-wah pedal and other timbral effects developed by Hendrix connect him to the legacy of African and African American experiments with timbre and added effects (such as the buzzing sound of the Shona *mbira* in Chapter 3, Gateway 9).

> AESTHETICS

> TECHNOLOGY

🔊)) Listen to Hendrix's lengthy solo on "All along the Watchtower" between 1:43 and 2:49 again, and pay attention to the use of the wah-wah pedal that begins at 2:15.

Hendrix's guitar playing and vocals are closely linked to the blues. He knew the recordings of blues guitarist and singer Robert Johnson (Chapter 9, Gateway 33), and call and response reminiscent of Johnson can be heard between his vocal phrases and his lead guitar lines, even though "All along the Watchtower" is a strophic song and not in a blues form. In addition to Johnson's acoustic guitar playing, Hendrix also knew the music of electric blues players Elmore James (1918–1963), T-Bone Walker (1910–1975), and others he heard in his early years. This wide range of blues influences can be heard as Hendrix performs the vocal and guitar melodies with a great deal of microtonality, a lot of sliding between pitches, and an emphasis on the blues scale. The vocal sensibilities of blues singers have influenced singers and instrumentalists in countless popular music genres, and Hendrix's vocals and guitar melodies on this recording and many others are particularly clear examples of how his music—and rock and roll and rock in general—is grounded in the blues.

> CULTURAL
> LINKAGES

Echoing Bessie Smith's "Backwater Blues," "All along the Watchtower" expresses frustration with the status quo and suggests an upending of established hierarchies in society. In the first four of the song's six verses, Bob Dylan's enigmatic lyrics describe a conversation between a joker and a thief. In verses 1 and 2 the joker is looking for a "way out of here"—"here" a world

> POLITICS

where businessmen benefit from the hard work of others. There seems to be confusion about values and priorities in the broader society. The thief replies in verses 3 and 4 that the value of human life is clear to them both (life is not a joke), and that the hour is late, implying a sense of drama and urgency. Hendrix's long guitar solo builds on this sense of drama until the final verses describe the watchtower of a castle, a symbol of the seat of power, about to be stormed by the thief and the joker amidst a howling wind and the sound of a growling wildcat.

The final section unleashes a final growling, howling guitar solo that reaches the highest pitch of the recording on guitar, sustained for more than a full eight-bar section and moving back and forth from the left channel to the right. Hendrix expresses the subversive meaning of the lyrics in his manipulation of melodic range, timbre, dynamics, and technology, making it clear that he and his listeners are aligned with the thief and the joker against the establishment. Hendrix's guitar solos amplified, literally, the countercultural themes of Dylan's lyrics, aimed at an audience loosely defined by opposition to U.S. involvement in the war in Vietnam and support of the civil rights movement, sexual freedom, communal living, psychedelic drugs, and hope for peace and justice. Hendrix, Dylan, and their audiences are imagining a world where the current power structures are broken down, their music a metaphor of social change. Rock music in the 1960s is closely related with these kinds of desires for social change, though its history and its roots in the rock and roll of the 1950s helps explain its cultural importance even more clearly.

 Listen one more time to "All along the Watchtower" from beginning to end, this time focusing on the various guitar solo sections. Notice the changes in each section, the musical elements that Hendrix uses to build and/or restrain intensity throughout the recording, and other ways his guitar playing and voice express the meaning of the song's lyrics.

What Is Its History?

CULTURAL
LINKAGES

The history of "All along the Watchtower," and of rock music in general, is rooted in the emergence of rock and roll as a genre in the mid-1950s. At that time, radio play and record sales fueled the popularity of country and western music primarily for white audiences and rhythm & blues for Black audiences. Big Mama Thornton (1926–1984), Muddy Waters, and Ruth Brown (1928–2006) were among the best-selling rhythm & blues artists in the early 1950s. With their showmanship, emphasis on the backbeat, and instrumentation of piano, electric guitar, bass, drums, and saxophone, their recordings and performances served as precursors of, and in some cases inspirations for, what would become rock and roll.

The term "rock and roll" itself comes from the common use of the words "rockin'" and "rollin'" in the lyrics of rhythm & blues songs and race records as references to sex. A radio disc jockey named Alan Freed (1922–1965) is usually credited with its first use as a commercial genre label to refer to rhythm & blues music that appealed to teenagers. In 1951, on his radio show in Cleveland, he started playing upbeat, guitar-based dance rhythm & blues records. Freed noticed that many white teenagers were calling in to request these songs. In the segregated society of time, he used the label "rock and roll" to increase the appeal of the music to a white audience. Radio disc jockeys, record companies, and the music trade press all over the country soon followed suit.

Freed began organizing concerts and tours of Black artists such as Chuck Berry (1926–2017), Fats Domino (1928–2017), LaVern Baker (1929–1997), and Little Richard (b. 1932) to perform for mixed-race audiences. These artists were all initially rhythm & blues performers whose music—marketed as rock and roll—became wildly popular among both Black and white audiences. One of the early rhythm & blues groups to appeal to both Black and white audiences was Louis Jordan and His Tympany Five. Formed in 1938 and initially released on race records, they inspired Chuck Berry in particular. Berry, a songwriter, guitarist, and vocalist, was probably more influential on the future of popular music than any other rock and roll musician. While the saxophone had been the primary soloing instrument on Freed's radio shows, Berry, along with the guitarist Bo Diddley (1928–2008), made the guitar the focal instrument of rock and roll. His recordings of such songs as "Johnny B. Goode" (1958), "Roll over Beethoven" (1956), and "Maybellene"

(1955) helped to establish rock and roll as a widely popular genre and influenced and inspired countless musicians in the 1950s and long afterwards. Though rock and roll was here to stay, in 1959 Freed was brought down by a scandal in which it was revealed that he accepted bribes, called payola, from record producers in exchange for featuring their songs on his radio show. Payola was common practice across the music industry at the time, so some have argued that Freed was taken down because he was supporting the indie record labels that were promoting African American artists and was a threat to the major record labels, who weren't.

Rock and roll became an age-group identity marker for a new generation of white teenagers born during and immediately after World War II during what is known as the baby boom. One of the ways they distinguished themselves from adults was in their musical taste. That white kids were going crazy at concerts and dances to the rhythmically energetic music of Black artists, especially male Black artists, performing in a genre named after synonyms for sex, was the perfect symbol of rebellion against the segregated and prudish social norms of 1950s American society. Many white adults hated the new music that was so different from the swing music and popular songs of the early 1950s. They found it sexually suggestive and even threatening in terms of Black male performers appealing to white girls. The more they expressed their disgust, however, the more young people clung to it as a symbol of their generation and its aspiration to break with out-of-date racist values and practices. The association of rock and roll, and later rock, with rebellion against social norms was sealed in these early years.

The popularity of rhythm & blues styles under the name rock and roll attracted many white artists, especially from the South, who might otherwise have become country singers. By dropping the fiddle and pedal steel guitar of country music and featuring the drums, piano, guitar, and saxophone of rhythm & blues bands, they were able to transcend their regional roots and cash in on the national popularity of rhythm & blues. They did so by producing **covers**, or new versions of existing rhythm & blues songs. Some covers closely imitated previous recordings, but others changed tempos, rhythms, and even lyrics to appeal to different or broader audiences. One of the most famous covers from this period is Elvis Presley's recording of "Hound Dog" in 1956, a song originally recorded in 1952 by Big Mama Thornton, an important bridge figure between the women blues singers of the 1920s and women rhythm & blues artists of the 1950s and 1960s. Thornton's recording draws on the blues in its microtonality, its shifting syncopation, and its lyrics that use double entendre to play with sexuality and gender expectations. It was a number one hit on the rhythm & blues charts for seven weeks in 1953. Presley's version features a faster tempo, a vocal style that includes rhythmic "hiccups" common in the style called "rockabilly" (a combination of rock and hillbilly), and cleaned-up lyrics that seem to make the song about a literal hound dog without any sexual metaphors. Presley's version reached number one on the pop, rhythm & blues, and country charts after its release.

The producer Sam Phillips (1923–2003), who owned Sun Records in Memphis, Tennessee, first recorded Presley in 1954 along with other young white artists, including Carl Perkins (1932–1998),

FIGURE 12.11
Chuck Berry
Source: Pickwick Records, Wikimedia Commons.

SOCIAL
BEHAVIOR

FIGURE 12.12
LaVern Baker
Source: Getty Images/Michael Ochs Archives/Stringer.

Jerry Lee Lewis (b. 1935), and Roy Orbison (1936–1988). These artists imitated the sound of Black singers and mimicked their dynamic, energetic performance style. Elvis Presley's energetic movements and hip-shaking dancing amplified the excitement, enthusiasm, and sexual energy of his performances. Both white and Black musicians and producers drew on influences from country music, African American and white gospel, the music of pop crooners of the time, rhythm & blues, and the blues to create a blend of styles appreciated by both Black and white audiences under the marketing category rock and roll.

Alongside rock and roll on the pop charts of the 1950s was a genre its fans called **folk music**. Performed in large part by urban intellectuals, and thus referred to by some critics as "urban folk," folk music drew on rural music and the Depression-era protest songs of Woody Guthrie (1912–1967). The most well-known folk music group in the 1950s was the Weavers, led by the banjo player and

POLITICS

singer Pete Seeger (1919–2014). In the early 1960s a younger generation of artists including Bob Dylan, Joan Baez, and Peter, Paul, and Mary performed folk music in a similar style. Their newly composed songs focused on social commentary, and their bands featured acoustic rather than electric guitars, which made it easier to hear their lyrics clearly. They looked down on rock and roll since it was primarily enjoyed for fun and socializing rather than for engaging with the serious issues of the day. In 1965, however, and in the wake of the success of the Beatles, Bob Dylan began recording and performing on electric guitar with a rock band, something he had aspired to as a high school student when he dreamed of playing in Little Richard's band. Although he continued to write about the serious themes characteristic of folk music in what became known as folk rock, many loyal fans of folk music were dismayed at Dylan's shift away from the genre's acoustic conventions. The injection of more "grownup" lyrical content into rock and roll was a sign that the teenagers of the 1950s were themselves becoming adults, ready for their music to mature along with them. That Hendrix recorded a version of Dylan's "All along the Watchtower" is a sign not only of Dylan's enormous influence on rock, but also that rock music was, by 1968, deeply engaged in the social challenges of its time. Not incidentally, Dylan admired Hendrix's version of the song and has said that Hendrix's version was not only an improvement on the song but also an inspiration for how Dylan has performed the song in subsequent live performances.

FIGURE 12.13
Elvis Presley
Source: INTERFOTO/Alamy Stock Photo.

Rock and roll's start along the path to engaging with social and political issues of its time began in 1964, when a new generation of white musicians from Britain brought rhythm & blues back to the United States. Like their white counterparts in the southern United States a decade earlier, many British rockers had been absorbing the electric guitar-based sound of Black rhythm & blues artists, even covering old recordings by blues legends like Robert Johnson and Muddy Waters, whose 1950 recording "Rollin' Stone" inspired both a new band's name and a new magazine devoted to music and politics. The first of the British groups to cross the Atlantic and hit it big in the United States was the Beatles, a band from Liverpool, England. After several years performing covers as a bar band, two members of the Beatles, bassist Paul McCartney (b. 1942) and rhythm guitarist John Lennon (1940–1980), began to compose their own songs in imitation of the styles of the day. Eventually lead guitarist George Harrison (1943–2001) and drummer Ringo Starr (b. 1940) joined in the songwriting effort. The Beatles first achieved success in Britain with their 1963 album *Please, Please Me*, and first toured the United States in 1964, exciting thousands of adoring fans.

FIGURE 12.14
Bob Dylan in 1966
Source: Pictorial Press Ltd/Alamy Stock Photo.

The success of the Beatles led to a "British Invasion" of similar groups drawing on Black American music. Some, like the Rolling Stones and the Who, had an enduring impact on American popular music. In 1966, after their third and last U.S. tour, the Beatles, in parallel with the American group the Beach Boys, began to experiment with new forms, textures, and timbres, which they created in recording studios. Both bands released **concept albums**, albums that were conceived as an integral whole, with interrelated songs arranged in a particular order. Instead of collections of songs, these and similar rock albums were viewed as large-scale works of art and popular musicians were viewed as artists. The Beach Boys released the first concept album, *Pet Sounds*, in 1966 and the Beatles released *Sgt. Pepper's Lonely Hearts Club Band* in 1967. After these two albums, the term "rock" replaced rock and roll. This name change reflected a more narrowly defined musical genre: bands that featured guitars and drums and

FIGURE 12.15
The Beatles in 1963
Source: Getty Images/Photoshot.

that wrote their own material, usually for full-album concepts rather than singles. More often than not, these bands comprised white male musicians.

AESTHETICS

CULTURAL LINKAGES

Jimi Hendrix was born in Seattle and moved to New York's Harlem neighborhood in 1963 at age twenty-one after serving for a time in the U.S. Army. In New York he worked as a guitarist locally and on tour for rhythm & blues acts like the Isley Brothers and Little Richard when they played the "chitlin circuit," an informal network of performance venues in the eastern half of the United States where Black performers entertained audiences, without fearing for their safety, during the Jim Crow era. After building a reputation as an excellent rhythm & blues guitarist, he began to perform with his own band in clubs in Greenwich Village. "The Village," as it is known, is a neighborhood in downtown Manhattan that was at the time a site of flourishing artistic activity and a home for many nightclubs that served the folk music, folk rock, jazz, and rock scenes. Greenwich Village audiences were largely white, but by 1965 the phenomenon of white teenage audiences adoring Black rock and roll stars like Chuck Berry was already a thing of the past. As a Black musician with extraordinary skills in blues and rhythm & blues styles, Hendrix did not seem to fit the image of what an American 1960s rock star should be.

In 1966 Chas Chandler (1938–1996), the original bass player of the British rhythm & blues and rock band the Animals, heard Hendrix play in Greenwich Village. Familiar with the scene in Britain, where great interest in rhythm & blues and the blues had persisted as audiences saw British rock bands succeeding in the United States and around the world, Chandler convinced Hendrix to come to London. Audiences there were thrilled to see and hear a Black American musician playing rock music that clearly drew on African American traditions like the blues. Hendrix and Chandler put together the Jimi Hendrix Experience, and Hendrix experienced his first large-scale success with the album *Are You Experienced?* (1967), which spent thirty-three weeks on the charts in the U.K.

Hendrix developed his own version of the stage antics of rhythm & blues performers and also extended their brilliant playing with his own groundbreaking virtuosity. In his performances he played his guitar with his teeth, stroked the guitar neck as if making love to it, and, on occasion, set his guitar on fire or destroyed it on stage. While drawing on long-established blues and rhythm & blues forms, styles, and melodies, he manipulated and transformed the sound of his guitar using a **fuzz box** (an effects pedal that distorts timbre), a wah-wah pedal, and other effects pedals along with feedback and stacked Marshall amplifiers turned up to maximum volume, producing the extreme loudness that is part of what distinguishes rock from other genres. **Feedback** happens when an audio input, like an electric guitar or a microphone, receives the sound from an audio output, like a speaker, in a loop. Often the result is a high-pitched screeching sound. Though the sound of guitar feedback in his time was typically avoided as undesirable, Hendrix's innovative use of it continues today in many subgenres of rock music.

FIGURE 12.16
Jimi Hendrix performing at Woodstock in 1969
Source: Getty Images/Barry Z Levine.

POLITICS

CULTURAL
LINKAGES

POLITICS

At the Woodstock Festival in 1969, where hundreds of thousands of young people gathered ostensibly in the name of peace and love to hear their favorite musicians, Hendrix performed a set of music featuring his songs, guitar improvisations, and influences from the blues and jazz. In the midst of the set, he unleashed perhaps his most famous single performance, a solo guitar rendition of the American national anthem complete with gritty, loud, and distorted effects that expressed iconically the violence of "the rockets' red glare, the bombs bursting in air." He combined the sonic symbolism of patriotism in the national anthem with the horrible sounds of war and captured the tension inherent in the times: most people at some level love their country, but many youth at the festival had come to despise their leaders, who had built a nuclear arsenal and had led the nation into a pointless and unjust war in Southeast Asia. It was as if Hendrix was reclaiming the national anthem for anti-war youth and musically redefining what it might mean to be an American.

An interest in alternative lifestyles led some rock bands and artists during the 1960s to create a subgenre called psychedelic rock, among them Big Brother and the Holding Company (featuring Janis Joplin [1943–1970]), the Grateful Dead, and Jefferson Airplane of the San Francisco scene, and the Beatles starting with their album *Revolver* (1966). Produced using new studio technologies and influenced by the enigmatic lyrics of Bob Dylan, their music seemed to replicate (and often accompanied) parts of the multisensory experience induced by psychedelic drugs such as LSD, which can include such sensations as "hearing colors" or "tasting sounds." In a nod to alternative religions, some psychedelic rock musicians incorporated the sounds of the North Indian *sitar* and *tabla* into their recordings. Among the most famous examples are the Beatles' "Love You To" from *Revolver* (1966) and the Rolling Stones' "Paint It Black" (1966) (see Chapter 4, Gateway 14).

Rock music continues to be an important part of the popular music scene today. During the last forty years the Irish band U2, the American Bruce Springsteen and his E Street Band, and the British band Radiohead, to name just a few, have all enjoyed tremendous commercial success performing diverse styles of rock, selling millions of albums, and filling stadiums the world over. Many of them have engaged with the political and social issues of their times. Springsteen, for example, has given voice to the plight of the working class, including Vietnam veterans, in the United States, affirming and honoring the dignity of their contribution to American society. Radiohead, realizing the negative effects that large-scale tours have on the environment, have curtailed their touring so that their carbon emissions and environmental impact are minimal.

Beyond the commercial mainstream, rock has taken a number of directions since the 1960s. Heavy metal and its countless subgenres emerged around 1970, and metal musicians have explored extremes in loudness, distortion, and guitar virtuosity, to the delight of their communities of fans. By the 1970s Tina Turner had begun covering rock songs by white bands such as the Beatles and the Rolling Stones, in a sense turning the tables on how white 1950s rock and roll artists had made hits out of their covers of songs by Black performers. She became a leading rock artist in the 1970s and 1980s, breaking out of the racialized constraints of categories such as rhythm & blues and soul. In the 1970s punk rock developed as a reaction against the elaborate performances of popular rock bands like Led Zeppelin and Pink Floyd. The music of punk bands like the Ramones and the Patti Smith Group from the United States and the Sex Pistols and the Clash from the U.K. featured a do-it-yourself ethic, stripped-down simple songs,

FIGURE 12.17
The Smashing Pumpkins in 1993. From left to right: D'Arcy Wretzky, Jimmy Chamberlin, Billy Corgan, and James Iha.
Source: Getty Images/Paul Bergen/Redferns.

and lyrics that were anti-establishment in nature. The independent record labels and underground scenes that developed in the wake of punk led to the umbrella term "alternative rock," which emerged in the 1980s and burst into the mainstream in the 1990s with the popularity of groups like the Seattle grunge bands Nirvana and Pearl Jam and the Chicago band Smashing Pumpkins.

Rock music was the dominant form of popular music from the mid-1950s to the mid-1970s, but it is no longer as central as it once was. Today it is one of many types of popular music enjoyed by wide audiences. Rock bands from the 1960s, 1970s, 1980s, and 1990s continue to re-form for reunion tours to perform for the fans who have aged with them and for new, younger fans who have become interested in their music. Beyond these reunion tours and the commercially successful artists and bands nominated for Grammys and other major awards in rock categories each year, smaller rock scenes have formed in cities around the world as people continue to find meaning and inspiration from the rock bands of today.

WHERE DO I GO FROM HERE?

- Listen to "Johnny B. Goode" by Chuck Berry for musical elements of the blues. Does the timbre of his electric guitar sound similar to the guitar timbres of any contemporary music that you know?

- Listen to Bob Dylan's original version of "All along the Watchtower" (1967) and compare it to Hendrix's version. How does Hendrix's version enhance (or detract from) the meaning of the song?

- Listen to "Voodoo Child (Slight Return)" or some other tracks from Hendrix's *Electric Ladyland*. How does his playing mark the music as psychedelic rock? Are there connections to the blues and rhythm & blues?

- Listen to some tracks from *Nevermind* (1991) by Nirvana, *Ten* (1991) by Pearl Jam, or *Siamese Dream* (1993) by Smashing Pumpkins. How do the musical elements, including the lyrics, build on, or depart from, the recordings and songwriting of Hendrix, Dylan, and others you might be familiar with?

- If you have a favorite group that might be considered an indie or alternative rock band, explore some of their interviews or social media activity and see if you can figure out how they are connected to their predecessors in rock music.

GATEWAY 48
NEW DIRECTIONS IN JAZZ

What Is It?

During the 1950s, 1960s, and 1970s, jazz musicians reacted in a variety of ways to bebop's innovations. Some wanted to simplify its harmonic complexities, while others wanted to push those harmonic complexities to their limits. Some wanted melodies rather than harmonies to structure improvisation, while others wanted to expand possibilities in rhythm and tempo. Still others wanted to explore overlaps between jazz and popular music in ways that were exciting to both musicians and audiences. Tenor saxophonist John Coltrane (1926–1967) was involved in several of these directions in jazz, and his recording titled "Acknowledgement," the opening part to his album *A Love Supreme* (released in 1965), is our gateway to jazz in this period. *A Love Supreme* is a suite in four parts: "Acknowledgement," "Resolution," "Pursuance," and "Psalm." This recording features Coltrane on tenor saxophone, Jimmy Garrison (1934–1976) on upright bass, Elvin Jones (1927–2004) on drums, and McCoy Tyner (b. 1938) on piano. From 1962 to 1965 this group of musicians constituted John Coltrane's regular quartet, which later became known in jazz circles as Coltrane's "Classic Quartet." One of the many reasons the quartet is "classic" is that *A Love Supreme* was a widely successful album with broad appeal beyond jazz audiences. It sold a half a million copies by 1970—a great deal more than was typical for jazz albums at the time—and many more since then.

 Listen to the first thirty seconds of the recording.

FIGURE 12.18
John Coltrane in the early 1960s
Source: Everett Collection Inc/Alamy Stock Photo.

How Does It Work?

Timbre

The sounds on this recording consist of John Coltrane's tenor saxophone, an upright bass, a piano, and a drum set with prominent cymbals (a gong also opens the recording). At the end of "Acknowledgement," John Coltrane's voice is heard, repeatedly singing the words "A Love Supreme."

Texture

The main texture here is solo saxophone with rhythm section accompaniment. The piano plays chords rhythmically, a process called **comping** (short for "accompanying," and possibly also associated with "to complement"), the bass plays either a four-note ostinato or an improvised bass line, and the drums provide a steady groove.

Rhythm

After a mostly nonmetrical introduction, a steady pulse is introduced by a bass ostinato and then picked up by the drums. At first the drums play a beat seemingly inspired by Afro-Latin sensibilities with elaborate syncopation in the ride cymbal. Throughout the recording, this type of groove continues, though Elvin Jones occasionally adds a slight swing feel on the ride cymbal. Coltrane's soloing sometimes lines up rhythmically with the rhythm section, but at other times he seems to be playing nonmetrically over the steady pulse.

Melody

The melodies of the saxophone are structured mostly around a minor pentatonic mode. The basis for many of the melodies Coltrane plays is a short, ascending three-note phrase that begins with an ascending minor third and an ascending whole step. He elaborates this phrase starting on various pitches at various times of the recording.

Harmony

For the most part, "Acknowledgement" is an example of improvisation over a particular mode, in this case a minor pentatonic. The musicians do not continue playing in this "home key" throughout the composition, but often modulate phrases and harmonies chromatically and to keys that are distantly related to this key. Near the end of the recording, the home key shifts down a step to set up a new harmonic structure for the following movement in the *A Love Supreme* suite.

Form

"Acknowledgement" begins with a nonmetrical introduction followed by a long, seemingly open-ended improvisation. With closer attention, however, it is evident that the improvisation is structured into five sections that are built of 4-, 8-, and 16-bar components.

Performance Techniques

The musicians can be heard responding to one another, increasing and decreasing rhythmic and dynamic intensity together, and sometimes playing in similar ranges to one another as they improvise over the structure of the composition.

🔊 Listen to the entire performance with these elements in mind while following the timed listening guide.

LISTENING GUIDE 12.3

TIME	SECTION	DESCRIPTION
0:00	Introduction	A gong, a piano chord, and a pedal tone on the bass open the recording. Coltrane enters playing nonmetrically, improvising over a pentatonic scale. He emphasizes intervals of a fourth while the drummer plays a roll on the cymbals and the piano plays a number of block chords ascending and descending through the range of the piano, also nonmetrically.
0:31		The bass enters playing a four-note ostinato. It establishes the tonality of the composition, moving from the tonic to the minor third, back to the tonic and up to the fourth. These are the first three pitches of the minor pentatonic scale.
0:40		The drums establish a pulse, playing a highly syncopated groove in an Afro-Latin style.
0:48		The piano enters, playing harmonies based on the interval of a fourth.
1:03	Section 1 (32 bars)	Even though Coltrane's improvisation may seem open ended and completely free-form, there is a fairly regular organized structure that the musicians are creating (and following) that can be heard. Coltrane begins this first section with a three-pitch arch-shaped phrase (A). This phrase is part of a pentatonic scale and forms the basis for much of his improvisation. Sometimes in this section he is playing rhythmically with the groove; at other times he is playing quickly and nonmetrically throughout a wide range of the saxophone. He ends this section with a sustained, accented high pitch.
2:05	Section 2 (48 bars)	Coltrane introduces several statements of a new, ascending three-pitch phrase (B) based on the pentatonic scale, though he also plays it in many keys outside of the pentatonic scale. The piano follows the solo, playing chords outside of the tonic key with Coltrane. In the middle of this section Coltrane ascends to another high pitch, played with a rough, strained timbre.
3:37	Section 3 (40 bars)	Coltrane plays phrase B and fragments of phrase A in a number of keys. He ascends to a number of repeating high pitches, playing with a rough timbre and bringing his solo to a climax. At the end of this section he descends into the middle and lower range of the saxophone, improvising not as rapidly, and mostly in the home key.
4:54	Section 4 (36 bars)	Coltrane plays the opening four-note ostinato twice in the home key before a long section where he only plays this ostinato, but modulates it into all twelve keys throughout much of the register of the saxophone and plays it in a number of rhythms as well as nonmetrically before returning to repeat it in the home key.
6:03	Section 5 (20 bars)	A strong chord in the piano announces this last section, where several overdubbed layers of Coltrane's voice sing the ostinato to the words "a love supreme." From here until the end of the recording, the drums intermix and sometimes alternate the polyrhythmic Afro-Latin groove with a swing feel—heard in swung subdivisions of the beat in the ride cymbal and a hi-hat closing on beats two and four. The bass also plays the ostinato as it did at the beginning of the recording and the home key shifts down a step for the whole band.
6:41	Coda	The vocal drops out, and the bass plays a three-note version of the ostinato, with the piano comping and the drums alternating between a swing feel and the Afro-Latin polyrhythmic groove. The piano and then the drums fade out, leaving the bass to a brief improvisation based on this three-note ostinato. The recording ends with the bass playing briefly in a rubato tempo before strumming an open fifth in the new home key.
7:41	End	

What Does It Mean?

There are many ways to understand "Acknowledgement" and *A Love Supreme*, but Coltrane provides a useful starting point in the liner notes to the album. He writes about a spiritual awakening in 1957 that led him to a rich, full, and productive life: "through the merciful hand of God, I do perceive and have been fully reinformed of his omnipotence. It is truly a love supreme." Coltrane was interested in a number of religions, and many believe that "Acknowledgement" points to his particular affinity for Islam. He does not specify a particular religion here, but he wants his listeners to know that this album is about a spiritual path. Its elements can be interpreted in light of that broad meaning, which also comes through in the title to each part.

ECONOMIC ACTIVITY

AESTHETICS

The form of "Acknowledgement" is organized around the way that Coltrane approaches three short melodic phrases: the four-note ostinato, three-note phrase A, and three-note phrase B. Though the ostinato in the bass is heard for the first time after the introduction, the full statement of the four-note phrase is not heard until the end of the recording in Section 5, where Coltrane's voice sings the ostinato with the words "a love supreme." His singing reveals that this four-note ostinato expresses this supreme spiritual love. In Section 4, Coltrane plays the "a love supreme" phrase without melodic embellishment in all keys and all around the range of the saxophone. This is the only time he performs this type of unembellished modulation of a given theme, which suggests that this is not spontaneously improvised, but part of a preconceived compositional structure.

Coltrane's saxophone solo, in broad strokes, starts with a brief fragment of the love supreme ostinato in Section 1, explores the possibilities of that fragment in search of the full statement of the ostinato in Sections 2 and 3, takes the ostinato into all possible keys in Section 4, and experiences a revelation of the full ostinato with text in Section 5. In one sense, this is an "Acknowledgement" that this spiritual "love supreme" is always present, often underlying everything he does, but only revealed in full after a period of searching and exploration. This love supreme is not only always present, but it is everywhere. It can be found in every key and it can be transformed into new and different forms. The form of "Acknowledgement" can also be understood as challenging the linear structure so often heard both in jazz when soloists improvise over a head or a repeating chord progression and in European classical music in forms like theme and variations or sonata form. Even though the bass performs the ostinato early on, the listener doesn't realize that it is the main theme, or head, until it appears at the end. This cyclical approach has antecedents in the blues and other African American forms, as well as in many African musical traditions (Central Africa in Chapter 1, Gateway 1, and Shona music in Chapter 3, Gateway 9). If the form of "Acknowledgement" is a cycle, from Coltrane's spiritual perspective it could be heard as a returning to the divine, the love supreme, over and over, with periods of search and exploration in between each return.

ECONOMIC ACTIVITY

Other musical elements suggest Coltrane's spiritual search in "Acknowledgement." On several occasions Coltrane performs in a high register with a rough or strained timbre. The high register of the saxophone, combined with the rough timbre, sounds as though Coltrane is exerting a lot of energy, in the same way that a singer would strain to sing or shout high pitches. It may be an expression of anguish or strife, or striving connected to overcoming the difficulties and hardships encountered in the search for spiritual wholeness. The rough timbre also is a continuation of the value African and African American musicians have placed on buzzing timbres in jazz, in Jimi Hendrix's guitar effects, and in the Shona *mbira dzavadzimu* (Chapter 3, Gateway 9), where added buzzing effects connected musicians and listeners to the spiritual world.

 Listen to "Acknowledgement" again, this time listening for appearances of the "A Love Supreme" ostinato and thinking about how Coltrane explores and transforms it before it is fully revealed when Coltrane's vocal enters.

AESTHETICS

"Acknowledgement" also demonstrates one way jazz musicians were responding to the harmonic complexities of bebop. It is called **modal jazz**, that is, jazz based on improvising over melodic modes rather than quickly moving chord progressions. Some musicians wondered what might be expressed if they improvised with a given mode as the underlying framework over long periods of time. In "Acknowledgement" the minor pentatonic provides this modal basis for improvisation. Coltrane, McCoy Tyner, and Jimmy Garrison take advantage of this underlying constant mode by not only experimenting with different harmonic and melodic formulations based on the pentatonic scale, but by venturing outside of that scale while some of the other musicians may continue in the "home key." Coltrane does this many times as he takes phrases A and B to other keys chromatically distant from the home key. Sometimes Tyner and Garrison follow him to these distant tonalities, but sometimes they remain in the home key. On a few occasions, the three musicians come back together in the home key after venturing out of it for a while, in another demonstration of cyclical motion that may be an icon of a spiritual journey.

What Is Its History?

Born in North Carolina, Coltrane first learned music in community and high school bands there and in Philadelphia, where he moved in his teens. After serving in the Navy at the end of World War II, he returned to Philadelphia where he honed his musical skills and studied jazz theory, before he moved to New York. There, he started playing with some of the leading figures in the bebop scene, including Thelonious Monk. In some of his music, Coltrane was interested in developing the harmonic complexities of bebop, which he did on one of his most-admired albums, *Giant Steps* (1960). The tempo of the recording of its title track, "Giant Steps," is nearly 300 beats per minute. The harmony changes every two beats for much of the form, sometimes between chords that are distantly related to one another in ways that would be unfamiliar to bebop players accustomed to improvising over jazz standards. This presents enormous difficulties for improvisers as they seek to play fluid lines informed by bebop sensibilities that move rapidly among harmonies that shift to distant key centers far more quickly than they typically would in bebop. Coltrane and others were pushing the conventions of bebop to its harmonic limits. "Giant Steps" still challenges students learning how to play jazz today to be able to improvise smoothly over quickly changing chord progressions.

Coltrane recorded *Giant Steps* in May, 1959, just a few weeks after recording the most well-known album of modal jazz titled *Kind of Blue* (1959) led by trumpet player Miles Davis. "So What," the first track from *Kind of Blue*, is a modal composition in AABA form. One mode underlies the entire form. The only change is that the B section is a half step higher than the A section. It maintains the head—solos—head overall form and the AABA form, both of which connect it to the common practices in form already established in jazz. Each of the other musicians performing on "So What" with Davis and Coltrane made significant contributions to various streams of jazz in this period beyond *Kind of Blue*: Paul Chambers on bass, Jimmy Cobb on drums, Bill Evans on piano, Julian "Cannonball" Adderley on alto saxophone.

In another reaction to the complexities of bebop, some jazz musicians brought elements of rhythm & blues, soul, and rock and roll into their music (Chapter 12, Gateways 46 and 47). **Hard bop** is a style of jazz that features the rhythms of gospel and rhythm & blues, memorable and simple bluesy melodies, and an aggressive, driving pulse in the drums that often accented beats two and four (the backbeat) in a four-beat measure. It departed from the virtuosic fast-tempo conventions of bebop, favoring instead slower tempos and simpler melodies, though it continued the head—solos—head form and complex harmonies for improvisation that characterized bebop. These elements arguably made hard bop recordings more understandable and appealing to larger audiences. Some of these recordings sold at a much higher rate than recordings in other jazz styles. "Soul-jazz" was a term some hard bop musicians embraced to reflect both a soulful feeling in their music from blues and gospel-related musical elements, like the sound of the Hammond B-3 organ, and pride in their African heritage and African American identity. John Coltrane's participation in hard bop, and his album *Blue Train* (1958) is considered to be among his most significant contributions to that style.

Other leading musicians playing hard bop in this period included the drummer Art Blakey (1919–1990) and the pianist Horace Silver (1928–2014), who together formed a group called the Jazz Messengers in 1953. Their style of hard bop emphasized bebop harmonic elements. In 1956 Horace Silver left the group to develop his own music emphasizing the rhythm & blues and gospel elements of hard bop and enjoyed commercial success with his album *Song for My Father* (1965). Art

AESTHETICS

FIGURE 12.19
Miles Davis in 1970
Source: Pictorial Press Ltd/Alamy Stock Photo.

FIGURE 12.20
Herbie Hancock in 1974
Source: Heritage Image Partnership Ltd/
Alamy Stock Photo.

FIGURE 12.21
Wayne Shorter in 1976
Source: Heritage Image Partnership Ltd/
Alamy Stock Photo.

Blakey and the Jazz Messengers continued to perform hard bop until Blakey's death in 1990, with a wide variety of musicians performing in the group in its many years of existence, including the trumpet player Wynton Marsalis (Chapter 13, Gateway 52). The group's recording "Moanin'" (1958) is a classic example of a bluesy, memorable hard bop head followed by bebop-oriented improvised solos.

Miles Davis, like his frequent collaborator Coltrane, was also active in the development of new styles during this period. He had performed in the bebop style with Charlie Parker and others and was at the forefront of the development of several other jazz styles: modal jazz with albums like *Kind of Blue* and *Milestones* (1958) recorded with his "First Great Quintet," some early iterations of hard bop, and in another style of jazz known as "cool jazz" typically associated with jazz musicians from the West Coast like the pianist Dave Brubeck (1920–2012) and the baritone saxophonist Gerry Mulligan (1927–1996), as well as East Coast-based musicians such as the pianist Lennie Tristano (1919–1978), the saxophonist Lee Konitz (b. 1927), and the pianist John Lewis and his Modern Jazz Quartet. Davis's so-called Second Great Quintet, with Wayne Shorter (b. 1933) on tenor saxophone, Herbie Hancock (b. 1940) on piano/keyboards, Tony Williams (1945–1997) on drums, and Ron Carter (b. 1937) on bass, included more open forms for improvisation that relied on a metric pulse but very little harmonic structure for improvisation on albums such as *Miles Smiles* (1966). Albums with some of the same musicians, *Filles de Kilimanjaro* (1968) and *In a Silent Way* (1969), began to explore electronic sounds and demonstrate a stylistic shift towards the rhythms and timbres of rock.

Davis's album *Bitches Brew* (1970) is the most famous example of how he combined elements of rock and jazz in what became known as **jazz fusion**, a genre label indicating how jazz styles were blended with rock and funk (though of course musicians have explored many other types of stylistic fusions with jazz). The rhythm section for *Bitches Brew* is extensive and includes two bass players, two to three drummers, two to three electric keyboard players, and a percussionist, plus many wind players, often all playing simultaneously. On the album Davis also employed new technologies common in rock, such as effects pedals and post-recording editing techniques where he spliced together and layered recorded materials on top of one another. In using these techniques, Davis took cues from innovations of the guitarist Jimi Hendrix, introduced to him by his wife (they were married from 1968 to 1969), rock artist Betty Davis (b. 1945). Though the album sold over a half million copies, some critics and audiences responded negatively to *Bitches Brew*, believing that it compromised the purity of jazz. But since jazz has always involved the overlap and influence of many musical styles and traditions, the search for some "pure" essence of jazz is likely futile. Many musicians were inspired to take jazz fusion further in the years after *Bitches Brew*. Herbie Hancock and Wayne Shorter both pursued projects in jazz fusion, Hancock with his album *Head Hunters* (1973) and many others (Chapter 1, Gateway 1), and Shorter with his band Weather Report, active in the 1970s and early 1980s.

After *A Love Supreme*, Coltrane pursued an even more avant-garde agenda in his albums *Meditations* (1966) and *Ascension* (1966), both of which continued his expression of the spiritual in music and experimented with improvisation over a loose harmonic framework, sometimes without a constant pulse. At the same time, other musicians began to question the common formal, harmonic, and rhythmic structures in jazz as they developed what was first known as the "New Thing," and later **free jazz**. Saxophonist Ornette Coleman (1930–2015) was prominent in this movement, and his 1961 album *Free Jazz* gave the style its name. His concept of "harmolodics" gives equal weight to melody, harmony, and rhythm in the development of improvised musical ideas. Often structuring his improvisation around melodic phrase shapes, he at times departed from the harmonic structures and steady pulse that had characterized jazz since its beginnings. Coltrane hints at this kind of approach in "Acknowledgement," in which his improvisation is based on transformations and permutations of phrases A and B rather than a particular harmonic structure. But Coleman took it further in the course of a long career that continued for nearly fifty years after Coltrane's tragic death from cancer at the age of forty.

Both individual musicians and so-called collectives developed the New Thing and free jazz during the 1960s and 1970s, chief among them the pianists Cecil Taylor (1929–2018) and Paul Bley (1932–2016), the saxophonist Albert Ayler (1936–1970), the Association for the Advancement of Creative Musicians (AACM), and the Art Ensemble of Chicago. Founded in 1965 on Chicago's South Side, the AACM and its members have experimented adventurously with combining avant-garde jazz, classical music, and music of various traditions of the world into new forms. In the context of the civil rights movement, the AACM was one of many examples of African American artists and communities coming together to forge pathways towards a world of equal rights. AACM cofounder and pianist-composer Muhal Richard Abrams (1930–2017) and early member trumpet player John Shenoy Jackson (1923–1985) stated in the early 1970s that part of the AACM's intention was "to show how the disadvantaged and the disenfranchised can come together and determine their own strategies for political and economic freedom, thereby determining their own destinies." The Art Ensemble of Chicago, affiliated with the AACM, did so in their lengthy performances that included improvisation, climactic moments featuring blues or other forms from past iterations of jazz, and performances on dozens of whistles, bells, and percussion instruments scattered all over the stage that referenced African music traditions. The musicians also used elaborate makeup and theatrical dress to show that the stage was a place where collective performance was a ritual of sorts, a special experience separate and different from everyday life.

FIGURE 12.22

The Ornette Coleman Quartet in New York in 1971. From left to right: drummer Ed Blackwell (1929–1992), tenor saxophonist Dewey Redman (1931–2006), Ornette Coleman, and bassist Charlie Haden (1937–2014).

Source: Getty Images/Val Wilmer/Redferns.

POLITICS

FIGURE 12.23
Art Ensemble of Chicago around 1980
Source: Getty Images/Tom Copi/Michael Ochs Archives.

FIGURE 12.24
Charles Mingus in the 1970s
Source: CSU Archives/Everett Collection Historical/
Alamy Stock Photo.

All this experimentation with the underpinnings of jazz seems like an indirect, implicit challenge to the authority of tradition being worked out explicitly by demonstrators on the streets of America. One jazz artist who explicitly referenced the politics of the period was bassist Charles Mingus (1922–1979) in a composition called "Fables of Faubus" (1959). It includes lyrics denouncing the Governor of Arkansas, Orval E. Faubus, who in 1957 had mobilized the Arkansas National Guard to prevent the integration of nine Black students into previously all-white Little Rock Central High School. In response, U.S. President Dwight Eisenhower ordered the 101st Airborne Division of the U.S. Army to protect and escort the "Little Rock Nine" to school. Mingus's composition uses humor, improvisation, and many elements of existing jazz styles to condemn Faubus's racism as "ridiculous," to use a word from the composition. Countless other recordings and performances in jazz during this period challenged racial injustice, among them Abbey Lincoln's stirring and powerful wordless vocals on "Triptych: Prayer/Protest/Peace" from Max Roach's *We Insist: Freedom Now Suite* (1960) and "Mississippi Goddam" (1964), "Backlash Blues" (1967), and other music by genre-defying pianist and vocalist Nina Simone.

John Coltrane was not himself as particularly politically active or vocal, but he did view his music as a conscious attempt to make change, whether that change was political, social, musical, or personal. His album *A Love Supreme* inspired many musicians, some of whom would take more overt political stances in the context of the New Thing and free jazz. Since Coltrane passed away in 1967, his life and music have touched countless musicians and audiences and the styles of jazz they enjoy as they connect music to other meaningful aspects of their lives.

WHERE DO I GO FROM HERE?

- Listen to "Pursuance" and "Psalm," two of the other three parts of the *A Love Supreme* suite. Listen for how the melody of "Pursuance" begins with statements of phrase A from "Acknowledgement," and sets up a clear 12-bar blues form at a fast tempo. The fourth part, "Psalm," has been interpreted as an expression of a poem that Coltrane wrote in the liner notes, also titled "A Love Supreme," in a recitation of the poem on saxophone, without words. Some have interpreted the way he expresses the words as melodies as analogous to how an African American preacher might phrase a line of text when addressing a congregation. Try reading Coltrane's poem along with "Psalm," beginning with the title "A Love Supreme," and match the text to the way he is expressing it on the saxophone.
- Listen to "Moanin'" by Art Blakey and the Jazz Messengers. How is the head influenced by the blues? What are the rhythmic and melodic elements that might have made this recording appealing to a wide audience? To what extent do the improvised solos share musical characteristics with bebop?
- Listen to all or part of *Bitches Brew* by Miles Davis. What are some of the elements that point to the fusion of jazz and rock in this recording?
- Find a recording of Ornette Coleman from any period. How do its harmonic structures, rhythms, pulse, or other musical elements suggest that this recording could be considered "free jazz"?
- Listen to "Fables of Faubus" by Charles Mingus, "Triptych Prayer/Protest/Peace" by Abbey Lincoln, and "Mississippi Goddam" by Nina Simone. Compare the musical elements the musicians use in their approaches to and expressions of protest of racial injustice.
- Read some excerpts from the book *John Coltrane: His Life and Music* by Lewis Porter, upon which much of this gateway is based. What other aspects of Coltrane's music and his life are interesting to you?

GATEWAY 49
EXPERIMENTAL MUSIC

What Is It?

In the middle of the twentieth century, some composers who were challenging the established conventions of classical concert music, as Debussy and Stravinsky had in the early twentieth century (Chapter 9, Gateways 32 and 36), began to describe their music as "experimental." These composers were pushing boundaries and testing the way the elements of music could be produced. Experimentalism in music of 1950–1975 encompasses a wide spectrum of practices. Composers experimented with expectations for audience behavior at concerts, with the ways music can create or transform social bonds between people, and with spiritual, ascetic practices of self-transformation in creating and performing music. In other cases the term "experimental" suggested a shift towards understanding the composer as a kind of scientist.

Composers of experimental music in this period were especially interested in the possibilities for new processes of composition and performance provided by the use of electronic technologies including newly invented computers. They were also interested in music that included improvisatory elements, where performers' interpretations of composer guidelines, as well as elements left to chance, could result in a variety of sonic outputs. Between 1950 and 1975, experimentalism was ascendent in classical music. Our gateway to this kind of music from 1950 to 1975 is *Stay On It*, composed by Julius Eastman (1940–1990) in 1973.

In *Stay On It*, one way that Julius Eastman experiments is by giving performers extensive opportunities to improvise in a classical music tradition where the faithful reproduction of the musical notation on a page was the rule. The main theme and its related variations in the piece are clearly pre-composed, since all of the musicians play these parts together. But when comparing multiple recordings of the piece, other elements of the music vary significantly. Soon after he composed it, Eastman participated in and recorded many performances of *Stay On It* as a pianist and vocalist. But after his death, scores or parts for the piece could not be found. Researchers and performers of the piece today have listened to recordings and interviewed musicians who performed the piece with Eastman in order to determine which elements of the piece are pre-composed and what kinds of guidelines performers were given for their improvisations. They found that the instrumentation and ensemble size varied in Eastman's performances, but that performances typically all contained piano, voice, and mallet percussion. They have reconstructed scores of the piece so that it can be performed by musicians today.

This recording of *Stay On It* is from a 2019 concert presented by Jacaranda Music. Jacaranda Music is a series of concerts of twentieth- and twenty-first-century classical compositions, presented in Santa Monica, California, since 2003. The performers in this recording are Seth Parker Woods (cello and ensemble leader), Zanaida Robles (soprano vocalist), Adam

FIGURE 12.25
Julius Eastman writing the manuscript of a composition c. 1970–1971
Source: D. W. Burkhardt.

FIGURE 12.26
The performance of Julius Eastman's *Stay On It* at Jacaranda Music in 2019
Source: Michael Baker.

Tendler (piano), Shalini Vijayan (violin), Max Opferkuch (clarinet), David Brennan (saxophone), Dustin Donohue (percussion), and Sidney Hopson (percussion).

 Listen to the first thirty seconds of the recording.

How Does It Work?

Timbre

The recording features the sound of the cello, violin, clarinet, marimba, tambourine, saxophone, and a woman vocalist, who varies her timbre widely.

Texture

The texture of the main theme and its variations is mostly homophonic, with all performers on the same rhythm, but on different pitches. Other heterophonic, polyphonic, and solo textures occur at various points in the recording.

Rhythm

The first two-thirds of the piece features a steady underlying beat. Sometimes this beat disappears in sections with prominent improvisation. These sections become nonmetrical or, in one case, adopt a new, faster beat. The rhythm of the main theme and its variations is highly syncopated and often features the habanera rhythm. The last third of the piece features a slower, rubato pulse, and then a faster steady beat played by the tambourine.

Melody

The melodies of this piece are mostly based on a major mode with a lowered seventh scale degree, especially the repeating main theme and its variations. Blues and pentatonic modes also occur frequently, as do fully chromatic melodies.

Harmony

The harmony of this piece is, at times, grounded in a sense of a sustained major tonality based on a major triad. Sometimes the harmony remains on a dominant seventh chord. The musicians improvise a variety of chords, especially the piano in the final sections, as well as combinations of pitches that sound dissonant and do not conform to a system of tonality.

Form

Stay On It experiments with the possibilities of the simple main theme. The first two-thirds of the piece explores variations on the theme. The ensemble adds a number of layers to each re-occurrence of the theme. The departure from the initially rigid main theme increases throughout the first two-thirds of the piece as the ensemble deconstructs it into what might be considered the sounds of a raucous street party. The last third of the piece is based on a rhythmic pattern containing elements of the main theme's rhythm in a slower, rubato tempo, closing with a tambourine playing a steady, faster, one-beat pattern.

Performance Techniques

When Eastman first wrote the piece, he gave a great deal of freedom to the performers. Instead of handing them a score that determined what they would play, as European composers had for centuries, he gave them fragments of approximate notation. He performed with the ensemble, and worked with the other musicians in rehearsals, coaching their interpretations of the music verbally and by example through his own playing and singing. This degree of freedom for performance, and dependency on Eastman's personal instructions, presents a challenge for musicians who want to perform *Stay On It* today. What Eastman had in mind for this improvisatory piece can, for the most part, only be discerned by talking with those who knew him and worked with him. The reconstructed scores of *Stay On It* that performers use today includes musical notation of short phrases, along with written instructions to musicians to perform certain parts "at their own discretion," to play "ad lib," or to choose from a number of phrases Eastman has composed. Musicians are directed to provide visual cues, or predetermined musical cues, to move from section to section, a game-like interaction that Eastman emphasized in public comments about the piece. The result is a composition that varies with each performance. This 2019 recording by Jacaranda reflects both Eastman's vision for the piece as well as sounds and understandings of the piece that the performers contribute.

Listen to the entire recording with these elements in mind while following this timed listening guide.

LISTENING GUIDE 12.4

TIME	SECTION	DESCRIPTION
0:00	A	The piece opens with four repetitions of a four-beat phrase by all instruments of the ensemble. The instruments play the syncopated rhythm in unison. They all play an arc-shaped stepwise melody in a major mode, but they start on different pitches, so they create a sense of harmony in a major key. The second half of the phrase is a repeated pitch on the habanera rhythm. After four repetitions of this theme, the vocalist enters, repeating the words "stay on it" on the fifth scale degree. Other members of the ensemble begin playing additional patterns that layer on top of and respond to the repeating theme. The vocalist joins the main theme, but also sings "stay on it" on the fifth and lowered seventh scale degrees, giving the piece its first reference to the blues.
2:24	B1	The main theme adds a second accented repeated pitch after the accent on beat one. After two repetitions of this modified main theme, the ensemble members add accented and sustained layers, with greater emphasis on the lowered seventh. The vocals feature notable slides in the vocals between the fifth and seventh, among other microtonal vocal styles of gospel and the blues.
3:36	B2	The main theme continues to repeat in a new variation, with a rhythmically compressed version of the first half of the initial theme, followed by a silence of varying durations, and then the habanera rhythm. The marimba enters on a sustained roll on a single pitch, the lowered seventh, during this section.
4:10	B3	The main theme repeats in another new variation, this time in a repeating cycle of five beats instead of four. The piano and vocalist play the first and second half of the rhythm, respectively, in a call-and-response pattern. The saxophone plays a sustained pitch, the lowered seventh, during this section.
4:59	B4	The texture thins and the ensemble performs quietly through this section, a delicate, highly syncopated variation on the theme in an eight-beat repeating cycle. At 5:30 the marimba enters with a strong roll on a sustained pitch (the fifth), which initiates a gradual thickening of the texture of the theme and an increase in volume leading into the next section.
5:45	C1	The original main theme returns followed by the adding of layers. At 6:26, the marimba introduces the first pitch outside of the mode of the piece, which is followed by other members of the ensemble playing outside of the mode. The rhythmic pattern, and tempo, change several times, and at 7:14, a faster, two-beat pattern sets in, with long sustained pitches.
7:57	C2	The original main theme returns followed by layered parts outside the mode of the theme. Eventually the theme becomes fragmented. As the vocalist sings in a gospel-soul style on vocables and the instrumentalists depart from the theme in many directions, the volume decreases and the texture becomes thinner until the ensemble is silent.
8:55	C3	The original main theme returns, layers are added, the beat disappears, and the volume decreases to silence.
9:42	C4	The original main theme returns again, with the vocalist entering at the end of the second repetition with a forceful repeating statement initially on the seventh scale degree that opens up into more gospel-soul melismas referencing the style of singers like Aretha Franklin. The others layer again and depart from the theme and its mode. This is the most raucous section yet, with some members of the ensemble emphasizing blues and gospel aesthetics, and others turning to more experimental techniques on their instruments such as **tone clusters** on the piano (many keys played simultaneously with the arm, elbow, or entire hand).

TIME	SECTION	DESCRIPTION
10:52	C5	The original main theme returns one last time with two strong repetitions. The ensemble layers and breaks down the beat and mode once again. Notable here is the vocalist singing a sustained "stay" on the tonic in a high register, slowing sliding the pitch up a half step and then a complete whole step. The saxophone joins her in a microtonal dissonance near her pitch several times, ascending higher before they gradually descend to lower pitches and decrease their volume. The ensemble becomes softer but does not totally die out.
12:00	D1	The piano begins playing a new rhythm in a repeating four-beat cycle reminiscent of a slow tango rhythm. The harmony oscillates generally between two different chords. Other instruments join the piano, gradually adding dissonance. Around 14:30 the piano departs from the rhythmic pattern and the harmony in an improvisatory manner. The other instruments slow the tempo and fade away, and the piano continues, improvising melodies and chords that gradually become more consonant.
16:34	D2	The piano returns to the repeating four-beat rhythmic pattern in a slow, rubato tempo, improvising the chords.
17:34	E	A tambourine joins the piano, playing a steady dance beat at a faster tempo than the piano, subdividing each beat into four with a slight swing. The piano slows and fades, until the tambourine is playing solo around 18:15. The tambourine continues its repeating pattern until the end of the recording.
19:40	End	

What Does It Mean?

Stay On It can be understood for the way it is situated within the social, political, and artistic iconoclasm of the 1950s, 1960s, and 1970s. After World War II the composers who enjoyed the most prestige used Arnold Schoenberg's twelve-tone serialism and its successor system, **total serialism**, the organization of all elements of music, including timbre, texture, rhythm, and dynamics, into series that provided the underlying material of the composition (Chapter 9, Gateway 36). These composers were creating a new equivalence among all these elements in a tradition that emphasized melody, harmony, and counterpoint more than all the other elements of music. Total serialism allowed composers to provide more detailed directions regarding many elements of a musical performance and to make the relationships among sounds in a piece of music extraordinarily complex. That complexity can be notated, seen, and explained on paper. Unfortunately, ordinary listeners find the music baffling because, except for the timbre of familiar instruments, little else is connected to previous musical experience. Predictable relationships among pitches, so crucial to most music, are avoided. Recognition of formal structure is almost impossible. And expressive devices such as dynamics are largely unpredictable.

Milton Babbitt (1916–2011) was the leading exponent of total serialism in the United States, and he approached composing music as an act of experimental science. He argued that music could be the subject of the same type of study as physics and mathematics. Just as quantum mechanics and the theory of relativity had placed the understanding of physics beyond the

FIGURE 12.27
Milton Babbitt with an electronic music synthesizer, c. 1965
Source: Getty Images/Keystone/Stringer.

capacity of all but a few specialists to understand, it should be possible, he argued, for compositions by an "informed composer" to reach that advanced stage.

Julius Eastman, together with another group of like-minded experimental composers,
rejected the total serialists' interest in complete control of musical elements. Instead, the composers sought ways for performers to join with them in the creation of music and experiment
with new ways of connecting to audiences. In 1964, the Center of the Creative and Performing
Arts was established at the State University of New York at Buffalo. Its aim was to decrease
the distance that had developed between composers, performers, and audiences in the twentieth century due to the increasing complexity of compositions. To achieve this aim, the Center
focused on attracting and funding a group of resident musicians and composers called "Creative
Associates." There were about twenty Creative Associates at any given time during the Center's existence (1964–1980), and these artists worked individually and collaboratively on new
projects. During a two-week festival of the arts put on by the Center in 1965, described in *Life*
magazine as "bigger and hipper than anything happening in Paris or New York," the Creative
Associates performed four sold-out concerts. The first concert turned away hundreds of people for
lack of space. Julius Eastman was a Creative Associate at the Center beginning in 1969. He
composed *Stay On It* for performance by an ensemble of Creative Associates, including him on
voice and piano.

Part of the appeal of *Stay On It* in 1973, and today, is its inclusion of known and familiar
musical sounds from a wide array of genres and styles. Its main theme returns repeatedly to the
sound of a major triad, a familiar sound to listeners of popular music, as well as jazz and classical
music. In this version of the piece, the vocalist and other musicians include a lowered seventh,
microtonality, and melismas in improvisations that bring in elements of blues, jazz, gospel, and
soul. The driving beat of *Stay On It* references popular music. Dennis Kahle, one of the percussionists in the piece's first performances, called the main theme a "riff"—a term common in
jazz and popular music—and interpreted it as influenced "almost entirely by soul/R&B music."
Other musicians recall discussions of the music of Motown's Diana Ross in rehearsals of *Stay
On It*, including Eastman's encouragement for players to include snippets of Diana Ross and the
Supremes' "Stop! In the Name of Love."

Stay On It also references disco, a genre of pop music that had, not incidentally, burst into
the mainstream in 1973. **Disco** is a soul-influenced music for dancing, typically featuring a regular beat in the bass (Chapter 13, Gateway 52). It originated in dance clubs called discothèques
or discos, underground venues in New York City where DJs played records in a continuous flow
for primarily Black, Latinx, and gay dancers. The beat in *Stay On It* connects it to disco, as do
the Latin American rhythms (for example, the habanera rhythm throughout the piece) and the
soul-influenced vocals. The beat pulsates incessantly through much of the piece, and one way
to understand the vocalist's repetitive command to "stay on it" is as an exhortation of the musicians to keep the beat going, the way DJs do when playing disco hits like the Bee Gees' "Stayin'
Alive" (1975), K.C. and the Sunshine Band's "Get Down Tonight" (1975), and Gloria Gaynor's "I
Will Survive" (1978). Though *Stay On It* was composed as concert music, many of its rhythmic
elements are oriented towards dance and often stimulate seated audiences to move their bodies. This is another way that Eastman, as an experimental musician and composer, challenges
conventions of classical music, by pushing the boundaries of expected audience behavior at
concerts.

The meaning of these musical elements of *Stay On It* can also be connected to Julius Eastman's personal identity. In a 1976 interview with the *Buffalo Evening News*, Eastman stated,
"What I am trying to achieve is to be what I am to the fullest: Black to the fullest, a musician to
the fullest, a homosexual to the fullest." In *Stay On It* Eastman directly references Black music,
such as soul, and gestures towards disco and its associations with gay nightlife. Musicians who
performed the piece with Eastman also suggested that the soloistic piano part that concludes
the piece (beginning at D1 in the listening guide) connects to sexuality as well. The piano in
this section is repetitive but also, when Eastman performed it (and in this recording), is full of
expression, introspection, and, the musicians suggested, sensuality. One of the recollections
of the early *Stay On It* performances from cellist David Gibson is that this section was often

CULTURAL
LINKAGES

SOCIAL
BEHAVIOR

performed as "musical lovemaking" between violinist Ben Hudson (who was also gay) and Eastman: "It got slower and it got sexier, and eyebrows and motions towards each other and flirting with each other. This piece is as much a theater piece as it is musical." While recorded or visual evidence of this interaction has proven difficult to find, this recollection is one of many examples where Eastman incorporated his personal identity into his work, a rarity at the time, and brought musicians and audiences face-to-face with erotic themes that were widely considered taboo in classical music performance.

What Is Its History?

AESTHETICS

One of the first composers in the classical music world to use the term "experimental" was John Cage (1912–1992), a Californian who, starting in the late 1940s, had articulated in his compositions and writings an extreme version of an experimentalist alternative to the traditions of European classical music. Born in Los Angeles, he studied composition with Arnold Schoenberg, who had moved to the United States from Vienna in the 1930s. Among Cage's inventions was the **prepared piano**, a piano into which screws and other objects are inserted between the strings to alter its timbre and emphasize its nature as a percussion instrument. Cage's *Sonatas and Interludes* for prepared piano (1946–1948) explore the resulting drum- and bell-like sounds in sixteen short "sonatas" mostly in AABB form and four "interludes."

In the 1940s Cage began to read Hindu and Zen Buddhist philosophy, whose search for quietness and stillness greatly affected his music. His most remarked-upon piece is called *4'33''*, first performed in 1952 at Maverick Concert Hall, a barn-like venue in a forested area near Woodstock, New York. The score called for the musician to perform three movements, all of them *tacet*, a traditional musical direction in Latin for performers to remain silent. The resulting performance, a kind of nonperformance, focuses listeners' attention on what are usually the extraneous and annoying sounds of a concert: the ambient noise of the lighting and heating systems, the audience coughing and moving in their seats, and so on. At a concert venue such as the Maverick Concert Hall, the sounds of the forest would have permeated the performance, including, perhaps, bird calls, the wind in the trees, rain splattering on the roof and windows, and, in the case of the premiere, murmurs of the audience. The composition is experimental in the sense that it questions the very nature of music and asks whether there is not also music, and thus lessons to be learned, in the seemingly random sounds of the environment, not just in the sounds that composers and performers intentionally organize in the name of music. Cage's compositions in this vein, like those of some other composers during this period, were engaged in an intense and deep questioning of fundamental assumptions about the separation of everyday life from art and music.

FIGURE 12.28
John Cage performing in 1966
Source: Getty Images/Rowland Scherman.

Recordings of music from around the world provided another inspiration for experimental music in this period. Composers borrowed instruments and ideas about tuning and scales from these traditions, and some invented their own instruments to play the new sounds and scales that interested them. If East Coast Ivy League colleges patronized the complexities of serialism and electronic music, the more laid-back culture of the West Coast, and California in particular, was home to many of these experiments. Henry Cowell (1897–1965), born in Menlo Park, California, wrote two concertos for Japanese *koto* (plucked zither) in the 1960s. Lou Harrison (1917–2003), born in Portland, Oregon, was a student of Cowell, of Arnold Schoenberg, and of K.R.T. Wasitodiningrat, an important Javanese composer who taught at the California Institute of the Arts. He wrote for combinations of Asian and European instruments and for Javanese gamelan. Harry Partch (1901–1974), born in Oakland and inspired by the microtonal pitch systems of Middle Eastern music, invented new musical instruments that could play a 43-pitch scale that he devised. His instruments included altered forms of the guitar, the Ancient Greek *kithara* (lyre), and the African marimba (xylophone), as well as whimsical percussion instruments made from cloud-chamber bowls used in physics labs and a set of suspended gourd bells he called a gourd tree.

Pauline Oliveros (1932–2016) was another composer active in experimental music on the West Coast at this time. Based in San Francisco from 1954 to 1967, and known as a performer and improviser on accordion, Oliveros was a leader in developing electronic and electroacoustic technologies in experimental music. She was one of the original members of the San Francisco (now Mills College) Tape Music Center, one of the centers of electronic music innovation on the West Coast in the 1960s. Her compositions in the 1960s often explored her interest in improvisation in relation to electronic music. *Bye Bye Butterfly* (1965) for oscillators, amplifiers, and tape, was fully improvised by Oliveros at the San Francisco Tape Music Center with these electronic technologies. The title of the piece refers to *Madame Butterfly* (1904), a popular opera by Giacomo Puccini, and is a play on the title of the then-recent Hollywood film musical *Bye Bye Birdie* (1963). Oliveros spontaneously incorporated a recording of the opera that happened to be on hand in the studio, manipulating it with her tape techniques. The piece encourages a farewell to the musical aesthetics and practices of nineteenth-century European classical music.

In this restless, searching, experimental cultural and artistic environment, some composers developed an approach to creating compositions that feature the ceaseless, pulsating repetition of a small number of musical elements. Beginning before Eastman's first compositions, La Monte Young (b. 1935), Terry Riley (b. 1935), Steve Reich (b. 1936) and Philip Glass (b. 1937) were among the first well-known composers of this style, which they developed as participants in a broader experimentalist Downtown Scene of 1960s New York. Because these Downtown composers' work seemed simple compared to the serialist music going on around them and the classical music that preceded them in the eighteenth and nineteenth centuries, it came to be labeled minimalism, even though the procedures they employed could be quite complex and the length of their works quite long. Musical **minimalism** emphasizes pulsating repetition of a small number of musical elements. In related movements in the 1960s, "minimal" and other styles of visual art reduced painting to color, shapes, and lines. In the 1960s and 1970s Steve Reich began studying African drumming traditions,

FIGURE 12.29
Harry Partch's Cloud-Chamber Bowls, a percussion instrument cut from large glass bottles
Source: HorsePunchKid, Wikimedia Commons.

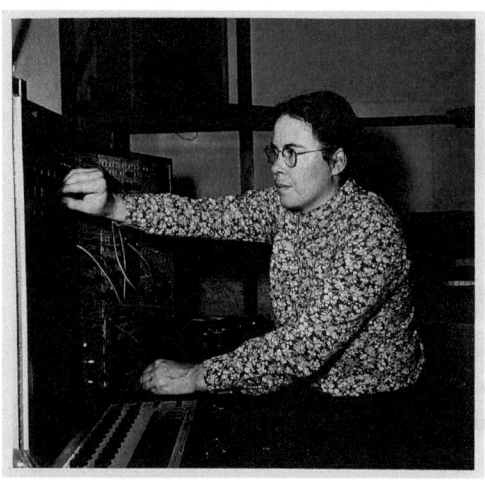

FIGURE 12.30
Pauline Oliveros in the studio at the Mills College Tape Music Center with Buchla 100-series modular synthesizers, 1966
Source: David Bernstein, photo courtesy of the Center for Contemporary Music Archive, Mills College.

traveled to Africa, and began to compose pieces for percussion ensemble influenced by the polyrhythms of African music. Philip Glass, inspired by the *tala*s of Indian classical music, wrote pieces with short repetitive melodies, simple harmonies, and repeated rhythms for his own ensemble.

The AACM (Chapter 21, Gateway 48), which had been founded in Chicago's virtually all-Black South Side in 1965, also became active in the New York experimental music world in the 1970s. Its members experimented with processes of improvisation, composition, and performance, as well as timbre, extended techniques, computer music technologies, and more, as their values of individual and collective self-production and promotion sought to challenge racialized limitations of African American musicians to Black-associated genres, such as jazz. AACM musicians in New York (and elsewhere)—such as Muhal Richard Abrams, Anthony Braxton,

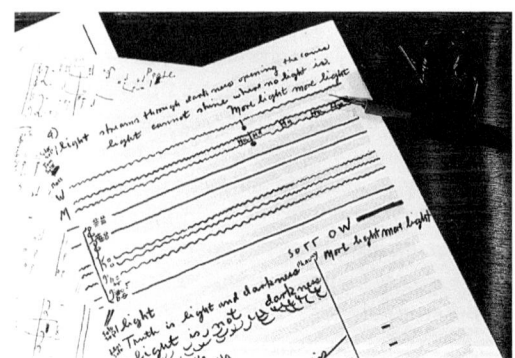

FIGURE 12.31A AND 12.31B
Two manuscripts of compositions Julius Eastman was working on c. 1970–1971
Source: D. W. Burkhardt.

Amina Claudine Myers, Henry Threadgill, and George Lewis—all contributed to various strands of experimental music and the many genres with which it intersects.

Julius Eastman entered this post-World War II world of experimentalism as a composer, pianist, and vocalist, having studied classical piano and composition in a conservatory (not an experimental) setting at the Curtis Institute of Music in Philadelphia, graduating in 1963. His music challenged both established conventions in classical music and many of the emerging practices of experimental composers such as Young, Reich, Glass, and Cage. The early minimalist compositions of Reich and Glass were often based on rigid pulse patterns that unfolded through repetition over long periods of time, resulting in almost mechanical music that was about process and control, with little reference to existing musical styles or external meanings. *Stay On It* and other Eastman compositions can be understood as critiques of this kind of minimalism, as they release control of repeating patterns, encourage improvisation, and reference popular music styles, as well as broader social and political ideas.

Eastman challenged the experimental work of John Cage in his performances of Cage's *Song Books (Solos for Voice 3–92)* (1970), a collection of pieces of four kinds: song, song with electronics, theater, and theater with electronics. The pieces of *Song Books* are filled with written instructions for performers, some of which ask them to create musical and theatrical elements on their own in advance, without telling the other performers what they had prepared. One of the sets of instructions reads:

> [I]n a situation with maximum amplification (no feedback), perform a disciplined action. With any interruptions. Fulfilling in whole or part an obligation to others. No attention to be given to the situation (electronic, musical, theatrical).

Eastman took a new approach to these instructions each time he performed the pieces. In the midst of a 1975 performance attended by Cage, Eastman presented a lecture on what he called a "new system of love," with a nude man and a semi-nude woman with him on stage. In an interview about the performance a year later, Eastman explained: "Well, it says 'perform a disciplined act,' so I gave this lecture on how to make love. What could be more disciplined? And with a pointer, I noted the various parts involved." The audience is reported to have admired the performance without significant shock; nudity on stage was not unprecedented, as thousands of people had seen the musical *Hair!* that had debuted on Broadway with on-stage nudity in 1968. But Cage was enraged, expressing disappointment and frustration that his work had been misunderstood.

Eastman's friends and some other writers have interpreted this performance as a challenge to the conspicuous absence of sexuality in the work of Cage, who was gay but did not discuss his sexuality publicly. Others view it as related to the broader struggle for gay rights. In 1969 a series of spontaneous demonstrations known as the Stonewall Uprising had occurred in response to

SOCIAL
BEHAVIOR

a police raid on a gay bar in New York City called the Stonewall Inn. The protests were a turning point for LGBTQ+ communities. The first pride march occurred at the first anniversary of the uprising, and within two years gay rights organizations had sprung up in major cities throughout the United States and many other parts of the world. Eastman's performance, six years after the Stonewall Uprising, demonstrates his awareness of the way society sought to control and limit people's sexuality by reclaiming and subverting this control in performance. Presenting his own anatomy lecture in a humorous, homoerotic performance piece, Eastman's experimentalism, in contrast to Cage's, engages with his personal identity in many of its dimensions, playing with audience perspectives and expectations, and challenging them to new understandings of music, and the world around them, as well.

After his time in Buffalo with the Creative Associates, Eastman lived in New York and participated in the Downtown scene, but never achieved the fame and financial success of minimalist composers such as Glass, who went on to enjoy a lucrative career composing music for operas, symphony orchestras, and films, among many other projects. Eastman toured Europe several times to perform his work and the work of other composers, including an international concert tour with the Creative Associates featuring *Stay On It* in 1974. Eastman's musical and artistic activity declined throughout the 1980s. He slipped in and out of homelessness; most of his scores were lost when he was evicted from an apartment he was living in; and he became disconnected from the social and artistic circles where he had previously collaborated so vibrantly. The extent to which this decline was due to structural factors such as racism and homophobia, or to Eastman's deliberate choices, remains subject to intense debate among scholars and those who knew and worked with him. After Eastman's death in 1990, his work remained mostly unknown and was rarely heard or performed until 2005, when the album *Unjust Malaise* (an anagram of his name), produced by Mary Jane Leach, was released by New World Records. The album features recordings of Eastman and the Creative Associates performing his pieces. Since then, an increasing interest in his music has led to more performances and recordings of his work, such as the recording of *Stay On It* from the Jacaranda concert series.

WHERE DO I GO FROM HERE?

- Listen to the 2021 version of *Stay On It* by Sō Percussion, MEDIAQUEER, Adam Tendler, Alex Sopp, Beth Meyers, Shelley Washington, and Grey Mcmurray. Some elements of this recording were recorded by remote collaboration due to the COVID-19 pandemic. Compare this recording to the Jacaranda Recording, or to the recording of it by Julius Eastman and his collaborators on the album *Unjust Malaise*. What musical possibilities and limitations are introduced by remote collaboration, either by necessity or by choice?

- If you decide to study more of Eastman's music, you will find that several of his compositions have titles with racist and homophobic slurs that can imply and perpetuate violence. Eastman's aim was to be provocative and, in part, to reclaim words whose original intent was to dehumanize and justify violence and murder. If you follow this path, we encourage respectful discussion in the classroom—and everywhere—about how words and language can cause harm. In your reading of press reviews or academic articles on these compositions, what do you learn about Eastman's reasons for titling his compositions in this way? How do the compositions, and the writing about them, confront audience and reader perspectives on race and sexuality? How do the titles relate to the musical sounds and meanings of the compositions?

- Read more about Pauline Oliveros and her work, and listen to *Bye Bye Butterfly* and her other compositions. What kinds of questions is she asking through her work about music, sound, listening, space, and the self?

GATEWAY 50
SALSA

What Is It?

Salsa first emerged in New York City in the 1960s and 1970s as a popular Latin American dance music. While it has roots in Cuban musical genres and influences from jazz, it was first popular

FIGURE 12.32
Tito Puente performing on the *timbales* with his band in 1985
Source: Getty Images/Robert Alexander.

among New York's Puerto Rican (or "Nuyorican") community. Its practitioners have come from a number of Latin American countries. As a result, salsa has broad appeal in a wide variety of music cultures. The word "salsa" can be used in a number of ways: as a musical genre or style, as a collection of musical genres or styles, or as a style of dance, not to mention its other common use in reference to a spicy sauce.

Our gateway to salsa is "Oye Como Va" by Nuyorican musician and international star Tito Puente (1923–2000), a song that contributed in part to the widespread popularity of salsa in the 1970s. "Oye Como Va" first appeared on Puente's 1963 album *El Rey: Bravo*. *El Rey* means "The King," and Puente was called "The King of the *timbales*" and "The King of Latin music" during his career. *Timbales* are single-headed drums with shallow metal bodies, usually tuned to higher pitches than the tom-toms of a drum set. During solos *timbaleros*, players of the *timbales*, produce a wide variety of timbres. When their role is to keep time, they play cowbells, cymbals, and the shell of the *timbales* rather than striking the drum heads. Traditionally *timbales* were played in sets of two, but Tito Puente added more drums to the set, and today up to seven or eight *timbales* of different sizes often appear together in a set. Although Tito Puente was associated with salsa for much of his career, he at times rejected the genre label, often instead preferring to consider himself a musician in the vein of Latin jazz or *mambo*, a dance music that developed in Cuba in the 1930s.

The phrase "oye como va" is a greeting that means something like "hey, how's it going?" but, together with the next line of text, it is an invitation to listeners and dancers to "listen to how my rhythm goes." It's no wonder, then, that rhythm is one of the most intriguing and captivating aspects of "Oye Como Va," and of salsa music more broadly.

 Listen to the first thirty seconds of the recording.

How Does It Work?

Timbre

Varied timbres are produced on the *timbales*, cowbell, *bongos* (small hand drums), and *congas* (barrel-shaped drums), along with male vocals, flute, saxophones, trombones, and trumpets.

Texture

The rhythm section provides a repetitive groove that supports polyphonic melodic lines and ostinatos in the flute, vocals, and saxophone and brass sections.

Rhythm

The rhythm of "Oye Como Va" is established by a repeating two-bar syncopated ostinato at the beginning of the recording. Each instrument or voice that enters introduces a new syncopated rhythm, creating a polyrhythm with many layers.

Melody

The melodies are mostly in minor and minor pentatonic modes.

Harmony

The harmony mostly alternates between a minor i chord and the IV chord, both with upper extensions of the chords.

Form

The form alternates between instrumental sections and a vocal refrain, called a *coro*, from the Spanish for "chorus."

Performance Techniques

Though much of the material is pre-composed, the flute seems to be improvising many of its phrases.

Listen to the first thirty seconds of the recording with these elements in mind.

Listen to the entire recording following this timed listening guide.

LISTENING GUIDE 12.5

TIME	SECTION	DESCRIPTION	LYRICS
0:00	Introduction	A piano and some soft wind instruments begin playing repeating block chords in a two-measure syncopated pattern. The harmony, a minor i chord in the first measure and a IV chord in the second measure, is also outlined in the bass, which plays a slightly different syncopated rhythm. The sound of hand claps and some drum sticks struck together play yet another rhythm.	
0:15		After a brief percussion fill, the *timbales*, *bongos*, and *congas* enter with more syncopated rhythms that repeat over the two-measure cycle. A trumpet and some trombones join the piano, playing its same rhythm and harmony.	
0:22		A flute enters playing a mostly stepwise minor melody that repeats over the two-measure cycle.	
0:38	Break	The polyrhythmic texture shifts to a homorhythmic one as the ensemble suddenly begins playing a syncopated rhythm all together for four measures.	
0:46	*Coro*	The polyrhythmic texture begins again (without the brass) and the vocals enter, singing a melody in a minor pentatonic mode. The flute answers each two-measure vocal phrase with a melody that begins with a descending one-octave jump.	Oye como va . . .
1:01	Break	A two-measure version of the homorhythmic break.	
1:05	Instrumental 1	The polyrhythmic texture in the piano, bass, and percussion begins again, this time with a melody in the saxophones that outlines a seventh chord on the first measure and resolves to a pitch in the IV chord. The accents in the melody create a syncopated rhythm.	
1:20		The trombones are added to the texture with yet another syncopated melody.	
1:36		The trumpet and flute are added to the texture with two additional syncopated melodies.	
1:52	Break	The two-measure version of the homorhythmic break.	
1:55	*Coro*	The *coro* returns as a nearly identical repeat of the first verse.	Oye como va . . .
2:12	Instrumental 2	The percussion, bass, and piano play repeating pulsating tones. At first only the lowest saxophone plays along with its own repeating eighth notes, but every two beats, a slightly higher pitch in the chord is added by a new instrument, creating a long crescendo and culminating with the final two beats of the four bars where everyone plays together with the flute on the highest pitch.	

TIME	SECTION	DESCRIPTION	LYRICS
2:20		A slightly different polyrhythm begins in the rhythm section, and the saxophones introduce a new syncopated melody that moves by leaps downward from the third scale degree of the minor mode. The flute plays what seems to be an improvised melody mostly in the minor mode. The vocalists interject a melody, along with whistling, shouting, and other party-like sounds.	
2:35		The trombones add a repeating figure that creates the effect of a polymeter where a triple meter happens over the existing duple meter.	
2:51		The trumpet adds a repeating figure, playing the ninth (an upper extension) of the i chord over and over in the high register.	
3:07	Break	The four-measure version of the homorhythmic break.	
3:15		The song seems to end, but is followed by many vocal sounds of cheering and shouting, whistling, some striking of the congas, and shouts of "one more time."	
3:27	Instrumental 3	The band seems to respond to the request to play it "one more time" and begins again at the beginning of Instrumental 2, playing it basically the same as the first time, but at a slightly quicker tempo and with different flute improvisations.	
4:29	End		

What Does It Mean?

AESTHETICS

As a dance music, salsa places a particular importance on rhythm. Each subgenre or dance style of salsa has its own distinct rhythm. "Oye Como Va" is a *cha-cha-chá*, a moderate-tempo dance named onomatopoeically for the repeating shuffle sound of three quick steps. At the beginning of the recording, the hand claps clearly outline the *cha-cha-chá* dance rhythm, which dancers start on beat 2 and can be felt as "2–3-cha-cha-cha, 2–3-cha-cha-cha." Over the two-measure repeating cycle, the rhythm would look something like this:

```
1   2   3   4   1   2   3   4   1

x   x   x   x x x   x   x   x x x
```

Concurrent with that hand clap pattern, the piano plays its own syncopated rhythm, a pattern that, as a result of the popularity of "Oye Como Va," has become a *cha-cha-chá* riff synonymous with the song. Its first two chords are on beats 1 and 2 of the first measure, and the last four occur on the offbeats:

```
Beats:  1   2   3   4   1   2   3   4
Piano:  x   x     x   x       x   x
```

The third thread in the texture at the beginning of the recording is the bass, which repeats a two-measure ostinato. The basic rhythm of the bass is known as a *tumbao*, in this rhythmic pattern:

```
Beats:  1   2   3   4   1   2   3   4
Bass:   x           x   x       x x   x
```

The *tumbao* in salsa music does not play on the first beat of the second measure, but rather anticipates it, playing the root of the chord of the second measure a half a beat early. (In some *tumbao* patterns, the bass anticipates every measure by up to a full beat, and never plays beat one.) When layered together, the hand claps, piano, and bass patterns form a polyrhythmic structure of interlocking beats:

Beats:	1	2	3	4	1	2	3	4
Claps:	x	x	x	x x x	x	x	x x	
Piano:	x	x	x	x		x	x	
Bass:	x			x	x		x x	x

In most salsa music, including the *cha-cha-chá*, yet another underlying rhythmic pattern, called **clave**, governs the performance of the entire ensemble. *Clave* is named after an instrument called *claves*, a pair of short, thick, resonant wooden rods that are struck together to produce a short, high-pitched sound. The *claves* often play the *clave* pattern, but sometimes, as in "Oye Como Va," the *clave* pattern is implied rather than heard. *Clave* can take two different rhythmic forms: a "2–3 *clave*" and a "3–2 *clave*." A 2–3 *clave* has two beats in the first half of the ostinato and three in the second half and vice versa for the 3–2 *clave*.

A 2–3 *clave*:

Beats:	1	2	3	4	1	2	3	4
Clave:		x	x		x		x	x

A 3–2 *clave*:

Beats:	1	2	3	4	1	2	3	4
Clave:	x		x		x		x	x

FIGURE 12.33
Salsa dancers
Source: Kumar Sriskandan/Alamy Stock Photo.

"Oye Como Va" is based on a 2–3 *clave*, though the *clave* is not very pronounced. It most closely corresponds to the piano part, where the first bar is relatively unsyncopated and the second bar is syncopated. If it were added to the texture at the beginning of the recording, a 2–3 *clave* would contribute yet another line to the polyrhythmic structure:

Beats:	1	2	3	4	1	2	3	4
Claps:	x	x	x	x x x	x	x	x x	
Piano:	x	x	x	x		x	x	
Bass:	x		x	x		x x	x	
Clave:		x	x		x		x	x

As the *timbales* take over, the hand claps and more and more instruments and rhythms are layered on top of this introductory texture, and the polyrhythm becomes more and more complex. Salsa musicians must orient their playing around the *clave* ostinato pattern, whether that pattern is heard or implied. When everyone is locked into the feel of the *clave*, it is said to produce just the right groove for the enjoyment of the musicians and for the dancers. Tellingly, the word *clave* means "key" or "code." It is the key to organizing and holding together a salsa groove.

 Listen again to "Oye Como Va" and try clapping along with the various rhythmic patterns of the instruments playing in the introduction. Try to clap the 2–3 clave and see if you can stick with it.

Salsa's polyrhythmic roots may be in African and Afro-Latin musical styles, but it also employs the harmonic sensibilities of jazz, especially the use of upper extensions that build on European-derived triadic harmony by adding desirable dissonances. For example, in the opening piano riff of "Oye Como Va," the piano can be heard switching between the minor i chord (A minor) and the IV chord (D major). On careful listening, the tonic (A) is the highest pitch in both chords, and the only pitch to change from one chord to the next is the lowest pitch (which moves from G to F♯). The pitches in the middle, though hard to hear individually, are G, E, A, C, and D. They stay consistent for each chord and add dissonances (such as the major second between C and D) and upper extensions (E is the ninth of the D major chord) to each one. Later in the song, at the end of the second instrumental (2:51) the trumpet adds the final layer in a polyphonic, polyrhythmic texture by playing a repeating figure on the note B, which is the ninth of the A minor chord and the thirteenth of the D major chord. Adding this upper extension to the harmony means that both chords contain the adjacent pitches A, B, C, D, and E at the same time. This kind of dissonant harmony is something that jazz musicians often value. Played by an ensemble of horns (saxophones, trombones, trumpet) derived from the jazz big band as part of a multi-layered polyrhythm based on *clave*, it makes sense that Tito Puente considered his music to be Latin jazz.

POLITICS

Listen to "Oye Como Va" one more time, listening this time for how the dissonances and the upper extensions are placed within the polyrhythmic structure, particularly in the trumpet at 2:51 as it creates a dissonance in its repeated pitch. Listen for the sound of the horns as a reflection of the influence of the big band sound.

Salsa musicians frequently include social commentary in the lyrics of their music. In the early twentieth century, thousands of Cubans and Puerto Ricans had settled in New York City, many in the upper Manhattan neighborhood of East Harlem, which became known as "Spanish Harlem." In the 1960s, a group of Puerto Rican activists called the Young Lords, inspired by the Black Panthers and the Black Power movement, began to take a stand against social inequalities and injustices experienced in this and other Spanish-speaking neighborhoods (*barrios*) in New York and other American cities. Nuyorican and other Puerto Rican and Latin American communities around the country, in the spirit of the social upheaval of the 1960s, were mobilized to achieve social and political goals and to resist cultural assimilation. Instead of assimilating, they took pride in their cultural roots and in their distinctive communities that had become embedded in the multicultural life of American cities. As musicians began including lyrics that commented on the realities of life in the *barrios*, critiqued American imperialism, and advocated for pan-Latin solidarity, the music that would become known as salsa began to serve as a social resource for individuals and communities. In salsa they experienced a musical performance of their complex and multifaceted identities in the form of energetic dance music.

CULTURAL LINKAGES

Nuyoricans and other Puerto Ricans in the 1960s and 1970s began to view salsa as an icon of their ethnic identity. Its nature as a sophisticated and cosmopolitan urban genre with influences from all over Latin America and elsewhere seemed to connect to their lived experience as Puerto Ricans living a cosmopolitan, urban life in New York City. Instead of a European-style musical nationalism based on rural folk music and cultivated by a state government to showcase a nation's distinctiveness, salsa expressed the national identity of urbanized Puerto Ricans and Nuyoricans as it emerged as a commercial music connecting them with other Latin American nationalities and across boundaries of age and class.

What Is Its History?

CULTURAL LINKAGES

This particular *clave* rhythmic pattern (in both 2–3 and 3–2 versions) is called *son clave* because it originates in a genre of music called Cuban *son* (sound, style). A genre of Afro-Cuban music, Cuban *son* (or *son cubano*) developed in the early twentieth century as a synthesis of musical elements with roots in both European and African music. The Spanish began colonizing Cuba in the early sixteenth century. Over the next two and a half centuries more than one million Africans were enslaved and brought to Cuba. The *son clave* of *son cubano* likely has roots in similar five-stroke patterns in much of sub-Saharan Africa, where iron bells play "bell patterns" to keep the beat in drum ensembles. In Cuba these patterns found their way into the Afro-Cuban syncretic religion called Santería (Chapter 6, Gateway 23) and eventually into all genres of Afro-Cuban popular music: *mambo*, *son montuno*, *rumba*, *bolero*, *guaguancó*, *guaracha*, and *danzón*, among others.

Salsa as a named music and dance genre emerged in the 1960s and 1970s in New York. But Latin American music was popular in the United States earlier, subsumed under the catch-all category "Latin music." Latin and Afro-Caribbean sounds were consistently featured in 1920s Broadway and Tin Pan Alley music. In the 1930s the Spanish-born Cuban Xavier Cugat (1900–1990), one of the first famous Latin bandleaders in the United States, appeared in many Hollywood films performing in a variety of Latin styles. In the 1940s Dizzy Gillespie and Cuban drummer Chano Pozo combined Afro-Cuban music with bebop to create Latin jazz. Cuban band leaders Frank "Machito" Grillo (1912–1984) and Mario Bauzá (1911–1993) mixed Cuban rhythms and big band jazz (Chapter 11, Gateway 43). The Cuban-style dance music *mambo* thrived in New York in the 1940s and 1950s. Puerto Rican bandleaders Machito (*c.* 1908–1984), Pablo "Tito" Rodriguez (1923–1973), and Tito Puente led featured acts at New York's Palladium Ballroom, the central hub of New York's Latin music and dance scene. Audiences at the Palladium were diverse: some nights attracted Puerto Ricans, other nights attracted African American audiences, and others attracted mixed audiences. Dancers active in the big band swing scene at the Savoy Ballroom often came to the Palladium, bringing with them their dance steps and contributing to the wide variety of cultural influences in the Latin music and dance scene.

By the 1960s, however, Latin music was experiencing a decline in popularity. Both big bands and large ensembles playing Latin music for dancing had fallen out of favor with the rise of rock and roll. The *mambo* craze had died out, the end of the era punctuated by the closing of the Palladium Ballroom in 1966. The intense interest in Cuban music that had fueled much of Latin music's development and popularity had also lost its connection to current music in Cuba due to the U.S. embargo against all imports from Cuba in 1962, a tactic designed to isolate the island nation economically, politically, and culturally in the wake of the Cuban Revolution and the ascendance of Fidel Castro's new government. Because they could no longer innovate alongside musicians arriving from Cuba, Latin musicians in New York in the 1960s began developing their music in their own ways. Instead of big bands, musicians formed smaller ensembles, some based on a small ensemble format called *conjunto*, which in the 1950s had been well established by many Cuban musicians in the New York scene. New York-born Puerto Rican pianist and bandleader Eddie Palmieri (b. 1936) established a *conjunto* that included piano, bass, percussion, flute, trumpets, prominent trombones, and vocals. This kind of *conjunto* ensemble, and others that were basically smaller versions of the large *mambo* orchestras, inspired what became salsa. Palmieri became one of the early stars of salsa on the way to a career that has spanned over six decades and resulted in worldwide fame and countless awards, including a number of Grammys.

Salsa's rise to fame around the world is inseparable from Fania Records. Fania chose the term "salsa" as a genre label to promote music rooted in Cuban *son*, interconnected with *mambo*, and developed in New York among musicians playing music from a variety of Caribbean and Latin American countries. The origins of salsa as a genre label are not clear. Some argue that Venezuelan radio DJ Phidia Danilo Escalona was the first to use the term in the early 1960s (not unlike the American DJ Alan Freed who popularized the genre label "rock and roll"). Others claim that a New York publisher named Izzy Sanabría first used the term in the late 1960s. Regardless of its origins, by the early 1970s salsa was the genre label in common use, due in no small part to

FIGURE 12.34

Salsa band and dancers at the Granada in Los Angeles (2004)
Source: Getty Images/Lawrence K. Ho/*Los Angeles Times*.

the many albums recorded and promoted by Fania Records. Founded in 1964 by Dominican-born bandleader Johnny Pacheco (b. 1935), Fania launched the careers of many salsa stars, whose recordings topped the charts not only in the *barrios* but also throughout Latin America. The label also put together a legendary supergroup, a gathering of the most successful salsa instrumentalists and singers into one band called the Fania All-Stars. In the 1970s the Fania All-Stars and the many individual salsa artists on the label sold millions of records and performed on tours throughout the Americas. Salsa exploded in popularity in the 1970s. Fania had played a significant role in transforming it from a music associated with the lower socio-economic classes of the *barrios* to one also celebrated and enjoyed by the middle and upper classes throughout the United States, Latin America, and the Caribbean.

One of Fania's earliest and most successful artists was the Nuyorican trombonist and composer Willie Colón (b. 1950), who signed with the label at age fifteen and two years later in 1967 released his first album, the bestselling *El Malo* (The Bad One). Colón's music is full of examples of lyrics about life in the *barrios*, such as his 1973 "Calle Luna Calle Sol," a cautionary tale that describes the dangers of the streets. It is also a clear example of a two-trombone instrumentation that had become common in salsa. This song, still a staple of salsa bands everywhere, first appeared on an album he recorded with the vocalist Héctor Lavoe (1946–1993) humorously and darkly titled *Lo Mato* (*Si No Compra Este LP*), which loosely means "I'll Kill You (If You Don't Buy This LP)." Colón also emphasized salsa's connection to Puerto Rico and Puerto Rican musicians by featuring the ten-stringed Puerto Rican *cuatro*, among other practices (Chapter 4, Gateway 13). Involved in social activism for most of his life, Colón often deals in his music with the complexities and challenges of life for Puerto Ricans in the United States, in particular on his 1993 album *Hecho en Puerto Rico* (Made in Puerto Rico).

POLITICS

One of Colón's many collaborators was the Panama-born musician and composer Rubén Blades (b. 1948), whose music also emphasizes social activism, including such themes as imperialism, environmentalism, and disarmament, along with critiques of capitalism and the conditions of *barrio* life. Their most successful collaboration was the 1978 album *Siembra* (Planting), arguably the best-selling salsa album of all time. On this album Blades's social commentary is particularly sharp on songs like "Plástico" (Plastic), a critique of capitalist materialism, and the now-classic "Pedro Navaja" (Pedro Knife), a grim story about *barrio* life where, in the end, a small-time criminal (Pedro Navaja) and a prostitute end up killing one another. A favorite son of Panama, Blades has been involved in acting and politics, and even ran for president in Panama in 1994, receiving 17 percent of the vote among seven candidates.

CULTURAL LINKAGES

Perhaps the most famous female salsa singer was Celia Cruz (1925–2003), "The Queen of Salsa." Born in Cuba, she was a well-known singer in the 1950s before moving to New York in 1959 in the aftermath of the Cuban Revolution. She worked extensively with Tito Puente before her 1974 album, with Fania co-founder Johnny Pacheco, titled *Celia y Johnny* (1974) launched her into stardom. The song "Quimbará" from the album became one of her classic hits, famously starting out with the line "*rumba* is calling out to me," and featuring Cruz shouting "Azúcar!" (Sugar!), a signature exclamation of hers that she often shouted during performances to rev up the audience. The most famous song of her later career, "La Vida es un Carnaval" (Life is a Carnival) from the 1998 album *Mi Vida Es Cantar* (My Life Is Singing), addressed hardships in life but focused on how celebration, singing, and a positive attitude can help someone survive difficult situations, serve as a powerful antidote to complainers and critics, and even be a force against the evils of war and disease.

FIGURE 12.35
Celia Cruz performing in Mexico City
Source: Keith Dannemiller/Alamy Stock Photo.

Tito Puente, like his close collaborator Celia Cruz, enjoyed wide renown long before salsa was an established genre. He was born to Puerto Rican parents in New York City, spent much of his childhood in Spanish Harlem, and began playing percussion at age ten. After serving in the U.S. Navy during World War II, he studied music formally at the Juilliard School. After that, he built his reputation as a performer and bandleader, becoming known as the King of the Timbales and the King of Mambo in the 1950s as he performed *rumba*, *son*, *cha-cha-chá*, and other genres for audiences who were going crazy for Latin dance music. He enjoyed many successful years as one of the featured acts at the Palladium Ballroom and other venues at the center of the Latin music scene in New York, though his popularity declined along with the popularity of Latin dance music in the 1960s.

He recorded frequently—in the early 1950s he was known to release a recording every week—and 1963's "Oye Como Va" was just one of many of his recordings from the 1960s that, initially, enjoyed only modest success among devotees of his and other Latin music. "Oye Como Va" became a mainstream hit after the Latin rock band Santana released a version of it on their second album, *Abraxas* (1970). Fronted by Mexican American guitarist Carlos Santana, the band became prominent after their performance at the Woodstock festival in 1969. For "Oye Como Va," Santana replaced the piano in the introduction with a Hammond B-3 organ and the flute with the distinctive electric guitar sound of Carlos Santana. He also took over the saxophone and brass lines, turning instrumental sections into guitar solos rooted in rock and the blues. The recording also features an energetic organ solo, soloistic percussion playing, and modified breaks. These elements, combined with Santana's significant popularity in rock, made "Oye Como Va" a hit and reignited Puente's popularity (and his bank account, with royalties paid to him as the songwriter). Santana's massively popular version of the song was a factor in the rise of salsa to popularity throughout the United States and Latin America.

Since Puente had enjoyed great success in the 1950s, before salsa was coined as a genre name, he was reluctant to embrace the term and call himself a salsa musician, though eventually he reconciled himself to the genre label, even working with Fania Records in his later years. By the 1990s Puente, like Cruz, was an icon of Latin music, and the two of them collaborated on hundreds of recordings and performances. Puente himself released over 100 albums and is credited with over 400 compositions. Some regard him as the most important figure of the twentieth century in all of Latin music. "Oye Como Va" had introduced salsa—and Puente—to much of the world, and the last album he recorded, *Mambo Birdland* (1999), featured the song as its final track. After his death in 2000, Latin pop stars that had emerged in the 1980s and 1990s, Gloria Estefan and Ricky Martin, joined Celia Cruz in a tribute performance to Tito Puente and his massive influence at the Latin Grammy Awards. The performance featured a band full of outstanding musicians, and even a video of Puente playing the *timbales*, whose sound was synced up with the band's performance. The performance began with Martin singing "Oye Como Va," a celebration of the enormous contributions of Tito Puente to Latin music, contributions that still resonate today.

WHERE DO I GO FROM HERE?

- Listen to Santana's version of "Oye Como Va" for the way the musical elements of the blues and rock combine with the polyrhythms of Tito Puente's original composition? Can you hear the *clave* in this case?

- Listen to "La Vida es un Carnaval" or "Quimbará" by Celia Cruz. Can you identify some of the musical elements of salsa in these recordings? Can you feel the *clave* pattern based on the way the rhythm fits together even if you can't hear it?

- Find the lyrics to "Plástico" by Rubén Blades and Willie Colón (and a translation if you need one) and listen to the recording. What other musical influences are obvious from the introduction to the song? What musical elements typical of salsa do you hear? Can you feel the *clave* pattern in this recording? To what extent does the social commentary of the song suit its social function as dance music?

- If you listen to contemporary Latin pop stars, choose a song by one of them and see if you can connect some of its musical elements to "Oye Como Va" or some of the other music mentioned in this gateway.

CLOSING

Musicians in the period between 1950 and 1975 responded, almost of necessity, to the powerful waves of social change and political unrest sweeping the United States and the world during this period. Rhythm & blues and soul brought African American communities together and contributed a hopeful soundtrack to the civil rights movement. Rock and roll helped a new, young generation of teenagers define themselves in contrast to older generations and express disenchantment with the world they were inheriting. Jazz musicians struggled against the boundaries of their tradition, some by combining it with rock and other popular genres to attract a young audience, some by rejecting the boundaries with avant-garde artistic expressions of ideologies related to the civil rights movement, and some by pushing the limits of older styles such as bebop. Composers of European classical music questioned the nature of music and experimented with new musical ideas at odds with hundreds of years of thinking about music. And salsa music exploded all over the world as Puerto Ricans and Latin Americans everywhere listened and danced to music that celebrated their multifaceted identities. With the end of the war in Vietnam, a new era of international peace seemed to be dawning. Musicians' attention would turn to absorbing and responding to the stylistic changes of this period and to confronting even more directly racial inequality and injustice at home and aboard.

THINGS TO THINK ABOUT

- Music takes a number of forms as protest or resistance music in this chapter. What do the various musical modes of resistance in the gateways to rhythm & blues and soul, rock, jazz, salsa, and classical music in this chapter share, and how are they different from one another? How are they similar to or different from music of protest and resistance today?

- Rock and roll, rock, and rhythm & blues music have long involved the contested crossing of boundaries of race and class, while salsa music exploded into a pan-Latin music that prided itself in crossing boundaries among Latin American communities. Compare these two cases. What are some of the historical and musical factors involved in how these kinds of boundaries are established and negotiated?

NEW TERMS

backbeat	folk music	prepared piano
bridge	free jazz	rock and roll
clave	funk	*timbales*
comping	fuzz box	tone clusters
concept album	hard bop	total serialism
cover	jazz fusion	wah-wah pedal
disco	minimalism	
feedback	modal jazz	

MUSIC AND COMMUNITY (1975–1994)

BETWEEN THE END of the Vietnam War in 1975 and 1994, 500 years of European colonialism, which began in 1492, came to an end with the dissolution of the last great European empire, the Soviet Union, and the end of white rule over an African majority in South Africa. The Cold War between the United States and the Soviet Union continued during this period (until the fall of the Soviet Union in 1991) and both countries plowed enormous sums of money into their nuclear weaponry and anti-ballistic missile systems. In the United States excessive military spending, along with an oil crisis initiated by Arab countries angered at American support for Israel, created a long-lasting economic recession with the highest unemployment rates since the Great Depression of the 1930s. The American auto industry, one of the country's most powerful economic engines, faced competition from carmakers in Japan. Unemployment and fear of a nuclear war fueled anger, anxiety, and hopelessness among lower- and middle-class white youth and probably account, in part at least, for the emergence of new aggressive genres of rock.

While the United States survived these economic and political upheavals, the Soviet Union did not. Destabilization in the Middle East, including an Islamic revolution in Iran in 1979, led the Soviet Union to invade and occupy Afghanistan. As it poured more and more money into the military sector of its economy, its citizens, along with those in the other communist countries of eastern Europe, became less and less satisfied with their standard of living compared to what they could see in western Europe. In 1989 communist governments fell across the whole of eastern Europe: in East Germany, Poland, Czechoslovakia, Hungary, Romania, and Bulgaria. In 1990 Yugoslavia dissolved, and war broke out among a number of its former federated republics. In 1991 the Soviet Union collapsed, the Cold War ended, and the communist world was reduced from nineteen countries to five: The People's Republic of China, North Korea, Vietnam, Laos, and Cuba.

In the so-called third world, African decolonization, begun in the 1950s, continued throughout this period. Angola and Mozambique in Southwestern Africa gained independence from Portugal in 1975, ending formal European colonial rule on the continent. However, in southern Africa white rule continued in the independent countries of Rhodesia and South Africa. Black resistance eventually brought democratic rule to Rhodesia, which changed its name to Zimbabwe in 1980, and to South Africa in 1994, when Nelson Mandela (1918–2013), a political prisoner for more than twenty-five years, was elected president. Many African musicians, by creating new styles and genres of music, joined political leaders, intellectuals, and educators in the creation of national identity and national sentiment.

The political successes in Africa existed in counterpoint with increasing poverty there. The global economy sucked more and more of the world's wealth into the industrialized world, creating economic misery across the world and pushing many to migrate from rural to urban areas and

DOI: 10.4324/9781003269304-17

FIGURE 13.1
Paul Simon performing with South African musicians from his *Graceland* album
Source: Getty Images/Rob Verhorst.

to leave their countries for the promise of greater prosperity abroad. Rural music traditions in many places were threatened, and new genres of urban music mixed local rural musical styles with elements of urban popular music. Immigrants brought increased ethnic diversity to growing cities, where interethnic musical fusions became commonplace, only partly fueled by the popularity of Paul Simon's best-selling 1986 album *Graceland*, on which he played with South African musicians. In 1987 record company executives in Britain settled on the genre label **world music** to describe hybrid musical performances that capitalized on the supposed authenticity of traditional music and the commercial appeal of popular music.

As the creation of the world music genre illustrates, not only did people migrate around the world, but their cultures did as well. The United States exported its film, music, and sports to every corner of the globe, and Americans, both long-standing residents and new immigrants, listened to music and viewed television shows from all over the world. New technology facilitated the easy passage of these cultural products across political borders and vast expanses of land. Audiocassettes that were cheap to produce and easy to pirate became available in the 1970s, and videocassettes soon followed in the 1980s. Personal computers became a necessity for many in the 1980s, and the internet debuted in the early 1990s, facilitating international communication and making knowledge of cultural and political activity in distant communities and nations as close as a click away.

Bob Marley, a Jamaican playing a genre called **reggae**, became a hero to working-class, Black Caribbean immigrants in Canada and the U.K. and, via recordings, to underprivileged Black populations in Brazil, South Africa, and the United States. The poor and oppressed in America and throughout the world learned about a new genre of Black popular music called **rap** from audiocassettes, radio, videotapes, and MTV, which launched in 1981 and played its first rap video in 1984. Rap music's chronicles of Black life in America inspired the poor and disaffected all over the world to adopt the genre for their own need to document their lives and protest the conditions in which they lived. Historians began to write about "the Black Atlantic," which encompasses networks of cultural exchange among Black musicians, writers, and other artists from Africa, the Caribbean, the United States and the U.K. Music is central to those flows of culture and, in addition to reggae and rap, other vigorous new popular music genres emerged along the Black Atlantic such as Afro-pop in Africa. These and other genres were inspired both by the independence of African countries from European colonial rule in the 1950s and 1960s and by the continued suffering of people of the African diaspora under repressive, racist political conditions around the world.

In the 1980s, the world was confronted with a new problem: HIV/AIDS, a deadly infectious virus that attacks the immune system. First identified in the United States in 1981, it spread around the world, with particularly devastating effects in Africa. It has caused an estimated thirty-six million deaths since then, and today an estimated thirty-eight million people are living with HIV/AIDS.

Although a lot of music in this period responded in one way or another to the political and economic crises of the time, not all of it did. The end of the Vietnam War had healed a gaping wound in American culture. Many social and political activists and hippies, having tuned in, turned on, and dropped out in the 1960s, dropped back in, cut their hair, and took mainstream jobs. The music industry geared up to take advantage of middle-class disposable income through a proliferation of subgenres of rock and popular music. And musicians all over the world tried to sell their styles of hybrid world music in the newly active global marketplace, which had given their efforts a name.

Much of the music performed and listened to today has its roots in this period. Classical composers returned to and revivified older musical styles. Some jazz musicians continued to seek a larger audience through their fusions with popular music styles, and others did so by honoring "classics" from the past of jazz. In addition to rap and a number of subgenres of rock, other genres of music that suffuse American popular music today got their start in this period, including electronic dance music (EDM), which first emerged as house music in Chicago and techno in Detroit as queer, Black communities of music lovers experimented with some of the possibilities created by developments in music technology.

GATEWAY 51
RAP AND HIP-HOP

What Is It?

Hip-hop has influenced popular music today arguably more than any other genre. It is enjoyed around the world by audiences of many cultural and class backgrounds and is a multibillion-dollar industry. Its impact can be heard in all types of popular music and stretches beyond music to film, television, fashion, politics, sports, video games, tourism industries, and many other sectors of society. Long before it was the big business it is today, however, hip-hop culture emerged in the 1970s among communities of African American, Latinx, and Caribbean American youth in economically struggling neighborhoods of the Bronx, located just north of Manhattan in New York City. At its inception **hip-hop culture** was a local phenomenon that included music (made by DJs and MCs), dance (breakdancing), and visual art (graffiti), as well as styles of dress and, later, the practice of producing percussive effects with the voice and mouth called beatboxing.

Hip-hop DJs (an abbreviation for "disc jockey") in the 1970s spun records (discs) for dancing at neighborhood parties, at dance clubs, and in other settings for partying in local communities. They found that dancers were excited by the instrumental "breaks" on funk and salsa recordings, where the vocals dropped out and the rhythm section was featured. Using turntable technology, they figured out ways to insert breaks from one record into the middle of another record and to loop a particular break over and over by playing two copies of the same record on their turntables and alternating from one to the other. First DJs, and later, MCs (an abbreviation for "master of ceremonies") would hype up and control the crowds at these parties not only by speaking on microphones, but also by performing improvised and pre-written rhymes over these so-called breakbeats, a practice that became known as **rapping** or **rap**. MCs relied on clever wordplay to boastfully introduce themselves, energize the crowd, describe dance moves, and tell humorous stories with references to local neighborhoods and social groups. Dancers developed an acrobatic style of improvised solo dance on breakbeats called **breakdancing**, with its young athletic dancers known as "B-boys" and "B-girls." Until the 1979 release of the first commercial hip-hop recording, "Rapper's Delight" by the Sugarhill Gang, rap music was heard mostly in live performance at parties as an element of hip-hop culture. The commercial success of "Rapper's Delight" introduced people across America and around the world to hip-hop and inspired the production of many more rap recordings.

By the late 1980s, rap music had blossomed into a major sector of the popular music industry. Because of this growing commercial success, the rapid innovation of the genre, its wide variety of themes, and the influence of recordings released at that time on future developments in hip-hop, the late 1980s and early 1990s are known as the "golden era" of hip-hop, especially with regard to rap on the East Coast. By this time a number of rappers and groups had begun to produce songs that described the social realities of life in poor urban African American communities and related issues of racism, violence, drugs, police brutality, and various forms of discrimination. A group leading the way in this kind of socially engaged hip-hop was Public Enemy from Long Island, New York. Formed in 1982, Public Enemy included MCs Chuck D (Carlton Ridenhour, b. 1960) and Flavor Flav (William Drayton, b. 1959), DJ Terminator X (Norman Lee Rogers, b. 1966), the "Minister of Information" Professor Griff (Richard Griffin, b. 1960), and a group of men referred to as "The S1W," which stands for "Security of the First World." Our

FIGURE 13.2
Public Enemy in 1987. From left to right: Terminator X, Flavor Flav, Professor Griff, and Chuck D.
Source: Getty Images/Jack Mitchell.

gateway to rap and hip-hop is their hit "Fight the Power" (1989) from their album *Fear of a Black Planet*, produced by their production team called the Bomb Squad (Hank Shocklee, Keith Shocklee, and Eric "Vietnam" Sadler). Like many of their recordings, "Fight the Power" addresses social issues in an aggressive style known as **hardcore rap**, which is typified by expressions of anger and confrontation. "Fight the Power" is regarded as one of the most significant recordings in the history of hip-hop and was written as the theme song for the film *Do the Right Thing* (1989), directed by Spike Lee.

 Listen to the first thirty seconds of the recording.

How Does It Work?

Timbre

Male voices are featured over a plethora of other sounds that mostly come from samples of previous recordings, including guitar, bass, drums, cymbals, turntable scratching, a synthesizer, and additional male and female voices.

Texture

Voices rapping over a thick, multi-layered texture of samples and other recorded sounds.

Rhythm

The track is in four with a steady tempo of around 106 bpm (beats per minute). The samples create dense polyrhythms forming underlying ostinatos for much of the rapping. Chuck D and Flavor Flav rap with a high degree of syncopation. They speed up and slow down, making spaces between words larger and smaller and adding additional layers to the polyrhythm of the samples.

Melody

Rap vocals are spoken but occupy an area between speech and song. Short melodic fragments that hint at minor pentatonic or major modes appear in a number of the samples.

Harmony

Harmonic aspects of this track are mainly grounded in the sampled bass ostinato that repeats the pitch D throughout. Various other harmonies are suggested by samples throughout the track.

Form

The form alternates between verses of rapping and choruses that feature a repetition of the song's title.

Performance Techniques

In addition to masterful rapping by Chuck D and Flavor Flav, this recording features two techniques that hip-hop DJs have developed. The first is **scratching**, where DJs spin a break on one turntable and, on the other turntable, move the vinyl record quickly backwards and forwards with one hand to create a rhythmic sound. Since the pitch of the scratching effect is higher when the record moves faster, the DJ can manipulate both rhythm and pitch through scratching, which is usually improvised. Sampling is the second technique. As recording technology developed in the 1980s, hip-hop producers began to create beats in the studio that sounded similar to the live breakbeats of the early DJs through the layering of **samples**, that is, short clips of existing recordings. By 1989 producers were using machines called samplers that created samples by converting recorded sound to digital files. Samplers take many different forms: keyboards, boxes with knobs and buttons, or, more common today, software programs that run on computers. Producers manipulate the speed, duration, pitch, and other timbral aspects of samples. They also reverse them and layer them on top of one another. Repeating a short sample is called a loop. Hip-hop producers layer loops of various lengths on top of one another to create the dense polyrhythmic textures that characterize this music. Public Enemy's production team, the Bomb Squad, used dozens of different samples to construct "Fight the Power."

Listen to the entire recording with these elements in mind while following this timed listening guide.

FIGURE 13.3
A DJ manipulating sounds using two turntables and a mixer, c. 1985
Source: Getty Images/Michael Ochs Archive/ Stringer.

LISTENING GUIDE 13.1

TIME	SECTION	DESCRIPTION	LYRICS
0:00	Introduction	The track opens with an excerpt from a speech by civil rights attorney and activist, Thomas N. Todd. Todd's original speech referred to the many Americans who refused to fight in the Vietnam War.	
0:16	Transition	This three-measure section introduces the tempo by way of a pulsing rhythm produced by a nearly unintelligible vocal that repeats six times. The words are "pump me up," sampled from a 1982 song of the same name by the band Trouble Funk—and played backwards. There is also a line of quickly moving notes that generally ascends a minor scale with accents every three notes. This line is heavily processed so that the source of the timbre is difficult to discern. A snare drum plays eight consecutive accents during the second measure, solidifying the steady tempo. Several other vocal samples are layered together in the third measure.	
0:23	Establishing the groove	These ten bars establish the main groove of the song through a complex layering of at least ten different samples, including the music of soul and funk artist James Brown. In this thick texture at least four vocal lines intertwine: one that repeats the phrase "give it," one that states "come on and get down," some of James Brown's characteristic grunts, and a few other moans and vocal gestures. Other layers include the bass ostinato, a funky repeating guitar riff, a number of different snare drum sounds, a single high pitch on a synthesizer, and various percussion samples.	
0:44	Verse 1	The groove continues as Chuck D raps the first verse and Flavor Flav inserts interjections and joins him on certain phrases. The first verse introduces the song as connected to funk and other African American popular music styles and connects freedom of speech to fighting the power.	1989 . . .
1:12	Chorus	The groove shifts as some samples are removed and others are added. On the second half of beat four of each measure, the "aah" sound sung in harmony is a sample of the word "I" from the chorus to "I Shot the Sheriff" by Bob Marley and the Wailers. Chuck D and Flavor Flav rap the title of the track, alternating between starting on beat one and starting on beat two.	Fight the power . . .
1:30	Verse 2	The original groove returns and additional samples layer on top of the groove to respond to and complement the rap at a number of points. The rap draws on themes such as Black pride, vigilance and awareness, and mental strength as necessary traits to fight the power.	As the rhythm . . .
2:07	Chorus	The chorus returns and is similar to the first chorus.	Fight the power . . .

TIME	SECTION	DESCRIPTION	LYRICS
2:25	Scratching	The main groove returns for an eight-bar break of turntable scratching. The turntable scratches eight short phrases, each one beginning with two quick pulses beginning on the second half of beat two.	
2:43	Chorus	The chorus repeats again in similar fashion to the first chorus.	Fight the power . . .
3:01	Verse 3	The main groove returns for verse three, again with the addition of samples that interact with the rap. Several times, most prominently at around 3:34, a highly processed voice sings "yeah." This is a sample from the classic 1982 hip-hop track "Planet Rock" by Afrika Bambaataa & Soulsonic Force. The rap here deals with the politics of representation (it refers to the lack of any Black heroes on postage stamps), challenges the prominence of Elvis Presley, and disparages the 1988 Bobby McFerrin hit "Don't Worry Be Happy."	Elvis . . .
3:41	Chorus	The chorus returns with a much thinner texture, this time including the bass line, the drum and percussion samples, the guitar riff, James Brown's grunts, and one other vocal sample.	Fight the power . . .
4:00	Instrumental break	The rap drops out and the texture becomes even thinner for these eight bars. The James Brown and other vocals are replaced by repetitions and syncopations of the "I Shot the Sheriff" sample. The second half of this section brings all of the samples together in a unison syncopated rhythm that repeats four times.	
4:18	Tag	A variation on the main groove begins, which includes the synthesizer sample and various iterations of the "Planet Rock" sample.	What we got to say . . .
4:36	Closing skit	The song closes with a short skit that sounds like a cut-off radio interview about the future of Public Enemy.	Yo check this out . . .
4:43	End		

What Does It Mean?

POLITICS

In "Fight the Power," many musical elements work together to communicate a political message that addresses racism, the lack of representation of African Americans in the public sphere, and freedom of speech. It advocates for Black pride and opposition to the white establishment in "fighting the powers that be." In producing the track, the Bomb Squad used over twenty samples, an unprecedented number in 1989. The ways they put these samples together with the rapping and scratching on "Fight the Power" both draws on the historical meanings of the existing samples and resituates those meanings in a way that makes the political message of the song even more powerful.

AESTHETICS

The main groove is a two-bar loop made of at least ten samples layered on top of one another. It repeats as the basis for the majority of the track. Though this kind of layering could only be achieved through the use of sampling technology in the studio, the effect it achieves is quite similar to that of the repeating breaks that hip-hop DJs began creating in the 1970s using turntabling techniques. With sampling and other studio technologies, producers of recorded hip-hop in the studio filled the role of the live DJ at a dance or street party. They maintained the aesthetics of hip-hop breaks ideal for rapping and dance and created new loops with sampling technologies. By including turntable scratching in the section after the second chorus, "Fight the Power" makes the sound of the DJ prominent and aligns the track closely with the sounds of hip-hop culture.

CULTURAL LINKAGES

A number of the samples in "Fight the Power" are taken from recordings by James Brown, who, through his innovative funk and soul music, helped set the stage for rap and hip-hop. In "Say It Loud—I'm Black and I'm Proud" (1968), an unofficial anthem of the Black Power movement, his vocal performance consists mostly of highly rhythmic speech performed over a repeating groove played by a live band, a forerunner to rapping. Brown's funk recordings feature musical elements that made them ideal sources for samples: syncopated, dance-oriented grooves; a prioritization of rhythm over harmony or melody; and his percussive characteristic shouts and grunts. His recordings were among the most commonly sampled by early hip-hop artists. The main groove of "Fight the Power" includes a number of Brown samples, including Brown grunting "uh!" and drums from a number of his recordings. One of the drum samples, performed by drummer Clyde Stubblefield on Brown's 1970 recording "Funky Drummer," is the most sampled drum break in hip-hop and in popular music overall. Public Enemy's indebtedness to Brown is clear in the verses that refer to the sound of the "funky drummer" and include the phrase "I'm Black and I'm proud." They draw on Brown's contagious, danceable grooves to build their own groove, and explicitly connect his political notions of Black pride to their own.

Two other samples connect "Fight the Power" to previous recordings by Black musicians. In the chorus and the final instrumental break, there is a brief sample from the opening seconds to "I Shot the Sheriff" (1973) by Jamaican reggae group Bob Marley and the Wailers (Chapter 13, Gateway 55). This sample might be difficult to recognize because it is so short, but listeners who know the Bob Marley and the Wailers recording may connect it to the narrative of the song, which is a nuanced comment on justice (and injustice), and to Marley's political views, which address the oppression of people of African descent the world over. The other sample that repeats several times is an electronically processed voice singing "yeah," taken from the game-changing hip-hop track "Planet Rock" (1982) by Afrika Bambaataa & Soulsonic Force. Every time the processed "yeah" is heard, it is as if a voice from hip-hop's past is encouraging Public Enemy. In the tag towards the end of "Fight the Power," Chuck D asks "What we got to say?" Before he and Flavor Flav can answer with "fight the power," there is an interjection of the electronic "yeah." In this multi-layered call and response, Public Enemy brings a highly regarded hip-hop track into a communal affirmation of its political message. Through these and the many other samples used in "Fight the Power," the voices of a number of Black musicians are brought together to create a sense of community and a rich, multi-dimensional message that challenges the powerful and addresses racial injustice.

Listen again to "Fight the Power" and see whether you can identify a number of layered samples, including James Brown's grunts, the "I" from "I Shot the Sheriff," the "yeah" from "Planet Rock," or any number of others, even if you don't know their source. Pay attention to the general effect that these multiple layers of samples seem to create.

The lyrics in rap are one of the genre's most important sources of meaning. In rap's early years they largely focused on creating an atmosphere for partying, but in the course of the history of hip-hop a wide range of themes have been covered, including the kind of social engagement heard in "Fight the Power." Chuck D's rap and Flavor Flav's responses and interjections evoke ideas of freedom of speech, Black pride, revolution, awareness, and mental clarity, as they invite others to fight the power with them. In verse two, Chuck D raps "people, people, we are the same," where "people, people" refers to lyrics from James Brown's 1974 recording "Funky President (People It's Bad)." The contradictory next line, "no we're not the same," suggests that while all humans are inherently equal, the structure of society is unequal. In verse three, Chuck D's rap disparages Elvis Presley, arguably for the way that he, as a white man, popularized and benefitted from the Black rhythm & blues styles in the rock and roll of the 1950s. While the lyrics in "Fight the Power" seem to attack Elvis directly, Chuck D in later years asserted that he and his contemporaries have always had great respect for Elvis, but that they have a problem with the way he is viewed as a singular icon at the expense of important Black musicians. Also in verse three, Chuck D and Flavor Flav mention Bobby McFerrin's 1988 number one hit "Don't Worry Be Happy." They disagree with the song's message. Chuck D invites the listener to "slap me right here" if he's caught saying its title phrase. Public Enemy's message is clear: this is not a time to live without worries and to be happy. It is a time to fight against oppression.

> **POLITICS**

Listen to "Fight the Power" again and focus on the lyrics of the rap by Chuck D and Flavor Flav and the way that they interact with one another. Notice the ideas that Flavor Flav adds with his interjections, the differences in timbre and pitch of the two voices, and any additional cultural, political, or musical references that you hear in the lyrics.

What Is Its History?

CULTURAL
LINKAGES

Hip-hop culture in the late 1970s in the Bronx emerged out of a number of existing musical practices. One of these was **disco**, a popular form of dance music in the 1970s enjoyed at nightclubs where audiences danced to continuous music played on records for hours at a time. By using a set of two turntables with adjustable speeds, disco DJs developed techniques of playing uninterrupted music, blending one song into the next without any breaks or abrupt changes in tempo. Early hip-hop DJs like Kool Herc (Clive Campbell, b. 1955, Jamaica), Grandmaster Flash (Joseph Saddler, b. 1958, Barbados), and Afrika Bambaataa (Kevin Donovan, b. 1960, the Bronx) built on disco turntabling techniques and adapted them to hip-hop contexts like neighborhood parties and dance clubs. Kool Herc was the first to adapt these techniques for smooth transitions between records, Grandmaster Flash refined them, and his protégé Grand Wizard Theodore (Theodore Livingston, b. 1963, the Bronx) invented the scratching technique.

Another precursor to hip-hop is **toasting**, a form of rhythmic storytelling with roots in West Africa and legacies in at least two parts of the Black Atlantic. In some American prison cultures it took the form of Black inmates bragging to one another about their exploits in rhyming poetic verse. In Jamaican popular culture beginning in the 1950s, DJs would improvise "toasts" over the music of mobile sound systems. DJ Kool Herc, born in Kingston, Jamaica, likely heard toasting in his youth and was one of the first to recite rhyming phrases over his breakbeats before that role became the domain of the MC.

TECHNOLOGY

After the Sugarhill Gang released their single "Rapper's Delight" in 1979, hip-hop began to shift from a local phenomenon to becoming well known as a genre with great commercial appeal. In the production of this and other early hip-hop recordings, rather than rapping over breaks put together by a DJ, MCs would rap over tracks that were pre-recorded in the studio by producers and studio musicians. These producers, like Sylvia Robinson (1935–2011), the producer of "Rapper's Delight" and other early hip-hop singles and co-founder of Sugar Hill Records, used new electronic music technologies such as drum machines and synthesizers in crafting the sounds of their tracks. Afrika Bambaataa & Soulsonic Force's "Planet Rock" (1982) famously uses a Roland TR-808 drum machine and its distinctive sounds; a vocoder, which electronically modifies the human voice (e.g., the "yeah" sampled in "Fight the Power"); and a synthesizer recreation of a melody from "Trans-Europe Express" (1977) by German electronic group Kraftwerk. "Planet Rock," especially its use of timbres of the 808 drum machine, became enormously influential not only in the production of hip-hop music, but it also served as an inspiration for innovators of concurrently emerging genres of electronic music like techno and house.

POLITICS

While early hip-hop recordings were generally oriented towards creating an environment for partying, "The Message" (1982), by Grandmaster Flash and the Furious Five and produced by Sylvia Robinson, broke new ground as the first hip-hop recording to describe the oppressive conditions of inner-city urban life in the United States. The chorus memorably states "don't push me 'cause I'm close to the edge" and "it's like a jungle sometimes; it makes me wonder how I keep from goin' under." The verses elaborate in detail on the economic struggles, violence, and failing public education that characterized the everyday experience of those living in urban poverty. The track includes mixed-in sounds of the street such as police sirens, and it closes with a skit in which the members of the group are harassed by a police officer and arrested for no apparent reason. "The Message" was a massive hit and paved the way for a whole stream of hip-hop music that dealt with oppression, marginalization, and struggle related to issues of race, class, drugs, and politics. During the 1980s, politically oriented hip-hop groups like Public Enemy followed in the footsteps of the social realism of "The Message," many of them in the aggressive style of hardcore rap. Public Enemy's albums *Yo! Bum Rush the Show* (1987), *It Takes a Nation* of *Millions to Hold Us Back* (1988), and *Fear of a Black Planet* (1990) sample quotes from speeches by Malcolm X, a leading African American activist noted for his fiery critique of white power, and other figures from the 1960s Black nationalist and civil rights movements.

On the West Coast, Snoop Dogg (Calvin Cordozar Broadus Jr., b. 1971), Tupac (2Pac) Shakur (Lesane Crooks, 1971–1996), and the group N.W.A popularized **gangsta rap**, a hip-hop subgenre that vividly chronicled the so-called gangsta lifestyle of the urban poor of Los Angeles: gang violence, sex, unemployment, and widespread crack cocaine use. N.W.A, with core members Ice Cube (O'Shea Jackson, b. 1969), Dr. Dre (Andre Young, b. 1965), and Eazy-E (Eric Wright, 1973–1995), plus DJ Yella (Antonie Carraby, b. 1967) and MC Ren (Lorenzo Patterson, b. 1969), recorded their first studio album, *Straight Outta Compton*, in 1988. In braggadocious and self-aggrandizing raps, they described in graphic terms life in gang-ridden South Central Los Angeles against a backdrop of the sounds of police sirens and gunshots along with funk (and other) samples, drum machine beats, and synthesizers. Rapping in a laid-back West Coast style, they cataloged police brutality and racial profiling ("Fuck tha Police"), the violence of the streets

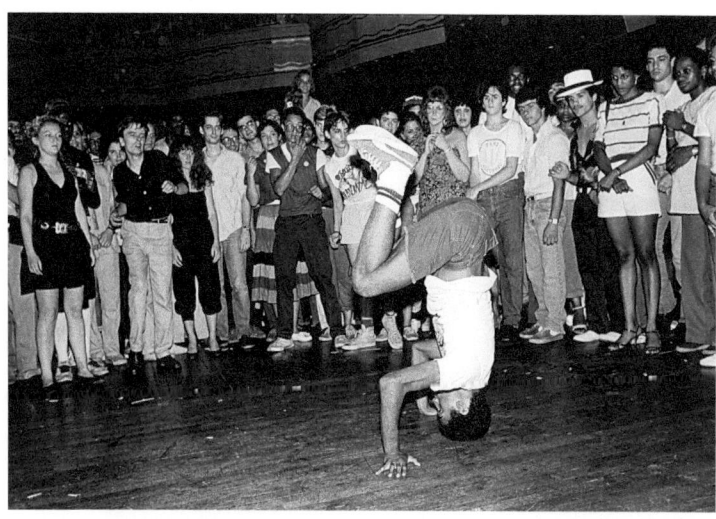

FIGURE 13.4

A member of one of hip-hop's early breakdancing groups, the Rock Steady Crew, breakdancing at a 1982 Soulsonic Force show in New York City

Source: Getty Images/Ebet Roberts/Contributor.

CULTURAL LINKAGES

("Gangsta Gangsta"), and the constraint that radio censorship places on rap artists ("Express Yourself"). *Straight Outta Compton* enjoyed massive success across lines of race and class, appealing to youth in urban Black communities and to youth in the white suburbs. Gangsta rap and its profanity-laced and violent lyrics set a new tone for commercial success in hip-hop, and many groups followed in the footsteps of N.W.A to produce their own music celebrating the gangsta lifestyle.

Straight Outta Compton had been released on Ruthless Records, a label co-founded by Eazy-E and manager Jerry Heller (1940–2016), which also released work by artists like Southern California all-women hip-hop group J.J. Fad, the singer Michel'le (Michel'le Toussaint, b. 1970), and, later, Bone Thugs-N-Harmony. After he left N.W.A in 1991, Dr. Dre co-founded Death Row Records, which released a series of multiplatinum-selling albums, including his first solo album *The Chronic* (1992), Snoop Dogg's debut *Doggystyle* (1993), and Tupac Shakur's *All Eyez on Me* (1996). Dr. Dre's productions departed from the thick, multi-layered sampling on Public Enemy's "Fight the Power." Instead, he often featured only two or three samples, a cleaner, pop-oriented style, slower grooves, and a smooth, laid-back style of rapping. This style was known as G-funk, a subgenre of gangsta rap that became widely popular in the hip-hop of the 1990s.

Other innovators in the golden era of hip-hop included East Coast hardcore group Run-DMC, which combined rock drum beats and guitar riffs with hip-hop conventions and attracted fans of rock. Their 1986 album *Raising Hell* included a new version of "Walk This Way" by the rock group Aerosmith, with vocals by Aerosmith vocalist Steven Tyler and the playing of Aerosmith

FIGURE 13.5

Sylvia Robinson in 1983

Source: Getty Images/Michael Ochs Archives.

FIGURE 13.6
N.W.A. From left to right: Dr. Dre, Eazy-E, MC Ren, and DJ Yella.
Source: Getty Images/Lynn Goldsmith.

guitarist Joe Perry. It and *Licensed to III* (1986), an album by the first successful white hip-hop group, the Beastie Boys, were the first two multi-platinum rap albums, both of which were produced by Rick Rubin (b. 1963) and released on his label Def Jam Records. In the late 1980s the rapper Rakim (William Michael Griffin Jr., b. 1968) was one of the first to introduce a smooth, laid-back style. His intricate rhyme schemes distinguished him from the more common energetic style of his peers like Chuck D and inspired a new generation of rappers. Rakim's legacy is heard today in the styles of rappers like Nas, Jay-Z, and Common. By the late 1980s women hip-hop groups began to break through to commercial success, with Salt-N-Pepa (Cheryl "Salt" James, Sandra "Pepa" Denton, and Deidra "DJ Spinderella" Roper, who replaced Latoya Hanson) making it first to the charts with their 1987 single "Push It." Queen Latifah (Dana Owens, b. 1970) also achieved commercial success as a hip-hop artist (before enjoying a successful career in film and television), releasing the first political commentary by a woman rapper. Her "Ladies First" (1989) responded to male rappers' negative stereotyping of female rappers.

One of the most influential groups of the 1990s was the hardcore group the Wu-Tang Clan, a collective of nine rappers from the projects of Staten Island, New York, whose first album was called *Enter the Wu-Tang (36 Chambers)* (1993). In addition to continuing to innovate within established conventions of hip-hop like sampling and the poetics of rapping about the realities of inner-city life, the Wu-Tang Clan connected their work to the world of Chinese martial arts. They sampled audio from martial arts films and referred to Staten Island as "Shaolin," a reference to the martial art called Shaolin Kung Fu and the Buddhist Shaolin Temple in China's Henan province, where it developed. Their recording contract allowed them to negotiate their own subsequent deals as solo artists with outside labels, with the caveat that a portion of the earnings from these projects would go back to the group. This new business model enabled the Wu-Tang Clan to pursue other business ventures such as a lucrative clothing line (Wu Wear) and a video game (*Shaolin Style*). The musical and entrepreneurial skills of the group changed the game in the business of hip-hop and set the stage for the further widespread development of the hip-hop industry beyond music.

New York and Los Angeles served as central locations for the development of hip-hop and the hip-hop industry, and in the mid-1990s the two scenes attracted even more attention as they became embroiled in a feud that resulted in the untimely deaths of East Coast rapper The Notorious B.I.G. (Christopher Wallace, aka Biggie Smalls or Biggie, 1972–1997) and West Coast rapper Tupac Shakur in anonymous drive-by shootings. Since the early 1980s hip-hop scenes have also developed around the United States and the world as rappers have found this now global music useful for commenting on local issues about social

FIGURE 13.7
Salt-N-Pepa in 1988. From left to right: Sandra Denton ("Pepa"), Deidra Roper ("DJ Spinderella"), and Cheryl James ("Salt").
Source: Getty Images/Janette Beckman.

marginalization and oppression, for entertainment and partying, and for fame and commercial gain. The best-selling hip-hop artist of all time, widely respected for his rap skills, is Eminem (Marshall Mathers, b. 1972), who was raised by a single mother as one of only a few white families in a predominantly Black neighborhood of Detroit. Canadian-born rapper Drake (Aubrey Drake Graham, b. 1986) has released the most hits in the history of the *Billboard* charts for all popular music (by 2022 over 250 songs of his had appeared on the *Billboard* Hot 100 Chart), and he has become one of the most celebrated rappers of today.

Since the mid-1990s a host of other extraordinary rappers have entertained audiences, including André 3000 and Big Boi of the group Outkast, Lil' Kim, Nas, Lauryn Hill, 50 Cent, Lil Wayne, Missy Elliot, Nicki Minaj, Kanye West, Jay-Z, Kendrick Lamar, and Cardi B. They have become some of the world's best-known celebrities with business operations across the entertainment industry and beyond. Singer and rapper Lauryn Hill (b. 1975) won the Grammy for Album of the Year for her debut album *The Miseducation of Lauryn Hill* in 1998, the first for a hip-hop album. (The only other has been Outkast's *Speakerboxxx/The Love Below* in 2004.) Jay-Z (Shawn Carter, b. 1969) controls a business empire that extends to fashion, professional sports, beverage companies, and the technology sector. Los Angeles rapper Kendrick Lamar's (b. 1987) "Alright" from his album *To Pimp a Butterfly* (2015) became an anthem for the Black Lives Matter movement, bringing socially conscious hip-hop into the mainstream once again. With contributions from jazz tenor saxophonist Kamasi Washington and jazz keyboardist Robert Glasper, the album connects hip-hop and jazz, exploring some of the two genres' common ground. Through their collaborations, complex use of samples, innovative musical production, entertaining humor, and expressive rapping, hip-hop artists look to the past and interpret the present as they mix and remix old and new sounds together, carrying themselves and their audiences into what they hope is a bright future.

FIGURE 13.8
The Wu-Tang Clan in 1997
Source: Getty Images/Bob Berg.

FIGURE 13.9
Kendrick Lamar performing at the 2016 Grammy Awards
Source: Getty Images/Larry Busacca.

WHERE DO I GO FROM HERE?

- Listen to James Brown's "Funky Drummer." Can you find the drum break used in "Fight the Power"?

- In a style called "battle rap," a rapper performs pre-composed or improvised freestyle verses full of insults and bragging, often in a live exchange with another rapper in an attempt to diss the opponent and prove superior skills. What is the earliest video example you can find of a rap battle? Where have you encountered it in popular culture? How many different forms of rap battle can you find? What are their characteristics?

- Listen to "Nuthin' but a 'G' Thang" by Dr. Dre featuring Snoop Doggy Dogg from *The Chronic*. What musical elements define Dr. Dre's G-funk production style? What themes do Dr. Dre and Snoop Dogg deal with in this rap?

- Compare "Fight the Power" with "Fuck tha Police" by N.W.A and "Alright" by Kendrick Lamar. Compare and contrast the ways these songs approach social issues in their lyrics and production.

GATEWAY 52
ELECTRONIC DANCE MUSIC

What Is It?

Electronic dance music is an umbrella term for a range of electronic music genres primarily produced for nightclubs, festivals, and large parties called raves. In these settings, DJs perform sets of continuous music by mixing one recorded song into the next, and sometimes by adding effects and electronically manipulating the music in real time. The sounds and experiences of electronic dance music were the key drivers of the mainstream popular music industry in much of the 2000s and 2010s, when the acronym EDM became a common term to describe the pop dance music of that time period. Electronic dance music first emerged in the early 1980s, notably in two Black communities of DJs and dancers located in cities of the American Midwest, Chicago and Detroit. These scenes continued and developed the practices and sounds of disco, where DJing continuous sets of music had begun. While these communities also called their music "electronic music" or "dance music," the music of the Chicago scene became known as house and the music of the Detroit scene became known as techno.

The gateway to electronic dance music comes from the Chicago house scene of the 1980s and is called "Your Love." Like hip-hop, Chicago house emerged from the collaborative practices of DJs and producers remixing, sampling, and adding electronic and other sounds to existing recordings. These new recordings were primarily experienced in clubs and on the radio, and the DJs and remixers, rather than the vocalists and recording artists, became well known figures in the scene. "Your Love" was first produced and recorded by Jamie Principle (b. 1960), with vocals by him and Adrienne Jett and additional production by Mark "Hot Rod" Trollan. It was frequently played in Chicago house clubs for at least a year before its first release in 1986. It has since come to be associated with Frankie Knuckles (1955–2014), one of the most prominent DJs and producers in the Chicago house scene, and one of its originators. While there are conflicting accounts about whether or not he collaborated with Principle on the production of the track, Knuckles played "Your Love" frequently as a club DJ, and re-released a version of it on Trax Records under his name in 1987.

 Listen to the first thirty seconds of the recording.

How Does It Work?

Timbre

The recording features the timbres of synthesizers, electronic drums, and spoken and sung vocals with significant reverb effects and the sound of breathing. A **synthesizer**, or **synth**, is an electronic musical instrument that generates sound by creating waveforms with electronic oscillators and manipulating their timbres with other electronic components. Synthesizers are typically played by keyboards.

Texture

Multiple layers of electronic sounds interlock to form the foundational texture of the recording. Sometimes the texture thins to a solo monophonic texture; sometimes a vocal or electronic part is more prominent than the other parts, which then assume an accompaniment role; and sometimes multiple melodies occur at the same time in a polyphonic texture.

FIGURE 13.10
Frankie Knuckles in the DJ booth at a club in New York City, 2003
Source: Getty Images/J. Countess/ WireImage.

Rhythm

A steady pulse of 118 beats per minute, ongoing even subdivisions, and syncopated vocals and bass lines are all prominent in the recording.

Melody

The melodies of the recording occur in the vocals and, sometimes, in a synth. Melodies are mostly in a minor key and typically have a narrow range.

Harmony

The harmony of the recording is relatively static. It sustains a harmony in a minor key (E minor) and sometimes moves through other chords closely related to that key. Over those harmonies, the repetitive percussive synth that opens the track simultaneously outlines a constant harmony in a major key (C major).

Form

The form features several sections of the perpetual repetitive synth, drum, and bass parts. Interspersed are sections where melodies are prominent either in the vocals or in a synth part. About two-thirds of the way through the track, a drum break section is followed by a breakdown, where all sounds stop other than the occasionally repeating bass line.

Performance Techniques

"Your Love," like most house and techno recordings, is intended to be played at a club or party by a DJ, seamlessly overlapping with previous and subsequent tracks to create a perpetual, ongoing dance beat. This means that the beginnings and endings of the recordings need to lend themselves to being combined with other recordings. As a result, they feature relatively static repeating patterns, as well as textures that do not change quickly or in any extreme manner.

Listen to the entire recording with these elements in mind while following this timed listening guide.

LISTENING GUIDE 13.2

TIME	SECTION	DESCRIPTION	LYRICS
0:00	Intro A	A bright percussive synthesizer begins repeating a three-pitch arpeggio outlining a major triad. This continues for much of the recording. It is joined by a bass playing a syncopated pattern suggesting a duple meter, which creates a polyrhythm. A mellow sustained synth sound called a synth pad joins, following the duple meter.	
0:41	Intro B	A drum pattern enters in the duple meter. At 1:10 the bass begins repeating pitches, and, together with the sustained synth, ascends through several harmonies twice. The bass drops out briefly to set up the next section.	
1:42	Intro C	The bass returns to its original pattern. An inhale and a sensual moan by a male vocalist are followed by spoken lyrics. At 1:51 an electronic snare drum sound that emulates a hand clap begins a repeating pattern on the backbeat, beats two and four.	Ahh, I can't let go.
2:07	Vocal A	A vocalist with a smooth timbre enters over the existing texture, singing in a syncopated rhythm but in a lyrical style, with very little accent.	When I'm with you . . .
2:56	Vocal B	Two vocalists sing a higher-pitched, more accented melody with a changing harmony in the underlying sampled and electronic textures.	Well, I need your love . . .
3:25	Interlude	The instrumental texture continues, with repetitions of the inhale and sensual moan and the spoken lyrics. The bass drops out 4:14 until the end of the section.	I can't let go . . .
4:28	Synth solo	The bass re-enters, and a bright synth sound called a "lead" plays a syncopated solo line over the rest of the texture. Its vibrato effect is produced by rotating a wheel on the keyboard called a modulation wheel.	
4:44	Drum break	Everything drops out other than drum sounds, and a gritty, sweeping electronic sound joins the drums on a number of downbeats.	

TIME	SECTION	DESCRIPTION	LYRICS
4:59	Breakdown	The original repeating bass pattern plays in a monophonic texture.	
5:17	Coda A	The bass continues and is joined by the bright syncopated synth lead and the rest of the instrumental texture, as well as the spoken vocals, inhales, and sensual moans.	I can't let go . . .
5:49	Coda B	A female vocal joins the texture, singing on ooh, aah, as well as on the lyrics, in an improvisatory and sometimes syncopated manner reminiscent of soul music. Starting at 6:37 the overall volume of the track gradually fades to silence.	I can't let go . . .
6:47	End		

What Does It Mean?

The sounds of "Your Love" reveal much about how house music and other genres of electronic dance music connect to the social worlds of these genres, to electronic technology, and to previous styles of African American music. Audiences of electronic dance music in nightclubs, at raves, and at festivals gather in open spaces to dance, to enjoy the experience of various drugs, to bond socially with others, and to connect with sexual partners. To keep the party going, it is important for the music to continue uninterrupted. It is also important for some elements of the music to remain constant but for others to provide some variety. Many house and other electronic dance music recordings feature a steady tempo and significant repetition throughout, such as the three-pitch repeating synth line at the opening of "Your Love" that continues for most of the track. This repetition, and the grooves that it helps create, provide audiences with a sense that the music around them is constant and not set up in a timeline with a beginning, middle, and end. As DJs string recordings together in a nightclub, audiences don't anticipate or focus on an ending or culmination of a recording but, instead, enjoy the present moment with others in the club or on the dancefloor. This is an important part of the club experience for many clubgoers, who join one another in an experience where time is suspended and where they can enjoy an alternative reality that is not constrained by structures like time schedules or by other social norms for behavior. They are often seeking a transcendent, perhaps spiritual, trance-like state on the dancefloor, and the repetitive nature of the rhythms of house music helps them achieve that state.

Even as they provide a static, repetitive sonic environment that suspends time for listeners, house and other EDM recordings also ebb and flow, providing changes in momentum through changes in rhythm, texture, melody, and other musical elements. DJs are very familiar with individual recordings and their shifts, and they select recordings to play to shape the momentum of a party in response to the current or desired mood of the crowd at any given time. "Your Love" features a gradual shift in texture over the course of the recording, moving generally towards a thick texture at the end of the recording where all the parts are heard at once: the bass line, the drum part, three or four synth parts, and two vocal parts. The recording introduces the elements of its texture one by one, familiarizing listeners with each of them. The end of the recording features more than half a dozen simultaneous, familiar, sounds that listeners can recognize (from earlier in the track), enjoy, and move their bodies to.

Several points in the track also feature sudden and gradual changes that build anticipation and direct listeners' attention towards various musical goals. For example, when the bass begins repeating pitches at 1:10, proceeding through two ascending patterns along with the sustained synth before dropping out briefly, it builds anticipation for the

FIGURE 13.11
A Moog Sub Phatty synthesizer with the modulation (mod) wheel and the pitch-bending wheel at the left.
Source: Jonny Avery.

entrance of the inhale, sensual moan, and spoken vocals that enter at 1:42. There, the bass and synth return to their grooves, which, along with the spoken vocal sounds, provides a sense of release. Another example of textural and rhythmic change that produces momentum in "Your Love" is the drum break followed by the breakdown. After a fast series of accents on a snare drum sound, the drum break brings the driving beat into focus, and the melodic and harmonic sounds of the recording disappear. This shifts the focus of the listener to particular rhythmic elements of the recording, which may affect the way dancers engage their bodies with the sound. After fifteen seconds, the drums cease and the bass line returns, repeating its pattern, which includes significant periods of silence. This monophonic texture, along with the silence, sets up a sense of anticipation for the contrasting thick texture that follows it and continues to the end of the track.

This building of anticipation and release, along with the sound of the vocals that are icons of sexual experience, points to one of the key elements of the social world of the scene where "Your Love" was experienced. House music in 1980s Chicago was developed in nightclubs where clubgoers were predominantly Black and gay, though, in many cases, the clubs fostered crowds that were also diverse racially and by sexuality. These clubs provided safe spaces for people to come together and feel free to be themselves without fear of judgment, violence, or other forms of discrimination. In these clubs, people could express their sexuality—and meet sexual partners through the intimacy of dance on the dancefloor—and the music facilitated this experience. The amplified breathing of a man, and his voice moaning and sexually whispering "I can't let go" after a build-up of texture and rhythmic activity, brings gay sexuality to the forefront of the recording. These sounds constitute an important part of the club experience, providing a sense of safety and support for people whose sexualities were not celebrated (or could put them in danger) in other settings of their everyday lives.

Listen again to "Your Love." Can you find any moments where the recording has a clear sense of direction or anticipation? Where do you hear a repetitive groove that focuses listeners' attention on an experience of the present?

Disco DJs had innovated the technique of using two adjustable-speed turntables to avoid abrupt tempo changes or breaks when transitioning between recordings. While a recording is playing through the sound system, a DJ typically listens on headphones to the next recording. The DJ adjusts the speeds of the two turntables so the tempos of the two recordings match, then moves the turntable of the next recording to a point near the beginning of the recording where the overlap of the two recordings sounds good. The DJ then slowly decreases the volume of the recording that is concluding, and increases the volume of the next recording, keeping the balance so the overall volume remains the same. House, techno, and other EDM recordings are usually made with an understanding that the recordings will overlap with other tracks in this way, since the recordings are made with the intention to be played in club, rave, and festival settings. "Your Love" is an example of this intersection of electronic technologies, social settings for music, and the sound of the music. The beginning and end of "Your Love" lend themselves to seamless and effective blending with other recordings. At the beginning of the track, the texture is thin, and notably does not have a drum beat until about forty seconds into the recording. This gives a DJ up to forty seconds to fade out the drum beat from any previous recording to avoid a rhythmic clash. The last minute or so of "Your Love" features many layers in a thicker texture. Adding additional parts from the subsequent track as it fades in provides an even thicker texture, which further amplifies the effect of polyrhythms and multiple melodies at the end of "Your Love."

Jamie Principle first brought "Your Love" to Frankie Knuckles on a cassette tape, and Knuckles played it in clubs on tape for about a year before it was released in any form. Knuckles was known for using technologies other than turntables in clubs when house and other EDM genres were first emerging in the late 1970s and early 1980s. Instead of records, he used tape that he played on a reel-to-reel tape player. He made his own remixes of existing tracks through cutting and splicing together tape that he would later play on the reel-to-reel player in the club. In his editing, based on what he thought would be best for the dancefloor, he would extend or

TECHNOLOGY

FIGURE 13.12
The front panel of a 1983 Roland TR-909 drum machine
Source: 909 bd at the English-language Wikipedia.

shorten introductions and dance breaks, and add new sections to existing recordings. Alongside playing the reel-to-reel tapes in the club, he would trigger drum sounds and loops on electronic drum machines. The sound of the bass drum on this version of "Your Love" is the bass drum sound on the Roland TR-909 drum machine, which was released by Roland in 1983 and became one of the key instruments in the production of the timbres and rhythms of house, techno, and other electronic music genres. The form of "Your Love," especially the duration of each section and the way the recording unfolds, demonstrates what Frankie Knuckles and Jamie Principle understood would work well on the dance floor.

"Your Love" also contains elements that relate to house music's roots in previous styles of African American music. Some examples of these elements include: samples of existing recordings, common in hip-hop (the bass part is taken from a sample of a 1982 disco recording called "Feels Good (Carrots and Beets)" by Electra featuring Tara Butler); repetitive bass lines and grooves that directly reference disco; and blues-inflected vocals full of melismas, referencing vocal styles of soul.

CULTURAL LINKAGES

In the 1980s, American cities continued to be racially segregated, the consequence of long-enduring forms of racial oppression, such as discriminatory policies for property ownership and other economic and spatial restrictions. In combination with homophobia, these racialized restrictions on the movement of human bodies meant that the dancefloor became a space for a temporary (if imagined) release from those restrictions, as people came together, moving their bodies to the steady, unceasing pulse of the party produced by African American producers and DJs. Frankie Knuckles, who was also gay, understood the significance of the space of the dancefloor, particularly for African American gay clubgoers. He described the nightclub as a "church" and himself as a "priest" of the dancefloor, partly because many Black gays who frequented house music parties were estranged from the churches they grew up in because of their sexuality. They found a spiritual transcendence on the dancefloor created by the repetitive grooves, the references to vocal styles of soul, and the shifting and dynamic timbres and textures of the music.

What Is Its History?

CULTURAL LINKAGES

The history of electronic dance music is strongly rooted in the practices and sounds of disco. Disco, which takes its name from the French word *discothèque*, first emerged in New York City in the 1970s in underground clubs as entertainment for primarily African American, Latino, and gay dancers. These audiences identified themselves as on the margins of mainstream society. In contrast to commercial radio and other popular music settings, the focus in disco was not on the individual recordings and recording artists, but rather on the presentation skills and style of a DJ, a focus that has continued throughout the history of electronic dance music. The persistent beat and repetitive groovy bass lines of disco kept dancers on the dancefloor, and recordings became hits based on heavy rotation in clubs. Some of the first influential disco tracks include "Soul Makossa" (1972) by Manu Dibango, "Do It ('Til You're Satisfied)" (1974) by B.T. Express, and "Rock the Boat" (1973) by the Hues Corporation (Karl Russell, H. Ann Kelley, and St. Clair Lee).

As disco grew in popularity beyond its original demographics through a proliferation of *discothèques* and increased radio play, it became commercialized in the mainstream. The apex of the commercialization of disco was the film *Saturday Night Fever* (1977) along with its soundtrack, featuring John Travolta and the music of British/Australian pop group the Bee Gees. The film obscures the social world of disco, as Travolta's character in the film and the Bee Gees are neither gay nor African American. Disco, like other African American dance musics such as 1930s swing and 1950s rock and roll, only gained mainstream acceptance as a music-and-dance culture after its widespread representation by non-Black performers. But as disco became a multimillion-dollar industry in the 1970s, established elements of the predominantly white, male, and straight pop/rock music industry began to increase their harsh criticism of the genre. This criticism was based in part on the association of disco with ethnic minorities and male homosexuality and in part on the fact that an overabundance of disco recordings were being released, many of them of low audio and production quality.

A turning point occurred in 1979, after Chicago rock radio DJ Steve Dahl launched a campaign dubbed "Disco Sucks!" on his radio show. The campaign, and its anti-Black and anti-gay undercurrents, came to a head when Dahl helped organize a promotional "Disco Demolition Night" at Comiskey Park, the home of the Chicago White Sox baseball team, where discounted tickets to a White Sox baseball game were offered to anyone who brought a disco record they wanted to destroy. Thousands of people came to burn their records, chanting "disco sucks!" and storming the field after Dahl and his associates used explosives to burn a giant box of records. They vandalized the field and the stadium to the extent that the game had to be forfeited. While this event certainly did not, on its own, precipitate the decline of disco's popularity, it was part of a broader trend in the mainstream to push disco back to the margins. By the early 1980s, disco had disappeared from discourse in the media, and the American popular music industry was investing its energy in genres like new wave, punk, hard rock, and rap.

After disco had declined in popularity, genres like house and techno emerged among communities that continued to value the aesthetics and social worlds of disco. They shaped the sound and meaning of the music through new technologies that some disco artists had already begun using. *Discothèques* started to become known as "clubs," and experimentation with electronic music technology alongside styles of disco, soul, and R&B became increasingly common in these settings. In Chicago, one of the clubs for primarily queer, Black, and Latino dancers to gather and party was called The Warehouse.

The Warehouse was located in a three-story former factory and operated between 1977 and 1982. The club served only juice, and, as an alcohol-free establishment, was able to stay open all night for all ages, unrestricted by a liquor license that would require it to close by 3 a.m. and to admit only those aged twenty-one and older. It was also members-only, which ensured it was a safe place for those in its core clientele to dance and experience the sense of belonging they were denied in other parts of their lives. By the time The Warehouse opened, there was already an active scene of gay Black and Latino dancers in Chicago centering on a circuit of house parties. These spaces for queer nightlife were created as safe havens for Black and Latino entertainment because, in many cases, gay nightclubs in Chicago were more favorable to white clubgoers. Frankie Knuckles, who had been active in New York's disco scene, relocated to Chicago and became the resident DJ at The Warehouse at the invitation of the club's main promoter, Robert Williams, another transplant from New York.

At The Warehouse and other party spaces, large sound systems that resonated with body-shaking bass frequencies and massive amplification capabilities made for an extraordinary sensory experience that typically began around 10:30 p.m. and lasted until morning

FIGURE 13.13
People flood the field at Chicago's Comiskey Park to destroy their disco records at Disco Demolition Night in 1979
Source: Fred Jewell/AP/Shutterstock.

or noon the following day. Knuckles's technique of splicing together tape mixes of disco, soul, R&B, and funk recordings by hand and adding live sounds from drum machines resonated with the DIY culture of the house parties, which had been part of the community's ecosystem before his arrival from New York. The mix of African American musical styles, the sounds of drum machines and synthesizers, and the deep bass sounds of the four-on-the-floor drum beat amplified by an enormous sound system became strongly associated with the social worlds of The Warehouse. While The Warehouse was also frequented by straight clubgoers, it was a place where people marginalized due to race, ethnicity, and sexuality could thrive. By the early 1980s, this music became known as house music, as either a reference to the name of The Warehouse, to the house party scene, or both. After The Warehouse closed in 1982, Williams and Knuckles each opened new venues where house music continued to increase in popularity, albeit among different audiences. Knuckles's The Power Plant attracted most of the gay clubgoers from The Warehouse parties, while Williams's The Music Box attracted most of its straight dancers. The appeal of house music began to spread among numerous demographics in and beyond Chicago, its popularity embodying what Frankie Knuckles later called "disco's revenge."

Early house music commercial recordings, such as "On & On" (1984) by DJ and producer Jesse Saunders, maintained the DIY aesthetic of the scene, but he and other producers and songwriters soon began to make recordings that sounded less DIY. Said Saunders, "I was combining all of these great genres together that I loved—new wave, reggae, funk, disco, and classic rock into a sound that could bring everyone together," both physically in the clubs and symbolically as well. "Screamin'" Rachael Cain, a singer and one of the few women (or white people) among regulars at The Warehouse in the 1980s, connected the DIY aesthetics of early house to those of punk and hip-hop on several recordings for Trax Records in Chicago. Her 1987 recording "Fun with Bad Boys," produced with Farley "Jackmaster" Funk and hip-hop innovator Afrika Bambaataa, brought hip-hop styles together with house and became a hit in clubs and a favorite track of hip-hop dancers. House music also included consistent influence from Latin American musical styles, especially percussion sounds. The vocalist Liz Torres (b. 1962), born in Puerto Rico and raised in Chicago from the age of three, was known as the Queen of House. Her music demonstrates more genre overlaps, between house, synth pop, various Latin American musical styles, and an electronic music genre called "Latin freestyle" that had developed in New York City in the 1980s. Her recording called "Loca (You Can Look, But Don't Touch)" (1989), was released in six different versions on one vinyl recording, including a "club mix," a "radio mix," a "Spanish version," and a "French & Spanish version," with the music in each version meant to suit a particular setting or to cater towards a particular language group or community.

While house music was developing in Chicago, a parallel but related electronic music was developing 250 miles to the east, in Detroit. Later called techno, this electronic music emerged from a scene similar to the one in Chicago. In the 1970s African American DJs such as Morris Mitchell and Ken Collier (a mentor to the first techno DJs) began spinning disco and bringing sounds and DJ techniques from New York and Chicago to Detroit. Collier's legendary DJ sets at an all-night club called Heaven attracted mainly Black gay men but also welcomed a crowd diverse by race, gender, and sexuality. Heaven and other clubs, as well as radio shows led by Charles "Electrifying Mojo" Johnson and Jeff Mills as the Wizard, also served middle-class African American youth who had, in the late 1970s, organized a network of exclusive social clubs in halls and nightclubs around the city. Typically named after Italian clubs and high-end fashion houses such as Giavante, Schiaparelli, and Charivari, the social clubs' parties featured a variety of dance music styles. Four young musicians active in this scene—Juan Atkins (b. 1962), Eddie Fowlkes (b. 1962), Derrick May (b. 1963), and Kevin Saunderson (b. 1964)—learned from established Detroit radio and nightlife DJs and traveled to Chicago to learn from Frankie Knuckles and other Chicago DJs. They were interested in a wide variety of music that influenced the emerging sound of techno: electronic groups like Kraftwerk, funk music like that of George Clinton and Parliament-Funkadelic, and soul by artists such as Sly and the Family Stone. In 1981 Atkins and Richard Davis (b. 1952) used the moniker Cybotron, a nod to their interest in futurism and technology, to release one of the first tracks of Detroit electronic music, "Alleys of Your Mind."

FIGURE 13.15
Juan Atkins performing in Los Angeles, 2017
Source: Getty Images/Michael Tullberg.

Techno went global when, in 1987, a British dance music entrepreneur and record collector named Neil Rushton visited Detroit and put together a compilation CD of electronic music tracks by Atkins, Fowlkes, May, Saunderson, and others called *Techno!: The New Dance Sound of Detroit*. Released in the UK in 1988, the CD, which included Derrick May's "Strings of Life," became a hit in the dance scene of the UK and for the first time "techno" was attached to the electronic music of Detroit. In the UK, sound system technologies used for reggae were used for parties featuring house, techno, and new subgenres like acid house being developed locally. People in the UK called large-scale all-night electronic music parties held at warehouses and in open fields on the outskirts of London raves. In 1987 MDMA (or "Ecstasy") entered the rave scene in the UK, enhancing the experience through heightened sensory perception, empathy, euphoria, and sociability. These UK raves inspired similar raves around the world, including back in Detroit and Chicago. By the early 1990s, house, techno, and raves had become common throughout the United States, primarily among middle-class, suburban, white, college-bound teenagers.

Electronic music cultures spread around the world in the 1990s, and a multiplicity of genres and subgenres have emerged, each with its own sonic sensibilities, devotees, dance styles, and social values. Among these are drum and bass, deep house, trance, UK garage, and countless others. Large music festivals and other music industry entities began to describe DJ-led dance events, no matter the style, as EDM. In the early 2000s, a genre called dubstep, which featured syncopated and triplet rhythm patterns, wobbly rhythmically oscillating bass tones, and "bass drops," emerged in the UK. In a bass drop, sometimes called a **drop**, the intensity of a track builds to a point where the percussive elements of a track pause (sometimes to silence), and then resume with a full sound of even greater intensity. In the late 2000s and early 2010s, dubstep enjoyed massive popularity in the United States, and it and other genres under the EDM umbrella significantly influenced the mainstream popular music industry, with artists such as Britney Spears ("Hold It Against Me," 2011), Taylor Swift ("I Knew You Were Trouble," 2012), and Rihanna (several tracks on her album *Rated R*, 2009) incorporating the sounds of dubstep into their music. At the peak of EDM's popularity in the early to mid 2010s, festivals featuring such DJs as Skrillex, Avicii, Deadmau5, Calvin Harris, and Tiësto attracted massive audiences.

Although its roots are in predominantly Black gay communities in Detroit and Chicago, electronic dance music is today a staple of the nightlife of most cities of the world across nearly every demographic imaginable. While it no longer dominates the popular music industry as it did in the 2010s, it remains widely popular and has, more than any other genre other than hip-hop, significantly influenced the sounds of mainstream popular music today, especially with regard to timbre, texture, and form. As people continue to dance and party at nightclubs, festivals, and raves around the world, electronic dance music will continue to transform in ways that entertain, bring people together, and foster community.

WHERE DO I GO FROM HERE?

- Compare the musical elements of "Your Love" to those of Cybotron's "Alleys of Your Mind" or Derrick May's "Strings of Life," two tracks by pioneers of techno. Which elements seem similar? Which elements seem different?

- Listen to "Baby Wants to Ride," another track by Frankie Knuckles and Jamie Principle. How do its musical elements express the spiritual, political, and erotic themes in the lyrics?

- Listen to a dubstep track such as "Scary Monsters and Sprites" by Skrillex and compare it to the second half of "Hold It Against Me" by Britney Spears, or to "I Knew You Were Trouble" by Taylor Swift.

GATEWAY 53
NEOTRADITIONAL JAZZ

What Is It?

A number of jazz musicians in the late 1970s and 1980s turned to various styles and sub-genres of jazz that had developed in previous times. This **neotraditionalism** in jazz focused on celebrating older styles and historical repertoire from earlier in the twentieth century. Probably the most well known of these jazz neotraditionalists is the New Orleans-born virtuoso trumpet player, composer, and bandleader Wynton Marsalis (b. 1961). Since the 1980s, Marsalis has been involved in many high-profile projects dedicated to preserving, sustaining, and continuing the jazz tradition as a significant aspect of American culture. Though he is interested in retaining tradition, Marsalis often presents music that might seem old in rather new ways. He recorded several albums of new arrangements of jazz standards in the 1980s and 1990s. Our gateway to jazz neotraditionalism is his recording of the jazz standard "Caravan" originally composed in 1936 by Duke Ellington and Ellington band trombonist Juan Tizol. It is the opening track to the album *Marsalis Standard Time Vol. 1* (1987), which, in addition to Marsalis on trumpet, features Marcus Roberts (b. 1963) on piano, Robert Leslie Hurst III (b. 1964) on upright bass, and Jeff "Tain" Watts (b. 1960) on drums.

 Listen to the first thirty seconds of the recording.

How Does It Work?

Timbre

This recording features the sound of Marsalis's trumpet. During the head he uses a mute, which gives the trumpet a covered timbre, and then plays with an unmuted, clear sound during his solo improvisations. The recording also features piano, upright bass, and drum set.

Texture

The texture is that of a typical jazz quartet. The trumpet plays a melodic line that interacts with the rhythm section of piano, bass, and drums. Sometimes the piano joins the trumpet to harmonize a melody, sometimes the piano plays a solo that interacts with the bass and drums, and sometimes the drums play solo.

Rhythm

The underlying rhythms of the drums, bass, and piano in the opening and some other sections of the recording come together to form a type

FIGURE 13.16
Wynton Marsalis
Source: Getty Images/Stephen J. Cohen.

of groove known generally as a New Orleans groove or feel. This groove features a habanera rhythm in the bass, accents on beats two and four in the drums (beat four gets a stronger accent than beat two), subdivided beats with a slight swing feel, and an active syncopated snare drum. At all other times, the rhythm section plays a straight-ahead swing feel. The bass plays a walking bass line and the drum set plays a heavy swing feel the ride cymbal, accents on two and four on the hi-hat, and occasional lighter fills and hits on the snare and bass drums. The tempo and meter of four are constant throughout this version of "Caravan."

Melody

The melody of the head is mostly in a minor mode, though in some instances it follows a chromatic scale. The melodies of the trumpet and piano improvisations for the most part correspond to the underlying harmonic chord progression outlined in the piano and bass.

Harmony

In the A section, the harmony does not change much, sustaining a V chord before resolving to the minor tonic. The bridge turns the minor tonic into a major chord and cycles briefly through four different major keys that lead back to the minor harmony of the A section.

Form

"Caravan" follows a 64-bar AABA form, with each section lasting sixteen bars rather than the more usual eight bars. This recording, after a short introduction in the drums and piano, follows a head—solos—head form as it repeats the AABA form over and over.

Performance Techniques

The musicians interact with one another constantly as they establish the groove and complement one another's playing during sections devoted to improvisation.

Listen to the first thirty seconds of the recording for the interlocking habanera rhythm of the bass and drums.

Listen to the entire recording following this timed listening guide.

TIME	SECTION	FORM	DESCRIPTION
0:00	Introduction		The drums play alone for four bars to set up the New Orleans groove. The bass and piano join for eight more bars, with the piano comping and the bass playing the habanera rhythm.
0:15	Head	A	Marsalis begins playing the head on the trumpet, with the piano playing along with him to create a two-part harmony and adding typical comping between melodic phrases. His version of the A section places many of the melody notes on the upbeat, creating a great deal of syncopation. During the final four bars of the A section, the bass displaces the habanera rhythm so that it begins on beat two instead of beat one, which creates a seemingly off-kilter polyrhythm. The A section is generally the same each time.
0:35		A	The A melody repeats.
0:54		B	In the first two measures of the B section, the groove stops as the rhythm section plays long notes together with the trumpet, though the steady pulse continues to be felt. When the rhythm section begins playing in time again at the start of the third measure, it launches into a swing feel. After the first four notes, instead of playing the melody of "Caravan," Marsalis improvises on the trumpet.

TIME	SECTION	FORM	DESCRIPTION
1:14		A	The A melody returns.
1:33	Chorus 1	A	Marsalis begins the first chorus of his improvised solo on some of the lowest pitches on the trumpet, and the rhythm section returns to the New Orleans feel. During the solos, the habanera rhythm continues in the bass throughout each A section without being displaced as it was during the head.
1:53		A	Throughout this A section and his entire solo, Marsalis outlines the underlying harmony and explores the full range of the trumpet, demonstrating his mastery of the instrument.
2:12		B	The rhythm section switches to the swing feel. At the end of the bridge, Marsalis plays a rhythm that emphasizes several upbeats in a row, referring back to his version of the A section of the head.
2:32		A	The New Orleans feel returns again, and Marsalis plays an ascending line from the lowest range of the trumpet to the instrument's high range in the last few bars of the chorus.
2:51	Chorus 2	A	As Marsalis and the rhythm section reach a high point in pitch and dynamics, a swing feel is played for the first time on an A section, which continues through the end of the bridge of this chorus.
3:11		A	
3:30		B	At the end of the bridge, Marsalis again plays a phrase consisting of all upbeats, referencing earlier moments in the solo as well as his version of the head.
3:50		A	The New Orleans feel returns again for Marsalis's final A section. His return to the low pitches of the trumpet from the beginning of the solo, and his and the rhythm section's gradual decrescendo together signal the end of his solo and sets up the beginning of the piano solo.
4:10	Chorus 3	A	Right from the start of the piano solo, the rhythm section plays the swing feel, which continues throughout the piano solo.
4:29		A	The piano outlines the harmonies of the chords, and also references melodic phrases from the head. For example, starting at 4:41 the piano repeats a three-note fragment of the head twice in a row.
4:49		B	During this bridge, the solo in the right hand of the piano interacts with the comping in the left hand of the piano particularly clearly, which sometimes produces a call-and-response effect.
5:09		A	The piano creates rhythmic excitement by playing a series of syncopated rhythms, to which the drummer responds with increasing rhythmic variety and activity.
5:28	Chorus 4	A	The piano solo continues with references to the head.
5:48		A	The solo features block chords.
6:07		B	The piano plays a series of full chords to start the bridge, and the drums and bass respond by playing much more loudly and actively.
6:27		A	As the piano descends and starts playing more sparsely in the last four bars, the habanera rhythm returns in the bass and the drums shift back to their part of the New Orleans groove.
6:47	Head	A	The head is restated, sounding mostly the same as the opening head.
7:06		A	The A melody repeats.
7:26		B	After starting the melody on the trumpet, Marsalis gives way to an improvised piano solo for the remainder of the bridge.
7:46		A	The final A ends with a tag where the band plays the final phrase of the head three times rather than once.
8:16	End		

What Does It Mean?

This recording of "Caravan" is neotraditional because it showcases musical elements in jazz that developed between the turn of the twentieth century and 1960. Its use of the traditional head—solos—head form common in jazz stays close to conventions of jazz performance established in the 1940s and 1950s. The AABA form of the head was common in Tin Pan Alley songs of the early twentieth century. By 1987 "Caravan" (composed by Ellington and Tizol, not by a Tin Pan Alley composer) was a well-established jazz standard. Marsalis's choice of this standard as the opening track on *Marsalis Standard Time Vol. 1* and his decision to maintain its original internal form, harmony, and melody can be understood as a tribute to Ellington and his significant place in jazz history and a way of Marsalis aligning himself with the tradition that Ellington helped establish.

CULTURAL
LINKAGES

The improvised solos by Marsalis and pianist Marcus Roberts are based on the underlying harmony and emphasize the dissonances produced by the upper extensions of chords, a bebop tradition. The way the soloists musically communicate with the other musicians and respond to one another's volume, rhythmic patterns, and overall intensity is reminiscent of the innovations of bebop and hard bop musicians in the 1940s and 1950s. In comparison to modal jazz, jazz fusion, and avant-garde and free jazz, this kind of improvisation sounds traditional, as it celebrates and hearkens back to jazz conventions developed in the 1940s and 1950s.

🔊 **Listen again to "Caravan" for the broader head—solos—head form (another long-standing tradition for the performance of standards) and the AABA form that repeats throughout the recording. Listen to the trumpet soloist and the piano soloist and compare the ways that they improvise and interact with the other musicians to Charlie Parker's improvisation on "Ko Ko" in the gateway to bebop (Chapter 11, Gateway 43).**

Wynton Marsalis' neotraditionalism, as his recording of "Caravan" illustrates, is richly layered historically. In addition to the Tin Pan Alley song form (AABA) of the 1920s, a jazz standard composed in the 1930s, and improvisatory and harmonic styles of the 1940s and 1950s, he draws on an even older layer of tradition by including the underlying New Orleans groove as a key part of its rhythm. Established by the drums and the habanera rhythm of the bass for many of the A sections in this recording, the New Orleans groove is most associated today with the music of New Orleans brass bands that perform in street parades, in clubs, and at concerts and festivals (Chapter 10, Gateway 38). This particular New Orleans groove, with its habanera rhythm, is an example of what Jelly Roll Morton called jazz's "Spanish tinge," part of a history that stretches back into the nineteenth century (Chapter 9, Gateway 35). Including this groove on his version of "Caravan" is a way for Marsalis to connect this recording to his and his family's own New Orleans roots and the roots of jazz in that city, and to create another historical layer to this example of neotraditionalism.

🔊 **Listen to "Caravan" again, paying close attention to the groove set up mostly by the bass and drums. Notice the shifts between the New Orleans groove and the swing feel in those instruments.**

What Is Its History?

By 1975 jazz musicians could choose from a wide range of stylistic options: bebop and hard bop featuring improvisation over repeating cycles of chord changes; modal jazz with improvisation over long stretches of static chords rather than harmonic motion; the "New Thing," which, as free jazz, had challenged many established jazz conventions; and jazz fusion's combinations of jazz with rock, funk, and other popular genres. Many of the musicians who had played on Miles Davis's groundbreaking jazz-rock fusion album *Bitches Brew* (1970) continued their own jazz fusion projects into the 1980s and 1990s, including Herbie Hancock, Wayne Shorter, Joe Zawinul, Chick Corea, and John McLaughlin. But neotraditionalists like Wynton Marsalis rejected

CULTURAL
LINKAGES

this approach. They believed that fusions were abandoning what they considered to be the "jazz tradition." In their view jazz was an art form that had developed historically through the creative work of particular master musicians such as Jelly Roll Morton, Louis Armstrong, and Charlie Parker. They believed that it was important to continue to perform jazz repertoires and styles that had developed among these great masters in the past. Given that jazz was no longer a genre with mass commercial appeal, neotraditionalists thought it was more important to maintain what they saw as traditional practices in jazz than to adapt the music to the commercial market in search of larger audiences and greater profits.

Wynton Marsalis is the most prominent of these neotraditionalists. He was born in New Orleans to a musical family. His father is the jazz pianist and educator Ellis Marsalis (1934–2020), and his most well-known sibling is the tenor saxophonist Branford Marsalis (b. 1960). A trumpet prodigy, Wynton came to national prominence in the 1980s through a number of recording projects. He is the only artist to win Grammy Awards for both jazz and classical music performance (he did so at age twenty-two in 1983 and again in 1984). In his early career, he was adamant that avant-garde jazz, free jazz, and fusion did not count as jazz, and he preferred to focus on the performance and celebration of styles and repertoires developed before 1960. Though he later softened that view, he has devoted much of his energy throughout his career to promoting earlier styles and repertoires of jazz, including tributes to Jelly Roll Morton, Thelonious Monk, Duke Ellington, Charles Mingus, and many others. His oratorio *Blood on the Fields* (1994) features big band instrumentation and includes many vocal and instrumental jazz styles. In the form of an oratorio, it embodies Marsalis's view that jazz is an art music. It also connects his expertise as a classical musician to his work promoting jazz in American society. The work received the 1997 Pulitzer Prize for Music, the first awarded to a jazz artist. In effect the Pulitzer jury, without saying so, was supporting the notion of jazz as "America's classical music," a notion that goes hand in hand with the work of Marsalis and other neotraditionalists.

Marsalis's award also marked a gradual shift in the Pulitzer Prize, which had previously only been awarded to compositions in the classical tradition, and whose board had notoriously rejected a suggestion to award a Special Citation to Duke Ellington for his work in 1965. After Marsalis's 1997 Pulitzer Prize, Ellington was posthumously awarded a Special Citation in 1999. And after the Pulitzer board issued a statement in 2004 that they wanted the annual Music Prize to now honor the "full range of distinguished American musical compositions," free jazz composer and saxophonist Ornette Coleman received the award in 2007 for his album *Sound Grammar,* as did

genre-crossing jazz experimenter Henry Threadgill (b. 1944) in 2016 for his album *In for a Penny, In for a Pound.* In 2018 rapper Kendrick Lamar received the Pulitzer for his album *Damn,* the first time a completely non-notated work, and one from popular music, had been recognized by the Pulitzer jury and board. The Pulitzer organization honored the work of these musicians in jazz and hip-hop as significant and excellent long after their audiences had recognized it as such. What these recent awards signify is not that these genres—long considered unworthy of recognition in the classical music world—are achieving greatness for the first time, but rather that institutions like the Pulitzer Prize are changing their understanding of what "great music" means.

Regardless of whether their music is receiving awards or recognition, jazz neotraditionalists, like aficionados of classical music, look to the past to admire what they regard as great

FIGURE 13.17
Wynton Marsalis with the Jazz at Lincoln Center Orchestra in 2017
Source: Getty Images/Stephen J. Cohen.

masterworks. Even though jazz has always welcomed influence from many parts of the world and musicians outside the United States have been performing music labeled as jazz since even before 1920, neotraditionalists have focused on celebrating jazz as a uniquely American cultural practice with a rich historical tradition.

Neotraditionalists recognized (and lamented) that, similar to classical music, jazz by the 1980s did not have broad commercial appeal. Many jazz musicians, instead of seeking to make the music more commercially accessible, began to build institutions during this period that could support jazz as an art form, institutions similar to (and sometimes connected with) institutions that support classical music. Wynton Marsalis has been a pillar of one such institution, Jazz at Lincoln Center (JALC), housed at Lincoln Center in New York City alongside the Metropolitan Opera, the New York Philharmonic, the New York City Ballet, and the Juilliard School. JALC began as a concert series in 1987, became an official constituent of Lincoln Center in 1996, and today boasts a facility with three concert

FIGURE 13.18
Herbie Hancock (left) with saxophonist Melissa Aldana, winner of the 2013 Thelonious Monk International Jazz Saxophone Competition, and Lee Godown, Global Public Policy staff of General Motors
Source: Getty Images/Paul Morigi.

venues designed specifically for jazz performance and an annual budget of over $50 million. JALC, with Marsalis as its Managing and Artistic Director, is committed to expanding the audience for jazz through performance (it typically presents over 500 concerts per year), extensive education programs, and public advocacy.

Another organization that emerged to support jazz in this period is the Herbie Hancock Institute of Jazz, originally founded as the Thelonious Monk Institute of Jazz in 1986. The Hancock Institute provides tuition-free educational programs, promotes jazz performance and education around the world, and sponsors a renowned annual international competition that focuses on a different instrument each year (or vocals) and has launched successful careers for many of its winners. Winners of the Herbie Hancock Institute of Jazz International Competition such as saxophonist Joshua Redman, trumpet player Ambrose Akinmusire, and vocalists Cécile McLorin Salvant and Gretchen Parlato enjoy successful careers as prominent jazz artists. Herbie Hancock serves as the chairman of the Institute's board of trustees and helps oversee the Hancock Institute for Jazz Performance, a tuition-free master of music program at the UCLA Herb Alpert School of Music.

In addition to independent institutions of performance and education like JALC and the Hancock Institute, jazz programs at colleges and universities proliferated in the United States and abroad during the period from 1975 to 1994. College-level jazz programs were first offered in the late 1940s, notably at North Texas State College (now the University of North Texas) and the Schillinger House in Boston (now the Berklee College of Music). Since the 1960s university schools of music have become more open to including jazz instruction alongside existing programs in classical performance and composition. By 1989, over 100 colleges and universities in the United States offered degrees in jazz studies, and hundreds of thousands of high school students were performing in school jazz ensembles. As jazz was becoming less commercially viable, it exploded in popularity in educational institutions, probably not unrelated to the view of jazz as America's classical music. Since the 1980s, classrooms and auditoriums at high schools and universities have emerged as among the main locations for teaching, learning, and performing jazz. Many—but not all—jazz programs developed curricula aligned with the views of jazz neotraditionalists, and they focused on training students in bebop and hard bop styles of performance, composition, and improvisation. Colleges and universities continue to attract students who are excited to develop their skills in jazz, and most active jazz musicians born since 1960 have studied in a university-level jazz program.

WHERE DO I GO FROM HERE?

- Listen to or watch some excerpts of *Blood on the Fields*, the Pulitzer Prize-winning oratorio by Wynton Marsalis. What styles of jazz can you hear in these excerpts? Why is this work called an oratorio?

- Find some recordings of tenor saxophonist Joshua Redman from the early 1990s. To what extent do these recordings sound like neotraditional jazz? Which musical elements can help us identify neotraditional aspects of the music?

- The jazz vocalist Jon Hendricks (1921–2017) had a long and prolific career and can be heard on *Blood on the Fields*. His work in the 1980s and early 1990s demonstrates a particularly innovative technique that he helped create called **vocalese**, a process in which instrumental compositions and well-known recorded improvisations are given lyrics and sung instead of played. Listen to his album *Freddie Freeloader* (1990). How do his vocal arrangements of well-known jazz recordings of the past compare with the original recordings on which they are modeled? How does this project compare to Wynton Marsalis's *Standard Time* albums as an example of neotraditional jazz?

GATEWAY 54
POSTMODERN CLASSICAL MUSIC

What Is It?

One of the significant social issues of the period between 1975 and 1994 was the HIV/AIDS epidemic, which has claimed approximately 700,000 lives in the United States and about thirty-six million worldwide. In addition to responses from the medical, scientific, and political communities, musicians and composers also engaged with this crisis in efforts to raise public awareness, garner support for those suffering from HIV/AIDS, and mourn those who had been lost. Our gateway to classical music of this period is the third movement, "Chaconne: Giulio's Song," of John Corigliano's Symphony No. 1, a composition written out of Corigliano's grief for those whose lives had been taken by AIDS. A *chaconne* is a Baroque-period triple-meter dance form with a short, repeated ostinato in the bass part over which others play melodic variations. The other movements of the symphony are "Apologue: Of Rage and Remembrance"; "Tarantella" (an Italian rural dance); and "Epilogue." Composed in 1988, Corigliano wrote in the program note in the score of the piece,

> During the past decade I have lost many friends and colleagues to the AIDS epidemic, and the cumulative effect of those losses has, naturally, deeply affected me. My Symphony No. 1 was generated by feelings of loss, anger, and frustration.

The Chicago Symphony Orchestra commissioned this work and gave its first performance in 1990. Leonard Slatkin conducts the National Symphony Orchestra in this recording.

 Listen to the quiet, somber opening of this movement.

How Does It Work?

Timbre

The full orchestra features two solo cellos and solos on woodwinds and horn.

Texture

The texture is varied but the two cellos playing in counterpoint figure prominently, as do instrumental solos over drone-like orchestral accompaniments.

FIGURE 13.19
John Corigliano with his Oscar for Best Original Score for the 1998 film *The Red Violin*
Source: Getty Images/HECTOR MATA.

Rhythm

The tempo is slow with long sustained tones. A sense of beat and meter comes and goes.

Melody

The principal melody, Giulio's song, ascends with disjunct leaps.

Harmony

The harmony is dissonant but drone-like.

Form

A single principal melody over a very slow, drone-like ostinato in the low strings is heard throughout.

Performance Techniques

The performance techniques are common to symphonic music.

 Listen for the entrance of Giulio's song and the drone-like texture for the first 1:30 of this performance.

What Does It Mean?

This movement memorializes Corigliano's friends who died of AIDS, including Giulio, an amateur cellist with whom Corigliano used to improvise, and Giulio's cello teacher. Giulio's song is based on a fragment of melody Giulio once improvised. The melodies for Corigliano's other friends, played by the woodwinds and horn, are the composer's settings of one-sentence eulogies he commissioned from a writer friend.

Listen to the entire performance following this timed listening guide.

LISTENING GUIDE 13.4

TIME	DESCRIPTION
0:00	The low strings (the basses, cellos, and violas) enter almost imperceptibly with a series of long sustained tones, which form the *chaconne*'s ostinato.
0:57	The cello enters with Giulio's song, an ascending, disjunct melody of sustained tones over the long, low pitches of the ostinato. A variant of the opening melodic ascent is played a number of times.
4:01	The second cello enters with a two-note stepwise descending motive and joins the first cello in counterpoint, an icon of a conversation (a lesson perhaps) between the two men.
4:39	The first cello replays Giulio's song and the second cello follows in imitative counterpoint, as if listening and understanding his friend's illness.
6:00	A high-pitched held tone announces a new section in which the whole orchestra enters with short melodies in the woodwinds and horn, indexing individual victims of AIDS.
7:05	The solo cello reintroduces Giulio's song, which joins in a chorus with other victims represented by the other instruments and the second cello, replete with the sounding of bell chimes imitating the death knell of church bells at their funerals.
8:57	The flute and other instruments join the cellos in Giulio's song, creating a new, brighter, perhaps more hopeful timbre, as if rejoicing in his life.
10:23	A crescendo leads to a long sustained tone on the trumpet followed by dramatic low-pitched thuds of a drum, icons of the final nails in the coffin perhaps, and dissonant forte chords in the brass expressing the anguish of those left behind. The steady drum beat, the bells, and the swirling instrumental lines echo the march to the gallows in Hector Berlioz's early nineteenth-century *Symphonie Fantastique* (Chapter 7, Gateway 25).
13:43	After a violent crescendo, the orchestra subsides to silence, leaving only the faint sound, and memory, of a solo cellist.
13:54	End

EMOTIONAL
RESONANCE

The HIV/AIDS epidemic, first reported and named in the early 1980s, devastated the arts community in the United States. Corigliano's Symphony No. 1 memorializes friends who had died or were dying of AIDS by referencing some of their favorite music. The first movement, in memory of a pianist, is called "Of Rage and Remembrance" and alternates an Argentine tango melody to signal nostalgia and remembrance with darker passages iconic of the rage many felt as the disease spread through their community. The second movement, for a music executive, is based on a traditional Italian dance, the *tarantella*. The fourth movement combines themes from the first three movements. The symphony won two Grammy Awards, and Corigliano went on to win the Pulitzer Prize for Music in 2001 for his Symphony No. 2.

AESTHETICS

Like Corigliano's Symphony No. 1, much of the classical music composed in the period from 1975 to 1994 is relatively accessible. Although it sounds modern rather than traditional, it often features appealing and widely understood tonal harmony, familiar forms and instrumental timbres like the symphony orchestra, and regular, often repetitive, meters and rhythms. Although the music contains plenty of unfamiliar, "modern," dissonant chords and chromatic scales, the composers hoped to attract listeners with iconic references to familiar music from the past of European classical music as well as to contemporary styles such as the tango of the first movement of Corigliano's Symphony No. 1 as well as styles of popular music and jazz. The most important trends in classical composition in this period can be described as **postmodernism** in the general sense that they reacted against the modernist musical styles of the 1950s and 1960s.

CULTURAL
LINKAGES

Postmodernism suffused all the arts in this period. European music, art, and architecture since the 1890s have generally been called "modern" for two reasons. First, modern art was

linked to "modern life" based on modern technologies like airplanes, computers, and electronic recordings. Second, modern art broke from nineteenth-century traditions, rejecting tonality in the case of music, figurative painting and sculpture in the case of art, and Baroque decoration and classic colonnaded façades in the case of architecture. In the 1970s some artists in all these disciplines turned their backs on the tenets and styles of modernism. Their art was dubbed postmodernism.

Fundamental to postmodernism is the rejection of the notion of progress in the arts. An earlier modernist ideology argued for continuous progress in the complexity of the arts. Postmodernists rejected this view and reclaimed, reordered, and reindexed the artistic styles of the past to create new art that had not been seen or heard before. Instead of progress, they proposed a kind of circularity or recycling. New postmodern work was at first criticized as vulgar, as it seemed to pander to a popular audience. In the case of music, postmodernism served to attract the audiences who had been alienated by the modernism of the 1950s and 1960s and its turn away from their expectations and understandings as listeners.

The term "postmodernism" was first used in the field of architecture, and the change in architectural style in the 1970s and 1980s illustrates visually the difference between modernism and postmodernism. Clean, repeating lines characterized modern architecture, whose archetypal representative is the skyscraper. Ludwig Mies van der Rohe (1886–1959), one of architectural modernism's founders and most respected figures, built unadorned, rectilinear prisms of steel and glass in Chicago in the 1950s and 1960s. Frank Lloyd Wright (1867–1959), another modernist, used a curvier, more sculptural, but nonetheless unadorned approach to the repetition of lines for the interior for the Guggenheim Museum in New York.

Postmodernism responded to the linear, repetitive quality of modern architecture by adding decorative elements borrowed from architectural styles of previous eras in a manner commonly called pastiche. In 1984 Philip Johnson (1906–2005) applied a postmodern sensibility to an otherwise rectilinear modernist skyscraper in New York City, his AT&T Building (now named by its address, 550 Madison Avenue). The triangular structure at the top is a whimsical

FIGURE 13.20
Mies van der Rohe's modernist AMA Plaza in Chicago
Source: Teemu008, Wikimedia Commons.

reference to similar structures, called pediments, on the top of colonnades in eighteenth-century classical-style architecture and on furniture designed in the so-called Chippendale style. Corigliano's use of the *chaconne* form and his echo of Berlioz's *Symphonie Fantastique* in his Symphony No. 1 are similar postmodern references to music of the past.

What Is Its History?

Postmodernism in music took four forms during the period from 1975 to 1994: postmodernism *per se*, minimalism, the use of familiar forms, and neo-Romanticism. Although much composition in this period is postmodernist in its turn away from modernist complexity and abstraction, the term "postmodernism" is often applied only to work that, like postmodern architecture, applies familiar styles and forms from the past to a modernist structure. John Corigliano, born to a musical family in New York in 1938 and a professor at the City University of New York (CUNY), was one of the most successful American composers to adopt the pastiche quality of postmodern architecture. In Symphony No. 1 he creates musical collages that paste a panoply of

FIGURE 13.21
Frank Lloyd Wright's modernist interior for the Guggenheim Museum in New York
Source: Evan-Amos, Wikimedia Commons.

historical styles onto an essentially modernist foundation. Critics and audiences have applauded his compositions for symphony orchestra and wind band, as well as his opera *The Ghosts of Versailles* (1991) and his score for the film *The Red Violin* (1998). Because of their accessibility, his work is performed relatively frequently today.

> AESTHETICS

Minimalism was another technique that became respectable in this period. What had begun on the fringes of the classical music scene in the 1960s has, over the last fifty years, entered its mainstream. To give just one example, in 1992 the Metropolitan Opera, perhaps the most prominent classical music institution in the United States, commissioned Philip Glass to write an opera called *The Voyage* to commemorate Columbus's sail to the West Indies 500 years earlier.

During this period John Adams (b. 1947) emerged as the most significant successor to the minimalist tradition. Born in Massachusetts and educated at Harvard, he taught at the San Francisco Conservatory of Music from 1972 to 1984 and has lived in California since then. Adams extended the limits of minimalism. While still writing music accessible to the general public, he extended the complexity of the minimalist tradition in ways that appealed to professional musicians and sophisticated listeners, some of whom found the repetition in early minimalist work boring. The title of his 1976 *Phrygian Gates* for solo piano refers to his use of a Medieval European church mode (Chapter 2, Gateway 5). "Gates" are a series of changes in texture that appear abruptly throughout the piece. These changes create a sense of progression and anticipation missing from earlier minimalist compositions. Adams joined Philip Glass in the composition of operas with his 1986 *Nixon in China*, premiered at the Houston Grand Opera. Typical of operas from the past, this opera deals with the personal dramas surrounding a major political event, in this case President Richard Nixon's surprising and unexpected diplomatic initiative toward communist China in the early 1970s. The music, although rooted in a minimalist sensibility, contains passages that link his work to the other two major trends of this period: references to late nineteenth-century composers (neo-Romanticism) and an eclectic collage of twentieth-century classical music styles and swing-era jazz (postmodernism).

FIGURE 13.22
The postmodernist 550 Madison Avenue building in New York
Source: David Shankbone, Wikimedia Commons.

FIGURE 13.23
Ellen Taaffe Zwilich
Source: Getty Images/Mark Kauffman.

A number of composers found ways to make their music accessible and understandable to listeners without resorting to the repetitions of minimalism by keeping certain elements, like texture or timbre, constant while varying other elements; by introducing tonality from time to time; or by revivifying traditional forms like sonata form and theme and variations. In the United States, Ellen Taaffe Zwilich, born in Florida in 1939 and a professor at Florida State University, used variation technique to such impressive effect in her Symphony No. 1 (1982) that, in 1983, she won the Pulitzer Prize for music, the first woman composer to do so. The seven-minute-long first movement begins quietly with an ascending third. This motive then reoccurs throughout the movement, reminding listeners of the motivic nature of Beethoven's Fifth Symphony (Chapter 6, Gateway 22) and providing audiences with a level of redundancy typical of virtually all music until the serialism, atonality, and experimentalism of the twentieth century. The rich orchestration, including bell chimes reminiscent of Berlioz's *Symphonie Fantastique*, and some short three- and four-note rhythmic motives, also offer pleasingly familiar anchors within a dissonant, rather static harmonic framework. Her technically sophisticated use of the orchestra in many of her works, including concertos for wind and brass instruments, have gained the favor of major orchestras in the United States.

Neo-Romanticism is a label applied to modern compositions that return in one way or another to nineteenth-century tonality and musical forms. The results are works that tradition-minded concertgoers find comprehensible and enjoyable because they contain so many icons of previous musical experience. George Rochberg (1918–2005), after embracing avant-garde styles early in his career, turned to Romantic-era and early twentieth-century styles during the 1970s when he found that he could not adequately express, with the compositional techniques he had been using, his grief after the death of his teenage son. Rochberg was born in New Jersey and taught for a number of years at the University of Pennsylvania. Each movement of his String Quartet No. 5 uses a style associated with a particular composer: some movements reference the tonality of nineteenth-century composers Ludwig van Beethoven, Franz Schubert (1797–1828), and Gustav Mahler. Other movements employ the challenging harmonies of early twentieth-century composers Béla Bartók (1881–1945) and Arnold Schoenberg.

Another neo-Romantic composer, David Del Tredici, born in California in 1937, worried that his reclamation of older tonal styles would not be well received by his composer colleagues, but he hoped that his appropriation of familiar musical icons would attract concert audiences to modern music. In 1976, after the Chicago Symphony premiered his work *Final Alice* to what one critic described as "the most enthusiastic reception of a new work I have ever heard at a symphony concert," Del Tredici captured, in an interview, both the challenge to modernism and the desire to reconnect with audiences through the emotional potential of Romantic-era musical expressiveness:

> I was terrified my colleagues would think I was an idiot. . . . For my generation, it is considered vulgar to have an audience really, really like a piece on a first hearing. But why are we writing music except to move people and to be expressive? To have what has moved us move somebody else? Right now, audiences just reject contemporary music. But if they start to like one thing, then they begin to have perspective. That will make a difference.

The work of all the postmodernists of this period reduced and recontextualized the complexities of modernism in ways that invited classical music audiences to listen and take seriously new work situated within the long tradition of European classical music and that responded to events in the world like the HIV/AIDS epidemic. Because of that search for connection to an audience, symphony orchestras and opera companies continue today to program many works of this period.

WHERE DO I GO FROM HERE?

- Listen to Corigliano's Symphony No. 1, Mvt. I, "Apologue: Of Rage and Remembrance." Which musical elements express his grief? How does this movement relate to the third movement, "Giulio's Song"?

- Listen to John Adams's *Phrygian Gates* for solo piano. Can you hear the various "gates" that the form passes through? How is the effect similar to and different from earlier examples of minimalism such as Julius Eastman's *Stay On It*?

- Listen to David Del Tredici's *Final Alice*. Do you find yourself responding in a similar manner as the audience at the premier? To what extent does your response, and the sound of the music, resonate with the quote from Del Tredici, above?

GATEWAY 55
REGGAE

What Is It?

Reggae is a style of music that emerged in Jamaica in the late 1960s. It became widely popular around the world, especially in Europe, the United States, and Africa, during the period from 1975 to 1994. Our gateway to reggae, "Buffalo Soldier," was recorded in 1978 by Bob Marley and the Wailers. Bob Marley (1945–1981) is arguably one of the world's most famous musicians and singer-songwriters. He co-wrote "Buffalo Soldier" with the Jamaican musician, DJ, and producer Noel "King Sporty" Williams (1943–2015), and the song was first released on the album *Confrontation* in 1983, after Marley's death.

The term "buffalo soldier" refers to African Americans serving in the segregated regiments of the U.S. Army during the late nineteenth century. The nickname was reportedly given to Black soldiers in such regiments by Native American tribes in the 1860s when they faced them in U.S. military campaigns to suppress Native American populations. In the song's lyrics, Marley transforms the definition of "buffalo soldier" by connecting African Americans to the contemporary plight and struggle of descendants of enslaved Africans throughout the African diaspora.

 Listen to the recording and focus on the lyrics. How does Marley redefine the "buffalo soldier"?

How Does It Work?

Timbre

Solo male and group vocals, a deep and heavy-sounding bass guitar, drum set, other percussion, electric guitars, a brass and saxophone horn section, organ, piano, and some other keyboards can all be heard in this recording. The timbres of the drum set feature short percussive sounds with rapid decay such as a tightly closed hi-hat, a punchy bass drum, and a high-pitched snare drum that sounds almost like *timbales*. Unlike most jazz and rock drumming, the resounding cymbals of the drum set are not heard.

Texture

The vocals and brass carry melody lines while a polyrhythmic groove created by the other instruments serves as an accompaniment.

Rhythm

This recording features a typical polyrhythmic reggae groove with a slight swing feel, an emphasis on beats two and four in some guitars and keyboards,

FIGURE 13.24
Bob Marley in 1978
Source: Trinity Mirror/Mirrorpix/Alamy Stock Photo.

and a bass drum on all four beats of nearly every measure. The bass and another guitar together play an ostinato that emphasizes many of the downbeats as well as the swing feel. The tempo, like in most reggae music, is moderate and relaxed.

Melody

The melody is in a major mode and spans a range of about an octave and a half.

Harmony

The harmony is tonal and mostly stays on the I chord, though it occasionally ventures briefly to a related minor chord and a few other chords.

Form

There are three distinct types of strophes (A, B, C) that repeat at various points of the song, sometimes with different words. A bridge section (D) appears once. The form of the song could be outlined like this: Intro—ABABACDACAC.

Performance Techniques

The horn section of brass and saxophones frequently interacts with the vocals in a call-and-response manner, echoing the call and response common in music throughout the African diaspora. The female choral responses share some features with African American gospel music.

Listen to the entire song, keeping in mind the musical elements described above and following the timed listening guide.

LISTENING GUIDE 13.5

TIME	SECTION	DESCRIPTION	LYRICS
0:00	Introduction	A brief drum fill on the high-pitched snare drum begins the recording, an opening gesture very common in reggae that signals the tempo and groove. A brief introduction with a melody in the horn section follows.	
0:08	A	The four-measure repeating groove begins, and Marley sings four nearly identical narrow-range melodic phrases that emphasize the third scale degree, each with different lyrics. The harmony centers on the I chord.	Buffalo soldier . . . Stolen from Africa . . .
0:39	B	In the first B section, the groove continues for two identical four-bar phrases with different harmonies than A. The melody Marley sings in B goes up to a higher range, focusing on the sixth scale degree and introducing a more strained vocal quality.	When I analyze . . .
0:55	A	The melody and harmony of A return, but the lyrics are slightly modified and the lyrical phrases occur in a new order. The horn section also answers some of the melodic phrases with their own melodies in the mode of call and response.	Taken from Africa . . . Buffalo soldier . . .
1:25	B	B returns with a new set of lyrics and background parts in the horns that alternate between sustained and syncopated notes.	If you know your history . . .
1:41	A	A returns with similar lyrics as previous iterations, but in a new order and with some additions.	Buffalo soldier . . . Fighting on arrival . . .
2:12	C	A new section, C, continues the groove and harmony of A, but has a new, higher melody, sung twice on vocables, that descends stepwise through the major scale and is repeated twice. The horn section again sets up a call-and-response pattern.	Woe yoy yoy . . .
2:28	D	Another new section, D, shifts the harmony to the key of the relative minor as Marley gestures towards the plight of the buffalo soldier, who is "trodding through the land."	Buffalo soldier trodding . . .
2:43	A	A returns again with some new lyrics.	Buffalo soldier . . .

TIME	SECTION	DESCRIPTION	LYRICS
			Fighting on arrival . . .
3:14	C	C repeats.	Woe yoy yoy . . .
3:29	A	A repeats one last time, this time with many new lyrics and a call-and-response pattern between the vocals and the horns on every line.	Troddin' through San Juan . . . Fighting on arrival . . .
4:00	C	C repeats and the recording fades out.	Woe yoy yoy . . .
4:16	End		

What Does It Mean?

Many of reggae's meanings are rooted in the **Rastafari Movement**, which emerged in Jamaica in the first half of the twentieth century. Not all reggae is associated with Rastafari, but the movement's emergence in the context of the colonization of Jamaica sheds some light on the Rastafari-related meaning of "Buffalo Soldier," especially that of its lyrics. Christopher Columbus landed in Jamaica in 1494, and the British captured the island a century and a half later in 1655. Relying on the labor of enslaved Africans, Jamaica became one of the largest sugar producers in the world. By the time Britain outlawed slavery in the 1830s, enslaved Africans outnumbered whites twenty to one in Jamaica. Jamaica achieved its independence from Britain in 1962 at the same time that African countries were becoming independent from Britain and other European countries.

> CULTURAL LINKAGES

Many Blacks in Jamaica turned to African culture and to African intellectuals for inspiration, fueled by frustration among the urban poor and a high murder rate in the capital city, Kingston. One of their heroes was Haile Selassie (1892–1975), the Emperor of Ethiopia from 1930 to 1974 and the first Black ruler in twentieth-century Africa. In the 1930s some Jamaicans came to regard him as the second coming of the biblical Messiah and as God himself, capable of leading Black people everywhere into a promised land of freedom, justice, equality, and prosperity. Taking Selassie's given name (Tafari) and princely title (Ras), they called their beliefs and practices, their "way of life" as they put it, the Rastafari Movement. Adherents use marijuana as a spiritual path, wear dreadlocks, and reject mainstream society, which they call Babylon because of its materialism and oppression. They hope to return one day to Zion, the Kingdom of God (whom they call "Jah"), which can refer literally to Ethiopia or Africa, or metaphorically to Africa as a state of mind where being of African descent is a point of pride and self-confidence.

Bob Marley, although raised a Catholic, became the most famous adherent of Rastafari in the 1960s and 1970s. Many of his songs directly reference Jah and Zion and are understood to reference people of African descent suffering in the oppressive world of Babylon. Marley includes Black history in the United States in this world by calling the buffalo soldiers a "dreadlock Rasta." In a subtle gesture by Marley, the melody of C comes from an American song called "Mammy's Little Baby Loves Shortnin' Bread" written in 1900 by a white poet in the Black dialect of minstrel shows. It quickly entered both Black and white folk traditions and suffused popular culture for much of the twentieth century. The Beach Boys recorded a version around the same time Marley recorded "Buffalo Soldier." By substituting African-derived vocables for the song's words, Marley reclaims this tune, for African Americans, from oppressive white stereotypes of their speech patterns.

> POLITICS

In the 1960s and 1970s, a growing sense of shared experience united the African diaspora across what came to be called the Black Atlantic. Descendants of enslaved Africans in the Americas and the Caribbean, Black immigrants from Jamaica and Trinidad to Britain, and other populations of African descent were all subject to similar and interrelated conditions of racial injustice. They also participated in networks of cultural exchange throughout this Black Atlantic. Musical exchanges of the Black Atlantic address oppression and bias in myriad ways. When Bob Marley sings about how it makes sense to him that the buffalo soldier is a dreadlock Rasta, he is connecting the struggles of Blacks in Jamaica with that of Blacks in the United States.

In the song's lyrics Marley both gives a history lesson and re-interprets history. He points out that one oppressed group, African Americans, were fighting for the cause of the United States in the oppression of another group, Native Americans. But he re-defines the buffalo soldier as someone "driven from the mainland [Africa]" to the heart of the Caribbean and the heart of America. After reminding listeners to learn their history, presumably about the African slave trade, Marley calls himself a buffalo soldier, uniting African Americans to himself and to the African diaspora once again. He repeats the phrase "fighting on arrival," to show that enslaved Africans and their descendants have been fighting to survive since they had arrived, even as they were fighting against Native Americans in the United States on behalf of the country that had enslaved them.

One of the characteristics of Rastafari is the way that it conflates and skews linear time, situating the past in the present and history as something that is not long gone but that is continually affecting the present. Historical themes of slavery, displacement from Africa ("the mainland"), Black survival, and the celebration of ordinary people, like the buffalo soldier and the dreadlock Rasta, are all brought into the present in this recording and in many other examples of reggae music. In "Buffalo Soldier" Marley presents historical events in seemingly random order, as if they are all happening together at once. For example, the lyrics of each repetition of the A section are in a different order or are replaced by new lyrics referencing some other historical event in nonchronological order. Marley returns repeatedly to certain lyrics, such as "buffalo soldier, dreadlock Rasta." Taken together, the lyrics suggest the unity of the Black Atlantic and its complex cyclical dynamics of oppression and hope.

AESTHETICS

The song's cyclical structure is also present in its repetition of a four-bar chord progression that occurs throughout the A and C sections. The progression begins on a I chord that is emphasized by a repeated note in the bass for two bars, departs briefly to other harmonies in the third bar, and returns, or cycles back, to the I chord for the fourth bar. This four-bar cycle occurs multiple times in each A and C section, for a total of twenty-six times in the course of the song, departing only briefly to the B and D sections, whose four-bar phrases repeat a total of only six times. This is not the first time that music of the African diaspora has challenged linear time with a cyclical approach. John Coltrane abandoned linear musical logic in *A Love Supreme* (Chapter 12, Gateway 48), and Trinidadian steel pan arrangers interrupt the linear flow of the theme and variations form with their sections called jams that suspend linear time with cyclical repetitions (Chapter 11, Gateway 45).

🔊 Listen again to "Buffalo Soldier," paying attention to how Marley's lyrics conflate historical time by bringing seemingly disparate events, people, and places together, and to the repeating four-bar cycle in the A and C sections.

Reggae is also remarkable for its distinctive rhythmic sensibilities. On just about every reggae song, there is a strong emphasis on beats two and four heard prominently in a repetitive, bright "chunk" sound on an electric guitar. In addition to the emphasis on two and four, the upbeats of each beat have an accent of their own. Many instruments play on these beats in the polyrhythmic texture. The most consistent is the organ, which can be heard faintly in the background playing every upbeat when the C section is first introduced. It reappears in all of the sections from the A section at 2:43 until the end of the recording. In combination with the strong accents on beats two and four, the upbeats in the organ and other louder instruments give "Buffalo Soldier" reggae's trademark "ga-CHUNK-ga" feel. This feel is related to one of reggae's precursors, **ska**, a genre that emerged in Jamaica around 1960 and that strongly emphasizes every offbeat, sometimes even leaving downbeats silent.

Because the rhythm is emphasized so strongly in the repeating upbeats and chords on beats two and four played by guitars and keyboard instruments in reggae, the bass is free to take other roles. In "Buffalo Soldier" the notes played in the bass are not particularly sustained.

On other Bob Marley recordings such as "Could You Be Loved" (1980) or "Is This Love" (1978), the bass plays even more freely, joining the melody at times and creating some of its own lines. This freedom in the bass contributes to an even more complex polyrhythm, which, along with call-and-response patterns, is a shared characteristic of much of the music that has roots in Africa and the African diaspora, including music of salsa, hip-hop, steel pan music, and all varieties of jazz.

Listen once more to "Buffalo Soldier." Identify some of the individual instruments playing the "ga-CHUNK-ga" rhythmic pattern throughout and identify other rhythms in the poly-rhythmic texture.

What Is Its History?

A number of musical genres and styles contributed to the development of reggae. One source is African-derived religious music traditions similar to Candomblé in Brazil, Santería in Cuba, and Vodou in Haiti (Chapter 6, Gateway 23). One of these, Kumina, coalesced as a religion in the mid-nineteenth century when, after the abolition of slavery, many Congolese were brought to Jamaica and worked as indentured servants or contract workers. Based in Congolese drumming styles, *kumina* drumming developed out of the religion of the same name and became a style of its own. It inspired drummers like Count Ossie (1926–1976) and other Rastafarians in the 1930s and 1940s. Another reggae precursor is a popular Jamaican folk genre called *mento*, which combined European dance forms with African musical sensibilities and, like Trinidadian calypso (Chapter 11, Gateway 45), was known for its topical songs commenting on social issues of everyday life, often with humor and wordplay. *Mento* set a precedent for social commentary in music, and it continues as a form of popular entertainment today.

> CULTURAL
> LINKAGES

During the 1950s, audiences in Jamaica were interested in hearing the latest music by American rhythm & blues acts blasted by powerful sound systems. But by the time independence was achieved in 1962, a new atmosphere encouraged the cultivation of distinctive forms of music and other arts, and musicians began experimenting with the rhythmic feel of rhythm & blues in their own music. In a gradual process, they developed a new type of groove that emphasized every **offbeat** (a beat in between two typically accented beats) in a 4/4 meter at a quick tempo, the characteristic sound of what became the genre ska. The swing shuffle feel of many rhythm & blues recordings includes a harmonic instrument such as a piano or guitar playing every upbeat, but not accented very strongly. In ska these upbeats were transformed into the most heavily accented beats in every measure, as heard in the influential recordings of a band called The Skatalites. Another genre, **rocksteady**, developed in the mid-1960s. It slowed down the tempo of ska, added an accented hit on beat three in the snare drum, and allowed musicians to experiment with different types of polyrhythms. Groups like the Techniques and the Heptones, influenced by American genres such as soul, created smooth, sweet-sounding melodies like the melody in the Techniques' recording "Queen Majesty" (1967).

Drawing on rocksteady, ska, *mento*, rhythm & blues, gospel, funk, and jazz, reggae emerged as a named genre after the term was first used in the title of the song "Do the Reggay," a 1968 recording by a Jamaican band called the Maytals, who sang in a close-harmony gospel style. Early reggae stars such as Jimmy Cliff (b. 1948) had been active in either ska or rocksteady (or both) before the naming of the reggae genre, a reminder that

FIGURE 13.25
A group of people setting up a Jamaican-style sound system at Notting Hill Carnival in London, 1983
Source: Getty Images/PYMCA/UIG.

the sonic distinctions between music genres can be quite subtle and that genre names might say more about how the music is marketed or the makeup of an audience than those sonic distinctions. Even Bob Marley's group, the Wailers, was originally a ska vocal group that he had formed with Peter Tosh (1944–1987) and Bunny Wailer (b. 1947) in 1963. Since the genre's inception, the lyrics of reggae have covered a range of topics from social commentary and Rastafari to the celebration of love and having a good time. Reggae's complex, contagious rhythm makes the body want to move and its often major-key melodies and harmonies remain consistent regardless of the subject of the lyrics. The dark political and social critiques of reggae can seem at odds with musical elements that often index a party mood, a juxtaposition not dissimilar to some salsa music (Chapter 12, Gateway 50). Perhaps the pleasant-sounding music helps listeners and dancers feel better about the struggles documented in its lyrics. And perhaps its infectious style draws in new listeners unfamiliar with the injustices expressed in the songs.

Bob Marley was born to an Afro-Jamaican mother and a white Jamaican father in central-northern Jamaica. At the age of twelve he moved with his mother to a neighborhood near Kingston called Trenchtown, a place he later referenced in songs such as "No Woman, No Cry" (1974), "Trenchtown Rock" (1971), and others. As a result of his work with the Wailers in the 1960s, he was already popular in Jamaica by the 1970s, and the group had released a number of albums. In 1973 Bob Marley and the Wailers released an album called *Burnin'* on Island Records, a large and influential record label with an international reach. It impressed not only reggae fans but also rock audiences in Britain and the United States. The first song on *Burnin'* is "Get Up, Stand Up," whose lyrics urge the oppressed with statements like "stand up for your rights" and "don't give up the fight" in the chorus. The second song evokes "Hallelujah Time," when the crying of children will turn to singing because "but though we bear our burdens now, all afflictions got to end somehow." Another song promises that, because of the poverty and brutality Blacks routinely face, "that's why we gonna be burnin' and lootin' tonight." The third song on the album, "I Shot the Sheriff," caught the attention of British rock guitarist Eric Clapton, whose 1974 cover version of the song became a number one hit in the United States and brought great attention to Marley and reggae in general in the United States and the U.K. (Its sampling in Public Enemy's "Fight the Power" is discussed in Gateway 51.)

POLITICS

Amid his massive worldwide fame in the 1970s, Marley remained ever passionate about Rastafari and addressing the struggles of Africans and the African diaspora, and about reggae as a vehicle for communicating these passions. In 1978 he performed a number of his hits as the featured artist at a concert in Kingston, Jamaica, with sixteen of reggae's most famous acts called the "One Love Peace Concert." The concert was organized by two imprisoned gangsters from opposing violent political factions who hoped that reggae could bring people together and end the violence between gangs armed by warring political parties, one led by Prime Minister Michael Manley and the other by his rival Edward Seaga. Both politicians were present at the concert. Marley performed "Jammin'," whose lyrics seem to be about musicians and music lovers "jammin'" together and having a good time. The lyrics also include references to Zion, Jah, poverty, Elvis (in the same vein as in "Fight the Power"), and other clues that Marley's concept of "jammin'" might be about a social and political sense of harmony as much as it is about a musical one. In the middle of the song, after singing lyrics like "I really wanna jam with you . . . I hope you like jammin' too," Marley began improvising lyrics invoking Emperor Haile Selassie and prayers to God and phrases like "show the people that you gonna unite." He then invited Manley and Seaga to the stage as the band continued to cycle through the groove of the song, joining the hands of these bitter rivals above his head as a hopeful icon for peace and unity and saying "love, prosperity, be with us all, Jah, Rastafari, Selassie." Though the crowd went wild as these political rivals were united physically onstage, the violence in Jamaica did not decrease. In 1980, during the election year when Seaga unseated Manley as prime minister, there were nearly 900 reported murders, more than double that of the previous year. Bob Marley died in 1981 of cancer, undoubtedly convinced that the fight against oppression and injustice was needed more than ever.

CULTURAL LINKAGES

Reggae's rise in global popularity during the 1970s has influenced popular music all around the world. One measure of reggae's continuing importance today is its status as a genre with its own Grammy Award "field" (others include pop, jazz, R&B, rap, country, American roots music, global music, Latin, classical, and rock). The Best Reggae Album Grammy was first awarded in 1985 and, since then, three of Bob Marley's children—Ziggy Marley (b. 1968), Stephen Marley (b. 1972), and Damien Marley (b. 1978)—have won the category thirteen times among them and another of his sons, Julian Marley (b. 1975), has also been nominated. As early as the late 1960s, adaptations of reggae's rhythmic groove could be heard in recordings like the Beatles' "Ob-La-Di, Ob-La-Da" (1968). Since reggae's explosion in popularity in the 1970s, musicians in other rock and popular music genres have embraced the style: the chorus of "Hotel California" (1976) by the American rock band the Eagles features a reggae-inflected rhythm; the first two hits of British rock band the Police, "Roxanne" (1978) and "I Can't Stand Losing You" (1978), are based on modified reggae grooves; and the hit Bobby McFerrin song "Don't Worry Be Happy" (1988), whose message Public Enemy rejected in "Fight the Power," recreates a reggae feel through percussive vocal singing and body percussion such as snapping. The infectious rhythmic sensibilities of reggae continue to inspire musicians today from Ariana Grande in her hit 2016 hit single "Side to Side" to Jay-Z (in collaboration with Damien Marley) on the song "Bam" from *4:44* (2017).

WHERE DO I GO FROM HERE?

- Listen to a few other Bob Marley songs, such as "Get Up, Stand Up," "No Woman, No Cry," and "Three Little Birds." What do these share in common with "Buffalo Soldier" in their lyrical themes, rhythmic grooves, and other musical elements? Where do they differ?
- Find the video of "Jammin'" from the 1978 One Love Peace Concert on YouTube and compare it to another recording of the song. How do the performances differ?
- Since the late 1970s the style of reggae popularized by Marley has been supplanted in popularity by a genre called "dancehall" in Jamaica, the Jamaican diaspora, and some sectors of mainstream pop. (Dancehall is sometimes loosely categorized as reggae, and Marley's style as "roots reggae.") Listen to some dancehall music from the 1980s or 1990s, and compare it to recent examples of pop music influenced by dancehall, such as "Work" (2016) by Rihanna, "One Dance" (2016) by Drake, or "Sorry" (2015) by Justin Bieber. What musical elements of dancehall do these pop artists exploit? How do these pop examples compare to the music of contemporary Jamaican dancehall artists like Sean Paul (b. 1971) or Shenseea (b. 1996)?

CLOSING

If there is a common theme in music from 1975 to 1994, it has to do with musicians seeking to connect with audiences and communities of listeners. Classical postmodernists and jazz neotraditionalists sought to create music that would interest and engage larger communities of listeners and those alienated from avant-garde styles of the previous period. Rappers began with community dance parties in their neighborhoods in the boroughs of New York and South Central Los Angeles and soon became, according to Chuck D of Public Enemy, "Black America's CNN," providing news and commentary on life and culture in America's cities. DJs and dancers in Chicago nurtured a scene that was a haven for queer Black and Latinx communities, and created house, a new genre of electronic music. Reggae artists understood themselves as speaking to a suffering community that stretched around the Black Atlantic. To engage their communities, musicians in all these genres and styles necessarily evoked musical histories of their traditions: neotraditionalism in jazz; neo-Romanticism in classical music; funk and other samples in rap and hip-hop; soul and disco in Chicago house; and the Ethiopian emperor, rhythm & blues, *mento*, ska, and *kumina* drumming in reggae. No matter the type of music they were making or whether they wanted to make art, make people think, or make them dance, musicians in this period were deeply committed to music as a social practice that brings people together.

THINGS TO THINK ABOUT

- In what ways can each of these gateway examples be considered postmodern? Are there similarities among all of them in this regard?
- What are the similarities and differences between neotraditionalism in jazz and postmodernism in classical music during the period from 1975 to 1994?
- Compare the ways that rap, electronic music, and reggae dealt with political and social issues facing Black communities during the period from 1975 to 1994.

NEW TERMS

breakdancing	neotraditionalism	scratching
disco	postmodernism	ska
drop	rap, rapping	synth pad
gangsta rap	Rastafari Movement	synthesizer, synth
hardcore rap	reggae	toasting
hip-hop culture	rocksteady	vocalese
neo-Romanticism	samples	world music

MUSIC TODAY

MUSIC IN EVERY PERIOD of time and every place in the world is embedded in the cultural, social, economic, political, and intellectual life of the society that makes and supports that music. Musicians, composers, and listeners respond, in one way or another, to the texture of cultural and social life. In some cases they try to influence or change culture and society through their music making and their musical taste. This claim has been true throughout history and is certainly true of music today.

Among the major currents tugging at American lives today are:

- the COVID-19 pandemic, the widespread illness and millions of deaths it has caused, and the corresponding changes it has brought to many aspects of life;
- a growing awareness of climate change and the specter of environmental disaster;
- a new acceptance of LGBTQ+ and other sexualities and gender identities, including the legalization of gay marriage;
- a renewed focus on standing against sexual harassment and advocating for equal rights for all genders in a patriarchal society;
- the concentration of wealth in the hands of the rich and the increasing poverty and lack of opportunity for the poor and the middle class;
- the effect of drugs in many forms on individual lives, on local communities, and on the broader social fabric;
- transnational migration and immigration due to poverty and war;
- racial injustice manifested in, among other ways, ongoing systemic discrimination and police violence; and
- the availability of images, news, and music from all over the world through social media, internet streaming services, and older media such as TV and film.

The gateway recordings in this chapter respond in one way or another to some of these themes in Americans' recent experience.

GATEWAY 56
POP MUSIC TODAY

What Is It?

Popular music today connects with audiences in countless ways, just as it has for decades. It helps people fall in love and deal with heartbreak. It entertains and makes people laugh. It distracts people from their trouble and helps them through it. It engages with social issues and serves as a vehicle for protest. It brings people together, providing ways for them to feel like they belong and take pride in their identities. Popular music today is popular in part because it connects with audiences in all of these ways and more.

DOI: 10.4324/9781003269304-18

FIGURE 14.1
Olivia Rodrigo performs, surrounded by dancers, in front of a camera at the 2021 MTV Video Music Awards in New York City
Source: Getty Images/Kevin Mazur/MTV VMAs 2021/ Contributor.

Our gateway to today's pop music, a genre of popular music that is made for commercial purposes and a wide, often young audience, is the song "Brutal" by Olivia Rodrigo (b. 2002). She, along with the song's producer Dan Nigro (b. 1982), composed it. The opening track on her debut full-length album *Sour* (2021), "Brutal" deals with the anxieties and insecurities of young people, specifically as they are experienced in the age of social media. The song's lyrics suggest that the mental health and other struggles of teenagers should be taken seriously, despite common notions that youth is the most carefree stage of life.

 Listen to the first thirty seconds of the recording.

How Does It Work?

Timbre

The recording's timbres include a solo female voice with various audio effects on it, drums, various guitars, bass, a small string ensemble, an electric piano, and some background vocals.

Texture

The texture varies to some extent, but at its densest it includes melody, chords played by guitars and bass, and a drum part.

Rhythm

The rhythm is in a meter of four beats per measure.

Melody

The melodies of most vocal phrases occupy a relatively narrow range and vary between sung and spoken pitches.

Harmony

The harmony is mostly based on unison bass lines and power chords. **Power chords** only include the root and the fifth and are commonly played on guitar in punk rock and heavy metal. The ending of the song includes chords that hint at a minor key.

Form

The form consists of a verse, a chorus (a section that recurs throughout the song with the same lyrics), and an instrumental section that recurs at various points of the song. The song generally follows a form common in popular music today: Verse 1, Verse 2, Chorus, Verse 3, with instrumental sections interspersed at various points as well as an introduction and outro section.

Performance Techniques

The vocals include speaking and singing that sometimes borders on shouting. Rodrigo's voice is often slightly distorted in a way that sounds like its volume and power are pushing the limits of the microphone or that she is singing very close to the microphone. The tempo is steady until it slows down dramatically during the final instrumental section.

Listen to the entire recording with these elements in mind while following this timed listening guide.

LISTENING GUIDE 14.1

TIME	SECTION	DESCRIPTION	LYRICS
0:00	Intro	A string section plays sustained pitches in a lyrical manner, with some electronic effects on the sound. A small crescendo precedes a complete break in the string sound, and Rodrigo is heard saying, as if in the background, "I want it to be, like, messy."	
0:14	Instrumental	Distorted guitars and bass enter together on a three-pitch repeating pattern that begins on the root of the song's key and descends by half steps. Drums play a simple rock beat with accents on the snare drum on beats two and four.	
0:21	Verse 1	The vocal enters singing lyrics based on the same repeating pattern descending by half steps, though it is partially sung and partially spoken. The only other sound with the vocal is an acoustic guitar, playing the repeating pattern.	I'm so insecure . . .
0:37	Verse 2	The vocals and guitar continue on new lyrics, joined by a synth bass on the repeating pattern. A bass drum plays accents on each beat, and cymbals play lightly on each beat.	I'm so sick of seventeen . . .
0:53	Chorus	The bass, drums, and guitars return to the timbre and texture of the instrumental section, and the vocal jumps to a higher octave. The lead vocal has a shout-like timbre, expressing a sense of frustration. Accented, playful background vocals sing "ah, ah, ah." The slight distortion on the vocal is more noticeable here.	All I did was try my best . . .
1:06	Chorus tag	The slightly distorted vocal speaks alone, with a serious, but slightly humorous, tone.	God, it's brutal out here.
1:08	Instrumental	This section is similar to the previous instrumental section, but with a few added background vocal sounds, some hand claps, and a high-pitched electric guitar sound at the end.	
1:16	Verse 3	The timbres, textures, and vocals are similar to those in Verse 2, but with different lyrics.	I feel like no one . . .
1:31	Chorus	This chorus is similar to the first chorus.	All I did was try my best . . .
1:45	Chorus tag		God, it's brutal out here.
1:47	Instrumental (twice)	The first instrumental here resembles the previous two instrumental sections. A highly distorted vocal states, sarcastically: "just having a really good time." On the repetition of the section the tempo slows down gradually, and a distorted electric guitar begins to slowly ascend. It lands on the root of the key in a high register, and adds more distortion as it leads into the outro.	
2:03	Outro	All guitars, bass, and drums drop out, and the vocalist sings with the string section, which plays the same material it played in the introduction. An electric piano adds chordal arpeggios. The vocals are clear, with no distortion, in a minor key about a broken heart, and not knowing where to start. Another voice whispers "it's brutal out here" twice in between the sung melodic lines.	Got a broken ego . . .
2:23	End		

What Does It Mean?

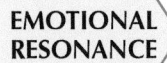

"Brutal" was released in May of 2021 after a year of lockdowns and social distancing restrictions due to the COVID-19 pandemic. It seems to express many of the anxieties about young people's return to in-person social interactions after many months of isolation, though it could signify, for listeners, any number of other anxieties that they perceive as "brutal." The lyrics, timbres, and rhythms of Rodrigo's vocals capture a common experience of her listeners and provide them with a vehicle to express, in a fun way, their emotions in solidarity with others. Her performance in the song provides reassurance for her listeners that they are not alone in their anxieties. And it may help reduce the intensity of any negative emotions they might be experiencing.

Some of the negative emotions experienced by teenagers in every time period include feelings of insecurity and anxiety related to how others perceive them, and Olivia Rodrigo expresses these feelings in the lyrics to "Brutal" from a first-person perspective, suggesting that living as a teenager today is a "brutal" rather than carefree experience. Phrases like "I'm so sick of seventeen," "I wish people liked me more," "I only have two real friends," and "I can't even parallel park" convey frustration, loneliness, desire, and several conflicting emotions. With her voice recorded closely into a microphone without any reverb effects that might provide the illusion of her singing in a large open space, the recording mimics the intimacy of a personal one-on-one conversation with a friend or, perhaps, listening to a friend ranting about why they are unhappy. Many people today listen to music on earbuds or headphones, and so Rodrigo's spoken/sung voice sounds like it is in the listener's head, alongside their own internal voice that may be expressing some of the same sentiments. Whether or not those sentiments are from Rodrigo's own experience, they connect with teens and other listeners who can identify with these statements from their current life or from their memories.

After the lyrics of the first two verses establish this connection, Rodrigo brings her voice into a higher register for the chorus, where her singing borders on shouting to anyone who will listen. The lyrics begin by expressing her frustration about trying her best but getting no appreciation in return. But they turn back to inner emotional thoughts that a person might not typically declare in a shout, shifting to the slightly detached "unrelentlessly upset" before stating "I wish I could disappear," an esoteric "ego crush is so severe," and finally, the playfully spoken phrase "God, it's brutal out here." The simple sung/shouted melodic line of the chorus that stays mostly on one pitch is easy for listeners to sing along to, or imagine themselves singing along to. The rhythm of the melody line also lines up precisely with the accented drums, guitar, and bass parts, providing a sense of power behind each word. Shouting in accented rhythms with Olivia Rodrigo about wanting to disappear and how life can feel like a brutal experience can provide a sense that there are others experiencing the same feelings.

The "brutality" Rodrigo is singing and shouting about may be the result of the ubiquity of social media in the social lives of young people today. Its use is known to contribute to increasing senses of loneliness and such mental health issues as depression and anxiety. When the social media personas of peers, friends, and public figures show them to be leading seemingly perfect, beautiful lives, it can stimulate destructive comparisons of the self to these highly mediated personas which, in turn, often results in low feelings of self-worth. Young people today also experience anxiety as they come of age in an era of uncertainties: increasing wealth inequality limits their economic opportunities and threatens their future livelihoods; a changing climate will have growing effects on all elements of their lives; and the COVID-19 pandemic is disrupting everything from education to food supplies and more. But this generation's pop music does not primarily address these anxieties head-on. In many ways, young people today do not see pop music as a way to face these immense global challenges that they have inherited from older generations. Instead, their pop music helps them deal with anxiety in more personal terms and provides them with diversions from the inescapable realities of life today.

TECHNOLOGY

Rodrigo's popularity has been greatly amplified by the way she has connected with her fans through social media and streaming platforms, including the video sharing app TikTok, a top platform for popular music since 2018. TikTok provides a user-friendly platform for anyone to make a video on their smartphone and upload it to the app's network of over a billion active users. It has become one of the most widely used social media platforms by members of Gen Z, the generation of people born between the mid-to-late 1990s and 2010. The app has a built-in library of countless recordings, and one of the typical ways users make videos is by selecting a recording and making an accompanying video featuring dance moves or other action on screen that adds meaning to the recording. Songs can become popular on TikTok if a dance, or other type of visual performance or effect, goes viral and large numbers of users begin imitating the dance or performing their personal take on it. The music industry tracks streams of songs on TikTok and other digital platforms (such as Spotify and YouTube) for its charts, and so a song that is part of a viral TikTok trend can result in massive popularity for its artist. As a result, many songs feature elements of their form that might lend themselves to short or catchy video trends. In "Brutal," one such section is the second half of the chorus, beginning with "they say these are the golden years" and ending with "God, it's brutal out here." With a duration of eight seconds, a dramatic texture shift on the word "God," and lyrics that express general emotions and mental states, this excerpt of the song has inspired users (sometimes with added text on the screen) to add their own interpretations of concepts like the golden years, of wanting to disappear, and of the experience of it being "brutal out here."

The music video of "Brutal" adds additional layers of meaning to the song. In the video, Rodrigo takes on a number of personas, many of which reference American pop culture of the late 1990s to early 2000s "Y2K" era, a time period whose fashion and other pop culture trends have been particularly resonant expressive resources for Gen Z. The video references several iconic looks from pop culture of the turn of the millennium. One of these references appears during the second verse, where she is shown in a school classroom wearing a plaid skirt, a reference to Britney Spears's iconic schoolgirl look in the music video of her 1998 song "Hit Me Baby One More Time." Some of the shots of Rodrigo walking down a school hallway and riding in a convertible with her two sidekicks reference the character Cher Horowitz from the 1995 movie *Clueless*. The orange bob haircut of one of her personas mimics the appearance of the character Leeloo from 1997 film *The Fifth Element*. These and the other elements of Y2K-era popular culture in the music video for "Brutal" demonstrate how Gen Z pop artists, and audiences, draw on this time period in meaningful ways.

> **CULTURAL LINKAGES**

While the music video to "Brutal" focuses on references to the late 1990s and early 2000s, it does so in a way that embeds them in contemporary uses of social media technologies. One of Rodrigo's personas is an Instagram influencer, who is shown singing the complete first chorus. She sings-shouts her inner thoughts on the screen of a smartphone, viewed by thousands of followers, some of whose comments can be seen scrolling on the left side of the screen. This persona's exaggerated, visually comical complaints about wanting to disappear, on a screen in front of her admiring followers, provides an ironic sense of levity. But it also addresses the serious challenges to mental health that having a presence on social media can have for anyone who uses it. In another reference to social media and smartphone technology, the video features a variety of face filters, which add virtual objects to an individual's face while on camera through digital augmented reality technology. Designed and drawn by Rodrigo, these face filters ground the video in the social media technology of today. This may signify that while young people of Gen Z today are drawn to fashion and music styles of an era before social media, they do so without casting aside the social media technologies that have enabled them to connect with these styles. The music video's visual elements enhance the way that "Brutal" brings out the conflict between the benefits of social media technology and its potential to facilitate harm and negative effects on users' well-being.

The distorted guitars, power chords, simple harmonies, and vocal styles of "Brutal" also reference popular music of late 1990s and the early 2000s, especially pop punk bands and artists such as Avril Lavigne and Blink 182, along with emo pop artists such as Paramore, Fallout Boy, and Panic! At the Disco. These genres often deal with adolescent frustration and express emotions in a confessional manner similar to "Brutal." Emo pop and pop punk also include such fashion elements as shredded T-shirts and plaid patterns, which appear in the video for "Brutal" and other performances by Rodrigo. The distorted guitar timbre and power chords of "Brutal" harken back to punk rock, the precursor of pop punk and emo. Punk emerged in the 1970s and 1980s as an anti-establishment musical and political movement challenging mainstream values from market capitalism to complexity and sophistication as a value in musical performance. In the 1990s the feminist punk movement called Riot Grrrl from the Pacific Northwest used similar musical elements in their political action and activism, with examples including "Rebel Girl" by Bikini Kill and "Gimme Brains" by Bratmobile.

Rodrigo's references in "Brutal" and "Good 4 U" to punk and pop punk musical style redirects those styles' associations with political activism, feminist ideals, and anti-establishment values to issues facing teens today. Her hits "Drivers License" and "Deja Vu" (each with their own viral trends on TikTok) are pop ballads about breakups with musical elements far from those of punk and related genres. She and her generation are comfortable drawing from a plethora of styles of the past to address the issues they face in their lives, from the trials of relationships shared by all generations to the new challenges of social media and the anxieties of being a teenager in the midst of political, economic, and environmental challenges that seem too big to face.

What Is Its History?

TECHNOLOGY

Since the advent of sound recordings in the late nineteenth century, music has been shaped in big and small ways by developments in recording and other audio technologies. As Olivia Rodrigo's music demonstrates, the popular music of the last few years has been significantly shaped by new technologies in streaming and social media. For most of the twentieth century, listening to a recording of music required listening to broadcast media (radio, TV) or purchasing a record, cassette tape, or CD. The music industry generated profits through the sales of recordings in these formats, and successful artists sold millions of their recordings to fans who wanted to listen to their music. By the mid-1990s, computers could store and play digital audio files in formats such as the MP3. The internet made it possible to quickly and easily transfer MP3 files from computer to computer. In 1999 a company called Napster began an internet file-sharing network for its millions of users to upload and download MP3 audio files for free. Record sales plummeted and, after a series of lawsuits by artists and record companies, Napster shut down in 2001. The music industry then developed a model of downloads for purchase. Online stores such as the Apple iTunes Store (launched in 2003) charged customers to download audio files to their computers, iPods, and later, smartphones. Despite these efforts, many consumers began to view recordings as something they accessed for free online, rather than something they paid to own.

By the mid-2000s internet technology allowed users to "stream" a high-quality recording or video without interruption and without downloading and saving it. YouTube, launched in 2005, quickly became one of the most influential sites for music consumption, and streaming services such as Pandora, Spotify, Apple Music, Amazon Music, and Tidal followed in its wake. Large record companies and other elements of the music industry gradually accepted that immediate access to recordings online through streaming was a convenience that the public had come to expect. They made agreements with streaming services to share profits, and began using algorithms and data collected from listeners to target their marketing of artists and to decide what kinds of artists and musical styles to promote. In 2013, Billboard began including data on YouTube streams to its "Hot 100" chart, which ranks the most popular songs in the United States, and started a chart called "Streaming Songs," which ranks the songs with the most streams across all platforms in the country.

Artists, record labels, and other players in the popular music industry have built on the interrelated capabilities of social media, streaming, and other digital technologies to position songs and their artists to "go viral" and move up the Billboard charts. Lil Nas X (Montero Lamar Hill, b. 1999), a rapper, singer, and songwriter, is one example of a pop artist who has built his popularity through skillful engagement with multiple digital platforms. Like others born since the late 1990s, he is a digital native, having grown up with social media and smartphones from a young age. Before he became a well-known musician, he ran a Twitter meme account with 30,000 followers and managed social media fan pages dedicated to the rapper Nicki Minaj. His first recording, "Old Town Road," seems almost designed for success in the age of music streaming. The song has a duration of less than two minutes, and, after a short intro, begins with a catchy chorus about thirteen seconds into the recording. This departure from typical pop song form (which almost always starts with one or two verses before a chorus) and duration (radio hits are usually about three minutes long) is related to shifts in the music industry's approach to streaming. On Spotify, if a recording is played longer than thirty seconds, it counts as one stream. With its early chorus that stretches almost to the thirty-second mark, streams of "Old Town Road" are guaranteed if listeners play only the chorus and the first line of the verse "horses in the back," which coincides with the introduction of a hip-hop bass line and drum beat. The track's shorter duration also means that it can rack up more streams, since shorter songs are streamed more. Lil Nas X released "Old Town Road" in December 2018 on his own, promoting it through memes on Twitter and other digital means, including using a fake account on the social news and entertainment site Reddit to ask the question, "What's the name of the song that goes 'take my horse to the old town road?'" The song's combination of timbres, lyrical themes, other musical elements of hip-hop and country, and a sample of a song by rock band Nine Inch Nails inspired many memes on TikTok, notably one where a person suddenly becomes transformed into a cowboy or cowgirl at the moment the chorus ends and the hip-hop beat drops to begin the verse. As a result, "Old Town Road" was the first song to become a #1 hit on the charts due to viral popularity on TikTok.

In the midst of the song's escalating success, *Billboard* removed it from its country charts, which stimulated debates about what makes a song "country" or not. The combination of plucked banjo sounds, rural-themed lyrics, country-style pronunciation, and hip-hop bass and drum sounds, fronted by a singing-rapping African American artist with no history of "paying dues" in the country music industry raised questions about the historical, and current, role of race in the genre labels promoted by the music industry, and about whether these genre labels are still relevant. Lil Nas X responded to the song's removal from the country charts by creating a remix of the song, with its own music video, featuring country star Billy Ray Cyrus (b. 1961), who had had a "viral" hit of his own in the 1990s with the song "Achy Breaky Heart." These events generated ongoing online dialogue about the song and about Lil Nas X, who continued to promote the song through social media memes and other posts. The song was #1 on the Hot 100 chart for a record-breaking nineteen weeks. Lil Nas X's internet savvy and blurring of genre boundaries had paid off with millions of listeners around the world embracing the song. At the height of the song's popularity, he came out as gay, placing himself outside of the straight sexuality typical of hip-hop and country music, the genres he so skillfully blends in the song. But he added to a long legacy of queer artists achieving success in pop music, including Elton John, Lady Gaga, Janelle Monáe, and Frank Ocean. In 2021, he began to incorporate his sexuality into his music more directly, and the music videos of his songs "Industry Baby" and "Montero (Call Me By Your Name)," included references to gay sex. This generated more online debate, more memes, more streams, and more fans.

Two women pop artists have also used social media to cast aside previous conventions in mainstream pop music: Billie Eilish (b. 2001) and Lizzo (Melissa Viviane Jefferson, b. 1988).

> CULTURAL
> LINKAGES

FIGURE 14.2
Lil Nas X performs "Old Town Road" with Billy Ray Cyrus at the 2020 Grammy Awards
Source: Getty Images/CBS Photo Archive/Contributor

FIGURE 14.3
Billie Eilish in 2019
Source: Lars Crommelinck Photography, Wikimedia Commons.

FIGURE 14.4
Lizzo performing in 2019
Source: Ralph_PH, Wikimedia Commons.

Eilish won seven Grammy awards by the age of eighteen, including Album of the Year for her album *When We All Fall Asleep, Where Do We Go?* (2019). When she was thirteen, she recorded "Ocean Eyes," a song written and produced by her brother Finneas. They uploaded the song to the online music sharing platform SoundCloud, where it quickly amassed hundreds of thousands of streams. Since then, Eilish has worked with record labels, publicists, and other music industry entities to shape her image and her music. Typically appearing in baggy clothing that conceals the shape of her own body, Eilish has embraced a style that rejects social media's unrealistic and digitally manipulated standards of beauty. This move has resonated with her teenage (and older) fans. While Instagram, TikTok, and other visually oriented social media platforms have promoted impossible standards of beauty, they have also given artists like Billie Eilish more power to represent themselves in photographs and videos on their (and their teams') terms.

Rapper, singer, songwriter, and flutist Lizzo has also promoted a message of body positivity in her music and in her public image. Her song "Good as Hell" (2016) embodies this message, with rapped and sung lyrics that encourage women to walk out on relationships that aren't working for them; a music video that features Lizzo and other women of color at a hair salon having fun getting their hair and nails done; and a call-and-response chorus that invites Lizzo's audiences to sing that they feel "good as hell" about their appearance and all aspects of themselves. Though Lizzo had been actively writing, performing, and releasing music since 2011, she achieved mainstream popularity in 2019 after her song "Truth Hurts" (2017) went viral on TikTok. Like in the case of "Old Town Road," a TikTok meme based on the opening of "Truth Hurts" became wildly popular and led to the song reaching #1 on the charts two years after it was initially released. Lizzo's renown spread internationally, and her messages of body positivity, inclusion, and confidence resonated broadly. As Nakkiah Lui, an actor, writer, and young leader in the Australian Aboriginal community, put it in her review of Lizzo's January 2020 performance at the Sydney Opera House:

> Lizzo doesn't just speak to me; her body looks like mine and that's something I've never seen in the public sphere before her. It's fat. It's a big belly and thighs that touch but most of all, it's beautiful and celebrated. . . . She's creating space for people to reclaim their worth in societies that have historically told them that they're worthless.

Olivia Rodrigo's rise to fame followed a trajectory typical in the entertainment industry during the era before TikTok and other social media platforms. At the age of thirteen, she performed the role of Paige Olvera, a guitarist, in *Bizaardvark*, a television series on the Disney Channel. At sixteen, she began playing the leading role in the Disney+ series *High School Musical: The Musical: The Series*, and wrote two songs for the soundtrack. As a result, when she began releasing music as a solo artist inspired by styles of those she admired, like Taylor Swift and Lorde, she already had a large base of young fans who followed her social media accounts. This built-in audience made it much less risky for record companies and other music industry entities to support her career, and she was signed to Interscope Records and Geffen Records, without having ever released a song of her own as a solo artist. The risk paid off, as her first ever single, "Drivers License," debuted at #1 on the *Billboard* Hot 100 chart, breaking several streaming records along the way.

Launching a solo artist's career in pop music by building on existing popularity is a long-running model in the popular music industry. Global pop stars Britney Spears (b. 1981), Christina Aguilera (b. 1980), and Justin Timberlake (b. 1981) were all, as children, cast members on the television series *The All-New Mickey Mouse Club*, which ran from 1989 to 1994. Before he was a successful solo artist, Timberlake also gained popularity as a member of the boy band NSYNC. Pop singers Demi Lovato (b. 1992), Selena Gomez (b. 1992), and Miley Cyrus (b. 1992) all starred in Disney Channel television series before they launched their careers as solo artists. Cyrus's Disney series *Hannah Montana* also starred her father, Billy Ray Cyrus (one of the co-producers of the show). One of today's biggest stars, Beyoncé (b. 1981), got her start as a child in the group Destiny's Child, which worked under various names and lineups from 1990 until 2006. Her solo career, which began with her 2003 album *Dangerously In Love*, has made her one of the most successful popular musical artists of all time, with more Grammy awards (twenty-eight) than any other individual other than orchestra conductor Georg Solti (thirty-one). In much of her work, such as her visual album *Lemonade* (2016), she pays tribute to Black culture and includes a plethora of African American and other Black musical styles. Her 2018 performance at the Coachella Music Festival (as the first African American woman to headline the festival), showcased the culture and traditions of historically Black colleges and universities (HBCUs), and featured a full marching band, majorette dancers, and step dancing in the style of Black fraternities and sororities.

Rodrigo's "Brutal" is a gateway into a music industry landscape that has changed dramatically since the mid-1990s. Music industry executives and record companies once controlled who fans of music got to hear through coveted but often exploitative contracts with performing artists. They continue to develop artists from the ranks of actors on children's television shows and through other popularity-generating mechanisms such as reality television singing competitions. And they work with social media companies and streaming internet services to promote certain artists over others. But these technologies have given artists today increased opportunities to reach potential fans and create music that manipulates the genre boundaries created by the music industry to sell records. Rodrigo and the other artists mentioned in this gateway have all benefited from this new media landscape.

> TECHNOLOGY

FIGURE 14.5
Beyoncé performing in 2011
Source: Asterio Tecson, Adabow, Wikimedia Commons.

WHERE DO I GO FROM HERE?

- Watch Olivia Rodrigo's music videos to "Drivers License" and "Good 4 U." Make a list of all the music styles or genres you can identify in these two recordings. Compare the songs to the music of Taylor Swift, one of Rodrigo's significant influences.

- Listen to various versions of "Old Town Road" by Lil Nas X, and find some TikTok trends based on the song. What musical elements do you think played into the song's success in the landscape of streaming and social media?

- Listen to several of Lizzo's songs about body positivity and confidence and find some positive and negative reactions to those songs online. How do the musical elements of the songs relate to reactions to them? How are the songs and their reactions related to mental health and well-being?

- Find some videos from Beyoncé's *Lemonade* or *Homecoming*, the documentary of her Coachella performance. Based on your own knowledge and experience, or on information you can find online, what are some of the African, African American, or other Black cultural references that she is celebrating?

FIGURE 14.6
esperanza spalding performing in Nice, France, in 2013
Source: Getty Images/Didier Baverel.

GATEWAY 57
JAZZ TODAY

What Is It?

Jazz today is performed and listened to by people all over the world, young and old, and from every background imaginable, as it has been for most of its history. Jazz musicians, for their part, take pride in the fact that jazz is a musical genre flexible enough to welcome influences from a wide variety of musical styles. Understanding the way they combine the musical elements of jazz with those from other styles is key to understanding what their music means to them and to their audiences.

Bassist, singer, composer, and producer esperanza spalding (who does not capitalize her name) combines the sounds of jazz with those of other genres in fascinating ways, often reminiscent of the jazz fusion of the 1970s. Our gateway to jazz today is "Black Gold," a song from spalding's 2012 album *Radio Music Society*. She is the composer, arranger, producer, bass player, and lead vocalist on the track. The song features the contemporary R&B singer Algebra Blessett (b. 1976), Benin-born guitarist and vocalist Lionel Loueke (b. 1973), the Savannah Children's Choir, Terri Lyne Carrington (b. 1965) on drums, and Raymond Angry on organ.

🔊 **Listen to the first thirty seconds of the recording to get an idea of its sound.**

How Does It Work?

Timbre

The timbres feature the clear vocals of esperanza spalding and Algebra Blessett along with electric bass, drum set, Hammond B-3 organ, guitar (sometimes in unison with vocables such as by the guitarist), and three horns (tenor saxophone and two trumpets). The organist plays in a way that manipulates the organ's timbre.

Texture

The texture features melodic lines in the vocals and guitar solos, a bass line, and a drum part, and accompanying parts in the organ, guitar, and horns. In "Black Gold" all of these parts interweave with one another in a sometimes dense and complex texture.

Rhythm

The rhythm in this recording is also quite complex with intricate interlocking polyrhythms over a four-beat meter in a steady tempo.

Melody

The vocal and instrumental melodies are mostly in a major key. They also include blue notes and some chromatic movement.

Harmony

Each section of the song is based on a different two-measure repeating harmonic cycle. Sometimes the chords last for four beats each, and sometimes they last for two beats each. The harmony is highly chromatic and full of chords with altered extensions.

Form

The form is organized into two sections: a chorus and a verse that itself has two parts, A and B. After a short nonmetrical introduction on the organ, the form proceeds like this: Chorus—ABAB—Chorus—Guitar Solo (over the Chorus)—B—Chorus—Chorus.

Performance Techniques

The organ's timbre and expressive qualities are notable performance techniques in this performance. In addition to the shifting timbres of the organ made possible by the drawbars of the Hammond B-3 organ (Chapter 12, Gateway 46), the sound at times also seems to shake or waver. This effect is produced on the Hammond B-3 organ by a complex spinning mechanism in a large box called a Leslie speaker that can be attached to the organ. This sound imitates two other sounds in music: vibrato, a pulsating slight raising and lowering of the pitch of a tone often heard in operatic singing, and **tremolo**, an electronic effect used on instruments like the electric guitar to quickly and repeatedly raise and lower the volume of the tone. The Leslie speaker combines vibrato and tremolo into a dramatic effect, which is part of the distinctive sound of the Hammond B-3 organ heard in gospel and many genres of popular music and jazz.

Listen to the first minute of this recording, identify the sound of each instrument, and notice the complex texture.

Listen to the entire recording following this timed listening guide.

LISTENING GUIDE 14.2

TIME	SECTION	DESCRIPTION	LYRICS
0:00	Introduction	A high shimmering sound begins the track. It seems to descend briefly, revealing that it is the sound of a Hammond B-3 organ.	
0:08	Chorus	Algebra Blessett sings the first phrase of the chorus, a bluesy descending line, accompanied by only the high frequencies of the organ carrying over from the introduction. esperanza spalding sings the second phrase with a similar melody and new lyrics, joined by gentle, pulsatile strikes of the cymbals of the drum set, a counter-melody in the guitar and vocals of Lionel Loueke, and the organ, now playing with a smoother timbre.	Hold your head . . .
0:19		For the second half of the chorus, Blessett and spalding sing together, and spalding adds a rhythmic bass line that interlocks with a new syncopated funk-based drum pattern and short accents played by the horn section.	You are . . .
0:32	A	The drums begin playing more sparsely, and spalding sings the first phrase of A, which is followed by a series of chords with altered extensions played rhythmically by the horns and accented by the drums and bass. Blessett sings the second phrase, followed again by the horns, drums, and bass, along with short improvisations in both the saxophone and spalding's vocals.	Now maybe . . .
0:56	B	The drums, bass, horns, organ, and guitar all begin playing short, syncopated rhythms to create another funk groove, with the bass and horns playing the same syncopated rhythm at certain points. Blessett begins the vocal lines and alternates phrases with spalding. The section ends with a break in the funk groove, over which Raymond Angry plays an improvised bluesy phrase on the organ.	With all the strength . . .
1:12	A	A repeats with new lyrics. It is similar to the first statement of A, but this time the vocal lines, saxophone, guitar, and organ perform in a more improvisatory manner.	They'll be folks . . .

TIME	SECTION	DESCRIPTION	LYRICS
1:36	B	B repeats with the same lyrics and texture, though spalding and Blessett begin to improvise on the melody and lyrics of the first B section. The end of this B section features a break but with no solo line as in the first B.	Think of all the strength . . .
2:02	Chorus	The funk groove continues in the drums, bass, and horns. The organ plays sustained chords and the guitar plays improvised countermelodies that contribute to the polyrhythmic funk groove.	Hold your head . . .
2:25	Guitar solo (Chorus)	Lionel Loueke plays an improvised solo, scat singing in unison with his guitar line. His improvisation outlines the harmonies and their upper extensions in the legacy of bebop musicians and other jazz musicians who have developed this kind of improvisation. The bass, organ, and drums continue the funk groove, with the addition of a on the ride cymbal, which has a long, sustained decay.	
2:48	B	With a smear of the organ and two syncopated hits in the bass, B repeats with its staccato funk groove and more improvisation by the vocalists. The Savannah Children's Choir joins in with gospel style interjections during the second half of this section.	Think of all the strength . . .
3:14	Chorus (extended)	Blessett begins the chorus vocals and spalding adds improvisatory lines on similar lyrics. After a few repetitions of the line "you are black gold," the children's choir joins in and the key modulates up a half step. Though the groove doesn't change much, the higher key and thicker texture increases the intensity and energy as the line "you are black gold" repeats eight times.	Hold your head . . .
4:11	Chorus (with tag)	The drums, bass, and horns drop out and the voices sing a version of the chorus accompanied by the organ. Blessett and spalding improvise over the lyrics with the melismas common in gospel and contemporary R&B styles. They are joined by Loueke as he sings and plays on the guitar his own overlapping improvised lines.	Hold your head . . .
5:14	End		

What Does It Mean?

CULTURAL LINKAGES

In 2012, when esperanza spalding released "Black Gold" as the first single from *Radio Music Society*, her press statement emphasized a central aspect of the song's meaning. She wrote:

> This song is singing to our African American heritage before slavery. Over the decades, so much of the strength in the African American community has seeded from resistance and endurance. I wanted to address the part of our heritage spanning back to pre-colonial Africa and the elements of Black pride that draw from our connection to our ancestors in their own land. I particularly wanted to create something that spoke to young boys.

In addition to the expressions of its lyrics, the meaning of "Black Gold" is carried in its combination of musical elements and in the broader context of *Radio Music Society* and spalding's other work.

AESTHETICS

As a contemporary example of jazz fusion, "Black Gold" includes some musical elements typical of jazz and others from a number of popular styles. Improvisation in the vocals, guitar, and saxophone all point to the long-standing prominence of improvisation in jazz. Lionel Loueke's guitar and vocal solo at 2:25 outlines the underlying harmony with angular phrases, chromaticism, and a reliance on altered extensions, characteristics that are all rooted in bebop. His clean guitar timbre, without distortion, feedback, or other timbral effects typical in rock and other genres, is common in jazz guitar. Many of his short improvised phrases at the end of the recording also connect to the blues as they emphasize bent pitches and blue notes. His scat singing in unison with his guitar playing suggest that the instrument is intimately connected to the human voice, in a way similar to the ways that musicians playing the blues (and other styles rooted in the blues like rock) have emulated vocal gestures on their instruments.

Listen again to Lionel Loueke's guitar solo at 2:25 for the way his improvisation references earlier styles of jazz and blues improvisation.

The musical elements of "Black Gold" also connect it to other popular genres such as gospel, funk, and soul. These elements position this recording as music that can be enjoyed and appreciated by a broad range of audiences in many different ways and for many different reasons. For example, the organ in "Black Gold," as in much gospel music, is an electric Hammond B-3 organ. At the beginning of the recording, the organist Raymond Angry sustains a single chord without changing any of the pitches while, using sliding drawbars on the instrument, he gradually changes the timbre from a shrill, bright sound featuring high frequencies to a duller sound for a brief moment before returning to the bright sound. Throughout the track, he manipulates the timbre and the vibrato-tremolo effect of the Leslie speaker as an expressive tool and to contribute to the texture in a variety of ways. Around 4:10, as the drums drop out and in preparation for the final chorus, he changes the timbre of the organ from a bright sound to a cooler or perhaps more mellow timbre. This allows the organ to take a supporting, background role behind the vocal and instrumental improvisations, in a way reminiscent of the kinds of extended, melismatic improvisations gospel soloists might perform with an organist at a church service or gospel concert. The Savannah Children's Choir adds a clear reference to gospel throughout the second half of the recording. All of these elements of gospel music connect "Black Gold" to gospel as a musical genre and are iconic of the music of a supportive church community. With its positive message geared towards children and teens, and the sounds of many people singing and playing music together in the gospel style, "Black Gold" delivers a powerful message of a community coming together to encourage young people to tap into their inner strength, build a sense of self-worth, and take pride in their heritage.

"Black Gold" also references other African American styles. The polyrhythmic danceable drum grooves of Terri Lyne Carrington, spalding's syncopated bass playing, the tight, percussive hits of the horn section, and the call-and-response improvisatory vocals are reminiscent of the funk and soul style of James Brown in recordings such as his classic song "I Got You (I Feel Good)" (1964). The melodic and active bass lines spalding plays often avoid the first beat of the measure and may have roots in the flowing bass lines of Jamaican reggae, which have inspired the bass parts of so many popular songs since the 1960s (Chapter 13, Gateway 55). This confluence of popular genres from Black musical traditions in "Black Gold" reinforces spalding's positioning of the song as a celebration of African heritage.

Listen one more time to "Black Gold" for the organ, choir, and other gospel influences and for elements that connect this recording to funk, soul, and reggae.

Other tracks on *Radio Music Society* demonstrate spalding's compelling combination of jazz and popular music genres. One of two covers on the album is "I Can't Help It," originally from *Off the Wall* (1979) by Michael Jackson (1958–2009) and composed by Stevie Wonder (b. 1950), two of the most critically and commercially acclaimed popular musicians of the late twentieth century. To set up a bebop-rooted improvisation by tenor saxophonist Joe Lovano (b. 1952), she begins the song with a Latin groove on the bass referencing Brazilian samba, bringing yet another style from the Black Atlantic into her fusion of jazz with other genres (Chapter 6, Gateway 23). Three other tracks on the album feature a full big band of high school students from the Portland, Oregon-based American Music Program, connecting her and her music to a younger generation of musicians and to the nearly 100-year-old legacy of the big band ensemble in jazz. The title of the album, *Radio Music Society*, hints at spalding's interest in jazz as a popular music, as she seems to be asserting that this broad combination of styles is music for the radio, that is, music that is meant for popular audiences.

FIGURE 14.7
esperanza spalding performing with Joe Lovano (saxophone), Jack DeJohnette (drums), and Leo Genovese (piano) in 2014 at the Barbican Centre in London
Source: Getty Images/Andy Sheppard.

In the pattern of a pop music single, spalding released a music video of "Black Gold" that illustrates the meaning of the lyrics and provides a visual image of spalding and Blessett trading vocal lines in an improvisatory manner. When the album was released in April 2012, it attracted many more listeners than a typical jazz album and debuted at #10 on the *Billboard* 200, a chart that tracks the popularity of albums of all genres in a given week.

SOCIAL BEHAVIOR

When reflecting on the history of jazz, it is a striking problem that most of the prominent jazz musicians have been men, especially jazz instrumentalists. The various styles of jazz have developed in twentieth-century societies where women have tended to be marginalized, excluded, or stereotyped as inferior. Compounding this problem are histories of jazz that have pushed women out of some of the central roles they have played in the story of jazz. Such histories imply that jazz is best performed by men. They offer few (if any) examples for aspiring women musicians that they can belong in jazz settings, other than in the typically female-gendered role of a vocalist. Since the 1990s, however, some of these gender expectations have begun to change in jazz, if ever so slightly. Jazz historians like Sherrie Tucker have undertaken and stimulated research on women jazz musicians throughout the history of jazz, bringing women's contributions into the historical narrative from which they had been excluded. Because of this kind of research, it is more common in histories of jazz today to encounter the work of musicians such as Bessie Smith, Lil Hardin Armstrong, Mary Lou Williams (the pianist and composer who served as a mentor of many of the first bebop musicians), and Melba Liston, the renowned arranger, composer, and trombonist who worked alongside Dizzy Gillespie and others.

In step with the struggle for equal opportunity, pay, and representation for all genders across many fields in American and other societies, an increasing number of women jazz musicians—both vocalists and instrumentalists—have become prominent in a number of streams of jazz. Diana Krall (b. 1964) and Norah Jones (b. 1979) became well known as jazz vocalists and pianists (in the 1990s and 2000s, respectively), and they have crossed over to popular music styles in a number of ways. More recently, the Chilean tenor saxophonist Melissa Aldana (b. 1988) won the Thelonious Monk Institute of Jazz International Saxophone Competition in 2013 and has become a well-known player in the New York and international scenes. Terri Lyne Carrington, the drummer on "Black Gold," has enjoyed an illustrious career spanning several decades. In 2018 she founded the Berklee College of Music Institute of Jazz and Gender Justice, an initiative in education, mentoring, and advocacy that focuses on equity in the field of jazz and the role that jazz plays in the larger struggle for gender justice and racial justice. Though adequate gender representation and inclusion in jazz is still a long way away, as these and other women and nonbinary musicians are recognized for their mastery, creativity, and excellence in jazz, they offer to audiences and to aspiring musicians a new vision for what jazz can look and sound like without patriarchy.

Sexual harassment where jazz is taught and performed has also contributed to the exclusion of women from jazz. In 2018 "We Have Voice," a collective of musicians involved in jazz, issued a comprehensive Code of Conduct for educational and performance institutions and for people working in the performing arts. It takes an unequivocal stance against gender discrimination and expresses zero tolerance for sexual harassment. In their campaign for "safe(r)" workplaces, the We Have Voice Collective challenges individuals and organizations to transform educational and work environments for all performers. This collective and its aligned musicians and institutions seek to cultivate spaces for collaborative music making that are safe for people of all genders. They believe that everyone should be able to participate in forms of music making they love without threats to their physical safety or discrimination based on gender.

What Is Its History?

As a genre rooted in the Black community of the United States, jazz has always responded to and dealt with racial injustice. Jazz today is no different. Despite the vision of a "post-racial" age in America in the wake of Barack Obama's election as the first Black president of the United States, police brutality against Black people and efforts to suppress the African American vote make the headlines and circulate in social media every day. While civil rights organizations and activist movements have never stopped advocating for equal rights and against racial violence, in this period new movements have added to this ongoing work. The most prominent has been Black Lives Matter, which emerged in 2013 in response to a seeming epidemic of police shootings of Black men. Musicians have also lent their voices to those of their predecessors in the struggle against these acts of racial violence and other forms of institutional racism in America. For example, the genre-crossing jazz pianist and vocalist Jon Batiste (b.1986) led a number of musical protest marches and concerts in New York City as part of the 2020 Black Lives Matter protests. Dozens of musicians gathered for the marches, leading large crowds in improvisational performances of jazz tunes like Duke Ellington's "Caravan," soul anthems like Aretha Franklin's "Respect," and the hymn "Lift Every Voice and Sing," which was written in 1900 by James Wheldon Johnson and his brother J. Rosamond Johnson and is often referred to as the Black national anthem of the United States.

> POLITICS

esperanza spalding, who released *Radio Music Society* a year before Black Lives Matter began, adds her voice to the long history of jazz musicians' engagement with racial oppression, stretching back as least as far as Bessie Smith, Ma Rainey, and other women blues singers who challenged the injustices of their world. Some of spalding's music on the album takes an activist stance. "Land of the Free" deals with the case of Cornelius Dupree, a Black man exonerated in 2011 after being imprisoned for thirty years for an aggravated robbery he did not commit. "Black Gold," as spalding asserts in her press release for the song, speaks to injustice from a different angle. She encourages a positive self-image among young Black men from a perspective akin to the Black Lives Matter movement and echoing James Brown's "Say It Loud—I'm Black and I'm Proud." With music grounded in jazz and connected to many styles of Black popular music, she joins a long tradition of jazz instrumentalists and singers who have promoted racial equality and celebrated Black culture.

FIGURE 14.8

esperanza spalding performing the material from *Emily's D+Evolution* in Brooklyn, NY

Source: Getty Images/Al Pereira.

Her biography sheds some light on how she, like many musicians of her generation, came to understand and adopt so many different overlapping stylistic approaches in her music. Born in Portland, Oregon, in 1984, she began playing musical instruments at a young age. She performed classical music on the violin in a community chamber orchestra starting when she was five years old. As a teenager, she began playing the bass and soon became active on the local club scene playing blues, funk, and hip-hop, styles that still pervade her music today. After finishing her high school studies at 16, she studied bass at Portland State University before attending the Berklee College of Music in Boston. Beyond the college education it provided, the Berklee environment

> CULTURAL
> LINKAGES

connected spalding to a community of established musicians, who began to hire her as a collaborator for live performances, tours, and recordings.

On her website, spalding's work is described as "grounded in jazz traditions but never bound by them." Her studio albums as a solo artist exemplify this description. In 2006 she released *Junjo*, her first solo album, which draws on jazz and a number of Brazilian and other Latin musical styles. She scat sings on many of the tracks and sings lyrics on others. The album also features her playing the upright bass along with a pianist and a drummer. Her second album, *Esperanza*, released in 2008, features her playing bass, scatting, and singing in English, Spanish, and Portuguese in many styles. The song "I Know You Know" is in a style of jazz-inflected soul; "Love in Time" is a jazz waltz with a swing feel; and "Cuerpo Y Alma" is a Spanish-language version of the jazz standard "Body and Soul." Contributions to the album by vocalist Gretchen Parlato and trumpet player Ambrose Akinmusire, both winners of the Thelonious Monk Institute of Jazz International Competition, align spalding with some of the other prominent jazz musicians of her generation. Her classical music roots surface on her 2010 album *Chamber Music Society*, where a small string section complements the jazz-based grooves. After *Radio Music Society* (2012), spalding released *Emily's D+Evolution* in 2016, which leans towards the overlap of jazz and rock.

Like many jazz musicians today, spalding has been involved in education initiatives. In addition to teaching at Berklee College of Music and, since 2017, at Harvard University, she served as the 2010 Artist in Residence for the Savannah Children's Choir, which appears on "Black Gold." As part of this program, she taught master classes for young chorus and orchestra students and worked with over 1000 school children. Her decision to record with the high school big band from the American Music Program for *Radio Music Society* connects her to her Portland roots as she supports the education of young musicians on what turned out to be an award-winning album.

spalding won the Grammy for Best New Artist in 2011, beating out Justin Bieber, Drake, Florence and the Machine, and Mumford and Sons. She has appeared in performances and on recordings with Prince, Bruno Mars, Alicia Keys, Janelle Monáe, and Herbie Hancock. She has performed at the White House and at the Academy Awards. In 2017 she live-streamed the production of an entire album for seventy-seven hours on social media, a project called *Exposure*. People all over the world could open her Facebook fan page and watch her and a studio full of musicians composing, arranging, and recording a full album project, issued as a limited release of 7777 copies. For her 2021 album *Songwrights Apothecary Lab*, she worked with other musicians, neuroscientists, and music therapists to create the album's twelve tracks, each designed to deal with specific emotions and stresses as a form of therapeutic healing. She and Wayne Shorter co-composed an opera *Iphigenia*, which also debuted in 2021. It features spalding, Shorter's jazz quartet, a full orchestra, operatic soloists, and chorus, and crosses all manner of stylistic and genre boundaries.

By working with many styles and musicians from within and beyond the boundaries of jazz and engaging with social media and other technology, spalding connects with audiences of all ages with diverse musical tastes. Her music reflects the unprecedented interconnectedness of the world today. She performs musical and social boundary crossing as she celebrates Black culture and engages with a plethora of themes and issues. Along with other jazz musicians today, she extends the long tradition of experimenting with new genre combinations in jazz to make music that connects with longtime fans of jazz as well as new audiences.

WHERE DO I GO FROM HERE?

- Watch the music video for "Black Gold." How does it enhance (or detract from) the meaning of the song for you? What are some of the narrative and visual elements that complement or enrich the song's meaning?
- Listen to "I Can't Help It" from *Radio Music Society* and compare it to the original version by Michael Jackson and written by Stevie Wonder. What has spalding added or taken away from the original version? How does her version deploy musical elements of jazz?
- Listen to a few tracks from her *Chamber Music Society*. What musical elements typical of classical music is spalding drawing on for this album? How do they fit together with the other musical styles on the album? Are there other fusions of classical music and jazz that you can find from any time in the 100 years since jazz began to emerge as a musical genre?
- Listen to some tracks from the album *Waiting Game* by Terri Lyne Carrington and Social Science or the album *Visions* by Melissa Aldana. What styles are they drawing on from jazz and other genres?

GATEWAY 58
CLASSICAL MUSIC TODAY

What Is It?

Composers of classical music today often write new and innovative music within genres that have existed for centuries in classical music: operas, string quartets, symphonies, and concertos. At the same time they engage with new technologies and multimedia, with musical styles from jazz and popular music, and with new challenging techniques on instruments that have long been common in classical music. Our gateway to classical music of the last two decades is an example of this kind of innovation within a classical genre: a movement called "Speech" from an oratorio titled *Anthracite Fields* by Julia Wolfe (b. 1958). The text of "Speech" is an excerpt from a speech that John L. Lewis, head of the United Mine Workers Union, gave to the Congressional House Labor Committee in 1947. The choir of the Mendelssohn Club of Philadelphia and an ensemble of musicians called the Bang on a Can All-Stars premiered the work in 2014. In 2015 *Anthracite Fields* was awarded the Pulitzer Prize for composition.

 Listen to the first thirty seconds of this recording to get a sense of its sound.

How Does It Work?

FIGURE 14.9
Julia Wolfe at the Grammy Awards in 2016
Source: Splash News/Alamy Stock Photo.

Timbre

The timbre consists of solo and choral singing by men's voices, bowed cello and bass played with a scratchy sound, strummed guitar, clarinet, drum set, and a synthesizer producing something like the scratchy static on old recordings.

Texture

The texture is varied. Sometimes the soloist and choir sing over a drone-like instrumental accompaniment. Sometimes the soloist's melody interacts with an instrumental melody.

Rhythm

The rhythm alternates between nonmetrical sections that mirror the rhythm of speech and sections with a constant pulse, often in a meter of four.

Melody

The composer uses melody sparingly, instead emphasizing drones and single pitches and chords in isolation.

Harmony

The men's chorus often sings in intervals of fifths and seconds.

Form

The form features alternating solo and choral men's voices.

Performance Techniques

The singing includes occasional slides between pitches and alternation of loud and soft either abruptly or with crescendos and decrescendos.

Listen to this recording with these elements in mind.

Listen to the entire recording following this timed listening guide.

LISTENING GUIDE 14.3

TIME	DESCRIPTION
0:00	The movement begins with a low-pitched, scratchy-sounding drone. A solo male singer begins the speech singing a melody on just a few pitches in a speech-like, nonmetrical rhythm: "If we must grind up human flesh in this industrial machine that we call modern America." A rhythmic pulse is introduced on the syllables "mo-dern A-mer-i-ca."
0:43	A chorus of men enters singing the same text and melody using harmonies based on the intervals of fifths and seconds. The drone texture thickens somewhat, adding a low-pitched clarinet, an electric guitar, and a drum set. Because they are played softly, these instruments may be difficult to hear.
1:10	The drone-like accompaniment changes character: a drum roll is clearly audible, as is the sound of the cello. The solo singer enters with these words, echoed by a two-part choral response using harmonic seconds: "then before God I assert that those who consume the coal." The electric guitar can be heard accompanying the singer, whose voice quality resembles that of a popular singer more than that of the typical classical choral or solo singer.
1:56	The soloist sings "because we live in comfort" on two very high, straining pitches. The chorus responds in harmony based on seconds: "that those who consume the coal and you and I who benefit from that service."
2:42	The soloist softly sings an ascending, stepwise melody accompanied by the guitar playing the same melody and a drone tone; in other words, the text becomes quite thin compared to what has come before: "we owe protection to those men and we owe the security to their families if they die." The chorus responds, repeating fragments of the text: "if they die," "those men," and "protection" in a thudding pulse aided by a low-pitched drum beat.
3:54	The soloist and chorus alternate singing the text, "I say it, I voice it, I proclaim it" in a constant pulse at a very loud volume, each phrase of the text on a single pitch.
4:53	The drone texture is abandoned as the soloist sings an ascending, stepwise melody in unison with the synthesizer on the words "And I care not who in heaven or hell opposes it."
5:11	The drone and the chorus return very loudly, singing and playing a drone in triple meter on the words, "That is what I believe. That is what I believe, I believe, I believe."
6:05	A brief pause and then the soloist, accompanied by the guitar in seconds, quietly concludes with a three-note ascending melody: "And the miners believe that."
6:23	End

What Does It Mean?

CULTURAL LINKAGES

Part of the meaning of "Speech" derives from its position among the four other movements in *Anthracite Fields*. The composer, Julia Wolfe, chose and created a set of texts that portray life in the anthracite coal-mining communities of Pennsylvania, where she grew up. Their related common themes unify the composition and express various points of view on the experience of coal mining. The first movement text, "Foundations," consists of selected names of coal miners killed in Pennsylvania mine accidents between 1869 and 1916 plus some geological descriptions of the region. The second movement text, "Breaker Boys," is a heart-rending first-person account of the horribly difficult work by children who picked debris from mined ore. The fourth movement text, "Flowers," is one woman's description of the beauty the women tried to create in their gardens above ground in a mining town while their husbands, sons, and fathers descended into the hell of the mines. The fifth-movement text, "Appliances," simply lists all the activities of daily life that depend on the energy generated by coal and by the hard and dangerous, sometimes fatal, work of coal miners: "bake a cake, go to the gym, blast your guitar, call your girlfriend on the phone." The oratorio's sixty-five-minute length in a concert setting requires a great deal of sustained attention. Within the national debate on the role of coal in our economy, in climate change, and in sustainable sources of clean energy, the composition sheds light on the human cost of mining.

Because of their association with a text, the musical elements in this piece can be interpreted for the way they express and reinforce the meaning of the words. For example, the solo singer is mimicking a speech by a single speaker or orator, an obvious connection to the real-world event on which the movement is based. Throughout the movement the men's chorus responds by repeating the soloist's words, their choral timbres representing the agreement of the miners' community with their union president's words. The vocal timbre of the soloist does not resemble the timbre of a classically trained singer. It is more like that of a singer of popular music. This aesthetic step away from the style of classical music, which is supported by wealthy and educated classes, and toward a "common" style, fits a text expressing the words of a working-class coal-mining community.

The nonmetrical quality of the soloist's singing mimics speech, while the pounding, pulsating, constant beat reinforces the miners' insistence on the truth that their leader is speaking.

The harmonies that the chorus sings are typically viewed as dissonant in European classical and American popular musical traditions. The dissonance of the harmony in this movement may disturb some listeners familiar mainly with those traditions. That disturbance, that dissonance, clearly matches the message of the text, which was meant, in 1947 and today, to disrupt the listener's complacency about the treatment of the men whose labor produces the creature comforts people enjoy and take for granted. The harmonic fifths sung by the choir may remind knowledgeable listeners of early polyphonic forms of Christian chant, lending a sacred quality, and a moral urgency, to a modern secular text.

FIGURE 14.10
Breaker boys from Pittston, Pennsylvania, in 1911
Source: Lewis Wickes Hine. Library of Congress. Wikimedia Commons.

FIGURE 14.11
A performance of *Anthracite Fields* with photographic projections in the background
Source: Getty Images/Carolyn Cole.

The alternations between softness and loudness express the contrast between a rational, if resigned, presentation of an intractable problem and the anger of the speaker and the miners at their fate and their desire to communicate resolutely their wish for fairer, more humane treatment and working conditions.

The instrumental accompaniment combines instruments and timbres associated with classical music (cello, string bass, clarinet, choral singing) with those from popular music (synthesizer, electric guitar, drum set, and the timbre of solo singing). The combination of these instruments from different categories, genres, and styles in one classical composition represents some of the breadth of contemporary American music. Fans of jazz or classical music or certain genres of popular music may bring to their listening experience specific ideas about what sounds authentic and appropriate in the genres they love. *Anthracite Fields* might be interpreted as a statement about the limits of musical genre in American culture today and the advantages of creative combinations that unify the musical and social divisions associated with categories, genres, and styles.

AESTHETICS

What Is Its History?

AESTHETICS

When twentieth- and twenty-first-century composers like Julia Wolfe contribute compositions relevant to their times to the repertoire of classical music, they often challenge the conventions of older music and the conventional expectations of their audience. In this piece Wolfe eschews traditional large or small ensembles of European classical instruments in favor of a unique combination of instruments and voices from classical and popular music. Wolfe also joins classical composers like Igor Stravinsky, Dmitri Shostakovich, and Julius Eastman who, for more than a century, had been exploring harmonic dissonance and drones as expressive devices in the context of a music culture that mainly values and experiences consonant harmonies. *Anthracite Fields* is part of this history of harmonic, timbral, and textural innovation in twentieth- and twenty-first-century classical music.

ECONOMIC ACTIVITY

One reason that classical composers today think twice about composing for symphony orchestras is that it is so expensive to do so. Even high-priced tickets are not enough to pay the bills of orchestras and opera companies. These organizations today have to turn to government grants and gifts from wealthy philanthropists to meet their expenses. In the United States, government support of the arts is woefully inadequate. On a per capita basis, Germany spends forty times as much on the arts as the United States does. This disparity speaks volumes about the value that these two governments place on the arts.

Government grants are a small part of government support for classical music. Far more comes from public schools, colleges, and universities, which offer music programs whose content consists mainly of exposure to European classical music. Many professional musicians get their starts in such programs, which are also important patrons of composers in this tradition. Since the ability of arts organizations to pay composers commissions for their works and royalties from music publishing are relatively limited, many composers enjoy full- or part-time employment as university professors. (**Commissions** are promises to pay composers for their work; the sources of funding are government and private granting agencies and wealthy donors.) In this economic context, many classical composers today favor works for small chamber ensembles, which are less expensive to stage and record than compositions for large symphonies and opera companies. *Anthracite Fields* falls into this pattern of patronage. Julia Wolfe is a professor of composition at New York University, and a number of private foundations and institutions supported her in the composition, performance, and recording of *Anthracite Fields*.

In addition to its history within the long history of European classical music, the history of *Anthracite Fields* has a history in the work of its composer, Julia Wolfe. Born and raised in Pennsylvania, Wolfe did not begin studying composition formally until after she finished her undergraduate degree at the University of Michigan. She studied piano as a child but was more interested in playing the music of Broadway musicals than classical music. She picked up the guitar in high school and became interested in folk songs in the vein of Canadian singer-songwriter Joni Mitchell. Soon after her undergraduate studies, in the early 1980s, she relocated to New York City and subsequently completed a master's degree in composition at Yale University in 1986. Like most composers of European-derived classical music today, she was trained as a composer in university settings and has continued to be involved with various institutions of higher education. She also completed a doctorate in composition at Princeton University in 2012, after she was already an established composer.

Anthracite Fields is part of a larger body of Wolfe's work that deals with American history and labor rights. For example, her 2009 composition *Steel Hammer* is a nine-movement work about John Henry, an African American folk hero renowned in the work of steel-driving, the hammering of a steel drill into rock to make holes for explosives, which were blown up to construct railroad tunnels. The most famous legend of John Henry is about a competition between him and a steam-powered steel drill, resulting in his victory and death from exhaustion. *Steel Hammer* explores the various versions of this human-versus-machine legend. Wolfe was also commissioned by the New York Philharmonic to compose the oratorio *Fire in My Mouth*, an oratorio for women's choir, girls' choir, and orchestra inspired by the 1911 Triangle Shirtwaist Factory Fire that claimed the lives of 146 garment workers in New York City, mostly young immigrant women. Like *Anthracite Fields*, the piece developed out of research into historical documents and interviews, and includes multimedia elements. This large-scale composition, premiered in 2019, demonstrates Wolfe's continuing interest in labor rights and American history, with an added consideration of gender and women's rights.

Unlike many composers today, Wolfe's career is intertwined with an organization that she helped co-found. This organization, called Bang on a Can, began in 1987 as a one-time event in New York organized by Wolfe and two friends of hers who had also studied composition at Yale in the early 1980s: Michael Gordon (b. 1956) and David Lang (b. 1957). At the time, classical music composition in New York was polarized into two camps. The first camp favored complicated, intellectualized systems for organizing musical sound and was typically performed in formal settings such as concert halls. This music had little appeal to audiences, and composers in this sphere (building on the aesthetics of the by now decades-long tradition of serialism) for the most part privileged rationality, austerity, and complexity of structure over enjoyment by audiences. The second camp rejected this rational, austere, and complicated approach, and instead favored a simpler, more engaging style full of the repetitions associated with minimalism. In New York City, this music, by Terry Riley, Philip Glass, Steve Reich, and others who got their start in the 1960s and 1970s, was typically performed in informal settings such as alternative art galleries and loft spaces in the Lower East Side and Greenwich Village neighborhoods.

> **AESTHETICS**

As young composers, Wolfe, Gordon, and Lang were attracted to some musical elements from each of these polarized scenes. But because of the pretensions of each of the scenes, and because they wanted to engage with popular culture in ways these scenes did not, they didn't feel at home in either one. Their response was to hold a twelve-hour marathon concert at an art gallery in New York's SoHo neighborhood titled "Bang on a Can," where they gathered a group of like-minded musicians to perform their compositions along with the music of composers from both of the polarized camps. Wolfe, Gordon, and Lang were seeking through this marathon to create opportunities for compositions in classical music to cross boundaries of style and genre.

The value of crossing boundaries has remained central to Bang on a Can's activities as it has grown from the 1987 one-day event to an organization today that features an ensemble dedicated to performing new compositions, the "Bang on a Can All-Stars," an annual summer festival devoted to the development of young composers and performers; a program to commission new compositions from emerging composers; and iterations of the original marathon concert in New York and elsewhere, among other endeavors. Bang on a Can provided a setting where composers of European classical music could incorporate elements of rock, folk, jazz, and pop, as Julia Wolfe has often done in her compositions.

As Bang on a Can developed, Wolfe's co-founders Michael Gordon and David Lang became well known and gained prestige in the world of classical composers earlier than she did. One could argue that this is due to the fact that composition in classical music in the United States and Europe (and elsewhere) is a male-dominated field. Audiences and critics have certain assumptions about composers, one of those being that a composer is typically a man. Other aspects of classical music are also associated with gender, including which genders tend to play certain instruments. Also conductors have typically been men. These associations do not demonstrate "natural" traits of men and women but rather are constructs based on factors such as associating a human's vocal range with an instrument's range or misguided assumptions about the physical abilities of women versus those of men. Similar to jazz, classical music has emerged from societies that were typically male-dominated and in which men typically played instruments and women typically sang. This musical division of labor by gender can even be observed in rural traditions like those in Bulgaria (Chapter 3, Gateway 10). Similar to jazz, efforts have been made in the last few decades to address classical music's gender problem. Blind auditions are now common for most symphony orchestras, preventing those assessing the musicians from making even subconscious judgments based on a person's gender (or race or other elements of their appearance). The result has been a much greater number of women in the world's orchestras. Granting organizations often have funds dedicated to supporting the work of women. OPERA America, the umbrella service organization for virtually all professional opera companies in the United States, has an ongoing grant program that financially supports women composers in the

> **SOCIAL BEHAVIOR**

development of new operas. Julia Wolfe and an increasing number of women composers today are challenging traditional norms in the field of classical composition, though a large majority of composers of European classical music today are still men.

WHERE DO I GO FROM HERE?

- Go to Julia Wolfe's website and listen to another movement, or all the movements, of *Anthracite Fields* or listen to another of her compositions. If you read musical notation, follow along with the score as you listen to Movement 3, "Speech" from *Anthracite Fields*.
- Read about Michael Gordon and David Lang, and listen to one of their compositions created, like *Anthracite Fields*, since 2010. Compare their work to Wolfe's.

GATEWAY 59
REGIONAL MEXICAN MUSIC

What Is It?

Regional Mexican music is an umbrella term that encompasses a number of genres, each with roots in the rural life of a region of Mexico. The roots of genres of regional Mexican music today span all of Mexico and the southwestern United States, and these genres include *mariachi, norteño, banda, tejano* (Tex-Mex), and *corridos tumbados*. Musical style varies widely among these genres, but they share in common a focus on telling stories about everyday life and, often, the challenges it can bring. The music industry began using the category "regional Mexican music" as a catch-all genre category and radio format in the 1990s. Today an entire radio industry is built around the regional Mexican music category, *Billboard* charts track regional Mexican music, Grammy and Latin Grammy categories are devoted to it, and Spotify playlists and other streaming technologies have led to a growing popularity of regional Mexican music and the genres it encompasses. Our gateway to regional Mexican music is a song from a genre called **música norteña** or **norteño**. The name refers to northern Mexico, where it developed. It is popular along the border between Mexico and the United States and with working-class Mexican Americans in California and other border states.

Our gateway recording is a song called "La Bala" (The Bullet) performed by Los Tigres del Norte (The Tigers of the North) from their 2014 album *Realidades* (Realities). A well-known band based in San Jose, California, their roots are in Sinaloa, Mexico. The song is about gang warfare that results in the death of an innocent child, an all-too-common reality in the United States. Such storytelling songs about real events are called **corridos**, possibly deriving from the Spanish word *corer* (to run), describing a running story or commentary. It may also be a cognate of the English word "courier," a way, like a newspaper, of carrying the news or reinforcing knowledge of familiar events, but in oral rather than written tradition.

🔊 Listen to the first thirty seconds of the recording.

FIGURE 14.12
Los Tigres del Norte at the 2011 Latin Grammy Awards
Source: Splash News/Alamy Stock Photo.

How Does It Work?

Timbre

"La Bala" is performed by a male singer to the accompaniment of a small combo called a ***conjunto*** (a group or grouping), in this case a *conjunto norteño*. It consists of a small button accordion, a twelve-string guitar called *bajo sexto* (bass of six strings), bass, and drum set.

Texture

The texture features a solo melody over alternating bass and chords.

Rhythm

This song is performed in a medium tempo duple meter.

Melody

The melody is based on a heptatonic scale with a range of about an octave and a half. The first three verses are sung in a minor mode, and the last four are in a major mode.

Harmony

The harmonies are triadic and frequently repeat in short cycles.

Form

The form is a variant of a strophic song. About halfway through "La Bala," the melody changes so that the form, instead of being AAAA (etc.) as in a normal strophic song, is AAA (minor mode) BB'BB' (major mode). Within the verses the A strophes are four lines long with the melodic form: abac. The B strophes introduce new melodies: B = defg and B = defgh.

Performance Techniques

The singer changes the timbre of his voice from relaxed and soft to loud and tense. The accordion player improvises occasional short melodies over the singer's voice and at the end of phrases and whole strophes.

Listen to the first thirty seconds of the recording for the sounds of these instruments and the singer's vocal timbre.

Listen to the entire recording following this timed listening guide.

LISTENING GUIDE 14.4

TIME	SECTION	DESCRIPTION	LYRICS	LYRICS (ENGLISH TRANSLATION)
0:00	Intro	The *conjunto* plays a syncopated introduction.		
0:12	A	The soloist enters in his low register, singing the first verse in a quiet, matter-of-fact way. The melody, in a minor mode, rises in pitch at the end of the strophe.	(a) *Ocho en punto y como siempre, parecía un día normal*	Eight o'clock and as always, it looked like a normal day
			(b) *dos hermanos y un destino, una madre y un papá*	Two brothers and one destiny, a mother and a father
			(a) *siete años tenía el niño, del que les vengo a cantar*	One child was seven years old, about whom I come to sing
			(c) *pero voy a regresarme una semana para atrás*	But I'm going back a week
0:34	A		*Mi hijo el de 18 años, se empezó a descarrilar*	My eighteen-year-old son started derailing

			su promedio era muy bajo, grosero con su mamá	His grade average was very low, rude to his mom
			cerraba el cuarto con llave, dizque su privacidad	I saw his locked room, signaling his privacy
			pero de armas en mi casa, él ocultaba un arsenal	He hid an arsenal of weapons in my house
0:57	A		*El jueves de esa semana, le conocí un par de amigos*	On Thursday of that week, I met a couple of his friends
			portaban otro semblante, no era gente de su tipo	They acted different, they weren't his type
			cosas raras me callaba, con tal yo de ser su amigo	I shut up about these strange things, I wanted to be his friend
			y por no verlo enojado, le cumplía cualquier capricho	And not to make him angry, I catered to his every whim
1:18	B	The singer changes to a major-mode melody for the next verse and sings in a more strained manner than in the first three strophes, ending on the fifth degree of the scale.	*(d) Y ese día fue el final*	And that day was the end
			(e) que el hijo más pequeño a la escuela iría a estudiar	[the last day] That my youngest son would go to study in school
			(f) los carteles de la mafia cuentas iban ajustar	The accounts of the mafia cartels were going to be settled
			(g) y con una bala perdida, me destrozaban mi hogar	And with a stray bullet, they destroyed my home
1:40	B'	The singer repeats the strophe, but adds a short, fifth phrase to end on the tonic.	*(d) La sorpresa es fatal*	The surprise is lethal
			(e) que el hijo el de 18 muy involucrado está	my eighteen-year-old son is very involved
			(f) con la muerte, con las drogas, participa en la crueldad	With death, with drugs, [and he] participates in cruelty
			(g) y en la muerte de su hermano	And in the death of his brother
			(h) fue el autor intelectual	he was the one who inspired the crime [the instigator]
2:02	B"	Instrumental interlude, a variant of the B melody, ending on the fifth degree of the scale.		
2:21	B		*Soy otro en la suma nada más*	I am nothing more than another in the total
			que es víctima del diario en la corrupta sociedad	of victims of the record of this corrupt society
			todo sabemos de alguien que hace daño a los demás	We all know of someone who hurts others
			y sus errores yo solía solapar	But I stayed silent about his misdeeds
2:41	B'		*Y hoy vengo a delatar*	And today I come to turn in
			al matón que anda en la calle, forma parte de mi hogar	The bully who walks in the street and is part of my home
			uno menos que ande suelto al mundo le servirá	One less that will have a place in the world
			si tú conoces un hijo igual al mío,	If you know a son like mine,
			por favor denuncia ya	please report him
3:17	End			

Credit: Song lyrics of "La Bala" courtesy of TN Ediciones Musicales.

What Does It Mean?

The meaning of a *corrido* is derived in large part from its lyrics. *Corridos* typically tell stories about themes and individuals (or character types) closely related to the lived experiences of musicians and their audiences. Some *corridos* are dedicated to contemporary or historical heroic figures and tell of their lives and legendary courageous deeds. Others deal with stories about the Mexican Revolution (1910–1917), political corruption, natural disasters, passionate love affairs and deceptions, and various injustices experienced by Mexicans at the hands of Americans, the wealthy, the Mexican government, or those involved in gang and drug-related violence. Today, *corridos* often touch on the injustices faced by poor Mexicans or Mexican Americans, such as discrimination and exploitation. At the same time they celebrate protagonists who exhibit courage, honor, and defiance in the face of these injustices. "La Bala" is a *corrido* that tells the story of the death of a child as a violent consequence of drug-related gang warfare.

CULTURAL LINKAGES

Like all *corridos*, "La Bala" is in the form of a strophic song, a song based on repeating strophes, or verses, that contain identical or similar melodies and harmonic chord progressions, but with new lyrics for each repetition of the verse. The story of "La Bala" can be broken into seven parts, each part corresponding to a strophe. The first three strophes are grouped together, and the final four strophes are grouped together in two pairs separated by an instrumental interlude. *Corridos* open with an introductory strophe that presents the characters, time, location, and theme of the story. The following central strophes of a *corrido* tell the events of the story, developing it to its climax and resolution, before the final strophe or strophes present a farewell and a moral lesson provided by the narrator of the story.

AESTHETICS

In "La Bala" the first strophe introduces the main characters (a family with two sons, a mother, and a father, who is the storyteller) and the time frame for the story (the important events take place on one particular day, but the story goes back a week to provide background information). It also hints that this particular day will be auspicious with the phrases "it looked like a normal day" and "two brothers and one destiny." The second and third strophes begin the story when the older son becomes involved in a gang and the father regrets not discouraging him from violence and gang activity. The fourth and fifth strophes tell of the death of the younger son as a result of the older son's gang membership. The sixth and seventh strophes present the conclusion and moral lesson: the father-narrator laments his previous silence, decides to turn his older son over to authorities, and urges others to do the same if they know, as he sings, "a son like mine." These formal elements—introduction, body of the story, and farewell/moral lesson—are present in all *corridos* as lyrics tell a story of a protagonist dealing with hardships, adversity, or violence. For "La Bala," the father seems to be the protagonist, and his complex act of courage is the turning in of his own son.

EMOTIONAL RESONANCE

Most strophic songs, and many *corridos*, employ basically the same harmony and melody for each strophe. The melody of "La Bala," however, makes a shift from a minor mode to a major mode after the third strophe, and introduces a new chord progression. This loosely corresponds to the narrative, where in the first three strophes the narrator is presenting the background to the story during the week leading up to the auspicious day, and the final four strophes tell of the death of the younger son and provide the moral lesson. In addition to the shift in harmony and melody after the third strophe, the vocalist begins to sing in a higher range and gives his voice a strained timbre. As he sings about the anguish of his younger son's death and his devastation at his older son's role in it, his voice is no longer low and relaxed as it was when he was providing the background for the story. The higher register and the strain and physical energy required express the emotions of the father, emotions that might similarly be communicated through the voice in crying or shouting.

The rhythmic structure of *corridos*, including "La Bala," is relatively simple. Historically many *corridos* have used a triple meter, though *corridos* in the *norteño* style like "La Bala" (and most of the songs by Los Tigres del Norte) typically use a duple meter. In "La Bala," the bass plays on the main accented beats, the downbeats. The *bajo sexto* and guitar play halfway between the main beats, on the upbeats. The drums play only on the beats and on the upbeats without adding any other accents or syncopation. This sparse rhythm allows the vocal and the text to stand out as the most prominent feature of the song, with the accordion and the melodic and chordal fills it plays complementing the melody and the lyrics. The vocal line also avoids rhythmic complexities and embellishments in favor of a clear and understandable presentation of the lyrics.

AESTHETICS

What Is Its History?

For the most part, "La Bala" is performed by and for the Mexican American community of the United States. Its history is connected to the Mexican American community, the history of Los Tigres del Norte, and the long history of the *corrido* in Mexico and throughout Latin America, part of which also includes the history of the *norteño* genre. These histories demonstrate the intersections of a number of musical styles with one another in the context of political events and social changes. The *corrido* has its roots in the *romance*, one of many Spanish genres brought to Mexico by Spanish colonists as early as the sixteenth century. The *romance*, like the *corrido*, often told long stories in a form called an epic ballad. *Corridos* focus more on contemporary events than the *romance* did. *Corridos* were likely sung as far back as the early nineteenth century in northern Mexico and the area of the border of Mexico and the United States. Like the *romance*, these early *corridos* told long stories in as many as twenty strophes. The basic form of the *corrido* as it exists today became fixed during the Mexican Revolution (1910–1917), when *corridos* dealt with such prominent figures of the revolution as Pancho Villa and Emiliano Zapata.

During the 1920s, the American recording industry began to recognize, as they did for race records and hillbilly music, the potential for a market among Mexican communities in California and the American southwest. Records featuring *corridos* were produced for, and sold to, a growing Spanish-language audience. By the 1960s recorded *corridos* had become much shorter in duration to fit the standard three-minute song length of records and commercial radio. The 3:10 duration of "La Bala's" seven strophes is evidence of this change in length from long *corridos* of many strophes to shorter ones.

Corridos can be performed in many styles and genres. In the *norteño* genre the accordion takes the lead, as it does in "La Bala." The accordion likely arrived in Mexico in the middle of the nineteenth century, introduced in western and northern Mexico and the borderlands by German immigrants. In addition to the accordion, Germans and other Europeans brought a variety of music and dance forms, many of which became associated with the music of *conjuntos*. These influences are still present today not only in the sound of the accordion but also in the two-beat duple meter of one of these dance forms, the polka, which became a widely popular meter for *corridos* and is still the most common meter for *corridos* in the *norteño* style. *Conjuntos* featuring the accordion have spread along with Mexican and Mexican American populations throughout the United States and Canada, and *corridos* have continued to tell stories about contemporary life and struggle. *Corridos* and the *norteño conjunto* also appear in other Latin American countries, and their influence is particularly strong in times and places experiencing political and social turmoil.

Los Tigres del Norte (or Los Tigres for short) was formed in the late 1960s by a group of brothers and cousins, all of whom had immigrated from the western Mexican state of Sinaloa to San Jose, California. Their fame spread beyond their local region after they recorded and released the song "Contrabando y Traición" (Smuggling and Betrayal) in 1974. This song is a *narcocorrido*, a type of *corrido* prevalent since the 1970s dealing with drug trafficking as its subject matter. *Narcocorridos* in many cases celebrate drug trafficking and drug traffickers, but Los Tigres have refrained from glorifying the drug trade or glamorizing criminal activity.

As their popularity has grown, Los Tigres del Norte have been one of the leading groups in bringing *norteño* and *corridos* to audiences far beyond the U.S.-Mexico border region. They have sold upwards of thirty million albums and have received seven Grammy awards (including Best Regional Mexican Music Album for *Realidades* in 2015). They maintain a rigorous tour schedule that typically includes more than 100 performances per year. Their popularity and critical acclaim are in no small part related to the ways their *corridos* and other songs touch the realities of life for Mexican Americans. For example, the album *Realidades* includes a

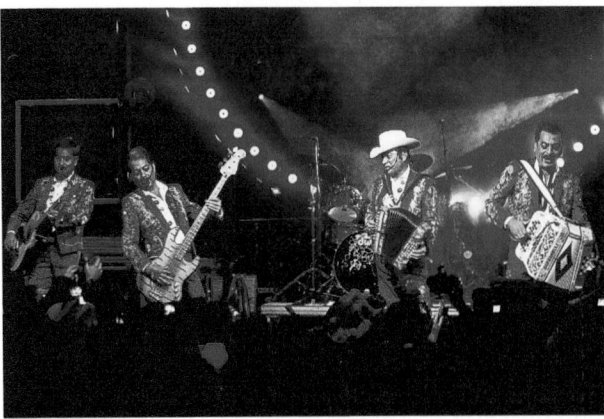

FIGURE 14.13

Los Tigres del Norte performing in Madrid, Spain, in 2009

Source: Getty Images/ Eduardo Parra.

song called "Era Diferente" (She Was Different) about a lesbian teenager falling in love with a close female friend. The *corrido* provides Los Tigres del Norte and other groups with an effective vehicle for dealing with complex issues facing the community. *Corridos* are, by definition, relevant to contemporary events and provide audiences with a musical way to navigate oppression, economic strife, violence close to home, and other struggles.

WHERE DO I GO FROM HERE?

- Watch the music video for "La Bala." To what extent does it reinforce the story told and the moral lesson? What position do the musicians hold in the music video? Are they part of the storyline or not? What effect does this have?
- Find other *norteño* bands, and artists from other regional Mexican genres such as *banda, tejano* (another border-crossing genre), or *corridos tumbados*, a new genre originating in Southern California that adds elements from hip-hop and trap and tells stories about urban life today. Compare their music to that of Los Tigres. Do they cover similar material? Is the instrumentation or musical style similar?
- The 1960s featured the rise of the Chicano Movement (or El Movimiento), the Mexican Farmworkers Movement, and civil rights leader Cesar Chavez. Can you find *corridos* related to Chavez and those movements? There are also *corridos* about nearly all important contemporary American political figures and events. What kinds of stories and moral lessons can you find in these kinds of *corridos*?

GATEWAY 60
K-POP

What Is It?

K-pop is a catch-all term that is regularly used for the popular music of South Korea. Outside Korea (all references to Korea in this gateway refer to South Korea) the best-known form of K-pop is made by so-called idols and idol groups; encompasses music, dance, and visual elements; and is associated with devoted fan communities. Korean idol groups today are typically either all women or all men. Almost all K-pop idols have been produced and promoted by large entertainment agencies in organized systems that train young performers and hone their skills and public images. K-pop and its idols have become increasingly popular outside of South Korea since the 1990s, and constitute a multibillion-dollar industry today. This spread of Korean popular culture internationally is known as *hallyu*, or the Korean wave. It includes K-pop as well as television dramas, films, cuisine, and "K-beauty" (skincare and makeup). Well-known examples of *hallyu* today include the Academy Award-winning film *Parasite* (2019) and the hit Netflix television series *Squid Game* (2021), both of which present harsh critiques of wealth inequality in Korea.

Blackpink is one of the most popular K-pop groups today with millions of fans all over the world. Formed by the agency YG Entertainment, the group debuted in 2016 with members Jisoo (Kim Ji-soo, b. 1995), Jennie (Jennie Kim, b. 1996), Rosé (Roseanne Park, b. 1997), and Lisa (Lalisa Manobal, b. Pranpriya Manobal, 1997). Our gateway to K-pop is their song "How You Like That" from *The Album* (2020), which reached #1 on the charts in several countries. Its music video, viewed eighty-six million times within twenty-four hours of release, set a record at the time and suggests the crucial role of music videos within K-pop.

FIGURE 14.14

Blackpink featured in a 2020 promotion for the video game PUBG Mobile. From left to right: Jennie, Lisa, Jisoo, and Rosé.

Source: PUBG Mobile/Blue Hole Studio/ Lori155, Wikimedia Commons.

Listen to the first thirty seconds of the recording.

How Does It Work?

Timbre

Female vocals and mostly electronic sounds constitute the timbres of the recording. The timbres of the electronic sounds range from bright buzzy synthesizers to deep, resonant bass lines and percussion.

Texture

Sung and rapped vocals are accompanied by rhythmic accompaniments and layers of synthesizers and percussion sounds, and sometimes by countermelodies.

Rhythm

The steady, danceable tempo is sometimes felt at 130 beats per minute, and sometimes felt in half-time at seventy-five beats per minute. The verse features phrases that start in between beats; the pre-chorus features phrases in triplet rhythms; and the chorus features accented rhythms squarely on the beat, with little syncopation.

Melody

The melody is in a minor mode in the verse and in a major mode in the pre-chorus. The chorus features a short melody that repeats a pitch followed by a descending then an ascending leap.

Harmony

The harmony is relatively static, featuring mostly consonant major and minor chords.

Form

The recording follows a version of a typical form in pop music: (Intro) verse, pre-chorus, chorus (and post-chorus), rap section, pre-chorus, chorus, bridge, outro. The bridge has a new melody, chord progression, and lyrics. Its rhythm creates an effect that the tempo is half as fast as previous sections.

Performance Techniques

Both singing and rapping alternate between Korean and English. This is common in K-pop, but the song has a higher proportion of English to Korean than is typical.

Listen to the entire recording with these elements in mind while following this timed listening guide.

LISTENING GUIDE 14.5

TIME	SECTION	DESCRIPTION	LYRICS
0:00	Intro	The track begins with sounds of trumpets, trombones, and other brass instruments playing short, accented chords in a minor key.	(Lisa) Blackpink in your area!
0:11	Verse	A synth with an accented attack and a mellow timbre outlines chords and provides a pulse underneath a vocal phrase. The vocal phrase follows the duple meter rather strictly, and leaps from a low pitch to a higher one and repeats once. Synthesized sustained sounds add to the texture.	(Jennie) Boran deusi muneojyeosseo . . . (Jisoo) Ot kkeutjarak . . .
0:27	Pre-chorus	The vocals with synth accompaniment texture continues, the rhythm of the vocal shifts to approximate triplets, and the vocals begin to add some English phrases to the lyrics. The end of the pre-chorus features a break, where only a percussive rattle is heard.	(Rosé) Dasi kamkamhan igose light up the sky . . .
0:41	Chorus	A sustained bass, hip-hop drums, and EDM-style synth sounds constitute the texture supporting the lead vocals, which sing a minor, angular melody that is sometimes also played by a synth with a nasal timbre.	(Jennie) Ha! How you like that . . .

TIME	SECTION	DESCRIPTION	LYRICS
0:56	Post-chorus	The harmony and texture of the chorus continue, but the sung melody is replaced by text rapped by Lisa and Jennie, with sung interjections on the angular part of the chorus melody, accompanied by a melodic synth line.	(Lisa) Now, look at you . . .
1:11	Rap	Lisa raps, alternating between English and Korean, and a plucked-string sounding instrument plays in a mode with an augmented second, reminiscent of the Arab *maqam* called *hijaz*.	(Lisa) Your girl need it all . . .
1:25	Pre-chorus	This pre-chorus is similar to the first pre-chorus, with a slightly more accented build-up to the chorus.	(Jennie) Deo kamkamhan igose shine like the stars
1:40	Chorus	This chorus resembles the initial chorus, though different individuals sing the various lines.	(Rosé) Ha, How you like that . . .
1:55	Post-chorus	The post-chorus is similar to the first post-chorus.	(Lisa) Now, look at you . . .
2:10	Bridge	With lyrical vocal melodies, a rhythm that makes the pulse feel half as fast, and a high-pitched counter melody in a synth with a smooth timbre, the bridge contrasts with the sections preceding it. The rhythm of the percussion sounds becomes more active at the end of the section to set up the outro, which begins with a drop.	(Rosé) Nalgae ilheun chaero churakhaetdeon nal . . .
2:25	Outro A	Synths and drum sounds with a driving beat dominate this section, which ends with a short, complete break.	Yeeeaaah . . .
2:39	Outro A'	During the break, the vocalists shout "Blackpink!" When the synths and drum sounds enter on beat one, the vocalists add rhythmic vocables on "ddu," interspersed with melodic statements of "how you like that."	Blackpink! Ddu, ddu, ddu, ddu-ddu-ddu . . .
3:02	End		

What Does It Mean?

CULTURAL LINKAGES

The musical elements of "How You Like That" assist in understanding two important aspects of the music of Blackpink and other K-pop artists: the relationships of fans to groups and to individual members, and the use of multiple musical styles, which help groups connect with global audiences. Both aspects are highlighted in the opening phrase of "How You Like That": six seconds in, the group proclaims in English, "Blackpink in your area." The motto, which appears in many of the group's recordings, lets audiences immediately identify the song as Blackpink's (a useful promotional tool). It expresses the idea that listeners anywhere in the world can embrace the group, their music, and the messages of their music. They are so present, and accessible through the internet, that they are constantly in "your" area, wherever that is. Fans of Blackpink, called "Blinks," pay close attention to which member of the group says this motto in each song. While Lisa says the catchphrase in "How You Like That" and in several other Blackpink recordings, Blinks often advocate for their favorite member to use the phrase, indicating a strong sense of fan identification with the individuals in the group. Fans of Jisoo were elated to learn that she had said the phrase for the first time in the 2020 song "Pretty Savage." Jisoo's use of a humorous post on Twitter to confirm that it is her voice on the recording highlights the role of social media in the intense idol-fan ecosystem of K-pop.

Fans of Blackpink and other K-pop groups also advocate for equal time for each group member to be featured in songs. The music video, and lyrics, for "How You Like That" introduce first Lisa, then Jennie, Jisoo, and Rosé before they all appear dancing together at the start of the first chorus. One fan-produced YouTube video tracks the line distribution among the group members in the video by how much time each person is singing, with the results showing Lisa (29.5 percent) with the most time singing, followed by Jennie (27 percent), Rosé (24.5 percent), and Jisoo (19 percent). The video is an example of the bias of fans for their favorite idols, with over four million views and nearly 9000 comments about the line distribution. Blinks, like many K-pop fans, want to see their favorite idol featured. They also believe that unequal line distributions could have a negative impact on the group members' relationships with one another. Part of the image that Blackpink has cultivated is that the members of the group are tight-knit and get along very well (and it appears they do), and fans of Blackpink want the group to maintain its positive and supportive relationships.

Many K-pop groups have relied on an aesthetic known as *aegyo*, a type of exaggerated cuteness, in their image and music. Blackpink combines *aegyo* with notions of being mature, cool, and confident, in Korea called a "girl crush concept." The group's name hints at this combination, drawing on associations in fashion of the color black with coolness and the color pink with stereotypical femininity. The lyrics of the chorus and outro sections repeat the text "how you like that," depicting an attitude of confidence and independence and hinting at revenge, or at least triumph, over those who might question or diminish an empowered young woman. The set of the music video features human-sized wings and several shots of Blackpink members standing in front of them to appear as if they have wings, an extension of their confidence. This references a trend that exploded in popularity on Instagram in 2014 when pop singer Taylor Swift posted a photo of her in front of a New York City mural of wings painted by artist Kelsey Montague. The chorus, the rap section, and outro can be understood as parts of the song where the members of Blackpink are flying with cool confidence. In the music video's chorus, post-chorus, and outro sections all members of the group dance together, embodying the self-assuredness of the lyrics in their movements and suggesting that independent young women triumphantly take flight together as supportive friends.

🔊 **Watch the music video of "How You Like That," paying attention to visual elements of the video as well as its musical elements, including its lyrics (translations to English appear throughout the video). How do these elements work together to present the individual members of Blackpink, and the group as a whole, as confident, mature, cute, and cool?**

AESTHETICS ▷

The musical elements of "How You Like That" bring together many styles. This is a typical feature of K-pop. It also helps extend the group's (and K-pop's) global reach and its appeal to a broad range of fans. One of the most prominent musical genres referenced in the song is hip-hop. The chorus, post-chorus, and outro feature deep rumbling bass lines, bass drum sounds from a Roland TR-808 drum machine, and varied rhythms on a crisp synthesized hi-hat, all of which are characteristics of **trap**, a hip-hop subgenre. Trap emerged in the American South in the 1990s and is also referenced in Lil Nas X's "Old Town Road" (Chapter 14, Gateway 56). Trap and its musical elements have been prominent in mainstream popular music in the United States and elsewhere since about 2015. These sounds, familiar to listeners of pop music globally, help Blackpink gain fans from among those who like the popular sound of trap. These sounds in "How You Like That" also position the group as "current" in the global pop music landscape and connect themes of coolness and confidence with musical elements common in pop music today.

CULTURAL LINKAGES ▷

K-pop groups have established strong links between K-pop and hip-hop. In the rap section of this recording, Lisa alternates between English and Korean. During her rap, the plucked-lute sounding instrument performs an arc-shaped melody twice in a mode similar to the Arab *maqam* called *hijaz*, with its characteristic augmented second. The music video during this section features Lisa, dressed in baggy pants and a bejeweled crop top typical of negative exoticizing stereotypes of the Arab world, walking through a set that evokes a Middle Eastern bazaar. She also is seen sitting on a plush, high-backed throne, a reference with numerous precedents in hip-hop. Fans of Blackpink reacted negatively to some elements of the video, especially a shot in this scene where a statue of the Hindu deity Ganesha rested on the floor as a background prop. Hindu fans and others found this disrespectful of the Hindu religion, since statues of Ganesha are meant to be placed in places of honor, not on the ground. The Blackpink India fan group, and many other fans, condemned the video for the way Ganesha was degraded. In response, YG Entertainment edited the video to remove shots that included Ganesha but used the YouTube interface to do so without removing the video from the site so that it could maintain its view count.

In addition to views on YouTube, forms of online engagement through social media are also an important part of K-pop. Fans are often uplifted by the generally positive and encouraging messages of K-pop songs, and inspired by the social media posts of their idols' daily lives. Many K-pop fan groups have self-organized to raise money for causes they believe in and to support protest movements through online action. But some fans have expressed their devotion in harmful ways as well, through cyberbullying those who critique their favorite idol. K-pop idols themselves are also subject to online bullying. Young women who are K-pop idols have been bullied online for not conforming to Korean ideals for traditional womanhood in actions such as not wearing a bra, not smiling in interviews, calling themselves feminists, or opening up about struggles with depression. In 2019, Sulli and Goo Hara, two K-pop artists who had experienced online bullying, took their own lives in separate incidents. Their suicides contributed to public debate in Korea about how mental health struggles are stigmatized, about the effects of the intense training programs undertaken by K-pop trainees, and about the impact of online bullying. A bill restricting cyberbullying nicknamed the "Sulli Act" was discussed in the wake of Sulli's death, but never signed into law.

The backgrounds of each member of Blackpink, well known by fans, contribute to an understanding of the group as both Korean and global. Lisa is from Thailand and her native language is Thai, but she raps mostly in English and Korean. She was the first non-ethnic Korean selected by YG Entertainment for its training program in 2011 and became its first non-ethnic Korean idol when Blackpink debuted in 2016. Lisa has become a superstar in Korea and Thailand and was the K-pop idol with the most followers on Instagram in 2021. Jennie, Rosé, and Jisoo, the same year, rounded out the top four K-pop idols on Instagram by number of followers. Rosé was born in Auckland, New Zealand to South Korean immigrant parents and raised through high school in Australia. At age fifteen she auditioned for YG Entertainment at a mass casting call in Sydney and moved to Seoul as part of their training program. Jennie was born in South Korea, but lived for part of her childhood in Auckland, before moving back to South Korea at age thirteen and auditioning there for YG. All four members of Blackpink are multilingual; in addition to Korean, languages they speak include English, Japanese, Chinese, and Thai.

In the music video of "How You Like That," Blackpink uses a cultural reference to a well-known Greek story to symbolize how they are confidently singing and dancing their way to worldwide fame, an example of how K-pop music videos commonly draw on numerous cultural and historical references. As the beat drops and the members of Blackpink metaphorically take flight like Superman to begin the outro, they are depicted first inside, then outside two Trojan horses, which Greek warriors hid inside and wheeled into the city of Troy to invade it. In front of a sprawling map of the entire northern hemisphere, the members of Blackpink perform as if having emerged from the Trojan horses, a vivid statement that they belong anywhere, are ever-present, and are always "in your area."

 Listen to "How You Like That" again and identify musical elements it shares with pop and hip-hop.

What Is Its History?

Girl groups have been part of Korean popular music since the first half of the twentieth century. The Jeogori Sisters (*jeogori* is the shirt in a typical two-piece traditional garment called *hanbok*) debuted in 1935, and featured Yi Nan-yeong, one of Korea's most famous vocalists. They performed *yuhaengga*, the popular music during the time of Japanese colonial rule in Korea (1915–1945), a genre which was influenced by musical styles of Korea, Japan, the United States, and Europe. During the 1950s Yi formed a new girl group, the Kim Sisters, originally consisting of her three daughters and later including her niece. Like many Korean groups and

FIGURE 14.15
The Kim Sisters with American entertainer Dean Martin
Source: Chick Sponder, Wikimedia Commons.

CULTURAL LINKAGES

bands, they found financial success singing American popular songs for U.S. troops during and after the Korean War (1950–1953). They signed a contract with American producer Tom Ball, and in 1959 they began performing in Las Vegas, on television programs like *The Ed Sullivan Show*, and in live performances.

During the 1960s and 1970s, Korean popular musicians continued to mix international styles in their music, but strict censorship laws during this period, and a focus of Park Chung-hee's (1917–1979) autocratic government on investing in industrial development, limited the styles, messages, and scope of the popular music industry. The two networks of the television broadcast system tightly controlled which musical artists appeared on weekend talent competitions. The radio networks promoted only the successful artists in those competitions, who performed mainly non-age-specific sentimental love ballads. Other styles were part of underground scenes that sought to resist and subvert government censorship. Park was assassinated in 1979. The democratic government established in 1987 loosened censorship laws and then eliminated them in the early 1990s. At that time, as the disposable income of young people grew significantly and international travel increased, mainstream pop in Korea became, for the first time, oriented towards youth cultures. Pop artists and producers targeted young audiences and began to include dance-oriented genres that appealed specifically to young audiences such as hip-hop, which was in the midst of its own golden era.

One of the first groups to introduce rap and hip-hop into Korean popular music was Seo Taiji & Boys, whose 1992 recording "Nan arayo" (I know) was among the first rap recordings to use the Korean language. The song's music video referenced dance, fashion, and visual aesthetics of music videos such as "Pump Up the Jam" (1990) by Technotronic, a Belgian group that had combined hip-hop with house music and featured Congolese-Belgian rapper Ya Kid K (Manuela Barbara Moasco Kamosi), who had been active in 1980s Chicago house (Chapter 13, Gateway 52). After Seo Taiji & Boys performed "Nan arayo" on a weekend televised talent show, the song became a smash hit. Its pop, rap, and dance elements paved the way for the many groups that followed. As democratic and censorship reforms continued, the dominance of the broadcast networks in the music industry also declined. During the 1990s the South Korean government began to view popular culture as a viable export to boost the national economy and started loosening regulations on popular music production. It incentivized large family-owned Korean business conglomerates called *chaebol* to invest in the entertainment industry, and many did so, including Samsung, Hyundai, and Daewoo. After the devastating effects of the 1997 Asian financial crisis, many of these companies pulled out of the risky business of film, television, and music. But their corporate structures endured in entertainment companies, including those focused on music.

ECONOMIC ACTIVITY ▷ Between 1995 and 1997, the first large-scale music entertainment companies took the place of the earlier state broadcast-network system. SM Entertainment (1995), YG Entertainment (1996), and JYP Entertainment (1997) and other conglomerates, to a greater extent than similar systems in U.S.-based companies such as Motown Records or Disney, encompassed all elements of the music industry: recruiting and training young performers; creating pop groups; producing and promoting the recordings, videos, tours, and public images of those groups and their members; and distributing their music. YG Entertainment, the company behind Blackpink, was founded by Yang Hyun-suk (b. 1970), a rapper, dancer, and songwriter, and one of the original members of Seo Taiji & Boys. The first Korean idols and groups produced by these companies in the late 1990s and early 2000s combined rap, pop, and dance, to the delight of fans in South Korea and in other parts of Asia. The first K-pop idol group, H.O.T., debuted with SM Entertainment in 1996 and found fame in South Korea, China, and Japan. In 1998, YG Entertainment launched the hip-hop group 1TYM (pronounced "One Time"). The group's leader and rapper, Teddy Park (b. 1978), later became an in-house producer for YG Entertainment and has been the main producer and co-songwriter for Blackpink.

Towards the end of the 2000s, the growth of social media coincided with increased government involvement in the profitable business of promoting Korean popular culture abroad. K-pop entertainment conglomerates pursued new markets in Southeast Asia, and gradually expanded into the Americas and Europe, taking advantage of social media and other digital technologies to promote its artists more broadly. In 2009, girl group Wonder Girls and solo idol BoA became the first K-pop artists to appear on the *Billboard* charts. "Gangnam Style" by YG Entertainment artist Psy topped the charts in over thirty countries in 2012, going viral with its catchy beat and entertaining music video, which became the first on YouTube to reach one billion views. Seven-member boy band BTS (originally Bangtan Sonyeondan, or Bulletproof Boy Scouts) debuted in 2013 under Big Hit Entertainment. The group has become one of the most popular in the world, with an enormous, passionate fanbase and multiple #1 hits on the *Billboard* charts, including the English-language hits "Dynamite" (2020) and "Butter" (2021), as well as the Korean-language "Life Goes On" (2020), which was written to be an uplifting song for fans during the COVID-19 pandemic.

Today the members of Blackpink, like other K-pop idols, continue to develop their already sizable fanbase through their music, videos, and social media. They performed at the Coachella Festival in 2019 and released a documentary on Netflix in 2020 called *Blackpink: Light Up the Sky*, its subtitle taken from the lyrics of "How You Like That." Jennie, Rosé, and Lisa have all released music as solo artists, and all members of the group endorse various fashion and cosmetics brands as models. Their growing fame, along with the many facets of *hallyu*, continues to broaden the influence of Korean popular culture around the world.

FIGURE 14.16
Wonder Girls performing in 2008
Source: AIKEN, Wikimedia Commons.

FIGURE 14.17
BTS in 2016
Source: Korean Culture and Information Service, Wikimedia Commons.

WHERE DO I GO FROM HERE?

- Watch the documentary *Blackpink: Light Up the Sky*. What kinds of narratives does it present about the members of Blackpink, and how do those narratives serve to cultivate a loyal fanbase? How does the documentary both reveal and mask the production processes of YG Entertainment?
- Compare a BTS #1 hit such as "Dynamite" or "Butter" to concurrently popular hits such as "Stay" (2021) by The Kid LAROI and Justin Bieber or "Blinding Lights" (2019) by The Weeknd. Using the list of musical elements in the gateways of this book, describe a similarity or difference between the two recordings (or video) in each category: timbre, texture, and so forth. Describe similarities and differences in visual style and dance style between the two videos.
- Learn more about K-pop girl groups such as S.E.S., Wonder Girls, Girls' Generation, and Blackpink. Compare the musical elements of their recordings and music videos, as well as their presentation of femininity and gender.

CLOSING

Categories and genres, whether large-scale ones like American popular music, European classical music, jazz, regional Mexican music, and K-pop or small-scale distinctions between the many kinds of rock music, are useful ways to make sense of the variety in the world of music.

But they cannot contain all that variety. Professional musicians have good reason to play within genres because it helps them to develop certain skills to high levels of excellence and to find an audience and sell their performances and recordings to them. But genre boundaries, reinforced by selective use of particular musical elements, are indefensible against musicians' creativity. Those who cross genre boundaries, like Olivia Rodrigo, Julia Wolfe, esperanza spalding, and Blackpink, do so for creative reasons, because they are excited by the music they hear on the other side of the boundary; for economic reasons, because they want to reach new audiences and markets; and for social reasons, because they want to act ethically and harmoniously with people different from themselves.

One of the most exciting aspects of musical life in the age of recordings has been the genre busters. These include jazz musicians who have embraced European classical music, African music, and American popular music; classical musicians who have connected to jazz and popular music; popular musicians who have used classical music, like string orchestras, to serve their purposes; and performers of musical traditions with roots in rural ways of life who understand themselves and their communities within a wide world of connections. Through their music making that moves beyond genre boundaries, these musicians show listeners new ways to imagine their worlds beyond the boundaries that can divide people. Their sympathy for a wide range of musical expressions demonstrates their interest in a wide range of human forms of linguistic and cultural expression. Whether they explicitly link their music to the social problems and conflicts facing the world today or they simply want listeners to enjoy their music and have some fun, their boundary-crossing music can challenge listeners to see (and hear) the world beyond their own horizons.

Some scholars and critics of classical music refer to it as "serious music," implying that other kinds of music are frivolous. Whether their music is for contemplation or for dancing and having fun, the musicians in this chapter's gateways are all making music that asks listeners to take it seriously. No matter the category of music they practice and love most, musicians and their audiences make sense of their worlds through music. They engage with the past; they celebrate, critique, and survive the present; and they envision a new and better future.

THINGS TO THINK ABOUT

- The gateways in this chapter provide examples of how music engages head-on with the challenges facing individuals and societies today. What are these issues? What other contemporary issues are musicians familiar to you dealing with? In addition to song texts, which elements of music do these musicians use to deal with these issues and how do they do that?

- Can music be both entertaining and fun and comment on serious issues facing musicians and their audiences? Is that a contradiction? If not, why not? If so, why?

NEW TERMS

commissions	*hallyu*	power chords
conjunto	K-pop	trap
corrido	*música norteña (norteño)*	tremolo (electronic)

WHERE WILL YOU GO FROM HERE?

IN THIS BOOK, YOU have taken the first few steps into sixty worlds of human music making. Each of these worlds invites you on a deeper and longer journey. We hope that by asking what it is, how it works, what it means, and what is its history to get you started on each of these journeys, you have gained a sense that you better understand music not only in these sixty particular instances but as a meaningful creative activity in every society, past, present, and future. And yet you surely know that there is so much more to explore. Happily, asking and answering these questions gives you the tools for continuing to deepen your understanding of these and other worlds of music. We hope we have inspired you to continue the journeys we began in this book, and to find new ones.

The paths to deeper understanding of music can lead us in several directions. One important journey heads into the future.

As you have learned, humans have, for millennia, responded musically to changing aesthetic, emotional, cultural, social, political, and economic circumstances. We can easily predict that this will continue for millennia. If you follow the path to deeper understanding into the future, you could do a number of things. You could watch out for the emergence of new musical artists in your favorite musical genres and ask if they are bringing anything new to the way music serves the audiences they hope to attract. If you think they are, then how are they doing that? In the lyrics? In the technologies they use? In their manipulation of the elements of music? In such performance practices as dance and dress?

You could also look for the emergence of new musical genres and styles and ask what aesthetic, cultural, social, or political purposes they serve. Do they drive a wedge between existing communities of listeners or do they bring together people with different tastes and experiences? Do they express something new that needs to be "said" but that older genres aren't saying? Is their purpose strictly commercial, or do they satisfy some other human need? In this book we have asked these questions repeatedly when looking at the emergence of new genres and styles such as spirituals, salsa, ragtime, *opera buffa*, gamelan *gong kebyar*, the blues, symphonies, bebop, mariachi, soul, electronic dance music, reggae, and rap, to name just a few. What will be the next new thing, and how will it serve its community or sector of society?

Yet another approach to understanding music in the future would be to follow new intellectual, cultural, social, political, economic, and ecological developments and ask whether and how musicians are responding to them. Climate change promises to be an inevitable part of the planet's future. Every day the news media seem to report on devastation somewhere in the world: whole societies forced to move from a disappearing atoll in the Pacific; melting permafrost in Siberia and Alaska; rising sea water in Bangladesh; desertification in the grasslands of Africa; and destructive fires, floods, and tornadoes across many parts of the United States. Surely musicians in these places are responding in some way to these disasters, and it would be interesting to understand how they are doing so in their music and whether music has any effect on human behavior in response to these crises.

DOI: 10.4324/9781003269304-19

At the time of this writing, some forty armed conflicts are going on around the world, and more will surely follow in the future. Each one of these has almost certainly had a profound effect on music and musicians. Some musicians will respond with songs in support of their side in the conflict; some will be killed for their support of one side or the other; and some will leave to save themselves and find more fertile ground elsewhere, in the process enriching the cultural life of their new homes. Understanding the role of music and the fate of musicians and their traditions in response to natural and human-made disasters are just two paths to follow toward a deeper understanding of music in the future.

This book has also documented the long history of human technological innovation in areas that affect musicians and music. These innovations will continue into the future. It would be fascinating to keep track of the way musicians and their audiences respond to them. For example, if the metaverse, with its augmented and virtual reality, blockchain and NFTs (non-fungible tokens), and artificial intelligence capabilities, becomes a widespread "thing," how will it affect music production, creativity, consumption, aesthetics, and the cultural, social, and political meanings that circulate in musical form through it?

Another journey heads into the past, into the histories of current music, following the many paths toward deeper understanding of musical genres and styles today whose histories are documented in notation and recordings. One path might take you deeper into an existing musical tradition. Another might involve a wider, panoramic view of a range of related current musical styles and their worlds and histories. If you went deeper into one of the traditions introduced in this book, you might listen to and read about all of Bach's Preludes and Fugues from his *Well-tempered Clavier*, all of esperanza spalding's recordings and stylistically diverse projects, all of the recordings of your favorite hip-hop artist or group, or the full range of music produced today on the island of Bali.

An alternate path might lead to a wider view of, say, the full range of compositions of a current composer like Julia Wolfe. She began composing in the 1980s, and her work since then includes other large-scale symphonic and operatic works as well as pieces for chamber ensembles, solo instruments, choir, wind ensemble, and other types of groups (even one for nine bagpipes). You might listen to and try to explain and understand the many new styles of jazz created just in the period from 1950 to 1975. You might look at a large category like rock and study some of its many subgenres with attention to differences in musical style (the elements of music and how they are combined) and to what fans of each subgenre like about this way of making music. You might look at all the different kinds of music performed today in China, the most populous country in the world. Or you might ask and answer questions about the musical elements, meanings, and histories of the latest popular song. Taylor Swift's "All Too Well (10 Minute Version) (Taylor's Version)" (2021) might inspire you to look more into the history of long-duration pop hits and the copyright issues behind Swift's re-recording of her past albums; "We Don't Talk about Bruno" (2021) from the Disney animated feature film *Encanto* might lead you to explore the song's Broadway and Latin American musical influences and the ways the song helps the film explore the theme of unresolved intergenerational trauma.

One other way of thinking about new and deeper paths into understanding and explaining music is to think both about musical styles and genres that are already familiar to you and about those that are unfamiliar and new to you. Because music is something we love, we often gravitate to the familiar. It feels comfortable, and it can be comforting to spend time listening to and thinking about songs, compositions, musicians, and styles that we know and love. But we hope that the paths we have taken through the histories of music in this book will stimulate you to be curious about all human music making and take frequent trips into new territory. As we hope you have learned, music is a gateway to new people, places, and times and to wonderful and rewarding experiences, both aesthetic and ethical. No matter which path you choose, asking and answering questions about how music works, about its meaning, and about its history will lead you into new understandings of the ways that people musically make sense of their worlds. Where will you go from here?

GLOSSARY

A

a cappella choral singing without instrumental accompaniment 4

accelerando increasing tempo 7

achieved status a society status or social role based on merit rather than heredity 4

additive meters meters that combine beats of two and three pulses that add up to meters of 5 (2+3), 7 (2+2+3), 9 (2+2+2+3), 11 (2+2+3+2+2), and so forth 3

aerophone an instrument whose sound is produced by a vibrating column of air 2

aesthetics the area of philosophy that deals with what is beautiful and appealing in the arts based on an analysis of the elements of the art I

alap in Indian music, a nonmetrical improvisation in a particular melodic mode 4

altered extensions chords that add the flat nine, the sharp eleven, and the flat thirteen 11

alto a low-pitched female voice or part 4

alto clef, C clef a five-line staff used for mid-pitched notes 2

antiphons newly composed chanted texts with more elaborate melodies than biblical chants 2

aria in opera, songs with clear melodies 5

arioso a vocal writing style in opera falling somewhere between the florid, melodic arias and the dry recitatives of Italian opera 8

arpeggio leaps through the pitches of a triad 5

articulation the separation of one note in a melody from another I

ascribed status a social status or social role based on heredity rather than achievement 4

atonality the refusal of a tonal center and predictable key relationships 9

attack the onset of a tone I

augmented second an interval of one and a half steps 3

authentic cadence a movement at the end of phrases and pieces from a triad built on the fifth degree of the scale (V) to a triad built on the first degree or tonic of the scale (I) 4

B

backbeat accents on beats 2 and 4 in a meter of 4, a common dance-oriented rhythmic practice in rhythm & blues 12

ballad a short song that tells a story 7

banjo a fretted, long-necked plucked lute with five strings running along the neck and a sixth, shorter string running halfway up the neck 7

bar in musical notation a group of beats I

Baroque a word for a misshapen pearl, used to refer to the elaborate style of art and music from 1600 to 1750 5

bass low-pitched male voice or part 4

bass clef, F clef the five-line staff used for low-pitched notes 2

basso continuo instrumental bass line and chords improvised by a keyboard or lute player 5

bebop a style of jazz featuring solo improvisation and harmonic complexity, at often very fast tempos 11

bel canto beautiful singing, a style of early nineteenth-century Italian opera 7

bell an idiophone with a depth greater than its surface diameter 5

big band a jazz ensemble with a typical instrumentation of five saxophones, four or five trombones, four or five trumpets, and a rhythm section typically including drums, bass, piano, and guitar 10

block chords a series of chords with the pitches sounding simultaneously 1

blue notes pitches on the third and seventh scale degree of the major scale that are lowered to the pitches of a minor mode; common in the blues 9

bluegrass a genre of rural American music from Appalachia consisting of songs and instrumental tunes played by an ensemble of mandolin, banjo, fiddle, guitar, and bass 7

blues a strophic song most typically in a repeating AAB form of twelve bars that originated in African American communities of the American South and that deals with the hardships and struggles of daily life 9

bourgeoisie city dwellers who provided professional services 7

break a term used in jazz and some popular music for a section of a performance when much of a rhythm section suddenly stops and other ensemble members continue playing (sometimes in solo improvisation) to a silent ongoing pulse 10

breakdancing acrobatic style of improvised solo dance developed as part of hip-hop culture 13

bridge (1) a section of a popular music or jazz form that typically departs from yet connects the sections that precede and follow it, such as the B in AABA form 11

bridge (2) in a song, a section that usually occurs only once connecting two repetitions of the chorus toward the end of the song 14

C

cabaletta the second part of a double aria in an early nineteenth-century Italian opera 7

cadence a musical gesture marking the end or a phrase of music 4

calypso a style of song that developed in Trinidad in the early twentieth century that provides social commentary on topical issues and events 11

Candomblé an African-derived Brazilian religion 6

canon a collection of works that scholars, critics, performers, and audiences have judged particularly worthy, important, influential, and possessing artistic value 6

cantabile the first part of a double aria in early nineteenth-century Italian opera 7

cantata multi-movement religious works for the Lutheran liturgy 5

cantus firmus a fixed song tune used as the basis for Renaissance sacred vocal polyphony 4

capitalist owners of enterprises that employ large numbers of workers 7

castrato a male singer castrated before puberty to prevent his voice from changing from soprano to tenor or bass 5

cavatina a character's introductory aria in early nineteenth-century Italian opera 7

chant, chanting religious melodies, religious singing 2

choir a group of singers supported by a church, school or other institution 2

chord three or more pitches performed simultaneously I

chord cluster a chord that includes many adjacent pitches sounding together 9

chordophones instruments with vibrating strings 3

chord progression the set of chords used to harmonize the melody of the head in a jazz performance 10

chorus (1) a group of singers 2

chorus (2) in a song, a section that repeats throughout the song with the same melody but different lyrics each time 2

chorus (3) the name given in jazz to one repetition of a form that serves as a basis for improvisation 10

chromatic scale a scale with twelve pitches to the octave 3

civic nationalism the notion that everyone living in a nation had the right to be full-fledged citizens regardless of their ethnic origins 8

civilization the culture of cities 2

classic blues blues usually sung by Black female singers accompanied by a band or a pianist 9

clave underlying rhythmic pattern in salsa music 12

clavichord a Baroque keyboard instrument with metal blades stopping the strings 5

clavier a generic term for keyboard in German 5

clawhammer style playing the banjo by striking strings with the fingernails of a curved hand 7

clef a sign at the beginning of the staff to indicate which pitches are assigned to which lines 2

coda the tail or ending added at the end of a musical composition or performance 3

collective improvisation simultaneous improvisation by two or more players, especially in jazz 10

coloratura a singer's display or ornamental creativity and virtuosity in opera 7

colotomic structure in Javanese gamelan music, the cycles of low-pitched gongs that "cut" the time into units of varying length 5

combo short for "combination," a small jazz ensemble 10

commissions promise to pay a composer for a composition 14

comping a term short for "accompanying" used in jazz for the way a guitarist or pianist plays in support of a soloist 12

compound duple meter a subdivision of beats in two-beat meter into three pulses per beat 8

concept album an album that is conceived as an integral whole, with interrelated songs arranged in a particular order 12

concerto an instrumental composition for soloist or a small group and orchestra 5

conjunct motion melodies that mainly move through adjacent pitches of a scale 2

conjunto in Latin music, a small group of musicians 14

consort an ensemble of musical instruments, particularly during the Renaissance 4

contrary motion when two polyphonic lines ascend and descend in opposite directions 4

corrido storytelling Mexican song 14

counterpoint, contrapuntal texture the simultaneous singing or playing of many melodic lines 4

Counter-Reformation a movement to restore the dignity and sanctity of the Roman Catholic Church in the wake of the Protestants' attacks on both 4

countertenor falsetto male voice 4

country blues a type of blues that emerged in rural areas that typically involved a male singer accompanying himself on the guitar 9

country music a commercial genre of popular music rooted in early twentieth-century rural music, mostly from white communities of the American South 11

course one string or a set of close-together strings tuned to the same pitch and stopped or pressed onto the fingerboard by one finger 3

cover in popular music, a new version of an existing song 12

crescendo increasing loudness in a musical phrase I

cyclical mass a mass with the same *cantus firmus* (fixed song) for each text in the ordinary of the mass 4

cymbal a metallic idiophone in the shape of a flat plate with no depth 5

D

decay the shape of a tone after the attack until it ends in silence I

decrescendo decreasing loudness in a musical phrase I

development the section in a sonata form where melodies modulate 6

diatonic scales scales consisting of whole steps and half steps 2

diegetic sound and music sound and music in a film or play that is heard by the characters and in the story world of the film or play 10

disco popular form of dance music in the 1970s enjoyed at nightclubs where audiences danced to continuous music played on records for hours at a time 12, 13

disjunct motion melodies that mainly employ large melodic intervals 2

dodecaphonic a scale of twelve pitches to the octave 3

dominant key the key on the fifth degree of the scale 5

dominant seventh chord a four-note chord on the fifth scale degree consisting of a major triad plus the flatted seventh degree of the scale 5

double aria an aria in two parts, each part separated by a brief orchestral *ritornello* 7

double reed two thin reeds striking one another to start the vibration in a tube 2

drop a pause, sometimes to silence, in the percussive elements of an electronic dance music track 13

Drum the circle of singers and drummers around a large bass drum 8

duple meter a regularly recurring two-beat meter counted 1-2-1-2-1-2 and so on I

dynamics change in the loudness and softness of music I

E

early music   European church, court, and concert music composed before 1750 5

English horn   a low-pitched cousin of the oboe 7

Enlightenment   an eighteenth-century political philosophy seeking freedom from autocracy and other forms of authority through the exercise of reason 6, 7

envelope   the shape of a tone from attack to decay I

episode   in a Baroque fugue, a polyphony section with imitative polyphony based on the subject 5

equal-tempered scale   a scale in which all the half steps of a 12-pitch scale are exactly the same size 3

ethnic nationalism   the notion that each ethnic groups is a "nationality" with the right to its own nation-state 8

explaining music   statements, descriptions, classifications, labels, analyses, interpretations, and claims about causes and effects that account in words (or diagrams, formulas, and graphs) for particular musical phenomena or set of facts in our musical experience I

exposition (1)   in a Baroque fugue, the opening section of imitative polyphony 5

exposition (2)   the opening section of sonata form 6

F

falsetto   a "false" voice that allows men, and women, to sing in a register above their normal, speaking vocal range 4

feedback   an effect that happens when an audio input, like an electric guitar or a microphone, receives the sound from an audio output, like a speaker, in a loop, which often results in a high-pitched screeching sound 12

fife   a small side-blown flute 9

final   the most important pitch of a mode, the pitch it ends on 2

flute   an instrument on which a sound wave in a vibrating column of air is initiated by blowing over an edge 1

folk music   a 1950s and 1960s genre featuring singers and acoustic guitarists, who drew on rural music and protest songs 12

folk songs   songs of rural peasants that were idealized as the ancient, unadulterated expression "national soul," in German *das Folk* (the people) 8

form, musical   the way a performance of music unfolds through time from beginning to end I

forte   a loud sound I

fortepiano   literally "loud-soft," a predecessor of the piano with a range of five or six octaves and a lighter, thinner sound than the modern piano 6

free jazz   a style of jazz that emerged in the 1960s seeking to break down conventions of rhythm, pulse, form, texture, and harmony, and departing from the harmonic structures and steady pulse that had long characterized jazz 12

fugue   a tightly organized piece featuring imitative counterpoint 5

fundamental   the slowest vibrating wave in a tone, the one with the longest wave form I

funk   a musical style that originated in the mid-1960s characterized by complex, multi-layered syncopation and grooves with driving, percussive bass lines, and guitar riffs featuring the wah-wah pedal in combination with percussive effects 12

fuzz box   an electronic effects pedal that distorts timbre 12

G

gamelan   in Java, a large orchestra of around forty instruments made of bronze gongs or metal keys, plus drums and a bowed fiddle 5

gamelan *gong kebyar*   the most popular type of Balinese gamelan orchestra, comprised of mostly bronze percussion instruments and typified by rhythmic complexity and excitement in performance 9

gangsta rap   a hip-hop subgenre that chronicles the lifestyle of the urban poor of Los Angeles 13

gat   the metrical section of a North Indian classical performance 4

gateway   a recording of music and a set of five questions asked of the recording that provide a portal to a world of music I

genre, musical   a way of labeling and categorizing music that is associated with a community of musicians and listeners I

Gesamtkunstwerk   Richard Wagner's concept of the "total artwork," where all of the elements of drama (poetry, music, stage design, and acting) were united in one work 8

gharana   a "house" or family of hereditary musicians and their students 4

glissando   a slide between two pitches 7

gong   an idiophone with a surface diameter greater than its depth 5

gospel quartets   four-part singing groups that performed gospel music; black gospel quartets first became popular in the 1930s 8

gospel songs   a genre of Christian religious songs that emerged in the late nineteenth century, characterized by their singability and relative simplicity compared to earlier hymns 8

Grand Staff   two parallel five-line staffs linked together, one with a treble and one with a bass clef 2

Gregorian chant   a label for monophonic Christian chant preserved in musical notation starting around the ninth century that acknowledges the influence of Pope Gregory I on the liturgy of the Catholic Church 2

groove   in jazz and popular music, a short, repeated musical pattern; ostinatos can be rhythmic, melodic, or chordal 11

guitarrón   a large guitar-shaped fretted lute 10

guru   a music teacher and spiritual guide 4

H

habanera rhythm   a Latin rhythm from Cuba characteristic of the tango 9

half step   the distance or interval between two adjacent keys on the piano 1

hallyu   the Korean wave, the spread of Korean popular culture internationally 14

hard bop   a style of jazz that features the rhythms of gospel and rhythm & blues 12

hardcore rap   a style of rap that arose in the East Coast scene in the 1980s that is typified by expressions of anger and confrontation 13

harmonic   the sound of an overtone rather than the fundamental of a tone 3

harmony   a combination of tones sounding simultaneously I

harpsichord   a Baroque keyboard instrument with quills plucking the strings 5

head   in jazz, a composition that serves as the main melody, usually appearing at the beginning and end of a given performance 10

heptatonic scale   a set of seven pitches arranged from low to high 1

heterophony, heterophonic texture   two or more instruments playing the same melody together, but slightly differently 3

hi-hat   two cymbals played with a pedal in a drum set 10

hillbilly records   recordings targeted at rural whites during the 1920s and the 1930s 11

hip-hop culture   music (made by DJs and MCs), dance (breakdancing), and visual art (graffiti) 13

honky-tonk music   a style of country music performed at "honky-tonk" bars 11

horn   a buzzed-lip aerophone with a curved tube 4

I

icon, iconic sign a sign type that links two phenomena by similarity or resemblance I

idée fixe an obsession, the recurring theme in all movements of Hector Berlioz's *Symphonie Fantastique* 7

idiophone an instrument whose wood or metal or other natural material vibrates 3

imitative polyphony a polyphonic texture in which each voice or part enters in succession on the same melody 4

impressionism an artistic movement in late nineteenth-century France 9

index, indexical sign a sign type that indexes or is associated with or is linked to something else I

Industrial Revolution a period of invention of machines that enabled the more efficient production and transportation of goods and the concentration of wealth in the hands of "industrialists" 7

inherent polyphony the experience of polyphony when a monophonic line is played 1

interval the distance between any two different pitches 1

J

jazz combo a small jazz ensemble including a rhythm section of drums, bass, and piano or guitar, often along with one or two other instrumental soloists 11

jazz fusion a broad genre label for styles that combine jazz with other styles such as rock and funk 12

jazz standard a song that is frequently used as a vehicle for jazz performance 10, 11

jukebox coin-operated record player 10

K

kettle drum a single-headed, bowl-shaped drum 4

keyboard a generic term used for all types of instruments that employ the layout of long, usually white, keys for the seven-pitch diatonic scale and short, usually black, keys for the five additional chromatic pitches of European music 5

kotekan a technique in Balinese gamelan where melodic and/or rhythmic figurations too fast to be played by one person are divided between two partners in a variety of configurations, sometimes involving a pattern where partners alternate playing every other note 9

K-pop a catch-all term regularly used for the popular music of South Korea 14

L

language sign a sign type that that conveys meaning in precise and clearly understood ways I

lap steel guitar a guitar set on the player's lap and played with metal picks on the fingers of the right hand and a steel bar in the left hand 11

leapwise motion melodies that mainly employ large melodic intervals 2

legato playing the tones of the melody with smooth connections between them I

Leitmotifs guiding or leading motives, a term coined by Richard Wagner 8

liturgies the ritual rules and practices for sacred services 2

loudness the perception of the amplitude of a tone's wave form I

lute (1) a generic name for a family of chordophones with a body and a neck 3

lute (2) a Renaissance plucked pear-shaped lute with a vaulted body (that is, a rounded back rather than a flat back) made from a set of thin wooden ribs glued together 4

lyre a stringed instrument with a resonating body and a frame holding five or six strings, which are plucked 2

M

madrigal a genre of polyphonic love songs in Italian and English that first appeared around 1530 4

major scale, major key a scale represented by the seven pitch names with a tonic on C (C D E F G A B) 5

major second the interval of a whole step between two adjacent scale degrees 5

major third the interval between, for example, C to E or G to B 4

major triad a chord consisting of three pitches: tonic, major third, and perfect fifth 5

maqam an Arab melodic mode that specifies intervals between pitches, characteristic melodic gestures, the addition of chromatic pitches, and typical modulations 2

mbira a Shona (Zimbabwe) twenty-two tuned, plucked metal keys mounted on a flat soundboard 3

measure in musical notation, a group of beats I

mehter an Ottoman band of valveless trumpets, reeds, and percussion 9

melisma, melismatic singing each syllable of the text is set to many pitches of the singing 2

melodic shape the movement of a melody, for example, ascending, descending, arc-shaped, undulating, flat I

melody, melodic line or part a series of pitches performed over time usually by a single voice or instrument I

membranophone instrument with stretched skins or "heads," often called drums 4

meter the organization of pulsation or beat I

metrical music with a beat or pulse I

microtone, microtonal interval an interval smaller than a half step 2

minimalism a genre label given to compositions that emphasize pulsating repetition of a small number of musical elements 12

minor scale, minor key a scale represented by the seven pitch names with a tonic on A (A B C D E F G) 5

minor second the interval of a half step between two adjacent scale degrees 5

minor third an interval between, for example, E to G or D to F 4

minstrel show white entertainers, masked in blackface, imitating and ridiculing both free and enslaved African Americans in ostensibly black styles of speech, dance, and music 7

minuet a middle movement of a Classical-period symphony or work for string quartet named for a slow, courtly dance in triple meter called a minuet; the trio is another minuet, often in a contrasting key 6

modal jazz a style of jazz where musicians improvise over melodic modes that last for long durations rather than over quickly changing harmonies 12

modernism the breaking of artistic boundaries, especially at the turn of the twentieth century 9

modes seven-pitch heptatonic scales with one pitch defined as the final or most important pitch 2

modulation changes in one or another element of music: a modal modulation, a key modulation, a metric modulation, and so forth 2

monody a vocal melody accompanied by bass and chords 5

monophony, monophonic texture a performance with a single line or melody I

motet a sacred work composed on a Latin text 4

motive a short melodic, rhythmic, or harmonic idea 6

music drama the term that Richard Wagner used to describe his works, in place of the term "opera" 8

música norteña (norteño) a musical style from northern Mexico 14

musical nationalism music composers wrote expressing nationalist sentiments in the hope of inspiring their people 8

N

nationalism in nineteenth-century Europe, the notion that each ethnic group has the right to its own nation-state 8

neoclassicism a style of twentieth-century classical music that includes references to elements of Classic-period music 11

neo-Romanticism modern compositions that return to nineteenth century tonality and musical forms 13

neotraditionalism in jazz a trend that values older styles and historical repertoire from earlier in the twentieth century 13

neumes a collection of graphic symbols written above the text of Christian chants to indicate the shape and character of a melody 2

New Orleans jazz a style of early jazz where a rhythm section backs up three melodic instruments (usually trumpet or cornet, clarinet, and trombone) that play in polyphony, improvising independent but interrelated melodic lines 10

nocturne evening serenade for piano 7

nonmetrical music without a beat or pulse I

note a visual representation of a tone in musical notation I

O

obbligato in band music, a second melody played simultaneously and in counterpoint with the main melody 9

oblique motion when one line stays at the same pitch while a second part ascends or descends 4

octave the interval between two pitches whose ratio of vibration is 2:1; perceived as "the same" pitch I

offbeat a beat in between two typically accented beats 13

opera a theatrical musical genre that tells stories through recitative, aria, instrumental music, acting, and dancing 5

opus (Op.) from the Latin for "work," a numerical designation used by Classical-period composers and publishers to identify their compositions in chronological order 6

oratorio a multi-movement composition that tells a biblical story in the vernacular (local) language rather than in the Latin of the Catholic liturgy 5

orchestration the art of composing for orchestral instruments singly and in combination 7

Ordinary of the Mass texts included in every celebration of mass 2

orixás a pantheon of male and female deities in *Candomblé* 6

ornamentation the addition of short tones to the main tones of a melody I

ostinato a short, repeated musical pattern; ostinatos can be rhythmic, melodic, or chordal 1

overtones waves in a waveform that vibrate faster than the fundamental I

overtone singing two sounds from one voice, one produced by the vocal cords and the other by resonating the overtones of the throat-produced drone tone in such a way as to create simultaneous high-pitched sounds 1

P

panpipe a flute that consists of a set of tubes of different lengths, each of which plays one pitch 1

parallel major and parallel minor keys keys that have the same tonic pitch 10

parallel motion two polyphonic voices that maintain the same interval between them 4

pedal steel guitar an electric zither played with picks on the right hand, a steel bar in the left hand, and a set of pedals and knee levers that adjust the pitches of strings 11

pentatonic scale a scale with five pitches to an octave 3

perfect fifths intervals with a frequency ratio of 3:2, for example, C to G 3

perfect fourths intervals with a frequency ratio of 4:3, for example, C to F 3

perspective in painting, the illusion, on two dimensions of the canvas, of three-dimensional human experience 4

piano (1) a soft sound I

piano (2) a keyboard instrument on which hammers attached to the keys strike the strings 6

pitch the perception of the rate of vibration of the fundamental frequency in a tone I

pizzicato plucking rather than bowing a violin, viola, cello, or bass 7

plagal cadence, amen cadence a movement at the end of phrases and pieces from a triad built on the fourth degree of the scale (IV) to a triad built on the first degree or tonic of the scale (I) 4

point of imitation a particular entrance of imitative polyphony 4

polymeter the simultaneous presence of two meters in a musical texture 1

polyphony, polyphonic texture a performance with many lines or parts I

polyrhythm a texture made of multiple, different, simultaneous rhythms 6, 9

polytonality the simultaneous employment of music in more than one key 9

postmodernism an artistic movement that reacted against the modernist styles of the 1950s and 1960s 13

power chords loud guitar chords containing only the root and the fifth 14

pow-wows intertribal gatherings of the Indigenous people of the United States and Canada that feature drumming and singing for social, contest, and exhibition dancing 8

prelude a piece of music before another piece of music; short, free-form pieces spun out from a single melodic or rhythmic idea 5

prepared piano a piano into which screws and other objects are inserted between the strings to alter its timbre and emphasize its nature as a percussion instrument 12

program a narrative expressed in music 7

program music, programmatic music music composed to express the emotions, moods, and meanings of an unperformed verbal narrative 5, 7

proletariat wage laborers in factories and industry 7

Proper of the Mass texts for particular days of the Christian calendar 2

psalms biblical poems in praise of God 2

push-ups the verses of a pow-wow song 8

Q

qin a Chinese zither consisting of a long piece of resonant, lacquered wood over which seven silk strings are stretched 3

R

race records   phonograph recordings produced between the 1920s and 1940s and marketed to African Americans 9

rag, raag, raga   an Indian melodic mode 4

ragtime   a style often played on the piano featuring a "ragged" or syncopated rhythm accompanied by a steady bass line with regular accents in duple meter 9

range   the distance between the highest and lowest pitches in a section or piece of music 2

rap, rapping   a genre emphasizing improvised rhymes 13

Rastafari Movement   a religious and social movement that arose in Jamaica in the first half of the twentieth century rooted in Abrahamic religious beliefs and centered on Africa as a spiritual homeland and destination. It takes many forms and is often associated with reggae 13

recapitulation   the section in sonata form where the opening themes return 6

recitative   in opera, melodic and rhythmic text recitation 5

recorder   a whistle flute with a beak that channels the player's breath over a sharp edge to produce the sound 4

reed instrument   a vibrating column of air is started either by a two thin pieces of cane or wood beating against one another (a double reed) or one piece of cane beating against a fixed stock (a single reed) 3

refrain   a melody that regularly returns during a performance 3

reggae   a popular music genre from Jamaica 13

relative major and minor   major and minor keys that share the same set of pitches 5

Renaissance   a period of rebirth of interest in Ancient Greek and Roman culture 4

rhapsody   a one-movement composition that has a free-flowing, improvisatory character and that often evokes national sentiment through the use of folk or newly composed folk-like melodies 10

rhythm (1)   the temporal dimension of music I

rhythm (2)   the organization of the duration of tones in a performance I

rhythm section   in jazz, the drums, bass, and piano or guitar in a combo or big band 11

ring shout   an early African American religious ritual featuring dancing in a circle, hand claps, and call-and-response singing 8

ritardando, ritard   slowing down 1

ritornello   returns of an instrumental melody in both instrumental and vocal genres 5

rock and roll   a genre label first used in the 1950s to describe rhythm & blues marketed to both black and white audiences and often featuring white musicians 12

rocksteady   a Jamaican genre developed in the mid-1960s 13

romances   twelfth-century Medieval stories written about mythical and legendary figures 8

Romanticism, Romantic   expressions in literature, music, and painting of interior experiences of passion, restlessness, longing, and striving; emerged in the nineteenth century 6, 7

rondo form   a form that alternates a fixed, returning melody (R) with excursions or episodes to other keys and other melodies (e.g., ARBRCR and so on) 3

rubato   ("robbed time" in Italian), an unsteady beat or pulse created by slightly holding some beats and slightly rushing others 7

S

sama'i   a composed instrumental form in a meter of ten beats 3

samba   songs with drumming for the pre-Lenten Carnival 6

samples   short clips of existing recordings that are often reproduced in loops and manipulated with any number of effects 13

scale   the arrangement of the pitches of a piece of music in ascending order from low to high 1

scale degree   the ordinal number of a pitch in ascending order 2

scat singing   a style of improvisation in jazz where singers use vocables, often in ways that imitate the sounds of musical instruments 10

scratching   a technique where a DJ moves a vinyl record quickly backwards and forwards with one hand on a turntable to create a rhythmic sound 13

sequence   a melodic phrase repeated at different pitch levels 3

serialism   a compositional technique that emerged in the early 1920s where various elements of music were organized into ordered sequences; most notably pitches were often ordered into twelve-tone rows 9

seventh chord   a triad plus a fourth note a major or minor third above the fifth degree of the scale 5

shawm   a loud, double-reed aerophone used in Medieval European music and a successor to the Turkish *zurna* 3, 9

sign, signal   an object or an action that has meaning to a person or a group of people I

Singspiel   a musical drama in German with spoken dialog rather than recitative 6

sitar   an Indian long-necked, fretted plucked lute with more than twenty strings 4

ska   a Jamaican genre of the 1960s that emphasizes every offbeat 13

solmization, solfege   a pedagogical system of syllables (do-re-mi-fa-sol-la-ti-do) on which singers can sing melodies 2

solo   a performance by a single performer I

sonata   an instrumental composition for a soloist or a small group of soloists 5

sonata form   the name given by nineteenth-century music theorists to a common Classical-period form, which includes an exposition, a development, and a recapitulation 6

soprano   high-pitched female voice or part 4

sousaphone   a version of the tuba invented by John Philip Sousa that marching band players support on their shoulders 9

spirituals   religious songs of African Americans from both during and after the time of slavery 8

staccato   playing the tones of a melody by shortening and leaving spaces between them I

staff   a set of horizontal lines and spaces on which notes are placed 2

steel pan   a pitched percussion instrument made from steel oil drums by pounding the surface into flat sections that can be tuned 11

steelbands   large ensembles of various sizes of steel pans plus a rhythm section known as the "engine room" consisting of non-pitched percussion instruments including a drum set, congas, large metal scrapers, and irons struck with metal rods 11

stepwise motion   melodies that mainly move through adjacent pitches of a scale 2

strain   the melody of each section in a march 9

stride piano   a style of piano playing that emerged in the first decades of the twentieth century among African American early jazz pianists which featured the left hand "striding" between bass notes and chords, along with heavy syncopation and many other virtuosic techniques 9

string quartet   an ensemble that consists of four players performing on instruments of the violin family: two violins, viola, and cello 6

strophe   the combination of a poetic stanza or verse with music 5

strophic song, strophic form   a song or song form that repeats the same melody for each verse 5

style, musical   the manner in which musical elements like melody and rhythm are deployed and combined in a large number of pieces or performances I

subject   in a Baroque fugue, the opening melody that is then treated to imitative polyphony 5

swing feel   beats are subdivided unequally with the first note longer than the second note 9

syllabic singing   each syllable of the text is set to one pitch of the melody 2

symbolist poets   a group of French poets in the late nineteenth century who were known for breaking the formal boundaries of poetic tradition in elusive, free-form, illogical poetry devoid of traditional poetic meters and rhyme schemes 9

sympathetic strings   strings that vibrate in response to a plucked pitch 4

symphonic poem   an instrumental composition that expresses emotion and tells a story 7

symphony   a multi-movement work for string orchestra with the addition of wind instruments and percussion that lacks the contrast between soloist and orchestra of a concerto 6

syncopation, syncopated   rhythmic accents between strong beats or on weak beats I

synth pad   a mellow sustained synthesizer sound 13

synthesizer (synth)   an electronic musical instrument that generates sound by creating waveforms with electronic oscillators and manipulating their timbres with other electronic components; typically played by keyboards 13

T

tabla   North Indian pair of kettle drums played with the hands 4

tablature   a notation method that indicates how an instrument is to be played 3

tal, taal, tala   an Indian rhythmic mode 4

tambura   North Indian plucked lute for playing drone accompaniments 4

taqsim   a nonmetrical improvisation in a particular melodic mode (*maqam* in Arabic) 3

tempo   the speed of a performance, which may be fast or slow or changing I

tenor   high-pitched male voice or part 4

tenor clef, C clef   a five-line staff used for mid-pitched notes 2

territory bands   big bands that performed in a geographic area within a day trip of their home city 10

text painting   musical icons for the ideas and sentiments in the text 4

texture   the way musical lines or parts are woven together in a musical performance I

theka   the basic pattern of strokes on the *tabla* in a given *tala* 4

theme   a melody appearing in sonata form 6

theme and variations   a form based on varied repetitions (in the melody, harmony, or timbre) of a melody 4

theorbo   a lute with an enormously long neck and fourteen courses of strings capable of playing low-pitched bass tones 5

throat-singing   a single singer produces a drone pitch and, at the same time, uses the mouth to amplify the set of overtones in the drone and produce a high-pitched melody 1

tihai   a highly syncopated rhythmic pattern played three times at the end of a *sitar* or *tabla* solo 4

timbales   single-headed drums with shallow metal bodies, usually tuned to higher pitches than the tom-toms of a drum set 12

timbre   differences in wave forms that allow us to distinguish one musical instrument or voice from others; tone quality; tone color I

timpani   single-headed, bowl-shaped kettle drums 3

toasting   a form of rhythmic storytelling from Jamaica 13

tonal harmony, tonality   harmony based on major and minor triads and other chords in a particular key with cadences that move from the chord on the fifth scale degree (V) to the tonic (I) 5

tone, musical   sounds that human beings make and interpret as musical consisting of five components: overtone structure, pitch, duration, envelope, and loudness I

tone clusters   many keys played simultaneously with the arm, elbow, or entire hand 12

tone poem   an instrumental composition that expresses emotion and tells a story 7

tone row   an ordered, non-repeating sequence of the twelve chromatic pitches where none of the pitches is more important than the other 9

tonic   the first degree of a scale 4

total serialism   the organization of all elements of music, including timbre, texture, rhythm, and dynamics, into "rows" that provide the underlying logic of a composition 12

trap   a hip-hop subgenre featuring deep bass lines, bass drum sounds from a Roland TR-808 drum machine, and varied rhythms on a crisp synthesized hi-hat 14

treble clef, G clef   the five-line staff used for high-pitched notes 2

tremolo (1)   on strings, short, rapid, back-and-forth bowing 9

tremolo (2)   an electronic effect used on instruments like the electric guitar to quickly and repeatedly raise and lower the volume of the tone 14

triad   A triad is a three-pitch cord build from low to high on the interval of a third, for example, A-C-E and C-E-G 4

triple meter   a regularly recurring three-beat meter counted 1-2-3-1-2-3-1-2-3 and so on I

triplets   the subdivision of a beat into three pulses 6

trombone   a buzzed-lip instrument made of metal with a slide to change the length, and thus the pitch, of tones played on it 4

troubadour   a Medieval singer of secular songs 4

trumpet   a generic term for a buzzed-lip aerophone made of metal 4

twelve-tone serialism   a compositional system in which twelve pitches are arranged in a series or "row" 11

U

'ud   a fretless, short-necked, pear-shaped, plucked lute with a vaulted (that is, rounded) back and a pegbox bent back at ninety degrees to the neck 3

underscore   music accompanying the action in a film 10

understanding music   finding music orderly rather than chaotic; pleasant rather than unpleasant; predictable rather than unpredictable; meaningful rather than meaningless; and familiar rather than unfamiliar I

unison   a performance with many performers singing the same pitch simultaneously I

upper extensions   in jazz, chord tones that extend above the octave such as the ninth, the eleventh, and the thirteenth 11

V

verse (1)   a group of lines in a poem, also called a stanza 5

verse (2)   a synonym for strophe 7

vibrato   a pulsating slight raising and lowering of the pitch of a tone 2

vihuela (1)   a sixteenth-century flat-backed waisted lute with gut frets tied around the neck and six double courses of gut strings plucked by the fingers 4

vihuela (2)   a small Mexican guitar-shaped fretted lute 10
viol   one of a family of waisted bowed lutes with frets 4
vocables   nonlexical syllables in song lyrics 1
vocalese   a process in which instrumental jazz compositions and well-known recorded improvisations are given lyrics and sung instead of played 13

W

wah-wah pedal   an electronic pedal that modifies the frequencies emphasized in a given tone in a way that, when it is rocked forwards and backwards, it mimics the sound of a human voice saying "wah-wah" 12
walking bass line   a mostly stepwise pulsatile line played by a plucked upright or electric bass in bebop and some other styles of jazz 11
waltz   a ballroom dance for couples in triple meter 7
waveform   a complex set of waves vibrating in air l
well-tempered   well-tuned and able to play in all keys of the tonal system 5

whole step   the distance or interval between every other key on the piano 1
whole-tone scales   an equidistant six-pitch (hexatonic) scale that eliminates half steps 9
world music   hybrid musical performances that combine traditional and popular music 13

X

xylophone   an idiophone with multiple struck wooden keys 3

Y

yodel, yodeling   alternation between chest-resonated tones and high-pitched, head-resonated tones 1

Z

zither   stringed instrument with a resonator but no added neck 3

SOURCES

Part opener image credits

Part I, The Yorck Project, Wikimedia Commons. http://warfare.gq/13/
Bayad-wa-Riyad-f10r.htm
Part II, Kyle Flubacker
Part III, Christian Bertrand/Shutterstock.

Introduction

The distinction between icons and indexes as sources of musical
emotion is indebted to Thomas Turino, *Music as Social Life: The Politics of Participation* (Chicago: University of Chicago Press, 2008).

Chapter 1

Gateway 1, Music of Foragers

This gateway is indebted to Michelle Kisliuk, *Seize the Dance! BaAka
Musical Life and the Ethnography of Performance* (New York:
Oxford University Press, 1998/2001).

Gateway 2, Music of Nomadic Pastoralists

"The river is alive. Rivers sing." Theodore Levin, with Tuvan researcher
Valentina Süzükei, *Where Rivers and Mountains Sing: Sound, Music,
and Nomadism in Tuva and Beyond* (Bloomington: Indiana University Press, 2006).
This gateway is based on Levin, *Where Rivers and Mountains Sing*, p. 29.

Gateway 3, Music of Horticultural Societies

This gateway is based on the research of French ethnomusicologist
Hugo Zemp. See, for example, Hugo Zemp, "Aspects of 'Are'are
Musical Theory," *Ethnomusicology 23*(1) (1978): 5–48.
Hugo Zemp details his experience of the music industry in "The/
An Ethnomusicologist in the Record Business," *Yearbook for Tradi-
tional Music 28* (1996): 36–55.

Chapter 2

Gateway 4, Buddhist Music

"sensually pleasing offering," from Ter Ellingson, *Mandala of Sound:
Concepts and Sound Structures in Tibetan Buddhism*, Ph.D. dissertation, University of Wisconsin, Madison, 1979.

"This music," one Tibetan monk said, "is more beneficial than a hundred years of meditation." Ellingson, p. xiii.
". . . according to their good and bad deeds," from Damien Keown,
Buddhism: A Very Short Introduction (New York: Oxford University
Press, 1996).
The discussion of the Four Noble Truths is derived from Keown,
pp. 46–48.
"the ultimate goal of Buddhism is to put an end to suffering and
rebirth . . . by fulfilling the human potential for goodness and happiness." Keown, p. 46.
The Bon religion acknowledged "nine vocal modulations," including
"*the dog's voice, barking and growling, . . . the beautiful voiced
parrot*" and "*the fluctuating voice of the lark.*" Ellingson, p. 101.
"body-cavity voice," Ellingson, p. 395.
"tone-color chants," Ellingson, p. 467; "voice of the hybrid yak-bull"
and the "*roaring voice of the* [*slayer of the*] *Lord of Death*," Ellingson, p. 400.
"They will rattle your bones." Mickey Hart in Frankie Wright, "Enchant-
ing Spirit of Buddhism," *Los Angeles Times*, November 16, 1991.
To understand melody as an aid to meditative visualization in Tibetan
Buddhist ritual liturgies, read Jeffrey W. Cupchik, "Buddhism as
Performing Art: Visualizing Music in the Tibetan Sacred Ritual
Music Liturgies," *Yale Journal of Music & Religion 1*(1) (2015):
31–62, https://doi.org/10.17132/2377–231X.1010.

Gateway 5, Christian Chant

This gateway is based in part on David Hiley, *Gregorian Chant* (Cambridge: Cambridge University Press, 2009).
Hildegard's biography is indebted to Sabina Flanagan, *Hildegard of
Bingen, 1098–1179: A Visionary Life* (New York: Routledge, 1989).
"the heavens were opened to me . . ." and "a low opinion (of myself)"
from Hildegard's autobiography, quoted in Flanagan, p. 4.
"Who does not bewail . . ." and "helpers . . . can produce . . ." Hiley,
p. 174.

Gateway 6, Qur'anic Chant

The Quran, trans. Maulana Wahiduddin Khan and Farida Khanam
(Chennai: Goodread Books, 2009).
"divine and inimitable beauty," Kristina Nelson, *The Art of Reciting
the Qur'an* (Austin: University of Texas Press, 1985), p. 13.
"calms the child and refreshes the camel on the long journey." Nelson, p. 43.
"the beautiful melody is a spirit from God which revives burning
hearts." Nelson, p. 44.

"extract" the meaning of verse "bring the listener closer to the Qur'an." Nelson, p. 64.

"If hell is so lovely and pleasant, take me to it." Nelson, p. 65.

"Ah, would that I had sent forth [good deeds] for [this] my [future] life" and quoted phrases in the next sentence. Nelson, p. 64.

Chapter 3

Opening

The data on urban populations in 1350 is from Tertius Chandler and Gerald Fox, *Three Thousand Years of Urban Growth* (New York: Academic Press, 1974).

Gateway 7, Music of China

Details on the *qin* and *qin* playing are based in part on Bell Yung, "Instruments: Qin," in Virginia Danielson, Scott Marcus, and Dwight Reynolds, eds., *Garland Encyclopedia of World Music: Volume 7: East Asia: China, Japan, and Korea* (New York: Routledge, 2002), pp. 157–165. This source also contains a transcription of a performance, different from the one in the gateway recording, of "Three Variations on Yang Pass."

The early theory of Chinese music is based in part on Chen Yingshi, "Theory and Notation in China," in Virginia Danielson, Scott Marcus, and Dwight Reynolds, eds., *Garland Encyclopedia of World Music: Volume 7: East Asia: China, Japan, and Korea* (New York: Routledge, 2002), pp. 115–126.

The life of Confucius and the discussion of Confucianism are based on D. Howard Smith, *Confucius* (New York: Charles Scribner's Sons, 1973).

Gateway 8, Music of the Middle East

The theory of emotion associated with specific *maqamat* is taken from Habib Hassan Touma, *The Music of the Arabs*, trans. Laurie Schwartz (Portland, OR: Amadeus Press, 1996).

The discussion of emotion and meaning in music is indebted to A. J. Racy, *Making Music in the Arab World: The Culture and Artistry of Tarab* (Cambridge: Cambridge University Press, 2003).

"an index of high Arab culture and a sign of musical pleasure as well as intellectual and scientific sophistication." Scheherazade Qassim Hassan, "Music Instruments of the Arab World," in Virginia Danielson, Scott Marcus, and Dwight Reynolds, eds., *Garland Encyclopedia of World Music, Volume 6: The Middle East* (New York: Routledge, 2002), p. 406.

Gateway 9, African Music

This gateway, including two short quotes, is based on Paul Berliner, *The Soul of Mbira: Music and Traditions of the Shona People of Zimbabwe* (Chicago: University of Chicago Press, 1993).

Chapter 4

Gateway 14, North Indian Classical Music

"could address a god or goddess, laud a king, express feelings of intimate romantic love, describe a season, transmit musicological knowledge, or deal with a metaphysical or religious concept." Bonnie C. Wade, "Hindustani Vocal Music," in Alison Arnold, ed., *The Garland Encyclopedia of World Music, Volume 5: South Asia: The Indian Subcontinent* (New York: Routledge, 2000), p. 164.

Chapter 5

Gateway 16, Baroque Orchestral Music

"about forty girls," from J. Peter Burkholder et al., *A History of Western Music*, 8th ed. (New York: W. W. Norton, 2010), p. 423, quoting from Charles de Brosses, *L'Italie il y a cent ans ou Lettres écrites d'Italie à quelques amis en 1739 et 1740*, ed. M. R. Colomb, vol. 1 (Paris: Alphonse Levavasseur, 1836), pp. 213–214.

Gateway 19, Javanese Court Music

This gateway is indebted in part to R. Anderson Sutton, "Java: Central and East Java," in Terry E. Miller and Sean Williams, eds., *The Garland Encyclopedia of World Music: Southeast Asia* (New York: Garland, 1998), pp. 631–685.

"Swept Away . . ." from Sumarsam, *Gamelan: Cultural Interaction and Musical Development in Central Java* (Chicago: University of Chicago Press, 1992, 1995), pp. 27, 60.

"Javanese music obeys laws of counterpoint . . ." from Richard Langham Smith, trans., *Debussy on Music* (New York: Knopf, 1977), published in 1913 in *Revue S.I.M.*

Chapter 6

Gateway 20, Classical-Period Chamber Music

"I barely managed to stay alive . . ." and "Not only did I have the encouragement of constant approval . . ." from Albert Christoph Dies and Georg August Griesinger, "Biographical Accounts of Joseph Haydn," in *Haydn: Two Contemporary Portraits*, trans. Vernon Gotwals (Milwaukee: University of Wisconsin Press, 1963), contains interviews Dies and Griesinger conducted with Haydn and published in 1810.

Gateway 21, Classical-Period Opera

"Useless people" and "beggars," Cliff Eisen and Simon P. Keefe, eds., *The Cambridge Mozart Encyclopedia* (Cambridge: Cambridge University Press, 2006), p. 268.

Gateway 22, Classical-Period Symphonies

"Joy follows sorrow, sunshine—rain . . ." in Friedrich Kerst and Henry Edward Krehbiel, eds., *Beethoven: The Man and the Artist, as Revealed in His Own Words*, trans. Henry Edward Krehbiel (Boston: IndyPublishing, 2008), p. 15.

Goethe quote: "That was a creation . . ." from Will Durant, *The Story of Civilization, Volume 10: Rousseau and Revolution* (New York: Simon & Schuster, 1967), p. 563.

Wordsworth quote: "the spontaneous overflow of powerful feelings," cited in Aidan Day, *Romanticism* (New York: Routledge, 1996), p. 2.

"Beethoven's music stirs the mists of fear . . ." from "'Beethoven's Instrumental Music,' translated from E. T. A. Hoffmann's Kreisleriana with an introductory note by Arthur Ware Locke," *Musical Quarterly* 3(1) (1917): 123–133.

Gateway 23, Music of the Atlantic Slave Trade

This gateway is indebted to Larry Crook, *Brazilian Music: Northeastern Traditions and the Heartbeat of a Modern Nation* (Santa Barbara, CA: ABC-Clio, 2005).

"the blacks divided by Nations . . ." Lucas Nicolau Parés, *The Formation of Candomblé: Vodun History and Ritual in Brazil* (Chapel Hill: University of North Carolina Press, 2013), p. 67.

Chapter 7

Gateway 24, Early Nineteenth-Century Opera

Many elements of this gateway are based on Emanuele Senici, ed., *The Cambridge Companion to Rossini* (Cambridge: Cambridge University Press, 2004).

"We know longer want or need any text . . .," from Nicholas Mathew, "On Being There in 1824," in Nicholas Mathew and Benjamin Walton, eds., *The Invention of Beethoven and Rossini* (Cambridge: Cambridge University Press, 2013), p. 186.

"I have never forgotten them . . .," from Richard Osborne, *Rossini: His Life and Works*, 2nd ed. (New York: Oxford University Press, 2007), p. 13. Rossini's biography in this gateway is indebted to this source.

The composer's "chief duty" . . . from Carolyn Abbate and Roger Parker, *A History of Opera* (New York: W. W. Norton, 2012), p. 208.

"I really believe so much in *bel canto* . . . " from Joseph McLellan, "Von Stade's Cinderella story," *Washington Post*, February 27, 1988; Mary Auen and Luiz Gazzola, "The exclusive *Opera Lively* interview with Frederica von Stade," *OperaLively*, March 6, 2013.

Gateway 25, Programmatic Orchestra Works

"I saw the giant form of Beethoven . . ." Hector Berlioz, *The Memoirs of Hector Berlioz*, translated by David Cairns (New York: Random House, 2002), p. 104.

Gateway 26, Romantic-Period Piano Music

"If the mighty autocrat in the north . . .," Robert Schumann, *Schumann on Music: A Selection from the Writings*, trans. and ed. Henry Pleasants (New York: Dover, 1988), p. 14.

"Music will perhaps become his [Felix's] profession . . .," Sebastian Hensel, *The Mendelssohn Family 1729–1847*, 4th rev. ed., 2 vols. (London: Sampson Low, 1884), vol. I, p. 82.

Gateway 27, Early American Popular Music

This gateway is indebted in part to Jacqueline Cogdell DjeDje, "The (Mis)Representation of African American Music: The Role of the Fiddle," *Journal of the Society for American Music* 10 (2016): 1–32.

"remarkably well on the violin." Theresa Jenoure, "The Afro-American Fiddler," *Contributions in Black Studies* 5 (2008): 68–81, quote from p. 69.

Chapter 8

Gateway 30, African American Religious Music

"There were many times when we didn't have a place to sleep or anything to eat . . ." Andrew Ward, *Dark Midnight When I Rise: The Story of the Jubilee Singers Who Introduced the World to the Music of Black America* (New York: Farrar, Strauss, and Giroux, 2000), p. 132.

"People came to despise . . ." Gustavus D. Pike, *The Jubilee Singers of Fisk University and Their Campaign for Twenty Thousand Dollars* (Boston: Lee and Shepard, 1873), pp. 107, 99, 77, 92, and 118–119, respectively.

"The permanency of the university was assured," Pike, *The Jubilee Singers*, p. 36.

"were sacred to our parents." Hollis Robbins and Henry Louis Gates Jr., eds., *Penguin Portable Nineteenth Century African American Women Writers* (New York: Penguin, 2017), p. 230.

Gateway 31, Native American Pow-wow Drumming, Singing, and Dancing

Much of this gateway is based on Tara Browner, *The Heartbeat of the People: Music and Dance of the Northern Pow-wow* (Urbana: University of Illinois Press, 2002).

All the quotes in this gateway come from John-Carlos Perea, *Intertribal American Music in the United States: Experiencing Music, Expressing Culture* (New York: Oxford University Press, 2014), another important source for this gateway. In order, the quotes appear on pp. 27 and 44 of Perea 2014.

The data on Apache land in Oklahoma is from Apache Tribe of Oklahoma, https://apachetribe.org/history/ (accessed December 17, 2021).

Chapter 9

Gateway 33, The Blues

Comments about flood relief efforts and the blues are indebted to Angela Davis, *Blues Legacies and Black Feminism: Gertrude "Ma" Rainey, Bessie Smith, and Billie Holiday* (New York: Vintage Books, 1998), pp. 109–110.

Details on Bessie Smith's biography as a performer are drawn from Michelle R. Scott, *Blues Empress in Black Chattanooga: Bessie Smith and the Emerging Urban South* (Urbana: University of Illinois Press, 2008), p. 120.

Gateway 34, American Band Music

"The Union Army is said to have . . . " is indebted to Larry Starr and Christopher Waterman, *American Popular Music: From Minstrelsy to MTV* (Oxford: Oxford University Press, 2003), p. 27.

Gateway 36, Classical Music in the New Century

Discussion of irregularity and unpredictability in rhythmic patterns in *The Rite of Spring* is indebted to Matthew McDonald, "*Jeux de Nombres*: Automated Rhythm in *The Rite of Spring*," *Journal of the American Musicological Society* 63(3) (2010): 499–551.

"In *The Rite of Spring* . . ." This paragraph is indebted to Richard Taruskin, *Stravinsky and the Russian Traditions: A Biography of the Works through Mavra* (Berkeley: University of California Press, 1996), pp. 849–966.

"Musicologist Richard Taruskin has even speculated . . ." is indebted to Richard Taruskin, "A Myth of the Twentieth Century: The Rite of Spring, the Tradition of the New, and 'The Music Itself,'" *Modernism/Modernity 2.1* (1995), p. 16.

Gateway 37, Balinese Gamelan

"On September 14, 1906 . . .," Debbie Guthrie Haer, Juliette Morillot, and Irene Toh, *Bali, a Traveller's Companion* (Paris: Editions Didier Millet, 2001), p. 38.

"In the area of culture and music the *puputan*s had three important consequences. First . . . " is indebted to Michael Tenzer, *Balinese Music* (Singapore: Periplus Editions, 1991), p. 23.

The paragraph beginning "Gamelan *gong kebyar* emerged between 1910 and 1915, not long after the Dutch colonized Bali . . . " is indebted to Michael Tenzer, *Gamelan Gong Kebyar: The Art of Twentieth-Century Balinese Music* (Chicago: University of Chicago Press, 2000), p. 86.

On cultural tourism in Bali, we are indebted to Elizabeth Clendinning, "Learning in the 'Global Village': Performing Arts Edutourism in Bali, Indonesia," *MUSICultures* 43(2) (2016).

Chapter 10

Opening

"Jazz was a slang word . . ." Lewis Porter, "Where Did 'Jazz,' the Word, Come From? Follow a Trail of Clues," *Deep Dive with Lewis Porter* (blog), WBGO.com, February 26, 2018, http://wbgo.org/post/where-did-jazz-word-come-follow-trail-clues-deep-dive-lewis-porter#stream/0 (accessed April 10, 2018).

Gateway 41, Mexican and Mexican American Mariachi Music

This gateway is indebted in part to Lauryn Salazar, *From Fiesta to Festival: Mariachi Music in California and the Southwestern United States*, Ph.D. dissertation, University of California, Los Angeles, 2011; and Daniel Sheehy, *Mariachi Music in America: Experiencing Music, Expressing Culture* (New York: Oxford University Press, 2006).

Chapter 12

Gateway 46, Rhythm & Blues and Soul

The discussion of the lyrics of "(You Make Me Feel Like) A Natural Woman" draws on Josefine Ramm Skaaning, *Respect for a Natural Woman: Representations of Femininities in Two Songs by Aretha Franklin*, M.A. thesis, University of Vienna, 2019.

The interpretation of Aretha Franklin's vocal timbre is indebted to Kate Heidemann, "A System for Describing Vocal Timbre in Popular Song," *Music Theory Online* 22(1) (2016).

The "What Is Its History" section of the gateway draws on several sources, in addition to the sources cited for specific sections. These include Emily J. Lordi, *The Meaning of Soul: Black Music and Resilience since the 1960s* (Durham, NC: Duke University Press, 2020); Portia K. Maultsby, "Rhythm and Blues/R&B," in Mellonee V. Burnim and Portia K. Maultsby, eds., *African American Music: An Introduction*, 2nd ed. (New York: Routledge, 2015), pp. 239–276; Portia K. Maultsby, "Soul," in Mellonee V. Burnim and Portia K. Maultsby, eds., *African American Music: An Introduction*, 2nd ed. (New York, Routledge, 2015), pp. 277–298; and Joel Rudinow, *Soul Music: Tracking the Spiritual Roots of Pop from Plato to Motown* (Ann Arbor: University of Michigan Press, 2010).

Descriptions of soul jazz by Lerone Bennett Jr. in a 1961 issue of *Ebony* magazine, quoted in David Brackett, *Categorizing Sound: Genre and Twentieth-Century Popular Music* (Berkeley: University of California Press, 2016), p. 268.

Aretha Franklin's statement "Well I believe that the black revolution . . . " quoted in Rickey Vincent, *Party Music: The Inside Story of the Black Panthers' Band and How Black Power Transformed Soul Music* (Chicago: Chicago Review Press, 2013), p. 156.

Gateway 47, Rock

Big Mama Thornton's role as a bridge figure between the women blues singers of the 1920s and women rhythm & blues artists of the 1950s and 1960s drawn from Maureen Mahon, *Black Diamond Queens: African American Women and Rock and Roll* (Durham, NC: Duke University Press, 2020), p. 30.

Discussion of Tina Turner drawn from Mahon, pp. 240–272.

Gateway 48, New Directions in Jazz

"to show how the disadvantaged and the disenfranchised . . . " Muhal Richard Abrams and John Shenoy Jackson. "Association for the Advancement of Creative Musicians," *Black World 23* (November 1973): 72.

Gateway 49, Experimental Music

Details on the Center of the Creative and Performance Arts are drawn from Renée Levine Packer, *This Life of Sounds: Evenings for New Music in Buffalo* (New York: Oxford University Press), 2010.

"bigger and hipper than . . . " from Rosalind Constable, "Can This Be Buffalo?" *Life*, April 23, 1965, p. 63.

Dennis Kahle quotation and other details from *Stay On It* musicians, from Matthew Mendez, "'That Piece Does Not Exist without Julius': Still Staying on *Stay On It*," in Renée Levine Packer and Mary Jane Leach, eds., *Gay Guerrilla: Julius Eastman and His Music* (Rochester, NY: Rochester University Press, 2015), pp. 151–78.

Julius Eastman statement ""What I am trying to achieve is . . . " from Renate Strauss, "Julius Eastman: Will the Real One Stand Up?" *Buffalo Evening News*, July 16, 1976, quoted in Matthew D. Morrison, "Julius Eastman: Gay Guerilla," *OUPblog*, May 28, 2015, https://blog.oup.com/2015/05/julius-eastman-gay-guerilla/. Morrison, "Julius Eastman," has also assisted in framing discussions throughout this gateway.

"It got slower and it got sexier . . . " quoted in Mendez, "'That Piece Does Not Exist without Julius,'" 161.

Information on AACM musicians from George E. Lewis, "Experimental Music in Black and White: The AACM in New York, 1970–1985," *Current Musicology* 71–73 (2002): 100–157.

"[I]n a situation with maximum . . . " quotation and details on Eastman's performance of *Song Books* from Ryan Dohoney, "John Cage, Julius Eastman, and the Homosexual Ego," in Benjamin Piekut, ed., *Tomorrow Is the Question: New Directions in Experimental Music Studies* (Ann Arbor: University of Michigan Press, 2014).

Julius Eastman quotation "Well, it says 'perform a disciplined act,' . . . " from Renée Levine Packer, "Julius Eastman, a Biography," in Renée Levine Packer and Mary Jane Leach, eds., *Gay Guerrilla: Julius Eastman and His Music* (Rochester, NY: Rochester University Press, 2015), 45–46.

Gateway 50, Salsa

Comments on Nuyorican and Puerto Rican national identity are indebted to Peter Manuel, "Puerto Rican Music and Cultural Identity: Creative Appropriation of Cuban *Sources* from Danza to Salsa," *Ethnomusicology 38* (1994): 249–280.

Chapter 13

Gateway 52, Electronic Dance Music

The co-presence of repetitive groove and goal-directed form is adapted from Robert Fink, "Goal-Directed Soul?: Analyzing Rhythmic Teleology in African American Popular Music," *Journal of the American Musicological Society 64*(1) (2011): 179–238.

The brief discussion of disco's history draws on Kai Fikentscher, "Disco and House," in Mellonee V. Burnim and Portia K. Maultsby, eds., *African American Music: An Introduction*, 2nd ed. (New York: Routledge, 2015), pp. 320–329.

Histories of house music draw on Micah Salkind, *Do You Remember House? Chicago's Queer of Color Undergrounds* (New York: Oxford University Press, 2019); and Jacob Arnold, "The Warehouse: The Place House Music Got Its Name," *Resident Advisor*, May 17, 2012, https://ra.co/features/1597 (accessed November 16, 2021).

Jesse Saunders quotation "I was combining all of these great genres together . . . " quoted in Jack Needham, "The Beautiful Black Gay History of Chicago House's Birth," *Dazed Digital*, May 11, 2017, https://www.dazeddigital.com/music/article/35892/1/chicago-house-lgbtq-history-documentary (accessed November 9, 2021).

Histories of Detroit techno are drawn from Dan Sicko, *Techno Rebels: The Renegades of Electronic Funk*, 2nd ed. (Detroit: Wayne State University Press, 2010); Denise Dalphond, "Detroit Techno," in Mellonee V. Burnim and Portia K. Maultsby, eds., *African American Music: An Introduction*, 2nd ed. (New York: Routledge, 2015), 335–353; citation, Simon Reynolds, *Energy Flash: A Journey through Rave Music and Dance Culture* (Berkeley, CA: Soft Skull Press, 2012); Luis Manuel-Garcia, "An Alternate History of Sexuality in Club Culture," *Resident Advisor*, January 28, 2014, https://www.residentadvisor.net/feature.aspx?1927 (accessed November 11, 2021).

Details on dubstep and the cultural politics of EDM as a genre label drawn from Mike D'Errico, "Electronic Dance Music in the Dubstep Era" (Oxford Handbooks Online, 2015), https://doi.org/10.1093/oxfordhb/9780199935321.013.74.

Gateway 54, Postmodern Classical Music

The section on neo-Romanticism, including the Del Tredici quote, is indebted to Barbara Russano Hanning, *Concise History of Western Music*, 4th ed. (New York: W. W. Norton, 2010), pp. 652–654.

Chapter 14

Gateway 56, Pop Music Today

"Lizzo doesn't just speak to me . . . " quotation from Nakkiah Lui, "Lizzo's Sydney Opera House performance was as close to transcendent as pop can get," *Guardian*, January 7, 2020, https://www.theguardian.com/music/2020/jan/07/lizzos-sydney-opera-house-performance-was-as-close-to-transcendent-as-pop-can-get (accessed November 24, 2021).

Gateway 57, Jazz Today

"This song is singing to our African American . . . " Patrick Jarenwattananon, "New Esperanza Spalding Song in Time for Black History Month," *National Public Radio*, February 2, 2012, https://www.npr.org/sections/ablogsupreme/2012/02/02/146287135/new-esperanza-spalding-song-in-time-for-black-history-month (accessed April 25, 2018).

Information on Jon Batiste-led protest marches comes from Alan Scherstuhl, "Jazz Is Built for Protests. Jon Batiste Is Taking It to the Streets," *New York Times*, June 24, 2020, https://www.nytimes.com/2020/06/24/arts/music/jon-batiste-jazz-protests.html (accessed January 1, 2022); and Elizabeth Kim, "Jon Batiste on the Soundtrack of Protest Movements," *Gothamist*, August 4, 2020, https://gothamist.com/arts-entertainment/jon-batiste-soundtrack-protest-movements (accessed January 1, 2022).

Gateway 59, Regional Mexican Music

Details on the regional Mexican music category are drawn from Melanie Josephine Morgan, *Regional Mexican Radio in the U.S.: Marketing Genre, Making Audiences*, Ph.D. dissertation, University of Texas at Austin, 2011.

Gateway 60, K-pop

The Blackpink line-distribution video and information are drawn from "BLACKPINK—How You Like That (Line Distribution + Lyrics Color Coded) [Updated]," June 27, 2020, posted by random_k, https://www.youtube.com/watch?v=buc9PvZefXo (accessed November 29, 2021).

Comment on K-pop music videos drawing on many cultural and historical references from CedarBough Saeji, "Thinking through Intertextuality in Korean Pop Music Videos," *Translation Review* 108(1) (2020): 48–63.

The "What Is Its History?" section for K-pop is based on Roald Maliangkay, "The Popularity of Individualism: The Seo Taiji Phenomenon in the 1990s," in *The Korean Popular Culture Reader*, edited by Kyung Hyun Kim and Youngmin Choe (Durham, NC: Duke University Press, 2014), 296–313; and Dal Yong Jin, New *Korean Wave: Transnational Cultural Power in the Age of Social Media* (Urbana: University of Illinois Press, 2016).

Discussion of the changes in the relationship of the South Korean state to the entertainment industry are drawn from Inkyu Kang, "The Political Economy of Idols: South Korea's Neoliberal Restructuring and Its Impact on the Entertainment Labour Force," in Jung-Bong Choi and Roald Maliangkay, eds., *K-pop: The International Rise of the Korean Music Industry* (New York: Routledge, 2014), pp. 51–65.

INDEX